gale
encyclopedia of
e-commerce

gale
encyclopedia of
e-commerce

Volume
2
J–Z

Jane A. Malonis, Editor

Foreword by Dr. Paula J. Haynes

GALE GROUP

THOMSON LEARNING ™

Detroit • New York • San Diego • San Francisco
Boston • New Haven, Conn. • Waterville, Maine
London • Munich

Staff

Editorial: Jane A. Malonis, *Senior Editor.* Erin Braun, *Managing Editor, Business Content.*
Jacqueline K. Mueckenheim, *Managing Editor, Business Product.* Paul Lewon, *Technical Training Specialist.*

Product Design: Cynthia Baldwin, Michelle DiMercurio, *Senior Art Directors.*

Composition and Electronic Prepress: Mary Beth Trimper, *Manager.* Evi Seoud, *Assistant Manager.*
Rhonda Williams, *Buyer.*

Library of Congress Cataloging-in-Publication Data

Gale encyclopedia of E-commerce / Jane A. Malonis, editor.
    p. cm.
Includes bibliographical references and index.
    ISBN 0-7876-5660-7 (set : hardcover) — ISBN 0-7876-5748-4 (vol. 1) —ISBN
0-7876-5749-2 (vol. 2)
    1. Electronic commerce—Encyclopedias. I. Malonis, Jane A.
    HF5548.32 .G35 2002
    381'.1—dc21

2001055543

ISBN 0-7876-5660-7 (set), ISBN 0-7876-5748-4 (Vol. 1), ISBN 0-7876-5749-2 (Vol. 2)

Printed in the United States of America

gale
encyclopedia of
e-commerce

J

Former Microsoft manager Naveen Jain is the founder, CEO, and chairman of InfoSpace, Inc., a provider of Internet services and content—including news, stock quotes, and yellow and white pages—to major World Wide Web portals like America Online, Lycos, Disney's GO Network, and Microsoft's MSN, as well as to various wireless networks. Sales at Info-Space grew nearly 200 percent to $215 million in 2000. That year, Jain's firm attained profitability for the first time, posting earnings of $46.2 million.

After earning an undergraduate degree in engineering from the University of Roorkee and an MBA from St. Xavier's School of Management, Jain emigrated to the U.S. from India in 1979. He was hired by Microsoft Corp. in 1989 to work on the firm's OS/2 platform. After working on early versions of the MS-DOS operating system, as well as on the more sophisticated Windows NT and Windows 95 platforms, Jain was put in charge of the Microsoft Network, which made its debut as part of Windows 95 to compete with online services such as Compuserve, Prodigy, and America Online. In March of 1996, Jain resigned from Microsoft and established his own business, InfoSpace.com. According to Jain's management profile on the InfoSpace Web site, while at Microsoft, "he noticed that the Internet failed to provide people with the useful and relevant real world information they needed." As a result, Jain developed a "vison of delivering real world content on the Internet—anytime, anywhere, and on any device."

When Jain first launched InfoSpace, it focused on offering virtual yellow page and white page services to other Web sites looking to enhance their offerings. Believing that Web site operators wanting to snag more traffic would likely embrace the chance to license additional content and services, Jain added to his offerings things like online classified advertising, message boards, and e-mail. Sales during InfoSpace's first full year of business totaled $1.6 million. They jumped to $9.4 million in 1998; that year, Jain hired Bernie Strom as president, appointed several other top managers, and took his company public.

In August 1999, Jain bought Inex Corp. to gain access to the Toronto, Ontario-based firm's e-merchant tools. The $42 million acquisition allowed InfoSpace to begin offering Web site conceptualization, construction, promotion, and operation services. The September purchase of Seattle, Washington-based upstart Union-Street.com brought with it technology that allowed InfoSpace to add chat services, visitor tracking capabilities, and other upgrades to existing Web sites. Later in the year, Jain added instant messaging to his firm's growing repository of content and services. By then, Netscape, AOL, Microsoft, Disney, and the Wall Street Journal were among Info-Space's 2,100 online clients. Sales grew more than threefold to $35 million, most of which came from the licensing fees InfoSpace charged its customers. By the year 2000, InfoSpace was valued at roughly $8 billion, and because Jain owned nearly one-third of the firm, his personal worth exceeded $2 billion.

Although Jain's earlier conviction that devices such as cellular phones would become Internet access tools had begun to pay off for the firm in the late 1990s, the larger rewards for his foresight came during 2000. In January, InfoSpace began licensing its wireless Internet services to Vodafone AirTouch, the world's mobile communications leader. To bolster its wireless offerings further, InfoSpace paid $58 million for IQorder.com, an Arizona-based firm that offered both wireless and traditional access to its online comparison shopping services. In April, Arun Sarin left his position as head of the U.S. and Asia Pacific regions of Vodafone AirTouch to takeover as CEO of InfoSpace. Together, Sarin and Jain, who remained chairman of his firm, oversaw the merger of InfoSpace with broadband service provider Go2Net Inc. in October. After the deal was finalized, Go2Net cofounder Russell Horowitz was named president of InfoSpace, Sarin remained CEO, and Jain continued as chairman. However, when Sarin resigned in February of 2001, to reportedly spend more time with family, Jain resumed CEO duties. Due to the weakening North American economy, which he believed would undercut sales of wireless devices, Jain brought his firm's spending to a near halt.

FURTHER READING:

Baker, Sharon M. "InfoSpace Isn't Done Acquiring." *Puget Sound Business Journal,* November 26, 1999.

"InfoSpace Completes Go2Net Acquisition." *Puget Sound Business Journal,* October 20, 2000.

InfoSpace Corp. "Management Profiles: CEO and Chairman." Bellevue, WA: InfoSpace Corp., 2001. Available from www.infospace.com.

"InfoSpace Inks Vodafone Deal." *Puget Sound Business Journal,* January 14, 2000.

"InfoSpace Names New Management, Reports Growth." *Electronic Information Report,* February 16, 2001.

"See Jain Gain." *Puget Sound Business Journal,* December 10, 1999.

SEE ALSO: Content Provider

JAVA

Java is a programming language that is widely used on the World Wide Web, both in Web pages (client side) and on Web servers (computers used to host or maintain Web sites). Therefore, it is an important technical component of e-commerce. Based on a high-level programming language called C++, the most popular, powerful aspect of Java is that it allows programmers to create programs that can be downloaded onto computers regardless of their operating systems (programs like Windows used for controlling a computer's basic operations). Additionally, because of its available security features, programs written in Java can be downloaded and run safely, eliminating concerns about viruses or damaged files.

Java is both simple and powerful, which makes it popular with programmers. Like C++, it is an object-oriented programming language. Object-oriented programming involves techniques that allow programmers to increase efficiency and reduce complexity. Java was developed by Sun Microsystems in 1991 for use in consumer devices. However, it soon found a place on the Web when Sun made it available for that purpose in the mid-1990s. In the early 2000s, Web browsers like Netscape Navigator, cellular phones, and personal digital assistants were being specifically designed to support the Java programming language.

HOW JAVA WORKS

Because it is an interpreted language, Java doesn't work alone. It relies on an interpreter called the Java Virtual Machine (JVM) to function. Many high-level programming languages, like C and C++, rely on programs called compilers or interpreters so they can be converted to the fundamental machine language (zeroes and ones) that a computer's hardware actually understands. However, instead of being translated directly into machine language, programs written in Java are compiled into bytecode—an intermediate language that can be interpreted by any computer running JVM. This is what gives the Java language the ability to run on any computer. While the Java programming language is available for free to programmers, the JVM requires a license for use.

Besides JVM, the Java language relies on another critical component known as the Java Platform. As David Flanagan explained in *Java in a Nutshell,* the Java platform consists of a set of classes. "A class is a module of Java code that defines a data structure and a set of methods (also called procedures, functions, or subroutines) that operate on that data." Classes are subsequently organized into groups called packages, which involve many functions, including networking, graphics, input/output, user-interface creation, and security.

When programs written in Java run from a Web page, they are referred to as applets. When they run on servers, they are referred to as servlets. Rather than running from a server, Web page applets actually get downloaded to a user's computer, sometimes in a matter of seconds. This frees up the server's resources so its efficiency is not affected. Many applets are available to Web site operators for free. Examples of applets include productivity tools like spread sheets, animation, mathematical applications like calculators, Web forms, and more. Many applets can be valuable tools on e-commerce sites. Because they are actual programs, applets allow Web site operators to expand the capabilities of their sites beyond that which is possible with hypertext markup language (HTML)—the authoring or presentation language used for creating the appearance of Web pages.

Like most programming languages, Java has evolved since it first came onto the scene. Since the mid-1990s, several improved versions have been released. Although other languages like Visual Basic were easier to learn, there was a very strong interest in Java during the early 2000s. At that time, hundreds of books had been written on the language, and it was poised to play an increasing role on the World Wide Web. Some industry professionals expected Java to become the dominant programming language of the 2000s.

FURTHER READING:

Appleman, Daniel. *How Computer Programming Works.* Berkeley: Apress. 2000.

Bull, Glen and Gina Bull "Java Applets." *Learning and Leading with Technology,* May, 2000.

Flanagan, David. *Java in a Nutshell.* Sebastopol, California: O'Reilly & Associates, Inc. 1999.

"Java." *NetLingo Inc,* January 31, 2001. Available from www.netlingo.com.

"Java." *Techencyclopedia,* March 7, 2001. Available from www.techweb.com/encyclopedia.

"The Origins of C and C++." *Cyberdiem,* January 30, 2001. Available from www.cyberdiem.com.

Tash, Jeff. "Java! Java! Java!" *Planet IT,* May 4, 1999. Available from www.planetit.com.

SEE ALSO: C; Programming Language; HTML

J.D. EDWARDS & COMPANY

J.D. Edwards & Company develops, produces, and markets software applications packages for business. It develops applications that can be used in every aspect of business, including supply, finance, human resources, manufacturing, and planning, and by most business sectors, such as chemicals, automobiles, arts and entertainment, and energy. Its flagship products, OneWorld and WorldSoftware, incorporate tools for enterprise resource planning (ERP), supply chain planning, knowledge management, and process integration. Services related to its software, such as training and consulting make up about 50 percent of J.D. Edwards' business.

In its software packages, J.D. Edwards made "interoperability" a byword. Beginning in the middle 1990s, J.D. Edwards began creating software that included all the essential functions needed by a business and allowed those functions to work together smoothly. This idea grew into a strategy the firm termed "c-commerce," or collaborative commerce. The c-commerce software packages it developed, in particular OneWorld, were suites of component with a variety of applications that could be used across a company or an industry. Diverse applications which previously were incompatible could "interoperate" in J.D. Edwards software. It threw up bridgeheads across networks, be they intranets, extranets or the Internet. Departments within a company could exchange data; as could companies collaborating on projects. It no longer mattered that their applications or even their computer systems were different.

J.D. Edwards' c-commerce approach offered many benefits. Some 60 percent of Fortune 500 businesses depended on three or more technology platforms. Software like OneWorld helped integrate these systems. Individual firms could exchange data about common projects, products, and services across systems efficiently in real-time. In summer 2000 J.D. Edwards intensified its commitment to c-commerce adopting a best-of-breed strategy for its software line. The firm's enabled a customer to select the best applications packages regardless of who produced them, rather than purchasing every application bundled together in a monolithic package from a single vendor. J.D. Edwards' software was able to integrate the diverse software into a seamlessly functioning system. Best-of-breed offered firm's an additional advantage—if it decided to alter or replace an application, it could do so without replacing its entire software system.

ONEWORLD

The OneWorld Suite is the flagship of J.D. Edwards' product line. It is a Web-enabled collection of business applications, a set of integrated components that can be assembled and disassembled to best serve the needs of a particular company. Released in 1997, OneWorld was designed from the ground up as a comprehensive component software architecture. It was one of the very first such systems on the market. OneWorld's architecture is a hierarchy comprised of six levels of components. Each level is constructed from the pieces in the next lower level. OneWorld's power and versatility come from its ability to combine its nearly 45,000 components to carry out a broad variety of business functions.

OneWorld's first level is comprised of about 30,000 predefined data elements, which constitute the building blocks of the system. The low-level components identify and store the most basic information and perform very simple calculations on that information. OneWorld users can also define new data elements. The second level is made up of tables and so-called business views, which assemble data from the first level and organize it into tables. Functions, such as joining or filtering, are also performed on the tables at this level to prepare them for the third level, business functions. There are nearly 3,000 business functions, each one of three types: field, line, or master. The nuts-and-bolts work of business is first apparent at this level. Field business functions control particular data fields in the application—price, for example. Line business functions control specific lines in a business form, for example, the third line of an invoice. Master business functions are set up to handle larger composite entities such as an entire purchase order.

Complex business functions, such as maintaining an accounting ledger, are performed in one of two modes, interactive and batch applications, at OneWorld's fourth level. The fifth level, OneWorld solutions, are programs that integrate all the lower-level business functions and application modes into complete, full-blown applications for different business activities, such as human resources, manufacturing, or finance. At the top-most level, OneWorld Vertical Market Suites, components are combined for the needs of specific industries, including energy, chemicals, engineering and construction, and public services.

OneWorld was designed to run on the Windows or UNIX operating systems, as well as on the IBM AS/400 platform, the system with which J.D. Edwards first made its name. A later version, OneWorld XE, included an "interoperability engine" that made it possible for users to integrate specific applications from different software or platforms, as well as from companies other than J.D. Edwards. A Hurwitz Group white paper on OneWorld called the package "a compelling choice for companies that recognize the importance of the technological and business cases for componentization."

HISTORY

J.D. Edwards was founded in 1977 by three employees at a Denver, Colorado accounting firm: Jack Thompson, Dan Gregory, and Ed McVaney. There was no J.D. Edwards—that was an amalgam of its founders' first names. The new company was set up to design business software for small and medium-sized computers. In the early 1980s it began specializing in software for IBM computers—first the IBM System/38, and in 1988 for the AS/400. WorldSoftware, a package of business applications introduced by J.D. Edwards in 1983, was the firm's leading product by the end of the 1980s. By 1992, the company was not only the world's largest producer of IBM midrange software, it was the 30th largest software company overall in the United States, averaging 15 percet annual growth for fifteen years running. By the early 1990s, 32 percent of J.D. Edwards' sales were overseas. More important, to achieve that astounding pattern of growth, it never needed to go public.

Edwards maintained its success through much of the 1990s. In 1996 it introduced OneWorld. Termed configurable network computing, OneWorld was the first shot in J.D. Edwards' c-commerce revolution. One year later, in August 1997, in the bull's rush for computer and Internet stocks, the firm launched a well-received stock offering. By the middle of the following year, the firm was worth nearly $1 billion and could boast an annual compound growth rate of 52 percent. As 1999 began, the ERP industry as a whole, and giants like SAP and Baan in particular, were reporting declines in profits; J.D. Edwards, however, nearly doubled its revenues. Flush with success, the company set its sights on overtaking the industry leader SAP within five years time.

In 1999, determined that its OneWorld package go head to head with high-end SAP and PeopleSoft offerings, J.D. Edwards moved all out into collaborative commerce. It acquired two companies, Premisys and Numetrix, whose technologies were essential to making OneWorld interoperable. However, the Year 2000 (Y2K) transition problem threw the entire ERP sector into a recession, and J.D. Edwards' fortunes took a major downturn in early 2000. In April CEO Doug Massingil left the company after less than a year and a half on the job, and was replaced by the man he had replaced, J.D. Edwards founder Ed McVaney. A month later the company announced that it would lay off around 13 percent of its workforce throughout the world, and its share price plunged from a high of $49 to a little over $10.

Struggling to recover, the firm announced OneWorld XPI—eXtended Process Integration. This best-of-breed software solution made it possible for J.D. Edwards' customers to incorporate diverse software applications into a single system that managed all operations and interconnected them. Technology licensed from Netfish Technologies and Active Software provided OneWorld XPI with its so-called interoperability engine. In January 2001, Edwards used the Internet for the first time to sell its systems directly to customers. Summer 2001 saw a chastened J.D. Edwards scaling back its ambitious plans to overtake SAP. The company refocused its attentions on the middle-sized companies that were always its bread and butter. In 2001, the company employed nearly 5,000 employees in 60 different offices throughout the world, and had approximately 6,000 customers in 113 countries.

FURTHER READING:

Everitt, Lisa Greim, ''JD Edwards & Co. Launches Direct Software Business.'' *Denver Rocky Mountain News,* January 6, 2000.

Howlett, Dennis, ''JD Edwards Attempts To Change To Try And Take On SAP.'' *Newswire* (VNU), May 20, 1999.

''IBM, J.D. Edwards Strike Global e-Business Pact.'' *Washington Technology,* April 2, 2001.

''JD Edwards Extends Oneworld With E-Business Vision.'' *Asia Computer Weekly,* May 31, 1999.

Koh, Cindy, ''New Strategy for JD Edwards.'' *New Straits Times,* June 29, 1998.

Manchester, Philip, ''A Seamless Electronic Environment.'' *Financial Times,* June 7, 2000.

Mun, Leong Khay, ''JD Edwards' Future Surrounds E-Commerce.'' *Asia Computer Weekly,* July 3, 2000.

Pardas, Aimie, ''JD Edwards in C-commerce Strategy.'' *New Straits Times - Computimes,* (Malaysia), June 26, 2000.

Stones, Lesley, ''Striking A Blow For Greybeards.'' *Business Day,* (South Africa), June 29, 2000.

Wild, Damian, ''JD Edwards Targets Mid-Market.'' *Accountancy Age,* June 21, 2001.

SEE ALSO: Enterprise Resource Planning (ERP); Integration; PeopleSoft Inc.

JOBS, STEVEN

As the founder and CEO of Apple Computer Co., the prolific Steve Jobs was at the very heart of the computer revolution. The early Apple computers played an integral part in opening the personal computer market. Through the years, as Jobs shifted his focus to his myriad side projects, Apple's market strength dissipated. By the 2000s, however, Jobs was back in command at Apple, and was busily positioning the company to regain its position atop the personal computer market.

EARLY LIFE, 1955-1975

Steven Paul Jobs was born on February 24, 1955, in San Francisco and raised by adoptive parents, Paul and Clara Jobs. The Jobs family moved in 1961 to Mountain View, California, the heart of what would become Silicon Valley. Jobs reportedly saw his first computer when he was about 12 years old. After graduating from high school, Jobs briefly attended Reed College in Oregon. He soon dropped out of college and led an alternative lifestyle, working for a time as a video game designer at Atari to finance a trip to India.

PROFESSIONAL LIFE BEGAN IN 1975

Jobs returned to California and the family home in Los Altos in 1975. He began attending meetings of the Homebrew Computer Club with other computer professionals and hobbyists, including his friend Steve Wozniak. In 1976 Jobs and Wozniak founded Apple Computer Co. Jobs handled most of the business aspects of the company, including marketing and sales, while Wozniak was responsible for computer and software design. They built computers in Jobs' parents' garage. Jobs and Wozniak began selling their first computer, the Apple I, in 1976. Like other computers of the time, it was too complex to be used by anyone but computer professionals.

It was the Apple II, introduced in 1977, that began the personal computer revolution. The Apple II was the first fully programmable, fully assembled desktop computer. Designed for computer novices and general users, it was smaller than other computers and included color graphics and a built-in keyboard, speaker, power supply, and case.

In 1984 Apple introduced the Macintosh, which featured a new operating system with a graphical user interface (GUI) instead of an operating system based strictly on text and text-based commands. The GUI used icons as well as text for commands and allowed users to point and click with a mouse. The first GUI was developed by Xerox Corp., but Apple was the first to apply it to a personal computer. The Macintosh was so easy to use that it came to be regarded as the first personal computer for the average person with no special computer training or knowledge.

JOBS SEPARATES FROM APPLE, 1985-1995

Jobs and Wozniak both left Apple in 1985 after Jobs hired John Sculley from PepsiCo to run the company. Jobs immediately started a new computer company, NeXT Computer Inc. At first NeXT built computers for colleges and universities. After the computers failed to become big sellers, the company turned to creating software. It developed an operating system, NextStep, which was soon overshadowed by Microsoft's Windows.

While continuing to run NeXT, Jobs became involved in another business. In 1986 he bought the special effects division of George Lucas's LucasFilm Ltd. for $10 million and renamed it Pixar. Under Jobs Pixar made workstations and software to enhance digital images. One of its notable software products was called RenderMan. It enabled computer graphic artists to add textures and color onto three-dimensional objects. One of the applications of RenderMan was to create the realistic skin and teeth on the dinosaurs in the 1993 film, *Jurassic Park.*

Another division of Pixar was involved in making short animated films. Although these films were designed to showcase Pixar's software, they began winning awards. The films were made under the direction of John Lasseter, who joined Pixar when it was a division of LucasFilm. In the early 1990's Lasseter and his colleagues teamed up with Walt Disney Co. to work on full-length animated feature films. Pixar developed a new way to create three-dimensional animation for use in film sequences, videos, CD-ROM games, and other applications.

Following the release of its first animated feature, *Toy Story,* in 1995, Pixar became financially successful. The company went public and followed up with two more hits, *A Bug's Life* in 1998 and *Toy Story 2* in 1999. Following these successes, Jobs' share of the company was worth more than $1 billion.

JOBS RETURNED TO APPLE, 1996-2001

As Windows became the dominant operating system in the 1990s, Apple was struggling with dwindling sales and market share. In December 1996 Jobs sold NeXT to Apple for $400 million and returned to the company as a consultant. After then-CEO Gilbert Amelio was forced out by Apple's board of directors, Jobs assumed an expanded role as a key advisor to the company. Morale at the company returned to a higher level because of Jobs' new role, and the company's loyal customers looked forward to new developments.

In September 1997 Jobs was named interim CEO of Apple. At the time Apple had only about 10 percent of the personal computer market, compared to 85 percent for Windows. As interim CEO Jobs took steps to refocus the company and cut costs. He eliminated Apple's licensing program so that other manufacturers could not make computers based on the Macintosh operating system. He refocused the company's product lines to better serve the education, home, and desktop publishing segments. He cut costs by outsourcing manufacturing, cutting the number of distributors, and reducing the amount of inventory on hand.

Jobs and Microsoft head Bill Gates were able to reach an agreement whereby Microsoft agreed to settle Apple's long-standing patent-infringement lawsuit and invest $150 million in Apple. Microsoft announced that it would develop software to run on the Macintosh platform, thus giving Mac users more choices in software.

In August 1998 Apple introduced a new line of computers, the iMac, that came in different colors and featured a new, rounded shape. A bold advertising campaign featuring the slogan, ''Think Different'' launched the iMac and helped it become an immediate sensation. Following the introduction of the iMac, Apple's financial performance improved. As the company posted solid gains in earnings its stock rose on Wall Street, reaching an all-time high of $118 in December 1999.

In January 2000 Jobs dropped ''interim'' from his title and became CEO of Apple, but 2000 would prove to be a difficult year for the company. Its stock fell to a low of $13, and its new Power Mac G4 Cube was not well received and was subsequently discontinued.

RETOOLING APPLE, 2001 AND BEYOND

In January 2001 Apple announced its first quarterly loss since Jobs returned to the company. For the quarter ending December 30, 2000, Apple reported a $247 million loss from operations, due largely to the poor performance of the G4 Cube. It was the end of a disappointing year for Apple. Critics noted that Apple had anticipated strong demand for video, building DVD drives into its computers and installing its critically acclaimed video editing software. Instead, 2000 was the year in which consumers, downloading digital music files and burning their own audio CDs, wanted more audio from their computers. Apple failed to anticipate that demand and, in fact, none of its computers came with installed read/write CD drives.

Apple computers were also equipped with slower processors than Intel-powered PCs. At the end of 2000 the fastest processor in an Apple computer was the 500-megahertz G4 chip in Macs for the professional market. By contrast, Intel-based chips were up to 1.5 gigahertz, three times the size of Apple's largest processor.

To retool the company and focus on innovation, Jobs directed several initiatives at Apple in the first half of 2001. He announced plans to open up to 25 retail stores by the end of the year, starting with outlets in Glendale, California, and Tysons Corner, Virginia. To lead Apple's retail team, Jobs recruited former Target Corp. merchandising executive Ron Johnson, who designed a 4,500-foot open space divided into subsections that focused more on what people do with their computers than the computers themselves. Apple expected the stores to become profitable by fiscal 2002.

Apple also introduced version 10.1 of its OS X operating system and updated versions of the iBook notebook computer and the Titanium PowerBook G4. Strong sales of the PowerBook in 2000 helped offset the Cube's poor sales. The new G4 PowerBook would come with a choice of three processors: a 733 MHz, 867 MHz, or a high-end version with dual 800 MHz processors.

Jobs was also determined to recapture lost market share in the education market, where Apple held more than 50 percent of the market in 1997. Through its low-priced PC program, Dell Computer Corp. had captured 34.3 percent of the U.S. education market, compared to Apple's 19 percent, by 2001.

Judging by a 25 percent increase in attendance at the mid-2001 Macworld Expo, consumer interest remained strong in Apple's innovative products. A major concern among consumers and professionals who managed networks of Macintosh computers for businesses and educational institutions was a lack of new software for Apple's new Unix-based OS X operating system. To address those concerns, Jobs displayed demo products from 10 software makers, including Adobe and Microsoft, that would be available later in the year for OS X, at the 2001 Macworld Expo.

Jobs, known as a charismatic leader and adept marketer, appeared committed to transforming Apple into a high-performance company. Even though Apple only had a 5 or 6 percent share of the personal computer market, Jobs told *Business Week,* "We only have to convince another 6 percent of PC buyers to buy from us and we can double the size of our company. That's exciting."

FURTHER READING:

"Apple." *Business Week,* July 31, 2000.

Bedell, Doug. "Ambitious Plan to Retool Apple Makes Jobs Lose Sleep." *Knight-Ridder/Tribune Business News,* July 18, 2001.

Clark, Ken. "Next Act for Apple: Stores." *Chain Store Age Executive with Shopping Center Age,* July 2001.

Deutschman, Alan. *The Second Coming of Steve Jobs.* New York: Broadway Books, 2000.

———. "Despite Recent Stock Slip, Jobs Isn't Finished with Apple." *Computer Reseller News,* October 16, 2000.

Fortt, Jon. "Jobs Trying to Revive Apple after Disappointing Year." *Knight-Ridder/Tribune Business News,* January 8, 2001.

"If the PC Doesn't Change, It'll Go the Way of the Dodo." *Business Week,* July 31, 2000.

Jobs, Steven. "Apple's One-Dollar-a-Year Man." *Fortune,* January 24, 2000.

Johnson, Cecil. "Warts-and-All Portrait of Steve Jobs a Valuable Account." *Knight-Ridder/Tribune Business News,* November 9, 2000.

"Steve Jobs' Apple Gets Way Cooler." *Fortune,* January 24, 2000.

SEE ALSO: Apple Computer; Wozniak, Steve

JUNO ONLINE SERVICES, INC.

New York-based Juno Online Services, Inc. was the third largest Internet service provider (ISP) in the U.S. prior to its merger with rival NetZero, Inc. In September of 2001, Juno Online Services and NetZero joined forces to become a new company, United Online. With more than 18 million registered accounts and 7 million active subscribers—those who access the Internet at least once a month—United Online surpassed Earthlink and became second only to America Online (AOL) among U.S. Internet access providers.

COMPANY HISTORY

Juno was founded in May of 1995 with the financial backing of David Shaw, an investment banker based in New York who once taught computer science at Columbia University. Other early investors in Juno included News Corp., Intel Corp., Prospect Street Ventures, and Sycamore Adventures. With four employees, the fledgling firm began offering its free email service eleven months later. Juno software was available via CD-ROM, or it could be downloaded from the firm's World Wide Web site; once users had loaded the software onto their machines, they could access Juno's servers by dialing a toll-free number. Juno marketed its free services in magazine advertisements and mailings that claimed, "E-mail was meant to be free." According to a January 2000 article in *BusinessWeek Online,* "A revolutionary, even audacious, idea at the time, Juno allowed its members to send and receive e-mail to or from anyone, anywhere on the Internet without charging a fee. The trade-off, as is the case with most free Net services, was that most users had to watch a series of ads in exchange for e-mail privileges. Although Juno members were only online long enough to download and upload messages, the company's proprietary technology kept pumping out a steady cycle of advertisers' pitches even as the users read or composed their e-mail offline." The ads appeared to customers as banners at the top of each page; users could then click on the banner to view more detailed information, and Juno could monitor the number of hits each advertisement received.

Many analysts considered the advertising business model upon which Juno was based promising. As a result, several competitors began to emerge, including NetZero, which was established in July of 1997. By mid-1998, more than five million users had signed up for Juno's free email services. In June of that year, Juno began offering its Premium Web service, which included full Internet access, for a $19.95 monthly fee. Management believed that as customers became more Web savvy, they would be willing to pay for enhanced services such as Premium Web. To differentiate itself from Juno, NetZero began offering free access to the Internet in October of 1998, prompting Juno to reduce its monthly Internet access fee to $9.95.

Subscribers grew to 6.5 million in early 1999. Juno conducted its initial public offering (IPO) that May. NetZero completed its IPO just a few months later, but with only 500,000 subscribers, the firm continued to lag far behind Juno. In December, Juno began offering full Internet access for free. The firm diversified into electronic commerce for the first time when it launched its Shop@Juno channel, which included links to Garden.com, Art.com, Bluefly, and 1-800-FLOWERS. This allowed the firm to add a third revenue source, a percentage of each sale originating at its shopping channel, to its business plan. However, advertising continued to bring in the bulk of sales, with subscriber fees making up most of the remainder. Sales grew 140 percent that year to $52 million.

Competition continued to intensify as several new ISPs—including BlueLight.com, owned by Kmart Corp.—began offering free email and Internet access. In April of 2000, QUALCOMM dumped $144 million into NetZero, and five months later, that firm's subscriber base reached 7 million. To boost its own subscriber base, Juno agreed to pay the bankrupt WorldSpy.com, another free ISP, to take over its 260,000 subscriber accounts. The firm also formed a strategic alliance with IBM Corp. by which IBM agreed to include Juno software on many of its personal computer (PC) lines. Also in 2000, Juno and broadband service provider Covad Communications launched Juno Express, the firm's digital subscriber line (DSL) service, a continual Internet connection roughly 21 times faster than a traditional modem-based connection. Within a few months, the high speed Internet access, which cost subscribers $49.95 per month, was available in more than 60 major markets in the U.S., including New York City; Milwaukee, Wisconsin; San Antonio, Texas; and Indianapolis, Indiana. Subscribers could also opt for high-speed mobile wireless access to the Internet, which Juno offered in conjunction with Metricom. Juno's sales grew 120 percent to $114 million that year, and subscribers exceeded the 12 million mark; however, the firm remained unprofitable, posting a $131.4 million loss.

Legal troubles with NetZero began in June of 2000 when Juno sued its competitor, alleging that NetZero infringed on its patent for technology that displays advertisements to users even when they are offline. Six months later, NetZero turned the tables and accused Juno of patent infringement, claiming that Juno had illegally copied portions of its ZeroPoint technology, which displays advertisements in a separate window.

Juno added a Games Channel to its online offerings in January 2001. Along with various types of games, including card, trivia, and simulation, the channel also included content from three leading game sites: Gamers.com, Boxerjam, and iEntertainment Network, Inc. Registered subscribers grew to 14 million. The release of Juno 5.0 included a mail assistant that allowed users to specify how they want e-mail messages sorted, integrated e-mail and Internet services, and an intelligent dialer that records the performance of all the access numbers used by each subscriber and selects the number most likely to offer a successful connection each time a user attempts to log on to Juno.

A BUSINESS MODEL CHALLENGED

Under mounting pressure from shareholders to produce profits, Juno began experimenting with ways to convince users to switch to fee-based services. According to a March 2001 article in *BusinessWeek Online,* the firm began making it more difficult for its most frequent users to log on to the free service. "The misconnects were no technical glitch. Juno was deliberately curbing heavy hitters' access to prod them into switching to its $14.95-a-month plan. The reason: A survey of its subscriber base revealed that a mere 5 percent of users of its free service accounted for most than half of Juno's online costs." Also forcing Juno to reexamine its free ISP model was the fact that the North American economic downturn in 2000 and 2001 prompted many firms, dot.com and otherwise, to tighten their online advertising budgets. With its main source of revenue drying up, Juno needed to find other sources of income.

By mid-2001, several of Juno's free ISP rivals had declared bankruptcy, and many analysts began to call into question the viability of the free ISP model. In June, Juno and NetZero announced their intent to merge; the deal was completed three months later. The newly merged firm, named United Online, was the second largest Internet access provider in the U.S. As stated by *Forbes.com* writer David Simons, "The haunting question is whether the merger creates a viable long-term business or just delays a fate already suffered by free Internet service providers around the world."

FURTHER READING:

Borrus, Amy. "Someone Has to Pay the Freight." *BusinessWeek Online,* March 26, 2001. Available from www.businessweek.com

Eads, Stefani. "Juno's Lesson: You Can't Give Everything Away." *BusinessWeek Online,* January 26, 2000. Available from www.businessweek.com

"Juno Launches Version 5.0 of its Internet Access Software." *Business Wire,* January 23, 2001.

"Juno's Broadband Service Now Available in 63 Markets; Juno Express DSL Expands into 39 New Markets." *Business Wire,* September 12, 2000.

Simons, David. "Marriage of Inconvenience." *Forbes,* June 11, 2001. Available from www.forbes.com.

Vargas, Alexia. "Digital New York." *Crain's New York Business,* July 17, 2000.

Verity, John. "Free E-Mail, But With a Catch." *BusinessWeek Online,* April 29, 1996. Available from www.businessweek.com.

SEE   Internet Service Provider (ISP)
ALSO:

JUPITER MEDIA METRIX

Jupiter Media Metrix is a leading market research and consulting firm that reports on the impact of the Internet and new technologies on commerce and marketing. Jupiter Media Metrix was formed in September 2000, when Media Metrix acquired Jupiter Communications for about $350 million in stock. The company's five business units were subsequently organized around its core competencies of measurement (Media Metrix), analysis (AdRelevance), intelligence (Jupiter Research), and events (Jupiter Events), with an international division (Jupiter Media Metrix International) focused on global expansion.

Jupiter Media Metrix provides audience measurement reports for Internet usage that are based on data collected from panels. The company's panels are randomly selected personal computer users, including at-home and at-work users, who are selected by random digit-dial telephone calls and direct mail. As of late 2001 the panel consisted of 50,000 individuals in the United States and another 50,000 located outside the U.S., all of whom were under continuous measurement. Through a proprietary metering system, the activity of each panel member's computer operating system and Web browser is monitored on a second-by-second basis.

The company's audience measurement database is then used to create a wide range of reports and services designed to help companies make intelligent business decisions regarding electronic commerce and the use of Internet and related technologies. A Key Measures report covers visitors and visitor demographics, among other measures, for all reportable Web sites by category. The database also tracks national and local market reach to show how national and local Web sites are performing within each of the top 38 local markets.

Other reports include the Q-Metrix Report, first introduced in 1999, which provides data on consumer media habits, product and service usage, lifestyle characteristics, and demographics. Among the specific areas covered in Q-Metrix Reports are banking and credit card activity, Internet shopping behavior, television viewing habits, and hobbies. The company's Online Shopping Report covers more than 500 Internet sites and the AOL Shopping Channel.

Another group of reports analyzes and reports on computer ownership and usage. The HardScan, SoftScan, and SoftUsage Reports produced by Jupiter Media Metrix cover hardware ownership, computer peripheral ownership, branding information, installed applications, and system software, including Internet browsers and the use of software applications. The company's Linkage Reports and its U.S. Consumer PC Report analyze the relationships between computer hardware, software, media, ownership, and usage.

In addition to publishing reports, Jupiter Media Metrix provides its clients with research services to help them make business decisions about Internet commerce and consumer and business use of the Internet and related new technologies. Using a wide range of data-gathering tools, Jupiter Media Metrix provides research services and products to help client companies set business and strategic goals, identify revenue opportunities, formulate and evaluate business models, develop and analyze marketing strategies, and determine which technologies and vendors are best suited to their needs.

Through its Jupiter Events division, Jupiter Media Metrix conducts numerous conferences and expositions focused on electronic commerce and new technologies for business. These two-to-three-day events provide the company with an opportunity to showcase its latest research and measurement products for clients and potential clients.

Jupiter Media Metrix operates globally. It maintains measurement panels and produces research products and services in nearly 15 countries in North and South America, Europe, and the Pacific Rim.

MEDIA METRIX AND JUPITER COMMUNICATIONS

Jupiter Media Metrix was formed in September 2000, when Media Metrix acquired Jupiter Communications. Established in 1986, Jupiter Communications was one of the first research firms to report on the dynamics of electronic commerce over the Internet. New York-based Media Metrix established itself as a leading measurement service for Internet usage in 1996, when it was spun off from market research firm the NPD Group. Media Metrix, which was originally named PC Meter, employed metering software to record the computer activity of its panelists. In 1997 the company changed its name to Media Metrix.

In 1998 Media Metrix acquired a major competitor, Relevant Knowledge, to form a comprehensive single source for reporting and analyzing Web usage. At the time Media Metrix was collecting data from about 30,000 panel members, while Relevant Knowledge had about 9,600 panelists. The two companies employed different methodologies, and Web advertisers hoped the merger would result in a single standard measurement system for Internet usage. Following the acquisition, Media Metrix had offices in New York, Atlanta, and San Francisco, and about 90 employees. The company built a client list of about 250 major companies and could measure 15,000 Web sites. Its major shareholder was the NPD Group.

Media Metrix went public in May 1999 with an initial public offering (IPO) that raised $51 million. During the year its client list grew to 500 companies, including major Internet players such as America Online and Yahoo!, large advertising agencies, and Wall Street firms. Media Metrix was a well-known brand and was frequently cited as a source of information on Internet usage and Web traffic. Following its IPO, Media Metrix sought to expand globally. With the help of local partners, it began supplying data on Internet usage in France, Germany, and the United Kingdom, to be followed by Australia, Japan, and Canada.

Media Metrix's primary competitor in 1999 was Nielsen/NetRatings, a joint venture formed by TV ratings giant Nielsen Media Research and NetRatings, an Internet research company spun off from Hitachi in July 1997. With a client list of 150 companies and some 33,000 panelists, Nielsen/NetRatings lagged behind Media Metrix, even as it attempted to distinguish itself by measuring ad banner traffic in addition to Web site usage. At the time Media Metrix was the only Internet measurement service that tracked Internet use in the workplace as well as at home. It was also the only service that tracked AOL subscribers. Toward the end of 1999 Media Metrix added the capability of measuring online ad traffic when it acquired AdRelevance, a research firm that tracked the results of online advertising.

MEDIA METRIX ACQUIRES JUPITER COMMUNICATIONS

In June 2000 Media Metrix announced it would acquire Jupiter Communications, an Internet research and consulting firm, for $414 million in stock. Following the announcement, however, Jupiter's stock fell by more than 8 percent, while Media Metrix's stock lost more than 17 percent, reducing the value of the stock-for-stock acquisition to about $350 million. The new company, called Jupiter Media Metrix, had more than 730 employees and 1,700 clients worldwide. Following the acquisition Jupiter Media Metrix reorganized into five divisions: Media Metrix, Ad-

Relevance, Jupiter Research, Jupiter Events, and Jupiter Media Metrix International. In addition to offering Internet audience measurement, the company also provided analyses of Internet trends and forecasts. Its consultants worked with clients to develop business models based on emerging trends in electronic commerce and Internet usage.

As it was for many other Internet companies, 2001 was a difficult year financially for Jupiter Media Metrix. The firm saw its stock decline to less than $1 a share by late 2001, down from $17.85 when Jupiter Media Metrix began trading as a single company in September 2000. The firm's long-time CEO, Tod Johnson, stepped down in March 2001. He was replaced later in the year by Robert Becker, an executive formerly with Infosis and the Thomson Corporation. Johnson remained as the company's chairman. In April the company laid off 18 percent of its staff and reported a net loss of $54.2 million for the quarter ending March 31, followed by a net loss of $48.2 million for the quarter ending June 30. It had to take a $25 million loan to remain in business while it sought a source of permanent funding. In October the company said it would eliminate another 180 workers, or 30 percent of its workforce, as part of its effort to trim $40 million in operating expenses. During the year Jupiter Media Metrix was also involved in patent infringement disputes with PC Data Online—which Jupiter won—and then with NetValue USA. While Jupiter Media Metrix added new services and enhanced existing ones in 2001, it was hard hit by the downturn in the Internet economy. By trimming its workforce and cutting costs, the company hoped to achieve profitability in the future.

FURTHER READING:

Flamm, Matthew. "A Merger's 1-2 Punch." *Crain's New York Business,* November 27, 2000.

Jupiter Media Metrix. "Corporate Fact Sheet." October 17, 2001. Available from www.jmm.com

Kerschbaumer, Ken. "Media Metrix, Jupiter Merge." *Broadcasting & Cable,* July 3, 2000.

Konicki, Steve. "Economic Slowdown Hits Hard at Analyst Firms." *InformationWeek,* September 10, 2001.

"Service Tracks Ad Relevance." *InternetWeek,* October 9, 2000.

Taylor, Catharine P. "Jupiter Enhances Tracking." *Advertising Age,* September 24, 2001.

———. "Jupiter Offers Vertical Reports for Nine Areas." *Advertising Age,* April 9, 2001.

———. "No More Hot Air: Panels, Not Parties, Mark Jupiter's Ad Confab." *Advertising Age,* August 13, 2001.

Wang, Nelson. "Merger to Unite Leaders in Audience Measurement." *Internet World,* October 19, 1998.

SEE Forrester Research Inv.; International Data Corp.
ALSO: (IDC); Internet Access, Tracking Growth of

K

KAPOR, MITCHELL D.

Mitchell D. Kapor is the founder of Lotus Development Corp. and co-developer of the Lotus 1-2-3 spreadsheet, considered the first "killer" software application. Many analysts credit 1-2-3 for being the catalyst that sparked widespread use of personal computers (PCs). Kapor served as CEO of Lotus until 1986, when he left to pursue other ventures, including the creation of network-utilities developer On Technology Inc. Kapor also went on to invest in several startups that evolved into major Internet players, including Uunet Technologies Inc, PSInet, and Real Networks.

After earning a degree in psychology from Yale University in 1974, Kapor worked as a disc jockey for WHCN-FM. In 1976, he began pursuing a graduate degree at the Sloan School of Business at the Massachusetts Institute of Technology (MIT). Kapor started developing his interest in computers at this time, and he purchased an Apple II machine. While working as a diskette librarian, he began tinkering with his first software product, a time series analysis application for the Apple II. Dubbed Tiny Troll, the program was modeled on the Troll mainframe system used by the National Bureau of Economic Research. Through friends Dan Bricklin and Bob Frankston—developers of VisiCalc, the first spreadsheet application for computers—Kapor met Dan Fylstra, founder of California-based Personal Software, which marketed VisiCalc products. Soon thereafter, Kapor decided to forgo his graduate studies. He moved to the West Coast and took a management position with Personal Software which eventually paid Kapor millions of dollars for his Tiny Troll program.

Kapor moved back to the East Coast in the early 1980s. He founded Lotus in 1982 to develop software programs for PCs. The following year, Kapor took Lotus public, selling more than 2 million shares for $18 each and raising nearly $41 million for research and development. That year, Jonathan Sachs and Kapor developed the first version of the Lotus 1-2-3 spreadsheet program. The program quickly surpassed VisiCalc as the top selling spreadsheet, and Kapor eventually bought out VisiCalc's founders. In fact, in less than a year, 1-2-3 propelled Lotus, with revenues of $53 million, to second place in the U.S. software manufacturing industry. Th impact of 1-2-3 was farther reaching than many realized, wrote *Computer Reseller News* columnist Lee Pender. Although the program offered the fastest and simplest calculation capabilities of any spreadsheet application to date, "1-2-3 would really come to mean much more to the industry. Its popularity would launch IBM Corp.'s fledgling personal computer, a device that had lacked the kind of practical application it needed to take off. 1-2-3 was the answer, and it and the applications that followed would put a PC on top of every desk in the business world."

As the growth of Lotus intensified, Kapor realized he needed management help. As a result, he hired James P. Manzi as president in 1984, retaining the position of chairman. That year, Lotus broadened its focus. For example, the firm began working on Symphony, which brought word processing and database management programs together with 1-2-3 in one of the first integrated software "suites." To develop Symphony, Kapor hired Ray Ozzie, agreeing to finance an idea of Ozzie's that would later evolve into the blockbuster Lotus Notes messaging system.

Because Lotus grew into a firm larger than he cared to manage, Kapor resigned from the company in 1986. His activities in the 1980s and 1990s included running various non-profit foundations, establishing new technology firms, and helping to fund Internet startups. In January 1999, venture capital firm Accel Partners named Kapor a partner. The technology pioneer also continues to publish articles in *Wired, Forbes,* and other leading publications.

FURTHER READING:

Hazlewood, Sara. "Lotus Founder Quietly Busy in the Venture Capital Arena." *The Business Journal,* February 11, 2000.

"Lotus Development Corp." In *Notable Corporate Chronologies.* Farmington Hills, MI: Gale Group, 1999.

Pender, Lee. "The Killer App Comes Alive—Lotus 1-2-3." *Computer Reseller News,* November 15, 1998.

Picarille, Lisa. "Where Are They Now?: Mitch Kapor: President, Electronic Frontier Foundation, San Francisco." *Computer Reseller News,* November 18, 1998.

Taft, Darryl K. "Mitch Kapor." *Computer Reseller News,* November 16, 1997.

SEE ALSO: Killer Applications; Lotus Development Corp.

KILLER APPLICATIONS

Having risen to prominence in the mid-1990s alongside the start of the Internet boom, "killer applications" (or "killer apps") is industry jargon for compelling uses for a technology. Technology developers and industry watchers deem an application "killer" when it drives high sales and wide adoption, possibly even creating whole new markets, paradigms, and categories of technology. In this sense, e-mail is commonly seen as one of the founding killer apps of the Internet because its speed, ease of use, and asynchronous nature appeal to everyone from scientists to high-school kids. The same could be said of graphical Web browsers. By contrast, technologies are often said to fail when they lack a killer app.

Yet part of the glory of a killer app is not simply wild success at the cash register, but relates to having a clearly defined, even narrow, purpose that makes the technology essential for a group of users, not just nice to have. So Internet, and especially Web, access became the killer apps of PC dial-up modems, even while the devices could also be used for peer networking with other PCs or for dialing into electronic bulletin board systems. Internet access became the defining use and made modems standard equipment on many PCs. However, the case isn't as clear with high-speed services like cable Internet and DSL. Certainly, these are also used for the same purposes as dial-up modems. But as yet, there's been no single, noteworthy use that distinguishes high-speed services, other than perhaps a vague notion of large file transfers for musical recordings, media clips, and so on. Thus everything tends to be faster, but for users sending e-mail and doing light Web browsing, the difference may be negligible. For many users in the early 2000s, at least, these benefits were only a moderate convenience relative to their costs.

Because having a killer app translates into having potential for brisk sales, technology analysts and strategists frequently speak of "the next killer app." At times the discussion is framed as a search to identify the next big application in a certain area of technology. An analyst, for instance, might lay out a description of the important technical features of a new piece of technology—say, wireless Internet access—and suggest what features have the most revolutionary potential for new applications. Other observers take more of a determinist view, naming the exact technology and perhaps forecasting how successful it will be in monetary terms. Of course, these predictions don't always pan out; unified messaging, or bringing together voice, e-mail, and fax capabilities, is one concept that has regularly been heralded as a killer app for various software and service providers, but one which has usually disappointed its advocates.

KILLER APPS THAT WEREN'T

Oftentimes the missing killer app is considered a harbinger of failure. A classic example comes from Apple Computer's Newton. Sophisticated and highly featured for its time, this handheld computer was unveiled with great fanfare in 1993 only to suffer disappointing sales and cancellation a few years later. Some attribute the Newton's demise to being too revolutionary, but its failure to catch on—as with other PDAs at the time—can also be traced to a dearth of clear, motivating benefits. It had a variety of uses, including an address book, a word processor, and a calendar, but for the most part didn't offer compelling new capabilities of wide interest.

More recent victims, lacking a killer app, may include DSL and cable Internet services, as suggested earlier. In the early 2000s, following a dash to roll out these high-bandwidth offerings, growth in new subscriptions began to taper off quickly and service providers faced losses and cash shortages in the wake of their heavy investments. Nonetheless they were far from failing altogether, and some believed that demand for high-speed services would rebound once a true killer app, such as movies on demand, reliable voice-over-Internet services, or new interactive video applications, took hold. Similarly, a driving application for wireless Internet services and devices, notably those offering Web browsing on handheld machines, has been called into question. Clearly these benefit certain types of businesses with personnel constantly on the move and in hard-to-network settings, but general devices were not meeting with overwhelming demand, at least in their early stages.

THE DEATH OF KILLER APPS?

What's more, if e-mail and the graphical Web are the quintessential killer apps, some question how easily developers can in fact turn out new killer apps. Many of the purported killer apps for technologies did not materialize, and it may reveal something about how difficult it is to develop an application that unleashes a new technological paradigm. DSL and cable Internet, absent new capabilities that set them apart from other connectivity technologies, were merely incremental improvements over dial-up access. Few things are as ubiquitous and natural in people's daily lives as simple text messaging—a new medium for interpersonal communications. And massive content systems like the Web take extraordinary time and cost to develop. As a result, some observers believe that most of the ''next'' killer apps will be much more limited in scope and effect than were these classic innovations of the information age; businesses will require strategies to cope when there are no killer apps in the making.

FURTHER READING:

''Broadband Waits for Killer App.'' *Internet Magazine,* July, 2001.

Hall, Karen. ''In Search of the Killer App.'' *Computer Dealer News,* August 3, 2001.

Ladley, Eric. ''Without 'Killer App' DSL is Doomed.'' *ISP Business News,* May 5, 2000.

Sanghi, Steve. ''Achieving Hyper Growth Without 'The Killer App.''' *Electronic News,* September 25, 2000.

Shaw, Russell. ''Stalking the Killer App.'' *Broadcasting & Cable,* January 15, 2001.

SEE ALSO: History of the Internet and World Wide Web (WWW)

KIOSKS

Web-enabled kiosks made their debut in 1996. One of the first retailers to make extensive use of in-store kiosks was outdoor sports retailer REI (Recreation Equipment Inc.), which had kiosks in 58 stores by fall 2000. Its in-store kiosks provided customers with access to 78,000 products available on its Web site.

At the end of 2000 kiosks were not widely deployed. Those that were installed seemed to attract little consumer interest. Forrester Research estimated that there were as many as 15,000 Internet kiosks internationally at the beginning of 2001, with some 100 companies planning to use them in retail settings. Forrester found that 80 percent of all major retailers planned to install kiosks by 2002.

It was reported that kiosks were beginning to make an impact in the retail sector at the beginning of 2001, albeit slowly. Among the issues retail stores needed to consider were whether the kiosks would be self-service or assisted, where they should be located, and what products and services would be listed on the kiosks.

Kiosk basics include a personal computer, a telephone connection, speakers, and a printer. By adding a credit-card reader and a touch screen, the kiosk becomes a sales channel. Additional features include scanners, which can be programmed to read a product's bar code and to provide additional information about the product.

Typically, kiosks link to the company's Web site but not to the wider Internet. They often have customized features. Retail applications and benefits include being able to list a wider range of products without having to add shelf space. Kiosks let customers find information on products and make comparisons. They can provide gift registries and credit applications as well as speed up customer service and help sales associates close a sale.

The content that a retailer puts on a kiosk can include more than a Web connection to the company's Web site. Kiosks are capable of carrying sound and video in addition to an Internet connection, thus making them potential multimedia displays. They have the capability of carrying multimedia presentations about the company, its stores, and special promotions and events.

KIOSKS OFFER BENEFITS TO CONSUMERS AND RETAILERS

Kiosks are used to offer information, provide Internet access, and allow customers to shop online. Web kiosks enable retailers to bring the Internet into their stores. While in the store, customers can shop online at the kiosk at the store's Web site. In-store kiosks can help sell a retailer's Web site and direct traffic there. Kiosks can also be a way to introduce non-Internet users to the Internet and encourage them to do more online shopping.

Kiosks are also a cost-effective way to increase the number of products available. They help retailers capture sales that might have been lost due to out-of-stock merchandise. If kiosks became widely accepted by consumers, retailers would be free to build smaller stores and let the kiosks provide access to a wider range of products.

Within the store, kiosks must be strategically placed and user-friendly. It is also helpful if they provide more information than is available at the retailer's Web site. They can be used as a source of additional product information, both by sales staff and by shoppers.

Compared to online shopping from home, kiosks offer several unique benefits to both consumers and retailers. Using an in-store kiosk allows customers to still touch and feel merchandise. At the same time, retailers can keep smaller quantities of merchandise in stock and let the kiosk offer customers access to products in a range of sizes and colors. For large items that are difficult to ship, such as furniture, customers can see floor samples in the store and order the merchandise online through the kiosk. Kiosks also offer more payment options than shopping online from home. Customers using an in-store kiosk are often given the option of paying for their order with cash or a check at the register.

RETAIL AND OTHER APPLICATIONS

Retailers with in-store kiosks included Bloomingdale's, where kiosks gave shoppers information on hot-selling items and prompted them to buy. The kiosks also displayed and sold catalog items. For the 2000 holiday shopping season, Bloomingdale's added second-generation software that enabled the company to produce its own editorial content and promote special events through live chats and other multimedia presentations. Bloomingdale's kiosks also had an e-mail feature that allowed customers to send e-mail postcards to their friends and attach digital photos of children with Santa Claus taken at the store. The kiosks also included store maps and could be customized for a particular location. Bloomingdale's considered its "eOsks" as empowering the consumer by providing them with convenience and expediency.

At the end of 2000 BlueLight.com, Kmart's e-commerce subsidiary, planned to roll out 3,500 Internet-enabled kiosks at about half of the 2,100 Kmart and Super K stores nationally. Customers in Kmart stores would be able to shop online at BlueLight.com and make payments either through a credit card, an alternative payment solution tied to their checking account, or by using a Kmart cash card. The in-store kiosks were located at customer service desks. They were intended to initiate consumers to the Internet. In addition, BlueLight.com passed out CDs that would provide customers with free Internet access. The kiosks represented a way for BlueLight.com to attract new customers as well as a new channel for Kmart to boost revenue. Orders received online and via kiosks were outsourced to SubmitOrder.com for fulfillment. Five months after the 3,500 BlueLight.com kiosks were installed in Kmart stores, the company reported that 20 percent of all BlueLight.com shoppers came from inside Kmart stores.

Kiosks were installed in 91 Store of Knowledge stores by publisher Dorling Kindersley in 2000. The Store of Knowledge retail chain sells educational toys, games, and books. Its kiosks enabled users to search for gifts according to the recipient's age and by type of merchandise. Users could also order gifts online, specify gift wrapping, and then pick up the gifts at a nearby store.

At the end of 2000, Service Merchandise, a discount jewelry and houseware retailer, was installing kiosks in its 220 stores as part of the firm's makeover following its reorganization. The kiosks were designed with the capability of printing coupons for consumers.

At Borders Books & Music, kiosks provide access to some 3 million items, while an individual Borders store could only carry some 200,000 items at a time. The kiosks featured a "Title Sleuth" that found books by title as well as store maps showing where a particular book was shelved. Similar kiosks at rival Barnes & Noble succeeded in driving traffic to Barnesandnoble.com, helping to push the Web site's book sales past those of Amazon.com in the first quarter of 2001.

By February 2001 office products retailer Staples had installed Web kiosks in all of its 954 stores. Staples' in-store kiosks provided customers with access to some 45,000 products listed at Staples.com, compared to 7,500 items carried in a typical store. The kiosks also provided customers with access to 10,000 downloadable software titles and a range of business services. Online purchases made through the kiosks could be paid for by cash, check, or credit card at the stores' registers.

Other retail chains with in-store kiosks included RadioShack, where Web-enabled kiosks provided sales staff and customers with a way to look up products, including many that were not in stock at the store. General Nutrition Center stores had small kiosks that provided information on food supplements.

Kiosks were also being deployed in banks and other financial institutions in 2001. Bank One Corp. installed two types of kiosks at different branches throughout the country. One type of kiosk, made by WingspanBank.com, was intended to attract new customers to Bank One's new Internet-only bank. The other bankone.com kiosks offered customers access to bankone.com's financial services, including online banking, bill payment, investing, and small business and commercial services.

Gas stations and convenience stores were emerging avenues for kiosks as well. The December 2000 NACS (National Association of Convenience Stores) convention featured a wide range of Internet kiosks. NCR displayed several Internet kiosk systems with different application development partners.

CONSUMER ACCEPTANCE KEY TO WIDER DEPLOYMENT

Experts admit that kiosks often fail for a variety of reasons, ranging from poor in-store location to technical problems with blank screens and printers that don't work. Retailers must be able to articulate why they want kiosks in their stores and integrate them into their retail strategy. After Hallmark installed kiosks that allowed customers to create their own greeting cards, the company found that consumers preferred to purchase stock greeting cards rather than create their own. Other problems included poor management, apathetic staff, and technological snafus.

While there are kiosk solution providers, the kiosk industry was fragmented in the early 2000s. Retailers typically purchased kiosk enclosures from one source, software from another, and possibly required a third vendor to maintain the kiosks. While some retailers successfully installed kiosks and found a profitable use for them, many others needed to develop a marketing plan to take full advantage of the possible benefits of maintaining in-store kiosks, including improved customer service, marketing and promotion, branding, and sales. Retailers needed to carefully plan to maximize the benefits of in-store kiosks. However, the driving force for wider deployment of kiosks remained consumer acceptance, and consumers will be more likely to accept and use kiosks if they are an integral part of a customer-focused retail strategy.

FURTHER READING:

Alexander, Brian. "The Kiosks, Where Brick Meets Click." *The New York Times,* December 13, 2000.

"The Box That Rocks." *Business Week,* June 4, 2001.

Cleary, Mike. "Box on the Rocks." *Interactive Week,* January 15, 2001.

Davis, Jessica. "Staples, Other Retailers Sign on to Web Kiosk Bandwagon." *InfoWorld,* February 5, 2001.

Enos, Lori. "E-Tail Invades the Real World." *E-Commerce Times,* February 12, 2001. Available from www.ecommercetimes.com.

Forman, Preston P. "Down to Business—Kiosks Becoming Retail's New Channel." *Computer Reseller News,* November 20, 2000.

Hickins, Michael. "Kmart's Online Hookup in Stores." *WWD,* December 27, 2000.

"In-Store Kiosks: Kick-Starting Web Sales?" *Display & Design Ideas,* October 2000.

Mearian, Lucas. "Staples Joins Kiosk Retailers." *Computerworld,* February 5, 2001.

O'Neill, Meaghan. "What's in Store Online?" *FamilyPC,* February 2001.

Ptacek, Megan J. "First Wingspan Kiosks; Now BankOne.com Kiosks Too." *American Banker,* March 23, 2001.

Reid, Keith. "Internet Everywhere at NACS." *National Petroleum News,* December 2000.

SEE ALSO: BlueLight.com LLC

KNIGHT-RIDDER INC.

Knight-Ridder is the third-largest U.S. newspaper publisher with sales of $3.2 billion, roughly 22,000 employees, daily circulation rates of 9 million, and Sunday circulation rates of 13 million. Behind both Gannett and Tribune Co. in print operations, the firm is considered a leader in online newspaper publishing. However, despite the success of the firm's Internet operations, the North American economic slowdown in 2000 and 2001 prompted Knight-Ridder to lay off roughly 16 percent of its Internet-related employees.

HISTORY OF RIDDER PUBLICATIONS

Knight-Ridder Inc. dates back to 1892, when Herman Ridder bought the *Staats-Zeitung,* a newspaper written for the German residents of New York City. Ridder expanded in 1926, acquiring the *Journal of Commerce.* In 1942, Ridder Publications incorporated in Delaware. Acquisitions that decade included *Post Tribune* in Gary, Indiana, and various newspapers in Washington and California. The firm also diversified into radio and television for the first time with the purchase of Minneapolis, Minnesota-based WCCO. In 1969, Ridder conducted its initial public offering and bought the *Daily Camera,* a newspaper published in Boulder, Colorado. Four years later, Ridder acquired Beacon Publishing Co. and the *Wichita Eagle.* Profits reached $14 million on sales of $166 million.

HISTORY OF KNIGHT NEWSPAPERS

In 1903, Charles Landon Knight exited the legal profession and bought the *Akron Beacon Journal.* By the late 1930s, Knight's sons had taken over the family business. They paid $2.25 million for the *Miami Herald* in 1937. The brothers also bought the competing *Miami Tribune* to gain access to its new printing press, as well as additional equipment and facilities. Eventually, the Knights stopped publishing the *Miami Tribune..* In 1939, they enhanced the *Miami Herald* with additional photographs, comic strips, and new columns.

By 1940, the Knight brothers had adopted the Knight Newspapers moniker. Accomplishments early in the decade included the acquisition of the *Detroit Free Press,* the $3 million purchase of the *Chicago Daily News,* and incorporation in Ohio. In 1946, *Miami Herald* editor Lee Hills launched the *Clipper Edition,* a consolidated version of the newspaper that was distributed to several Latin American countries. A fire destroyed the Miami newsprint warehouse in 1949. The following year, the *Miami Herald* was awarded its first Pulitzer Prize for uncovering government corruption in Southern Florida. Knight Newspapers added the *Charlotte Observer* to its lineup in 1956. Three years later, it purchased rival *The Charlotte News.* The *Chicago Daily News* was divested to Marshall Field for $17 million.

CEO James Knight brought Alvah H. Chapman Jr. on board as his assistant in 1960. It was Chapman who first spearheaded the use of computers for tasks ranging from administration and advertising to layout, typesetting, and production. In 1965, the *Tallahassee Democrat* was acquired. That purchase was followed by four more in 1969: the *The Philadelphia News,* the *Philadelphia Inquirer,* the *Macon Telegraph,* and the *Macon News.* The strategy of owning more than one newspaper in a given market worked to eradicate competition for Knight. By the end of the decade, daily circulation had exceeded 2 million, and the company had conducted its initial public offering. Sales in the early 1970s reached $350 million, with profits of roughly $23 million. Knight added another five daily newspapers to its holdings, including two in Columbus, Georgia, two in Lexington, Kentucky, and one in Florida.

OPERATING AS KNIGHT-RIDDER INC.

In November of 1974, Knight Newspapers merged with Ridder Publications to form Knight-Ridder Newspapers, the largest newspaper publisher in the United States with 35 papers in 25 cities and a total daily circulation of 3.8 million and a Sunday circulation of 4.2 million. To receive Federal Communications Commission approval for the merger,

Ridder had agreed to sell off its radio and television operations. In 1976, Knight-Ridder Newspapers changed its name to Knight-Ridder Inc. Two years later, the firm purchased VHF stations in Michigan, New York, and Rhode Island. Acquisitions in 1979 included Adams Inc., Fisher Publishing Inc., and Nittany Printing and Publishing Co.

Knight-Ridder diversified into cable television in 1981 via a joint venture with Denver, Colorado-based Tele-Communications Inc. The firm also bought a television station in Norfolk, Virginia. A pioneer in making information available online, Knight-Ridder launched an electronic library retrieval system, called VU/TEXT, in 1982. The following year, Knight-Ridder created a business information services division; acquired WNGE-TV in Nashville, Tennessee; and created Viewdata Corp. to offer news and financial services on home computers. In 1985, the online Knight-Ridder Graphics Network was put in place to serve Knight-Ridder newspapers. The firm paid $311 million for the six newspapers owned by Columbia, South Carolina-based State Record Co. in 1986. That year, the Knight-Ridder Graphics Network began selling its service to competing papers for $50 to $300 a month, depending on circulation rates, and the Viewdata unit was shuttered due to minimal demand. Knight-Ridder paid $353 million for Lockheed Corp.'s Dialog Information Services in 1988. The firm found that its Business Information Services division was growing at threefold the rate of newspaper operations, although newspapers still accounted for nearly 90 percent of sales. By the end of the decade, the company had divested its television broadcasting arm.

INCREASED FOCUS ON ONLINE TECHNOLOGY

In 1991, Knight-Ridder and Tribune Co. formed a joint venture to electronically deliver business news to personal computer users. The firm's Dialog unit unveiled technology that allowed users to purchase a license while online and avoid copyright law infringement. Knight-Ridder published *The San Jose Mercury News* on America Online in May of 1993, marking the debut of the first newspaper published in its entirety online. A wide-area network (WAN), put in place by MCI Telecommunications Corp. in 1994, allowed Knight-Ridder to link all of its offices via email and also to centralize its human resources operations. Economist Group bought the *Journal of Commerce* for $115 million in 1995. That year, Knight-Ridder acquired a stake in an Internet-based newspaper service known as InfiNet; published the *The San Jose Mercury News* on the World Wide Web; and joined forces with four other firms to acquire an 11-percent stake in Netscape Communications Corp. Other purchases included Carl Corp., Uncover Co., and Lesher Communications. Knight-Ridder sold its cable holdings back to TeleCommunications Inc. in 1996. It also became the first leading newspaper publisher to make all of its newspapers available online.

After deciding in 1997 to refocus on its newspaper operations, both print and online, the firm paid $1.65 billion to Walt Disney Co.'s ABC for four newspapers. That year, Knight-Ridder also replaced its WAN with a World Wide Web-based intranet, which it used to streamline procurement procedures. A major online advertising campaign began in January of 1998, when Knight-Ridder began developing its Real Cities series of regional information Web sites. By that time the company was already considered a major contender in the online classified advertising market. Knight-Ridder also eliminated the hyphen from its official name and moved headquarters from Miami, Florida, to San Jose, California. In November of 1999, Knight-Ridder folded the Internet-based operations of its daily newspapers into a new unit, dubbed KnightRidder.com.

In 2000, Yahoo! contracted Knight-Ridder to provide local and regional news on its My Yahoo! customized Web pages. To distance itself from the dot-com fallout, the firm changed the name of its KnightRidder.com unit to Knight-Ridder Digital in 2001. Cost cutting measures, including layoffs, continued as Knight-Ridder strove to improve its earnings despite the economic downturn in North America.

FURTHER READING:

"History of Knight-Ridder, Inc." San Jose, California: 2001. Available from www.kri.com.

"Knight-Ridder Inc." In *Notable Corporate Chronologies.* Farmington Hills, MI: Gale Group, 1999.

"Knight-Ridder Plans Net Venture." *Phildelphia Business Journal.* November 12, 1999.

Moses, Lucia. "Knight-Ridder Into Spirit of the Season." *Editor & Publisher.* January 1, 2001.

Sliwa, Carol. "Intranet Helps Knight-Ridder Centralize Buys." *Computerworld.* December 29, 1997.

Violino, Bob. "Technology on the Front Page." *InformationWeek.* September 14, 1998.

SEE ALSO: Content Provider; Electronic Publishing; Wide Area Network (WAN)

KNOWLEDGE MANAGEMENT

Although knowledge management assumes a variety of meanings depending on the context, the most basic idea behind knowledge management is the sharing of knowledge and information in an efficient and productive manner. As the Information Age, and particularly the Internet, dramatically expanded the wealth of information available and necessary to companies' operations, the efficiency of information and knowledge flow, through and between firms, in the knowledge-centered economy grew into a paramount concern. Computer and information technology developed in the 1980s and 1990s forced a shift of the field of competition to these grounds, and thus firms hoping to remain competitive needed to take account of how their knowledge is used within their organizations.

Knowledge management emerged as a central concern among businesses in the late 1980s and early 1990s, although the field itself dated back to the 1970s, when researchers at Stanford University and the Massachusetts Institute of Technology collaborated on a study of information transfer within organizations. By the late 1980s, the field had developed to such an extent that industry observers grew increasingly aware that businesses needed to take notice in order to utilize their resources efficiently and remain competitive. The increasingly global nature of major companies, along with corporate downsizing and restructuring, also brought with it a massive turn toward knowledge management as companies strove to eliminate redundancy and coordinate its efforts over a broader area. Knowledge management, by the turn of the 21st century, had emerged as one of the chief concerns of most major companies, with more than half of the *Fortune* 1000 firms expected to implement knowledge-management systems by 2003, according to the Gartner Group, and with many of these companies devising new positions within their ranks for knowledge managers.

In the field of knowledge management, theorists distinguish between information and knowledge. Information and data are the unprocessed mass of material available to a company for scrutiny, while knowledge has been processed and put to a practical use. Thus, information cannot be used to solve a problem until it has been intelligently processed and converted into knowledge. For example, a company may design a database to extract knowledge from a mass of information; knowledge management then seeks to implement that knowledge in the best possible manner to advance the company, determining how that knowledge can continue to be accessed, used, and manipulated.

Knowledge management aims at the elimination of redundancy in the company, as when two employees in different departments duplicate each other's actions by devising solutions to the same problem. By pooling the company's resources and working to retain knowledge within the company and enhance the flow of information, firms can realize substantial gains in an area to which investors were paying increasing attention.

As knowledge management proved an increasingly central concern among companies and IT managers, it spawned a vibrant industry of software builders and service providers designed to help businesses make the best use of their intellectual capital and capitalize on its promise. At the most basic level, companies install identical, or at least compatible, software on their computers, particularly for communications applications, and install an intranet (sometimes described as a network linking the computers), within a company to a central server.

Companies typically build knowledge management systems around this centralized network, which sorts and makes accessible to its employees all the available repositories of knowledge in searchable and sharable formats. In this way, particular problems require solving only once, after which employees in different departments or divisions need only access the knowledge-management network and search for a particular kind of solution, thereby eliminating the duplication of efforts. Moreover, employees can build on accumulated knowledge bank to devise solutions to new problems, rather than being continually forced to start from scratch. To aid this process, companies may wish to quantify and classify their problem-solving techniques and approaches to various business situations, and take an inventory of the kinds of expertise existing among the employee ranks. In addition, many companies establish an entire digital library to store all vital documents and the available knowledge accumulated through these means.

Knowledge management is not, however, just a series of technological innovations. For a company to truly reap the benefits of knowledge management, it must be an integral part of the corporate culture. That is, the internal practices, communications, structures, habits, and atmosphere of the company must be conducive to the kind of knowledge sharing on which knowledge management depends. Employees must be encouraged to share knowledge between them, either informally or by having them work in teams that continually interact, and employers must remain open to accepting ideas from and continually interacting with their subordinates. In short, the company must feel comfortable with the sharing of knowledge, and individuals must feel that they will be rewarded even if their ideas are disseminated throughout the company.

FURTHER READING:

Birkinshaw, Julian. "Making Sense of Knowledge Management." *Ivey Business Journal,* March/April, 2001.

Doucet, Kristin. "Know What You Know." *CMA Management,* March, 2001.

Johne, Marjo. "What Do You Know?" *CMA Management,* March, 2001.

Krogh, Georg von, and Johan Roos, eds. *Managing Knowledge.* London: Sage Publications, 1996.

Ruber, Peter. "Keep the Knowledge You're Paying For." *Information Week,* October 30, 2000.

SEE ALSO: Data Mining; Intellectual Capital

KNOWLEDGE WORKER

The Industrial Revolution gave birth to a large base of manufacturing jobs. These often required physical labor but little thought on the part of workers: employees repetitively operated machines and performed a limited range of physical tasks. During the latter half of the 20th century, however, information began to play a more central role in the world of work, particularly in advanced industrial economies. This process shifted the job base away from manufacturing and toward new forms of labor. With the introduction of computers, it became possible for companies to process, analyze, and share vast amounts of data. As the processing speed and memory capacity of computers increased and the number of users connected to networks grew, the role of knowledge and information also grew in importance.

The term "knowledge worker" describes workers whose roles involve making decisions and analyzing information. It is sometimes used in the wider context of knowledge management, which refers to how companies manage and use intellectual capital, or what their employees know. Although many assume the term "knowledge worker" is new, it actually was coined by well-known business commentator Peter Drucker in his 1959 book *Landmarks of Tomorrow.* It not only includes people in technical fields, but extends to other professionals and students in fields like science, law, and education.

A variety of tasks are central to the role of a knowledge worker including planning, marketing, researching, analyzing, strategizing, communicating, organizing, and negotiating. According to The Kudos Partnership Ltd., a U.K.-based provider of information and human resources services, knowledge workers are defined by three broad characteristics: being part of real or virtual teams; using information technology for everyday tasks; and working with information that provides a business advantage and that impacts results. *Automotive Manufacturing & Production* explains that there are different classes of knowledge workers: those who perform specialty knowledge work; those with more portable knowledge, including those with graduate degrees in business; and those who focus on the creation of knowledge and innovation like engineers and programmers.

In the early 2000s formal training was available for those interested in harnessing the full potential of knowledge work. The Innovation Management Institute offered the Knowledge Management Certification Program "designed to provide education and support to serious KM practitioners." Complying with standards established by the Knowledge Management Certification Board, the program was used by more than 1,000 professionals from organizations like IBM, Xerox, Compaq, Pfizer, the U.S. Navy, and AT&T Solutions.

FURTHER READING:

Dove, Rick. "The Knowledge Worker." *Automotive Manufacturing & Production*. June 1998.

"Enter the Knowledge Worker." The Kudos Partnership Ltd. June 13, 2001. Available from www.kudos-uk.com.

"KM Certification Training Program Overview." Innovation Management Institute. June 13, 2001. Available from www.eknowledgecenter.com.

SEE
ALSO:
Information Revolution vs. Industrial Revolution; Intellectual Capital; Knowledge Management; Workforce, E-commerce

KOOGLE, TIMOTHY

Timothy Koogle is CEO of Yahoo! Inc., the most heavily trafficked Internet portal in the world with roughly 100 million visitors every month. For free, Yahoo! browsers can do everything from sending and receiving email and searching for old classmates to booking airline flights and car rentals and creating online photo albums. Koogle oversaw Yahoo!'s growth from a small upstart Internet search engine company in 1995 into an online powerhouse that offers more than 400 different services to its individual and business customers. Koogle is also credited for parlaying the firm into one of the few dot.com ventures to actually earn a profit. Although he announced plans to step down as CEO Yahoo! in 2001, Koogle will remain chairman.

After completing his undergraduate work in mechanical engineering at the University of Virginia in 1973, Koogle began pursuing a graduate degree at Stanford University. He earned a Master's degree in electrical engineering in 1975 and a Ph.D. in mathe-

matics a few years later. Koogle paid for school by working as an automobile mechanic for his fellow students. An attempt to create his own robotics company fizzled in 1982, and Motorola Corp. hired him a year later as a management executive. In 1992, Koogle was named president at Intermec, a data communications firm based in Seattle, Washington, known for creating bar-code technology.

In early 1995, Yahoo!'s young founders, 27-year-old Jerry Yang and 30-year-old David Filo, began searching for a seasoned executive to run the business that had started with a simple list of favorite World Wide Web sites. Yang and Filo knew they lacked the management experience to run a company, and they sought someone with an entrepreneurial spirit who could also lend the fledgling firm credibility. When they asked the 49-year-old Koogle to head up Yahoo!, he was still working for Intermec, which was owned by Litton Industries. His frustrations there over Litton's reticence to let him pursue rapid growth outweighed his uncertainty about the viability of a Web-based business. Koogle agreed to run Yahoo! in May of 1995. The firm's lucrative initial public offering in April 1996 allowed Koogle to launch an acquisition spree that would eventually exceed $10 billion. In September of 1997, Yahoo! bought a news delivery service, as well as technology that allowed it to add people-searching and e-mail capabilities to its free online services. Purchases in the following year allowed Yahoo! users to play games and shop. Koogle also oversaw two major deals in 1999: the $4 billion acquisition of Geocities and the $5.7 billion acquisition of video service provider Broadcast.com. Koogle's reason for the bold growth strategy was simple: the more features, services, and content Yahoo! offered, the more visitors it would attract. More visitors meant more advertising dollars.

Advertising is what allowed Yahoo! to set itself apart from other dot.com upstarts because it was advertising that enabled Yahoo! to achieve profitability. The firm developed technology that allowed it to monitor a visitor's online activity and also control what banner bars and button ads are displayed on the pages that visitor is browsing. Yahoo! is also able to monitor how many hits an advertisement receives, a valuable tool for determining an advertisement's reach.

Business Week named Koogle one of the "Top 25 Executives of the Year" in 1999. That year, Yahoo! became the only Internet-based venture besides America Online to be listed on Standard & Poor's 500 stock index. Yahoo! stock reached a high of $237.50 per share in January 2000. Like most other Internet-based ventures, though, Yahoo! saw its share prices begin to crumble when the U.S. economy slowed down later in the year. The firm was hit particularly hard because its advertising revenue came mainly from the dot.com ventures that were forced to slash their advertising budgets as they fought to stay afloat. Yahoo! began securing advertising from bricks and mortar firms; because they were also tightening their advertising budgets, though, Yahoo! was unable to line up new customers as quickly as Koogle had hoped. To reduce the firm's reliance on advertising, which accounted for roughly 85 percent of annual sales in 2000, Koogle began steering Yahoo! into new fee-based services for consumers, such as online bill paying and auctioning objects for sale. New services for corporate clients included e-store management services.

Koogle's efforts failed to turn Yahoo! around quickly enough to satisfy investors. In 2001, when rumors began to circulate that Yahoo! was vulnerable to a takeover, the firm implemented a poison pill, which is a shareholders' rights program that makes a hostile takeover very costly for a buyer. In March of that year, with Yahoo's stock hovering at roughly $21 per share, Koogle announced his intent to step down as CEO of Yahoo! as soon as a replacement was found.

FURTHER READING:

''A Class Act at Yahoo!'' *BusinessWeek Online,* January 10, 2000, Available from www.businessweek.com.

Hardy, Quentin. ''Building Yahoo!'s Arcade.'' *Forbes,* December 11, 2000.

———. ''The Killer Ad Machine.'' *Forbes,* December 11, 2000.

Konrad, Rachel, and Paul Festa. ''Koogle To Let New Chief Overhaul Yahoo's Engine.'' *CNET News.com,* March 7, 2001. Available from news.cnet.com.

Tessler, Joelle. ''Yahoo Struggles to Survive: Dot-Com Shake-out Forces New Direction.'' *San Jose Mercury News,* March 8, 2001.

Umberto, Tosi. ''Yahoo!'s Tim Koogle.'' *Forbes,* October 7, 1996.

SEE ALSO: Yahoo! Inc.

L

LANDSEND.COM

LandsEnd.com was launched in 1995 by catalog apparel firm Lands' End Inc. The site, which started out selling 100 items, grew to include all Lands' End catalog items and was visited by 38 million World Wide Web surfers in 2000. Profitable since its inception, LandsEnd.com was considered the number one online apparel site, having secured $218 million in sales in fiscal 2001.

A direct merchant of casual apparel, luggage, and traditional home furnishings, Lands' End was founded in 1963 by Gary C. Comer. By the mid-1990s, the company had gone public and expanded into the United Kingdom and Japan, selling its merchandise through catalogs as well as outlet stores. Known for his innovative approach to business— Lands' End had been the first to offer a toll-free 800 number in 1978—Comer continually looked for new technology to bolster his business.

Eyeing the Internet's potential as a lucrative sales channel, Lands' End launched its company Web site in 1995 as a means of complimenting its catalog and outlet store sales. In the first month of operation, the site recorded just $160 in online sales, offering approximately 100 different items from the Lands' End catalog. It soon proved to be a success, however, securing a profit in its first year of operation.

The demographics of typical Lands' End shoppers fit well with the company's e-business strategy and left management confident that the Web site would become as popular as the catalogs. According to the firm, a large portion of its customer base owned a personal computer and was twice as likely to have online access than the rest of the population. A typical Lands' End shopper was between the ages of 35 and 54, with an average household income of $60,000. Nearly 88 percent had earned a college degree, and two-thirds were employed in a professional or managerial position.

In 1998, sales from Web operations reached $18 million. Reflecting its commitment to its Web-based business, Lands' End began to advertise its site in print ads and on television. In April, Lands' End added technology to its site, allowing shoppers to mix and match apparel. Entitled Outfits Online, the tool enabled online customers to coordinate 4,750 different outfits. The company also introduced Your Personal Model, which allowed users to create a 3-D model of their body shape. The tool then suggested clothing that was appropriate for that body type. The firm also began utilizing technology that enabled shoppers to create personal accounts that would store billing and shipping information to make future online purchasing quicker and easier. By December 1998, over 1,000 shoppers had opened accounts.

LandsEnd.com also deployed internal technology that proved effective. While warmer weather in the U.S. during the fall season of 1998 left many apparel retailers overstocked with winter outerwear, technology used by the firm allowed it to manipulate its merchandise mix in a timely fashion on the Web site to reflect the changing weather. LandsEnd.com also added three additional servers to speed up order-processing time on its site during that year's holiday season. According to monitoring firm Keynote Systems, the LandsEnd.com site was one of the best operating sites during the 1998 holiday season.

The company's foray onto the Web continued to pay off as online sales grew to $61 million in fiscal 1999. However, while Internet operations appeared to be booming, other business efforts by Lands' End were falling short. High expenses and lackluster catalog sales began taking their toll on the firm's bottom line. As a result, the company announced that it would pare back its catalog mailings and begin to focus additional efforts on Internet sales. Wanting to secure a larger portion of total company sales from its Web business, Lands' End began to bolster its customer service offerings on its site.

By the end of 1999, LandsEnd.com was known throughout the industry for its innovative Web site. In November of that year, the firm launched Lands' End Live, which provided online shoppers with real-time personal assistance twenty-fours hours a day, seven days a week. LandsEnd.com shoppers were also introduced to Shop With a Friend, which enabled people in different locations to shop online together.

Lands' End continued its focus on e-business into the new millennium. Having been successful in selling to consumers, the firm began targeting business customers. In March 2000, LandsEnd.com began offering customized Web sites for businesses such as General Motor's Saturn division and RadioShack. The sites allowed employees to order corporate merchandise online. The Lands' End site also featured Logo SnapShot, a tool that enabled business customers to view different corporate logos on various types of merchandise. The firm focused on international efforts as well. With sites already available to shoppers in the U.K., Germany, and Japan, LandsEnd.com expanded its reach to Ireland, France, and Italy in the fall of 2000.

LandsEnd.com experienced continued success in fiscal 2000. Sales reached $138 million—10.5 percent of total Lands' End sales—and the site logged over 38 million visits. The firm's focus on customer service continued to garner industry attention as well. According to a September 2000 *BusinessWeek Online* article, Lands' End had "blazed the path towards blending people and technology in Web shopping." That year, *Smart Business* magazine ranked LandsEnd.com one of the most successful online retail sites for its customer service and Web-based technology.

While a slowing economy began to wreak havoc on many Internet-based firms in 2001, LandsEnd.com continued to secure positive sales results. That year, LandsEnd.com recorded $218 million in sales, roughly 16 percent of Lands' End total revenues. However, Lands' End continued to falter due to catalog related expenses. In an attempt to shift more of its catalog-related telephone sales to Web-based sales, the company began aggressively promoting LandsEnd.com to encourage online purchasing. To cut costs, the firm also mailed out smaller than usual catalogs to its online customers.

In early 2001, reports had surfaced that Comer—owner of 55 percent of the firm—was looking for a buyer for Lands' End. Its successful Internet business made it an attractive acquisition target; however, by mid-2001, those reports remained only speculation. While LandsEnd.com continued to prosper, management of the bricks and mortar firm remained focused on reducing costs and making Internet sales an even larger portion of total revenues.

FURTHER READING:

Abend, Jules. "Lands' End Uses Internet to Expand Sales, Personalize Customer Service." *Bobbin*. June, 1999.

Berner, Robert. "Will Lands' End Land a Buyer?" *BusinessWeek Online*. May 18, 2001. Available from www.businessweek.com.

Hajweski, Doris. "Lands' End to Send Fewer Catalog Pages to Online Customers." *E-Commerce Times*. May 17, 2001. Available from www.ecommercetimes.com.

"Lands' End Introduces New Collaborative Shopping Aids." *Direct Marketing*. November, 1999.

Messmer, Ellen. "Lands' End Builds Custom Web Sites." *Network World*. March 27, 2000.

Prior, Molly. "Lands' End Crosses the Threshold of Internet Retailing Excellence." *DSN Retailing Today*. November 6, 2000 6.

Zimmermann, Kim Ann. "A Model for Lands' End." *WWD*. November 25, 1998.

SEE ALSO: E-tailing

LEGAL ISSUES

The rise of the Internet has impacted virtually every branch of law and is expected to revolutionize the relationship between law, government, and technology. Central questions concerning Internet-related legal issues include: If cyberspace constitutes a separate legal domain, should there be a separate branch of "cyberlaw" to regulate it? Or should existing laws be reinterpreted to adapt to the special legal circumstances of the electronic world? Alternatively, should the Internet remain free of regulation altogether? How will the Internet affect fundamental principles of civil liberties, commercial relations, and international law?

The terrain of cyberspace creates unique legal dilemmas. The Internet transcends all geographic and political borders, potentially rendering obsolete one of the fundamental tenets of modern law: that laws are created and enforced within discrete, political territories. When users can access online services and information or communicate with individuals all over the world, which legal jurisdiction takes responsibility for disputes that may arise? To what extent should the laws of differing nations—which cover topics as varied as intellectual property and freedom of speech—be harmonized, especially to facilitate international e-commerce?

The branches of law most under discussion at the turn of the millennium included intellectual property, criminal law, conflict of jurisdiction, and the civil liberties issues of privacy and freedom of expression.

INTELLECTUAL PROPERTY

Intellectual property (IP)—inventions, artistic creations, and commercial symbols, for example—falls under the branch of law covering protections and rights such as copyrights, patents, trademarks, and trade secrets. Ideally, IP laws balance the rights holder's ability to derive profit from creations with society's interest in the free flow of information. However, the Internet makes it possible to generate numerous, flawless reproductions of digitized information and instantaneously transmit those copies anywhere in the world. This imperils the ability of the rights holder to control how and by whom that information is used. However, erecting stricter protections around intellectual property rights (through, for example, encryption or licensing requirements) might stifle both creative expression and commercial innovation. Copyright and trademark form the nucleus of contested cyberspace-related intellectual property issues.

The U.S. Constitution grants Congress the power to regulate copyright. The basic statute is the Copyright Act of 1976, which protects traditional creative works and online text, image, and sound files. Copyright violations can be prosecuted as civil or criminal offenses, depending on the circumstances, and those committing unintentional or contributory infringement may also incur liability. Subsequent legislation directly addressing copyright in cyberspace included the Copyright Felony Act (1992), which addressed software piracy as a felony; the Digital Performance Right Act (1996), governing inclusion of non-original music on Web sites; the No Electronic Theft Act (1997), which abolished the requirement that a violation had to be committed for financial gain in order to be prosecutable; and the Digital Millennium Copyright Act (1998), which harmonized American copyright law with international law as embodied in the World Intellectual Property Organization's Copyright Treaty. Among other things, DMCA prohibits the circumvention of technology used to block unauthorized access to protected digital content.

In the U.S., the states also regulate copyright. In particular, the Uniform Computer Information Transactions Act (USCITA), introduced in 1999, was adopted by Virginia and Maryland and was under consideration in many other states in the early 2000s. It strictly limits permitted (''fair'') free use of copyrighted digital materials, and has been opposed by many groups who fear it could erase copyright exceptions that currently permit unauthorized use of works for scholarly, news, and critical purposes.

Within trademark law, the intellectual-property status of domain names emerged as the leading cyber-law dilemma. The practice of ''cyber-squatting,'' the bad-faith registration of domain names in the hopes that the namesake will later purchase the name back, spurred new guidelines for registration of domain names. WIPO implemented a swift arbitration procedure to handle international domain-name disputes.

Many international treaties govern IP, including the Berne Convention, the WIPO Copyright Treaty, and the Trade-Related Aspects of Intellectual Property Rights (TRIPs) Agreement. Most industrialized nations provide stronger IP protections than the U.S. Experts predict that e-commerce, globalization, and IP piracy will prompt increased standardization of international IP laws, perhaps at the expense of developing nations.

CRIMINAL LAW

Crimes committed in connection with the Internet (commonly called ''cybercrimes'') have attracted widespread attention. Cybercrime encompasses an enormous range of offenses, from hacking to online fraud to child pornography. Generally, cybercrimes either involve traditional crimes committed with computers or crimes in which the computer serves as the ''victim'' of the illegal act, as in hacking or virus attacks.

The Internet has made certain kinds of criminal activities much more attractive, since cyberspace possesses unique characteristics that may actually encourage the commission of criminal acts. For example, identifying and apprehending an offender is more difficult in cyberspace than in real space; cybercrimes are often far cheaper to carry out than traditional offenses; the physical risk and expense required to commit crimes are often reduced when they occur in cyberspace; and the impersonality of the Internet may diminish the perpetrator's perception of the impact his or her actions have on the victim of the crime, as well as limit the opportunities that victim has for retaliation. Finally, computers cloak the identity and location of the perpetrator and erasure and encryption software can obliterate virtual evidence. Cybercrimes may also implicate third parties, such as Internet service providers (ISPs).

Though reliable statistics are hard to find since cybercrime incidents are under-reported, many believe cybercrime is accelerating. Recorded computer security breaches increased from six in 1988 to more than 8,000 in 1999, while ten to 15 new viruses appeared daily by the early 2000s. In 2000, the U.S. Department of Defense recorded over 22,000 attacks against its computers.

The basic federal statute, the Federal Computer Fraud and Abuse Act, prohibits unauthorized access to any "protected" computer (basically any computer connected to the Internet) for purposes of espionage, accessing unauthorized information, fraud, and damaging the computers. Online dissemination of child pornography was the focus of much controversial federal legislation, including the Child Pornography Prevention Act (1996). Many state laws criminalize various cybercrimes, among them e-mail crimes and cyber-stalking. The attacks on the World Trade Center and Pentagon on September 11, 2001 swiftly drew international attention to the threat of cyber-terrorism, and the Bush administration enacted sweeping online-surveillance legislation that supporters argued was essential for enhanced national security, but that critics charged ran roughshod over fundamental civil liberties.

European nations were moving toward more comprehensive, anti-cybercrime legislation by 2000. The EU's controversial proposed cybercrime treaty, made public in April 2000, was designed to harmonize European criminal laws on a wide range of computer-related offenses. Any nation's enforcement officials could gain online access to other states to pursue cybercrime investigations. The treaty would also grant European governments extensive powers regarding wiretapping, real-time collection of traffic data, and the search and seizure of digital information.

The global interconnectedness of computer systems and the specter of international terrorism prompted calls for greater cooperation in the fight against cybercrime. In 1998 Britain, Canada, France, Germany, Italy, Japan, Russia, and the U.S. agreed to coordinate efforts to investigate and prosecute cyber-crimes. Proposed solutions included a broad, international treaty that could bring all domestic anti-cybercrime laws into agreement. But nations differed on the extent to which data encryption should be permitted, since it simultaneously protects the privacy of individual and business information, but may aid cyber-criminals in hiding their activities. They also debated increased governmental surveillance of online communications, a particularly sensitive topic in the aftermath of the World Trade Center and Pentagon attacks of 2001. Such monitoring could help identify cyber-criminals and terrorists, but was construed by privacy advocates and members of various ethic and racial groups as a means of fostering the growth of "police" states and the illegal targeting of specific groups ("profiling"). Finally, digital-content regulation, which might help suppress hate speech or child pornography, is seen as endangering freedom of expression and promoting state-sponsored censorship.

JURISDICTION AND SOVEREIGNTY

Because the Internet enables information to be delivered nearly anywhere in the world, irrespective of the physical locations of the sender, service provider, or recipient, territorial boundaries become virtually meaningless in cyberspace. This creates a basic legal dilemma, however, because historically most laws have been understood to function along territorial lines. Legal sovereignty has traditionally followed national borders and legal jurisdictions have recognized, geographic borders as well. A conflict arises concerning how, and whether, to legally regulate the border-free realm of cyberspace according to territorially bound laws. Furthermore, in an Internet-related dispute, which jurisdiction can claim legal cognizance of the matter when the parties involved can be situated in different parts of the world? Domestic and international laws were a long way from clear solutions in the early 2000s.

CONSTITUTIONAL ISSUES: PRIVACY AND FREEDOM OF EXPRESSION

The U.S. Constitution contains no explicit guarantee of privacy. However, case law establishes privacy rights implicit in the provisions of the Bill of Rights and Fourteenth Amendment. The spread of e-commerce has led many consumers to make their sensitive personal information available on the Web. In the U.S., the security of such information is generally guaranteed by voluntary privacy policies enacted by Web sites themselves and by industry self-policing. Technologies, such as "cookies" track users online habits to compile user profiles. Personal data can be transferred or sold to third parties without an individual's consent or even knowledge.

Some U.S. online privacy-protection laws do exist, such as the Children's Online Privacy Protection Act and the Health Insurance Portability and Accountability Act of 1996, but they have been difficult to implement.

Many European nations possess data-protection laws that govern an individual's rights over the use of personal information stored in computers. The European Union's Data Protection Act (1998) mandates that Web sites gathering personal information about users must notify individuals of this practice and user consent is required to collect sensitive, personal data. In addition, member states are directed to block data transmissions to other countries, including the U.S., if they are deemed to lack adequate privacy protection laws.

The U.S. and the EU worked out a compromise, "safe-harbor" agreement to resolve the problem. American companies can transmit data online to EU members as long as their privacy policies accord with certain EU privacy-protection principles. Participation is voluntary, with the American businesses registering their compliance with the U.S. Department of Commerce.

Online marketers and law-enforcement agencies often oppose enhanced privacy protection, because it impedes their ability to gather data in cyberspace. New technologies, such as IPV6, may further erode the anonymity of Internet users by using expanded IP addresses that include the unique serial number of each computer's network-connection hardware, imprinting each data transmission with a user's "electronic fingerprint."

Monitoring of digital communications had been a touchy subject, but after September 11, 2001, governmental leaders moved quickly to reinforce the security of information networks and to deploy greater Internet surveillance in hopes of identifying and tracking suspected terrorists. In October 2001, the Bush administration passed anti-terrorism legislation that established the basis for a massive, domestic intelligence-gathering system incorporating the FBI, CIA, and Treasury Department law enforcement agencies. It decreased legal privacy safeguards in place since Watergate, and permitted governmental agencies freer rein in gathering electronic information and financial records and monitoring Internet communications, sometimes even without a warrant. The move set off alarms among critics concerned about the erosion of privacy rights.

The other constitutional issue at the forefront of cyberlaw debates was the extent to which expression should be regulated online. The founding vision of the Internet was as an untrammeled information superhighway. To a great extent, First Amendment free-speech guarantees fostered this attitude in the U.S., where online content has not been highly regulated. The exceptions concerned speech considered harmful to minors, which was addressed by the 1996 Communications Decency Act and the 1998 Child Online Protection Act; both laws faced First Amendment challenges. Filtering software has also been used to shield certain users from undesirable online content.

Other countries showed less reluctance to regulate online content, particularly hate speech directed against specific groups. Many EU members, such as Germany and France, prohibit Web sites from featuring pro-Nazi messages, for example. And China erected a "Great Firewall" that blocks access to unacceptable sites worldwide. This approach generated wide disagreement between many nations and the U.S., home to many sites deemed "undesirable" or "harmful."

In 2000, the Supreme Court ruled that computer source code qualified as protected speech under the First Amendment. However, the court also recognized the government's legitimate interest in regulating source code, especially in circumstances where national security interests were at stake.

CONCEPTIONS OF CYBERLAW

Some observers have asserted that cyberlaw does not exist, since few of the legal issues raised by the Internet are novel and few branches of law are determined by technology. However, others argue that cyberspace should be considered different from real space, as far as legal issues are concerned. Furthermore, since the Internet transcends territorial boundaries, it renders territorially based laws obsolete. They predict that cyberlaw will become a new form of transnational law, ushering in greater standardization of Internet-related legal regulations worldwide to accommodate e-commerce, globalization, and the spread of western, democratic ideals. Some view this as the opportunity for greater freedoms, security, and prosperity to be extended to more people around the globe. Others, however, fear that such a trend will infringe on national sovereignty and legal jurisdictions. Finally, they caution that cyberlaw will benefit the interests of large, multinational businesses and police surveillance, rather than the civil liberties of individual citizens.

FURTHER READING:

Gilden, Michael. "Jurisdiction and the Internet: The Real World Meets Cyberspace." *ILSA Journal of International & Comparative Law,* Fall 2000.

"The Internet and the Law: Stop Signs on the Web." *Economist,* January 13, 2001.

Johnson, David and David G. Post. "Law and Borders: The Rise of Law in Cyberspace." *Stanford Law Review,* vol. 48, 1996. Available from www.temple.edu/lawschool.

Kaplan, Carl. "How to Govern Cyperspace: Frontier Justice or Legal Precedent?" *New York Times Cyberlaw Journal,* 1998.

Katyal, Neal Kumar. "Criminal Law in Cyberspace." *University of Pennsylvania Law Review,* April 2001.

Hongju Koh, Harold. "The Globalization of Freedom." *Yale Journal of International Law,* Summer 2001.

Lessig, Lawrence. *Code and Other Laws of Cyberspace.* New York: Basic Books, 1999.

Sommer, Joseph. "Against Cyberlaw." *Berkeley Technology Law Journal,* Fall 2000.

Tsesis, Alexander. ''Hate in Cyberspace: Regulating Hate Speech on the Internet.'' *San Diego Law Review,* Summer 2001.

SEE ALSO: Children and the Internet; Computer Crime; Cyber-squatting; Encryption; Fraud, Internet; Intellectual Property; Privacy; World Intellectual Property Organization (WIPO)

LEVIS.COM

Levis.com was launched by fashion retailer Levi Strauss & Co. in 1996 as an informative company Web site that included pages on the firm's history and current operations, culture, and fashion. Two years later, the Web site became a sales outlet for more than 120 clothing items in 3,000 different styles. However, in 1999 Levi Strauss pulled the plug on its online sales efforts, using the Levis.com site instead to promote the firm's brand image.

Apparel retailer Levi Strauss was established in the 1850s and became known throughout the fashion industry for its name brand clothing including jeans, casual and dress pants, shirts, jackets, and accessories. Seeing the Internet as a potential marketing channel, the firm developed an Internet strategy in the mid-1990s. Launched to cater to both U.S. and European customers, the site included pages on the company's history, as well as product and marketing information. Levis.com also featured pages, dedicated to its target audience of 15-to-24-year-olds, that covered fashion and cultural issues. Shortly after the Web site's debut, Levi Strauss introduced a new marketing scheme entitled I-candy. The interactive advertising was available on various Web sites, including music sites MTV and Addicted to Noise, in the form of a blinking eye. When Web surfers clicked on the eye, an interactive commercial appeared, touting the Levi's brand.

While Levi Strauss continued to utilize the Levis.com Web site for marketing purposes, company management eventually set plans in motion to turn the popular site into a shopping destination. The firm's market share had slipped from 30 percent in 1990 to 17 percent in 1998, and Levi Strauss planned to use its online efforts to regain a hold on the apparel market. The company also was prompted to begin e-tailing when customers began complaining about not begin able to order Levi's brand products online or by telephone. As a result, an e-commerce plan was developed and in November of 1998 Levis.com began selling 120 items from the Levi's branded apparel line. The site featured a tool entitled Style Finder, which asked online shoppers a series of questions related to fashion, music, and entertainment, and then made apparel suggestions based on the shoppers re-sponses. According to Digital Marketing Director Jay Thomas, as cited in a 1998 *Digital Age* article, the move into e-commerce reflected Levis.com's ''single-minded goal. . .to make it easier to shop and buy our products.''

While customers applauded the firm's entrance into the online selling arena, its retailers were less than thrilled. When Levis.com began selling branded products, Levi Strauss retained exclusive online rights to both the Levi's and Dockers brands. This move prevented retailers—including Sears, Roebuck & Co. and J.C. Penney—from selling Levi's branded products online. At the time, retailers accounted for a large portion of company sales, and some analysts believed the online site might undercut these sales and undermine the firm's relationship with retailers.

Levis.com faced many problems and did not fare well in its first year as an online shopping destination. The transition from selling large quantities to retail outlets versus shipping to individual consumers proved to be costly. The site did not sell the famous Levi's 501 Blues line until March 1999, worried that Asian and European customers, who could not buy the jeans online and were paying more than U.S.-based customers, would boycott the firm. Many customers continued to shop at retail outlets to avoid on-line shipping charges. In addition, the online return policy also was discouraging to customers because merchandise bought on Levis.com could not be returned at retail stores.

At the same time, Levi Strauss was in turmoil. Long-time company president Peter Jacobi retired in January 1999. Having cut its workforce by 40 percent over the previous three years, the firm was struggling with distribution issues, often unable to keep supplies of its products in stores. Sales during 1998 fell by 13 percent, which forced Levi's to cut costs, including those related to e-commerce efforts. Consequently, Levis.com's advertising budget was slashed. With little support from Levi Strauss, the site did not attract the Web traffic necessary to make it a successful venture, and without a substantial Web audience Levis.com did not garner enough attention to effectively compete with major competitors. Many of the Web site's technology staff members began seeking employment with other Internet-based firms.

Continued losses at Levi Strauss forced the company to take further action. In November of 1999, it announced that Levis.com would no longer sell Levi's branded apparel online after the holiday season. The company stated in a 1999 *E-Commerce Times* article that ''during the past year, it became clear to us that the cost of running a truly world-class e-commerce business is unaffordable right now as we look at other competing priorities.'' Levis.com remained online, however, and was once again primarily used for marketing and communications efforts. Levis.com's exit from e-tailing also strengthened the firm's relationship with retailers. After the announcement, retailers J.C. Penney and Macy's were given the go-ahead to start selling Levi's branded apparel on their Web sites. The move proved effective, as the J.C. Penney Web site sold 50 percent more Levi's branded apparel in six weeks than Levis.com had sold in 12 weeks.

Philip Marineau, the new CEO of Levi Strauss, also was confident that Levis.com's exit from e-tailing was a good move. In a February 2000 *Daily News Record* article, he commented, ''I view the Internet as a key asset. But we're not fulfilling goods on a mass level, let alone one at a time. I'm trying to improve retail partnerships, not drive a stake through them.'' After shuttering the e-tailing operations, Marineau put plans in motion to improve the use of Levis.com as a marketing tool. The firm shifted control of its Web operations in-house from an outside agency in early 2000. The site's new focus was to promote the Levi's brand image and to encourage Web surfers to purchase Levi's apparel from its retailers' Web sites.

By 2001, users across Europe, South America, Asia Pacific, and Latin America were able to access Levis.com. Along with information on Levi's apparel for men, women, and children, the site also featured company commercials and fashion information, as well as the firm's Original Spin program, which allowed consumers to order customized jeans at certain Levi Strauss stores. As Levi Strauss focused on improving its bottom line, the company continued to use Levis.com as a strategic communication and marketing tool.

FURTHER READING:

Cuneo, Alice Z. ''Levi Strauss Begins 1st Online Sales Effort.'' *Advertising Age*. November 23, 1998.

DeSalvo, Kathy. ''501 Reasons to Check Out Levi's Online.'' *Shoot*. February 9, 1996.

Dugan, Sean M. ''Net Prophet: Levi Strauss & Co. Site Doesn't Pan Out, but the Rush Isn't Over Yet.'' *InfoWorld*. November 22, 1999.

Forseter, Murray. ''Levi's Weaves a Tangled Web.'' *Chain Store Age Executive with Shopping Center Age*. January 1999.

Greenberg, Paul A. ''Levi's to Bow Out of E-Commerce.'' *E-Commerce Times*. October 29, 1999. Available from www.ecommercetimes.com.

————. ''Manufacturers Beset by E-Commerce 'Channel Conflict.''' *E-Commerce Times*. January 7, 2000. Available from www.ecommercetimes.com.

Hye, Jeanette. ''Levi's Good Fit: In-House Control.'' *WWD*. January 5, 2000.

Knight, Molly. ''Levi's Closes Year With 13 Percent Decline in Sales.'' *Daily News Record*. February 23, 2001.

Kroll, Lisa. ''Denim Disaster.'' *Forbes*. November 29, 1999.

————. ''Digital Denim.'' *Forbes*. December 28, 1998.

''Levi's Launches I-Candy, New Ad for Internet.'' *WWD*. July 10, 1996.

Malone, Scott. ''Levi's Comeback Above Plan.'' *WWD*. January 11, 2001.

Summerfield, Gideon. ''Levis Invests in Getting Onto the Net with a Surf-Friendly, Worldwide Site.'' *Campaign*. February 23, 1996.

SEE ALSO: E-tailing; Mass Customization

LINUX

A freely distributed operating system that functions on many different platforms, Linux is important to e-commerce because of its increasing use as an operating system for Web servers. The system thrives in multi-user, networked environments and runs on a range of hardware configurations, including PCs, Macintoshes, high-end workstations, and many servers and network devices. Besides its compatibility with different platforms, Linux has also attracted widespread attention because many consider it faster, more robust, and more economical compared to other operating systems.

Linux is open-source software, meaning that the system's code has been developed over time by many different individuals working collaboratively. Although in the early 2000s it wasn't the dominant operating system for e-commerce, Linux was making steady gains on more commonly used systems like Windows 2000, OS/400, HP-UX, Solaris, and AIX. According to *Informationweek,* Dell Computer CEO Michael Dell predicted that, by 2003, his company would sell 27 percent of its servers with Linux preinstalled. In the same issue, Hewlett-Packard Chief Scientist Joel Birnbaum noted that Linux could become the preferred operating system for many users by 2010.

Although it once held a predominantly cult status, Linux was gaining wider acceptance among many corporate users in the early 2000s, especially those in academia, financial services, telecommunications and the government. The system's acceptance in the financial industry is especially important for its long-term success in the area of e-commerce because Web sites in that industry are among the busiest and most demanding, especially for processing transactions.

The Linux kernel, or the program's essential core, was created in the early 1990s by Linus Torvalds, a Finnish computer science student. According to writer Gerry Dorman, Torvalds developed Linux as an alternative to the Unix operating system, which he found to be expensive and incompatible with PCs. Torvalds based his creation on a Unix-like program called Minix. Because it adheres to a number of Unix standards and architectures, Linux is often seen as part of the Unix lineage, as a particular implementation of Unix.

The resulting stability and adaptability have carried Linux far. "One of the things that fascinates us about Linux is that it was designed to be hardware-independent," explained Scott Handy, director of Linux solutions marketing for IBM in a *Planet IT* article by Anne Zieger. "Porting Linux from platform to platform is very simple." IBM's backing of Linux is in fact one of the fledgling system's greatest achievements from a marketing standpoint. In late 2000, IBM Chairman Louis Gerstner, pointing out that Linux was growing at twice the rate of Windows NT, announced the computer giant would invest $1 billion in the system's development. "Some estimate it will become even more prevalent than NT by 2004," he said in the December 12, 2000 issue of *Planet IT*. "This is a big issue for every server company."

FURTHER READING:

Burke, Steven. "IBM Stakes $1 Billion Bet On Linux." *Planet IT,* December 12, 2000. Available from www.PlanetIT.com.

Dorman, Gerry. "Linux—Overview and Installation." *Planet IT,* June 3, 1999. Available from www.PlanetIT.com.

McDougall, Paul, Elisabeth Goodridge, and Tony Kontzer. "Dell, HP, and IBM Step Up Linux Efforts." *Informationweek,* August 21, 2000.

Radding, Alan. "Linux in Stealth Mode on Wall Street." *Planet IT,* October 23, 2000. Available from www.PlanetIT.com.

Yager, Tom. "Is Linux Ready for E-Commerce?" *InfoWorld.* March 27, 2000.

Zieger, Anne. "IBM Embraces Linux Throughout Its Line." *Planet IT,* December 27, 2000. Available from www.PlanetIT.com.

SEE ALSO: Unix

LOCAL AREA NETWORK (LAN)

Local area networks, more commonly known as LANs, typically connect a geographically restricted group of clients, such as a group of employees in an office building, to a server. Clients simply are stand-alone personal computers (PCs) or other types of workstations, while servers are faster computers that house the programs and data distributed to the workstations. Servers either can be mainframe computers or sophisticated PCs. Several network operating systems exist, including Microsoft Windows NT, Macintosh's AppleTalk, and Novell's NetWare. These systems are housed directly within the machine acting as the server. Related software within each client allows it to access programs and data on the server, just as if the applications and files were actually on the hard drive of the client's machine. Some LANs also allow clients to communicate with each another via e-mail messages or real-time chat programs. Particularly large LANs may require several dedicated servers, while smaller LANs may actually be nothing more than a peer-to-peer network, in which a few workstations act as servers by allowing the users at each station to access files and applications on one another's machines.

In some cases, clients must access a server for all the software applications and data files they need. However, LANs also can be set up with servers that only provide select applications to clients. For example, some workstations equipped with their own printers may access their LAN each time they perform a word processing or data processing function, yet not need the LAN when actually printing documents. Other LANs may link printers directly to servers to allow a single printer to be shared by several workstations, a cost saving technique used by many corporations, libraries, schools, and other institutions.

To actually transfer data, LANs use protocols like IBM's Token Ring, which typically arranges computers in a ring or star shape to facilitate connection. Ethernet, which was developed by Bob Metcalfe and Xerox Corp. in the early 1970s, is the most common LAN protocol. It uses coaxial cables or twisted pair wires to connect machines arranged most commonly in a bus layout, where all computers are connected to a central line. Another protocol, Fiber Distributed-Data Interface (FDDI), uses fiber optic lines to connect up to thousands of workstations as far as 124 miles apart. Networks much bigger than this typically begin to connect LANs together to form a wide-area network, or WAN. Data transmission speeds for these technologies range from roughly 1 million bytes per second for Ethernet and Token Ring to 10 million bytes per second for FDDI. Efforts to improve network speed have resulted in the creation of new technologies like Fast Ethernet, the even faster Gigabit Ethernet, and Fast Token Ring.

FURTHER READING:

"Ethernet." In *Ecommerce Webopedia.* Darien, CT: Internet.com, 2001. Available from e-comm.webopedia.com.

"Ethernet." In *WhatIs.com.* Needham, MA: TechTarget.com Inc., 2000. Available from whatis.techtarget.com.

"Fiber Distributed-Data Interface." In *WhatIs.com*. Needham, MA: TechTarget.com Inc., 2000. Available from whatis.techtarget.com.

"LAN." In *Techencyclopedia*. Point Pleasant, PA: Computer Language Co., 2001. Available from www.techweb.com/encyclopedia.

"Local-Area Network." In *Ecommerce Webopedia*. Darien, CT: Internet.com, 2001. Available from e-comm.webopedia.com.

"Local Area Network." In *WhatIs.com*. Needham, MA: TechTarget.com Inc., 2000. Available from whatis.techtarget.com.

"Token Ring." In *WhatIs.com*. Needham, MA: TechTarget.com Inc., 2000. Available from whatis.techtarget.com.

SEE ALSO: Communication Protocols; Wide Area Network (WAN)

LOCK-IN

Over time, companies invest a great deal of effort and money in the computer systems they rely on to manage their many business functions. Not only do the systems themselves cost money (in terms of hardware, software, and other network infrastructure), they also require a substantial investment of human capital. Employees, customers, and business partners spend many hours learning to use such systems. Additionally, there are costs associated with maintaining these systems from day to day and performing various infrastructure and system upgrades. Considering all this, it's easy to see why giving up one system for something newer or better is difficult at best, and often represents significant cost and frustration. The term lock-in is used to describe this very real business challenge, which many companies face as they attempt to adapt different systems, some of which are very old (sometimes referred to as legacy systems), to the cutting-edge world of e-commerce.

Lock-in can have very negative effects. Not only does this phenomenon make it difficult for companies to switch over to newer systems, it also can stifle competition and hinder progress. When large companies, entire industries, or even the public at large become dependent on technologies or platforms from a mere handful of companies, it can be extremely difficult for new competitors and more innovative products and services to enter the marketplace. This is sometimes referred to as the network effect, whereby a company's sheer size and dominance keeps the competition at bay, and keeps the majority hooked on one system for the sake of compatibility.

Software manufacturer Microsoft Corp. was one company that received a great deal of negative press in the late 1990s and early 2000s for just this reason, culminating in a lawsuit raised by U.S. anti-trust regulators. This stemmed from the monolithic firm's practice of packaging its Web browser with its pervasive Windows operating system, causing rival Netscape to lose market share. Many industry professionals have expressed frustration concerning Microsoft's lock-in practices. In *Linux Today*, Brian Pfaffenberger argued: "Virtually all of the firm's products contain features designed so that customers cannot enjoy the product's full feature set unless they purchase additional products made by the same company." While such practices increase profits for software vendors, they generally tend to cost companies more money in the long run and increase their dependence on one vendor's technology.

FURTHER READING:

Enos, Lori. "FTC: Antitrust Enforcement Critical to High-Tech Growth." *E-Commerce Times,* June 16, 2000. Available from www.ecommercetimes.com.

Pfaffenberger, Bryan. "Linux Journal—The Linux Advantage: Locking Out the Lock-in Artists." *Linux Today,* July 8, 2000. Available from www.linuxtoday.com.

Saliba, Clare. "EU Signs Off on E-Signature Initiative." *E-Commerce Times,* August 1, 2001. Available from www.ecommercetimes.com.

LOTUS DEVELOPMENT CORP.

One of the world's largest software developers, Lotus Development Corp. operates as a subsidiary of computing giant IBM Corp. The firm is best known for its Lotus 1-2-3 spreadsheet program and its Lotus Notes messaging system, which holds a 51 percent share of the e-mail software market, compared to the 27.7 percent held by Microsoft Corp.'s Exchange program. In 2001, after Lotus cut 183 jobs, analysts began to speculate that IBM would take greater control of the Cambridge, Massachusetts-based company.

Mitchell D. Kapor created Lotus in 1982 to develop software applications for the fledgling personal computer (PC) industry. Operations launched with eight employees. Kapor took his firm public in 1983, raising roughly $41 million in fresh capital via the sale of more than 2 million shares at $18 apiece. That year, Jonathan Sachs worked with Kapor to create the first version of Lotus 1-2-3, a spreadsheet application for PCs that converted numerical data into graphs. Within a year of its launch, Lotus 1-2-3 boosted Lotus to the number two spot among software makers. Sales grew to $53 million, and employees totaled 300.

The firm's intense pace of growth prompted Kapor to bring in outside management; he hired James P. Manzi as president in 1984, taking on the role of chairman for himself. Wanting to reduce its reliance on 1-2-3, Lotus began to invest in software startups and new programs, such as Symphony, which added word processing and database management applications to 1-2-3. These integrated programs, which allowed for networking between computers, formed one of the first software application ''suites.'' Because customers found Symphony difficult to use, sales of the suite fell short of management expectations. Total year revenues reached $157 million, and the firm's workforce more than doubled to 700.

Lotus continued its efforts to diversify via acquisition of firms and of software programs in 1985. For example, the company paid $800,000 for Software Arts. A strategic alliance with Apple Computer resulted in the creation of Jazz, a spreadsheet program targeting new computer users. The product was the first Macintosh-compatible application developed by Lotus programmers, who struggled with the new code. Although they eventually resolved several glitches, consumer response to Jazz remained cool. Kapor resigned from Lotus in 1986, leaving Manzi at the helm. That year, Lotus sold 750,000 copies of 1-2-3. To compete with Microsoft's Excel, a spreadsheet program created for the Macintosh market, Lotus began working on an upgraded version of 1-2-3. The firm also began marketing its products in Japan and agreed to develop a version of 1-2-3 for IBM Corp.'s mainframe computers.

Lotus's early move into Japan paid off as 1-2-3 outperformed competitors there by five-to-one in 1987. Although the newest version of 1-2-3 was delayed several times, Lotus maintained a 70 percent share of the spreadsheet market, which was valued at $500 million in 1988. However, the holdups eventually undermined the firm's public image. As a result, W. Frank King III, a former IBM executive, was hired to improve the software-development department's performance. The third version of 1-2-3 was finally shipped in 1989, as were 26 other applications, such as the long-awaited spreadsheet programs for mainframes, as well as those for minicomputers and workstations. Increasingly hostile relations with Microsoft prompted Lotus to decline invitations to develop products compatible with Microsoft's new Windows platform; this decision was later viewed as a poor one as the firm fell behind competitors in making its products compatible with what became the leading PC operating system. That year, Lotus also purchased a stake in database software maker Sybase Inc.

In 1990, a blockbuster merger agreement with Novell Inc., the leading U.S. computer networking firm, fell through when Lotus failed to ease Novell's

fear that the deal was not a merger of equals. Lotus worked with Apple, Novell, Microsoft and other leading software makers to create an electronic message tampering encryption program that would allow messages transferred over PCs dependable enough to serve as legal contracts, records, etc. That year, finally acknowledging the success of Microsoft's Windows platform, Lotus began developing products for use with the graphical system. However, these efforts were delayed after Lotus invested in the new OS/2 operating system, which failed to emerge as a major contender to Windows. When Borland International launched its Quattro Pro spreadsheet, Lotus filed suit against Borland for copyright infringement of the 1-2-3 program. Lotus also paid $65 million for Samna Corp. Earnings grew to $23 million on revenues of $692 million.

Several small glitches with the first version of 1-2-3 for Windows forced Lotus to begin tweaking its new release in 1991. Less than 250,000 copies of the program sold that year. As a result, the firm cut its workforce by 10 percent, or roughly 400 employees. Lotus diversified into the e-mail market in 1991 with the release of a mail forwarding application known as Open Messaging Interface, which allowed users to send messages without exiting other programs first. Both IBM and Apple began using the program on their machines. Lotus then developed Notes, part of a new category of messaging software called Groupware, which enabled computer users to communicate from distant locations. Within several months of its release, more than 112,000 copies of notes were sold to General Motors Corp., Metropolitan Life Insurance, and other large firms. IBM began using another new Lotus program, cc:Mail, as part of the networking system it recommended to clients. Lotus also finally released a version of 1-2-3 for Macintosh machines. Other new products included Windows, OS/2, and DOS versions of Freelance Graphics, a new graphics program.

Sales reached $900 million in 1992. More than 1.5 million copies of cc:Mail were sold that year, and Lotus pulled ahead of its rivals in the networking industry. Lotus, Borland, Novell, and Apple began drafting a set of electronic messaging standards for both businesses and individuals. Despite the success of its networking software, the firm's inability to capture more than 30 percent of the Windows market for its other programs undercut earnings. In 1994, Lotus paid $84 million in stock for software maker Iris Associates. The firm decided to halt its Macintosh software development efforts. A major reorganization took place in 1995 as Lotus reduced expenses, eliminated employees, and reshuffled products. The firm's word processing program, which remained in third place behind Microsoft Word and WordPerfect, changed its name from Ami Pro to Word Pro. That year, Lotus agreed to be acquired by IBM for roughly $3.5 billion. According to the terms of the deal, IBM would allow Lotus to operate fairly autonomously. Manzi resigned, and Michael D. Zisman and Jeffrey Papows were named co-presidents. Papows eventually took over as CEO.

When the friendly takeover was completed, Lotus made its new focus the Internet, a key component of which was the Notes messaging system. The firm's SmartSuite program, which included Word Pro and 1-2-3, was adopted by IBM, replacing the computer-industry giant's own StarOffice suite. In 1996, Lotus unveiled the Component Starter Pack, a program that granted Notes users access to spreadsheet, client, data-query, drawing, and project-scheduling applications. The firm also started developing its Web Information Manager program and Domino, a Web page design program with the application development capabilities of Notes. Along with restructuring itself around Internet-based software, Lotus spent its first few years as an IBM subsidiary undergoing several reorganizations as IBM struggled with how to best manage its new unit from afar.

Late in 1997, Lotus released business application package eSuite, one of the first products on the market to offer Java-based applications, including email, word processing, presentations, and spreadsheets. Notes 5.0 and Domino 5.0, both released in 1998, were designed to allow for ''easier access to information on the Internet,'' wrote *PC Week*. The new Notes application looked more like a World Wide Web browser, while the latest version of Domino departed from its traditional ''database-centric model'' to offer upgraded searching abilities that allowed users to comb through several databases, including the Web.

Papows was succeeded in 2000 by Al Zollar, a long-time executive at IBM. In 2001, Lotus announced its intent to include wireless access capabilities with its next release of the Domino software, dubbed Lotus Domino Everyplace. According to a June 2001 article in *eWeek*, Lotus was also working on transforming its software into Web-based services. ''The Cambridge, Mass. IBM subsidiary is creating tools that will make it easier to extend its Domino-based messaging and collaboration applications to the Web, a move that follows Microsoft Corp.'s similar efforts around Exchange and.Net.''

FURTHER READING:

Burke, Steven. ''Lotus' New Frontier-Poised for the Wireless World.'' *Computer Reseller News,* April 16, 2001.

Gonsalves, Antone. ''Notes Worthy?—Lotus is Delivering Its Long-Awaited Knowledge Management Products, But Now May Be a Tough Time to Sell Them.'' *InformationWeek,* June 25, 2001.

''Lotus Development Corp.'' In *Notable Corporate Chronologies.* Farmington Hills, MI: Gale Research, 1999.

Luening, Erich. ''Lotus Restructuring May Lead to Tighter IBM Control.'' *CNET News.com,* January 8, 2001. Available from news.cnet.com.

McCright, John S. ''Lotus Pushes Domino Services—Company Aims to Ease Web Collaboration; Follows.Net, Exchange Model.'' *eWeek,* June 11, 2001.

Peterson, Scot. ''IBM's Lotus Story Never Ends.'' *eWeek,* March 5, 2001.

Walker, Christy. ''Webward Ho!'' *PC Week.* January 26, 1998.

SEE
ALSO: Apple Computer Inc.; IBM Inc.; Kapor, Mitchell D.; Microsoft Corp.; Novell, Inc.

LOUDCLOUD, INC.

Loudcloud, Inc. was founded in September 1999 by some of the Internet's earliest innovators, including Netscape Communications Corp. co-founder Marc Andreessen and former Netscape and America Online (AOL) executive Ben Horowitz. Other members of the founding team included Tim Howes, who co-invented the Lightweight Directory Access Protocol (LDAP), which became the Internet standard for directories; and Sik Rhee, who designed the Kiva application server. All four members of the founding team worked together at Netscape and then at AOL after Netscape was acquired by AOL and Sun Microsystems. Horowitz was the executive in charge of AOL's e-commerce platform division and oversaw the development of Shop@AOL, the Internet's largest shopping destination.

Loudcloud offers a complete solutions package for companies to outsource their global Internet operations. The company stresses that it is not simply an Internet consulting firm, an application service provider (ASP), or a data center provider. Rather, it describes itself as a software infrastructure service provider. Beyond hosting or managing services, Loudcloud provides the technology to automate the operations environment to give customers reliability, efficiency, and performance in a single solution. Thus, while Loudcloud sells a service, it is the company's own Opsware automation technology that makes its service so powerful; and the Opsware software is not sold as packaged software.

Companies who have outsourced some or all of their Internet operations to Loudcloud include America Online (AOL), for whom Loudcloud is a preferred provider of e-commerce technologies, including the merchant portion of AOL's QuickCheckout wallet technology and future shopping technologies. In March 2001 Loudcloud announced that the News Corporation—owned Web sites Foxsports.com, Foxnews.com, and Fox.com would be deployed, scaled, managed, and monitored using Loudcloud's Opsware automation technology. That same month Loudcloud added USAToday.com to its list of customers.

By providing solutions for outsourcing global Internet operations, Loudcloud enables its customers to focus on the key business decisions that will give them a competitive advantage instead of spending their time making thousands of technical decisions. While data centers provide basic Web-hosting services and Internet consulting firms help companies design their top-level customer application, Loudcloud provides a complete infrastructure solution. Outsourcing their Internet operations to Loudcloud frees companies from the need to hire talented operations personnel to manage their Web site; the need to procure the right hardware, software, storage, and networking components; the need to deploy a secure operational environment; the need to monitor the site on a 24/7 basis and keep it up and running; and the need to scale the site by adding capacity and functionality as business grows.

LOUDCLOUD'S CORE SOLUTION

Loudcloud's core solution is called the Loudcloud Operational Environment (LOE). The LOE includes all of the technology, expertise, and services necessary to architect, deploy, manage, and continually grow a customer's Internet operations. Loudcloud has organized the LOE into four components: Readiness Services, Deployment Services, Global Support Services, and Opsware automation technology.

Readiness services include everything a company needs to create a reliable, scalable, and secure architecture. Client companies benefit from Loudcloud's expertise in product selection, which utilizes technologies and services approved by the Loudcloud Research team. Sites that are designed by Loudcloud and built on technologies certified by Loudcloud Research are backed by a 100 percent scheduled-uptime guarantee.

Deployment services include the configuration, preparation, testing, and implementation services needed to deploy a client's Web site within the LOE. Loudcloud provides customers with a single point of contact for project management by assigning a dedicated project engineer to each customer deployment. The project engineer, in turn, coordinates a team of experts that includes a consulting engineer, a network engineer, a database administrator, a systems administrator, a systems engineer, an account manager, and a site operations engineer. Loudcloud's deployment services can take a new operational environment live in as little as six weeks.

The next basic component, global support services, keeps the client's site running on a 24/7 basis

through Loudcloud's Network Operations Center (NOC). Service level agreements (SLAs) are provided to ensure that NOC engineers not only monitor Internet operations, they also take immediate action to remedy any outstanding problems.

The core foundation of the LOE is Loudcloud's proprietary Opsware automation technology. Opsware automates many of the tasks associated with the deployment, support, and growth of Internet infrastructure. The software integrates several functional components into a single technology, including server provisioning and configuration, network provisioning and configuration, monitoring and security framework, change management and maintenance, code deployment, failure recovery, operational audit, and more.

SMART CLOUD EXPANDS THE LOUDCLOUD OPERATIONAL ENVIRONMENT

Loudcloud also offers client companies a choice of four optional Smart Clouds that expand the LOE. Each Smart Cloud includes licenses, hardware, software, deployment, and 24/7 monitoring and management. They include industry-leading technologies and services that have been certified by Loudcloud Research. Customers can purchase the appropriate combination of Smart Clouds to match their own needs. The four Smart Clouds are Enhanced Environment, Enhanced Performance, Enhanced Development, and Enhanced Risk Management.

Enhanced Environment Smart Clouds allow customers to increase the scalability, security, and functionality of their Internet operations. The core operational components include Web servers, application servers, database servers, storage, staging, and integration services. Benefits to customers include rapid response to market, architecture that eliminates single points of failure, and seamless scalability. Enhanced environment services include the following Clouds: Web, Application, Database, Storage, Staging, Directory, Integration, and Enhanced General Support.

Enhanced Development Smart Clouds provide customers with development and evaluation tools that enable them to develop, test, and qualify their Web site applications and code. Loudcloud offers customers the RapidBuild Cloud, which provides them with a solid development environment for testing and qualifying new content and code, as well as the Stress Cloud, which enables customers to test if their site can withstand the pressure and demands of different levels of Internet traffic.

Enhanced Performance Smart Clouds provide client companies with performance evaluation tools to help them improve their end-users' Web site experience. Included among this group of Smart Clouds is the Global Response Cloud, which lets customers monitor and measure their site performance from up to 50 metropolitan areas around the world. The Transaction Response Cloud gives customers the ability to monitor and measure the performance of their site in real time. The Content Distribution Cloud accelerates site performance by caching static media on geographically dispersed servers which, in effect, put content closer to end-users. The Streaming Cloud allows customers to provide high-quality video-on-demand content on their sites.

Enhanced Risk Management Smart Clouds are a collection of enhanced security tools for customers with specialized needs. Among the areas for which enhanced security tools are offered are access control, e-mail, global recovery, and file transfers.

Loudcloud's solutions support most of the major platforms and software applications used for large-scale Internet sites. Supported operating systems include Linux, Microsoft Windows NT, Microsoft Windows 2000, and Sun Solaris. Supported Web servers include Apache, Microsoft IIS, and iPlanet (Netscape) Enterprise.

LOUDCLOUD GOES PUBLIC

When Loudcloud officially opened for business in February 2000, it had seven customers and $68 million in venture capital financing. By mid-2000 the company had raised another $120 million in capital. In September 2000 Loudcloud expanded into the European market by opening offices in London, Paris, and Munich.

On March 9, 2001, Loudcloud held its initial public offering (IPO). The investment climate for Internet-based companies was not favorable, however, and the company had to lower its initial offering price. Instead of selling 10 million shares at $10 to $12 a share, Loudcloud had to sell 25 million shares at an offering price of $6 in order to raise the necessary $150 million.

For the fiscal year ending January 31, 2001, Loudcloud reported revenue of $15.5 million. Its pro-forma net loss for the year was $94.7 million, excluding non-cash amortization associated with deferred employee stock compensation and a non-cash preferred stock dividend. The company's fourth quarter revenue increased 94 percent over third quarter revenue, from $4.6 million to $8.9 million.

At the end of the first quarter of fiscal 2002 Loudcloud announced initiatives to achieve a fully-funded business plan. Cost-cutting measures that were taken included a workforce reduction of 19 percent, representing 122 employees and resulting in a scaled back workforce of 507 employees. Following the cutbacks the company planned to continue to focus on customer sales, support, and satisfaction, as well as its core research and development efforts, while scaling back on other Internet support functions.

FURTHER READING:

''All Together Now.'' *The Economist (U.S.),* April 14, 2001.

''Andreessen Launches Loudcloud.'' *The Business Journal,* February 11, 2000.

Brown, Eryn. ''The Internet's Alphabet Soup Is Getting Messy.'' *Fortune,* December 18, 2000.

Byron, Christopher. ''Netscape Founder Offers a New Cash-Burning Dot-Com.'' *Los Angeles Business Journal,* February 26, 2001.

Darrow, Barbara, and Amy Rogers. ''Loudcloud-The Secret Is Out-Goal: Become Infrastructure Provider to B2B Stars.'' *Computer Reseller News,* February 7, 2000.

Leger, Dimitry Elias. ''Behind Every Great Man is a Great Manager.'' *Fortune,* October 16, 2000.

Loudcloud, Inc. May 2001. Available from www.loudcloud.com.

Mardesich, Jodi. ''Andreessen Starts It Up.'' *Fortune,* November 22, 1999.

''A Pioneer Once More.'' *Business Week,* February 28, 2000.

Roberts-Witt, Sarah L. ''Loudcloud.'' *Internet World,* July 1, 2000.

Spangler, Todd. ''Andreessen's Loudcloud: Techies for Hire.'' *Inter@ctive Week,* February 14, 2000.

SEE ALSO: Andreessen, Marc; Service Level Agreement (SLA)

LOYALTY

E-merchants, like merchants in traditional retailing, are interested not only in attracting new customers to their Web sites, but developing a base of loyal old customers who return to a site regularly. Web sites that inspire customer loyalty are said to be ''sticky.'' The stickiest, most successful retail sites, such as Amazon.com, have shown that the characteristics that make a Web site sticky are frequently the same ones that keep customers coming back to bricks-and-mortar establishments: quality merchandise, low prices, and good customer service.

As the age of the World Wide Web was dawning, it was assumed that crucial differences in e-commerce would result in a different yardstick for the loyalty of customers. In fact, customer loyalty was expected to be so completely up for grabs on the Web as to be nonexistent. Unlike traditional shopping, consumers on the Web were always ''just a mouse click away'' from any merchant and every competitor. Established economic theory suggested that the ease of comparison shopping on the Web would encourage shoppers to seek out the lowest possible price on any purchase. In the end, Web shoppers would be loyal primarily to their own pocketbooks.

By the beginning of the 2000s, however, it seemed that something was seriously awry in these theoretical predictions. A 2001 study by Erik Brynjolfsson and Michael D. Smith found that online shoppers maintained a loyalty to brand names, even when prices were higher. Shoppers who used shopbots—online engines that compare the prices of similar goods at a variety of online sources—also tended to limit their shopping to familiar sites, even when they could plainly see that an item was available at a lower price elsewhere. The same study revealed that brand-name online retailers could charge more than their competition, and that shoppers were willing to pay more at sites they had already visited.

The latter finding was confirmed in a study of online shopping patterns conducted by Professor Eric J. Johnson and others. Johnson discovered that, despite being just a click away, Internet consumers do very little comparison shopping. The average shopper, he found, visits an average of only 1.1 book sites, 1.2 CD sites, and 1.8 travel sites in any month, and furthermore the number of sites visited did not increase as shoppers gained experience using the Web. Although Web shoppers tended to be more affluent and less conscious of price than traditional shoppers, Johnson provided evidence that loyalty to a single site was rooted in a phenomenon called cognitive lock-in. Learning to use a Web site is an investment of time and energy for shoppers. They must learn their way around each new site they visit, much like learning to find groceries in the aisles of a supermarket. Once shoppers are familiar with a particular online site (or supermarket), they are much less likely to switch to a new site whose individual, perhaps idiosyncratic, navigational features they would have to learn from scratch. Cognitive lock-in is so powerful that most Web shoppers are willing to pay more at sites they know rather than switch.

The implications for designers of e-commerce sites are clear. First, a Web site that is easy to use will be stickier—consumers will be likely to keep coming back. Second, when updating a site, Webmasters should revise content but keep navigational features. New pages on a site should use the same familiar navigational features. Finally, new sites benefit by actively copying the navigational features of the most successful e-commerce sites. It is still an open question precisely which features make a Web site easy to use. It is also unclear how many shoppers stick with the first Web site they shop at regardless how easy or difficult it is to use.

Like traditional retailers such as gas stations and supermarkets, e-retailers feature special promotions, so-called ''loyalty programs,'' meant to boost customer loyalty. A variety of programs exist, similar to the old idea of frequent flier miles—surfers who use a Web site are awarded points which are collected and then exchanged for goods or services. Some Web sites, such as Dell Computers and American Airlines, have mounted their own loyalty programs. In contrast, so-called ''loyalty vendors'' develop programs in which many businesses, online and offline, can participate. In the programs developed by beenz, iPoints, Webrewards, and MyPoints, for example, consumers collect points at participating sites and can swap the points for merchandise at the same site or others—sometimes even at bricks-and-mortar stores. How shoppers qualify for points varies from program to program. Beenz, for example, awards points to surfers who visit or shop at participating sites; MyPoints gives points to surfers who take part in various marketing schemes, such as reading marketing e-mails, filling out surveys, visiting Web sites, making referrals to friends, taking advantage of trial offers, as well as shopping. The impact of these programs in influencing actual customer loyalty is in question. A study by Jupiter Communications, an Internet research firm, found that nearly 70 percent of online shoppers participate in such programs, but only 22 percent felt the programs influence their online shopping habits. The same study found that 72 percent of shoppers ranked the quality of online customer service as the deciding factor.

Another scheme for increasing online stickiness is the use of information about consumers to generate personalized marketing e-mails targeted at individual interests. Amazon.com, for example, tracks its customers' purchases and later notifies them of interesting new books. Some marketers believe that this sort of database mining—collecting as much information on individual consumers interests and pervious purchases—is the key to developing strong online loyalty. However, a survey reported in the *Guardian,* an English newspaper, found many consumers are suspicious of such ''personal relationships'' when initiated by e-merchants. Half the respondents believed the point of such a relationship was to earn the e-merchant more money. Less than five percent were interested in a relationship that involved revealing their preferences to online businesses.

Jupiter Communications developed a list of recommendations for Web-based merchants interested in strengthening the loyalty of their customer base, most of which apply equally to non-Web businesses:

1) Improve customer service;

2) Develop a site that is easy to navigate;

3) Provide more product information;

4) Improve product selection and availability, provide easy returns, and get the most out of information about users.

FURTHER READING:

Brynjolfsson, Erik, and Michael D. Smith. ''The Great Equalizer? Consumer Choice Behavior at Internet Shopbots.'' May 2000, (Revised: April 13, 2001) Available at ebusiness.mit.edu/papers.

''E-Collaboration Raises Revenues, Lowers Costs.'' *Asia Computer Weekly,* November 6, 2000.

Enos, Lori. ''E-tailers Itemize Customer Loyalty Needs.'' *E-Commerce Times Online,* May 23, 2001. Available at www.ecommercetimes.com.

Fry, Jason. ''Why Shoppers' Loyalty To Familiar Web Sites Isn't So Crazy After All.'' *Wall Street Journal,* August 13, 2001.

Hilsdon, John. ''How to Satisfy the Customer.'' *Guardian* (London), October 30, 2000.

Johnson, Eric J., Gerald L. Lohse, and Naomi Mandel. ''Designing Marketplaces of the Artificial: Four Approaches to Understanding Consumer Behavior in Electronic Environments.'' July 27, 1999. Available from hops.wharton.upenn.edu.

———, Steven Bellman, and Gerald L. Lohse. ''What Makes a Web Site Sticky?: Cognitive Lock In and the Power Law of Practice.'' October 4, 2000. Available from ecom.gsb.columbia.edu.

———, Wendy Moe, Peter Fader, Steven Bellman, and Jerry Lohse. ''On the Depth and Dynamics of Online Search Behavior.'' June 26, 2000. Available from www.cebiz.org/Papers.

Macaluso, Nora. ''E-Shoppers Not Swayed by Loyalty Programs.'' *E-Commerce Times,* May 1, 2000. Available at www.ecommercetimes.com.

Murphy, David. ''Developing Rules to Build Online Loyalty.'' *Marketing,* June 22, 2000.

Seben, Larry. ''Pitfalls in the Customer Loyalty Quest.'' *CRM Daily.com/ E-Commerce Times,* May 18, 2001. Available at www.crmdaily.com.

Spiegel, Rob. ''Amazon.com and American Airlines Top Internet Customer Loyalty List.'' *E-Commerce Times,* October 13, 1999. Available at www.ecommercetimes.com.

Strom, David. ''E-commerce is All About E-mail.'' *Daily Yomiuri* (Tokyo), December 7, 1999.

Tobin, Mark. ''Attractive Sites,'' *New Media Age,* April 20, 2000.

SEE ALSO: Churn

LUCENT TECHNOLOGIES

Lucent Technologies Inc.'s core businesses involved the design, development, and manufacture of communications systems, software, and products. The company supplied public and private communication systems and software to most of the world's largest communications network operators and service providers.

Since the time it was formed in 1995 as part of AT&T's restructuring, Lucent was also involved in other communications-related businesses, ranging from consumer products to microelectronics. It left the consumer products market in 1999 and 2000 by selling off its wireless handset unit and other consumer products businesses. To better focus on its core businesses and raise much-needed cash, Lucent sold or spun off significant portions of its operations in 2000 and 2001. In September 2000 Lucent spun off its enterprise networks business, which included voice and data solutions for business and government enterprises, into a separate and independent company, Avaya Inc. At the end of March 2001 Lucent spun off its microelectronics business, which included the manufacture of integrated circuits (ICs) and optoelectronics components, into a separate public company known as Agere Systems Inc. For much of 2001 Lucent was in merger talks with French telecommunications provider Alcatel. After the talks collapsed, Lucent sold its optical fiber and cable unit to Furukawa Electric of Japan.

While Lucent enjoyed strong revenue growth from 1995 to 1999, many of Lucent's businesses were affected by a global downturn in the telecommunications industry in 2000 and 2001. The company was also burdened with debt as the result of numerous acquisitions. In the 12 months preceding September 2001, Lucent's stock fell from around $40 a share to around $6, losing some 85 percent of its market value. The company reported quarterly losses of more than $3 billion for two successive quarters in fiscal 2001. As a result of layoffs and divestitures, Lucent's workforce was reduced by 44 percent from 155,000 employees in mid-2000 to 87,000 in mid-2001.

LUCENT SPUN OFF FROM AT&T

Lucent was incorporated in November 1995 in the wake of AT&T's restructuring. AT&T sold 17.6 percent of Lucent to the public on April 10, 1996. The $3 billion initial public offering was the largest U.S. history. The remaining 82.4 percent of Lucent was distributed to AT&T shareholders later in 1996. Lucent is the corporate descendant of AT&T's Western

Electric manufacturing division that AT&T bought in 1881. Bell Laboratories was also made part of Lucent. Bell Laboratories is known as the inventor of the transistor, the communications satellite, the laser, the cellular phone, and electronic telephone switching. From the time it was founded until the time it was incorporated into Lucent, Bell Laboratories averaged one patent a day.

In its first nine months as a public company, Lucent reported revenue of $15.9 billion. From 1997 to 1999 Lucent spent $32 billion on some 30 acquisitions. Its largest acquisition during this period was Ascend Communications in 1999 for more than $21 billion. Ascend was the leading manufacturer of ATM switches that were used by telephone carriers to link old voice circuits with new data lines. In 1999 Lucent also spent $1.5 billion to acquire Excel Switching Corp., which made telecommunications network switching products, and $1.5 billion on Kenan Systems Corp., which made customer service software.

In 1999 the company realigned its businesses into four main operating groups in addition to Bell Labs. Service Provider Networks consisted of optical networking, switching and access solutions, wireless networks, and communications software, plus businesses focused on serving cable TV operators and other service providers. Enterprise Networks was responsible for voice and data solutions for business and government enterprises. NetworkCare Professional Services offered a complete range of network services, including planning, design, implementation, operations, maintenance, education, and software. Lucent's Microelectronics and Communications Technologies group included the company's microelectronics business, network products, new ventures, and intellectual property. Its products included integrated circuits, optoelectronic components, power systems, optical fiber, cable, and connectivity solutions.

For much of its history Lucent's stock was popular with investors. From the time of its IPO in 1996 to the end of 1999, its stock increased in value 11 times, or 1,100 percent. With 4.6 million shareholders, Lucent became America's most widely held stock, surpassing AT&T in that regard. Like other technology companies, though, Lucent was affected by the stock market's volatility. When the company's first quarter results for fiscal 2000 fell short of analysts' expectations, its stock lost 28 percent of its value in one day, January 5, 2000.

ACQUISITIONS AND DIVESTITURES MARKED 2000

Lucent continued to pursue acquisitions in 2000 as well as to sell off non-core businesses. It continued to divest its consumer products units, selling its consumer telephone manufacturing business in the United States to Hong Kong-based VTech Holdings for $113 million. Lucent's first major acquisition in 2000 was Ortel Corp. for $2.95 billion. Ortel developed opto-electronic components for cable TV networks and was a market leader for lasers that increased the bandwidth of existing cable networks. The acquisition strengthened Lucent's ability to build high-capacity networks for cable TV operators.

Lucent hoped to strengthen its position in supplying fiber-optic networks with a $4.75 billion acquisition of Chromatis Networks Inc. Chromatis was a two-year-old start-up company that had yet to sell a single product. The company was involved in developing optical networking technology known as DWDM (dense wavelength division multiplexing). The company hoped to link long-haul networks with the so-called ''last-mile'' of high-speed telecommunications networks. However, the acquisition did not prove fruitful, and Lucent closed down Chromatis Networks in August 2001.

Other significant acquisitions in 2000 included Spring Tide Networks, a vendor of network switches and Internet protocol (IP) products, for $1.3 billion, and Hermann Technology Inc., a supplier of next-generation optical network devices, for $438 million.

Lucent completed the spinoff of its enterprise networks business in 2000. The new company was called Avaya Inc. It began with 34,000 employees in 90 countries and was expected to have revenue of $8 billion annually. Its core business was the manufacture and marketing of traditional telecommunications equipment, which included Lucent's enterprise switching business and call center equipment and software. Lucent remained active in the enterprise market by focusing on corporate demand for hosted Web and e-commerce applications. Its NetworkCare Professional Services division would also continue to provide network planning and integration services.

Although Lucent was the leading vendor of power supplies in the United States and internationally, the company decided to put its power systems business up for sale in 2000. Lucent Power Systems generated revenue of $1 billion in the United States and $1.2 billion internationally. Late in 2000 it was sold to Tyco International Ltd. for $2.5 billion.

LOSSES MOUNTED DURING 2001

In March 2001 Lucent announced it was seeking buyers for its fiber and cable business unit, one of its core businesses. At the time Lucent was the second largest producer of optical fiber in the world behind Corning. The unit's revenue grew to nearly $2 billion in 2000. French telecommunications giant Alcatel SA made a bid for the fiber-optic business, then entered into talks with Lucent about a possible merger. At the end of May 2001 *The Washington Post* reported that Alcatel and Lucent were finalizing an agreement to merge, with Alcatel acquiring Lucent for $32 billion in stock. The next day it was announced that talks had collapsed, reportedly over issues of control. Lucent announced it would proceed with its own turnaround plan, which included laying off 10,000 workers and reducing annual expenses by $2 billion. Lucent subsequently sold its fiber-optic business to Furukawa Electric Co. of Japan for $2.5 billion, with Corning paying an additional $225 million for Lucent's interest in two joint ventures in China.

LUCENT'S GOAL: RETURN TO PROFITABILITY

The years 2000 and 2001 were difficult for Lucent. The company sold or spun off several revenue-producing units. At first it appeared that Lucent wanted to sell its non-core business assets and strengthen its core businesses. Later it became apparent that the cash-hungry company was burdened with a significant amount of debt, which caused it to sell more revenue-producing businesses, such as its fiber optic solutions unit, in 2001.

Lucent also faced a slowdown in the telecommunications market, which caused some of its customers to go out of business. The combination of a debt-laden balance sheet and a slowdown in spending by its customers made the company desperate for cash. For the quarter ending December 31, 2000—the first quarter of Lucent's 2001 fiscal year—Lucent lost $1 billion and experienced a 26 percent decrease in revenue from the same quarter of the previous year. Revenue from continuing operations declined 18 percent in the second quarter compared to the previous year, and Lucent's loss rose to $3.7 billion. In the third quarter Lucent posted a $3.25 billion loss as it accelerated its cost-cutting program by offering buyouts to some 10,000 employees. Other cost reduction measures included closing manufacturing plants and reducing the number of products. Lucent also planned to trim an additional 15,000 to 20,000 jobs by the end of 2001. Its goal was to return to profitability in fiscal 2002.

FURTHER READING:

"Acquiring Company of the Year." *Mergers & Acquisitions,* January 2000.

"Back to the Drawing Board: Schacht Speeds up Lucent's Turnaround Effort." *Telephony,* June 11, 2001.

Bucholtz, Chris. "Avaya Takes Flight." *VARbusiness,* January 8, 2001.

Drozdiak, William, and Greg Schneider. "Lucent Merger Talks Collapse." *The Washington Post,* May 30, 2001.

Feduschak, Natalia A. "Lucent Buys Ortel for $2.95B." *Multichannel News,* February 14, 2000.

Garretson, Rob, and John Schwartz. "For $4.75 Billion, Lucent Gets Tiny Va. Firm and a Big Idea." *The Washington Post,* June 1, 2000.

"Loose Ends." *Orlando Business Journal,* July 27, 2001.

"Lucent: Suddenly, the Hole Is Even Deeper." *Business Week,* June 11, 2001.

Miller, Elizabeth Starr. "Download: Whale Watching." *Telephony,* February 26, 2001.

Schaff, William. "Reeling Lucent Pushes Spin-Off Despite Chilly IPO Market." *InformationWeek,* March 26, 2001.

SEE ALSO: Fiber Optics; Optical Switching; Photonics

M

For companies engaging in e-commerce, downtime can mean missed business opportunities, lost revenue, and compromised customer service. The costs are significant; according to *Business Communications Review,* the Infonetics Research WAN Downtime Study put annual costs of wide area network problems at almost $8 million for organizations with more than 1,000 employees. Management Service Providers (MSPs) are third-party vendors to whom companies outsource different functions related to information technology (IT) management, usually for a monthly fee. They are able to measure, monitor, assess, and provide feedback on the performance of the many different applications and systems companies use during the course of doing business, including networks and servers (computers used to host Web sites).

Many different MSPs existed in the early 2000s. In terms of specialization, some provided service to e-businesses (relatively new companies), while others provided solutions to companies with enterprise or legacy systems. Companies falling into the latter category often have made investments over the years in many different computer systems that were not designed to work together, which can create complicated scenarios. Some MSPs were full-service, while others were self-service or somewhere in between.

Although MSPs varied in terms of focus, most were able to provide the same types of general services. These included simulating the experiences customers have when visiting a client's Web site, providing data management services, testing the security of a company's Web site, and so on. Developing adequate systems that perform critical tasks such as these can be a challenge for any company. As *Business Communications Review,* explained, the process involves many steps including evaluating, buying, installing, integrating, testing, and finding the right people (operators and systems analysts). For this reason, the turnkey solutions offered by MSPs were an attractive alternative for many companies, especially small and medium-sized organizations for which employing expensive IT staff was difficult or impossible. They also were valuable to companies doing business strictly on the Internet who require such expertise around the clock.

According to *Information Systems Management,* ''Organizations have an increasingly complex, expanding infrastructure to manage. . .If sites are not as or more available than the competition, organizations are no longer in business. So companies realize that management and availability have gone from being a competitive advantage to a mission-critical necessity.''

In addition to cost savings, MSPs were able to provide companies with other benefits in the early 2000s, including the necessary software to manage IT needs. Although this came at the expense of control and flexibility for some companies, staying abreast of developments in the area of network and systems management software was beyond the grasp of many organizations. Fast implementation was another benefit, since MSPs had the knowledge and skills to step in and provide immediate benefits to clients who otherwise would have to recruit scarce human resources for the same purpose. The drawbacks to using MSPs included limited capabilities and the fact that some did not offer services to fix the IT problems they identified, leaving that task to the contracting organization.

Strong growth potential was projected for MSPs in the early 2000s. *Information Systems Management* revealed that, according to industry analysts, by 2005 MSPs would create more than $4 billion in revenue. This was a significant increase over the $90 million analysts expected in 2000. *InformationWeek* cited information from International Data Corp. that predicted a similarly bright outlook for MSPs, projecting a 61-percent compound annual growth rate from 2000 to 2004.

Austin, Texas-based NetSolve was one leading enterprise-focused MSP during the early 2000s. Formed in 1995, its clients included national companies like Bally Total Fitness, Pinkerton Security, American Medical Response, and Wyndham Hotels. The company offered a suite of services under the name ProWatch that pertained to Internet security, local area networks (LANs), and wide area networks (WANs). According to NetSolve, its ProWatch services did more than just monitor its customer's networks; repair functions also were available.

As MSPs grew in number, a trade association was formed to meet their needs. An international consortium of companies called the MSP Association was created in June 2000. Based in Wakefield, Massachusetts, its mission is "to define and promote the management service provider market through education, research and definition of standards and best practices. To accomplish this, the Association will serve as a forum for discussion of issues, sponsor industry research, develop open standards and guidelines, and promote best practices, among other activities." Less than a year after it was founded, the MSP Association had more than 100 members who were able to take advantage of events, conferences, and other industry-specific resources.

FURTHER READING:

"About NetSolve." NetSolve. June 28, 2001. Available from www.netsolve.com.

Butler, Janet. "The Management Service Provider Option." *Information Systems Management,* Fall 2000.

"Management Service Provider (MSP) Association Strikes Membership Milestone With 100 Members." Management Service Provider (MSP) Association. March 2, 2001. Available from www.mspassociation.org.

"ProWatch Services." NetSolve. June 28, 2001. Available from www.netsolve.com.

Sevcik, Peter. "The MSP Movement is Launched." *Business Communications Review,* May 2000.

Shea, Billie. "MSPs Help Manage IT Assets." *InformationWeek,* October 30, 2000.

MANDL, ALEX J.

Alex J. Mandl served as the CEO of Teligent, Inc., a Virginia-based telecommunications upstart, from August 1996 to April 2001. He left his post as president and COO of AT&T Corp. to head up the new competitive local exchange carrier (CLEC), which uses its own high-frequency microwave and broadband SmartWave networks to offer local and long-distance phone services, Internet access, World Wide Web hosting, and similar services to small and mid-sized businesses. With Mandl at the reins, Teligent grew into a firm with $152 million in 2000 sales, and services in 43 U.S. cities, as well as in Argentina, Spain, France, and Germany. When long-distance provider IDT bought Teligent in April of 2001, Mandl resigned.

Mandl began his career in 1969 at Boise Cascade Corp., where he worked as a merger and acquisition analyst until 1980, when he accepted the position of senior vice president of finance at Seaboard Coast Line Industries. In 1988, Sea-Land Service tapped Mandl as chairman and CEO. Three years later, he moved to AT&T as chief financial officer, a position he retained until 1993, when he was named executive vice president and CEO of the firm's communications service division. In January of 1996, Mandl became president and chief operating officer of AT&T. According to *Telephony* columnist Jason Meyers, "Mandl accomplished every major task asked of him during his five-year tenure. . .his legacy includes AT&T's successful acquisition of McCaw Cellular Communications and its classification as a non-dominant carrier by the Federal Communications Commission." The McCaw purchase was particularly important to AT&T because its ill-fated takeover of NCR Corp. in 1991 had cost the company roughly $4 billion in losses when the anticipated synergies between communications and computers failed to materialize. As AT&T began seeking non-computer avenues of expansion and analysts began to sing the praises of bundled communication services, Mandl recognized that AT&T's lack of cellular services was a major shortcoming. When negotiations launched between AT&T and McCaw, he pushed AT&T's CEO, Allen Robert, to buy the cellular firm outright. The $12.6 billion purchase resulted in the formation of AT&T Wireless, which evolved into the largest wireless services provider in the U.S.

A relatively unknown firm, Associated Group, coaxed Mandl away from AT&T in August of 1996, offering him a $20 million signing bonus and an 18 percent stake in a new wireless service provider that would compete with local exchange carriers, Associated Communications. Since the early 1990s, Associated Group had owned licenses to sell wireless services in 31 U.S. markets. The deregulation of the telecommunications industry in 1996, which permitted competition in the U.S. local telephone carrier market, prompted Associated Group to make use of its licenses via Associated Communications, which Mandl agreed to manage. The upstart became known as Teligent when Mandl took it public in November of 1997.

To prepare Teligent for the launch of its services, Mandl spent most of 1997 and 1998 developing the firm's infrastructure and securing permission for it to operate as a CLEC. Teligent's technology offered several advantages over competitors like WinStar Communications. For example, its low 18 GHz frequency extended the coverage and capacity of Teligent's digital microwave networks. In contrast to the costly copper and fiber networks typically used by local carriers, Teligent relied on digital signals transferred from home base sites to antennas mounted on the roofs of office buildings housing clients. The cost savings allowed Teligent to undercut competitors' prices by 25 percent.

Services were activated in ten U.S. cities in October of 1998, and by the end of 1999, Teligent was operating in 40 major markets. Sales reached $31 million, yet losses totaled $539 million. In 2000, although revenues grew to $152 million, losses of $808 million and the firm's $1 billion debt started to concern investors. The telecommunications industry as a whole began experiencing a downturn, and despite Mandl's cost cutting efforts, which included laying off employees and scaling back growth, shareholders began dumping stock and funding disappeared. Long-distance firm IDT purchased a 54 percent stake in Teligent in April of 2001. Shortly thereafter, Mandl resigned. In May, Teligent filed for Chapter 11 bankruptcy protection, and analysts began to speculate about where the former AT&T executive might land next.

FURTHER READING:

Andrejczak, Matt. "Former AT&T Head Takes Teligent Public." *Baltimore Business Journal.* October 24, 1997.

Dix, Denise. "Teligent's Mandl Sizes Up a Tough Market." *Network World.* March 6, 2000.

Elstrom, Peter. "Telecom Meltdown." *BusinessWeek Online.* April 23, 2001. Available from www.businessweek.com.

Haynes, Peter. "Teligent's Test." *Forbes.* March 9, 1998, 202.

Meyers, Jason. "Mandl Forgoes Goliath for Would-Be David." *Telephony.* August 26, 1996.

Swartz, Nikki. "InTeligent Challenger." *Wireless Review.* March 31, 1999.

"Teligent Files for Chapter 11 Bankruptcy." *Fiber Optic News.* May 28, 2001.

"Teligent Reports $152 Million in 2000 Revenues; Records Nearly 400 Percent Growth in Second Full Year of Operations." *Business Wire.* February 28, 2001.

"Teligent Scales Back Telecom Effort." *The Business Journal.* December 1, 2000.

"Turning to Chapter 11; Teligent Declares Bankruptcy." *Telephony.* May 28, 2001.

Warner, Bernhard. "Alex Mandl." *Brandwek.* October 7, 1996.

SEE ALSO: Teligent Inc.

MANUFACTURER MODEL

Connectivity is what gives the Internet its power. Ever since consumers widely adopted the World Wide Web, new possibilities have existed for buying and selling goods and services. Companies that already sold products directly to consumers gained another channel for doing so, and companies that relied on wholesalers and distributors to sell their products via different retail outlets suddenly were able to eliminate, partially or completely, those parties from their distribution channels. Selling directly, via the manufacturer model, often resulted in higher profits for manufacturers and more savings for consumers. Selling products or services directly to consumers is at the heart of the business model known as the manufacturer model.

UNDERSTANDING BUSINESS MODELS

Business models describe how companies generate revenue from their efforts by detailing the ways products, information, and other elements are utilized for commercial activity. Companies can generate revenue in a number of different ways. For example, some only sell products and services to consumers, some sell to other businesses, and some sell through both of these channels. Third-party organizations, including distributors or online marketplaces, enable transactions between companies and other businesses or consumers.

Business models often involve multiple levels within supply chains or value chains, which companies review and analyze regularly to remain optimally efficient. Value chains define the different steps involved in creating value along the spectrum of supply and demand. At one end of this spectrum are the raw materials used during manufacturing. At the other end are finished products used for direct consumption or as components by other manufacturers.

Because of the widespread variation in the marketplace, many different business models exist, ranging from those that are simple like the manufacturer model, to the more complex. In addition, some companies rely on a combination of different business models, and even within one industry may rely on very different approaches.

General business models are good tools for painting pictures of the way enterprises profit in the marketplace. With that in mind, they normally do not go into descriptions of detailed strategies. For that purpose, companies rely on a special kind of business model called a marketing plan. Marketing plans identify the specific situation a company finds itself in within a particular marketplace, the differentials that set a company apart from its competitors, the marketing tactics used to accomplish strategic objectives, and so on.

TRADITIONAL VERSUS ELECTRONIC BUSINESS MODELS

Long-established business models used in the physical world may or may not be meaningful for e-commerce. Some, including manufacturer models, subscription models, mail-order models, advertising models, free-trial models, and direct-marketing models, work well on the Internet. Furthermore, some business models have no place in the physical world and are native to electronic markets. Focusing heavily on the movement of electronic information, these include information-barter models, digital-delivery models, and freeware models.

Just because a company relies on an established online business model does not mean that it will be successful. Many other factors are responsible for the success or failure of an enterprise, online or offline. According to Jeffrey F. Rayport, "Every e-commerce business is either viable or not viable. They hardly qualify for the paint-by-number prescriptions that business people seem to expect. Business models themselves do not offer solutions; rather, how each business is run determines its success. So the success of e-commerce businesses will hinge largely on the art of management even as it is enabled by the science of technology."

SELLING DIRECT

The use of direct sales channels was expected to significantly increase in the early 2000s, boding well for companies using a manufacturer model. Stamford, Conn.-based Peppers and Rogers Group and the Menlo, Calif.-based Institute for the Future conducted a study that forecast revenues for consumer direct sales to grow from $190 billion in 1998 to $1.1 trillion by 2010. The study also predicted that the number of consumers using the direct sales channel would triple during that timeframe from 11 percent to 33 percent.

By eliminating third party intermediaries like distributors and wholesalers, consumers are supposed to benefit with lower prices. However, some third-party groups have made successful attempts to protect their survival. Among them are the National Automotive Dealers Association, the Wine Wholesalers Association, the National Association of Travel Agents, and the National Association of Realtors. Their efforts have made it impossible for automobile manufacturers to sell directly to consumers, and for wineries to sell wine via the Web. Efforts such as these were considered roadblocks by some manufacturers. However, others encouraged the involvement of third parties in their supply chains because they were able to offer added services that manufacturers found valuable. One such area was logistics, which can include services related to warehousing, storage, inventory management, and shipping.

While leading companies like Mattel, Nabisco, and Polo Ralph Lauren were selling some products directly to consumers in the early 2000s, they did not do so exclusively. Companies like Austin, Texas-based Dell Computer Corp. relied more heavily on the manufacturer model. In 1984, Michael Dell founded the company in a Texas dorm room with the goal of understanding the unique needs of customers and building computers that met those needs. Through a direct sales approach, the company put a premium on in-person relationships. Based on customer specifications, the company manufactured computers individually at locations in Texas, Tennessee, Brazil, China, Ireland, and Malaysia. In addition to consumers, Dell also sold computers to the corporate, education, and government sectors. It received about half of its orders and technical support requests via its Web site. Dell is proof that the manufacturer model works. The company achieved rapid growth, surpassing IBM in global market share in 1999 and climbing to the top of the overall world market in the first quarter of 2001.

The manufacturer model isn't limited to the technology industry. Airborne Direct manufactured bicycles for consumers based on their custom specifications, much like Dell did with computers. At its Web site, consumers were able to choose different types of bicycles and customize the components they wanted. The company used a "Bike Wizard" to help customers pick the right bike. Based on a number of different questions related to riding experience and body size, the wizard was able to select the right bike for each customer. If components were selected that might not be compatible with the bike, or that might delay a fast shipment, the Web site displayed special warning icons. Salespeople were available by phone or e-mail to assist customers with their orders prior to purchase. Additionally, Airborne allowed cyclists to store their custom bike designs in "online hangars" for 90 days to put bikes on display for viewing or to set up a gift registry. While most leading bicycle manufacturers remained loyal to their large networks of dealers, Yeti Cycles also sold custom bikes via the Internet. Mongoose used a combination of the two approaches to sell its line of titanium bikes, giving local retailers credit for bikes it sold online.

Flowerbud.com was another example of a company using the manufacturer model. This company sold flowers through its Web site. Founded by Mark and Alice Hayes, who operated a bulb farm near Portland, Oregon, orders sent to Flowerbud.com were filled by a handful of select growers across the United States, as opposed to florists. These growers shipped flowers in special packages via FedEx next-day service hours after being cut to ensure maximum freshness.

FURTHER READING:

Bambury, Paul. "A Taxonomy of Internet Commerce." *First-Monday,* 1998. Available from www.firstmonday.dk.

"Consumer Direct Sales To Explode." *Web Trend Watch,* July 14, 1999. Available from www.mediainfo.com.

"Direct to the Top: Dell Ranks No. 1 in Global Market Share for First Time." Dell Computer Corp. April 19, 2001. Available from www.dell.com.

Donahue, Sean. "Lock In Your Online Subs." *Business 2.0,* January 12, 2001. Available from www.business2.co.uk.

Lindsey, Joe. "Click and Buy to Ship on the Fly Internet Bike Sales Speed Up." *BikeZone.com,* May 5, 2001. Available from www.airborne.net.

McDowell, Dagen. "Dear Dagen: Business Models Explained." *TheStreet.com,* September 13, 1999. Available from www.thestreet.com.

"Progressive Policy Institute: Middlemen Hampering E-commerce." *Nua Internet Surveys,* February 1, 2001. Available from www.nua.ie/surveys.

Rappa, Michael. "Business Models On The Web." April 9, 2001. Available from www.academic.uofs.edu/faculty.

Rayport, Jeffrey F. "The Truth About Internet Business Models." *Strategy+Business,* Third Quarter, 1999. Available from www.strategy-business.com.

"Return of the Middleman." *Nua Internet Surveys,* December 5, 2001. Available from www.nua.ie/surveys.

Timmers, Paul. "Business Models for Electronic Markets." *Electronic Markets,* April, 1998. Available from www.electronicmarkets.org.

Vincent, Adam. "Are Web Sales Inevitable? Retailers Worry About Who's Next On The Internet." *Bicycle Retailer,* May 1, 1999. Available from www.airborne.net.

SEE ALSO: Business Models

MARKET RESEARCH

Market research is a tool used by businesses of all kinds to assist with decisions regarding things like product development, marketing campaigns, expansion efforts, pricing, and even overall strategy. The world's largest market researcher, AC Nielsen Corp., is best known for its Nielsen ratings, which provide information regarding a television show's viewers. Advertisers quite often use this information to target a particular demographic group with a television commercial. In the e-commerce world, online advertisers use market research to determine the efficacy of their online campaigns. Technology firms might use market research when deciding what new features to include in the newest version of a product. Many firms looking to move into e-commerce for the first time rely on market research when developing an online strategy. In fact, the Internet revolution of the late 1990s spawned a new niche for market researchers. As a result, established market researchers found themselves competing with upstarts as they jostled for position in the burgeoning Internet-related market research industries.

NETRATINGS INC.

One market research upstart, NetRatings, was founded in the summer of 1996 by David Toth, a vice president for the software arm of Hitachi. Toth used $3 million in venture capital from Hitachi to get the Internet demographics information provider up and running. The firm gathered its information on how World Wide Web surfers used the Internet by compiling panels of regular Internet users willing to install NetRatings tracking software on their personal computers (PCs).

In 1998, NetRatings and ACNielsen jointly created Nielsen/NetRating, a service that measured Internet usage, including audience demographics and advertising, in the U.S. and Canada. The following year, ACNielsen and NetRating created ACNielsen eRatings.com, which monitored Internet usage in Europe, Latin America, the Middle East, Africa, and Asia. According to an August 2001 *Business Wire* release, the combined services track "the entire spectrum of Internet user behavior: who's online, where they're going, what ads they're viewing and clicking on and how much time they spend." In October of 2001, NetRatings announced its intent to buy competitor Jupiter Media Metrix for $71.2 million. The purchase was scheduled for completion in early 2002.

GARTNER, INC.

An established market researcher competing against rivals like Jupiter Media Metrix and NetRatings was Gartner Inc., which employed roughly 800 consultants and served a client base of nearly 10,000 businesses, institutions, and other organizations that used outside experts for advice on decisions regarding computer hardware and software, communications devices, and other technology-related topics. The firm was founded in 1979 as Gartner Group by partners Gideon Gartner and David Stein. Its original focus was providing research and analysis of the information technology (IT) industry to buyers and sellers of computers and related devices. Six years later, the firm founded Gartner Group Securities, a unit serving the investment community with IT recommendations and information. Sales reached $40 million in 1988, and earnings exceeded $2 million.

By the early 1990s, operations spanned 20 countries, and sales exceeded $120 million. To generate capital for an acquisition spree, Gartner Group listed its shares publicly for the first time in 1994. Purchases that year included information technology (IT) system evaluator Real Decisions and IT research and analysis provider New Science. In 1995, Gartner Group bought IT market researcher Dataquest, Inc., which made a large portion of its data, including statistics, charts, and analysis, available online. The firm paid $2.5 million for project management software consultant Productivity Management Group Inc. in 1996. Gartner also purchased a 40 percent stake in Web content provider EC Cubed. The following year, the company acquired a 32 percent stake in Jupiter Communications, LLC, an online market researcher that would grow to be one of Gartner's largest competitors.

Growth via acquisition continued in 1998 as the firm worked to strengthen its position as a leading IT consultant both domestically and abroad. The firm's focus on looming Y2K problems proved problematic in 1999 as analysts began pointing to Gartner's lack of attention to the emerging e-business industry. According to an August 2001 article in *The Industry Standard,* ''The technology market researcher had spent so much effort warning the world about the looming Y2K disaster that it seemingly missed the biggest tech story of the decade. Upstart firms Forrester Research and Jupiter Communications grabbed the spotlight—and pots of money—by advising Web-struck managers about the e-business future.'' As a result, the firm began funneling millions of dollars into e-business market research services. To this end, Gartner acquired INTECO Corp., a research firm focused on Internet and e-commerce technology. The company also bought a 70 percent stake in cPulse, LLC, which developed an e-business application that tracked the satisfaction level of online customers.

Gartner hired 441 new employees, including 24 e-business consultants, in the first half of 2000 as part of a $10 million employee recruitment and retention program. The firm also paid $80 million for TechRepublic, Inc., a Web site for IT professionals. Four months later, the firm launched its eMetrix service, a real-time e-business monitor that cautions IT managers and other executives if a major supply chain problem appears imminent. Despite these efforts, Gartner continued to struggle with its online operations. A Web site overhaul in January 2001 drew criticism from both industry analysts and clients when several glitches remained unresolved for months. In June, Gartner released Gartner G2, a research service designed to assist non-technology executives utilize technology already in place within their company to improve operations. This new service marked the first attempt by Gartner to target non-technology professionals. Ironically, while Gartner continued to expand into new areas, it was the firm's core research and analysis that helped it weather both the dot.com fallout and economic downtown at the turn of the century better than its rivals.

FORRESTER RESEARCH INC.

Forrester Research Inc. is one of the leading market research firms covering the Internet and related technology. Its early focus on Internet technology, which began in 1995, helped bolster the firm's image as an Internet industry expert able to predict future trends in technology, business practices, and customer behavior. Unlike its rivals who base their projections on statistical data analysis, Forrester conducts surveys of major corporations. The firm's market research services—which range in cost from $5,000 to $10,000—target senior managers, marketing and technology executives, and business strategists at major corporations.

Forrester's products and services include two types of strategy research: Market Focus and Core Skills. Market Focus reports and briefs analyze the trends and industries related to a particular topic and make forecasts based on that information. Core Skills reports and briefs cover the issues involved in operating an e-business. Forrester also gathers Consumer Technographics data by querying over 400,000 households in North America and Europe regarding their use of technology for entertainment, shopping, and money management. Business Technographics data is pulled from interviews, regarding technology procurement, with executives of more than 2,500 corporations with annual sales exceeding $1 billion. The Advisory Services component of Forrester's offerings includes four programs: Web & Commerce Site Review, Web Site Review Boot Camp, Research Inquiry, and the Partners Program, which assigns a team of analysts to work with a business to develop and monitor some aspect of its corporate strategy. One final product, Forrester's eBusiness TechRankings assessment tool, evaluates emerging technologies for clients.

Forrester was founded in 1983 by George Forrester Colony, who spent five years at rival Yankee Group conducting telecommunications and office automation market research. After initially focusing on telecommunications market research, Forrester eventually moved into the PC and networking markets. As stated in the October 1996 issue of *Marketing Computers,* ''Colony, credited with coining the term 'client/server,' practically defined the course of network technology in the late '80s and '90s, and led many through its dark alleyways as the technology developed.'' New technology continued to emerge, fueling the need for market research. Forrester continued working to stay abreast of major technological developments, eventually becoming a ''leading prognosticator on Internet computing, having recognized early the effects that the Internet would have on business.'' Integral to Forrester's Internet expertise was its New Media Research Group, created in 1995 to focus on World Wide Web site analysis, new Internet-based technologies, and the demographics of Web surfers.

In 1999, Forrester launched its PowerRankings service, which listed the best e-commerce sites among different categories of online retailers. To compile its list, Forrester surveyed nearly 20,000 online customers and also conducted its own anonymous shopping tests at a variety of leading sites selling product ranging from airline tickets, apparel, books, and music to computer hardware and software. The e-tailers were evaluated for six different criteria: cost, customer service, delivery, features, transacting, and usability. Also that year, to boost its international operations, Forrester acquired London, England-based Fletcher Research, a two-year-old market analysis firm covering Internet usage in the United Kingdom.

Forrester teamed up with Information Resources Inc. in June of 2000 to create Netquity, a brand marketing research service targeting brand managers selling products on the Internet. A few months later, BuyerZone.com and Forrester began offering market analysis reports to small and medium-sized businesses. In November, the firm began working with the National Association of Purchasing Management to monitor the utilization of Internet-based procurement by various businesses. The dot.com meltdown in 2000 began to undermine the e-business market research industry by 2001. When Forrester's sales slowed, it laid off 111 employees, roughly 15 percent of its workforce.

YANKEE GROUP

Yankee Group is a leading market researcher focused on Internet-related industries, such as e-commerce, telecommunications, and wireless. The communication industry's first research and advisory services firm, Yankee Group was founded by Harvard Business School graduate Howard Anderson in 1970. Eventually, the firm's focus shifted to networking technology, particularly enterprise applications and data communications networks. In 1986, Yankee Group began using the Technologically Advanced Family Survey to query U.S. households with regard to their use and perception of new technology products and services. Four years later, the firm launched its Mobile User Survey, seeking data regarding mobile technology use across North America.

Annual growth during the early 1990s exceeded 20 percent. During that time, the firm expanded into Canada, establishing a research and consulting unit in Ontario named Canadian Market Strategies. The Global Network Strategies Survey was first utilized in 1992, to gather information from corporate network administrators regarding network usage. In August of 1996, Primark Corp. acquired Yankee Group from Anderson for roughly $65 million. The company expanded into Brazil by opening an office in Sao Paulo in 1999; the number of World Wide Web users there, approximately 3.5 million, was expected to nearly double over the next two years. This growth prompted firms like MCI Communications Corp., Sprint Corp., and Bell Canada to move into the country, and Yankee Group believed a market for its services would exist there as well. As a result, the firm also launched its Internet Strategies Latin America Planning Service, which analyzed the regional Internet Service Provider (ISP) strategies, broadband Internet access development, business-to-business (B2) e-commerce initiatives, and Web hosting services among Latin American businesses.

It was during 1999 that Yankee Group also began to retool itself as an Internet industry expert. Not only did the Internet become a key focus of Yankee Group's research—along with wireless and communications industries—but the firm also began working to offer its Internet industry analysis on a global scale, reaching Europe, the Pacific Rim, and Latin America. YankeeTek was created to invest in small dot.com startups, which would receive strategic planning services from Yankee Group, as well as access to Yankee's research.

Yankee Group launched two new programs—Online Financial Strategies (OFS) Planning Service and Online Retail Strategies (ORS) Planning Service—in 2000. The OFS service analyzed the Internet's influence on the financial services industry in terms of consumer behavior, new products, marketplace requirements, and business issues. The ORS service analyzed the behavior and attitudes of online shoppers, the business models used by online retailers, online shopping services, and fulfillment. Yankee Group also assisted clients within either industry to develop appropriate business strategies. Reuters plc, one of the world's leading information firms with $35 billion in market capitalization, bought for Yankee Group from Primark for $72.5 million in June. Yankee Group remained an autonomous entity, operating out of its parent's newly created global information business arm, known as Reuters Enterprise. The firm released its ''Yankee Group Stars'' list of the best online retailers in early 2001. That year, Yankee created a new Global Regulatory Strategies service to cover the regulatory issues surrounding international e-business.

FURTHER READING:

Barlas, Pete. ''Small Firm Has Big Plans for Net Ratings.'' *The Business Journal,* December 15, 1997.

Fattah, Hassan. ''Would Wall Street Muzzle George Colony?'' *Marketing Computers,* October 1996.

''Forrester Research and the National Association of Purchasing Management Collaborate to Generate a Quarterly Report on eBusiness.'' *Business Wire,* November 6, 2000.

''Forrester Research's Creative Thinker.'' *InformationWeek,* November 15, 1999.

''Gartner Rises Again.'' *The Industry Standard,* August 2001. Available from www.thestandard.com.

Greene, Tim. ''Yankee Group to Focus on e-Business.'' *Network World,* November 15, 1999.

''IRI, Forrester Research Launch Netquity.'' *Chain Drug Review,* June 5, 2000.

Judge, Paul C. ''Forrester Research: Sassy, Quirky, and Rich.'' *BusinessWeek Online,* May 26, 1997. Available from www.businessweek.com.

Konicki, Steve. ''Economic Slowdown Hits Hard at Analyst Firms.'' *InformationWeek,* September 10, 2001.

McGee, Marianne K. ''The Specialists: Finding Their Own Niche.'' *InformationWeek,* November 15, 1999.

''Nielsen/Net Ratings is Launched in Argentina.'' *Business Wire,* August 21, 2001.

Tanzillo, Kevin. ''Howard Anderson's Forward Thinking.'' *Communications News,* December 1996.

SEE ALSO: Forrester Research; Gartner Inc.; International Data Corp. (IDC); Jupiter Media Metrix; Yankee Group

MARKETING, INTERNET

Internet marketing is the practice of using the Internet as a medium for a marketing campaign. An Internet marketing campaign can involve several different types of advertisements, including the banner bars that formed of core of online advertising efforts in the late 1990s, a newsletter distributed via e-mail, an interactive pop-up window, links to one World Wide Web site from another, and a Web site itself. Internet marketing efforts can be designed to push direct sales, build or solidify a brand, encourage repeat business, and garner customer information. Quite often, the Internet is just one of several mediums—including television, radio, and print—that companies use in their marketing campaigns.

HISTORY OF INTERNET MARKETING

Spending on Internet advertising in 1996 totaled $301 million in the U.S. While significant compared to the zero dollars spent in 1994, the figure paled in comparison to the $175 billion spent on traditional advertising as a whole that year. As the number of Internet surfers continued to rise, however, interest in the Internet as a mass-media vehicle increased. Online advertising grew to an industry worth nearly $1 billion in 1997. The Internet became increasingly popular in the late 1990s, and the viability of the Internet as a marketing medium emerged as more than mere speculation. Millions of surfers logged on to the Web each day, and many businesses were determined to reach this new audience. Web sites emerged for companies in nearly every industry, ranging from household cleaning products and cosmetics to electronics and automobiles. At the same time, many firms realized that simply creating a Web site wasn't enough to create a solid Internet presence; they also needed to drive traffic either to their sites or to their specific advertisements.

For example, drug company Bristol-Myers Squibb Co. launched an Internet marketing campaign designed to build brand awareness for Excedrin. For 30 days during the 1997 tax season, the firm proclaimed Excedrin to be the ''tax headache medicine'' on a variety of financial Web sites. To entice surfers to click on the advertisement, Bristol-Myers offered a free sample of Excedrin to anyone who entered their name and address. According to *Business Week* writer Linda Himelstein, ''The response was as good as any elixir. In just one month, Bristol-Myers added 30,000 new names to its customer list—some 1,000 per day and triple the company's best-case scenario. What's more, the cost of obtaining those names was only half that of traditional marketing methods.''

Hoping for similar results, many traditional firms began incorporating the Internet into their existing marketing plans. Even technology industry giants like IBM Corp. and Microsoft Corp. began dumping millions of dollars into Internet marketing efforts. Many smaller firms, including Internet upstarts, turned to highly trafficked sites like Internet portal Yahoo!, paying for advertisements such as banner bars. In fact, Yahoo! was one of the few Internet-based firms actually able to earn a profit from online advertising. By developing technology that allowed it to track a visitor's online activity and control what banner bars and button ads that visitor saw, Yahoo! was able to target its messages in a manner never before seen by the marketing industry. Yahoo! could also monitor the number of hits each advertisement received as a means of evaluating an ad's effectiveness. This innovative technology, coupled with the site's intense traffic levels, attracted dot.com upstarts hoping to reach as many Internet users as possible.

However, like most other ventures reliant on dot-com businesses, Yahoo! saw its customer base dwindle when the U.S. economy began to cool in 2000 and many dot.com firms were forced to tighten advertising budgets as they fought to stay afloat. Making matters worse, many industry analysts began to argue that online advertisements like banner bars were simply ineffective more often than not. Despite the dot.com fallout, though, the $8.2 billion online advertising industry did not disappear. The fact remained that millions of people were surfing the Internet on a regular basis, and businesses were not willing to turn a blind eye to this mass market.

INTERNET MARKETING IN THE TWENTY-FIRST CENTURY

Although banner bars had fallen out of favor by the 21st century, many other forms of online advertising were playing an increased role in the marketing plans of various companies. For example, many businesses began to use online newsletters, transmitted via e-mail, to communicate new product developments to existing customers, solidify brand awareness, and announce special promotions. Some even began to sell advertising in their newsletters. According to a 2001 study conducted by *Opt-in News,* one out of three online newsletter publishers use the newsletter to generate advertising revenue. In many cases, according to Forrester Research, advertising in online newsletters is more effective than placing a banner ad on a Web site; a Forrester study revealed that advertisements in e-mail newsletters had an average response rate of 18 percent in 2000, versus a banner ad click through rate—the number of times someone clicks on an ad—of less than one percent. Michele Slack, an advertising executive for Jupiter Research, stated in a March 2000 *CNET News* article, "online players either have e-mail newsletters or are going to have them, and it's partially driven by competition. Newsletters are a way to lock in your consumers and remind them on a periodic basis of the value you provide."

Some firms began taking advantage of high-speed Internet connections to create things like short films to advertise their goods. For example, BMW spent millions of dollars to create a series of five-minute films available exclusively at BMW-films.com. The marketing campaign targeted men with incomes of more than $75,000, the same demographic that makes up the majority of individuals with high-speed access to the Internet. BMW advertised the films in magazines, movie theaters, and television. In June of 2001, roughly 1.1 million browsers paid a visit to BMWfilms.com.

Despite successes like those realized by BMW, the six largest advertising firms in the U.S. spent less than one percent of their budgets on Internet marketing in 2000. The reason for this, according to a July 2001 article in *BusinessWeek Online,* is that "the Web is still a developing medium, with no firmly established standards for either presenting advertising or measuring its effectiveness." The traditional firms who did begin to focus on the Internet, like BMW, focused "on ways to reinvent Web advertising in the image of its offline cousins—complete with more sophisticated presentation and broader standards for measuring success." In mid-2001, many traditional marketing firms began purchasing online advertising ventures, which they could acquire for rock bottom prices thanks to the dot.com meltdown. For example, European giant Havas Advertising acquired Circle.com, an interactive advertising agency based in Baltimore, Maryland.

Many established brick-and-mortar firms like General Motors Corp. came to see the Internet as one medium among many. For example, rather than simply deciding to use the Internet as a marketing tool, marketing executives at General Motors first identify the objectives of the marketing campaign in question. If the audience they are trying to reach is present on the Internet, they then decide which medium is going to play a major role, and which mediums will play supporting roles. In some cases, print and television ads might be used to market a campaign that is primarily online. In other cases, the Web might be used to supplement a television or print campaign, or an event of some sort. Typically, the automaker uses print and television when the marketing goal is building a brand; however, the firm believes the Internet is particularly valuable for the generation of leads. For example, General Motors can use the Web to send new vehicle launch information to anyone who is interested in a new car, essentially including those individuals in the launch campaign.

Despite the negative press regarding banner advertisements in recent years, General Motors opted for a banner advertisement to generate general interest in the Vibe, a new vehicle under production in 2001.

Targeting the young individuals it hopes will be interested in the Vibe, General Motors is allowing Web surfers who click on its banner ad to suggest color names for the various hues in which the car will be available. According to GM's director of interactive marketing, as quoted in a September 2001 issue of *E-Commerce Times,* "We thought, why should we come up with funky names for colors that we think people will like? Why not just ask them and build a contest around it? Then, we had our objective, and the Web was the obvious channel to accomplish this."

Enterprise resource planning software vendor PeopleSoft Inc. also views the Internet as one of many tools at the disposal of marketing professionals. The firm's marketing staff selects its target audience before deciding which medium to use. While it doesn't believe the Internet is well suited to creating initial brand awareness, it does use the medium to support existing brands, as well as to generate sales leads and determine interest levels. The firm enjoyed success with e-mail newsletters, believing that the key to success with this type of advertisement is ensuring the newsletters are mailed to the appropriate customers or potential customers. Also important is the inclusion of a specific offer in each newsletter, as well as a link allowing newsletter readers to instantly connect to the site.

Software giant Oracle Corp. believes Internet marketing has reduced its overall marketing expenditures. According to chief marketing officer Mark Jarvis, as quoted in a November 2001 article in *E-Commerce Times,* "You can do a great deal of marketing on the Internet without spending a dime. You put up a Web site with good content on it and customers will come, they'll register, and you can generate leads for your sales force without ever having to do outbound marketing." While some analysts might also attribute this success to Oracle's established product base and technologically savvy clients, the fact remains that the Internet has allowed Oracle to reduce its annual marketing expenses from $500 million in 1997 to $300 million in 2001. One way the firm has done this is by replacing direct mailing advertisements—which involve paper, printing, and postage costs—with e-mails. The firm sends roughly 100,000 marketing e-mails each day. While it continues to use print and television advertisements to create brand awareness, many of its lead generation activities revolve around the Internet. For example, Oracle uses banner ads that offer free software or a free information package in response to information like a visitor's name and email address. Referring to Internet marketing as "completely unchartered territory," Jarvis believes most companies are better off using their own experience to determine how the Internet can best serve them as a marketing medium.

The success of future Internet marketing efforts may well depend on the industry's ability to develop credible methods for measuring the success of online marketing campaigns. As the number of Internet users continues to rise, though, efforts to target those users are likely to grow with or without tools for measuring impact. Forrester Research predicts that by 2005, Internet marketing will be worth $42 billion, or 9.5 percent of total marketing expenditures.

FURTHER READING:

"Ad Model Not Dead, Just Evolving for Online Information Providers." *Electronic Information Report,* February 23, 2001.

Himmelstein, Linda. "Web Ads Start to Click." *Business Week,* October 6, 1997.

"It's a Shop-Eat-Shop World." *BusinessWeek Online,* July 12, 2001. Available from www.businessweek.com

Lindorff, Dave. "Draw More Business With an Online Newsletter." *BusinessWeek Online,* February 18, 2000. Available from www.businessweek.com.

Macaluso, Nora. "I-Marketing Interview: PeopleSoft." *E-Commerce Times,* October 23, 2001. Available from www.ecommertimes.com.

Olsen, Stefanie. "Newsletter Authors Reap Banner Profits." *CNET News,* March 30, 2000. Available from news.cnet.com.

"Online Advertising: It's Just the Beginning." *BusinessWeek Online,* July 12, 2001. Available from www.businessweek.com

Owens, Jennifer. "Study: E-Newsletters Drive Site Traffic." *Adweek,* April 2, 2001. Available from www.adweek.com.

Saliba, Clare. "I-Marketing Interview: Oracle." *E-Commerce Times,* November 13, 2001. Available from www.ecommertimes.com.

Vigoroso, Mark W. "I-Marketing Interview: General Motors." *E-Commerce Times,* September 20, 2001. Available from www.ecommertimes.com.

SEE ALSO: Advertising, Online; Affiliate Model; Banner Ads; E-mail Marketing; Marketing Plan, Creating a

MARKETING PLAN, CREATING A

A marketing plan is a key component of a business plan, a document written by an individual or group of individuals interested in launching a new business. Creating a marketing plan allows new business owners to understand their customer base, determine exactly how products or services will meet the needs of a customer base, and devise promotional and sales strategies to target that specific market. Marketing plans can also be written throughout the life of a business to determine appropriate strategies for things like public relations campaigns designed to raise the general awareness level of a company or advertising efforts designed to position products and services as superior to those of competitors. Although many businesses create marketing plans to detail their firm's overall marketing strategy, some use more focused marketing plans for specific brands or products.

In the late 1990s, as World Wide Web-based advertising began its surge in popularity, many traditional companies scrambled to gain a presence online. Web sites for all sorts of companies, as well as for specific brands, began to emerge. When traffic to many of these sites failed to materialize, some industry experts pointed to a lack of planning as the culprit. Companies had built the sites before establishing goals or figuring out who they were targeting. Along similar lines, many dot.com upstarts launched operations with no concrete marketing plan because speed to market was the top priority. When the stock market plummeted in 2000, and dot.coms began disappearing as quickly as they emerged, the business climate changed and surviving companies began investing time and effort in traditional business development tools like marketing plans. Fledgling firms began pulling together marketing plans to guide overall marketing strategy, while more established firms began to update their original marketing plans to include specifics on the addition of a new channel, the Internet, to existing marketing efforts.

By 2001, many firms, including automotive giant General Motors Corp., had started to view the Internet as one of many marketing channels. When creating a marketing plan, whether it will include Internet-based initiatives or not, General Motors executives first identify concrete goals for the plan before choosing a channel or group of channels, such as television, radio, and print. For example, they might decide their goal is to generate a specified number of leads for a new vehicle launch. Once the goal is in place, one of the next major planning decisions concerns target audience. For example, if the target audience of a new product—such as GM's Vibe, which was under production in 2001—is young professionals, a marketing plan can specify how the firm might best reach those individuals. If the audience GM is trying to reach is present on the Internet, the firm can then decide if that medium is going to play a major role or simply a supporting role. Because General Motors executives believe the Internet is particularly well suited to lead generation campaigns, the firm might choose Web-based marketing as the focal point of its lead generation campaign for Vibe. Television, radio, and prints ads might then be used to publicize Web-based promotions.

Telecommunications services provider Verizon also uses the Internet as one of many channels. According to Julie Weitzner, a marketing executive for Verizon quoted in the August 2001 issue of *E-Commerce Times,* the firm establishes specific, measurable goals for nearly all of its marketing efforts, both online and offline. It then determines if the goal is something that might be best handled via the Internet, like a lead generation campaign, or if it is something Verizon believes is better suited to more traditional mediums, such as a brand-building initiative. Having selected the channels, the firm then begins to address questions surrounding audience. ''What we try to do is view [the Internet] like any other medium. We define our target audience and we usually have multiple targets, which the Web allows you to segment. For instance, with our DSL, we can focus on gamers, people who download a lot of video or music as a key target audience.''

Marketing plans, even those created within a single company, can vary in scope, format, length, and level of detail; however, they typically include similar types of information. In addition, regardless of a firm's online activities or lack thereof, marketing plan developers tend to follow similar steps when creating a marketing plan.

DEFINING GOALS

Concrete goals are a key component of all marketing plans. Goals help to steer the development of all marketing activities, including promotions, advertising campaigns, and press related activities. Examples of specific and measurable goals include increasing market share by two percentage points over a 12-month period, doubling sales of a particular product in six months, and increasing customer retention by 25 percent from one holiday season to the next. Less specific goals might include increasing a company's visibility within a marketplace or differentiating a company from its rivals.

CONDUCTING MARKET RESEARCH

Like those preparing to write a business plan, one of the first things marketing plan developers do after establishing goals is conduct market research. Some might make a trip to the library, while others might use focus groups or purchase research from an established market researcher like Gartner, Inc. or Forrester Research Inc. Another key source of information, of course, is the Internet.

Marketing plans include extensive information about target market, such as the existing size and the anticipated growth rate of the market and the level of demand for the product or service offered. Marketing plans also quite often include descriptions of potential customers, including their gender, age, level of education, marital status, how they make purchases, and the reasons behind those purchases. When clothing retailer Lands' End began planning for its new Landsend.com site, the firm had already determined that a large portion of its customer base owned a personal computer and was twice as likely to have online access than the rest of the population. A typical Lands' End shopper was between 35 and 54 years of age and reported an average household income of at least $60,000. Nearly 88 percent had earned a college degree, and 66 percent were employed in a professional or managerial position. Incorporated into a marketing plan, all of this information would allow executives to make a wide variety of informed marketing decisions.

Discussions of target market also provide information on the history of the market, as well as various trends within the market. While marketers planning to target an emerging market might be unable to produce historical data about that market, they might be able to make comparisons to a similar industry. For example, although Amazon.com founder Jeff Bezos was unable to research the online consumer book industry—which for all practical purposes did not exist prior to Amazon's launch—he was able to use the traditional book industry as a basis for extrapolation when analyzing his target market. In fact, it was only after investigating 20 different products that he believed could be sold via the Internet—including magazines, CDs, and computer software—that Bezos settled on books, guessing that this sizable market, with its wide range of purchase choices, would be well served by the electronic searching and organizing capabilities of the Web.

Market research also includes a thorough analysis of competition. Marketing plans require information regarding the strengths and weaknesses of rivals, as well as information about their market share, profitability, and pricing strategies. Prior to choosing books as Amazon's initial focus, Bezos analyzed his competition and realized that market share was distributed among many leading book publishers. In fact, industry leader Barnes & Noble held less than 12 percent of the $25 billion book retailing market. This market fragmentation, Bezos believed, left room for upstarts. Along with describing the competition, marketing plan writers often explain how they plan to gain a competitive advantage over rivals. In the case of Amazon, Bezos planned to wrest market share from traditional book retailers by offering a wider selection and undercutting prices by 10 to 30 percent. Online travel discounter Hotwire.com planned to compete with its well established rival, the name-your-own-price giant Priceline.com, by offering improved services to customers. For example, online shoppers who purchased airline tickets on Hotwire.com would be granted access to their specific dates of travel, their estimated number of layovers, and the exact purchase price before they actually completed a transaction. In comparison, shoppers on Priceline.com were required to commit to a purchase when they submitted a desired price or price range, should that price be available, without always knowing the exact travel dates or approximate number of layovers.

According to a July 2000 issue of *Catalog Age,* the market research section of a marketing plan for pure play e-commerce vendors—those without a brick-and-mortar counterpart—might also require additional information. ''For instance, a print catalog selling camping supplies competes directly with other camping catalogs, and to some extent, local camping stores. But a pure-play Web site of camping products competes with other pure-plays, as well as catalogers and retailers that also have sites, and manufacturers that may have started selling direct to the consumer online. It's not just that there's more competition on the Web. An online consumer may find a tent he wants on your site, and then many search for a better or cheaper version elsewhere in cyberspace. These differences need to be noted, quantified, and attended to in the marketing plan.''

CHOOSING MARKETING ACTIVITIES

Once marketers have a sound understanding of the market they are targeting, they can begin selecting the marketing activities that will allow them to achieve their goals. Questions of budget typically arise at this point; some firms plan to spend a certain percentage of sales on marketing efforts, while others specify a set dollar amount, and budget limitations can factor into the selection of activities. Along with traditional forms of advertising, such as television, radio, newspaper, and magazine advertisements, marketers can also choose from less conventional promotional materials including online banner bars and buttons, as well as both print and online newsletters, and press releases. Regardless of the activities selected, ''the major task in developing effective advertising is to make sure the ads reflect the specific marketing goals and objectives,'' wrote *Agency Sales Magazine* columnist John R. Graham in a September 1998 article.

Trade show exhibits, seminars, special events, charitable activities, and even things like letterhead and business cards can all factor into a marketing plan, as can strategic alliances with other firms. One of online services powerhouse America Online's (AOL) most lauded marketing tactics was its 1996 deal with Microsoft Corp. which required the software giant to include AOL software on its Windows 95 operating system. In a similar move, dot.com startups could include as a major marketing strategy in their plans the securing of links from heavily trafficked sites like Yahoo! and Amazon to their sites.

Many firms also include in their marketing plan an explanation of how the effectiveness of marketing activities will be measured. Ideally, marketing executives are able to review their plans periodically, allowing for the discontinuation of those tactics that prove ineffective. Conversely, those activities that worked well might be continued and also used in future marketing plans.

FURTHER READING:

Beech, Wendy M. "Crafting Your Sales Technique: With a Marketing Plan, You Can Put Your Sales and Promotion Strategies in Place." *Black Enterprise,* December 1997.

Fridstein, Stan. "Marketing Plan." *Catalog Age,* July 2000.

Graham, John R. "Working With a Marketing Plan." *Agency Sales Magazine,* September 1998.

Holly, Tricia A. "Marketing Magic." *Travel Agent,* September 3, 2001.

Regan, Keith. "I-Marketing Interview: Verizon." *E-Commerce Times,* August 16, 2001. Available from www.ecommercetimes.com.

Vigoroso, Mark W. "I-Marketing Interview: General Motors." *E-Commerce Times,* September 20, 2001. Available from www.ecommercetimes.com.

SEE ALSO: Advertising, Online; Business Plan

MASS CUSTOMIZATION

The prevalence of customized goods has waned since the industrial revolution in favor of mass-produced goods, and for good economic reasons. Since industrial technology allowed for the mass production of virtually identical goods, the input costs for each unit declined, allowing firms to allocate their resources more efficiently via mass production rather than paying the extra cost per unit involved in tailoring each item toward customized specifications. Thus, mass production allowed companies to achieve economies of scale, a key to keeping prices low and gaining an edge on their competitors.

Mass customization, however, uses advances in information technology (IT) and computerized manufacturing to reverse this trend and once again bring customized goods to the forefront. It signals a shift from a product-centered approach to manufacturing—where the customer buys whatever the company decides to make—to a customer-centered approach—where the company makes exactly what the customer wishes to buy. Mass customization in manufacturing combines build-to-order assembly, just-in-time inventory control, high-tech database marketing, and IT-enhanced order-fulfillment systems to enable firms to take advantage of mass production's economy of scale while creating a product to individual specifications. In other words, thanks chiefly to breakthroughs in IT, companies can make individualized products without substantially increasing their per-unit costs. This helps keep prices down and enables manufacturers to continue to reap profits while providing greater value to the customer.

Mass customization is a reversal of the manufacturing logic symbolized in the early 20th century by Henry Ford, whose moving assembly-line model revolutionized manufacturing, further severing it from the individualized processes and customization of previous years toward a more or less monolithic manufacturing process centered around the product, not the customer. This ethos was crystallized in Ford's classic quip, "People can have the Model T in any color—so long as it's black."

THE DEVELOPMENT OF MASS CUSTOMIZATION

One of the first companies to dive into mass customization was Dell Computer in the mid-1980s. The company allowed customers to pick and choose specifications, including design, computer power, and software, from a predetermined list of available options, after which the components, some already pre-assembled, would be assembled to build the finished product.

The Internet, however, ultimately proved the greatest means toward mass customization for a number of reasons. First, the Internet dramatically enhanced the ability of companies to compile detailed information on individual customers and create comprehensive customer profiles. These profiles enabled firms to reach customers with a degree of customization already in hand and provided an avenue toward appealing to the customer for greater customization. Relatedly, the Internet provides customers with a mechanism for easy, personalized communication with companies. Finally, the Internet and related IT systems afford companies the ability to integrate their customer-profiling, customer-outreach, order-handling, and inventory-control systems more or less seamlessly, thereby minimizing costs and speeding the entire process. Manufacturers and managers can respond quickly to shifting order needs through the use of computerized systems, and customer-relationship agents can rapidly receive orders and attend to customer concerns while feeding the information along to other parts of the organization.

Enthusiasts of mass customization point out that it gives special advantages to smaller customers and helps level the playing field. Where once customization was confined more or less to high-value customers, it is now available to a much wider audience. And mass customization isn't simply a business-to-consumer phenomenon; it is also increasingly popular in business-to-business transactions.

THE PRODUCTION PROCESS

Above all, mass customization demands that the individual parts of a given good be produced separately and then assembled together at the end of the process, rather than continuously building and adding to the original skeleton from the ground up. Whether it's automobiles or clothing, firms are fragmenting their production processes so that, when customers communicate their orders via the Internet or other means to the manufacturer, a minimum amount of production slowdown and reordering is required to fulfill the order's specifications. In more production-intensive industries, breaking up production is the key to keeping a steady stream of products coming while also allowing for mass customization, all at a relatively low cost to the firm. Postponing the finished product is another key to reaping all the potential value from mass customization. This pushes the final stages of production as late as possible in the chain of production and delivery. Third-party logistics services increasingly offer late-stage assembly as part of their services, moving some production into the distribution channel and allowing greater flexibility to customize products.

Particularly when many stages of the production process are outsourced to other firms, an increasingly common configuration by the 21st century, the need for all levels of the production and distribution chain to be adequately wired together in a seamless fashion is paramount. But because manufacturing operations require a high degree of capital investment and back-end overhaul, relatively few had yet integrated mass customization architecture by the early 2000s.

Although in the ideal mass-customization environment production wouldn't even begin until the customer's order was submitted, for most industries that's simply not practical. They need to have the supplies handy and some level of production underway in order to keep their facilities moving and in order to get their entire range of products to their point of delivery in a timely fashion. Thus fracturing the assembly process proved the best compromise, allowing firms the flexibility of producing standard, mass-production models while also remaining capable of fulfilling custom orders as they arise.

Clothing and apparel manufacturers from Nike to Levi Strauss implemented mass customization tech-

nology to take body measurements, color preferences, and design specifications directly from customers over the Internet and feed them to the assembly line, while Mattel, according to *Business Week,* introduced mass customization to allow consumers to purchase its Barbie-theme dolls with their own unique hair style, skin color, and accessories.

THE CUSTOMER

The Internet is driving the mass customization trend in another way as well. As shoppers grow accustomed to making purchases on the Web, they come to expect getting exactly what they want, thereby opening a new field of competition for companies.

But in order to make mass customization technologies pay off, firms must get their customers excited about personalizing their purchases. Customizing, for all its benefits, does entail extra work for the buyer at the beginning of the shopping experience, and shoppers taking advantage of the Internet specifically for speed and convenience may stop short if their shopping entails lengthy forms or questionnaires. If customers are simply used to and comfortable with buying mass-produced products off the rack, then companies may need to put forth extra effort to prod customers into taking advantage of customization. This could include anything from marketing campaigns to concerted efforts to make the experience of customizing itself more attractive; in other words, firms may need to create an atmosphere around the customization process that in itself adds value for the customer.

THE COMPANY

Offering custom products has clear advantages for businesses. Since acquiring new customers is more expensive than retaining existing ones, firms would prefer to go on building customer relationships over time rather than continuously marketing to an indistinguishable mass. Mass customization is tailor-made for this kind of retention. Even where customized products are marginally more expensive to produce, the savings generated, in terms of marketing and outreach, by boosting customer satisfaction and developing long-term loyalty, can more than make up the difference.

Mass customization also tends to foster an alternate method of measuring a firm's success. Rather than looking at market share, which measures the percentage of the total market that is captured by one firm without distinguishing individual customers from each other, under mass customization, according to Ward Hanson of Stanford Business School, firms place greater weight on the lifetime value of individual customers. In other words, the company with the greatest number of customers may have a higher cost structure than a competitor which has the greatest customer loyalty, placing the share leader at a long-term disadvantage. Since customization places greater emphasis on customer profiles and outreach, the cost of acquiring and retaining a customer becomes paramount.

FURTHER READING:

Alexander, Steve. ''Mass Customization.'' *Computer World,* September 6, 1999.

''All Yours.'' *The Economist,* April 1, 2000.

Brady, Diane. ''Customizing for the Masses.'' *Business Week,* March 20, 2000.

Krizner, Ken. ''Individuality Extends Into Manufacturing.'' *Frontline Solutions,* March 2001

Schrage, Michael. ''Mine, All Mine.'' *MC Technology Marketing Intelligence,* August 1999.

Schwartz, Ephraim. ''Build-to-Order Drives Change.'' *InfoWorld,* September 27, 1999.

Zeiger, Ari. ''Customization Nation.'' *Incentive,* May 1999.

SEE ALSO: Customer Relationship Management (CRM); Economies of Scale; Levis.com

MCKELVEY, ANDREW J.

Andrew McKelvey is the founder, chairman, and CEO of TMP Worldwide, the world's largest seller of yellow page ads. TMP is also owner and operator of Monster.com, the number one job placement World Wide Web site and one of the 100 most visited Web sites. With sales of more than $1 billion and earnings of nearly $57 million, online recruitment powerhouse TMP is also a top recruitment advertising services firm and executive search and selection agent.

McKelvey earned his undergraduate degree from Westminster College. After borrowing $18,000, he founded the New York-based Telephone Marketing Program (TMP) in 1967 by offering to place local yellow page advertisements for national companies. McKelvey spent the next two decades growing his business through strategic alliances and acquisitions. By 1985, TMP held a 30 percent share of the yellow page advertisements market. The firm changed its name to TMP Worldwide in 1992. The following year, McKelvey decided to diversify into recruitment advertising by purchasing two recruitment agencies.

TMP made its first move toward the Internet in 1995 when it acquired two leading career Web sites:

Monsterboard and Online Career Center. To fund his firm's aggressive expansion, McKelvey conducted an initial public offering in December of 1996. He used the fresh capital to bolster recruitment operations with the purchase of 12 recruitment agencies, including one in Australia. Austin Knight Ltd., the world's third-largest recruitment agency, was added to TMP's holdings in 1997, as were U.S.-based Johnson Recruitment Advertising and two U.K.-based firms, MSL Group and Lonsdale Advertising. The following year, McKelvey found himself at the helm of the largest recruitment-advertising agency in the world and a leading Web-based publisher. The Monsterboard site, by then the leading career Web site, earned its first profit.

Afer merging Monsterboard with Online Career Center, McKelvey launched Monster.com in January of 1999. According to Doug Donovan, writer for *Forbes,* it was Monster's success that allowed McKelvey to achieve billionaire status. ''He ended up making more money in three years than in the three previous decades.'' By 2000, Monster.com had grown into an online career gateway with a series of Web sites in the U.S., Canada, Australia, Belgium, England, France, Germany, Hong Kong, India, Italy, Ireland, Luxembourg, the Netherlands, Singapore, Spain, and New Zealand. More than seven million users had registered at the site.

Each Monster site offers real-time job posting, company profiling, and resume screening and routing services to employers. Job seekers are able to store several versions of their resume in Monster's database. They can also participate on message boards and in chat rooms. Personal job search agents are available to assist with job seeking. Monster makes money by charging companies for access to its database of resumes—which total roughly 1.5 million—and to list their job openings on the site.

Hoping to further the success of his Internet powerhouse, McKelvey oversaw the acquisition of several of Monster's rivals, including Hotjobs.com and FlipDog.com, in 2001. He remains at the helm of parent company TMP.

FURTHER READING:

Donovan, Doug. ''Captive Monster.'' *Forbes,* July 5, 1999.

Monster.com. ''About Monster.com.'' Maynard, MA: Monster.com, 2001. Available from www.monster.com.

''Monster.com Acquires Rival Job Site.'' *United Press International,* July 3, 2001.

Stone, Amey. ''TMP Worldwide: A Safe Internet Play?'' *BusinessWeek Online,* March 12, 1998. Available from www.businessweekonline.com.

''TMP Worldwide Inc. Acquires HW Group PLC; Global Expansion Continues to Increase Distribution Channels and Strengthen Offerings in Selection Services.'' *Business Wire,* February 17, 2000.

TMP Worldwide Inc. ''Andrew J. McKelvey.'' New York: TMP Worldwide Inc., 2001. Available from www.tmp.com.

TMP Worldwide Inc. ''Milestones.'' New York: TMP Worldwide Inc., 2001. Available from www.tmp.com.

SEE ALSO: Monster.com

MCNEALY, SCOTT

Scott McNealy is the founder and CEO of Sun Microsystems Inc., the world's largest network computing firm. Sun's Java programming language and network servers account for most of its $14 billion in annual sales. Known for his declaration in the late 1980s that ''the network is the computer,'' McNealy is considered one of the world's most important figures in the development of technology as a whole, as well as in the rise of e-commerce.

After earning his undergraduate degree in economics at Harvard University, McNealy began working on his MBA at Stanford University. In 1982, shortly after his graduate work was completed, McNealy joined forces with Stanford graduate student Andreas Bechtolsheim, and Vinod Khosla to found Sun Microsystems Inc. CAD systems supplier Computer Vision contracted Sun to build a new operating system for its software applications in 1983. McNealy took over as president and CEO in 1984, after Khosla left the fledgling firm. McNealy took Sun public in 1986. By the end of the following year, Sun had emerged as the top U.S. workstation manufacturer. Sales exceeded $1 billion in 1988, and Sun began working with AT&T Corp. to upgrade the UNIX operating system.

Earnings dipped in 1989 as McNealy struggled to manage his firm's explosive growth. To bolster profits, he put in place a plan to develop the Sun OS operating system, a version of UNIX able to run on a wide variety of computers, including those with Intel microprocessors. McNealy also oversaw international expansion into Moscow in 1992 and the development of an enhanced customer support program in 1993. The following year, he refocused Sun on developing Internet access and security tools, including encryption devices, searching applications, and online telephone directories.

In 1995, the Internet revolution began in earnest. As a result, Sun's sales jumped to nearly $6 billion. McNealy made sure his firm was involved in as many aspects of Internet technology as possible. Sun developed Java, an object oriented programming language for the Internet, and McNealy convinced Microsoft Corp. to begin licensing it that year. Sales jumped another 21 percent in 1997. The following year, Sun usurped Hewlett-Packard as the top manufacturer of Unix servers in the United States. It also strengthened its foothold in the Internet software industry by acquiring NetDynamics, a World Wide Web application software maker.

Sales continued to climb, reaching $15.7 billion in 2000. Earnings grew to $1.9 billion. According to a May 2001 article in *Fortune,* McNealy ''rode the Internet craze for all it was worth. Whether it was e-commerce firms, telecommunications service providers, or traditional companies, if there was a Web application to run, the odds were that a Sun computer was running it.'' However, growth slowed dramatically for Sun when dot-com firms began declaring bankruptcy and information technology spending slowed in the fall of 2000. Fortunately for Sun, McNealy recognized the impending economic downturn and immediately launched modest cost cutting efforts that included curbing travel expenses, reducing the number of new hires, and suspending work on new facilities. As a result, the firm was able to survive the first half of 2001 without laying off employees, a fact which set it apart from competitors like Cisco Systems, which cut roughly 8,500 positions. In 2001, *BusinessWeek Online* named McNealy as a member of the ''e.biz 25,'' a listing of the 25 individuals most influential in the development of e-commerce early in the twenty-first century.

FURTHER READING:

Nee, Eric. ''Sun Microsystems: Life After Dot-Coms.'' *Fortune.* May 28, 2001.

''Executive Bios: Scott McNealy, Chairman and CEO.'' Palo Alto, California: Sun Microsystems Inc., 2001. Available from www.sun.com.

''The e.biz 25: Scott McNealy.'' *BusinessWeek Online.* May 14, 2001. Available from www.businessweek.com.

SEE ALSO: AT&T Corp.; Hewlett-Packard Co.; Java; Microsoft Corp.; Sun Microsystems; UNIX

MERCHANT DISCOUNT

A merchant is a business—or in terms of e-commerce, a Web site—that accepts credit or debit cards in exchange for goods or services. In order to accept credit cards as a method of payment, a merchant must first establish a merchant account by forming a relationship with an acquiring financial institution (or ''acquiring bank''). This relationship enables the merchant to process transactions and obtain cash from credit card purchases. A merchant discount, or discount rate, is the percentage of sales that a merchant pays to the acquiring bank to process credit card transactions.

The merchant discount rate is based on sales volume, average ticket size, industry, and risk. The rate is determined by multiplying the total credit card volume by a percentage charged by the bank. Most rates fall between one and three percent and are based on the rate requirements of a credit card company, such as Visa or Mastercard.

Online merchants, those that do business via the Internet, have a higher merchant discount rate than retail merchants. For example, USA Bankcards' online merchant discount rate was 2.39 percent in August 2001, while its discount rate for traditional retail merchants was 1.59 percent. In a traditional retail transaction, the merchant typically makes contact with both the credit card and the consumer and, as a result, is not held responsible for potential fraud. An online transaction, however, is completed without the customer or credit card present, leaving the online merchant accountable for any wrongdoing. Consequently, both the merchant and the credit card company become vulnerable to charge-backs, which happen when a consumer disputes a credit card transaction. If a charge-back is issued, the credit card company is responsible for pulling the payment back from the merchant and crediting that amount to the customer's account. An online merchant that continually receives charge-back requests is considered high-risk and may find its authorization to process credit cards suspended.

Most online merchants typically strive to make online purchasing at their site as safe as possible in order to reduce their merchant discount rate. Many utilize secure electronic transaction (SET) specifications that support credit card payments over the Web. Address verification service (AVS) is also used by online merchants. This security device checks U.S.-based billing addresses—the first four numbers of a street address and zip code—that are given to the online merchant by the consumer at the time of purchase. Shoppers who give a billing address that does not match their credit card billing address are unable to complete their purchase. Another online credit-card fraud deterrent, FraudScreenNet, was developed by merchant services and credit card processing firm Merchant Express LLC. This security service was used by 40 of the top 50 Visa and MasterCard credit card issuers in the United States in 2001. It not only verifies addresses, but also reviews the purchaser's e-mail address activity, shipping method history, product purchasing pattern, payment method history, work and telephone number patterns, time of day purchases are typically made, and purchasing frequency in order

to pinpoint unusual activity and reduce the occurrence of fraud.

As online spending increases, credit card transaction security continues to be a major concern for merchants. In order to lower their merchant discount rates, online merchants will, no doubt, continue to utilize security measures designed to decrease credit card fraud.

FURTHER READING:

ePay Management LLC. "Merchant Accounts." Mesa, AZ: ePay Management LLC, 2001. Available from www.epayinternet.com.

Shop.org. "Statistics: U.S. Online Shoppers." Washington, DC: Shop.org, 2001. Available from www.shop.org.

Webcom. "Getting a Merchant Account." Santa Cruz, CA: Webcom, 2001. Available from www.webcom.com.

SEE ALSO: Acquiring Bank; Charge-back; Merchant Model

MERCHANT MODEL

The merchant model of e-commerce involves the establishment of an electronic storefront on the World Wide Web, an information-technology infrastructure capable of receiving and processing orders, appropriate security measures to assure the safety, secrecy, and authenticity of transaction information, and means for procuring payments—either online or in the physical world—and completing orders via shipping and delivery. Under this broad outline, however, there are myriad considerations dependent on market conditions, financial ability, and technological capabilities.

The most important first step in implementing a successful e-commerce merchant strategy is drawing visitors to the company's Web site, and then turning those visitors into customers—preferably repeat customers. There are several ways a merchant may go about achieving this. One very popular method in the late 1990s was for merchants to contract with affiliate Web sites to place advertisements on the affiliates' pages. These advertisements, such as banners—the equivalent of cyberspace billboards—are clickable graphics or links that direct users to the merchant's site. In such an arrangement, the merchant agrees to pay the affiliate for posting the advertisement—either a flat fee or a tiny commission for each visit or sale based on a user clicking through from the affiliate's site. However, this method was losing favor in the early 2000s, as studies showed that the click-through model and banner advertisements were generating paltry returns. Increasingly, savvy marketing schemes were another favored method of drawing traffic to e-merchants' sites.

To maintain users and turn them into content shoppers, e-merchants need to give great consideration to the design of their Web sites, striking the right balance between aesthetic attractiveness, user-friendliness, and simplicity. For example, sites with heavy graphics and complex layout schemes may please some Web designers, but if a customer gets lost trying to purchase a product, they may be unlikely to return to the site. The general rule of thumb holds that customers should be able to find or purchase whatever they want in as few clicks as possible.

Perhaps the most heavily prized value-added component of online shopping for which merchants strive is the personalized shopping experience. Virtually unavailable at any large physical outlet, personalized shopping was the special purview of the e-merchant. In the late 1990s and 2000s, e-merchants invested heavily in technologies and applications that allow them to create sophisticated user profiles—or have customers create them themselves—which can then be fed to an application that tailors the online shopping experience to those specific customers. This was obviously a primary means of generating repeat business, and of taking maximum advantage of the kind of convenience the Web offers.

The late 1990s and early 2000s saw the rapid escalation but slower maturation of the merchant model. The dot-com craze propelled online merchants to the forefront of the e-commerce revolution, but the merchant model was plagued by a number of serious problems that culminated in the 2000 dot-com bust in the stock market, which forced e-commerce merchants to rethink their strategies and business models.

THE MERCHANT MODEL ADAPTS TO A TOUGHER ENVIRONMENT

The merchant model was challenged in the late 1990s by the industry dynamic of competing directly with established, bricks-and-mortar businesses. As a result, the merchant model was largely characterized by a number of unorthodox strategies. Perhaps the most dramatic of these were the competitive pricing schemes, whereby dot-com merchants sought to undercut their competitors—sometimes drastically—in order to draw customers to their sites, in hopes that the sheer volume of sales would enable them to stay afloat and increase their chances of attracting future venture financing, or find them favor in the stock market. However, as e-commerce merchants soon found, to their dismay, this business strategy, while for a time successful in gaining customers, wasn't much of a money maker, since the sale prices were often so low they barely covered the costs of the goods sold. At the most general level, one myth that proved untenable as bricks-and-mortar merchants began to shore up their Internet strategies was the idea that dot-com merchants were immune from traditional business rules, that e-commerce somehow transcended the standard economic wisdom. Thus, strategies such as these had to be overhauled to reflect a more stable scheme for turning a profit in the longterm.

One of the most pressing problems facing the e-commerce merchant model in the early 2000s was the issue of credit card fraud and chargebacks—the transactions enacted to remedy bogus charges. According to Visa International, chargebacks occur in Internet transactions three times as often as in all other credit-card processing mediums combined. If a chargeback occurs, it is the sole responsibility of the merchant. In the early 2000s, the major credit card companies were bringing pressure to bear on e-merchants to shore up their defenses against credit card fraud. According to Meridian Research, about 10 percent of all 1999 Internet sales involved credit-card fraud of some kind, which, without some sort of intervention, would cost U.S. e-merchants $30 billion by 2005.

Another major difficulty facing e-merchants in the late 1990s and early 2000s was order fulfillment. While merchants were often highly successful at drawing traffic to their sites and generating customers eager to take advantage of their low prices and innovative offerings, getting the products to those customers via the dot-com infrastructure proved much harder than anyone realized. Since much of the dot-com merchant model relied on the elimination of as much inventory as possible, combined with a heavy reliance on logistics outsourcing, e-merchants frequently exercised little direct control over their order-fulfillment capacities, and the relative newness of this approach in the Internet world made for complicated and bumpy relationships, as well as large numbers of dissatisfied customers. In this case, too, established bricks-and-mortar firms building their merchant Web operations enjoyed a distinct advantage over their pure-play dot-com competition by virtue of the former's ability to leverage their existing networks, rather than building, and relying so heavily on, brand new ones.

In addition, customer expectations of online shopping matured rapidly. When e-retailing picked up in the mid-1990s, the experience and convenience of making purchases over the Internet was often enough to keep customers visiting a merchant's site. By the end of the decade, however, convenience wasn't enough; online merchants were expected to make online shopping a value-added experience. In other words, customers demanded features in their online shopping experience—other than convenience—that they just couldn't get at a physical retail outlet.

In the early 2000s, the merchant sector witnessed a slow convergence between the maintenance of company warehouses and logistics operations incorporating sophisticated information technology for supply-chain management; improved and streamlined relationships between merchants and logistics specialists; and a greatly enhanced focus on customer relations to ensure that once customers are drawn to a site, they are enticed to stay by quality order fulfillment and overall service.

FURTHER READING:

Kemp, Ted. "Back To Retail Basics—E-Merchants Regroup." *InternetWeek,* January 29, 2001.

Mack, Ann. "E-Tailers Transfer Shelf Space into Cyberspace." *Adweek,* November 6, 2000.

Radcliff, Deborah. "E-merchant Beware." *Computerworld,* June 18, 2001.

Wilder, Clinton. "The Complete Package." *InformationWeek,* October 16, 2000.

SEE   Affiliate Model; Charge-back; E-tailing; Fraud, Inter-
ALSO: net; Fulfillment Problems; Order Fulfillment; Shake-out, E-commerce; Storefront Builders; Transaction Issues; Web Site Basics

MERGERS AND ACQUISITIONS

The rapid growth of dot.com upstarts in the latter half of the 1990s proved a fertile breeding ground for mergers and acquisitions. For example, between 1996 and 1997 the number of Internet service providers (ISPs) in operation skyrocketed from roughly 1,500 to nearly 4,000. Because smaller ISPs were able to serve local markets less expensively than larger rivals, the top contenders in the U.S. ISP market began consolidating in an effort to cut costs. America Online Inc. (AOL) played a key role with its September 1997 purchase of the consumer online service of CompuServe Corp. from WorldCom Inc. The acquisition boosted AOL's subscriber base to over 10 million, pushing rivals like Microsoft Network, AT WorldNet, and Prodigy to a distance second place. AOL's rapid growth allowed it to lower its prices to better compete with the upstarts. In turn, this prompted several upstarts to join forces in an effort to compete with industry leaders in terms of market share.

ISPs were not the only Internet players feeling pressure to grow via mergers and acquisitions, however. The intense competition between World Wide Web browser-makers Microsoft Corp. and Netscape Communications Corp. prompted both companies to seek Internet-related acquisitions as a means of keeping pace with the industry's continually evolving technology. Purchasing new technology meant neither firm had to spend the time and money necessary to develop its own products. In 1997, Netscape bought high-end Web server manufacturer KIVA Software Corp.; Internet commerce solutions provider Actra; Web graphics tools maker Digital Style Corp.; and messaging server technology vendor Portola Communications, Inc. That year, Microsoft Corp. acquired award-winning Web-based free e-mail service Hotmail; video streaming technology maker Vxtreme Inc; Java-based multimedia tools manufacturer Dimension X Inc.; Internet usage monitoring software vendor Interse Corp.; and WebTV Networks Inc.

In 1998, Netscape watched its share of the Web browser market fall from 62 percent to less than 40 percent. Microsoft's decision in 1995, when Netscape's share of the browser market had hovered around 80 percent, to bundle its Internet Explorer browser with its Windows 95 platform had been effective. People who bought new computers used Internet Explorer, simply because it was the browser software already available to them. In November of 1998, America Online (AOL) offered $4.2 billion in stock for the struggling Netscape. Netscape's managers believed a merger with AOL could potentially boost Netscape's share of the browser market, especially if AOL changed its default browser from Internet Explorer to Netscape Navigator. The deal would also increase both firms' positions in the e-commerce industry, which analysts predicted would be worth an estimated $4 billion by 2002. Netscape's Netcenter was already one of the leading full-service Web sites, offering users a gateway to the Internet, as well as online shopping and entertainment services, areas where AOL was looking to expand. Microsoft was also expected to compete extensively in these markets, and the merger would create a company that could potentially hold its own against the giant. The deal was completed in early 1999.

Mergers and acquisitions continued to take place as the e-commerce industry matured. Some companies continued to use acquisitions to gain quick access to new technology. For example, KB Toys purchased Brianplay.com in July 1999 rather than build its own online sales operation. Others merged with rivals as a means of gaining increased market share, as was the case with online auction powerhouse eBay, which bought Paris-based iBazar for $112 million in early 2001 to expand its presence in Europe. One of the largest Internet-related mergers, the $183 billion joining of AOL and Time Warner Inc. to form AOL Time Warner Inc., helped to ensure AOL's position as a leading Internet player in the future. Despite the varying reasons for mergers and acquisitions among e-commerce players, the majority of deals fell into one of two categories: mergers between dot.coms looking to increase their competitiveness and buyouts of floundering dot.coms by traditional brick and mortar firms.

JOINING FORCES TO COMPETE WITH INDUSTRY GIANTS

EGGHEAD.COM'S MERGER WITH ONSALE INC. Egghead, a traditional software retailer that converted all operations to the Internet in 1998, initiated merger negotiations with Internet auctioneer OnSale in July of 1999. Troubled by the decision by Amazon.com to diversify into both software sales and auctioning, the two firms believed a merger would allow them to better compete against the retailing giant. Along with giving the two firms access to one another's customers and allowing for cost cutting via layoffs, the deal would also enhance Egghead's site by adding auction functionality. OnSale and Egghead completed their merger in November, becoming an online retailer and auctioneer of discounted computer software, hardware, and related technology. The newly merged firm retained Egghead's more recognized name.

Although the merger fueled Egghead's growth into a leader in online software and consumer electronics sales by mid-2000, it wasn't enough to propel the firm to profitability. In the wake of the dot.com meltdown, Egghead's stock price began to tumble. At the same time, spending in the technology industry began to wane, slowing Egghead's sales. Cost cutting efforts included layoffs that eventually trimmed the firm's workforce by more than 65 percent. However, despite these measures, as well as $20 million in funding from IBM Corp., Egghead failed to stay afloat. The company declared bankruptcy in August of 2001.

JUNO ONLINE SERVICES INC.'S MERGER WITH NETZERO INC. Under mounting pressure from shareholders to produce profits, Juno Online, an ISP known for pioneering free Internet access, began testing methods for persuading users to convert to fee-based services in 2000. For example, the firm began making it more difficult for its most frequent users to log on to the free service, hoping they might decide to pay for more reliable premium service. Also forcing Juno to reexamine its free ISP model was the fact that the North American economic downturn in 2000 and 2001 had prompted many firms, dot.com and otherwise, to tighten their online advertising budgets. With its main source of revenue drying up, Juno needed to find other sources of income.

In June 2001, Juno and rival NetZero announced their intent to merge. The $70 million deal was completed three months later. The newly merged firm, named United Online, was the second largest Internet access provider in the U.S., behind AOL. Because many free ISP rivals like Free Inet and 1stUp had declared bankruptcy, the only viable free ISP competitor to United Online was Bluelight.com, operated by Kmart Corp., which admitted that the free ISP model was inherently flawed. Analysts speculated about whether or not the newly merged firm would abandon the increasingly criticized free ISP model altogether in favor of a fee-based service.

SEEKING REFUGE WITH A LARGER PARTNER

PEAPOD INC.'S TAKEOVER BY ROYAL AHOLD N.V. Founded in 1989, Peapod eventually evolved into an online grocer that allowed users to shop for groceries online and have the purchases delivered to their home. Although it got its start much earlier than most other Internet-based firms, Peapod found itself susceptible to the dot.com meltdown early in 2000. In March, the online grocer's stock was worth nearly 75 percent less than its peak price in 1999. Peapod's CEO resigned and investors balked at the idea of pumping more money into the unprofitable venture. As a result, Peapod was nearly out of cash.

In April, European brick-and-mortar grocery giant Royal Ahold agreed to pay $73 million for a 52 percent stake in Peapod. The reason for the bailout was simple, according to *InternetWeek* writer Scott Tillett. "To start its own U.S. online operation from scratch, Ahold would likely have spent more money over a longer period of time. Instead, its purchase of Peapod secured for Ahold 24 order fulfillment warehouses, 130,000 established customers, 1,000 employees, and existing information technology infrastructure. Peapod's sales in 2000 grew 28 percent $93 million, although its losses grew to $57 million, compared to $29 million the year earlier. However, Peapod's ability to use the warehouses serving Ahold's existing U.S. supermarket chains, such as Stop & Shop, allowed Peapod to cut its procurement costs in 2001. As a result, the firm's Chicago operation operated in the black for the first time ever, prompting management to predict that by 2004, Peapod would be the first online grocer to achieve profitability.

CDNOW'S TAKEOVER BY BERTELSMANN Despite leading online music retailer CDNow's rapid growth in the late 1990s, rivals like Amazon.com and barnesandnoble.com began undercutting the firm's sales. In fact, Amazon surpassed CDNow in music sales in 2000 mainly because CDNow lacked the resources to compete with Amazon's customer service savvy and vast customer base. Merger plans with Columbia House, made public mid-1999, dissolved in March of 2000, and many analysts pointed to the bursting of the dot.com bubble and CDNow's subsequent stock price nosedive as the culprits. Others believed that Columbia House had balked at CDNow's $30 million debt, as well as the fact that the online music retailer had lost roughly $200 million since its 1994 founding. At any rate, news of the cancelled plans caused share prices to fall another 28 percent. Reports that the firm might run out of cash by September pushed stock to a record low of $3.50. CDNow was seen "as struggling to keep pace with market leader Amazon.com and as scrambling to find a partner with deep pockets before it runs out of money," wrote Brian Garrity in the March 2000 issue of *Billboard.*

To make itself more appealing to potential partners, CDNow pared down its advertising costs and shuttered its London unit. Rather than relying mainly on the sale of CDs, the firm also began pushing sales of advertisements on its site. To retain customers, CDNow launched reward and incentive programs. In July of 2000, German media giant Bertelsmann offered to pay roughly $117 million, or $3 per share, for CDNow. Bertelsmann had been growing its e-commerce operations since 1998, when it paid $200 million for a 50 percent stake in BarnesandNoble.com; the firm used its new assets to develop an online retail book site to compete with Amazon in Europe. By mid-2000, Bertelsmann had spent nearly $13 billion on its Internet arm. One of its investments—Terra Lycos, created when Spain-based Terra Networks paid $12.5 billion for U.S.-based Web portal Lycos—secured Bertelsmann access to the 50 million customers already using either Terra Networks or Lycos. Many analysts believed that Bertelsmann's extensive reach would increase CDNow's ability to compete with rivals like Amazon.

In October 2000, CDNow joined the newly formed Bertelsmann eCommerce Group. In the months following its takeover, CDNow continued to grow. For example, via deals with ViaFone Inc. and Sprint PCS, the online music retailer began offering wireless access to its site. In addition, things like film reviews and best seller lists bolstered the content at its Video Shop and video offerings were expanded to more than 70,000 titles. As a result, CDNow's video sales nearly doubled by early 2001.

FUTURE MERGER AND ACQUISITION ACTIVITY

Many analysts predicted that the pace of merger and acquisition activity would remain steady, if not increase, throughout the early 2000s. According to an October 2001 article in *E-Commerce Times,* "With stock prices at bargain basement levels, these and other dot.coms like them could make good partners for brick-and-mortar companies seeking to add online operations to their existing businesses."

FURTHER READING:

"Bertelsmann to Acquire CDNow." *Direct Marketing,* October 2000.

"CDNow's Movie Sales More Than Double in One Year Since Launch of New Store." *PR Newswire,* February 26, 2001.

Davis, Jessica. "Dot-com Bargains Mean Mergers Ahead." *InfoWorld,* October 9, 2000.

"Egghead.com Merger Complete." *InformationWeek,* November 29, 1999.

"Egghead.com Rated No. 1 Online Consumer Electronics Retailer by Nielsen/NetRatings; Top Rankings Also Awarded by PC Data Online and Gomez.com." *Business Wire,* March 29, 2000.

"Egghead.com Shows Signs of Cracking." *Chain Store Age Executive with Shopping Center Age,* May 2001.

Garrity, Brian, and Don Jeffrey. "What Now for Col. House, CDNow?" *Billboard,* March 25, 2000.

Gillen, Marilyn A. "Bertelsmann Gains Web Hub with Purchase of CDNow." *Billboard,* July 29, 2000.

Macaluso, Nora. "Merger Mania Could Include Many E-Commerce Buyouts, Analysts Say." *E-Commerce Times,* October 8, 2001. Available from www.ecommercetimes.com.

Murphy, H. Lee. "Peapod's Single-Market Profit Seen As Signal Event." *Crain's Chicago Business,* May 28, 2001.

Sheldon, AnnaMarie L. "America Online and Netscape." In *Cases in Corporate Acquisitions, Buyouts, Mergers, & Takeovers.* Farmington Hills, MI: Gale Group, 1999.

Simons, David. "Marriage of Inconvenience." *Forbes,* June 11, 2001. Available from www.forbes.com.

Tillett, Scott L. "Shortcut to the Web." *InternetWeek,* April 24, 2000.

"A Web of M&A Activity." *Catalog Age,* September 1999.

SEE ALSO: AOL Time Warner Inc.; AT&T Corp.

METCALFE'S LAW

The Internet is a giant network of many smaller computer networks throughout the world. Its power and value stems from the fact that it connects millions of people. As more organizations and individuals use the Internet, the cost to access it decreases and more funds are invested that ultimately advance Internet technologies and infrastructure. If only a few people had access to the connections that form the Internet, its power and value would decrease significantly. The same could be said of many other technologies, including the telephone and television networks. In order for society to benefit from them, these tools must be used by more than just a handful of people. This concept is at the heart of Metcalfe's Law.

Metcalfe's Law is named after an observation of Robert Metcalfe, who founded 3Com Corp. in 1981 and played a major role in discovering and designing Ethernet technology—a leading way to access local area networks (LAN). Author George Gilder applied the term Metcalfe's Law to Metcalfe's observation in his 1993 article "Telecosm: Metcalfe's Law and Legacy," which was published in *Forbes ASAP.* According to 3Com, Metcalfe's Law "states that the economic value of a network increases like the square of the number of its nodes, or the law of increasing returns. Usually, when people share a piece of equipment, the return diminishes. When more people are engaged in the network, more value is returned to the user."

FURTHER READING:

"3Com CTO John Hart Foresees Access To Internet As A Basic Human Right." 3Com Corp., March 24, 1999. Available from www.3com.com.

Gilder, George. "Telecosm: Metcalfe's Law and Legacy." *Forbes ASAP,* September 13, 1993.

Metcalfe, Bob. "Metcalfe's Law: A Network Becomes More Valuable as it Reaches More Users." *InfoWorld,* October 2, 1995.

"Metcalfe's Law." *Tech Encyclopedia,* May 30, 2001. Available from www.techweb.com/encyclopedia.

SEE ALSO: Moore's Law

MICRO-PAYMENTS

Micro-payments are online transactions of low value, ranging from several pennies to approximately $10.00. Micro-payments are commonly used to pay for downloads of newspaper articles, electronic books, music clips, or software, but could be used for virtually any low-priced item for sale on the Internet.

Because the cost of accepting credit cards for small purchases is prohibitively expensive, some companies involved in e-commerce have turned to third party vendors to manage the billing and collection of micro-payments. Such vendors normally receive a percentage of each transaction as compensation.

According to *Computerworld,* the micropayment concept was especially popular in the early days of the World Wide Web. However, the popularity waned because the process of working with third-party vendors was considered too cumbersome by those involved. For example, in order to participate companies and consumers often had to install special software on their systems or fill out forms. Problems also surfaced when companies and consumers were registered with different third-party vendors. Finally, the issue of privacy was a factor that contributed to consumers' reluctance.

Both Forrester Research and the Gartner Group expected person-to-person micro-payments to grow in popularity. *Communications International* also expected the concept of mobile commerce to take off, where mobile phones and wireless devices like personal digital assistants (PDAs) are used to make micro-payments. In the early 2000s, Andersen Consulting developed prototype technology called Mobile Micropayments that had many potential uses. According to *InformationWeek,* the technology enabled consumers to receive special offers from merchants in their immediate location via their wireless device. For example, a consumer who walks past a vending machine might be presented with a range of selections on the display of his or her PDA, which could be purchased immediately.

Micro-payments represent a large amount of revenue. According to *Communications International,* Visa International estimates worldwide payments for items less than $10.00 to be $1.8 trillion annually. With the overall growth in e-commerce, it's unlikely the concept of micro-payments will disappear. For handling traditional online transactions of this kind, Internet service providers and telephone companies were poised to play a larger role in the early 2000s, according to *EContent.* Because these companies already have established financial relationships with large numbers of customers, it is possible for them to offer Internet payment services as an added benefit. Not only does this reduce the need for special software, it also reduces security concerns, since trusted financial information remains with the ISP or phone company.

FURTHER READING:

Caulfield, Brian. "The Technology's Here—But are Net Businesses Ready to Use It?" *Internet World,* October 1, 2000.

Nelson, Matthew. "Innovation: A Remote Control for E-commerce." *InformationWeek,* October 30, 2000.

Raffray, Nathalie. "Who Will Get the Credit?" *Communications International,* October, 2000.

Short, Sharon Gwyn. "Beyond Digital Wallets: Internet Payment Services as Ecommerce Boom or Bust?" *EContent,* April/May, 2000.

Solomon, Melissa. "Micropayments." *Computerworld,* May 1, 2000.

Weiner, Stuart E. ''Electronic Payments in the U.S. Economy: An Overview.'' *Government Finance Review.* April, 2000.

SEE ALSO: Electronic Payment; Personal Digital Assistant (PDA)

MICROPROCESSOR

Microprocessors are silicon chips that contain a computer's central processing unit (CPU)—the device that executes commands entered into the computer. Along with clocks and main memory, CPUs are among a computer's main components. The terms CPU and microprocessor often are used interchangeably. Essentially, microprocessors are responsible for manipulating data and performing numeric calculations and logical comparisons. At the heart of microprocessors are tiny electronic switches called transistors, which allow digital computers to process information in the form of electrical signals. These signals are in one of two states (on or off), and are represented by ones and zeroes, respectively. High-level programming languages like Java or C++, used to write popular software programs, eventually are translated to the machine language of ones and zeroes that computers understand.

Intel was the first company to produce a microprocessor for commercial use. Called the 4004, it was released in the early 1970s and contained slightly more than 2,000 transistors. By the early 2000s, microprocessors contained more than 5 million transistors on a single silicon chip. The more transistors a chip has, the more quickly it can process information. A microprocessor's clock speed defines the number of instructions it can carry out per second. This figure is expressed in Megahertz (MHz) or Gigahertz (GHz). In 2001 the processing speeds of some microprocessors exceeded 1.7 GHz.

In 1965, Intel Co-Founder Gordon E. Moore predicted the number of transistors manufacturers could fit onto a silicon chip would double every 18 months. Because his prediction proved to be accurate over time, it came to be known as Moore's Law. The law eventually will expire when it becomes physically impossible for manufacturers to fit any more transistors onto a single chip. This is expected to happen somewhere around 2017 or 2020 when transistors are atom-sized. At that time, a new computing architecture will be necessary. One possibility is quantum computing, which relies on atomic properties instead of transistors to determine the ones and zeros a computer understands. According to *InfoWorld*, ''quantum computers rely on a particle's traits, such as the direction of its spin, for creating a state. For example,

when the spin is up, a particle could be read as 'one,' and when its spin is down, the partide would be read as 'zero.'''

In mid-2001 Intel announced experimental technology that it called ''Wireless-Internet-On-A-Chip.'' Essentially, the technology consisted of a silicon chip that held a microprocessor, as well as analog communication circuits and flash memory. According to Intel, the technology potentially would lead to the development of more powerful wireless Internet devices. Around the same time, Intel and Hewlett-Packard announced the launch of the Itanium Processor, a new generation of microprocessor the companies co-developed for use in servers and workstation computers.

FURTHER READING:

Borck, James R. ''Life After Moore's Law: Quantum Computing.'' *InfoWorld,* October 16, 2000.

Intel Corp. ''Intel Creates Technology To Enable 'Wireless-Internet-On-A-Chip.''' Intel Corp., May 17, 2001. Available from www.intel.com/pressroom/archive.

———. ''Gordon E. Moore.'' Intel Corp., May 29, 2001. Available from www.intel.com/pressroom.

———. ''How Microprocessors Work.'' Intel Corp., May 29, 2001. Available from www.intel.com/education.

———. ''How Transistors Work.'' Intel Corp., May 29, 2001. Available from www.intel.com/education.

''Microprocessor.'' *Ecommerce Webopedia,* May 25, 2001. Available from www.e-comm.webopedia.com.

''Microprocessor.'' *Tech Encyclopedia,* May 25, 2001. Available from www.techweb.com.

SEE ALSO: Hardware; Intel Corp.; Moore, Gordon; Moore's Law; Programming Languages

MICROSOFT CORP.

Microsoft Corp. is the world's largest software firm, with annual sales of roughly $23 billion and more than 39,000 employees. Its Windows operating system boasts a worldwide personal computer (PC) market share of 92 percent. The firm's word processing, spreadsheet, and presentation software suite known as Microsoft Office brings in roughly $9 billion each year—more than any other Microsoft product. While Windows and Office continue to account for a major portion of Microsoft's revenues, the company has started reshaping its software packages and creating new technology to meet the growing needs of businesses and consumers online. The firm is also starting to focus on Internet-based services. In mid-2001, Microsoft continued to appeal a U.S. district court ruling that ordered the alleged ''monopolist'' to split in two.

EARLY HISTORY

In February of 1975, nineteen-year-old Harvard University student William H. Gates and twenty-one-year-old Honeywell employee Paul Allen created a version of the computer language known as BASIC (Beginner's All-Purpose Symbolic Instruction Code) for Altair, the world's first personal computer, which was manufactured in Albuquerque, New Mexico, by MITS. Because BASIC had never been copyrighted or patented by its developers—Dartmouth College mathematics professors Thomas Kurtz and John G. Kemeny—several variations had cropped up, including the one developed by Allen and Gates, who had been childhood friends in their hometown of Seattle, Washington. Eventually, Gates also created DiskBASIC, a disk management program. Along with dreaming up new ways to use BASIC, one of Gates' first major innovations was a legal contract by which a hardware developer could utilize and market versions of a software language owned by the creator of the language; this contract became the model upon which future software licensing agreements were based. On April 4th, Gates and Allen officially founded Microsoft. The next year, Gates left Harvard, opting to work full-time at the new company. He established a headquarters office in Albuquerque, New Mexico, and hired four programmers.

Microsoft released a software product based on a version of the Fortran programming language in July of 1977. Roughly one year later, a product based on COBOL-80 was launched. The firm also licensed its BASIC software to Radio Shack and Apple Computer and made its first international move when it established an office in Japan. Sales reached $1 million. When companies like Sirius, Zenith Electronics, Sharp, and Texas Instruments started using Microsoft products in conjunction with the CP/M operating system, Microsoft became the largest U.S. distributor of microcomputer languages.

It was in 1979 that Microsoft left New Mexico to establish its headquarters in Bellevue, Washington. A more sophisticated version of FORTRAN was developed for a new chip that could handle additional memory. With 25 employees and revenues of $2.5 million, Microsoft sold its one millionth copy of BASIC. In November of 1980, IBM Corp. asked Microsoft to develop four languages, as well as an operating system, for its new PCs. That year, the firm also released Softcard, which allowed Microsoft BASIC to operate on Apple II machines.

Gates and Allen incorporated their business on June 25, 1981. Gates was appointed president and chairman of the board, while Allen was named executive vice president. In August, IBM began selling PCs powered by Microsoft's new operating system, known as MS-DOS. Within in several months, more than 50 microcomputer manufacturers had licensed MS-DOS. Microsoft moved into Europe by creating a subsidiary in England in 1982. That year, the firm unveiled Multiplan Electronic Worksheet, which became *InfoWorld* magazine's "Software Product of the Year." Employees reached roughly 200.

INTENSE GROWTH AS A SOFTWARE MANUFACTURER

Several major products were developed in 1983. Microsoft Mouse, a small hand-held device used to manipulate a cursor on a computer screen was shipped early that year. In September, the firm unveiled its first word processing program, called Microsoft Word. Although the program did poorly in the U.S. at first, European sales were strong. Also, in perhaps its most important product launch ever, Microsoft introduced a new program, called Windows, in November. Based on the MS-DOS operating system, Windows offered users a graphical user interface (GUI). Within one month of its launch, more than 500,000 copies of Windows had been sold. Revenues reached $70 million, and international expansion was fueled with the establishment of units in France and Germany.

Microsoft began developing software, including a version of Microsoft Word, for the Apple Macintosh computer in 1984. By then, roughly 200 microcomputer manufacturers had licensed MS-DOS. Microsoft Word's popularity in the U.S. increased, and the firm began selling nearly 20,000 copies per month. In 1985, Microsoft opened its first international manufacturing plant in Ireland. By the end of the year, the firm had started distributing Windows to retailers for sale to consumers. Microsoft spearheaded an alliance with IBM's competitors—including Compaq, Hewlett-Packard, Texas Instruments, and Digital Equipment—in an effort to undermine IBM's monopoly on PC standards development. As a result, IBM began to work with Microsoft's competitors on software programs. Despite its increasingly rocky relationship with IBM and the fact that several problems had emerged with the earliest version of Windows, Microsoft convinced IBM to use an upgraded version of Windows on its next line of PCs.

In February of 1986, Microsoft moved its headquarters to Redmond, Washington. One month later, the firm conducted its initial public offering, offerings its shares at $21 each. The IPO raised $61 million in capital. Within a year, shares were selling for $84.75, making the 31-year-old Gates a billionaire. A third version of Microsoft Word was released, and it soon became Microsoft's best selling product. The Windows-based spreadsheet software known as Excel was introduced in October of 1987.

Apple Computers filed a lawsuit against Microsoft in 1988, alleging that the firm had used the appearance of the Macintosh operating system as the basis for its Windows program. Apple's lawyers requested that Microsoft either pay royalties or stop simply selling Windows. By then, Microsoft had grown into the leading U.S. maker of PC software and had also diversified into network software. By the end of the decade, revenues had neared the $800 million mark, and more than two million copies of Windows 3.0 had been sold. Employees totaled roughly 4,000.

Revenues exceeded $1 billion for the first time in 1990. The firm's relationship with IBM worsened, resulting in a price war between Microsoft's DOS 5.0 and IBM's competitor to DOS, OS/2. In 1991, in what was viewed by many analysts as a plan to wrest market share back from Microsoft, IBM and Apple forged an alliance to develop a new operating system that would not only make computers easier to use, but also facilitate compatibility between IBM and Apple machines. By then, roughly 90 percent of worldwide PCs used the MS-DOS platform, and Apple had broadened its litigation against Microsoft. In 1992, the firm diversified into desktop publishing software and launched its first television commercial. Microsoft won the case against Apple after a judge decreed that the appearance of the Macintosh operating system was not protected by Apple's copyrights; therefore, Microsoft's Windows platform, though very similar to Macintosh in appearance, was not in violation of copyright law. Apple appealed the decision.

By 1993, Microsoft had a market valuation of $25 billion. The Microsoft Encarta multimedia CD-ROM, which housed all 29 volumes of *Funk & Wagnall's New Encyclopedia*, including graphics, was awarded the Consumer Disc Product of the Year. The firm also launched Windows NT, an operating system for the network servers of large corporations. Microsoft's meteoric growth brought with it increased scrutiny and continued legal troubles. For example, after receiving complaints regarding alleged unfair and monopolistic trade practices by Microsoft, the U.S. Department of Justice launched an investigation of the firm. In 1994, to resolve the ongoing antitrust investigation, Microsoft volunteered to change its marketing tactics, a proposal the Justice Department accepted. However, critics of the settlement asserted that it did nothing to address several of the firm's alleged anticompetitive activities. As a result, U.S. District Judge Stanley Sporkin agreed to revisit the settlement.

To compete with Navigator, a World Wide Web browser released by upstart Netscape Communications Corp. in September of 1994, Microsoft licensed technology from Spyglass in an effort to speed its own browser to market. The firm also unveiled its Windows NT BackOffice suite, which bundled various server applications, such as SQL Server. Sony Corp. and Microsoft began jointly developing multimedia software and hardware in early 1995. The Supreme Court refused to hear Apple's appeal regarding the case against Microsoft; however, Microsoft's legal woes continued when Judge Sporkin ruled that the Department of Justice's antitrust settlement with Microsoft failed to address two key issues: licensing policies for computer operating systems and nondisclosure agreements. In response, the Department of Justice and Microsoft both filed appeals. Eventually, the U.S. Court of Appeals reinstated the initial settlement. In April, Microsoft's plan to acquire Intuit Inc. for $2.1 billion was blocked by the Justice Department due to antitrust concerns.

FOCUS ON INTERNET TECHNOLOGY

In mid-1995, believing that it had fallen behind Netscape and Sun Microsystems in the Internet arena while it had worked to develop its long awaited Windows 95 operating system, the company switched its primary focus from PC operating systems to Internet technology. In August, the firm finally released Windows 95, which included software for the Microsoft Network—a new online service competing with the likes of Compuserve, Prodigy, and America Online— and the Internet Explorer browser. The product release was one of the most highly anticipated to date in the technology sector. In November, Microsoft recruited Michael Kinsley to create *Slate*, an online magazine first published the following June. The firm also introduced Internet Explorer 2.0 to compete with the second version of Netscape's Navigator browser. NBC and Microsoft announced their intent to create an online news source, a plan which eventually culminated in the creation of MSNBC.

In January of 1996, MCI Communications Corp., known as the most competitive advertiser in the telecommunication industry, agreed to promote the Microsoft Network. Two months later, the Microsoft Network secured its one millionth customer; however, its worldwide reach continued to pale in comparison to industry leader America Online. To further facilitate its focus on Internet technology, Microsoft condensed its four platform groups into three divisions. Brad Silverberg was named head of the new Internet Platform and Tools Division. In a major coup against rival Netscape, Microsoft convinced America Online to license its Internet Explorer browser, rather than Netscape Navigator. Internet Explorer 3.0 was released shortly thereafter to complete with upgraded releases of Navigator. When sales of Windows NT, which competed with the UNIX-based servers on which corporate networks operated, surged 86 percent in 1996, Microsoft turned its attention to the network server market, which was being fueled by increased Internet usage and e-commerce activity. ''Forget Internet browsers, forget MSNBC, forget multimedia, Slate, and the Microsoft Network,'' wrote *Fortune* columnist David Kirkpatrick in May of 1997. ''Gates's strategy is to extend Microsoft's hegemony from the desktop into the windowless rooms housing the servers, minicomputers, and mainframes that are still central to business data processing. If he succeeds, Microsoft could dominate information technology well into the next decade.''

Despite the manpower and research and development dollars it was devoting to Windows NT, and its BackOffice applications, Microsoft did maintain its other Internet initiatives, albeit at a slower pace for a while. After an eighteen-month acquisition spree, which resulted in the purchase of Vxtreme Inc. and many other upstart Internet technology firms, spending came to a halt in mid-1997. Internet Explorer 4.0 was shipped, resulting in a suit filed by Sun Microsystems, which alleged that Microsoft had violated an agreement with Sun by using incompatible Java source code. Sun asked the courts to force Microsoft to remove the ''Java Compatible'' logo from the new version of Explorer. Legal pressures mounted when the Justice Dept. began investigating complaints regarding Microsoft's bundling of its Internet Explorer with Windows 95 as a way of stealing market share from Netscape. Allegations also emerged that Microsoft had threatened to pull Windows licenses from computer manufacturers who were unwilling to install Explorer on their machines in place of Netscape's Navigator. After examining the case, a U.S. District Court judge ordered the firm to sell a version of Windows 95 unbundled from Internet Explorer. When Microsoft refused to do this, asserting that it would cause problems for the operating system, the Justice Dept. asked the U.S. District Court to hold Microsoft in contempt. Eventually, to avoid such charges, Microsoft agreed to let PC makers sell Windows 95 without Internet Explorer.

Acquisitions resumed in early 1998 when Microsoft purchased Hotmail, which became the leading free e-mail service on the Web. Sales that year surged by 30 percent, or roughly $3 billion. With a market capitalization of $466 billion, Microsoft was the world's most valuable company. It operated several Web sites, including Carpoint, Home Advisor, the Sidewalk city guides, the Expedia virtual travel agency, Microsoft Investor, and online bill payment service MSFDC. Despite the firm's phenomenal success, however, growth began to slow in the late 1990s. With more than half of its annual sales coming from international operations, recessionary economic conditions in Asia cut growth by three percent in 1999. The firm also faced saturation in two of its major markets: PC operating systems and application suites like Office. In addition, Microsoft's plans to dominate the network server market were hampered by several de-

lays in the release of Windows NT 5.0, one of the most complex programs ever developed by the company. Perhaps most troubling of all was the fact that several of Microsoft's Internet endeavors had simply fallen short of expectations. By 1998, Internet-based technology accounted for only $548 million of Microsoft's $14.5 billion in total revenues, a fact which revealed the firm's continued reliance on the PC industry.

Early in 1999, Microsoft initiated a major reorganization, moving from product segments to five customer-based divisions: corporate systems customers; programmers; knowledge workers; ordinary Windows customers; and consumers interested in digitized content, entertainment, and shopping. The restructuring was spearheaded by Steven Ballmer, a former Harvard classmate of Gates who had been appointed Microsoft's president in 1998. Ballmer recognized that Microsoft needed to pay more attention to its clients in order to attract the large corporate accounts it hoped to secure with Windows NT; these enterprises typically demanded a level of service Microsoft had admitted it wasn't used to providing. According to *Fortune* columnist Eric Nee, Ballmer also realized that as Microsoft was ''trying to reach beyond the desktop and keep pace with the Internet Age,'' it would need to retool itself to be more like the most successful Internet-based firms, which relied on continually evolving alliances with other businesses. ''Witness Amazon.com., which helped gain dominance and bolster its brand name by signing up 200,000 'associate' Web sites that refer customers to Amazon in return for a share of the revenues. Microsoft, by contrast, has succeeded thus far by building (Expedia), buying (Hotmail), or crushing (Netscape)—the moves of a PC-industry survivor that prefers to go it alone.''

One industry in which Microsoft had already attempted to forge various alliances was cable television. In 1997, the firm had invested roughly $1 billion in Comcast, and in 1999, it had dumped $500 million into United Kingdom-based NTL Inc. and $300 million into Netherlands-based UPC Cable Co. Believing that cable television technology would be an integral part of future Internet operations Microsoft also agreed to invest $5 million in AT&T Corp., which was merging with cable behemoth [M|MediaOne]. Consequently, AT&T agreed to purchase Microsoft software for its cable and Internet applications.

Microsoft also began retooling the Microsoft Network, which changed its name to MSN.com, as an Internet gateway that integrated all of the firm's Web sites. In January of 2000, Gates appointed Ballmer CEO, retaining his role as chairman and taking on the additional role of chief software architect. One month later, the firm shipped its long awaited new version of Windows NT, named Windows 2000, which had taken five years to complete. Windows 2000 was designed to serve as the platform on which businesses, including e-commerce companies like BarnesandNoble.com and Buy.com, could operate.

In April of 2000, the longstanding antitrust investigation of Microsoft came to a head when a judge ruled that the firm was a monopoly that dominated nearly all PC operating systems and did, in fact, cause injury to consumers. The Justice Department and 17 states issued a landmark proposal that Microsoft split into two separate companies, one based on the Office software applications, and the other based on the Windows operating system. Microsoft quickly appealed the verdict, and by mid-2001, many industry analysts believed that an appeals court would find in Microsoft's favor.

Despite its legal battles, Microsoft continued to beef up its Internet technology and services. The firm completed its largest acquisition ever, the $1.1 billion purchase of small and mid-sized enterprise management software maker Great Plains Corp. It also launched bCentral, which offers e-business hosting services to small companies lacking the resources to construct their own e-business infrastructure. In June of 2001, the firm unveiled its new version of the Office suite, dubbed Office XP, and also announced its intent to launch Windows XP, the firm's largest new product in five years, in October. According to USA Today writer Byron Acohido, the latest version of Microsoft's operating system is more than just another upgrade. "Microsoft has fashioned XP into its weapon of choice for subjugating the Internet, just as it conquered desktop PCs." The new operating system is a key component of a new Microsoft strategy known as.Net, which the firm envisions as "a framework of software programs and services connecting every computing device to the Internet and to each other. With Windows XP as the dominant operating system, Microsoft could touch virtually every transaction." While the viability of this strategy remains to be seen, most analysts agree that Microsoft will likely emerge as a leading Internet technology and services provider.

FURTHER READING:

Acohido, Byron. "Microsoft Aims to Conquer Net." *USA Today*. June 6, 2001. Available from www.usetoday.com.

"At War with Microsoft." *The Economist*. May 23, 1998.

Baker, Sharon M. "Microsoft Pushing Ahead on Many Fronts." *Puget Sounds Business Journal*. March 12, 1999.

"Bill's Big Roll-Out." *The Economist*. September 18, 1999.

Kirkpatrick, David. "He Wants All of Your Business—And He's Starting to Get It." *Fortune*. May 26, 1997.

———. "Microsoft: Is Your Company Its Next Meal?" *Fortune*. April 27, 1998.

———. "The New Face of Microsoft: The Management Change Is Just the First Step." *Fortune*. February 7, 2000.

"Microsoft: The Beast Is Back." *Fortune*. June 11, 2001.

"Microsoft Corp." In *Notable Corporate Chronologies*. Farmington Hills, MI: Gale Group, 1999.

Mitchell, Russ. "Microsoft's Midlife Crisis." *U.S. News & World Report*. October 19, 1998.

Nee, Eric. "Microsoft Gets Ready to Play a New Game." *Fortune*. April 26, 1999.

Nocera, Joseph. "The Men Who Would Be King: Case Has Content. Gates Has Software. The Internet Will Be Their Battleground." *Fortune*. February 7, 2000.

SEE ALSO: Allen, Paul; Ballmer, Steve; Gates, William (Bill); Microsoft Network (MSN); Microsoft Windows

MICROSOFT NETWORK (MSN)

The Microsoft Network—MSN for short—is an online service owned by the Microsoft Corporation. MSN.com is a multi-service web portal, comparable to America Online (AOL) or Yahoo, which offers a number of free features to surfers of the Web, including email from Hotmail, news from MSNBC and Newsweek magazine, a variety of financial and shopping services, and MSN Web Communities, a network of chat rooms and online communities.

MSN derives its revenue from a combination of subscription fees, advertising, and e-retailing agreements. MSN's millions of subscribers can use MSN to access the Internet and the proprietary portions of MSN.com. The service has forged strategic alliances with firms, such as AltaVista, John Hancock Mutual Life Insurance Co., Merrill Lynch & Company Inc., Unilever PLC, and Barnes & Noble Inc., which in turn sponsor a number of individual services on the MSN site. The site has become a nexus of e-tailing with stores like Barnes & Noble and The Discovery Shop represented. According to MSN, in late 2001 it had agreements with over 10,000 businesses that brought in some $6 billion in e-commerce every year.

By 2001, its burgeoning partnership, its slowly growing subscriber list, and the pure glitter of the Microsoft name had helped raise MSN to the number two spot among online services, second only to AOL. Reaching that level, however, was an achievement fraught with missteps, turnarounds, and failure that only a company with the size, power, and deep pockets of the Microsoft Corporation could have survived. And though it was number two in September 2001, MSN was a distant second, its 6.9 million subscribers well behind over 31 million at AOL. In fact, AOL managed to sign up 7 million new members in 2001 alone—more than MSN's entire subscriber base.

MICROSOFT BUILDS ITS ONLINE SERVICE

When Bill Gates decided in 1993 that Microsoft should launch its own online service, it was conceived as a private dial-up service on the order of CompuServe or Prodigy at the time. In such a "closed" system, all content—databases, bulletin boards, etc.—was stored on a private network and could only be accessed by paying subscribers via local dial-up numbers. In 1994, however, while Microsoft was designing MSN, the online world underwent a momentous change. The Internet, an incomparably larger network, was opened to the public. For the cost of a browser and a modest monthly charge, users could surf the vast network. The Internet rapidly began displacing the old private dial-up networks. Microsoft, however, was unable to react quickly to the change. When the Microsoft Network debuted in August 1995, it did not yet offer Internet access—a feature its primary competitors, like AOL and CompuServe, had already implemented. Nonetheless, because MSN bore the Microsoft name, most observers expected it to be a rousing success.

Microsoft was hard at work developing a Web browser and other software for MSN, and it planned to install them all on Windows 95, the new version of its best-selling operating system, due for release around the time MSN was going online. Microsoft's plan to integrate MSN into Windows created more problems, in particular an icon on the Windows desktop which enabled computer users to sign up with the MSN service with the click of a mouse. Competitors, like AOL, maintained that this amounted to an antitrust violation and asked the Justice Department to intervene. It was alleged at the same time that Microsoft intended to track MSN users' visits to competing software makers in order to follow up with advertising of its own. Three weeks before MSN's debut, the Justice Department announced its investigation.

The first reactions to the service were mixed at best. Its complicated graphics were slow to load, critics said. Its on-screen interface was a virtual carbon copy of Windows, which would be off-putting to some users. There was very little brand-name content, and most of that had to be paid for. Finally, by 1995 it seemed inconceivable that a service from Microsoft would not include general Internet access. Microsoft put a browser together—but it was only available in a special version of Windows 95 or with extra software that cost about $50.

When Microsoft Network opened its virtual doors Microsoft admitted that it expected the service to lose money during its first year of operations. By the end of 1995, MSN had more than half a million subscribers, which placed the service up with the industry leaders. Industry observers predicted that the service would grow quickly to three million or more subscribers by the end of 1996. However, MSN's early growth was staggeringly slow, considering that some 7 million copies of Windows 95 had been sold, each offering the ease of one-click access to MSN. The slow start led some of MSN's content partners to cancel agreements with the service. It also caused the Goldman Sachs Group., an investment firm, to remove Microsoft from its list of recommended stocks, sending the shares into decline.

MSN WORKS TO FIND ITS FOCUS

In an attempt to shore up its loses, eight months after its debut, in March 1996, Microsoft inaugurated the first of a series of major makeovers at MSN. Microsoft put the entire "closed" service on the Internet. MSN still had a full range of features, including shopping, news, business and finance pages, chat rooms, etc—but made them available free of charge. The facelift was intended to make MSN more attractive, but one of the signals it and later changes sent was that Microsoft really had no vision for MSN, that it was merely reacting. The change to the Internet had another serious short-term impact. It alienated most of MSN's 400 information providers, companies like NBC that spent millions of dollars to develop material for the old MSN. The switch to Web-based operations meant they had to go back to the drawing board to design product offerings for the new MSN. The transition to the Web was completed in October 1996.

In April 1996, MSN made a huge advance in terms of brand-name content, when Microsoft announced a major partnership with NBC. The two firms intended to produce a variety of news, sports, finance and entertainment products for the Web and cable TV. Part of NBC's contribution was developing a 24-hour, New York-based cable news network to be called MSNBC. Microsoft built a large newsroom at its headquarters in Redmond, Washington, and with NBC began generating news content which would be posted free on MSN.com.

The alliance with NBC pushed MSN into its second large-scale makeover at the end of 1996, just two months after its transformation to a Web-based service. The Microsoft Network as newly conceived would radically expand the model of a standard Web portal and Internet service provider. While it continued to develop what would later be considered "traditional" online content—the series of arts and entertainment guides for various American cities called Sidewalk, the Internet Gaming Zone, or the MSNBC news stories—MSN would at the same time begin morphing into a full-blown media company. A production studio, Microsoft Multimedia Productions, was founded for it where some 20 online comedies, dramas, and soap operas went into production.

MSN introduced *Slate*, an upscale online magazine modeled on the *New Yorker* or *Vanity Fair.* MSN hoped its radical new focus would pump up its subscriber base to 3 million by summer 1997 and enable it to overtake CompuServe as the number two online service.

Only two and a half months later, however, the strategy seemed to be failing. Microsoft announced the layoff of hundreds of part-time workers who had been hired to develop content for the new MSN. It cancelled half the newly formed MSN programs. New programming was on the way, the company said, that would be "light years better," a blunt reflection on the quality of the cancelled content. Things were falling apart on all fronts in April 1997. MSN was plagued by apparently irresolvable billing problems. Worse, overloaded servers shut down its email system on various occasions, depriving MSN subscribers service for days at a time. E-mail remained MSN's Achilles tendon until January 1998 when it purchased Hotmail, the free email service, for about $395 million. The purchase gave MSN a tried and true email technology along with instant access to nearly ten million Hotmail subscribers. By that time although MSN had 2.3 million users, it was still number 3. According to reports, MSN was not making money on subscriptions or advertising, and had lost hundreds of millions of dollars. One effect of the Hotmail acquisition was to put an end to a buzz in the online industry that Microsoft intended to cut its losses and sell MSN off once and for all.

Whatever, MSN's difficulties, the power of Microsoft was enough to make it attractive attract new corporate partners. AltaVista Search Service, Infoseek Corp., Lycos Inc., and Snap Internet Portal Service chipped in $60 million for the right to be the featured search engines on MSN. Barnes & Noble Booksellers allied with MSN in hopes of catching Amazon.com. One effect of these partnerships, combined with the new popularity of service-oriented Web sites such as Yahoo!, was to nudge MSN back into its previous incarnation. In August 1998 it abandoned its attempt to become an online entertainment powerhouse altogether and transformed itself back to a simple Web portal, offering news, information, email, bulletin boards, and online shopping. The change increased traffic at the MSN site, but further distanced advertisers who were losing confidence in Microsoft to develop and stick with a plan for MSN.

If advertisers suspected a lack of vision at MSN, they may have been right. MSN redesigned its entire site again, first in 1999 when it shifted its direction to focus on online communications, and again in early 2000, when the service returned to Microsoft's functional roots in software and set itself up as a toolkit for the Internet that assembled resources to make Web-based activities, like shopping, investing, and communicating, easier for consumers. MSN launched a series of expensive media blitzes in 2000 and 2001 that included nationwide TV commercials, massive CD-ROM mailings, and even rebates up to $400 on computer purchases to customers willing to commit to MSN service for a year or more. It was a desperate and ultimately futile effort to make headway on AOL. The promotional campaigns added another $1 billion to the $1.5 billion Microsoft had already sunk into MSN, yet by spring 2000 MSN still had only 2.5 million members compared to AOL's 22 million. By the end of 2001, Microsoft Network was once again a basic Internet portal, much like AOL's.

The MSN-AOL competition frequently broke into open conflict. Microsoft's decision to rig Windows in favor of MSN drew a long Justice Department investigation largely at AOL's behest. In 1999 AOL protested publicly and loudly that MSN Messenger, the network's instant messaging tool, had been improperly set up to communicate with AOL's members-only instant message system. What's more, AOL users who had Windows versions that included MSN Messenger found that MSN Messenger ran automatically when they tried to send messages, and blocked or completely disabled the AOL version. AOL also accused Microsoft of planning to program its new Windows XP system so that only MSN would be able to run on it—a threat 19 state attorneys general took seriously enough to jointly bring suit against Microsoft. Eventually Microsoft agreed to allow dealers to place on the Windows desktop any Internet provider as long as an MSN icon was there too.

FURTHER READING:

Andrews, Paul. "Microsoft places $1 billion Net Bet." *Seattle Times,* October 26, 2000.

Buck, Richard. "Online With Microsoft—Network To Change The Structure Of How Services Operate." *Seattle Times,* July 24, 1995.

Hansell, Saul. "Where Does Microsoft Want You To Go Today?" *New York Times,* November 16, 1998.

Healy, Jon. "AOL, Microsoft Continue Battle Over Instant-Messaging Software." *San Jose Mercury News,* July 29, 1999.

Helmore, Ed. "Web of Legality Over Software Threatens Microsoft's March." *Independent* (London), August 2, 1995.

Lohr, Steve. "Again, It's Microsoft vs. the World." *New York Times,* February 13, 2000.

O'Leary, Mick. "Microsoft Goes Online." *Online Magazine,* March 1996.

Rebello, Kathy. "Microsoft's Online Timing May Be Off." *Business Week,* July 17, 1995.

"Special Report: The Microsoft Network." *Interactive Age,* August 14, 1995.

SEE ALSO: AOL Time Warner Inc.; Microsoft Corp.; Microsoft Windows

MICROSOFT WINDOWS

In the early 2000s, Microsoft Windows was the dominant operating system for home and business computer users. Operating systems (OS) are programs responsible for running computers. In addition to Windows, other OS in the 2000s included Linux, Unix, and Macintosh. Microsoft Windows provides users with a graphical environment, meaning that it allows them to issue commands to a computer by clicking on icons with a mouse or by typing commands into graphical forms.

Before Microsoft announced the creation of Windows in November of 1983, most computing was done by typing very specific text-based commands into an OS at a command prompt; not by clicking on user-friendly graphical icons. Many early computer systems ran on the Microsoft Disk Operating System (MS-DOS), introduced in August of 1981. After Apple Computer released the Macintosh in 1984, which included a graphical interface, Microsoft followed with several versions of Windows, including Windows 1.0 in 1985; Windows 2.0 in 1987; and Windows 3.0 in 1990. The latter release marked the beginning of the system's widespread popularity and adoption. Two years later, the release of Windows 3.1 was especially well received.

The popularity of Windows 3.0 had much to do with the elimination of the DOS interface. Users still had to boot Windows from DOS (it didn't automatically start when the computer was turned on as would later versions of Windows), but the end result was a more intuitive environment consisting of what resembled a virtual desktop. Several main programs made up the operating system. The Program Manager was responsible for launching programs. Users relied on the File Manager to view and organize their files and to move them between different media like floppy disks and the computer's hard drive. A Clipboard application allowed text from one program to be copied or cut and then pasted into another application. The appearance of the Windows system could be altered or customized on the Control Panel. The Print Manager was responsible for printing information from various applications. Finally, Windows came with a variety of other programs, including Write and Paintbrush, which were basic productivity applications.

With the release of Windows 95 in 1995, the system interface took on a totally new look that more closely resembled the Apple Macintosh. Windows 95 booted automatically when the computer was turned on, eliminating the scenario of Windows running on top of DOS. In addition to graphic file, folder, and program icons residing on the desktop, users also could access programs, documents, and settings via the Start Button, which also could be used for several other purposes. A taskbar allowed users to multi-task by running several applications at once and switching between them more easily. It also made the addition of peripheral devices easier than had been the case with Windows 3.1.

Three years after the introduction of Windows 95, Windows 98 was introduced. It included solutions to bugs and other imperfections found in Windows 95 and made the Internet Explorer Web browser a more integrated part of the desktop. A major improvement was made to the OS with Windows Millennium Edition. Released in September 2000, the upgrade included improved multimedia features and system protection capabilities that restored the OS to an earlier state in the event of a crash. It also allowed for more-user-friendly home networking.

Microsoft planned to release Windows XP on Oct. 25, 2001. According to the company, the new version of Windows was to have a new look and was "built on an enhanced Windows 2000 engine and enables exciting experiences that gives users the freedom to create, connect and communicate in new ways. Windows XP also establishes a new standard in power, reliability, security and simplicity." Two versions were to be released, one for home users and another for business users.

In addition to the Windows OS for home PC users, several other varieties of Windows were developed for other kinds of users. Windows NT was designed for use on servers and networked workstation computers. It was first released in 1993. Windows 2000 was released in February 2000 and was more suitable for use on laptop and desktop computers than its predecessor, Windows NT 4.0. Windows CE, an OS for handheld computers, was released in 1996. Windows CE 2.1 for palm-sized computers came out two years later.

In the late 1990s Microsoft fell under increasing scrutiny of U.S. anti-trust regulators, partly from its competition with Netscape, which lost market share when Microsoft aggressively pushed its Internet Explorer Web browser along with the Windows OS. The Justice Department appeared adamant that Microsoft change its practices and took the company to court. In June of 2000 Judge Thomas Penfield Jackson ordered that Microsoft be broken up into two companies. The ruling was appealed and the historic anti-trust case moved to the Court of Appeals for the D.C. Circuit in 2001.

FURTHER READING:

''Computer History. History of Microsoft Windows.'' *Computer Hope Newsletter*. May 24, 2001. Available from www.computerhope.com.

Crawford Greenburg, Jan. ''Appeals Court Hits Judge's Comments in Microsoft trial.'' *Chicago Tribune*. February 28, 2001. Available from www.chicagotribune.com.

Introducing Microsoft Windows 95. Redmond, Washington: Microsoft Press. 1995.

''Microsoft Windows History.'' *Frank Condron's World O'Windows*. March 22, 2001. Available from www.worldowindows.com.

''Windows Evolution.'' *Tech Encyclopedia.*. May 24, 2001. Available from www.techweb.com.

Wolverton, Van and Michael Boom. *Van Wolverton's Guide To Windows 3.1*. New York: Random House Electronic Publishing, 1992.

SEE ALSO: Microsoft Corp.

MIDDLEWARE

In the corporate world, companies often operate using a patchwork of different computer systems across various departments or divisions, in which they have invested considerable resources over the years. Many of these systems and software applications weren't designed for use on the World Wide Web. However, in order to engage in e-commerce companies must find a way to enable them for this purpose, and to integrate them so they function together seamlessly.

One solution is middleware—a kind of software that resides between applications on one computer system, such as a Web server (computers used to host Web sites) and many different client applications (including Web browsers like Microsoft's Internet Explorer), functioning as a translation layer. Middleware comes in several forms, each with a different focus. Some forms deal specifically with databases, while others connect applications or deliver messages across different networks between programs and systems.

Middleware, especially the application-server and database varieties, is critical to e-commerce because of the many different company databases and applications involved. For example, when middleware is used on a company's Web site it can take customer data entered on a single Web page form—like credit card numbers or shipping addresses—and distribute it to the appropriate databases within the company. It also can allow someone to query or search for information found in different company databases—like price and inventory—from one easy-to-use interface like a Web page. On the front end these processes are hidden from the customer's view, but on the back end data may get transferred across several networks, among many different databases in the accounting, shipping, marketing and customer service departments.

Middleware can be created on a custom basis for a company's unique needs or purchased pre-packaged from software companies like IBM. Even if a company buys an off-the-shelf form of middleware, adjustments, analysis, and fine-tuning are almost always needed before it will work correctly. In the early 2000s, software companies were taking steps to make it easier for end-users without backgrounds in computer programming to purchase pre-packaged programs and tailor them to their company's needs.

Middleware also is useful for delivering Web site content to people who use wireless Internet devices like personal digital assistants (PDAs). Because such devices don't always use the same wireless language, a company that delivers content in one language and not another could limit the number of people who are able to access its site. Middleware enables Web sites to adjust content so it can be read by both regular desktop computers and many different kinds of wireless devices.

FURTHER READING:

Baum, David. ''Middleware.'' *InfoWorld*, November 30, 1992.

———. ''Middleware to the Rescue.'' *Computerworld*, May 10, 1993.

Meehan, Michael. ''Vendors Try to Make Middleware More User-friendly.'' *Computerworld*, May 15, 2000.

''Middleware.'' *Tech Encyclopedia*, February 23, 2001. Available from www.techweb.com.

Pappo, Nicky. ''Middleware Bridges Internet, Wireless.'' *Telecommunications*, May 2000.

Rosencrance, Linda. ''Middleware.'' *Computerworld*, October 9, 2000.

Sliwa, Carol. ''Plot your B2B Integration.'' *Computerworld*, January 1, 2001.

SEE ALSO: Software

MIME/SMIME

In its most primitive, text-only form, e-mail is a powerful communications tool for both businesses and consumers. The ability to add picture, audio, and video attachments makes it even more powerful—especially for e-marketers. Multipurpose Internet Mail Extensions (MIME) allow these many different kinds of files to be exchanged online. MIME is an extension of the Simple Mail Transfer Protocol (SMTP), which specifies the format of e-mail messages. Originally, MIME was created to send ASCII text files. However, it evolved to support the many different types of files that were being widely used for e-commerce.

MIME works through the use of headers, which servers (computers used to host Web sites, e-mail systems, or applications) insert into all mail transmissions as they are sent. Client applications like Web browsers or e-mail programs are then able to read the information contained in the headers and determine what kind of file has been sent and how to display or run a file's contents. MIME supports a large number of different file types in the realms of video, audio, images, text, and application files. Among these many file types are JPEG, TIFF, GIF, Postscript, MPEG, and QuickTime files.

Before it became a standard, MIME was first proposed to the Internet Engineering Task Force (IETF) in the early 1990s by Bellcore's Nathan Borenstein. The IETF is ''a large open international community of network designers, operators, vendors, and researchers concerned with the evolution of the Internet architecture and the smooth operation of the Internet.'' A secure version of MIME, called S/MIME, allows messages to be encrypted between sender and receiver. S/MIME relies on a form of encryption called Rivest-Shamir-Adleman, created by Redwood City, California-based RSA Data Security Inc. Encryption is a process that allows messages to be sent securely from one party to another, and intends to prevent unauthorized parties from reading the message's contents.

Despite the increased capabilities MIME provides to e-mail users, it is not universally popular. In *Network World,* Scott Bradner of Harvard's University Information Systems department called the standard annoying, and criticized it for causing problems with message readability and size, as well as software compatibility. Bradner pointed out that if the receiving party to a message does not have the right software application for opening and viewing a file, the receiver receives a file filled with garbled text, which can be both frustrating and confusing.

FURTHER READING:

Au, Yoris A. and Robert J. Kauffman. ''Should We Wait? Network Externalities and Electronic Billing Adoption.'' Working paper, University of Minnesota Management Information Systems Research Center, 2000-2001. Available from misrc.umn.edu.

Baker, Steven. ''MIME: A Richer Shade of Mail.'' *UNIX Review,* July 1993.

Bradner, Scott. ''If You Send Me Mail, Make it Plain.'' *Network World,* February 26, 2001.

SEE ALSO: E-mail; Encryption

MIRROR SITES

For companies that rely on the Internet to generate revenue, obtain new customers and investors, and maintain or build relationships with existing customers and investors, slow connections and crashes can spell disaster. Mirror sites are cloned or alternate versions of the same Web site. Companies that receive heavy traffic often create mirror sites to resolve potential problems caused by excess demand on one or several servers—the computers used to host Web sites. They also create mirror sites as part of disaster-recovery plans for the sake of preserving all of the information contained on their Web site in the event a server crashes or is damaged.

Mirror sites can be accessed in different ways. In one case, visitors to a Web site might be automatically directed to the mirror site when traffic exceeds a certain level or the main server crashes. This process is usually unnoticeable to the visitor. If a company's local server crashes in Chicago, it could have a second server running at the same physical location that takes over, or one in Minneapolis or Boston that immediately accepts traffic in the event of a problem. Visitors also may be given an option to choose one of several different mirror sites depending on their geographic location, especially in the case of international Web sites. For example, a British company might host several servers in the United States to improve ease of accessibility for U.S. customers. This is because the path from the user's computer (client) may be closer to one of a company's Web servers than another, meaning faster access. Visitors are often given an option to access one of several mirror sites when downloading files or programs via the Internet.

In addition to serving as fail-over tools and backups, the term mirror site also can be used to describe Web sites used for malicious purposes by hackers or disgruntled individuals. In this scenario, a phony version of a legitimate Web site is created, with inaccurate, harmful, libelous, or scandalous information about the company and its employees, plans, products, or services. By the time the imposters are caught and shut down, a great deal of damage already may have been done. Besides creating public relations disasters for the target company, fraudulent mirror sites also have the potential to deflate or increase the value of a company's stock and positively or negatively impact its bottom line in other ways.

One example of a malicious mirror site involved an engineer at PairGain Technologies Inc. According to *Legal Assistant Today,* the engineer posted a false Web page announcing that his company was going to be acquired by an Israeli telecommunications firm. Resembling the physical look of a leading news service, the page created an investment spurt that resulted in a 31-percent stock price increase for PairGain. Because of schemes like these, it is no surprise that the Worldwide E-Commerce Fraud Prevention Network found 50 percent of U.S. businesses saw online fraud as a significant problem, as reported in Nua Internet Surveys. Ten percent of the companies surveyed identified fraud as the most significant problem they faced.

To alleviate the potential risk of malicious mirror sites, *Across the Board* cited suggestions from *Director's Monthly* encouraging companies to buy Web site addresses that were very similar to their own (to prevent them from falling into unscrupulous hands); take steps to maintain good relations with employees, who hold the potential to cause sabotage; and to weigh the merits of going after imposters when discovered, since increased attention can cause unwanted traffic and attention to the phony site.

FURTHER READING:

Allen, Kelley L. ''Mirror, Mirror on the Web.'' *Across the Board,* February 2000.

Blankenhorn, Dana. ''Web Sites Starting to See Need for Backup.'' *Advertising Age's Business Marketing,* May 1998.

Greenspan, Robyn. ''Mirror, Mirror on the Web.'' *Insights—ECTips,* May 18, 2000. Available from ecommerce.internet.com.

''Mirror Site.'' *Ecommerce Webopedia,* June 26, 2001. Available from e-comm.webopedia.com.

''Mirror Site.'' *TechEncyclopedia,* June 26, 2001. Available from www.techweb.com/encyclopedia.

Schwartz, Jeffrey. ''Schwab Outage: IT Wake-Up Call.'' *InternetWeek,* February 26, 1999. Available from www.internetweek.com.

Tyburski, Genie. ''Honest Mistakes, Deceptive Facts.'' *Legal Assistant Today,* March/April 2000.

''Worldwide E-Commerce Fraud Prevention Network: US Firms Concerned About Online Fraud.'' *Nua Internet Surveys,* April 10, 2001. Available from www.nua.ie.

SEE ALSO: Global Presence, Becoming a

MISINFORMATION ONLINE

While the Internet was hailed by business leaders, activists, researchers, and policy makers alike for proliferating and democratizing information as never before, many observers remained cognizant of a danger inherent in such rapid and widespread movement of information; namely, the potential for misinformation to cause serious damage. Misinformation online assumes myriad forms, such as phony business rumors to spur stock activity, bogus quotations or actions attributed to public figures, fabricated medical breakthroughs citing names of respected or nonexistent researchers, social statistics citing anonymous government reports, malicious rumors designed to defame individuals, vengeful flames against companies from disgruntled customers or employees, urban legends, and so on. Tools of the Internet misinformation trade include Web sites, emails, postings on message boards, chat rooms, cybersquatting, and other methods.

Providing individuals with a nearly limitless reservoir of information just a mouse-click away, the power of the Internet for altering social life has been undisputed. The danger, however, is that left unchecked that power could produce extremely negative effects if the information that is shared and acted upon happens to be false, slanderous, malicious, or mere rumor. The old adage that ''a lie can travel halfway around the world before the truth has got its boots on'' was often cited as a summary of online misinformation, and in many cases the metaphor rang true, as strategically placed misinformation was established as truth by the time the affected parties were even made aware of it.

The anonymity of the Internet was a primary impetus to misinformation, since accountability is minimal comparable to print media, and being a vastly younger medium, the Internet has yet to produce clear mechanisms for making critical distinctions and methods for checking credibility. Legitimacy is often garnered by the simple measures of professional-looking Web page design and sophisticated graphics, which, while clearly a mark of know-how, were well within reach of virtually any Internet user. Since anyone with access can make a claim on the Internet without restraint, the potential for misinformation to be posted and spread is greatly expanded.

Journalism as a profession suffered numerous setbacks as a result of online misinformation, as reporters found it all too easy to build their reporting and columns on the basis of information, often ambiguous or outright false, they retrieved off the Internet. One widely publicized incident occurred when a *Bos-*

511

ton Globe columnist was suspended from his post for four months for printing an article without disclosing that he had simply reprinted the contents of an e-mail that was being widely distributed on the Internet at the time; to make matters worse, the information therein, about the fate of the signers of the Declaration of Independence, was filled with factual errors.

Since information on the Internet comes in all varieties, from official documents to gossip, researchers, journalists, and others needed to develop discriminatory skills for retrieving and disseminating news and facts derived from the Internet. In the print, radio, and television worlds, getting information to masses of people quickly requires an enormous amount of capital backing. But one of the Web's most highly touted virtues—its exceptionally low barriers to entry—was also one of the main ingredients in the proliferation of online misinformation. With little invested in their information and with the Internet's anonymity negating the necessity of maintaining a solid reputation, intentional purveyors of misinformation have little to lose, and often find much to gain, in spreading false information.

Time being of the essence in journalism, the temptation for journalists to conduct their research on the Internet rather than go through private libraries—and many newspapers and magazines have closed down their libraries in recent years in favor of the Web—is particularly strong, since it enables them to track down information in seconds or minutes that it might take hours or days to accumulate through traditional channels. Clear guidelines and professional scrutiny are all-important in these cases, however, since the Internet can just as quickly lead to the spread of misinformation. This often means that journalists must combine Internet research with traditional methods, such as calling original sources for verification or consulting books from public libraries.

The Securities and Exchange Commission (SEC), meanwhile, busied itself in the late 1990s and early 2000s with developing new investigative methods to crack down on individuals, companies, and investors who were attempting to deceive online investors by engaging in securities fraud. There were numerous reports through this period, for instance, of individual investors getting rich by floating a rumor about certain stocks early in the day on investing-related Web sites, allowing the fabrication to mushroom and spur other investors to act accordingly, then buying or selling those same stocks later in the day to their advantage; in other words, defrauding other investors and relying on herd-like investment patterns to profit from intentional misinformation. One of the most infamous such cases resulted in the arrest of a 23-year-old El Segundo, California man who made $242,724 in profits by issuing a fabricated press re-

lease about the Costa Mesa firm Emulex Corp., which resulted in bad publicity that caused the firm's stock to plunge by 62 percent.

The dissemination of business and financial data on the World Wide Web troubled business leaders worried about the potential for misinformation to spread and accumulate damage as its effects on investors and others move through the economic system. To counter such potential threats, the International Accounting Standards Committee (IASC) issued a study titled "Business Reporting on the Internet," in which, having scrutinized 660 corporations in Europe, Asia-Pacific, North America, and South America, it called for codes of conduct to be applied to the publishing of business and financial information online.

The study reported that "the idiosyncrasies of the electronic medium will create problems in financial reporting that were not conceivable under the print medium." These idiosyncrasies included the ability for instantaneous reproduction and dissemination across wide geographical territory. Under these conditions, any misinformation, intentional or otherwise, especially when combined with perpetual access to rapidly shifting financial and business markets in a global economy, could rapidly produce a ripple effect that disrupts the efficient workings of economic systems, potentially with drastic effects. Thus the study encouraged securities regulators, national and international accounting firms and standards organizations, software companies, business publishers, and information intermediaries to collaborate on the development of stringent global language and criteria for electronic business reporting.

FURTHER READING:

Cannon, Carl M. "The Real Computer Virus." *American Journalism Review,* April, 2001.

Ebbinghouse, Carol. "Deliberate Misinformation on the Internet!? Tell Me it Ain't So!" *Searcher,* May, 2000.

Figg, J. "Study Urges Online Reporting Standards." *Internal Auditor,* February, 2000.

"Gossip on the Web: Truth, Lies, and Cyberspace." *Economist,* April 24, 1999.

Mendell, Ronald L. "Is the Internet Just a Web of Misinformation?" *Security Management,* June, 1999.

SEE ALSO: Cybersquatting; Fraud, Internet; Spam

MIT AND THE GALACTIC NETWORK

The concept of the Galactic Network was created by J.C.R. Licklider, a Massachusetts Institute of

Technology (MIT) researcher and professor. Licklider's vision of a Galactic Network—a network of computers that allows users to gather data and access programs anywhere in the world—was detailed in a series of memos. The first, *Man-Computer Symbiosis,* was written in 1960 and detailed Licklider's thoughts on the development of interaction between humans and computers. The second memo, *On-Line Man Computer Communication,* was published two years later and took the Galactic Network idea further, promoting the concept of social interaction through the networking of computers. In 1968, Licklider co-authored *The Computer as a Communication Device* with researcher Robert Taylor. The memo discussed the idea of using online communities and systems as an efficient method of human communication. Both the Galactic Network concept and research headed by MIT proved to be influential in early development of the ARPANET, the predecessor to the Internet.

An important milestone in the progression of Licklider's ideas was the creation of the Advanced Research Projects Agency (ARPA). The agency was developed by the U.S. government after the Soviet Union's launch of Sputnik I, the first satellite to orbit around the earth. ARPA was responsible for funding projects that would bring cutting-edge technology to the U.S. military. In 1962, ARPA created the Information Processing Techniques Office (IPTO) and selected Licklider to head up research dedicated to the advancement of information processing.

Upon taking control of IPTO, Licklider immediately began supporting research groups at educational institutions, especially MIT. The focus of research became a new concept called time-sharing, which would bring the idea of a Galactic Network one step closer to realization. Batch processing, the method of computing being used by researchers, was a time consuming process that allowed only one programmer at a time to use a computer system by feeding in stacks of program cards or tape. Howard Rheingold stated in his book *Tools for Thought* that "time-sharing was to be the first, most important step in the transition from batch processing to the threshold of personal computing (i.e., one person to one machine). The idea was to create computer systems capable of interacting with many programmers at the same time, instead of forcing them to wait in line with their cards or tapes."

As such, MIT laboratories were given additional funding to pursue time-sharing research efforts. By that time, Licklider had convinced several key MIT researchers that the creation of the Galactic Network should be pursued. Ivan Sutherland, a Ph.D. graduate from MIT—now considered a pioneer of the computer graphics industry—had caught the eye of ARPA management. In 1964, he took over as director of the IPTO and continued focusing on Licklider's ideas.

The following year, Sutherland awarded the industry's first networking contract to Lawrence G. Roberts, an MIT researcher.

While working on the contract, Roberts proved that a packet switching theory developed by Leonard Kleinrock, another MIT researcher, was completely necessary for computer networks. In a 1961 paper entitled *Information Flow in Large Communication Nets,* Kleinrock described packet switching as information that was broken down into packets of data, addressed to a receiver, transferred from one computer to another via a computer network, and then reassembled upon delivery to the receiver. In 1965, Roberts connected a TX-2 MIT computer to a Q-32 computer in California using a telephone line, creating the world's first wide-area computer network using Kleinrock's packets rather than circuits.

The progression of Licklider's ideas when Roberts was named the IPTO chief scientist in the late 1960s. It was then that he started developing ARPANET, created to develop and explore computer research sharing and packet switched communications. The ARPANET became an early version of the Internet in 1969 when computers at the University of California-Los Angeles, University of California-Santa Barbara, Stanford Research Institute, and the University of Utah were the first to be connected to the online network. They were later joined by MIT, Harvard, Systems Development Corp., and consulting firm Bolt, Beranek & Newman—a firm for whom Licklider once worked.

Licklider's foresight—he predicted millions of people would be using a Galactic Network by 2000—and the research efforts of those at MIT and various other educational institutions paved the way for the development of the ARPANET and, eventually, the Internet. According to Michael and Rhonda Hauben in *Netizens: On the History and Impact of Usenet and the Internet,* "Licklider's vision of an 'intergalactic network' connecting people represented an important conceptual shift in computer science. This vision guided the researchers who created the ARPANET. After the ARPANET was functioning, the computer scientists using it realized that assisting human communication was a major fundamental advance that the ARPANET made possible."

FURTHER READING:

Clark, David D., Cerf, Vinton G., et al. "A Brief History of the Internet." Reston, VA: The Internet Society, August 4, 2000. Available from www.isoc.org.

Hauben, Michael, and Ronda Hauben. *Netizens: On the History and Impact of Usenet and the Internet.* Los Alamitos, CA: IEEE Computer Society, May 1997.

Rheingold, Howard. *Tools for Thought.* Cambridge, MA: MIT Press, 2000.

SEE ALSO: ARPAnet; History of the Internet and World Wide Web (WWW)

MONSTER.COM

Monster.com, the leading career-related Web site, was formed in January 1999 by the merger of two online recruiting companies, The Monster Board and the Online Career Center. Both companies were owned by New York-based recruitment firm TMP Worldwide, a publicly-traded company with nearly $1.5 billion in annual revenue in 2001. Since 1999 Monster.com has spent hundreds of millions of dollars to build its brand. With funds provided by its parent company Monster.com also acquired other online job-search firms. For $100 million Monster.com entered into a four-year strategic relationship with America Online and gained its own keyword there. Monster.com was TMP Worldwide's best-performing subsidiary, and it claimed to be the only profitable business in its field.

Monster.com is considered an innovator in the field of online recruitment and employment. It was the first to develop a database of resumes with user names and passwords. It was also the first to develop a job-search agent, which has become a standard in the industry. It introduced a talent auction for free agents, allowing them to offer their services to the highest bidder. It was the first online employment service to develop a special area for executive-level positions.

By 2001 Monster.com was a market-share leader with more than 50 percent of the market in nearly every category. Its database of resumes surpassed 10 million in 2001, and the company expected to increase the database to 20 or 30 million resumes. More than 100,000 employers used Monster.com to post job openings and search for recruits, including more than 800 of the Fortune 1000. During the first half of 2001, Monster.com had about 6 million unique visitors going to its Web site about 25 million times a month, with the average user going to the site about once a week. The company boasted about 500 million page views per month, with the average user looking at 25 to 30 pages per month.

BUILDING THE BRAND

One of the key factors in Monster.com's success was the brand recognition it was able to achieve. Jeff Taylor, Monster.com's CEO and founder of The Monster Board, is regarded as an innovative marketer.

He estimated that Monster.com would spend about $250 million around the world to build the company's brand in 2001. The company did its first Super Bowl ad in 1999, when it introduced its ''What I want to be when I grow up'' advertising theme, which it used for about two years. Immediately after the ad, traffic at Monster.com increased by 450 percent. The results encouraged the company to spend more on TV advertising and brand building. Taylor estimated that Monster.com spent about $45 million on branding in 1999, with about 65 percent of the budget going to television advertising. The company's ads ran more than 500,000 times during 1999. During this time the company doubled in size, in part as a result of renaming the business Monster.com, advertising on the Super Bowl, and then developing its partnership with America Online. By the end of 1999 Monster.com was easily the most-visited online job search site.

Monster.com also built its brand in other ways. The company owned two blimps, which it flew over major sporting events. The company also had a presence at major events ranging from Mardi Gras to the Daytona 500. The firm's monster mascot, named Trumpasaurus, went to events and ran in marathons. Taylor himself spoke at about 75 events a year. In 2001 Monster.com produced a 30-minute infomercial called ''The Monster Show,'' which was shown on unused media time the company bought on off-peak, non-network programming. The company also bought time on about 100 radio stations, with CEO Taylor going on air to be a guest or host a special program where people could call in and ask questions or talk about finding a job.

ACQUISITIONS AND PARTNERSHIPS ENHANCE LEADERSHIP POSITION

Jeff Taylor started The Monster Board in 1994 with three employees in Maynard, Massachusetts. The company's interactive Web site allowed people to post resumes and look for job openings, primarily in the Northeast. Recruiters also used the site to fill open positions. A year after it was founded, The Monster Board was acquired by TMP Worldwide for $900,000. In 1996 TMP Worldwide went public and raised about $54 million through its initial public offering. For the next two years Monster developed nearly 100 co-branded career sites with partners such as Lycos and *USA Today*. When traffic coming to Monster from those sites flattened out, the company shifted its focus to developing the Monster.com brand, starting in 1999.

At the end of 1998, just before merging with Indianapolis-based Online Career Center to form Monster.com, The Monster Board was receiving about 5 million visitors a month and listed jobs from about

50,000 employers. Anticipating increased traffic in 1999, the company invested about $1 million in new servers to allow it to scale up its business. By mid-1999 Monster.com had a database of 1 million resumes—none of them more than a year old—and an estimated 180,000 job postings—none of them more than 2 months old. Under one package recruiters paid $7,900 to Monster.com for up to 30 job postings for 60 days, access to the resume database for one year, a company profile on Monster.com, and 5 skill screens per job. *PC Magazine* rated Monster.com the best online job search site, writing "None can beat Monster.com's impressive combination of ease of use and power for both job seekers and employers."

In mid-1999 Monster.com launched Monster Talent Market 1.0, an auction service for independent contractors and other free agents. Monster.com charged freelancers a small fee and also received a percentage from companies that signed them to a contract. Under the service independent contractors could post their experience, fees, and projects they were interested in, while employers would use the service to locate and hire temporary worker on a contract basis.

At the beginning of 2000 Monster.com had 2 million resumes posted at its site and an average of 260,000 job openings. According to *PC Week,* 1.3 million of the resumes posted at Monster.com were in the information technology (IT) field. For its 2000 Super Bowl ad, the company adapted the Robert Frost poem, "The Road Not Taken." After the ad was shown, Monster.com reported more than 4.4 million job searches on the day after, compared to 1.7 million on a day prior to the Super Bowl.

Internationally, the company also committed $20 million for a pan-European advertising campaign, where Monster.com operated sites in the United Kingdom, France, Germany, Belgium, the Netherlands, and Ireland. Although the company considered expanding into Eastern Europe, it eventually decided to focus on key countries in Western Europe. Its best results were obtained in the United Kingdom, France, and Germany. A Spanish site was launched in September 2000, followed by one in Italy in October. For 2001 the company planned to spend $70 to $75 million building its brand in Europe. In 2001 it also announced it would acquire Europe's largest online professional search company, Jobline International, for about $115 million, and gain sites in Sweden, Norway, Denmark, Switzerland, and Finland. Monster.com's Asia-Pacific strategy began with sites in Australia and New Zealand, a small presence in Singapore and Hong Kong, and the launch of a site in India in March 2001.

Monster.com announced its executive search service in September 2000 and launched it in January 2001. Called ChiefMonster, it targeted executive positions at the vice president level and above. Candidates could post their resumes for free, but they had to pass a screening test. Companies could post an unlimited number of executive positions for about $1,000 per year. Employers and recruiters also had to pay a fee to search the resume database.

Other initiatives for 2001 included an alliance with ESPN to create a Web site for sports jobs. The agreement gave Monster.com advertising time on ABC Sports' college football Bowl Championship Series and access to ESPN's audience of 18-to-34-year-old males. Through another agreement with the U.S. Department of Labor, Monster.com began to share listings and information with the federally run America's Job Bank.

Monster.com and its parent TMP Worldwide became more aggressive about acquiring competing firms and new technologies in 2001. Monster.com also added new services, including a moving and relocation site called Monstermoving.com. Among the technology companies acquired in 2001 were Hiring-Tools, which made Web-based human resources software, and Simpatix, which produced a Web-user interface desktop for recruiters. Career sites acquired in 2001, in addition to the European company Jobline International, included Utah-based FlipDog, which used a Web crawler to find jobs at internal employer postings. The firm's largest acquisition of 2001—if it passed regulatory approval—was a $460 million bid for HotJobs.com, which parent company TMP Worldwide said would continue to operate as a standalone brand. HotJobs.com and FlipDog were considered the number two and three online job search sites, respectively. That left Career Builder, a joint venture owned by Knight-Ridder and the Tribune Co., as Monster.com's principal competitor. In spite of Career Builder's $200 million bid for Headhunter.net, analysts believed that Monster.com was so far ahead of its competition that it would remain the top online recruiter for the foreseeable future.

FURTHER READING:

"AOL's Monster Accord." *Washington Business Journal,* December 10, 1999.

Cole-Gomolski, Barb. "Site to Collect Bids for Contract Workers." *Computerworld,* June 28, 1999.

DeLong, Daniel F. "Analysts: Monster Will Remain Top Online Recruiter." *E-Commerce Times,* August 31, 2001. Available from www.ecommercetimes.com

"The Life of the Party." *Business Week,* June 4, 2001.

Mateyaschuk, Jennifer. "Career Opportunities for IT." *InformationWeek,* May 31, 1999.

Mollinson, Caitlin. "The Internet World Interview: Jeff Taylor." *Internet World,* May 1, 2001.

"Monster.com." *PC Magazine,* May 25, 1999.

Neil, Stephanie. ''The Monster Match Focuses on Quality.'' *PC Week,* January 17, 2000.

Regan, Keith. ''Is Monster.com a Monster.'' *E-Commerce Times,* July 6, 2001. Available from www.ecommercetimes.com

''Rivals of Monster.com Say Online Recruiting Site Isn't Unstoppable.'' *Knight-Ridder/Tribune Business News,* August 23, 2001.

Sweeney, Phil. ''Monster.com Expanding by Eating up Competition.'' *Business First-Columbus,* August 31, 2001.

Wasserman, Todd. ''Jeff Taylor.'' *Brandweek,* November 8, 1999.

Willmott, Don. ''PC Magazine Editor's Choice: Monster.com.'' *PC Magazine,* January 16, 2001.

MOORE, GORDON E.

Gordon E. Moore is co-founder of Intel Corp., the world's largest maker of microprocessors and one of the five most profitable manufacturing companies of any business sector. Moore served as CEO of Intel from 1975 until 1987. His prediction, made in the mid-1960s, that computer chip capacity would double every year and a half eventually became known as ''Moore's Law.'' It is viewed by many as the guidepost by which most chip manufacturers of the 1980s and 1990s gauged their success. For that foresight, Moore was awarded a National Medal of Technology from President George Bush in 1990. Having served Intel as chairman since 1979, Moore was appointed chairman emeritus in 1997, a role he retained until May of 2001, when he officially resigned from Intel's board at the age of 72. With an estimated worth of $26 billion, Moore is one of the five wealthiest men in the U.S.

Moore earned a B.S. degree in Chemistry from the University of California at Berkeley. His graduate work, which culminated in a Ph.D. in chemistry and physics, took place at the California Institute of Technology. After finishing his studies in 1955, Moore went to work for Dr. William Shockley—a Nobel Prize winner for his work on the world's first transistor—at a semiconductor upstart in Mountain View, California, known as Shockley Laboratory. After finding it difficult to work with the eccentric researcher, Moore and seven colleagues, including Dr. Robert Noyce, left Shockley Laboratory in 1957 to establish Fairchild Semiconductor, which was owned by parent Fairchild Camera and Instrument. Moore served as head of research, and it was there that he made the projection that became known as Moore's law: a computer chip's power, measured by the number of transistors it could handle, would double every eighteen months. According to *Fortune* columnist Brian O'Reilly, it was with Noyce serving as vice president and Moore overseeing research that ''Fairchild came up with inventions that laid the groundwork for the chip industry, including making chips by etching and printing components in layers, and the 'integrated circuit,' in which components with different functions were etched and connected on the same sliver of silicon.''

Although Fairchild Semiconductor eventually became the largest semiconductor company in the world, due in large part to its development of computer chip industry production technology known as the planar process, Moore and Noyce found themselves dissatisfied with the level of financial support they were receiving from their owners. In 1968, they left Fairchild Semiconductor to found their own company, NM Electronics, which was based on a one-page business plan developed by Noyce. NM Electronics was later renamed Intel, from the first syllables of ''integrated electronics.'' Its first products included LSI semiconductor memories, a new high-speed RAM device, and a metal oxide semiconductor chip. With Noyce at the helm, Moore first served Intel as executive vice president.

In 1974, Intel released the 8088, the world's first general purpose microprocessor, which quickly became an industry standard. One year later, Moore was appointed president and CEO of Intel. Sales at that time totaled $135 million. Moore named Andrew S. Grove president in 1979 and also took on the chairmanship of Intel's board. Both Moore and Grove were instrumental in persuading IBM to select the 8088 chip for its new personal computer line in 1980. Together, they also began to discontinue memory chip operations in the mid-1980s, instead focusing Intel on the more profitable microprocessor market. In 1987, Grove took over as CEO from Moore, who remained chairman. By the end of the decade, Intel had grown into the third-largest private semiconductor maker in the world.

Moore continued to serve as chairman of Intel until 1997, when he scaled back his daily responsibilities and took on the role of chairman emeritus. It was at this time that PC growth began to slow and Intel began reducing its emphasis on central processing units in favor of burgeoning networking technology markets such as flash memory chips and cell phone processors. Intel also began offering Internet services, such as World Wide Web hosting. While the Internet revolution had helped to boost the success of the firm Moore co-founded, by prompting hordes of consumers to become PC owners, it also spawned the technology that eventually allowed those same consumers to access the Internet without their PCs. In the late

1990s, just as Moore's career at Intel began to wind down, the firm began to gear up, hoping to reinvent itself as a networking technology and Internet services powerhouse.

FURTHER READING:

Clancy, Heather. "Gordon Moore—The Intelligence of Intel." *Computer Reseller News.* November 13, 2000.

Intel Corp. "Gordon E. Moore." Santa Clara, CA: Intel Corp., 2001. Available from www.intel.com.

Manners, David. "Hero of Our Time." *Electronics Weekly.* March 26, 1997.

"Moore Leaves Intel, But Legacy Remains Set in Law." *Info-World.* May 28, 2001.

O'Reilly, Brian. "From Intel to the Amazon: Gordon Moore's Incredible Journey." *Fortune.* April 26, 1999.

Ross, Philip E. "Moore's Second Law." *Forbes.* March 25, 1996.

SEE ALSO: Grove, Andrew; Intel Corp.; Moore's Law; Noyce, Robert

MOORE, J. STUART

J. Stuart Moore is the co-founder and co-CEO of Sapient Corp., an Internet integration services provider—one of the leading such firms in the U.S.—whose clients include traditional businesses like WalMart and Staples, as well as Internet firms like iwon.com. Moore oversees the internal operations of Sapient, including employee recruiting and retention and corporate strategy, while Jerry Greenberg, the firm's other co-founder and co-CEO, handles the more external components of operations such as sales, marketing, and public relations. In 1999, both men made *Fortune* magazine's list of the 40 wealthiest Americans under the age of 40. With revenues of more than $500 million in the year 2000, Sapient became the first Internet integration services provider to be added to the Standard & Poor's 500-stock index. Moore and Greenberg each own 18 percent of the firm.

Moore earned a bachelor's degree in computer science from the University of California at Berkeley. Upon graduation, he began working in the information technology industry, eventually making his way to Cambridge Technology Partners, where he met Greenberg. In 1991, Moore and Greenberg—at 29 and 25 years of age, respectively—created their own company, Sapient Corp., in Cambridge, Massachusetts. Rather than attempt to secure funding from outside venture capitalists, the partners used $40,000 of their own savings and charged nearly $70,000 on their credit cards. Sapient's initial contracts focused on client-server integration. Moore and Greenberg worked to set themselves apart from competitors by not only assisting clients in determining how technology could eradicate problems and boost operational efficiencies, but also by creating, executing, and supporting whatever applications they decide to use. Moore and Greenberg were also unique for offering set fees and deadline schedules at the onset of a project and connecting employee pay, including their own, to customer satisfaction.

The number of employees jumped from 95 in 1994 to 213 in 1995, and revenues and earnings both doubled. Moore and Greenberg, each retaining roughly 36 percent of the firm's stock, took Sapient public in April of 1996. The $33 million raised was funneled into expansion efforts. After realizing that an increasing number of Sapient's clients were delving into e-commerce, Moore and Greenberg began repositioning the firm to offer e-business integration services. Four small acquisitions—including Adjacency and Studio Archetype, two World Wide Web design firms—augmented Sapient's offerings. To make the best use of Sapient's new holdings, Moore began to reorganize the firm into smaller, more autonomous, industry-based divisions. Eventually, Sapient was able to offer a full range of e-commerce services that included the planning and creation of online stores. Unlike many e-business service firms emerging in the late 1990s, Sapient kept its advertising budget in check, careful not to spend more than it could afford. Moore and Greenberg saw their efforts pay off as Sapient's growing profitability set the firm apart from rivals. In 1998, Sapient earned $9.4 million on sales of $165 million. Those numbers were upped to $30.3 million in profits and $277 million in sales in 1999. According to a November 2000 article in *Computer Reseller News,* Moore and Greenberg successfully transformed "a nine-year-old consulting and integration company grounded in client/server computing into one of the foremost Web integrators on the scene."

Roughly 2,600 employees staffed 18 offices around the world by the end of 2000. Despite Sapient's strength, however, recessionary economic conditions in North America, along with a slowdown in the e-commerce sector, did undercut the firm's profits in the first quarter of 2001. As a result, Moore and Greenberg announced that the workforce would be reduced by 20 percent, the office in Sydney, Australia, closed, and U.S. operations consolidated.

FURTHER READING:

Mulqueen, John T. "Young Company Flourishes." *CommunicationsWeek,* June 17, 1996.

Rosa, Jerry. "Eleven—Jerry Greenberg—The Stalwart." *Computer Reseller News,* November 13, 2000.

"Sapient Corp." *Advertising Age,* June 19, 2000.

Sapient Corp. ''J. Stuart Moore.'' Cambridge, MA: Sapient Corp., 2001.

''U.S. Business Brief: Sapient Cuts 720 Jobs, Warns of Losses.'' *Futures World News,* May 7, 2001.

Whitford, David. ''The Two-Headed Manager: Sapient Co-CEOs Jerry Greenberg and Stuart Moore Have (Almost) Nothing in Common. That Helps Explain Why Their Relationship Works.'' *Fortune,* January 24, 2000.

SEE   Greenberg, Jerry; Integration; Sapient Corp.
ALSO:

MOORE'S LAW

Moore's Law was expounded in a 1965 *Electronics Magazine* article by Gordon Moore, who was then the research director at Fairchild Semiconductor. Moore noted that since the invention of the integrated circuit, the number of transistors per square inch on those circuits had doubled each year. Moore, who co-founded Intel Corp. in 1968, projected that this doubling would continue into the foreseeable future. This proved essentially correct, with subsequent data density doubling about every 18 months.

In 1975, Moore modified his law, stating that the increasing technical difficulties associated with the production of enhanced microchips would cause the number of devices located on a chip to double every two years, another prediction born out by industry trends. He noted that as microprocessor circuits get smaller, future silicon chips could contain the modem, graphic, and memory-control functions previously housed on discrete hardware in computers. Among other things, Moore's Law explains why computer technology drops in price so rapidly and so quickly becomes obsolete, giving the average computer a competitive life span of only three years.

Among the technical difficulties linked to producing shrinking chips containing ever more options is the inclusion of dopant impurities mixed into silicon to increase its capacity to hold electric-charges. As transistors get smaller, they still must hold the same charge. Thus, the silicon must include a higher percentage of dopants. But at a certain limit, dopant atoms conglomerate into electrically inert clumps. Chips manufactured by 2000 were reaching that limit of operability. The ''gates'' that regulate electron flow in chips posed another problem. They had grown so minute that they were susceptible to a quantum effect in which electrons burrow through the gates even when closed. If the gates fail to block the electron stream completely, chips won't function.

In 1995, Moore presciently observed that although such technical difficulties could hamper the sustained pace of microprocessor growth, increasing manufacturing costs could prove an even bigger obstacle. Though processing equipment cost about $12,000 when Moore founded Intel, by 1995 it had risen to about $12 million, while productive output remained constant. As chip technology becomes more sophisticated, the cost of manufacturing chip grows exponentially. As capital costs outstrip income, eventually it will no longer be financially feasible to produce ever-more complex chips. This observation became known as Moore's Second Law.

Moore prophesied the end of his law in 2000 at an Intel Developer Forum, pronouncing that the technical ability to downsize microprocessors would soon collide with the finite size of atomic particles. Unless microprocessing technology changed dramatically, this would eventually halt the growth of microprocessor capacity. Moore predicted that the industry could reach such physical limitations by 2017.

FURTHER READING:

Kanellos, Michael. ''Moore Says Moore's Law to Hit Wall.'' *CNET News.com,* September 30, 1997. Available from news.cnet.com.

Mann, Charles. ''The End of Moore's Law?'' *Technology Review,* May/June 2000.

SEE   Intel Corp.; Metcalfe's Law; Microprocessor; Moore,
ALSO: Gordon E.

MOTLEY FOOL INC., THE

In 1993, The Motley Fool Inc. was established by brothers David and Tom Gardner and their friend, Erik Rydholm, as a 16-page newsletter offering investment information with a humorous twist. By the end of the decade, the newsletter operation had evolved into a multimedia personal finance company with a World Wide Web site, online store, a nationally syndicated newspaper column and radio show, a monthly magazine, and a series of published books. By 2001, The Motley Fool reached 30 million people per month through its multimedia channels.

EARLY HISTORY

After graduating from college with English degrees, David and Tom Gardner, along with Rydholm, teamed up to write a newsletter that mixed humor with investment information. The Gardner brothers had been exposed to their father's laid back and humorous philosophy toward business and investing throughout their childhood, and that set the tone for the newsletter. The Motley Fool name stemmed from Shakespearean literature and was based on the concept that only the Fool could speak the truth and go against what was the norm, without being beheaded for his ideas.

Using wedding invitation lists from friends and family, the trio mailed out their first issues in hopes of securing subscriptions to their fledgling publication. After receiving only a few dozen orders, the partners began to realize that marketing and selling a publication was not an easy task. The Gardners, who had been answering investment questions online via their Prodigy account, decided that utilizing the Internet would give them access to customers across the country. The pair began using America Online (AOL) to advertise their newsletter and solicit investment questions from fellow AOL members.

The Gardners' big break came in 1994 when AOL invited The Motley Fool to become a featured part of its home page. Using funds secured from the contract with AOL, the company moved into an office in Alexandria, Virginia, and established the ''Fool Portfolio.'' AOL members were then encouraged to use the stock portfolio as a learning device and were able to track The Motley Fool's investment successes and failures. The Gardners' laid-back approach to personal investing gained in popularity rather quickly. Their habit of making public appearances wearing suits and jester hats garnered industry attention as well. The Motley Fool's unconventional mission—to educate, enrich, and amuse individual investors around the world—soon earned it a leading position among online investment forums.

The company's focus on the individual investor was also a key factor in its success on the Internet. By 1996, the company's investment forum on AOL was securing 275,000 visitors per month. According to a 1996 *Computerworld* article, ''The Motley Fool founders have become cult figures because of their investment philosophy, which pumps up the abilities of individual investors instead of the powerful investment establishment of brokers and firms.'' In April 1997, when its contract with AOL expired, the company developed its own Web site. By then, it was offering its investment advice to over 500,000 surfers each month.

EXPANSION

As the firm's success on the Internet continued, the Gardners found themselves expanding offline as well. With the help of Gary Hill—the company's chief financial officer hired in 1996—the firm partnered with Simon and Schuster and published its first book, *The Motley Fool Investment Guide*, which became a New York Times bestseller. It also teamed up with Andrews McMeel Universal (AMU) to develop a nationally syndicated weekly newspaper column. In 1998, The Motley Fool began a nationally syndicated radio show. That year, the company expanded internationally by establishing Fool U.K.

The Gardners continued expanding by tapping into any media channel that was available. In 1999, the *Motley Fool Monthly* magazine was launched. The company also formed a strategic alliance with Reuters Ltd. As part of the deal, Reuters supplied financial news to The Motley Fool Web site and advertised the firm on its News Network. The company also developed FoolMart, an online store that operated as a subsidiary by selling e-mail subscriptions, detailed investment information, and company reports. That year, the firm secured $26.5 million in venture capital from Maveron and the Mayfield Fund, funds it used to beef up marketing efforts and upgrade The Motley Fool Web site.

Growth efforts continued into the new millennium. After nearly a year of searching for the perfect CEO candidate, the Gardners hired seasoned marketing executive C. Patrick Garner in May of 2000. Garner began to oversee the firm's growth efforts, which were focused on Europe and Asia, while the Gardner brothers remained co-chairmen and chief strategists. That month, the firm launched a new monthly subscription-based publication entitled *The Motley Fool Select*. The new publication replaced company research reports and detailed the Fool's top investment ideas. The stocks covered were divided into three categories: the highly profitable companies, or Rule Makers; the emerging firms, or Rule Breakers; and the smaller startups, or Small-Cap Foolish 8.

To fund expansion, the firm secured a second round of financing—$30 million from Softbank Finance Group, AOL Time Warner Ventures, Maveron, and the Mayfield Fund—in early 2001. At the same time, The Motley Fool signed a content distribution agreement with MSNBC.com, an Internet-based news site. The agreement allowed MSNBC.com to feature Fool information on its network. The successes of the company were overshadowed, however, by the downturn of the dot.com industry. As a result, The Motley Fool was forced to lay off 115 employees. The Gardners blamed a drop in advertising revenues, along with a weakening U.S. economy, for the cutbacks. In June of 2001, the firm continued with its downsizing and cut 45 additional jobs. The layoffs weighed heavily on the founders, who took pride in operating a close-knit organization. Co-founder Rydholm, the chief operating officer of the firm, stated in *Institutional Investor* that, ''it was one of the most difficult things I've ever had to do. But you owe it to your investors to perform.'' As part of the restructuring, The

Motley Fool also divided its business into six different units including Publishing, Electronic Media, Consumer Internet, Corporate Solutions, Fool U.K., and Fool Japan.

FURTHER READING:

Bruno, Michael P. "The Motley Fool Gains a Chief Ringleader." *Newsbytes,* May 2, 2000.

Deck, Stewart. "A Fool's Paradise." *Computerworld,* October 21, 1996.

Gittlen, Sandra. "Motley Fooling Around With Electronic Commerce." *Network World,* September 14, 1998.

Harper, Philipp. "A Fool's Paradise." *Forbes,* February 19, 2001.

Johnson, Cory. "Silicon Babylon: Do the Motley Fools Still Matter?" *TheStreet.com,* June 18, 1998. Available from www.thestandard.com.

Linafelt, Tom. "AMU Taking Financial Jesters to Papers." *The Kansas City Business Journal,* July 25, 1997.

Lux, Hal. "Fool's Gold." *Institutional Investor,* March 2001.

The Motley Fool Inc. "The History of The Motley Fool." Alexandria, VA: The Motley Fool Inc., 2001. Available from www.fool.com.

Mullaney, Timothy J. "Clicks & Misses." *BusinessWeekOnline,* September 17, 1999. Available from www.businessweek.com.

Wilson, Korey A. "Nobody's Fool." *Black Enterprise,* November 1999.

SEE ALSO: Investing, Online; New Economy; Volatility

MOTOROLA, INC.

Motorola Inc. is known for its pioneering efforts in the car radio, pager, and cellular phone industries. With sales of $37.5 billion, it is the world's second largest manufacturer of mobile phones which, along with pagers and other communications devices, bring in nearly 33 percent of revenues. Semiconductors account for another 20 percent in sales. In the late 1990s, the Schaumburg, Illinois-based firm began laying off employees in an attempt to improve its bottom line. Various cost cutting measures continued into 2001, when Motorola closed its largest U.S. cellular phone factory and eliminated 2,500 positions.

EARLY HISTORY

The foundation for Motorola was laid when Illinois residents Paul V. Galvin and Edward Stewart founded a storage battery company in 1921. Although the U.S. government shut the new business down in 1923 for failure to pay excise taxes, operations continued when Stewart opened a new storage battery firm, named Stewart Storage Battery Co., in 1926. When the growing popularity of electric power undercut battery sales, Steward devised the "battery eliminator," a converter that allowed a battery-operated radio to plug into a wall outlet. The new product wasn't enough to keep the firm from insolvency; however, Galvin and his brother acquired the battery eliminator operations from the bankrupt firm, and they later incorporated the business as Galvin Manufacturing Corp.

Galvin began working on a new car radio receiver in 1929. The following year, the firm introduced the world's first commercially viable car radio. The product was named Motorola, a combination of the words of "motor" and "victrola." Motorola continued to lead the U.S. automobile radio industry into the 1930s. After a trip to Europe in 1936, Galvin recognized the likelihood of war and began preparing his firm for such an event. For example, he oversaw the development of the "Police Cruiser," a radio designed to receive police broadcasts. The firm diversified into home radios in 1937; at that time, more than half of all American households owned radios. B. F. Goodrich Co. became the first national Motorola dealer that year.

Galvin Manufacturing launched its first major advertising campaign, which included print ads, billboards, and road signs, in 1938. Two years later, the company created a hand-held, two-way radio, known as the "handie-talkie," for the U.S. military. Believing that radio communication products would be increasingly called upon to enhance military efforts, Galvin created a separate communications products division. Sales that year reached nearly $10 million.

In 1941, the company established Motorola Communications and Electronics, Inc. as its sales subsidiary. The first two-way FM radio communications products, which offered increased range and quieter operation, were introduced. Galvin Manufacturing completed its initial public offering in 1943, selling its share for $8.50 each. That year, Researcher Dan Noble developed the first portable two-way FM radio, known as the "walkie-talkie." Both the "walkie-talkie" and the "handie-talkie" played an integral role in U.S. military field communications during World War II. When the war ended, the firm renewed its development of electronic products for consumers.

Galvin Manufacturing officially adopted the Motorola name in 1947. The firm also purchased Detrola, a supplier of car radios to Ford Motor Co. Other major car radio clients included Chrysler and General Motors. Motorola diversified into televisions in 1948 with the launch of the Golden View VT71. Priced at $179, more than 100,000 unit were sold by the end of the year. As a result, Motorola became the fourth-largest television manufacturer in the nation. In 1949, the company established a research and development facility, headed by Dan Noble, in Phoenix, Arizona. By focusing on transistors, Noble played a major role Motorola's emergence as a leader in the worldwide semiconductor industry. Motorola also released a two-way FM radio communications equipment line which made us of the increased number of radio frequencies.

Developments during the early 1950s included a three-amp power transistor and a color television set, which proved problematic. The set was criticized for technical glitches and its high price. Limited color programming from broadcasters also posed a problem at the time. In 1956, the firm pulled its color television from shelves. A small car radio was the first commercial Motorola product to use transistors. The firm also unveiled a small radio receiver, called a pager, which was used mainly by hospitals. The first fully transistorized two-way radio was shipped in 1959; it became one of the firm's best selling products. Motorola unveiled its first portable transistor radio at roughly the same time. Competition heated up as several foreign radio manufacturers begin gaining market share.

INTERNATIONAL EXPANSION AND DIVERSIFICATION

Sales reached $300 million by 1960. International expansion efforts were initiated in 1961 with the establishment of an office in Japan. The firm's auto products division began producing alternators, a move which marked the beginning of Motorola's role as an auto industry electronics supplier. National Video and Motorola worked together in the mid-1960s to create the first rectangular picture tube for color televisions, a product that eventually became a standard in the color television industry. During the same period, Ford, RCA, and Motorola jointly developed the first eight-track tape player for automobiles. The falling cost of semiconductors fueled their increased use in consumer electronic products; to take advantage of the growing market, Motorola developed a line of low-cost, plastic encapsulated transistors. Other new product releases included a line of color receivers, a portable FM radio that was half the size and weight of previous radios, and the first all-transistor color television set sold in the U.S. International expansion continued.

Motorola began making components for battery powered quartz watches in 1972. As a result, the firm gained familiarity with integrated circuits, quartz crystals, and miniature motors. Two years later, Mat-sushita Electric Industrial Co. bought Motorola's television operations. Acquisitions during the late 1970s included data communications network systems maker Codex Corp. and communications equipment manufacturer Universal Data Systems. The firm also added advanced integrated circuits to all of its radio communications products. Making its first foray into the microprocessor industry, Motorola launched a 16-bit microprocessor in 1979; the new product was first used in electronic components for the auto industry.

Sales reached $3 billion in 1980. Motorola paid $253 million for computer system maker Four-Phase Systems, Inc. in 1982. Nippon Telegraph and Telephone ordered roughly 43,000 Pocket Bell pagers from Motorola that year. Four-Phase, Codex, and Universal Data were combined to form a new Information Systems division, which launched a 32-bit microprocessor in 1984. Motorola's paging division constructed a new plant in Boynton Beach, Florida; it also began transforming the devices from one-way receivers into two-way appliances able to handle various data formats. By then, the firm was also supplying cellular phone systems—technology it had first developed in the mid-1960s—to New York, Philadelphia, Beijing, and Hong Kong. As part of a major shift in focus, Motorola exited the car radio industry. The following year, Congress awarded the first Malcolm Baldridge National Quality Award to Motorola. The firm created Motorola Lighting Inc. to manufacture electronic ballasts for the lighting industry. It also unveiled the world's smallest cellular phone, the Micro-TAC, which became the industry's best selling product. Motorola's success in the cellular phone market was marred by its losses in computer systems, however, which reached roughly $200 million in the late 1980s.

Motorola created Iridium Inc. in 1991 to oversee a satellite communications system that allowed mobile telephones to operate worldwide; however, the unit's poor performance eventually cost the firm millions of dollars in writeoffs. Unisys Corp. and Motorola forged a semiconductor technology alliance in 1992. The firm also created Motorola-Nortel Communications in conjunction with Northern Telecom as a joint cellular network marketing venture. International expansion continued with new plants in China and India. In 1994, Motorola landed a contract to construct the first digital mobile phone system in Russia. The firm diversified into digital modems in 1995. The following year, the firm discovered that cable television lines could be used to offer Internet access to home computer users and began investigating ways to capitalize on this new market. Intense competition in the U.S. cellular telephone industry undercut sales, prompting the firm to lay off 225 employees. To bolster its cellular phone sales, the firm launched the StarTAC phone in 1996. Although the StarTAC was initially highly successful, digital technology had already begun to replace the analog technology that powered StarTAC, a fact that later earned Motorola sharp criticism from shareholders.

In the mid-1990s, Apple, IBM, and Motorola joined forces to create PowerPC, a microprocessor chip designed to compete with those manufactured and marketed by Intel Corp. However, PowerPC failed to penetrate the mainstream market. In 1997, Motorola established an Internet software division. By the late 1990s, semiconductor sales growth had ground to a near halt, and the firm's share of the U.S. cellular phone market fell to 41 percent from a high of 54 percent. Losses in 1998 totaled roughly $1 billion. In an effort to recapture lost market share, Motorola finally created a line of digital phones, known as the V-Series, in 1999. The firm also acquired Software Corporation of America, Inc. and the portion of wafer manufacturer Tohoku Semiconductor Corp. it did not already own.

In January of 2000, Motorola paid $17 billion for General Instrument Corp., which it folded into its newly established Motorola Broadband Communications Sector. The purchase gave Motorola access to General Instrument subsidiary Next Level—a high-speed Internet access provider—as well as to the alliances General Instrument had forged with TCI, the cable arm of AT&T Corp. Other acquisitions that year included network processor developer C-Port Corp., printer acceleration specialist WaveMark Technologies, Inc., and software development tools maker HI-WARE AG. The firm also divested its lighting unit. While sales of both personal communications devices and semiconductors declined that year, sales of cable modems and digital set-top boxes increased by roughly 50 percent. The broadband unit accounted for 8.4 percent of total revenues, a figure which Motorola planned to bolster in coming years.

FURTHER READING:

''Motorola, Inc.'' In *Notable Corporate Chronologies.* Farmington Hills, MI: Gale Group, 1999.

Roth, Daniel. ''From Poster Boy to Whipping Boy: Burying Motorola.'' *Fortune,* July 6, 1998.

———. ''Motorola Lives!'' *Fortune,* September 27, 1999.

Schaff, William. ''A Merger That Makes Sense.'' *InformationWeek,* September 27, 1999.

Tatge, Mark. ''Major Hang Up.'' *Forbes,* March 5, 2001.

Tetzeli, Rick. ''And Now For Motorola's Next Trick.'' *Fortune,* April 28, 1997.

SEE ALSO: Broadband Technology; Microprocessor

MULTIMEDIA

By the mid-1990s the processing speed and memory capacity of computers had advanced considerably, enabling users to do more than ever before on their PCs. It became possible to run applications like video games that combined text, sounds, video, and graphic animation in exciting ways. The combination of these different media elements came to be known as multimedia. In addition to multimedia software, the use of multimedia technology began to increase on the World Wide Web. Consumers were able listen to music and news via Internet audio technology, such as that offered by RealNetworks; and view streaming video clips, films, and Web casts.

Multimedia technology was a powerful tool for companies engaging in e-commerce. First, it allowed marketers to show and describe products on the Web or CD-ROM with static text and pictures. However, it also allowed them to create more exciting promotional efforts that incorporated video and sound. For example, a hotel chain could allow potential visitors to take virtual tours that included previews of rooms, restaurants, and entertainment offerings at different properties. An online music store could provide sample songs from CDs prior to purchase. Multimedia technology also made inroads in the area of e-mail marketing. In the early 2000s, Radical Communications provided technology to leading companies like 20th Century Fox, the National Football League, Dell, Old Navy, and Kraft that allowed them to deliver audio and video to consumers via e-mail. It did this through a product called RadicalMail.

Despite rapid advancements in multimedia technology and the speeds at which consumers connected to the Internet, a survey conducted by Keynote Systems Inc. in October 2000 revealed that the quality of Web-based audio and video was still quite poor. The organization expected conditions to improve as streaming technologies evolved and more users relied on high-speed connections to access the Internet. Bandwidth, or the amount of data that a network connection is able to carry, is important for multimedia transmission quality. According to Dataquest, the number of households with high-speed access was expected to reach 28 million by 2004, increasing from 6 million at the end of 2000.

FURTHER READING:

''Dataquest: Broadband to Connect 28 Million U.S. Households.'' *Nua Internet Surveys,* November 21, 2000. Available from www.nua.ie.

''Keynote Systems: Web Multimedia Still Low-Grade.'' *Nua Internet Surveys,* October 25, 2000. Available from www.nua.ie.

"Multimedia." *Ecommerce Webopedia,* May 25, 2001. Available from www.e-comm.webopedia.com.

"Multimedia." *Tech Encyclopedia,* May 25, 2001. Available from www.techweb.com.

SEE Bandwidth; Streaming Media
ALSO:

MUSK, ELON

Elon Musk founded Zip2 Corp., a Web-based city and community guide firm, in 1995 and X.com, a now defunct online financial services provider, in 1999. In February of 1999, Musk sold Zip2 to Compaq Computer Corp. for $305 million; it now helps to power the Alta Vista search engine owned by Compaq. Although he decided to shutter the original X.com banking and investment services operations in October of 2000, Musk still plays an integral role in PayPal, the firm X.com merged with shortly after its inception.

In his twenties, Musk earned a degree in physics from the University of Pennsylvania and a degree in business from the Wharton School. After dropping out of the Ph.D. program in energy physics at Stanford University, Musk founded Zip2 at the age of 24. Via agreements with the likes of the *Chicago Tribune* and the *New York Times,* his new company began providing both local and national news, entertainment, and related online content to various metropolitan communities. A planned merger with CitySearch fell through in April of 1998. Less than a year later, Musk sold Zip2 to Compaq Computer for $305 million in a deal proclaimed one of the largest Internet-based cash payments to date. Compaq used the customization features of Zip2 to create MyAltaVista, a personalized version its popular Web portal.

Once the deal with Compaq was completed, the young millionaire began pursuing his next venture: X.com. Initially, Musk founded X.com with plans to grow it into a full-scale financial services site that offered everything from checking accounts to insurance and investment options. To help him run his new venture, Musk hired investment banker John Story as executive vice president and Bill Harris—the CEO behind Intuit Corp.'s aggressive Internet push—as president and CEO. Musk appointed himself chairman. Investments from Musk, Harris, and Sequoia Capital totaled $25 million.

Launched in December of 1999, X.com began offering $20 to anyone who opened a free online checking account in an effort to secure its first customers. Musk also put in place a referral program, giving $10 to any member who signed up a new customer. He planned to make money in the same way that traditional lenders did by relying on the interest rate spreads. Within two months of its launch, X.com had secured 100,000 customers, coming close to matching the client base of its largest competitor, Etrade Telebank, which had 130,000 customers. While the firm's growth was impressive relative to its rivals, convincing customers to trust virtual banking proved difficult. This problem was exacerbated when X.com was forced to make public the fact that hackers had been able to illegally transfer funds to its accounts. As a result, the firm began requesting cancelled checks before accepting transfers from outside accounts.

In March of 2000, Musk orchestrated the merger of X.com and PayPal, an online payment services provider that had been operating since late 1999. Successful in the person-to-person (P2P) online payment industry, with nearly 15,000 new clients signing up each day, PayPal began looking to business-to-consumer (B2C) and business-to-business (B2B) markets shortly after the merger was completed. Customers willing to deposit money into an X.com account by electronic fund transfer, credit card transfer, or check were able to make instant payments, via email, to participating PayPal businesses.

Management disputes between Musk and Harris resulted in the resignation of Harris after a short six-month tenure. Musk announced a dramatic shift in focus in October. According to Megan J. Ptacek, a writer for *American Banker,* Musk decided that "rather than offer a wide range of banking and related services," his firm would "become solely a global payment system." Soon thereafter, X.com changed its name to PayPal. The firm spent the latter half of 2000, as well as most of 2001, focusing on international expansion efforts, as well as on increasing its B2B and B2C operations.

FURTHER READING:

Carlsen, Clifford. "PayPal Lands $90M in Funding." *TheDeal.com.* March 6, 2001. Available from www.TheDeal.com.

Corcoran, Elizabeth. "Something Better Than Free." *Forbes.* February 21, 2000.

PayPal.com. Company Information. Available from www.paypal.com. July 2001.

Perry, Joellen. "Settling Debts Online: A New Tool for E-mailers." *U.S. News and World Report.* April 17, 2000.

Ptacek, Megan J. "X.com Scraps Bank Strategy to Focus on PayPal System." *American Banker.* October 11, 2000.

Toonkel, Jessica. "Electronic Commerce: X.com Moving In to B-to-B Online Payments." *American Banker.* August 9, 2000.

"Zip2 Founder Launches 2nd Firm: Readies Financial Supersite." *Computergram International.* August 30, 1999.

SEE   AltaVista Co.; Compaq Computer Corp.; PayPal;
ALSO: X.com

MYSIMON.COM

MySimon.com, a wholly owned subsidiary of CNET Networks, is a leading comparison shopping site on the Internet. Through its proprietary Virtual Learning Agent (VLA) technology, users are able to shop for products at more than 2,000 online merchants—including online auctions and classified ads—and find the lowest prices. Orders can then be placed directly with the online sellers. MySimon does not sell or ship any products and does not provide customer service support for orders. MySimon is free to use and generates revenue from advertising and merchant affiliates. Merchants may join MySimon's BOLD (Building Online Demand) program and pay a fee to have their name or icon highlighted in search results.

EASY-TO-USE SERVICE

MySimon is considered easy to use. The site's home page offers several search options, including a keyword search for a specific product and a list of 17 product categories called "Shopping Departments" that are further divided into subcategories. Users can browse and search within these categories and enter selection criteria as well as minimum and maximum prices. Although it is not necessary to register to use MySimon.com, those who do so gain access to such features as saved searches and e-mail updates.

Search results appear in a table that lists the products, prices, manufacturers, merchants, and merchant ratings. Users can learn what other shoppers think of specific products and merchants and have the opportunity to write their own reviews. The search results can be sorted by any of the data fields. Clicking on a product's name takes the user to the merchant's Web page.

Purchases are made by clicking on the Buy button next to the product's name. MySimon frames merchant pages with its own name and logo, so it may appear that purchases are made through MySimon. In actuality, they are made directly with the seller over a secure connection.

A mobile version of MySimon is available for wireless devices, including cell phones and Palm and Blackberry handheld devices. Information on obtaining MySimon over a wireless device is available by clicking on MySimon Mobile at the bottom of the site's home page.

PROPRIETARY TECHNOLOGY DEVELOPED IN 1998

MySimon obtains price and product information through its proprietary, patent-pending VLA technology, which sends intelligent agents across the World Wide Web. Developed in 1998 by MySimon cofounder Yeogirl Yun, VLA is a highly scalable, intelligent information retrieval system that is capable of scanning thousands of Web sites and returning precise data instantly. VLA employs next-generation intelligent agent and advanced parallel search technologies to automatically search online sites for price and product information and then present it in an easy-to-read format.

Founded in April 1998 by Michael Yang and Yeogirl Yun, MySimon.com was launched later in the year as a comparison shopping engine. At first the company planned to license its technology to Web portals and other sites. However, competition in licensing became more difficult when Inktomi acquired rival C2B Technologies. In addition, portals began charging higher fees, raising the cost to MySimon to reach a broad audience through them.

Under the direction of president and CEO Joshua Goodman, MySimon refocused in 1999 to become a shopping destination site. At the time MySimon was one of the few independent shopping bots. It was able to search about 1,200 merchants, more than any other service, because some merchants blocked comparative shopping engines that were owned by their competitors. MySimon.com's revenue came from advertising, affiliate program fees, and promotional opportunities it offered merchants, such as enhanced listings.

In mid-1999 a redesigned MySimon was launched to coincide with a multimillion-dollar advertising campaign that was built around the phrase, "The future of shopping is here." A humorous character named Simon was created for the campaign to personify MySimon's shopping bot technology. Through an agreement with Active Research, informative content on products was added to MySimon through the Active Buyer's Guide. During the 1999 holiday shopping season comparative shopping sites experienced heavy traffic, and MySimon's traffic increased by 146 percent from November through December.

In January 2000 MySimon.com was acquired by CNET for $736 million in stock. CNET was in the process of transforming itself from an online publisher into an e-commerce company. During the year MySimon added more content about products, including reviews from users and editorial recommendations, and more product categories. MySimon also included merchant ratings supplied by Gomez Advisors that assessed each merchant's reliability. Through an arrangement with *Billboard* magazine, visitors to MySimon.com could access the top titles on various *Billboard* charts and conduct comparative price searches for them.

MySimon.com enjoyed a record fourth quarter at the end of 2000 in terms of audience growth, page views, and leads. In December it was the number one pure-play consumer comparison shopping site that was not a portal. It had more than 1 million more unique visitors than its nearest competitor, based on traffic as reported by both Nielsen/Net Ratings and Media Metrix. MySimon generated more than half of CNET Networks' total leads to merchants in the fourth quarter, and more than half of MySimon's leads represented non-technology products.

FURTHER READING:

"And All the Price Trimmings." *Business Week,* December 18, 2000.

"CNET: Can a Tech Guru Handle Wine, Too?" *Business Week,* October 30, 2000.

Kemp, Ted. "MySimon: Customers Are Inventory." *Internet-Week,* July 24, 2000.

Kuchinskas, Susan. "MySimon Puts Price Power in Users' Hands." *Brandweek,* May 24, 1999.

Lucas, Sloane. "Lycos, mySimon Tout New User Guides." *Brandweek,* August 9, 1999.

"MySimon Adds Billboard Charts to Internet-Shopping Service." *Billboard,* February 19, 2000.

Pack, Thomas. "Intelligent Shopping Agents." *Link-Up,* March-April 2001.

Wang, Nelson. "Shopping Tool Aspires to Evolve into Hot Web Site." *Internet World,* April 5, 1999.

SEE ALSO: CNET Networks Inc.; Shopping Bots

N

NAPSTER

Napster achieved widespread celebrity as a peer-to-peer file-sharing service that allowed people to trade compressed MP3 computer files for a wide range of popular music. Napster's browser software, which was installed on more than 40 percent of the world's personal computers in early 2001, enabled users to locate, share, and swap compressed MP3 music files. Users simply sent in a request for a song. Napster software then checked its database and located the MP3 file with the song on another user's hard drive. The MP3 file containing the song was then sent from one user to the other.

Napster's file-sharing system can be credited, at the very least, with motivating the major record labels that effectively control the distribution of popular music to find alternatives to their hard copy, full-price music distribution system. Napster's popularity made the recording industry realize that it would need to find a way to distribute music to consumers in other formats, notably online over the Internet, while still protecting its intellectual property.

Napster's wildly popular service was also credited with boosting the sales of a wide range of computer gear, including CD burners, portable MP3 players, and personal computers equipped with fancy speakers. By 2001 CD burners had become standard equipment on 70 percent of all computers sold, according to *The Washington Post*. Napster was also a factor in the growth of broadband services, such as cable and DSL Internet service, which grew by 150 percent in 2000. A broadband connection made it possible to download songs much faster than with a dial-up modem. The Consumer Electronics Association, in support of Napster, argued that closing Napster would discourage innovation in the marketplace.

NAPSTER SOFTWARE DEVELOPED BY SHAWN FANNING

Before the advent of Napster it was very difficult to locate and copy music files on the Internet. MP3 technology, which made it possible to compress audio tracks on CD into digital computer files that were small enough to copy and download, was invented in 1987. While MP3 files existed on the Internet, there was no central directory, and copying the files—once they were located—was a cumbersome process.

In early 1999 Shawn Fanning, a student at Northeastern University, dropped out of school to complete work on a software program that would simplify the process of finding and downloading MP3 files on the Internet. His program combined the instant messaging capability of Internet Relay Chat; the file sharing capability of Windows; and the search capabilities of Internet search engines. Contributing ideas to the development of Fanning's software were Internet friends Sean Parker and Jordan Ritter.

When it was introduced in mid-1999, Napster software could be downloaded for free from Napster's Web site. The software would automatically search hard drives where MP3 files were located and add them to a centralized database of available music. Napster's Web site also featured chat rooms where people could discuss music, thus helping to create a community of users.

Fanning initially distributed his software to 30 computer and music friends and asked them not to share it. Within a week, however, the popular software had been downloaded by 15,000 people. In August 1999 Fanning announced that the number of users quintupled in one week on the file-sharing service. It was the beginning of a landslide of music fans coming to Napster to download music whenever they wanted to, at no charge. While consumers may have thought they had wrested control of the music's distribution from the record labels, two groups would rise up to oppose Napster's song-swapping service. One group included artists whose copyrighted songs were being downloaded. They felt they were entitled to some form of compensation, according to existing copyright laws. The second group consisted of the major record labels and the recording industry, as represented by the Recording Industry Association of America (RIAA).

RECORD INDUSTRY OPPOSES THE CONTROVERSIAL SERVICE, 1999-2001

In December 1999 the major record labels—including Universal (a subsidiary of Vivendi), Sony Music, Warner Music, EMI Group, and BMG Entertainment (the music division of Bertelsmann AG)—together with the RIAA, brought a lawsuit against Napster claiming copyright infringement. The RIAA listed among its concerns the non-payment of royalties and the loss of revenue through lost sales of CDs. The RIAA claimed that the loss of financial incentives would prevent musicians from creating new songs.

Napster's position was that it only provided the software for people to share music files. No copyrighted material ever appeared on Napster's computers. Rather, the MP3 files were swapped directly from one user's computer to another. Napster also argued that the added exposure of certain songs would actually increase CD sales for some artists.

While the lawsuit worked its way through the courts, Napster was the fastest-growing home application for the first half of 2000, according to Media Metrix (now Jupiter Media Metrix). The number of Napster users grew from just over 1 million users daily in January 2000 to 6.7 million in August 2000.

In April 2000 heavy metal rock group Metallica and rap artist Dr. Dre filed separate lawsuits against Napster for copyright infringement. In May federal Judge Marilyn Hall Patel ruled that Napster was not entitled to "safe harbor" under the Digital Millennium Copyright Act. In July Judge Patel granted the RIAA's request for a preliminary injunction against Napster and ordered Napster to shut down. Two days later, the 9th Circuit Court of Appeals stayed Judge Patel's injunction, allowing Napster to stay in business. After hearing oral arguments in October, the appeals court would not issue a ruling until February 2001.

Meanwhile, Napster gained support from an unexpected quarter. Breaking ranks with the other major record labels, Bertelsmann AG formed an alliance with Napster in Octboer 2000 and became its chief financial backer. Under the alliance Bertelsmann agreed to help Napster develop a legitimate version of its service, such as a subscription or fee-based service. Once a new version of Napster was developed, BMG Entertainment would drop its copyright infringement suit against Napster and make its recording catalog available to the service. At the time Napster had about 38 million users. Commenting on the alliance, Bertelsmann chairman and CEO Thomas Middelhoff said, "Napster has pointed the way for a new direction for music distribution. We believe it will form the basis of important and exciting new business models for the future of the music industry." Some analysts believed the alliance would accelerate the recording industry's acceptance of legitimate file-sharing services.

In January 2001 Napster added a link to CDNow, which was owned by Bertelsmann, in part to blunt criticism that MP3 downloading was hurting CD sales. Napster also added instant messaging and message boards to promote the use of Napster as a community to discuss music as well as to share files.

According to a report from PC Pitstop, Napster's integrated browser and communication tool was installed on 38 percent of all personal computers worldwide in March 2001. That marked a decline from February, when it was to be found on 40.5 percent of all PCs, the highest level of penetration achieved by Napster. A year previously, in April 2000, Napster software was to be found on nearly 15 percent of all PCs worldwide. The study found that the leading alternatives to Napster in 2001 were AudioGalaxy and BearShare.

On February 12, 2001, the appeals court ruled that Napster must halt the trading of copyrighted songs. A week later Napster announced it was willing to pay $1 billion to license the content of copyrighted songs, an offer that was dismissed by the RIAA. The appeals court sent the injunction for revision back to Judge Patel, who had ruled that Napster might be liable for knowingly encouraging and assisting large-scale copyright infringement by its users. The appeals court also asked the record labels to provide Napster with a list of songs that must be removed from its directory.

In March Judge Patel issued a preliminary injunction against Napster that required it to block copyrighted song files. Napster complied with the order by barring the trading of copyrighted songs on its service. Over the next several months the service experienced a sharp drop in usage, from an estimated 2.79 billion songs downloaded in February 2001 to

360 million in May. Later, on July 2, Napster voluntarily suspended file-sharing and shut down to fix technical problems related to its latest filter upgrade. At the time it shut down, Napster's usage had declined from an average of 220 songs shared per user in February 2001 to an average of 1.5 songs per user. Former Napster users were simply going to other song-swapping services.

At first Napster attempted to filter copyrighted songs by blocking them based on song titles. However, misspellings and other errors meant that many copyrighted songs were not being blocked. Following criticism of the blocking system by the recording industry, Napster upgraded its efforts to screen copyrighted songs by using digital fingerprints. Each downloadable song was given a unique fingerprint when it was added to Napster's database. If Napster's software did not find the fingerprint, the song could not be downloaded. Napster claimed that its new filtering system was ''99 percent'' effective in blocking the downloading of copyrighted songs for which it did not have permission to use, but technical problems with the filtering upgrade caused the service to shut down on July 2, 2001.

Meanwhile, there were other developments in the online distribution of music. In April 2001 the music industry announced a new music subscription venture called MusicNet. Participating companies included RealNetworks Inc., AOL Time Warner Music, EMI Group PLC, and Bertelsmann AG's BMG division. MusicNet was created as an intermediary to license the music of AOL Time Warner Music, EMI, and BMG, using RealNetworks' secure technology. America Online and RealNetworks were MusicNet's first two licensing affiliates. Duet, formed by Vivendi Universal and Sony Music, was another recording industry service that was created as an alternative to Napster.

In June, Napster became the third distribution partner for MusicNet. The three participating major labels agreed to permit their content to be carried on Napster, once the music-swapping service found a way not to infringe on copyrighted material. Napster said that MusicNet would be one of several options offered by Napster once it launched its new fee-based service. At the time Napster had more than 70 million users.

Also in June, Napster signed a worldwide licensing agreement with the United Kingdom's Association of Independent Music (AIM) and the Independent Music Companies Association (IMPALA). The agreement authorized Napster's use of hundreds of thousands of songs belonging to more than 150 independent record labels in the United Kingdom and Europe. Prior to Napster's July 2 shutdown, it had permission to share more than 800,000 titles with its users.

In mid-July Napster settled the suits brought against it by rock group Metallica and rap artist Dr. Dre. The settlement gave the artists final say over which song files could be traded over the Napster system. However, the RIAA vowed to continue its legal battle with Napster until it fully complied with copyright laws.

ONCE A MAVERICK, NAPSTER'S FUTURE TIED TO RECORD INDUSTRY

In July 2001 Napster named a new CEO, Konrad Hilbers, an executive with Bertelsmann AG. Hilbers replaced Hank Barry, who was Napster's interim CEO since May 2000. Hilbers was formerly executive vice president and chief administrative officer at BMG Entertainment. He also had experience managing the AOL, Netscape, and Compuserve brands in Europe from 1996 to 2000.

Hilbers' immediate challenge was to rebuild Napster as a fee-based service. A report from Jupiter Media Metrix found that worldwide use of Napster fell 65 percent between February 2001 and June 2001, in terms of number of minutes online. Napster's significant brand recognition made it likely that once the company developed its fee-based service, it would recapture many of its lost users. In August Hilbers said the song swap service would cost about $5 a month when it was ready to go live. Recording industry attorneys requested an October 1 hearing for a final judgment from U.S. District Judge Marilyn Hall Patel. Meanwhile, Napster's future hung in the balance.

FURTHER READING:

Centeno, Cerelle. ''Napster Clinches MusicNet Deal Amid Label Discord.'' *eMarketer,* June 23, 2001. Available from www.emarketer.com.

———. ''Worldwide Napstered PCs.'' *eMarketer,* May 4, 2001. Available from www.emarketer.com.

Eliscu, Jenny. ''Is Napster Signing Off for Good?'' *Rolling Stone,* March 29, 2001.

Enos, Lori. ''Napster UK Deal Advances Paid Online Music.'' *E-Commerce Times,* June 26, 2001. Available from www.ecommercetimes.com.

Evangelista, Benny. ''Record Group Calls Napster Filter Archaic.'' *E-Commerce Times,* March 28, 2001. Available from www.ecommercetimes.com.

Markoff, John. ''Record Companies Seek Fees for Net Music.'' *The New York Times,* April 3, 2001.

''A New Hope for Napster, but the Recording Industry Empire Strikes Back.'' *eMarketer Weekly Newsletter,* August 22, 2001.

Quinn, Andrew. ''Napster Settles Metallica Suit, Vows to Fight On.'' *Reuters,* July 12, 2001.

Regan, Keith. ''Napster Unveils E-Commerce Link.'' *E-Commerce Times,* January 12, 2001. Available from www.ecommercetimes.com

Saliba, Clare. "Napster, Bertelsmann to Develop Paid Service." *E-Commerce Times,* November 1, 2000. Available from www.ecommercetimes.com

"Shawn Fanning." *Biography Today: Scientists & Inventors Series, Volume 3.* Detroit: Omnigraphics, 2001.

Stern, Christopher. "With Napster, Industry Hears Future." *The Washington Post,* March 2, 2001.

SEE ALSO: Intellectual Property; Legal Issues; Peer-to-Peer Technology

NARROWCASTING

Since the earliest days of advertising, it has been challenging for marketers to reach highly targeted groups with promotional messages about products and services. Printed publications represent one long-established channel for doing this. Television initially was very broad in its reach, and it was necessary for advertisers to time communications based on the groups that were most likely to watch during different timeframes (women during the day, families during the evening, and so on). The emergence of cable television eventually made it possible for marketers to be more specific about where they concentrated their messages. Subscription-based channels became very focused on specific areas of interest or ethnicity. Reaching audiences via this targeted approach is known as narrowcasting.

Narrowcasting is a technique that translates well to the Internet and has strong implications for e-commerce. Although the Internet itself is generally broad in nature, in terms of access to information, it also can be a very targeted medium for marketers. When consumers provide demographic information about themselves, it becomes possible for marketers to customize the advertising and content they see or receive. For example, although thousands of people may listen to the very same Internet radio broadcast, the commercials they hear can be tailored based on details they have provided regarding ethnicity, geography, income, sex, hobbies, occupation, and more. Fewer marketing messages are directed toward people who have no interest in hearing or seeing them. Permission-based e-mail marketing is another means of narrowcasting. In this scenario, companies build lists of individuals who want to receive promotional information via e-mail, and communications are sent accordingly.

As technology evolves and more Internet users switch to high-speed broadband connections, the value of the Internet as a multimedia promotional tool grows. It is becoming increasingly feasible for marketers to use targeted streaming video and audio messages, as opposed to static banner ads or text-only e-mail messages. Short streaming video films, for example, have evolved into a growing form of entertainment for many Internet users, and a source of lucrative marketing opportunities for companies.

FURTHER READING:

Brady, Mick. "Lights, Camera, E-Commerce!" *E-Commerce Times,* March 23, 2000. Available from www.ecommercetimes.com.

Lounsbury, Erik. "Transforming a Transparent Eyeball." *Customer Inter@Ction,* March 2001.

"Streaming Ad Market to Take Off with Broadband Adoption." *CyberAtlas,* June 21, 2001. Available from www.turboads.com.

SEE ALSO: Advertising, Online

NASDAQ STOCK MARKET

Often referred to as the pulse of the New Economy, the Nasdaq Stock Market, operated by the National Association of Securities Dealers (NASD), is divided into two separate markets: the Nasdaq National Market, comprised of over 4,000 of the largest and most heavily traded Nasdaq securities and featuring heavy financing, capitalization, and corporate governance standards for listed companies; and the Nasdaq SmallCap Market, which caters to smaller, emerging companies and maintains more relaxed listing requirements. The general course of stock movement is to graduate from the SmallCap Market to the National Market. Nasdaq's listings are comprised most notably of companies operating in various sectors of high technology, including Internet companies and others devoted to aspects of the Internet architecture.

Nasdaq began trading in 1971, ten years after the U.S. Securities and Exchange Commission (SEC) charged the NASD with implementing a solution to what the U.S. Congress called a fragmentation in the over-the-counter securities market. Only in the closing decade of the 20th century, however, did Nasdaq truly emerge as a major benchmark by which the U.S. economy was monitored. Between 1997 and 2000, Nasdaq brought 1,649 companies public, according to NASD. With the Internet producing profound changes in economic life and the high-tech sector in which Nasdaq specializes leading the dramatic U.S. economic growth, the Nasdaq Stock Market became one of the most-watched stock indexes, alongside that of the New York Stock Exchange and major benchmarks like the Standard & Poor's 500 Index and the Dow Jones Industrial Average. It was on Nasdaq more than the others, moreover, that the hotshots of the Internet age were listed and on which New Economy investors focused their attention.

Nasdaq, like the New York Stock Exchange, runs trades through market makers, middlemen who work on the trading floors—or, in Nasdaq's case, at computer terminals that receive instantaneous market information and on which they place buy and sell bids—and are generally backed by major securities firms such as Merrill Lynch and Goldman Sachs. When a stock finds no buyer, market makers use their own capital to purchase it. Later, they turn around and sell the stock at a higher price, and the spread between the buy and sell price constitutes their profit.

In addition to the market makers, Nasdaq allows electronic communications networks (ECNs) to implement electronic orders from their own diverse clientele. With these two brands of market participants, Nasdaq purports to increase the opportunities for its listed companies to have their stock bought and sold, thereby granting them greater access to capital and greater market visibility.

Prior to 1997, Nasdaq stocks were listed by quotations. In other words, stock prices listed on the screen represented the buy and sell bids of the market makers. Investors brought a class-action lawsuit against Nasdaq after a study reported that Nasdaq market makers were in the habit of stretching their profit margins by conspiring to keep the trading spreads-the difference between the buy and sell prices-artificially wide. Although collusion was never proven and the market makers settled out of court, the Securities and Exchange Commission (SEC) ordered Nasdaq to alter their order-handling rules so as to require market makers to list ECN quotes that beat the market maker's prices.

In spring 2001, Nasdaq switched its price listings to decimals, eliminating the fractions it had always employed. Immediately, and as expected, the spreads between the market makers' buy and sell bids diminished, particularly for the most heavily traded stocks. However, not all traders were eager to jump to decimalization; in the weeks before the proposed switch, the 7,700-member Security Traders Association (STA) petitioned the Securities and Exchange Commission (SEC) to postpone the deadline by at least three months, claiming that the tighter schedule would leave them unprepared and unduly upset their businesses.

LIFE IN THE DOT-COM ERA

The late-1990s tech- and Internet-fueled boom in the U.S. economy gave Nasdaq a prominence in the trading world that it hadn't before enjoyed. For years in the shadow of the older and more prestigious New York Stock Exchange, the close of the 20th century watched the Nasdaq emerge as the trendiest and most-watched market in financial circles. In the 16 months beginning January 1999, for instance, the 4,600 companies listed on Nasdaq watched their market capitalization skyrocket 150 percent to $6.6 trillion. Nasdaq rode the strength of such high-tech stalwarts as Microsoft, Intel, and Cisco, as well as the fleet of dot-com startups, to position itself as the market of the future and the financial hub of the New Economy, where the companies engineering economic growth were listed.

However, as a barometer of the dot-com economy, the Nasdaq was a bearer of bad news in the early 2000s. Following the dot-com crash of March 2000 and the subsequent nosedive of the Nasdaq—the market lost 40 percent of its value in 2000&mdahs;-a number of Internet companies were in danger of being delisted from Nasdaq due to stock prices that dipped below minimum requirements. Since the investment funds that were filtered through Nasdaq were so vital to most of the Internet companies, delistings could spell more doom and gloom for dot-coms. Other companies, such as the online brokerage E*Trade Group Inc., lost confidence in Nasdaq and defected to the rival New York Stock Exchange, citing the limits of company growth in the Nasdaq field as well as the excessive degree of volatility found on Nasdaq.

Compared with the New York Stock Exchange, Nasdaq was especially volatile, marked by rapid fluctuations, even in its glory days in the late 1990s and early 2000s, largely due to the dearth of dot-com and other high-tech stocks traded on that system. Since these sectors were the primary engines behind the dramatic growth in the U.S. economy in the late 1990s, Nasdaq was marked by heavy trading from investors hoping to profit from the strong economy, but buying and selling were rapid and often erratic as market information shifted quickly.

RIVALRY WITH ECNS AND SUPERMONTAGE

In the late 1990s, Nasdaq was challenged by a new breed of trading entities known as electronic communication networks (ECNs). ECNs spearheaded the public's zest for electronic trading, and their astonishing success led many Wall Street analysts to believe that they were the wave of the stock market's future. ECNs claimed to democratize investing by making it cheaper and bringing it directly to the public at large, reducing the reliance on large brokerage firms. While the rapid turn-around of the dot-com economy in the early 2000s also served to sour the revolutionary prospects for many ECNs—to the point that many, including Island ECN, were turning into exchanges themselves—there was little doubt that these upstarts greatly accelerated innovation and modernization among the major exchanges, particularly Nasdaq. For instance, ECNs led the way in opening after-hours trading and listing share prices in the more accurate (and less fraud-prone) decimals, rather than in fractions. Having adopted much of the ECN-driven innovation, and with a vastly greater economy of scale, Nasdaq was expected to make it much more difficult for its one-time rivals to compete.

For instance, one practice for which ECNs roundly criticized Nasdaq was its refusal to offer customers information such as comparative pricing for individual stocks, which would then allow customers to get the best deal. In the early 2000s, however, that changed with the introduction of Nasdaq's Super-Montage, a quote aggregation and execution system. SuperMontage was a serious blow to the ECN competition, since it offered most of the same functions that distinguished ECNs. Nasdaq spent the early 2000s pushing SuperMontage through the SEC approval stages. Because of its similarities to the ECN model, SuperMontage raised the ire of ECNs, who claimed that the system would effectively amount to an ECN that enjoyed government-mandated liquidity, putting ECNs at a hopeless disadvantage, and worse, turning their regulator into a competitor.

FOREIGN EXPANSION

The NASD announced in 1999 its intentions to spend generously on Internet technology for the purposes of staving off competition from ECNs and, simultaneously, to expand globally. Its ultimate goal was a globally integrated securities market under its purview. Nasdaq launched its London-based European exchange in late 2000. Around the same time, Nasdaq established its own Japanese board in conjunction with the Japanese Internet investment company Softbank, linking Japanese investors seamlessly to Nasdaq's U.S. and European markets. This added to Nasdaq's existing Internet Web service in partnership with the Stock Exchange of Hong Kong, which offers information service on various markets to investors across the globe. Nasdaq won praise from analysts for its success in integrating various trading cultures into its own system.

FURTHER READING:

Guerra, Anthony. "NASDAQ Rolls Back the Curtain on Supermontage." *Wall Street & Technology,* October, 2000.

Hanes, Kathryn. "Japan: NASDAQ's Next Frontier." *Global Finance,* April, 2000.

Henry, David. "What Else Can Go Wrong at NASDAQ? Well..." *Business Week,* April 30, 2001.

Nasdaq Stock Market, Inc. "About Nasdaq." New York: Nasdaq Stock Market, Inc., 2001. Available from www.nasdaq.com.

Radcliff, Deborah. "Trading Nets Give Exchanges a Run for Their Money." *Computerworld,* December 18, 2000.

Trombly, Maria. "Nasdaq Begins Trading Stocks in Decimals." *Computerworld,* April 16, 2001.

SEE ALSO: Day Trading; Electronic Communications Networks (ECNs); Investing, Online; Volatility

NATIONAL COMMITTEE FOR INFORMATION TECHNOLOGY STANDARDS (NCITS)

The need for common standards is obvious to anyone who has ever traveled with an electric hair dryer and learned that it needed a special adapter to be used in Europe, or who once tried to purchase a typewriter ribbon only to find thirty or forty incompatible types from which to choose. The need for standards is even more apparent in electronic commerce, which presupposes the rapid, accurate, technically problem-free exchange of data between computers via the World Wide Web. The National Committee for Information Technology Standards (NCITS) takes a leading role in establishing IT standards for the United States and in representing American interests in groups that set international standards.

The mission of NCITS—pronounced "insights"—is to establish standards in the areas of multimedia, such as JPEG and MPEG, intercommunication among various computers and information systems, storage media such as hard disks and floppies, database technology, security, and programming languages. In early 2001, the organization added electronic commerce to its agenda of interests. From its formation in 1961 as the Accredited Standards Committee X3, Information Technology of the Computer and Business Equipment Association (now ITI, the Information Technology Industry Council) until autumn 2001, NCITS promulgated 612 separate technical standards related to information technology. ITI, a private, nonprofit trade group, continues to sponsor the work of NCITS. The group operates under the rules of the American National Standards Institute (ANSI), which were written to guarantee that standards were developed by the parties who had a direct and material interest in them.

Some 1,700 organizations from around the world are members of NCITS. They include leading companies from the computer, telecommunications, and Internet industries, such as Microsoft, Hewlett-Packard, IBM, and Bell Laboratories; defense industries such as Northrop Grumman; government and quasi-governmental bodies such as the Defense Department, Los Alamos National Laboratory, and the U.S. Postal Service; and universities like the University of Illinois. Members pay an annual membership fee, plus an additional fee to procure voting rights on any of NCITS' 40 Technical Committees (TCs). The TCs are where the main work of NCITS are done. They research, study, and hammer out standards for the IT industry. There are TCs devoted to most conceivable categories of the IT realm, ranging from the apparently mundane, like computer paper and forms, office equipment, and storage media such as disk drives and floppies, to high level specialties such as the various programming languages, character sets, security, I/O interfaces, text processing, and database technologies.

TCs carry out three main functions. First, within the limits of their assigned technical scope, they study and draft proposed new standards for hardware and software. Second, they recommend new standards-related projects for study to NCITS. Third, they act as technical advisors for or on behalf of NCITS at meetings of international standards-setting organizations. Some special NCITS projects are also assigned to special study groups or ad hoc groups as the need arises.

Establishing a new standard at NCITS is a process that can take from 6 to 18 months at its most rapid, or years and years at its slowest. The work on the second revision of the COBOL programming language, for example, has been in committee since the mid-1980s. Once NCITS accepts a standard, compliance is strictly voluntary, even by the group's members. A critical standard in which NCITS had a hand at establishing was the size of floppy disks. The five-inch floppy is universal today, and the easy transfer of data between computers is a fact of life. In the 1980s NCITS was instrumental in the development of the National Standard Code for Information Exchange, the well-known ANSI character set. The group's most important achievement of the 1990s was probably the development of the SQL language, which helped make possible present-day database technology. In the wake of the terrorist attacks on the World Trade Center and the Pentagon in September 2001, NCITS turned its attention to the establishment of common standards for biometrics—the measurement and analysis of biological data. If an international standard for taking and transmitting electronic fingerprints had been in place after the attack, for example, it would have been much easier to track terrorists across international borders because fingerprints could have been exchanged by law enforcement agencies instantaneously.

In January 2001, NCITS established a new Technical Committee to develop standards to codify the technology of e-commerce. V3, as the committee is called, proposes standards in a broad range of e-commerce areas, including the transportation of freight, traffic management, entertainment, financial instruments, healthcare management, distribution, and manufacturing. The committee's early work was divided into four phases: to identify necessary conditions for making e-commerce economically and technically viable; to catalog any relevant existing standards; to catalog current e-commerce practices; and to determine areas where standards can be developed. In its first two meetings, the committee pinpointed software safety, fault tolerance, and application reliability as three areas where standards were lacking. As of October 2001, the V3 committee had not proposed any new standards.

FURTHER READING:

"NCITS, National Committee for Information Technology Standards." Washington, D.C.: National Committee for Information Technology Standards, 2001. Available from www.ncits.org/.

SEE ALSO: American National Standards Institute (ANSI); Biometrics

NATIONAL INFORMATION INFRASTRUCTURE PROTECTION ACT (NIIPA) OF 1996

The National Information Infrastructure Protection Act (NIIPA), signed into law in October 1996, was a significant revision of U.S. computer crime law. It provides federal criminal liability for theft of trade secrets and for "anyone who intentionally accesses a protected computer without authorization, and as a result of such conduct, recklessly causes damage." The NIIPA is one of a number of laws enacted by the U.S. government to address the array of new cybercrimes that have emerged with the ongoing expansion and development of the Internet. The NIIPA represents the most ambitious amendments to the Computer Fraud and Abuse Act of 1984, which had previously been modified in 1986 and 1994.

The U.S. national information infrastructure (NII) is composed of computer networks, data storage and generating equipment, the connections between these components, and the networks that support them: the Internet and public switched telephone (PSTN), satellite communication, and private networks. With the commercialization of the Internet in the early 1990s, use of these systems burgeoned and led to the creation of the NII. Many industries and private users, as well as the government, increasingly rely on the NII to conduct their business.

However, the NII's dependence on public telecommunications lines and its myriad points of access also render it vulnerable. Thus, in the 1990s the U.S. government had to determine how to reinforce NII security while retaining its availability to the public and to the business sector. Particularly critical areas in need of added protection were identified as telecommunications, energy, transportation, essential human services, and especially national defense. These areas, while still susceptible to traditional forms of physical attack—such as foreign or domestic entities exploiting weaknesses in the electronic infrastructure—were thought to require new modes of security. Many involved in reviewing NII security, both in government and in the private sector, believe successful protection of the NII requires the cooperation of the government, the public, and industry.

Two types of threats menace the NII—traditional physical threats and newer, electronic threats. The former encompass the damage inflicted to the NII via conventional or unconventional weapons, while the latter stem from electronic, radio-frequency or computer-based attacks on the information or communications components that control critical infrastructures.

The NIIPA contains several major subsections, each targeting a separate offense. First, it criminalizes unauthorized access of computer files that results in transmission of classified government information. Second, it prohibits the extraction of information from financial institutions, the U.S. government, or private-sector computers that are used in interstate commerce. Third, it disallows the intentional and unauthorized access of non-public computers in U.S. governmental departments or agencies. Fourth, it bans accessing protected computers without permission for the purposes of defrauding or obtaining material of value, unless a defendant can prove the resulting damages amounted to less than $5,000.

Another section of NIIPA concerns hacking. It outlaws the intentional transmission of any program, code, or command that could result in damage to a protected computer, regardless of whether or not access to that computer was authorized. This stipulation permits prosecution of authorized company, department, or agency users who might inflict harm on a computer system. Furthermore, any damage caused recklessly or negligently is also liable to prosecution, thus facilitating prosecution of hackers who may transfer malevolent software without intending any specific harm.

Elsewhere, NIIPA forbids the knowledgeable trafficking of passwords with intent to defraud, where such conduct would enable someone to access a protected computer without permission. Finally, the law also criminalizes the interstate or foreign transmission of threats to damage a protected computer so that something of value is extorted. This provision addresses, among other things, the possibility of hackers

threatening to disable a system unless they were accorded system access.

NIIPA distinguishes actions that constitute improper access or a threat to privacy from those in which the defendant uses access for pernicious purposes. It does so by making such conduct a felony, rather than a misdemeanor, if it is committed for financial gain, to further a criminal or civil infraction, or if it results in the gathering of information worth more than $5,000.

In addition, NIIPA encourages victims to report cyber offenses by permitting them to claim civil remedies for intentional computer crimes. It punishes attempted crimes to the same extent as completed offenses. Finally, the act extends the right to investigate to the U.S. Secret Service, along with all other authorized agencies.

NIIPA cut off many arguments that defendants could claim under prior legislation. For example, earlier law required that the computer affected be of "federal interest;" hence, one could not be charged under federal law for accessing private-sector, non-financial computers to commit intrastate fraud. However, defendants may still argue under NIIPA that they did not obtain anything of value or that their actions did not create damage in excess of $5,000.

Finally, NIIPA also modified the sentencing guidelines of earlier laws, which only permitted repeat offenders to receive enhanced sentences if they were convicted of exactly duplicating a previous violation. NIIPA permits those who violate any of its subsections to be treated as recidivists.

Among the agencies responsible for overseeing the NII are the Department of Defense; the National Telecommunications and Information Administration at the Commerce Department, which coordinates aspects of NII policy that don't involve national security concerns; and the National Security Telecommunications and Information Systems Security Committee, which supervises all activities involving the NII which affect national security.

FURTHER READING:

Dillon, Sheri, Douglas Groene, and Todd Hayward. "Computer Crimes." *American Criminal Law Review,* Spring 1998, 503.

Nicholson, Laura, Tom Shebar, and Meredith Weinberg. "Computer Crimes." *American Criminal Law Review,* Spring 2000, 207.

Persico, Brian. "Under Siege: The Jurisdictional and Interagency Problems of Protecting the National Information Infrastructure." *CommLaw Conspectus,* Winter 1999, 153.

U.S. Department of Justice. "The National Information Infrastructure Protection Act of 1996: Legislative Analysis." Washington: GPO, June 18, 1998. Available from www.usdoj.gov.

SEE ALSO: Computer Crime; Computer Fraud and Abuse Act of 1986; Fraud, Internet

NATIONAL INFRASTRUCTURE PROTECTION CENTER (NIPC)

A federal agency based in Washington, D.C., the National Infrastructure Protection Center (NIPC) is the primary governmental organization charged with safeguarding the infrastructure networks and systems of the United States from attack, including computer-generated attacks such as hacking and viruses. The NIPC, housed in the headquarters of the Federal Bureau of Investigations (FBI), defends from compromise everything from telecommunications networks and financial systems to energy, transportation, and governmental infrastructures. As more and more of the nation's infrastructure, as well as the management of industrial and financial activities, comes under the control of computer networks and information technology, the government has recognized the need to build new lines of defense to stave off threats to the nation's critical infrastructures from the next generations of attack. The NICP thus spots vulnerabilities in existing infrastructures with an eye toward their eventual fortification.

NIPC was founded in February 1998 on the heels of the 1997 report on the President's Commission on Critical Infrastructure Protection, also known as the Marsh Report after commission chairman Robert Marsh, a former Air Force General. The Marsh Commission itself grew out of a recommendation by the Critical Infrastructure Working Group (CWIG) that new vulnerabilities in the nation's infrastructure be studied and addressed. The Marsh Report identified computer-based infrastructure attacks as a new and serious threat, issuing a proposal for a government-industry partnership to protect key infrastructures.

The agency was built out of a conglomeration of elements of several federal agencies that maintained key roles in the defense of the national infrastructure, including the departments of Transportation, Energy, and Defense, along with the National Security Agency, the CIA, and the FBI. The NIPC also brought into closer coordination the intelligence and security operations of the FBI and the U.S. military. In addition, since the bulk of the national infrastructure was in the hands of private corporations, they were also invited into the fold to form a public-private governmental agency.

NIPC is divided into three divisions: Computer Investigations and Operations; Training, Administration, and Outreach; and Analysis and Warning. These organizations cover the wide range of NIPC's responsibilities pertaining to infrastructure protection, which include spotting incoming threats, identifying existing systems to pinpoint vulnerabilities, devising response strategies to particular threats as they happen, fostering preventive awareness and technologies, and investigating attacks and helping bring perpetrators to justice. In addition, the NIPC was charged with devising training programs for state and local agencies for the detection, tracking, and investigation of cyberattacks in their jurisdiction.

NIPC's first two years were particularly embattled as a number of high-profile viruses swept computer networks, propelling NIPC into action to try to find those responsible. In May 1999, even the FBI's and Senate's Web sites were hacked into, the perpetrators leaving behind messages directly challenging the FBI. NIPC director Michael Vatis was convinced that the nation's infrastructure was likely to fall victim to more frequent and more sophisticated cyberattacks in the future. Hackers and even national enemies aiming to attack the United States, in these scenarios, will target major infrastructure computer systems, thereby shutting down vital elements of U.S. society, rather than simply breaking into and disrupting Web sites or email servers.

NIPC's investigative procedures, however, came under fire in the early 2000s, as critics inside and outside the government criticized the agency for its alleged unwillingness to work with other organizations and share information about particular investigations. In addition, NIPC was attacked for its failure to issue prompt warnings to prevent the spreading of the crippling "I Love You" virus in May 2000. These kinds of criticisms generated more widespread consideration of just what role the NIPC should play in investigations and how it should relate not only to the rest of the government but to private companies as well. For instance, since NIPC, in the course of its investigations, needed to access the internal workings of company systems, firms were increasingly concerned about their ability to avoid having their own secrets compromised.

Another area of tension was the availability of strong and complex encryption systems. While the NIPC and the federal government generally was reticent about allowing such encryptions schemes into the general public for fear that they would be harder pressed to decode criminal transmissions, industry groups increasingly coveted state-of-the-art encryption schemes in order to secure e-commerce transactions and alleviate public fears over engaging in online commerce.

FURTHER READING:

Berners-Lee, Tim, and Mark Fischetti. *Weaving the Web: The Original Design and Ultimate Destiny of the World Wide Web by its Inventor.* San Francisco, CA: HarperCollins, 1999.

Messmer, Ellen. "Feds Fine-Tune Infowar Plan." *Network World,* September 14, 1998.

Rapaport, Richard. "Cyberwars: The Feds Strike Back." *Forbes,* August 23, 1999.

U.S. Federal Bureau of Investigations. National Infrastructure Protection Center. "National Infrastructure Protection Center (NPIC)—About NPIC-Welcome." Washington, D.C.: National Infrastructure Protection Center, 2001. Available from www.nipc.gov.

Verton, Dan. "Bush Eyes Overhaul of E-security." *Computerworld,* December 18, 2000.

SEE ALSO: Computer Crime; Computer Fraud and Abuse Act of 1986; Encryption; Viruses

NATIONAL TELECOMMUNICATIONS AND INFORMATION ADMINISTRATION (NTIA)

Few Americans know of the National Telecommunications and Information Administration (NTIA). But to the extent that they use radio, television, cell phones, computers, and the Internet, or watch public television, listen to public radio, or travel by plane, the agency has a great impact on everyone's life. The NTIA, a division of the U.S. Department of Commerce, serves as the principal advisor to the President on telecommunications and information policy in both domestic and international affairs—the sole federal body that deals exclusively with these questions. Its 280 employees work out of two locations, the agency headquarters on Washington D.C., and the Institute for Telecommunication Sciences, its laboratory in Boulder Colorado.

The NTIA was created by an act of Congress and an Executive order that combined the White House Office of Telecommunications Policy (OTP) and the Department of Commerce's Office of Telecommunications in 1978. The post of Assistant Secretary for Communications and Information, responsible directly to the Commerce Secretary, was created at the same time to head the new office. The mission of the NTIA is the promotion of an efficient telecommunications infrastructure that will contribute to the economic welfare of the American people and enhance American competitiveness abroad. Another task the agency describes as key is "to ensure that government does not obstruct private sector innovation and the rapid deployment of telecommunications technology."

A number of specific responsibilities fall to the NTIA. It acts as an advisor to the President on developing and implementing domestic and international telecommunications policy. In this context, the agency frequently works with other agencies of the executive branch on issues that affect telecommunications. For example, it has worked closely with the Justice Department and the Securities and Exchange Commission on problems connected with the increasing concentration of ownership in the media and telecommunications industries.

On the international front, the NTIA develops and presents U.S. viewpoints at conferences on communications. It advocates the adoption of liberalized, deregulated telecommunications policies by foreign governments. For example, following the World Trade Agreement on basic telecommunications services of 1997, the NTIA worked with American negotiators to ensure that the nearly 70 other signatories understood the mechanisms of liberalization and enforcement contained in the Agreement. The agency also represents the interests of the Defense Department and the American business community in negotiations with foreign governments over the radio spectrum.

One of the NTIA's most important duties is overseeing the federal government's use of the radio spectrum. In this regard its activities parallel those of the Federal Communications Commission (FCC) in the public-commercial broadcasting sector. The NTIA is responsible for assigning frequencies to government-wned users of the radio spectrum, in particular the Defense Department and the Federal Aviation Administration. The NTIA also cooperates with the FCC in the formulation of a coherent, unified "spectrum management vision." The agency also participates in policy for the development of the nation's communications satellite system.

The NTIA administers the Technology Opportunities Program which awards grants to projects intended to promote and expand the availability of digital telecommunications technologies. For example, there are grants to support the expansion of the Internet into urban and rural locales with lower than average access, in particular schools and libraries. Other grants, such as the Public Telecommunications Facilities Program, support the changeover of the public television network from analog to digital technology, which is required to take place by 2006, as well as the availability of affordable phone and cable service for all Americans. Finally, through its Colorado laboratory, the NTIA actively develops new telecommunications technologies.

During its existence, the NTIA has been involved with a variety of important issues in the telecommunications and information technology field. It was the first agency to propose in 1989 the introduction of "spectrum auctions," at which broadcast frequencies would be awarded through a competitive bidding process, a procedure eventually adopted by the FCC. Later it helped develop a system of electronic auctions.

As the new century begins, the NTIA was busy responding to the explosion in wireless communication technologies, such as cell phones, by studying ways of allocating frequencies to private mobile communications companies that balance the needs of the public with those of national security. It was conducting research into ultra-wideband technology as a communications medium, and attempting to find ways to avoid possible interference with the global satellite positioning system used by the telecommunications industry and the defense sector while issuing as many licenses for the use of ultra-wideband frequencies as possible to private companies. Finally, although it has not released an official policy, the NTIA is looking at ways to bring broadband technologies and high-speed Internet access to as broad a segment of the population as possible.

FURTHER READING:

U.S. Department of Commerce. National Telecommunications and Information Administration. ''Facts About the NTIA.'' Washington, D.C.: National Technology and Information Administration, 2001. Available from www.ntia.doc.gov.

SEE ALSO: Internet Infrastructure

NEGROPONTE, NICHOLAS

Computer-aided design expert Nicholas Negroponte is the founder of the Massachusetts Institute of Technology (MIT) Media Laboratory, a leading $35 million research facility funded by MIT itself and several governmental bodies, as well as by more than 175 corporations across the globe. The lab focuses its efforts on communications methods of the future. Its programs include Information and Entertainment Systems, Schools of the Future, and Television of Tomorrow. Negroponte is also the Jerome B. Wiesner Professor of Media Technology at MIT, a member of Motorola Inc.'s board of directors, and a columnist for *Wired* magazine, which he co-founded in 1993. In 2000, at the age of 56, Negroponte began reducing his activities at the lab and spending more time on other ventures, including Webswappers.com, a European online swapping site in which he had invested heavily, and Protos LLC, an investment fund which he created with CCBN.com CEO Jeff Parker, Harvard Business School professor Bill Sahlman, and venture capitalist Thomas Grant.

Negroponte has served as a faculty member of MIT since 1966. When he first enrolled there as a student, Negroponte was interested in studying architec-

ture. However, by the time he graduated he had become more intrigued by the fledgling concept of computer-aided design, which became the topic of his thesis. In 1968, Negroponte established the Architecture Machine Group at MIT, a research group focused on developing new types of interactions between humans and computers. Throughout the 1970s and 1980s, Negroponte also taught courses at Yale University, the University of Michigan, and the University of California at Berkeley. At the time, he was considered a bit of a fanatic by many of his colleagues for his ideas about how computers, telephones, and televisions might one day work together to offer something called ''multimedia.''

Negroponte was named the first chairman of the Computers in Everyday Life subgroup of the International Federation of Information Processing Societies in 1980. The World Center for Personal Computation and Human Development, based in Paris, appointed him executive director in 1982. Three years later, Negroponte co-founded the MIT Media Laboratory with Jerome Weisner, a former president of MIT. The new research center began studying things like artificial intelligence, a topic considered radical by many critics. As a result, the lab generated unanticipated publicity, which allowed Negroponte to secure more corporate funding than he otherwise might have obtained with the lab's unusual sponsorship model. Rather than offer corporate sponsors rights to any new technological developments or allow them to control the direction of research, Negroponte and his cohorts decided to simply allow sponsors access to the lab, where they could interact with any of the researchers there by asking questions, making suggestions, and so on. According to a September 2000 article in *Technology Review*, although corporations would receive no tangible reward from funding research at the lab, ''Negroponte proved remarkably adept at selling the proposition, bolstered by the growing perception that something magical was happening.''

In 1995, Negroponte published his book *Being Digital,* which lingered on the bestseller list for more than a year and eventually was translated into more than 40 languages. According to Jennifer O'Connell in a July 2000 issue of *The Sunday Business Post,* it was this book that ''transformed Negroponte from an obscure Bostonian professor to the leading authority on tomorrow's world.'' His predictions about the growth of online traffic (1 billion people by the year 2000) and Internet-based commerce ($1 trillion by 2001) became commonly used benchmarks in technology circles, and Negroponte became known as one of the most electronically connected individuals in the world—one who refused to use a traditional telephone phone and shunned paper and pens in favor of e-mail.

By the late 1990s, Negroponte's lab had started to outgrow the model of intimate collaboration that had worked so well to foster innovation. Decisions like the one to establish MediaLab Europe in Dublin, Ireland—one of the largest investments in Ireland's e-business infrastructure to date—forced Negroponte and his colleagues to begin rethinking the strategy that would best cultivate future ingenuity. Also impacting the lab was the ease with which Internet-based startups were securing funding from venture capitalists. Recognizing that his lab could benefit from access to such funding, Negroponte began meeting with officials at MIT in an effort to secure approval for the lab to begin pursuing deals with venture capitalists. In 2000, just as the lab was poised to launch the most dramatic restructuring in its 15-year history, Negroponte began delegating many management tasks to his colleagues. While some industry observers believed Negroponte's absence would leave the lab floundering, others saw the upcoming management transitions as essential for the lab to successfully reinvent itself in the rapidly shifting technological landscape of the twenty-first century.

FURTHER READING:

Freedman, David H. "The Media Lab Crossroads." *Technology Review.* September 2000.

"The Importance of Being Digital." *Industry Week.* February 19, 1996.

O'Connell, Jennifer. "Digital Evangelist." *The Sunday Business Post.* July 30, 2000. Available from www.sbpost.ie.

SEE ALSO: MIT and the Galactic Network

NELSON, TED

Ted Nelson is known for creating the term "hypertext." Although his Xanadu software project, conceived in the 1960s, had not yet come to fruition by the turn of the century, Nelson's ideas for developing an information handling system that would allow for a highly complex level of linked data had a profound impact on programmers throughout the personal computer (PC) and Internet revolutions.

Nelson earned his undergraduate degree in philosophy from Swarthmore College and launched his graduate studies in sociology at Harvard in 1960. While taking a course on computers for the humanities, he began using the Assembler computer language in an attempt to develop a text management system that would allow users to manipulate their work in a variety of ways. Nelson envisioned a system complete with saving, editing, and printing capabilities. Although his early efforts to create what is now

known as a word processing application failed, Nelson continued working to flesh out his abstract ideas. He completed his master of arts degree in 1963. Two years later, he presented a paper at the Association of Computing Machinery annual convention, where he first made public his vision of hypertext.

In 1974, Nelson published *Dream Machines,* in which he described his vision of a software system that would use hypertext technology to link all kinds of information in highly sophisticated ways. The software project eventually became known as Xanadu, and more than 50,000 copies of *Dream Machines* were sold, mainly to computer programmers who embraced Nelson's belief that computer technology was going to change the way the world communicated. According to Gary Wolf in *The Curse of Xanadu,* "Nelson's writing and presentations inspired some of the most visionary computer programmers, managers, and executives—including Autodesk Inc. founder John Walker—to pour millions of dollars and years of effort into the project. Xanadu was meant to be a universal library, a worldwide hypertext publishing tool, a system to resolve copyright disputes, and a meritocratic forum for discussion and debate. By putting all information within reach of all people, Xanadu was meant to eliminate scientific ignorance and cure political misunderstandings."

Nelson spent the latter half of the decade working for publisher Harcourt, Brace as a computer technology advisor. He persuaded a few colleagues to invest in the Xanadu project and hired programmer Cal Daniels from Minicomputer Systems Inc. to develop a rudimentary Xanadu program to run on a Nova computer he was renting. Before Daniels was able to display his work to additional investors, however, Nelson ran out of money and could no longer afford to rent the Nova. In 1974, he published *Computer Lib,* an eccentric compiling of statistics, lists, quotations, and thoughts with no table of contents or index to help readers locate specific passages. The book was republished by Microsoft Press through 1987.

Programmer Roger Gregory and Yale University student Mark Miller joined Nelson in Pennsylvania in the summer of 1979 to work on developing code for Xanadu. At first, they used a Sol 20 machine, and later upgraded to an Onyx with a 10MB hard drive. Nelson published *Literary Machines,* which housed a detailed explanation of hypertext, in 1981. During the early 1980s, it was Gregory who spent most of his time working on Xanadu, while Miller and Nelson ended up in San Antonio, Texas, working for networking technology powerhouse Datapoint. In 1982, Gregory became the fist individual without institutional backing to purchase a Sun computer, which cost $26,000. The machine was the first one truly capable of handling the code he was writing for Xanadu.

When Datapoint dissolved in the midst of a financial scandal, Nelson again found himself low on cash and work on Xanadu ground to a near halt. The project caught the attention of John Walker, founder of Autodesk, in 1987. Walker, who had parlayed his $15,000 computer-aided design startup into the $54 million maker of AutoCAD software, believed that Nelson's ideas were worth pursuing. Consequently, he helped to found the Xanadu Operating Co. in 1988. After a period of intense negotiations, Walker ended up owning 80 percent of the new firm, while Nelson retained rights to the Xanadu name and to any publishing system that might result from the alliance.

Autodesk's plans to complete work on Xanadu by the end of 1989 never materialized, and Autodesk eventually sold its stake in Xanadu Operating Co. Nelson attempted to regain managerial control of the project, but was blocked by programmers who felt his eccentricities would hinder progress. By the mid-1990s, after several battles for control of the project, all work on Xanadu had ceased. Nelson moved to Japan and took a position as visiting professor of environmental information at Keio University. He views the World Wide Web as a simplistic version of his vision of the capabilities of hypertext and believes that, one day, some form of the Xanadu project will be completed.

FURTHER READING:

Keep, Christopher, McLaughlin, Tim, and Robin Parmar. "Ted Nelson and Xanadu." 2000. Available from www.iath.virginia.edu.

Wolf, Gary. "The Curse of Xanadu." *Wired*. June 1995. Available from www.wired.com.

SEE ALSO: HTML; World Wide Web (WWW)

NETCENTIVES INC.

Netcentives Inc. was founded in 1996 by MBA students Eric Tilenius and Elliot Ng. Two years later, the pair launched their ClickRewards program, which allowed members to earn ClickMiles for purchases made on participating merchant Web sites. In just a few short years, ClickRewards had grown to include more than 4 million members and was the only loyalty network that had exclusive contracts with 10 major airlines to provide frequent flyer miles in exchange for ClickMiles. More than 240 companies including American Express Co., Eddie Bauer Inc., Gap.com, IBM Corp., Hewlett-Packard Co., Nortel Networks, OfficeMax.com, and Victoria's Secret used Netcen-

tives' loyalty marketing programs, e-mail marketing services, and professional services including consulting and marketing plan development.

EARLY HISTORY

Netcentives Inc. was the brainchild of Ng, a former Microsoft Corp. employee and Harvard Business School student, and Tilenius, who attended Stanford Business School and had worked for both Oracle Corp. and Intuit Inc. In 1995, Tilenius and Ng began developing ideas for an Internet start-up company and zeroed in on the idea of creating an Internet rewards program similar to the rewards programs used by major airlines. In April of that year, the partners read an article in *The Wall Street Journal* that claimed frequent flyer miles were becoming the "second national currency." In an October 1998 *Business 2.0* article, Tilenius stated: "seeing that article set off a roller coaster of emotions. We were scared to death that someone else would beat us to it."

In June of 1996, Netcentives was incorporated and the duo immediately began promoting their idea to venture capitalists. By November, Information Technology Ventures had invested in the firm; a second round of financing followed in September of the next year. Tilenius and Ng then chose West Shell III, a seasoned marketing executive, to head up the new company. Testing of the rewards program, called ClickRewards, began in December 1997 and the site was officially launched in March of 1998.

The ClickRewards program was set up to reward online shoppers and to foster brand loyalty. As part of the program, Netcentives purchased frequent flyer miles from airline companies and then sold the miles to e-merchants such as 1-800-Flowers and BarnesandNoble.com. Those merchants then used the miles to entice online shoppers. The shoppers earned ClickMiles for making online purchases and used the ClickRewards Web site to redeem the ClickMiles for airline tickets, as well as other merchandise. By the time the program was launched, Netcentives had secured exclusive supplier agreements with American Airlines, British Airways, Continental Airlines, Delta Air Lines, Marriott Hotels and Resorts, Northwest Airlines, US Airways, and Westin Hotels & Resorts. Its merchant network included Broderbund Software, Burke Marketing Research, CNET Direct's BUYDIRECT, Golfweb, Macy's, Wells Fargo, and Yahoo!.

During December of 1998, merchants in the ClickRewards network secured more than $50 million in sales. By early 1999, nearly 655,000 consumers had become ClickRewards members. At that time, the network's merchant base had grown to 50 companies and Netcentives had awarded close to 1 million frequent flyer miles. The success of the start-up was due in part to the innovative management style of Tilenius and Ng. Wanting their executive staff to have the best possible management advice, the pair gave out extra shares of Netcentives to the staff. The executives could then give the shares to the mentor of their choice, in exchange for five hours per month of confidential business advice. The six-month program proved to be successful for both the executives and the company. Mentors from Visa, Intuit, and Wells Fargo were so impressed with the program that they signed up for Netcentives' services.

EXPANSION

While ClickRewards became increasingly popular, CEO Shell focused on expanding Netcentives' other offerings. In late 1998, the Panttaja Consulting Group Inc. was acquired and folded into the Netcentives Professional Services unit, which offered consulting services to e-commerce merchants. In May of 1999, the company also introduced its Enterprise Incentive Solutions program entitled ClickRewards@ Work. By using Netcentives' technology, enterprises were able to set up Web-enabled employee reward programs. Companies including Microsoft, Cisco Systems, and EventSource.com used the program to reward and motivate employees. In July, Netcentives also introduced its Custom Loyalty network through which businesses were able to set up customized incentive programs.

In October of 1999, Netcentives went public, offering 6 million shares and raising $72 million. By the end of the year, the ClickRewards program had nearly 2.5 million consumer members and 85 merchant members. The company also had secured a leading position among those in the promotional industry.

Netcentives entered the new millennium intent on continuing its growth. The firm made three key acquisitions during the year that were designed to bolster its product offerings. MaxMiles Inc., a producer of technology that enabled customers to view their reward and frequent flyer information online, was purchased in January 2000 in order to beef up Netcentives' technology platform. That purchase was followed by the March acquisition of UVN Holdings Inc., a leading collector of consumer shopping trend analysis. The deal also included an equity stake in Golden Retriever Systems, which provided information on 90 percent of U.S.-based payment card transactions. In April, Netcentives purchased Post Communications as part of its plans to combine its incentive programs with direct e-mail marketing.

The firm expanded through strategic alliances as well. In January of 2000, it teamed up with American Express to launch BlueLoot, an incentive program designed to reward American Express Blue credit card holders. That month, America Online (AOL) bought a stake in Netcentives. As part of the deal, Netcentives provided the infrastructure necessary to operate AOL AAdvantage, a frequent flyer program owned by AOL and American Airlines, and also created a rewards program for ICQ, AOL's Web-based chat community.

Netcentives also secured several lucrative contracts in 2000. E-marketing firm Coolsavings.com Inc. hired the firm to develop and operate a rewards program. In December, 3Com Corp. contracted the company to develop a customized incentive program to reward its business partners. Novell Inc. and CNN also chose Netcentives to operate their incentive programs. Revenue rose to $43 million, an increase of 447 percent over the previous year. However, despite its impressive revenue figures and powerful client list, Netcentives' stock price faltered. Shares trading at $80 at the end of 1999 fell to just $9 in April of 2000, and down to 69 cents in June 2001. Like many firms in the dot-com industry, Netcentives was hit hard by the slowing U.S. economy and a lack of investor confidence. At the same time, two key management figures left the firm unexpectedly. In May of 2001, Shell stepped down as chairman, and the firm's chief financial officer, Jack Longinotti, left to pursue other opportunities.

Nevertheless, Netcentives continued to provide products and services designed to optimize customer, partner, and employee relationships. With more than 4 million ClickRewards members and business relationships with more than 240 companies, Netcentives' management remained focused on future growth.

FURTHER READING:

"About Us." San Francisco, CA: Netcentives Inc., 2001. Available from www.netcentives.com.

"Buyin' and Flyin'." *Computer Reseller News.* September 14, 1998.

Conlin, Robert. "AOL Acquires Stake in Netcentives." *E-Commerce Times.* January 31, 2000. Available from www.ecommercetimes.com.

———. "High-Flyer Netcentives Signs Agreement with TWA." *E-Commerce Times.* May 11, 1999. Available from www.ecommercetimes.com.

Doan, Amy. "Wanted: Coaches." *Forbes.* February 8, 1999.

Feuerstein, Adam. "Netcentives Buys Chicago's MaxMiles." *San Francisco Business Times.* February 11, 2000.

Kuchinskas, Susan. "Netcentive Aids Amex with Rewards Program." *Brandweek.* January 24, 2000.

Patsuris, Penelope. "More Points for Netcentives." *Forbes.* April 11, 2000. Available from www.forbes.com.

Poole, Gary Andrew. "Just Rewards." *Business 2.0.* October 10, 1998. Available from www.business2.com.

SEE ALSO: AOL Time Warner Inc.; BarnesandNoble.com; Business-to-Consumer (B2C) E-Commerce; Marketing, Internet

NETIQUETTE

Shorthand for Internet etiquette, netiquette was the key to civility on Internet newsgroups, e-mail, listservs, chat rooms, and other Internet communications. Like etiquette, there was no official enforcement of netiquette; rather, Internet users were generally expected to abide by these basic rules—and were likely to be castigated by fellow users if they deviated from them.

The two key reasons for the development of netiquette protocol were speed and anonymity. Because the Internet was so fast, typing, pointing, and clicking often resulted in careless sloppiness, unintentional blunders, or hasty belligerence. The rules of netiquette were designed to slow people down and help them ensure that the message they plan to send is in fact the message they mean to convey. The anonymity of the Internet provided ample opportunity for users to be rude and insensitive, and the goal of netiquette was to provide a basic framework for minimizing this temptation.

Typing in all capital letters, for instance, was considered akin to "shouting" on the Internet, and was as discouraged on the Internet as yelling was in daily conversation. Informal language, humor, and sarcasm, according to the rules of netiquette, were best left for messages between those who know each other very well, since the spin a writer may have intended to apply may not be the one the reader derives. However, sometimes it was still necessary or advisable to influence the reading of a message through the demonstration of emotions. Since vocal inflections, gestures, and other clues to the emotions and semantics of conversation don't translate over the Internet, users developed a series of "emoticons," or "smileys," to relate emotions and give readers a clue as to the interpretation of a message. For instance, should a user wish to convey a light-hearted tone to a sentence, he or she could append certain characters to indicate a smile; conversely, there were also ways to indicate displeasure, via characters that indicated a frown.

On the most basic level, netiquette asks that users pay attention to ordinary rules of grammar, spelling, and other letter-writing decorum. The Internet's speed is, of course, one of its most prized benefits, but the downside is that many users tend to fire off messages without checking them over for readability. On listservs and newsgroups, in particular, such attention is important in order to establish one's credibility.

Users of newsgroups and listservs are also discouraged from posting chain letters as well as messages that are off the topic to which the group or list is devoted. Perhaps most bothersome to newsgroup and listserv members, and to ordinary e-mail recipients in general, is "spam," or junk e-mail (usually unsolicited commercial e-mail).

Extremely aggressive attacks over e-mail or in newsgroups are known as "flames," which take cover in the anonymity of the Internet to heap electronic abuse on an individual. While flaming is strongly discouraged, it is impossible to control completely, and thus netiquette rules encourage victims of a flame attack to avoid the temptation to get even by reciprocating the flame and launching a "flame war," which, like military warfare, can quickly escalate in scale and draw in more participants.

Some rules of netiquette have had less to do with content and tone than with consideration of technological capabilities. For instance, before sending off an e-mail with a large attachment, polite Internet users should consider the time it will take for the recipient to download it, and how much space in his or her mailbox or hard drive the attachment would fill. This is especially true when sending messages to a list, where the recipients' capacities vary greatly.

The online sins that netiquette was intended to prevent fall into two categories: the intended and the unintended. The former, of course, were those blunders that, however innocent, carry negative consequences for those involved, as when a user accidentally sends a personal e-mail to a listserv or fails to indicate that a message was meant to be taken as a joke. The latter included the uglier forms of Internet communications, such as sending obscene, insulting, or threatening content under the cover of the Internet's anonymity. In both cases, netiquette's primary utility was the nurturing of a civilized, orderly space for individuals, communities, and businesses to feel free to maximize the Internet's potential value.

FURTHER READING:

Harper, Doug. "How's Your Netiquette?" *Industrial Distribution,* November, 1999.

Selway, Mark. "Netiquette for Beginners." *Accountancy,* April, 1999.

Sloboda, Brian. "'Netiquette'—New Rules and Policies for the Information Age." *Management Quarterly,* Winter 1999.

Solomon, Gilbert. "E-mail Etiquette." *Medical Economics,* April 23, 2001.

SEE ALSO: Spam

NETSCAPE COMMUNICATIONS CORP.

Netscape Communications Corp. was co-founded in 1994 by James H. (Jim) Clark and Marc Andreessen. Clark, a former associate professor of computer science at Stanford University, had founded Silicon Graphics Inc. (SGI) in 1982. Having left SGI earlier in the year, Clark contacted Andreessen with a proposal to start a new company to develop an improved version of Mosaic. Mosaic was a graphical user interface (GUI) for the World Wide Web that integrated text, graphics, and sound. It made the Web accessible to a wide range of users and was responsible for a 10,000-fold increase in Web users over a period of two years. When Mosaic was made available for free over the Internet in 1993, more than 2 million copies were downloaded in the first year.

Andreessen had been part of the team of programmers that developed Mosaic in 1993 at the National Center for Supercomputing Applications (NCSA) at the University of Illinois at Champaign-Urbana, where he was attending college. Andreessen had recently graduated from college when he was contacted by Clark, and the two decided to combine Andreessen's technical know-how with Clark's business expertise to launch their own company. Established in April 1994 with $4 million in start-up capital from Clark, the company was first called Mosaic Communications Corp. However, NCSA, which held the copyright to the Mosaic software, objected and the company was renamed Netscape Communications Corp. later in the year. Andreessen, then 22 years old, became Netscape's vice president of technology. His job was to make the Web browser Mosaic faster and more interactive. He persuaded several NCSA team members to join him at Netscape, and the company soon released its new browser. While the development team wanted to call it Mozilla, short for Mosaic Killer, the company's marketing executives insisted on calling it Netscape Navigator. Netscape Navigator shipped in December 1994. Jim Barksdale, formerly with AT&T's McCaw Cellular division and Federal Express, was hired as the company's CEO in January 1995.

WEB BROWSER MADE INTERNET MORE ACCESSIBLE

Like Mosaic before it, Netscape Navigator was distributed for free over the Internet. Interested users could simply download it using a modem. It was an immediate hit, and Netscape claimed to have captured 70 to 75 percent of the browser market. Netscape Navigator featured an open architecture that enabled it to work with all kinds of computers and operating systems. The open architecture concept, known as TCP/IP (Transmission Control Protocol/Internet Protocol), was the same concept upon which the Internet was based. Netscape also sold an improved version of Netscape Navigator for $40. The company signed up resale partners, including Apple, AT&T, Hewlett-Packard, IBM, and others, and by 1996 was selling products in 29 countries. By early 1996 it had signed up more than 1,000 Internet service providers to distribute Navigator to their customers.

The easy availability of the Web browser created a lot of goodwill for Netscape, which the company hoped to capitalize on by selling high-priced software and Web servers that were used to build and run Web sites. Version 1.0 of Netscape's NetSite Web Server was released in December 1994. Netscape's Web servers, which sold for between $1,500 and $50,000 each, enabled companies to create online or "virtual" stores where customers could view products and purchase them online with credit cards. It was a time when electronic commerce over the Internet was in its infancy, and Netscape was providing a key element that would help it to achieve explosive growth in the coming years. Netscape also marketed its servers to corporate customers for their corporate intranets, where orders could run into the hundreds of thousands of dollars. Large companies found that Netscape's Web servers could communicate easily with outside networks, and Netscape gained a 70-percent market share among the Global *Fortune* 100 companies in the lucrative corporate intranet market. The first officially branded Netscape Enterprise Server product, version 2.0, was released in March 1996, and corporate sales accounted for some 80 percent of Netscape's revenue that year.

The development and introduction of Netscape Navigator drained nearly all of Netscape's capital. In order to raise more capital, the company sold an 11-percent interest to a consortium of media and computer companies that included Adobe Systems, International Data Group (IDG), Knight-Ridder, TCI, and Times Mirror. The next step was to raise money in the public equity market by going public. Without having turned a profit, Netscape went public on August 9, 1995. Its initial public offering (IPO) was one of the hottest of the 1990s and one of the first for Internet-based companies. The success of Netscape's IPO has been credited with starting the investor craze for Internet start-ups that lasted until the end of the decade. Netscape's stock was first offered at $28 a share. However, it was worth $75 after one day of trading and peaked at $171 on December 5, 1995. The company's first-day market capitalization was $2.2 billion.

Netscape enjoyed phenomenal growth from 1994 to 1996, with sales rising from $1 million in 1994 to

$81 million in 1995 and $346 million in 1996. In April 1996 Netscape announced it had its best quarter to date, with earnings of $4.7 million on revenue of $55 million. Netscape improved on that later in the year with a quarterly profit of $7.7 million on revenue of $100 million. Barksdale commented that the company made too much money and should have used more revenue to build its business. After reporting losses in 1994 and 1995, the company turned a $21 million profit in 1996.

INVOLVED IN OTHER E-COMMERCE INITIATIVES

Netscape also was involved in other initiatives that helped the development of e-commerce. One problem hindering such development in 1995 was the lack of a secure payment system that would enable customers to make credit card payments over the Internet. Netscape joined forces with MasterCard to develop the Secure Courier encryption standard, while Microsoft and Visa developed the Secure Transaction Technology. Netscape teamed with Verifone, the largest credit card transaction processor, to develop a credit card payment system for the Internet using the Secure Courier technology in January 1996. Netscape was all too aware of security issues, having suffered a security breach in September 1995 when two hackers at the University of California at Berkeley cracked the security code in Netscape Navigator. Netscape corrected the problem and posted warnings on the Internet. The company also established a ''Bugs Bounty'' program, giving prizes to users who identified flaws and potential security problems with the browser.

In 1995 and 1996, Netscape also entered into several strategic alliances. America Online (AOL), the nation's largest provider of online services, agreed to offer improved Internet access by using Netscape Navigator. Both Netscape and Microsoft worked with Hewlett-Packard to develop a Hypertext Markup Language (HTML) that could be printed as seen on screen. Netscape also worked with Sun Microsystems Inc. on the development of JavaScript language, which allowed programs to be imbedded in Web pages.

Netscape was expanding its technological base by acquiring other software companies. In January 1996 it acquired software developer Callabra Software Inc. for $108.7 million. Callabra's main product was Share, a system that enabled simultaneous e-mail discussions and document sharing among network users. In February 1996 Netscape acquired Paper Software Inc. and its 3-D programs for the Internet. During 1997 Netscape improved its position in the business software market by acquiring Digital-Style, which made Web graphics tools, and Portola Communications, which made messaging systems.

In 1996 and 1997, Netscape continued to form joint ventures. Actra Business Systems was created by Netscape and GE Information Services (GEIS) to develop e-commerce software. Netscape bought out GEIS' interest in November 1997 for $56.1 million and assumed full ownership of Actra. Together with Novell, it established Novonyx, and Netscape and Oracle formed the joint venture Navio Communications Inc. to produce consumer-oriented Internet software. Oracle purchased Navio from Netscape for $60 million in May 1997.

CONFLICT WITH MICROSOFT

In January 1997 Netscape joined an alliance with Oracle, IBM, and Sun Microsystems to develop common standards for all of the company's software products. The NOIS alliance, as it came to be known, was seen as a response to Microsoft's growing dominance in several key sectors of the software market. Netscape also released Communicator, the successor to Netscape Navigator.

By 1997 Netscape's leadership position in the browser market was dwindling. Early in the year it still had about 70 percent of the market but was losing market share to Microsoft's Internet Explorer. Microsoft had introduced Internet Explorer 2.0 in 1995 after the company had licensed Mosaic from Spyglass Inc., which had obtained the rights to the Internet browser from the University of Illinois. In August 1996 Microsoft shipped Explorer 3.0, which was considered to be the equal of Navigator. However, it was the introduction of Internet Explorer 4.0 in 1997 with Windows that caused the most serious erosion of Netscape's position. By bundling Internet Explorer with its operating system, Microsoft made the Internet accessible from the computer user's desktop and, at the same time, eliminated the need for a separate Web browser.

The U.S. Department of Justice, with the support of Netscape, complained that Microsoft was guilty of anticompetitive behavior in marketing its browser and asked a federal court to fine the company $1 million per day. A November 1997 survey of corporate information technology (IT) managers by the magazine *Computerworld* revealed that 59 percent of them felt that tying Explorer to the operating system gave Microsoft an unfair advantage. While most of the survey respondents were using Navigator, more than half said they would switch to Explorer in 1998. By April 1998 Microsoft had captured some 40 percent of the browser market, while Netscape's share had shrunk to 60 percent. Netscape's share of the browser market would decline even further, and Netscape CEO Jim Barksdale became more vocal in accusing Microsoft of unfair competition. When the Department of Justice filed an antitrust suit against Microsoft in 1998, Barksdale was the first witness to be called.

ACQUISITION BY AOL AND SUN

Although Netcape's annual revenue reached $534 million in 1997, the company reported a surprising $88 million loss. It laid off 300 workers. Reports soon began to appear that the company was for sale, and Netscape did nothing to dispel the rumors. Netscape's stock had fallen dramatically, but the company had $261 million in the bank. With no debt, it appeared to be a desirable takeover target, and IBM, Oracle, Sun Microsystems, and AOL were all reported to be potential suitors.

In April 1998 Netscape acquired Kiva Software, strengthening its position in the Web server market. Later in the year it acquired AtWeb, which provided automated Web site management and marketing services, and NewHoo, a directory-based search service. These acquisitions would enhance Netcenter, Netscape's portal to the Internet.

After nine months of takeover rumors, AOL announced in November 1998 that it would acquire Netscape for $4.2 billion in a stock-for-stock transaction. By this time Netscape's share of the browser market had fallen to 41 percent, compared to Microsoft's 44 percent market share. After passing regulatory approval in March 1999, the transaction was completed, creating what *The Economist* called the ''world's most powerful Internet company.'' As part of the deal, Sun Microsystems would pay $350 million over three years to license Netscape's software, and AOL agreed to purchase $500 million worth of servers from Sun. The terms of the three-way deal made it clear that AOL was primarily interested in the consumer side of Netscape's business, which included Netcenter and the company's Web browser, while Sun Microsystems would benefit from Netscape's server business for corporate intranets and e-commerce.

Following the sale of Netscape, Marc Andreessen was named AOL's chief technology officer, but he left after six months to form a new Internet services company, Loudcloud Inc. Jim Barksdale, who realized $700 million from the sale of Netscape, departed to focus on Internet-related investments and philanthropy. Netscape co-founder Jim Clark was involved with other Internet start-ups, including the vertical portals Healtheon and myCFO.

SUN-NETSCAPE ALLIANCE

In mid-1999 the Sun-Netscape Alliance adopted a new brand name, iPlanet, which would be used on such products as the Netscape Application Server and the Netscape Web Server. In August 1999 the alliance introduced the iPlanet Commerce Integration Suite, which enabled companies to build online trading communities. *PC Week's* review of the alliance's new iPlanet Web Server Enterprise Edition 4.0 said it ''has cemented its position as a top-of-the-line enterprise Web server, providing the power, scalability and features needed to run the busiest and most complex Web sites.'' *Infoworld* noted that the Web server was capable of meeting the challenges associated with ensuring reliable uptime, strong security, and acceptable performance.

The Sun-Netscape Alliance also was forming partnerships that would make it a key technology provider for companies that wanted to outsource their e-mail networks. In August it made an agreement with Frontier Corp. whereby Frontier would build an e-mail outsourcing service using Sun-Netscape servers that would support millions of simultaneous users. Frontier also planned to offer calendaring and scheduling features based on software from Sun-Netscape. A similar agreement was made with USA.net, a leading provider of hosted mailboxes.

By the end of 1999 Sun-Netscape was competing in the consolidated electronic billing market. It offered iPlanet BillerXpert Consolidator Edition software as a way for retail banks and other organizations to adopt consolidated electronic billing. Such organization could realize considerable savings over paper-based billing systems by using a single system to issue bills electronically. At this time no other single method or system was available for issuing bills electronically.

New Web servers were released in the first half of 2000, including the iPlanet Web Server, Enterprise Edition 4.1, which upgraded the Netscape Enterprise Server 2.01. Sun-Netscape also unveiled the iPlanet Wireless Server, which offered wireless access to e-mail, directory, and calendar services. In February Sun-Netscape introduced its iPlanet Portal Server, which gave companies an out-of-the-box package for deploying portals. The package included membership services, personalization services, security, and integration services. The product was aimed at e-commerce portals and came in three versions.

NETSCAPE 2000-2001

AOL's Netscape division released a beta version of Netscape 6, the successor to Netscape Communicator, in April 2000 at the Internet World conference. Netscape 6 included a new browsing engine nicknamed Gecko, which increased the speed at which Web pages were displayed. Until this time, Netscape had made only minor revisions to Communicator 4.5, which shipped in October 1998. After three beta versions were released during 2001, the commercial version of Netscape 6 was finally released at the Comdex show in fall 2000. Estimates of Netscape's share of the browser market ranged from 20 percent to as low as 12 percent. This was compared to between 80 and 88 percent for Microsoft's Internet Explorer. Netscape 6.01 was released in May 2001 to make the browser more stable and fix some glitches that had been discovered.

Traffic at Netcenter lagged well behind that of other portals. In January 2000 Netcenter had 347,000 unique visitors, compared to 37 million for Yahoo!, 26.2 million for AOL.com, 15.6 million for Go.com, 13.8 million for Lycos, and 9.9 million for AltaVista. America Online, in the process of completing its merger with Time Warner, announced an advertising campaign designed to recast Netscape Netcenter as a business professional's portal. In addition to adding AOL features to Netcenter, such as instant messaging and e-mail services, AOL was integrating content from Time Warner into the site. Netcenter's new default pages for categories such as news, sports, and money, would become CNN, *Sports Illustrated,* and *Money.* Time Warner-owned CNN also became Netcenter's premier broadcast news partner, replacing Walt Disney Co.'s ABC after ABC's contract with Netscape expired in December 1999.

In Fall 2000 AOL unveiled its new Netscape Netbusiness service, which was designed to help small businesses build Web-based storefronts and engage in business-to-business e-commerce. AOL formed a partnership with Las Vegas-based marketplace developer PurchasePro to develop Netscape Netbusiness. Organized in three sections—My Industry, My Business, and My Life—Netscape Netbusiness Marketplace included e-mail, a business version of Netscape Instant Messenger, industry-specific news, market research, expert opinions, maps and directions to member businesses, and community tools for sharing information. In late 2000 and early 2001 AOL entered into several alliances designed to strengthen its Netscape Netbusiness division, including an agreement with Hewlett-Packard that would link the HP Business Store to Netbusiness and give HP access to the 140,000 mostly small businesses that were using the Netbusiness hub. Other new partners included BroadVision Inc., which would offer personalized e-commerce software; CD-ROM replicator Viva Magnetics; online agricultural marketplace eFruit; and ProfitScape, which handled business-to-business transactions. Monster.com agreed to develop a recruitment industry marketplace for Netbusiness.

The introduction in 2000 of a new version of Netscape's browser and the launch of Netscape Netbusiness indicated AOL Time Warner's commitment to its Netscape division. When AOL was in the process of merging with Time Warner, some analysts thought Netscape would be neglected, disappear, or be sold off. Instead, it appears that Netscape, one of the original enablers of e-commerce, will continue to impact the way e-commerce is conducted for the foreseeable future.

FURTHER READING:

Biggs, Maggie. "iPlanet Pushes the Web Envelope." *InfoWorld.* October 4, 1999.

Chandrasekaran, Rajiv. "Netscape's Boy Wonder Looks Beyond the Browser." *Washington Post.* March 25, 1997.

Corcoran, Elizabeth. "Inside Netscape." *The Washington Post.* June 2, 1996.

Du Bois, Grant. "Netscape 6 Is a Head-Turner." *PC Week.* April 10, 2000.

———. "Portal Opens for Small Businesses." *eWeek.* September 25, 2000.

Finnie, Scot. "Fall Comdex: Netscape 6 Hits the Web." *WinMag.com.* November 15, 2000.

Holzinger, Albert G. "Netscape's Founder Points, and It Clicks." *Nation's Business.* January 1996.

Kaplan, David A. "Nothing but Net." *Newsweek.* December 25, 1995.

Malloy, Amy. "Microsoft vs. Netscape." *Computerworld.* November 10, 1997.

Moschella, David. "Figuring the Odds on Netscape." *Computerworld.* February 16, 1998.

Musgrove, Mike. "Netscape 6 Browser Unveiled." *The Washington Post.* April 6, 2000.

Regan, Keith. "AOL Rolls out 10 New E-Commerce Partnerships." *E-Commerce Times.* March 28, 2001. Available from www.ecommercetimes.com.

Sager, Ira. "A New Cyber Order." *Business Week.* December 7, 1998.

Sandberg, Jared. "Net Gain." *Newsweek.* December 7, 1998.

"Spinning a Golden Web." *People Weekly.* September 11, 1995.

Streitfeld, David. "An Awkward Anniversary." *The Washington Post.* March 17, 2000.

SEE ALSO: AOL Time Warner; Andreessen, Marc; Barksdale, Jim; Clark, Jim; Loudcloud; Microsoft Corp.; Sun Microsystems

NETWORK EXTERNALITIES

When the value of a technology, product, or service depends upon the number of other entities using it, the phenomenon is called network externality. Direct network externalities involve the value aspect of things like telephone systems, computing platforms, and especially the Internet and e-commerce. Additionally, indirect externalities involve related items like devices (telephones, fax machines, or software applications) becoming cheaper and more accessible as the number of overall users increases. This may also extend to things like service or parts.

Simply put, e-commerce in general becomes more valuable for both sellers and buyers as the overall number of connected entities grows. This kind of growth also means that information can be distributed to more entities for less money. One example of where network externalities play a role in e-commerce is the insurance industry. Certain kinds of insurance have low face values and high overhead costs associated with them. Among these products are travel and burial insurance. By selling these forms of insurance online where sales transactions cost less, insurers are able to offer them at lower prices.

Electronic billing is another area where network externalities have played a central role. In the early 2000s, it was possible for consumers to handle banking and pay many of their bills online. However, the practice of electronic bill payment and presentment (EBPP) was not widely used. Findings from the Gartner Group indicated that in order for consumers to become interested in and use EBPP, it was necessary for banks or bill consolidators (third parties who gather bills from different billers present them to consumers) to offer consumers the ability to pay most or all of their bills at one, convenient online location. Information from Jupiter Research indicated that less than one million U.S. households took advantage of EBPP in late 2000, but projected that number to reach 40 million by 2005. As the number of billers and payers grows, the value for all parties will likely increase.

Network externalities also have a large impact on the international aspect of e-commerce. Although there are many Internet users, which creates significant value for all, infrastructure issues prevent this value from being distributed evenly throughout the world. According to *InformationWeek,* in March 2001 approximately 100 million computers were connected to the Internet. However, the total accounted for less than two percent of the world's population. Additionally, the publication indicated that most (88 percent) Internet users resided in industrialized nations.

Part of this problem can be attributed to quality issues. In some developing nations like India, the telecommunication systems are not pervasive, and those that do exist often are in poor condition. However, these types of issues even challenge more developed nations. For example, *Newsbytes* cited a report from the Australian Productivity Commission that indicated the nation's outdated copper wire network limited the speeds at which most Australians connected to the Internet. The report revealed that, at both home and work, only 73 percent of Australian Internet users connected at speeds of at least 28.8 kbps.

In many ways, the heart of the Internet's infrastructure resides in the United States. As Kenneth Neil Cukier explained in *Communications Week International,* "The high demand for U.S.-based content, the lack of regional infrastructure such as low-cost and high-speed international circuits, and the lack of dominant interconnection points to exchange traffic all serve as both causes and embodiments of the underlying problem: an Internet that is not global, but centered in the United States. This leads to inefficient Internet traffic routing between countries outside the United States, and results in requiring ISPs that handle e-commerce traffic to pay U.S. carriers for access to the Internet."

Although it was improving in the early 2000s, this situation means that the value of the Internet is disproportionately greater for U.S. residents than it is for consumers in many foreign countries. Because the United States has been the center Internet activity and e-commerce, many foreign companies have opted to host their e-business operations there because of superior Internet connections. This allows more global consumers to access the company's Web site in more optimal ways than if it were hosted abroad, where the infrastructure is not as good.

FURTHER READING:

Au, Yoris A., and Robert J. Kauffman. "Should We Wait? Network Externalities and Electronic Billing Adoption." Working paper. University of Minnesota Management Information Systems Research Center, 2000-2001. Available from misrc.umn.edu.

Cukier, Kenneth. "Bandwidth Colonialism? The Implications of Internet Infrastructure on International E-Commerce." *Communications Week International,* 1999. Available from www.isoc.org.

"University Technology Transfer—Questions and Answers." The Regents of the University of California, 2001. Available from www.ucop.edu.

SEE ALSO: Internet Infrastructure

NETWORK SOLUTIONS

Computer networks, including the Internet, play critical roles in business and communications. Without them, it would be impossible for companies to engage in e-commerce and the vast majority of business systems would come to a complete standstill. Therefore, by enabling real-time relationships between many parties, networks in many ways become synonymous with the individuals and businesses they connect. Networks provide speed, connectivity, and ultimately value to their members and provide solutions to business challenges and problems that otherwise would not be possible.

Over time, businesses make large investments in computer systems used to manage different functions, such as accounting, human resources, customer service, purchasing, inventory management, and so on. These hefty investments make it difficult to totally replace old systems with new ones. Beyond the purely financial costs involved, doing so often requires retraining thousands of employees and making changes to long-established systems and processes. Therefore, it is common to find patchworks of older legacy systems connected together within large companies.

Integrated, networked systems are at the very heart of e-commerce. In a perfect world, companies would be able to network all of their underlying computer systems, both new and old, together in a seamless fashion. Employees, customers, and business partners would have instant, real-time access to the information contained in these systems and would be able to access and share it easily. Unfortunately, many legacy systems were not designed to be used with other systems, or to be accessed via the Internet. One of the biggest challenges facing businesses and entire industries is connecting applications and networks together at the company and industry level and getting them to work reliably.

NETWORK SOLUTION RESOURCES

In the early 2000s, companies relied on in-house technical employees, consultants, and a variety of information technology-based tools (hardware and software) to plan, execute, and manage network solutions at both the technical and the strategic levels. While the largest organizations had the luxury of employing staff devoted to exclusively to information technology, smaller and medium-sized organizations often found it more cost effective to contract with third parties for many network-related services. Larger companies also followed this approach in situations where services were highly specialized and hiring or training in-house staff was deemed too expensive. For example, a study conducted by People3 found that among 104 different information technology (IT) jobs, network architect positions took the longest for companies to fill (4.2 months). For reasons like these, outsourcing was a popular option. According to a CommerceNet survey, in early 2001 almost 75 percent of e-commerce firms outsourced some of their work or were considering doing so.

In order to obtain expert advice quickly, companies and industries often turn to large consulting firms. Such consultancies are able to use their vast, broad experience and resources to help clients plan and implement network solutions that they can't affordably develop in-house. This not only involves a tremendous amount of specialized knowledge and experience, it also requires continually staying current about the latest developments in technology. KPMG

Consulting was one leading consultancy in the early 2000s. One of KPMG's clients was the Union Bank of California, for whom it helped build a large, company-wide network solution. As *InformationWeek* explained, KMPG helped the bank "build and implement a retail sales, marketing, and relationship-tracking application for the bank's 250 branches. The application, which will link more than 1,000 sales and support personnel via Web browsers, will let bank employees instantly access consumers' financial profiles, as well as deposit, investment, and loan-account data."

Although consultants were a powerful resource for many organizations, there were disadvantages to using them. Published accounts of consultants relying on unethical business practices were not uncommon in the early 2000s. One approach used by some consultants was to draw out projects and continually recommend additional services or devices. Another approach was known as the "bait and switch." In this scenario, consultancies secure IT projects by sending in bona fide experts to close deals with clients. Companies are willing to pay handsomely for this expertise, and expect the consultants to be directly involved in their project. However, instead of the experts, recent college graduates are sent in to perform the actual work, at a lower cost to the consultant. Consultants also have been known to overcharge clients for a variety of reasons. Although some of these practices have resulted in highly publicized lawsuits, many go unreported when discovered by clients, who remain silent instead of revealing the expensive blunders to senior management or the company's board of directors.

Like any system or tool that provides value to users, networks require monitoring and maintenance. In addition to the advice of consultants, network management software and systems were powerful tools organizations used to keep their solutions up and running. These were useful for avoiding network problems and inefficiencies that cost companies large sums of money, including traffic bottlenecks; downtime; poor Web site, application, workstation, and server performance; and compromised security. In the early 2000s, network management systems varied in cost and complexity, depending on their range of capabilities. Such systems were able to issue wide varieties of reports and notify network administrators of problems. Historically, one challenge administrators faced was finding a way to tie multiple network management systems together so they had access to one streamlined view of all activities. However, special software packages eventually were developed to address this issue, which stemmed from networks that were growing in complexity and sophistication.

A NETWORK SOLUTION IN ACTION

One company that was highly successful at leveraging the power of networked systems as a business advantage was Walgreen Co., which in 2001 was the largest U.S. drugstore chain with 3,446 stores operating in 43 states and Puerto Rico. The company began using networks as a solution to business challenges in 1981. At that time, it connected its pharmacies together via satellite and unveiled a computer system called Intercom. Since then, its computer systems and networks have continued to evolve. The next generation of Intercom was Intercom Plus, which Walgreens described as an advanced "pharmacy computer and workflow system."

Intercom Plus provided a variety of benefits to staff and customers. One of the system's features allowed patients to request prescription refills and pick-up times by phone and have the data fed directly into Walgreen's system. Consumers also could access Intercom Plus via Walgreen's full-service online pharmacy. Because the same system is used via the Web, telephone, or at physical store locations, Walgreen always has one consistent, real-time view of its operations, and is able to realize benefits through increased efficiencies.

In August of 2000, Walgreens took advantage of its seamless network to make e-commerce even easier for its customers when it gave them the ability to register for its online pharmacy by simply providing their e-mail address to staff at any physical retail location. Staff then took the address and integrated it with information that was already on file for that customer in Walgreen's database. This eliminated the need for customers to re-key the information online. Once their e-mail addresses were added to Walgreen's system, customers automatically received a username, password, and PIN number via e-mail, allowing them to use their new online account.

FURTHER READING:

Botelho, Jay. "The Latest Look in Systems Management." *Telephony,* June 5, 2000.

"KPMG Adapts to Being On Its Own." *InformationWeek,* April 30, 2001.

Liebmann, Lenny. "Network Management Goes Open Source." *Communications News,* April 2001.

Nash, Kim S. "Users Say Consultants Play Role in IT Disasters." *Computerworld,* November 6, 2000.

Walgreen Co. "Background on Electronic Prescriptions." Walgreen Co. July 28, 2000. Available from www.walgreens.com.

SEE   E-commerce Consultants; E-commerce Solutions
ALSO:

NEW ECONOMY

As the U.S. economy surged into overdrive between the mid-1990s and early 2000s, delivering skyrocketing profit margins and profound technological development, economists, business leaders, policy makers, and everyday observers debated the idea of a New Economy. Were there characteristics about the new economic environment that set it apart qualitatively from historical economic conditions? Had there been a fundamental break from the periodic disjunctions and crises of yesteryear? Was the development of new technologies, particularly sophisticated information technology (IT) and telecommunications breakthroughs, responsible for generating unprecedented—and, perhaps, unending—economic growth and prosperity? These and other questions generated fierce debate and passions, producing New Economy devotees and skeptics alike.

Some analysts warmly and enthusiastically embraced the idea of a New Economy, encouraging others to shed their antiquated Old Economy ways and adapt to the exciting and inevitable future. At the other extreme, critics scoffed at any thought of a New Economy and insisted that the engines driving the supposed new era were irrational exuberance over much-hyped new technologies, fueled by a strong upswing in the business cycle and an extended bull market. Particularly following the tech-market bust in the early 2000s, sober analysts tended to situate themselves somewhere between the two extremes, holding that technological innovations had indeed produced substantial alterations in the productive engines of the U.S. economy, but eschewing the idea that traditional economic laws had been forever suspended.

DEFINING THE NEW ECONOMY

The concept of a New Economy wasn't born with the dot-com craze or the 1990s economic boom. The idea surfaced years earlier, particularly in the early 1980s when sophisticated computers began to effect sweeping changes both in the factory, where computer automation overhauled production processes, and in consumer markets, with households rapidly purchasing personal computers for their homes.

Pinpointing a clear definition of the New Economy was difficult, as so many commentators weighed in with various and often-contradictory definitions. For example, some viewed the entire economic spectrum as wholly transformed, while others conceived of the New Economy as a sector that coexisted with other, traditional economic sectors. Still others simply viewed the New Economy as a set of practices and approaches to doing business that was fundamentally distinguished from those of the Old Economy.

Loosely, however, the business sectors that the New Economy claims as its base include high-technology equipment and consumer products, e-commerce in all its forms, innovative IT-led financial services, high-tech telecommunications, and other IT goods and services. What follows are some general characteristics proposed by enthusiasts of the New Economy.

RADICALLY ALTERED BUSINESS ENVIRONMENT. New Economy proponents energetically proclaimed that computer automation, the Internet, high-speed tele-communications, and IT were creating an economic revolution on a scale similar to those wrought in previous eras by the introduction of electricity or the automobile. In other words, the New Economy was placed on a scale with the Industrial Revolution, creating an Information Revolution in terms of acting as a historical marker or turning point. These structural changes were wrought by the implementation of technological innovations into the structure of economic production, particularly in the 1980s and 1990s, bringing greater means of precise control over production and exchange. For example, the movement of exchange and payment systems into electronic format and the attendant speed and efficiency of processing and recording transactions overhauled traditional practices and assumptions of economic exchange.

Other factors complementing the dramatically fortified technological infrastructure included the forces of economic globalization and the more or less worldwide trend toward deregulation of markets, allowing businesses and capital greater mobility to seek out the most cost-effective and profitable methods of conducting business and forcing local business and labor markets to compete with each other for investment. The end results included sharply lowered prices, particularly for high-technology goods for both the business and consumer markets.

THE BUSINESS CYCLE. One of the boldest, albeit widespread, claims about the New Economy was that it had propelled capitalism past the era of the business cycle, in which periods of economic growth were punctuated by periodic recessions, during which time the excesses of the expansion period were weeded out and conditions were prepared for renewed growth. Most economic theory, and history, holds that this cycle takes place within the space of a decade. According to many commentators, the New Economy was immune from this cycle, which frequently produced political and social upheaval and occasionally severe economic depressions such as that suffered by much of the industrialized world in the 1930s. The unprecedented 10-year uninterrupted U.S. economic expansion between 1991 and 2001 gave considerable fuel to such New Economy arguments, and the accel-

eration of investment and profit levels following the explosion of the Internet in the mid-1990s greatly boosted their confidence.

ECONOMIC SAFEGUARDS VIA TECHNOLOGICAL DEVELOPMENT. The sheer pace of IT development and evolution was another defining characteristic of the New Economy, producing hyperspeed innovation that fed on itself, bleeding into adjacent industries for a snowball effect on technological efficiency. This high-speed development carried an additional benefit, according to many New Economy enthusiasts. Because information technology developed so quickly, the latest, most cutting-edge technology, while immediately necessary in order to keep up with competitors, would be obsolete within a few years, requiring a new round of investment in order to remain competitive. In this way, according to such analysts, the IT sector of the economy could weather any slowdown elsewhere in the economy, and keep new money pouring in, because of the inherent nature of the business.

COMPANY VALUATION AND BUSINESS PRACTICES. Another feature of the New Economy, and one that may largely have fueled its attendant outstanding growth, was the notion that old methods of valuating company stocks—such as seeking out sound fundamentals, profits, and long-term growth strategies—no longer applied. By the late 1990s, cartloads of dot-com start-ups defied all market logic by generating fantastic share prices without ever having made a profit, and with little evidence that they would one day be in the black. Nonetheless, companies such as Yahoo!, which sober-minded analysts in 1997 swore was grossly overvalued, saw their stocks continue to run up through the rest of the decade; investors who had listened to those analysts and pulled out of Yahoo! stocks would have missed extraordinary returns on their investments. As a result, such traditional analysts and companies, and their valuation logic, were increasingly derided as outdated and ''Old Economy.''

ECONOMIC GROWTH. At the heart of the New Economy claims, however, was the enhanced rate of productivity growth that its enthusiasts insisted was a feature of the IT-driven economy. Fueled by information technology throughout their productive and managerial systems, companies were able to lead the United States to economic expansion while keeping inflation in check, generate tremendous profits for continued investment, and boost the gross domestic product and create a budget surplus for the first time in decades. This feature of the New Economy was hotly debated within the economics profession, however, with divergent researchers disagreeing on how much of the growth in productivity could be directly attributed to IT development and how much was simply an intrinsic component of the upswing in the business cycle.

Historical comparisons floated many proponents' claims. The 1950s and 1960s were characterized by staggering annual productivity growth rates of about 3 percent, fueled by a combination of factors: pent-up demand stemming from the war and depression years, the integration of military-based technological developments into the commercial sector, and boosted trade and production from the Marshall Plan's U.S.-based reconstruction of the war-torn industrial economies. By comparison, the 1970s and, to a lesser extent, the 1980s were a disappointment, with annual productivity growth averaging between 1 and 2 percent. The unique post-war circumstances had by that time played themselves out, while new challenges, such as skyrocketing energy prices, took their toll, leading many economists to suspect that the 2-percent annual growth rate was just about as much as a highly developed country could hope for. When annual growth rates leaped to the 3-percent mark again in the late 1990s, however, economists tried to explain the phenomena; one such explanation was rooted in the concept of the New Economy.

History seemed to vindicate New Economy proponents in another economic category as well. While the 1950s and 1960s are often called the Golden Years of capitalism because of the fantastic rate of growth, the period was also characterized by steady inflation. The annual growth rate long considered by economists to be the limit for containing runaway inflation was about 2 and one-half percent. Yet between 1995 and 2000, the U.S. economy grew at an annual average of about 3 percent with little inflation to show for it, while simultaneously keeping unemployment levels remarkably low. As a result, as the 20th century drew to a close, New Economy theorization and commentary gradually won over skeptics and assumed prominence, if not hegemony, in economic and popular literature.

SKEPTICS ABOUND

While the booming economy proceeded and commentators routinely chalked it up to the breakthroughs in technological development, there did exist the many, though much quieter, killjoys who insisted that the boom, as large and prolonged as it was, represented nothing evidently new as much as it represented a traditional stock-market bubble, a run-up of investment fueled by unsound predictions of lucrative returns and can't-miss myths that would, eventually, crash on itself. For instance, e-commerce itself, despite its tremendous publicity, was a very small factor in the surge in productivity and economic growth

in the late 1990s. Both business-to-consumer and business-to-business e-commerce sales in 2000 accounted for only about one percent of total U.S. sales in those categories.

The first empirical challenges to the New Economy thesis came with the tech-market bust of spring 2000. Through the rest of the year, tech stocks sank. In late 2000 and 2001, moreover, the economy was certainly slowing, and analysts debated whether the United States was heading for recession. The Nasdaq high-tech stock market index, the benchmark of the New Economy, plunged through much of 2000 and early 2001, most glaringly in the realm of dot-com start-ups, and profits of Internet giants, such as Cisco, fell off dramatically. The rose-colored predictions by equity analysts in late 2000 of sustained long-term profits growth of 19 percent, according to *The Economist,* just months later sounded like wishful fantasies. By 2001, with the U.S. economy slowing and unemployment on the rise, the idea of a New Economy immune from the capitalist business cycle was transformed into a laughable notion that few were willing to admit to having entertained. When the technology markets began to retrench in 2000, major IT firms, such as Cisco, Sun, and Nortel, long remained certain that they could soundly weather the storm without any substantial decline in earnings. In the end, however, such companies ended up lowering earnings projections, stinging many New Economy faithful into accepting that one of their cherished assumptions was unsound.

While dot-coms and other Internet companies rejoiced in what they saw as the New Economy's abandonment of economic laws, many acted as though the Internet Age brought the suspension of labor laws as well. While a tight labor market and a seemingly endless supply of venture capital turned many hotshot dot-coms into attractive places to work, once the financial bottom fell out of the market and these firms scrambled for cover or closed their doors, many neglected to adequately honor their employee agreements, resulting in drastically thickened caseloads for employment-law firms across the country, particularly in New Economy hotbeds like California. Failure to adequately warn employees of, or compensate them for, mass layoffs was the most common blanket claim against such firms, encompassing negligence on agreements, loosely worded contracts, and even misuse of 401(k) withholdings. As companies surged ahead to take advantage of the hot dot-com economy, according to *Business Week,* many left clear human-resources policies and contract language on the back burner. When stock options, health benefits, and even back pay were increasingly pulled out from under employees as the Internet economy cooled, employees turned to litigation.

Another claim of the New Economy enthusiasts also suffered from embarrassing realities in the early 2000s. According to *The Economist,* IT-based inventory control systems and the widespread adoption of just-in-time inventory techniques were supposed to ensure that production across companies' diverse operations, even across international borders, would be so systematically and expertly controlled that large inventories would never be permitted to swell up due to excess production relative to sales figures and projections, thus avoiding the massive inventory stockpiling that helped generate earlier recessions. The evidence across many IT-saturated industries by 2001, however, suggested otherwise, with companies that implemented the latest cutting-edge software forced to scale back workforces due to excessive production.

In the end, the Internet blitz followed the pattern of other major technological innovations, such as railroads and electricity, before investors, awed by the new technology and its potential, poured money into the industry and sent stock prices soaring, only to watch the market plunge as economic reality began to catch up. Between spring 2000 and 2001, according to Laura D'Andrea Tyson, dean of the Haas School of Business at the University of California at Berkeley and writing in *Business Week,* more than half of the previous five years' astonishing gains in the high-tech sector were obliterated by the stock-market plunge, resulting in an unprecedented cycle of wealth creation and destruction.

WHICH WAY FOR THE NEW ECONOMY?

While the end of the business cycle, the discarding of old valuation methods, dot-com mania, or profoundly altered economic laws may be consigned to relics of 1990s over-excitement, many analysts still insist that, minus these extravagances, there's still much to be said for the New Economy, and that it isn't going away. Generally, these analyses focus on the transformative power of information technology and the Internet, which have yielded, and will continue to yield, greatly enhanced productivity and efficiency to businesses across many sectors of the economy, particularly, of course, in high technology but in Old Economy sectors as well.

Meanwhile, brick-and-mortar firms were hardly retreating from the Internet in the wake of the dot-com bust. Rather, established firms were busy sifting through the wreckage of the Internet shakeout, swallowing up Internet-based firms in order to take advantage of their diversified leverage to make a quick inroad into the Internet market. While overall corporate IT investment retrenched substantially in the early 2000s as the U.S. economy (contrary to the ex-

pectations of many New Economy promoters) backtracked, the continuation of e-commerce was assured, albeit at a more measured pace of evolution.

The New Economy, at least its tremendous growth in IT investment, may be hard to revive even after the early 2000s slowdown irons itself out, in large part because the quadrupling IT investment of the late 1990s is extremely unlikely to repeat itself, although investment in such technology is expected to pick up again. In order to reignite the kind of growth about which economists, investors, and business leaders were so excited, it will be necessary for the New Economy to shift its main engines of growth away from the boom in IT investment, perhaps towards a greater surge in e-commerce. The latter possibility was certainly in the cards, as Internet penetration increases, bandwidth improves, interbusiness networks are implemented and the novelty of online shopping graduates into common practice.

While the New Economy's sputtering in the early 2000s certainly gave skeptics the long-awaited opportunity to say ''I told you so,'' several key features of economic organization lingered. As *Computer World* explained, the economy of most of the 20th century was built on a particular mode of business organization—the vertically organized corporation—and a physical infrastructure of storefronts, roads, railroads, and power grids. With the advent of late-20th century IT, and particularly the Internet, the traditional business model was being supplanted by more diffusely organized entities connected over sophisticated electronic networks irrespective of geographical boundaries, while the Internet infrastructure allowed for tremendous access to comparative information, networking, and shopping without regard for geography. In the process, the New Economy created tremendous—and ultimately superior—methods of competition, cost reduction, and wealth creation. Moreover, the New Economy model, according to Don Tapscott in *Computer World,* wasn't limited to high-tech or Internet firms. Instead of the business sector a company worked in, it was the kind of business thinking and organization a company engineered for itself that determined whether it was New Economy or Old Economy.

FURTHER READING:

''Amid the Euphoria, a Note of Caution.'' *Business Week,* December 27, 1999, 220.

Brandt, John. ''Here's to the New New Economy.'' *Chief Executive,* April 2001.

D'Andrea Tyson, Laura. ''Why the New Economy is Here to Stay.'' *Business Week,* April 30, 2001.

Landefeld, J. Steven, and Barbara M. Fraumeni. ''Measuring the New Economy.'' *Survey of Current Business,* March 2001.

Means, Grady E. ''Rebirth of the New Economy.'' *Computer World,* March/April 2001.

"Nasdaq Crashed. The New Economy Didn't." *Business Week,* January 22, 2001.

"The New Economy's New Reality." *Business Week,* March 12, 2001.

"Still the Same Old Economy, Stupid." *Euromoney,* December 2000.

Tapscott, Don. "Don't Doubt the Future of the New Economy." *Computer World,* February 19, 2001.

Taylor, Timothy. "Thinking About a 'New Economy.'" *Public Interest,* Spring 2001.

"What's Left?" *The Economist,* May 12, 2001.

SEE ALSO: Dot-com; Information Revolution vs. Industrial Revolution; Nasdaq Stock Market; Shakeout, Dot-com; Start-Ups

NEWSLETTERS, ONLINE

Online newsletters, also known as electronic newsletters, became popular during the late 1990s. As the number of World Wide Web surfers using the Internet for gathering information and making purchases increased, many businesses began using online newsletters to promote company Web sites, products, and services; to provide information; and as an additional source of revenue through advertising.

According to a 2000 *BusinessWeek Online* article, online newsletters can accomplish the same things as traditional print counterparts. "They remind customers you're there, spark repeat business, and help attract new clients." The article also points out some benefits of producing an online newsletter versus a traditional print version. As well as being environmentally friendly, online newsletters save the publisher time and cut costs by reducing postage, paper, and other mailing supplies costs.

Along with being less expensive and easier to produce, online newsletters can also reach a much larger customer base. While many online newsletters are available on a publisher's Web site, the most popular method of delivery for many newsletters is through email. Whether free or fee-based, Web surfers can sign up to receive newsletters that are sent directly to their email accounts. For example, CNET.com, an informative Web site catering to the computer and technology industry, has over 40 free online newsletters such as the *Enterprise Weekly Newsletter* and the *News.com Daily Dispatch.* The Motley Fool, known for its humorous investment advice, also offers its members free newsletters via email, including *FoolWatch Weekly* and *Investing Basics.* Both newsletters are sent to the subscriber's e-mail address on a weekly basis and contain investing information and news. In June of 2001, Japan's Prime Minister, Junichiro Koizumi, launched an online newsletter entitled *Lion Heart,* which covered political and technological issues. In its first week, over one million people subscribed to it, and just two weeks later, the newsletter had secured over 1.82 million readers.

While many newsletters exist solely as an information source and do not utilize advertising, many others are published as a source of revenue. A 2001 study done by *Opt-in News* reported that one out of three online newsletter publishers used the newsletter to generate advertising revenue. Twenty-eight percent of those publishers used outside firms to garner advertising sales. Another study done by Clientize, a Florida-based market research firm, found that 207 of the top 500 magazines had free online newsletters. While most magazine publishers polled thought the online newsletter was an excellent tool for generating traffic on their Web sites, 21 percent rated them as an excellent source of additional revenue.

With an increasing number of online newsletters in circulation and online traffic increasing, businesses began viewing the electronic medium as an attractive place to advertise. In fact, advertising in online newsletters is often more effective than placing a banner ad on a Web site. According to Forrester Research, advertisements in email newsletters had an average response rate of 18 percent in 2000, versus a banner ad click through rate—the number of times someone clicks on an ad—of less than one percent.

As advertising in online newsletters grows more commonplace, many marketing firms began touting services that helped businesses advertise in electronic media. In 2001, interactive media firm Engage Inc. offered a business-to-business (B2B) e-mail newsletter sponsorship program that allowed companies to place ads in B2B newsletters. 24/7 Media Inc., another interactive marketing firm, offered similar programs that were targeted towards newsletter advertising.

With Internet use predicted to continue rising, the number of online newsletters will, no doubt, continue to increase along with it. Forrester predicts that by 2002, businesses will send 250 billion e-mail newsletters, and by 2004, most firms will have tripled their e-mail budgets. Michele Slack, an advertising executive with Jupiter Research, stated in a March 2000 *CNET News* article, "online players either have e-mail newsletters or are going to have them, and it's partially driven by competition. Newsletters are a way to lock in your consumers and remind them on a periodic basis of the value you provide."

FURTHER READING:

Brady, Diane. "Six Parties a Night? It's a Living." *BusinessWeek Online,* April 3, 2000. Available from www.businessweek.com.

Lindorff, Dave. "Draw More Business With an Online Newsletter." *BusinessWeek Online,* February 18, 2000. Available from www.businessweek.com.

Olsen, Stefanie. "Newsletter Authors Reap Banner Profits." *CNET News,* March 30, 2000. Available from news.cnet.com.

Owens, Jennifer. "Study: E-Newsletters Drive Site Traffic." *Adweek,* April 2, 2001. Available from www.adweek.com.

Wimpsett, Kim. "Newsletter Know-How." *CNET News,* December 1, 2000. Available from news.cnet.com.

SEE ALSO: Electronic Publishing

NEXT GENERATION INTERNET INITIATIVE (NGI)

The Next Generation Internet Initiative (NGI) is a conglomeration of projects funded by the United States government under the rubric of creating an Internet capable of accommodating the demands placed on it in the advanced world of business, consumer, research, and communication networking in the 21st century. The initiative's three primary goals are: the expansion of bandwidth capabilities to create universal high-performance Internet connectivity; the construction of sophisticated distributed applications for areas as diverse as digital libraries, telemedicine, and manufacturing systems; and the development of easy-to-use, secure networking technologies.

Officially launched in 1997, the NGI was designed as a five-year project, during which time the government would remain the primary coordinator of the networks and associated technology. After the five years were up, the fruits of the initiative would be turned over to the stewardship of the private sector and services would proliferate throughout the networked world. Still, the government was adamant that the companies involved in assisting in the development of NGI begin implementing the technologies, applications, and processes they develop from their work on NGI as quickly as possible. Among the tasks charged to the NGI was the coordination of next-generation network capabilities and next-generation applications, whereby the technical requirements of highly touted applications can enjoy proper support from the networks on which they operate.

The NGI Initiative had its genesis under the Clinton administration, which launched NGI as a supplement to the existing high-speed initiatives Backbone Network Service (vBNS) and Internet2 (I2). At the time, the promise of NGI included transmission speeds a million times greater than those offered by contemporary modems. The National Science Foundation (NSF) sponsored vBNS as a testing ground for emerging high-speed Internet systems. I2, meanwhile, was the fruit of the collaboration between 100 universities, and served as a support system for experimental applications that required extensive bandwidth. I2 was geared more specifically toward educational purposes. With universities as the primary actors driving I2, this program was designed to enhance the research capabilities at educational institutions across the United States, facilitate such advanced teaching and research collaboration tools as full-screen distance learning and real-time, long-distance project coordination.

Perhaps the defining characteristic of the NGI is speed; the initiative was launched primarily to accommodate increasing traffic and skyrocketing bandwidth demand to enable instantaneous Internet speeds. By converting the backbone of the Internet network into a fiber-optic system, download times were shrinking rapidly in the early 2000s. The biggest challenge was in what telecommunications experts refer to as the last mile—the telecommunications infrastructure that brought the signals from the Internet backbone directly into the residential areas where PCs are used. These infrastructures generally relied on older electronic systems that required a conversion of the photonic signals employed by the backbone into electronics, thereby slowing the transmission of data. The NGI aims at the conversion of the last mile to a compatible photonic system to allow the capabilities of the telecommunications breakthroughs to be realized. In addition to addressing the prevalent complaints from average users of excessive delays in download speeds, dial-up busy signals, and poor-quality video and audio streams, NGI was expected to clear the path for sophisticated applications that were expected to drive the Internet in the early 2000s, including advanced business applications such as video teleconferencing.

The government's initiative called for five testbed networks, each supported by a federal agency, including the National Aeronautics and Space Administration (NASA), the National Science Foundation (NSF), the Department of Energy (DOE), the National Institute of Health (NIH) and the Department of Defense (DOD). The Defense Department agency most responsible for NGI development was the Defense Advanced Research Projects Agency (DARPA), the same agency under which the Internet's first two decades of development took place.

NGI enjoyed widespread support in the telecommunications industry, which not only hoped to implement the new initiatives but also stood to derive technological spinoffs from the government-sponsored research. Internet backbone stalwarts such as Bell Atlantic, MCI WorldCom (later renamed WorldCom), and Sprint offered parts of their commercial networks to various NGI projects. In this way, NGI projects such as experimenting with expanded-bandwidth techniques could proceed immediately without necessitating the laying of thousands of miles of new cables and supporting infrastructure.

Thus, the plan for the NGI was similar to the course of development of the original Internet. That is, after extensive government-led research and investment, the technology would become commercialized and fall under control of private companies that would assume the responsibility for its construction, refinement, and ownership. This time around, however, private industry, with considerable background in the Internet already, is involved from the very beginning, thereby resulting in commercial products more quickly.

FURTHER READING:

Abernathy, Donna J. "Internet 2: The Next Generation." *Training & Development,* February, 1999.

Anderson, Neil. "Next Generation Internet: Work in Progress." *Network World,* June 14, 1999.

Scannell, Ed. "NGI On the Brain." *InfoWorld,* December 4, 2000.

Swartz, Jon. "Need for Speed Spawns 2 Internetlets." *San Francisco Chronicle,* July 28, 1997.

Tweney, Dylan. "Network Necessities for Next-Generation I-Commerce: It's More Than Just Bandwidth." *InfoWorld,* November 2, 1998.

SEE   History of the Internet and World Wide Web (WWW);
ALSO: Optical Switching; Photonics

NOKIA CORP.

Nokia Corp. is the world's largest cell phone manufacturer with sales of $27 billion, profits of $3.5 billion, and a 31-percent share of the worldwide mobile phone market. Believing that mobile products will one day replace PCs as the most popular method for gaining Internet access, the Finland-based firm began focusing on developing wireless Internet devices in the late 1990s.

EARLY HISTORY

Oy Nokia Ab was established in 1865 to sell paper and other products that would result from har-

vesting the forests that grew near the small town of Nokia, Finland. When the rebuilding of Europe following World War II spurred demand for construction materials, Nokia found itself operating as a major exporter of paper and wood products. To increase its international presence, Nokia began to diversify by purchasing other companies.

In 1966, Nokia merged with Finnish Rubber Works, a rubber products manufacturer created in 1898, and Finnish Cable Works, a power transmission cable and phone line manufacturer founded in 1912. The new firm was renamed Nokia Corp., and operations were restructured into four units: pulp, paper, and power; Finnish Rubber Works; Finnish Cable Works; and Nokia Electronics. The following year, Nokia created a fifth unit, hoping to move into the areas of data processing, industrial automation, and communications systems. By the early 1970s, the Soviet Union accounted for 12 percent of Nokia's sales. Most of the firm's business with the Soviet Union was done via trade, as lumber products and machinery were exchanged for petroleum.

FOCUS ON ELECTRONICS

Kari Kairamo took over as CEO in 1975 and shifted Nokia's focus from forest products to consumer electronics. He also began consolidating Nokia's Scandinavian operations in an effort to increase operations throughout the remainder of Europe. Two years later, Nokia acquired Oy Kymamo, which formed the core of the firm's sixth operating unit, Nokia Plastics. The company's first foray into telecommunications came in 1981, when it purchased a 51-percent stake in Finland's state-owned telecommunications company, which was eventually renamed Telenokia. It was then that Finland began developing its cellular system, which developed into the world's most heavily trafficked cellular network, a major factor in Nokia's rise to dominance in the cellular phone industry. The following year, Nokia designed a digital switching system for Finnish telephone companies and purchased Finnish mobile phone company Mobira, which gave the firm entrance to what would become an exploding mobile phone market. Nokia continued to expand its electronics holdings in 1984, acquiring Luxor, Sweden's state-owned electronics and computer firm, and an 18.3-percent stake in Salora, the second-largest manufacturer of televisions in Scandinavia. By then, Nokia had forged several original equipment manufacture deals, agreeing to manufacture electronic equipment under the brand names of other firms.

The later half of the 1980s was marked by the launch of the Nokia brand name when the firm began to manufacture Nokia mobile phones. In 1986, the largest electrical products wholesaler in Finland, Sahkoliikkeiden, was added to Nokia's growing list of holdings. Purchases the following year included German consumer electronics manufacturer Standard Elektrik Lorenz AG, Swiss cable manufacturer Maillefer, and a French manufacturer of consumer electronics, Oceanic. Nokia also listed its shares on the London stock exchange. Nokia became Scandinavia's largest information technology company in 1988 when it purchased the data systems division of Sweden-based Ericsson Group. The company also acquired Great Britain's Deeko PLC and Renucci SA of France. Tire producing operations were rolled into a new subsidiary, dubbed Nokia Tyres Ltd. Divestitures that year included paper pulp producer Metsa-Botnia Oy.

Reportedly feeling intense pressure to boost profit margins, Kairamo committed suicide in 1988. He was succeeded by Simo S. Vuorilehto. Mobile phone operations continued to grow as Nokia forged joint ventures to produce mobile phones in the United States with Tandy Corp., and in France with Matra. The following year, Nokia sold off the bulk of its conveyor belt, technical, and flooring operations interests, as well as a circuit board plant in Germany.

In 1990, Nokia agreed to merge its European soft-tissue paper operations with those of United States-based James River Corp. and Italy-based Ferruzzi Group. The firm also worked with the telephone authority in Moscow, Russia, to establish ATM there. Acquisitions included Finnish electrical equipment wholesaler Suomen Sahkotukku Oy and a 51-percent stake in NKF Holding NV, which owned the Dutch telecommunications and cable manufacturer NFK Kabel. Cellular phone assets grew in 1991 with the purchase of Britain's Technophone Ltd., a mobile phone manufacturer. Also that year, Nokia sold its Nokia Data unit, and Kymmene Corp. agreed to merge its chemical operations with Nokia. The firm purchased television manufacturer Finlux in 1992. By then, Nokia had grown into the leading corporation in Finland. The diversified giant also was the sixth-largest manufacturer of electrical cables in Europe, as well as a leading television maker. Nokia also was the world's top cable machinery and winter tires maker. However, despite the firm's impressive growth, it had lost $213 million over the previous two years. Jorma Ollila took over as CEO that year, and he refocused the company on telecommunications.

FOCUS ON TELECOMMUNICATIONS

Sales in 1993 reached $2.1 billion. Ollila sold off the firm's cable manufacturing operations. Nokia released its blockbuster 2100 mobile phone series that year, selling 20 million units. To raise capital, the firm

listed its shares on the New York Stock Exchange in 1994. The tire division was spun off into a separate company in 1995, and in 1996 television operations were brought to a halt. By 1996, Nokia had become the second-largest maker of mobile phones. In fact, roughly 70 percent of annual sales came from telecommunications operations. Employees totaled 32,000, and operations spanned 40 countries. Despite efforts to diversify, European sales still accounted for roughly 70 percent of total revenues.

Thailand's Total Access Communications Inc. awarded Nokia a $30 million contract in 1997 to build a fiber optic transmission system named SYNFONET, as well as a network management system, and to provide technical support services. Sales grew to $8.7 billion. Capturing a 25-percent share of the market, Nokia surpassed Motorola Corp., which had a 20-percent share, as the leading mobile phone maker in 1998. That year, Ericsson, Nokia, and Motorola created Symbian, a company focused on developing wireless technology with messaging, information access, and Internet capabilities. In 1999, sales grew 48 percent, nearing the $20 billion mark, and earnings jumped 57 percent to nearly $4 billion. IBM Corp. and Nokia forged an alliance to hasten the growth of the wireless Internet. The two companies agreed to work together to develop enterprise wireless application protocol (WAP) solutions that would allow customers to immediately begin extending e-business beyond the PC to a variety of mobile devices. With the cellular phone markets in many nations nearing saturation, Nokia had started looking to the Internet as a way to ensure future sales, believing that wireless devices would replace PCs as the most popular method for accessing the Net.

In September of 2000, Nokia released a WAP-enabled mobile phone. The firm also established a systems integration center in France to support mobile Internet applications for its business and individual customers. Nokia and RealNetworks Inc. began working together to develop technology designed to deliver Internet audio and video content to future mobile devices. According to a May 2000 article in *Fortune*, "To achieve its goal of brining the Internet to our pockets, Nokia is taking off in many directions. It isn't just making wireless application protocol (WAP) phones that can surf an abridged version of the Internet; it's also making the WAP servers upon which that abridged Net will run. It's building wireless Internet connections for cars; developing products for Bluetooth, a new standard for high bandwidth wireless connections inside a house or office; and working on wireless videophones and all sorts of other gee-whiz stuff." To oversee its wide range of Internet products, the firm created Nokia Internet Communications.

Telecommunications spending slowed dramatically as economies in both North America and Europe slumped in late 2000 and continued their downturns in 2001. As a result, spending on the new general packet radio networks, known as 2.5G and 3G, that Nokia was relying upon for its wireless Internet products came to a near halt. According to a June 2001 *BusinessWeek Online* article, "with nearly three-quarters of its revenues coming from handsets, Nokia had big hopes that existing customers would upgrade their phones to get speedier Internet access complete with services from mobile air ticketing to driving directions. But as Europe's phone companies have been forced to scale back spending on 2.5G and 3G networks, the resultant delays are cooling a once torrid market." Despite the slowdown, Nokia continued to develop its wireless Internet devices.

FURTHER READING:

Capell, Kerry. "Surprise! Nokia Doesn't Walk on Water." *BusinessWeek Online.* June 25, 2001. Available from www.businessweek.com.

Crum, Rex. "Nokia Keeps on Keeping on." *Upside Today.* September 19, 2001. Available from www.upside.com.

Fox, Justin. "Nokia's Secret Code." *Fortune.* May 1, 2000.

Jacob, Rahul. "Nokia Fumbles, But Don't Count It Out." *Fortune.* February 19, 1996.

McClenahen, John S. "CEO of the Year." *Industry Week.* November 20, 2000.

Morais, Richard C. "Damn the Torpedoes." *Forbes.* May 14, 2001.

"Nokia Corp." In *Notable Corporate Chronologies.* Farmington Hills, MI: Gale Research, 1999.

SEE ALSO: Communication Protocols; IBM Inc.; Motorola; Real-Networks; Telephony

NOORDA, RAYMOND J.

Raymond J. Noorda, more than any other individual, is widely recognized as the man primarily responsible for the advent of networked personal computers (PCs) in the business environment, shifting PCs from stand-alone tools to interlinked nodes in a larger, more fluid network. While Noorda didn't invent the local area network (LAN), he is considered the figure who created the organization—and the market—in which LANs could achieve critical mass.

Born in Ogden, Utah and raised in the Great Depression by Dutch Mormon immigrants, Noorda worked in various manual labor jobs for several years, contributing to his famous work ethic and frugal living habits; according to *Computer Reseller News,* even as a multibillionaire Noorda maintained a tiny office and flew coach class. After fighting with the U.S. Navy in World War II, Noorda received an engineering degree from the University of Utah and went to work for General Electric. By 1970, Noorda felt he'd accumulated enough experience to strike out on his own, and launched a consulting firm catering to struggling firms.

An electrical engineer by training, Noorda made his name by taking struggling companies and turning them into successful industry powerhouses. Beginning in the 1970s, Noorda rescued a number of notable players, including System Industries, Inc. and Boschert Inc. But he achieved his greatest fame and success at Provo, Utah-based Novell Inc. In 1983, investors coaxed Noorda to serve as chief executive of the troubled three-year-old firm. Noorda quickly took Novell to the forefront of the burgeoning network-software industry, expanding the company beyond its original PC-components manufacturing operations. Novell's bread and butter through the 1980s and early 1990s was its software for local area networks, which allowed companies and organizations to wire their personal computers in networks and reduce their reliance on expensive and bulky back-office mainframes. Novell's nosediving stock price prompted Noorda to retire in 1994, but he maintained a hefty stake in the company's shares, which contributed greatly to his financial health in the late 1990s as Novell shot back up the stock market. In late 1999 *Forbes* estimated the 75-year-old Noorda's wealth at $1.1 billion.

In the early 1990s, Noorda was notorious in industry circles for his very fierce and very outspoken criticism of, and feud with, Microsoft chairman Bill Gates. Noorda's distaste for Gates and Microsoft stemmed from his perception that Microsoft's aggressive tactics in the software industry were greatly harming not only Novell but the industry as a whole, as well as adjacent industries and their consumers. Indeed, Novell was one of the major players responsible for the highly publicized government antitrust investigation of Microsoft in the 1990s. The animosity between Novell—and Noorda in particular—and Microsoft was not without its nuances. In fact, Novell twice attempted to merge with Microsoft, but was rebuffed.

After retiring from Novell, Noorda busied himself with a variety of projects. In the late 1990s and early 2000s, Noorda's activities were channeled primarily through his investment organization, Canopy Group. He invested heavily in several companies aiming to compete with Microsoft by building alternative operating systems to Microsoft's Windows. In September 1999, Canopy Group brought to life Center 7, an electronic business application service provider

(ASP) providing companies with e-commerce tools ranging from databases, Web-based storefronts, and procurement management.

FURTHER READING:

"Beware a Billionaire Scorned." *Economist* (U.S.), March 18, 1995.

Buchok, James. "A Novell Sunset," *Computing Canada,* April 6, 2001.

"Kings of the Code: Rich Computer Programmers," *Fortune,* October 11, 1999.

"Noorda, Ray." *Computer Reseller News,* November 16, 1997.

SEE   Gates, William (Bill); Local Area Network (LAN);
ALSO: Microsoft Corp.; Novell, Inc.; Personal Computer
        (PC), Introduction of the

NORTEL NETWORKS CORP.

Nortel Networks Corp. is world's second largest manufacturer of telecommunications equipment. The Ontario, Canada-based firm spent billions of dollars in the late 1990s investing in Internet technology. The telecommunications industry slowdown that began in North America in 2000 prompted Nortel to take a $19.2 billion loss—the second-largest quarterly loss in worldwide corporate history—in the second of quarter of 2001. The firm also laid off nearly 30,000 employees, cutting its work force by nearly one third.

EARLY HISTORY

In 1882, the Bell Telephone Company of Canada, based in Montreal, founded a manufacturing arm to develop telephone equipment for the company. The new unit had 13 employees. Three years later, the Northern Electric & Manufacturing Co., Ltd. was founded in Canada. Northern Electric took over the making of telephone equipment for Bell Telephone in 1895. Western Electric Co. acquired a minority stake in Northern Electric & Manufacturing in 1906, and seven years later, Northern Electric and Western Electric Co. agreed to share patents.

Northern Electric & Manufacturing Co. merged with Imperial Wire and Cable Co. to form Northern Electric Company, Ltd. in 1914. Bell Telephone retained a 50 percent stake in the new firm, while Western Electric held the remaining shares. Northern Electric continued to grow as a telephone equipment provider throughout the 1920s and 1930s. In the late 1940s, the firm erected a facility to manufacture electronic switchboard and key equipment. Bell repur-

chased the shares of Northern Electric from Western Electric in 1962; as a result, Northern Electric began to operate as a wholly owned subsidiary of Bell. Northern Electric extended its reach overseas for the first time in 1967, when it established a plant in Turkey. The firm also began developing its first switching systems.

EMERGENCE AS A WORLDWIDE TELECOMMUNICATIONS LEADER

In 1971, Northern Electric founded Northern Telecom Inc. as a wholly owned subsidiary to make and market telecommunications equipment in the U.S. The following year, Northern Telecom opened its first U.S. manufacturing plant, a unit in Port Huron, Michigan, that produced telephone sets, key systems, and related equipment. Northern Electric began listing its shares on the New York Stock Exchange in 1975, roughly two years after completing its initial public offering. Northern Electric also expanded its international operations with the creation of Northern Electric of Canada (U.K.) in London, England. Northern Electric Export Corp. was created that year as well. Northern Electric changed its name to Northern Telecom Ltd. in 1976. All of the firm's subsidiaries also changed their names. By the end of the decade, revenues had surpassed $1.5 billion. According to an October 1998 article in *The Financial Post*, the 1970s proved to be a turning point for the firm when its parent company ordered the firm to develop a line of digital switching equipment in an extraordinarily short amount of time. "Bell's customers were telling it that the time had come to switch from analogue to digital technology, which transmits voice traffic after first translating it into the computer language of ones and zeros. Nortel's success in responding to Bell's marching orders ultimately put it on the map as a telecom pioneer, with the world's first complete line of fully digital telecom equipment." The new product line was dubbed Digital World.

In 1981, Northern Telecom launched Displayphone, a telephone model which permitted both voice and data communications to take place in a single unit. That year, the firm began working with AT&T Corp. to develop the DMS-200 system, a long-distance switching system which routed both direct dial and operator-assisted calls between cities. The new system was designed for use in the Bell Telephone network. In January of 1983, MCI purchased 62,000 miles of fiberoptic cable from Northern Telecom to augment its long-distance service between New York and Washington, D.C. The deal marked the largest fiberoptic supply agreement ever reached with a single company. In 1985, when Nippon Telegraph and Telephone contracted Northern Telecom for $250 million worth of DMS-10 switching systems, Northern Telecom became the first non-Japanese telecommunications equipment vendor to serve Japan's public telephone system.

Northern Telecom forged its first major computer-related deal in January of 1986 when the firm began supplying networking equipment for Apple Computer's Macintosh machines. The following year, it acquired a 24 percent stake in British communications and information systems supplier STC. PacTel Communications Co. and Northern Telecom established PacTel Meridian Systems, a joint venture selling and servicing Northern Telecom's Meridian line in California and Nevada, in 1988. The firm strengthened its foothold in Asia that year via an alliance with China's Tong Guang Electronics Corp.

The lines between the telecommunications and computer industries began to blur for Northern Telecom in the early 1990s as the firm began developing products that targeted both markets. For example, Northern Telecom unveiled Meridian TeleCenter, a software productivity tool that linked its digital lines with Macintosh machines, allowing users to use their computers for phone calls. In 1991, Northern Telecom, South Central Bell, Apple, IBM Corp., and ADC Telecommunications began working on a distance learning project dubbed the Mississippi 2000; eventually, the program connected four high schools to institutes of higher learning to allow video-based computer instruction over the public telephone network. The firm also acquired the shares of STC plc it did not already own. The following year, Motorola Corp. and Northern Telecom agreed to work together to sell and service cellular telephone networks in Canada, Central and South America, the Caribbean, and the U.S.

The Republic of Tunisia awarded a $40 million telecommunications equipment contract to Northern Telecom in 1994. The firm also secured a $100 million telecommunications equipment contract from the builders of a personal communications systems (PCS) network in the U.K. Northern Telecom changed its name to Nortel in 1995; eventually research and development design groups were consolidated into a single division, Nortel Technology. International growth continued with the creation of a unit in Moscow, Russia. In a contract valued at $1 billion, Sprint Spectrum LP hired Nortel in 1996 to develop PCS networks. The following year, Telewest Communications PLC hired Nortel to produce digital hierarchy transmission equipment.

FOCUS ON THE INTERNET

When CEO John A. Roth took the reins of Nortel in 1997, the firm "was in danger of being eclipsed by fleet-footed rivals serving up Net gear," wrote *Busi-*

nessWeek Online columnist Joseph Weber. Recognizing this, Roth began working to transform the telecommunications equipment giant into a maker of cutting edge Internet equipment. Nortel launched an acquisition spree in 1998, buying Broadband Networks Inc., Aptis Communications, Inc., and Cambrian Systems Corp. The firm also completed its largest deal to date, paying $6.9 billion for Bay Networks, Inc., the world's third largest data and Internet networking equipment vendor. According to Weber, "Bay brought Nortel top-notch technology, setting it up to compete in a brave new world where phone and data networks are fast converging."

In the late 1990s, Nortel began to release several Internet-based products. For example, the Meg-1 modem allowed telephone companies to offer high-speed Internet access to consumers. The firm's Succession system combined traditional telephone equipment with Internet gear, appealing to clients wanting to gradually increase their Internet capabilities. E-commerce products and services included online configuration, as well as ordering and support. In 1999, Nortel added Shasta Networks, Inc., X-CEL Communications, Ltd., and Periphonics Corp. to its holdings. The firm also paid $2.1 billion for Clarify Inc., a customer relationship management software manufacturer. In an effort to boost electronic sales of its products and services, Nortel revamped its Web site. That year, Sweden's national telephone company, Telia, hired Nortel over rival Cisco Systems Inc. to develop Internet-based voice and data equipment for a national network. Similarly, Nortel beat out Lucent Technologies Inc. to supply equipment for a fiber network Jazz Telecom Inc. was erecting in Spain. Purchases continued into 2000 with the acquisition of Dimension Enterprises, Inc., an engineering and business strategy consulting firm; Australian-based Photonic Technologies; Xros, Inc., a switching concern; and CoreTek, Inc., an optical components firm. The $7.8 billion purchase of Alteon WebSystems brought with it the Web switching equipment many analysts predicted would be in great demand. In May of that year, Bell Telephone sold off its remaining 35 percent stake in Nortel to a newly formed holding company, Nortel Networks Corp.

STMicroelectronics paid $100 million for Nortel's semiconductor manufacturing operations in 2001. Nortel revealed plans to increase its European workforce by 10 percent, creating 2,000 high-technology jobs, primarily in the U.K., Ireland, France, Germany, Italy, and Spain. However, when telecommunications spending slowed drastically later that year, the firm actually began cutting jobs. The inventory Nortel had been building in anticipation of increased growth suddenly became a major liability. In the second quarter of 2001, Nortel posted a $19.2 billion loss as it wrote off billions of dollars in excess inventory. The number of layoffs eventually reached 30,000, and Nortel began selling off non-core units, such as its Access Solutions high-speed Internet access products. Like most other telecommunications firms, Nortel planned to outlast the industry downturn, which was predicted to continue well into 2002.

FURTHER READING:

Boyd, Jade. ''September 25, 2000—Nortel's Pain.'' *Internet-Week,* June 25, 2001.

Hochmuth, Phil. ''Nortel's Alteon Play Gets Mixed Results.'' *Network World,* July 30, 2001.

Hooper, Larry. ''Is the Sky Falling at Nortel.'' *Computer Reseller News,* June 18, 2001.

''Nortel Goes from Fab Four to Gaynor.'' *Fiber Optics News,* July 30, 2001.

''Nortel Networks Corp.'' In *Notable Corporate Chronologies.* Farmington Hills, MI: Gale Research, 1999.

''Nortel Pays Price for Dotcom Folly.'' *South China Morning Post,* June 17, 2001.

''Nortel's Pain Deepens; $19.2 Billion Loss for Second Quarter Takes Suffering to a New Level.'' *Telephony,* June 25, 2001.

''Nortel's Web Sights—Part 2.'' *The Financial Post,* October 17, 1998.

Weber, Joseph. ''Racing Ahead at Nortel.'' *BusinessWeek Online,* November 8, 1999. Available from www.businessweek.com.

NOVELL INC.

Novell Inc. is best known for its network server platform, Netware, which links desktop computers with corporate networks. Throughout the 1980s and early 1990s, Novell's NetWare was the leading server platform, eventually gaining a 65-percent market share. However, competition from Microsoft Corp.'s Windows NT, and from Linux—a network operating system created by volunteers—had pushed Netware into third place by the late 1990s. Novell currently is working on Netware 6, which will offer increased Internet storage management functions. It plans to finalize a shift in focus to Web-based solutions in 2002.

Novell Data Systems Inc. was founded as a personal computer (PC) manufacturer in 1980. The fledgling company spent the majority of its capital on hardware design, leaving minimal funds for advertising. Within two years, Novell found itself near bankruptcy. Realizing that it would be unable to afford leasing a booth at Comdex, the premier tradeshow of the computer industry, the firm instead displayed its products in a hotel room. Impressed by Novell's products, 58-year-old electronics engineer Raymond J. Noorda invested $125,000 of his personal savings and borrowed $1.3 million from investors to purchase a 33-percent stake in the young company. The long-time General Electric executive also took over as president. Believing Novell's most promising product was an operating system that enabled PCs to share peripherals such as printers and disk drives on a local area network (LAN), Noorda refocused the firm on networking technology. After changing its named to Novell Inc., the company developed Btrieve, the first multi-user database application for LANs. It also released a software package for UNIX-based computers.

In 1984, Novell released software for networks using Ethernet, a system created by Xerox Corp. and manufactured by rival 3Com Corp. The firm completed its first acquisition with the 1985 purchase of Microsource Inc. That year, Novell also developed networking technology for Microsoft's new DOS 3.1 platform, introduced software that allowed Apple's Macintosh computers to run on Ethernet networks, and conducted its initial public offering. Novell paid $4.1 million for Santa Clara Systems Inc., a data storage systems and LAN products maker, in 1986. The acquisition brought Novell closer to its goal of offering comprehensive network systems. In 1987, sales reached $222 million. Two years later, the firm released its blockbuster Netware 386 network server, which was compatible with Windows, UNIX, and Macintosh platforms.

Merger negotiations with PC software giant Lotus Development Corp. fell through in 1990. That year, Novell established Novell Japan Ltd., a joint venture with Canon Inc., Fujitsu Ltd., NEC Corp., Sony Corp., and Toshiba Corp. that sold NetWare products in Japan. Novell benefited from strained relations between IBM and Microsoft in 1991, when IBM agreed to market Netware in an effort to limit Microsoft's increasing control over PC standards. In other deals, both Hewlett-Packard Corp. and Compaq Computer Corp. agreed to work with Novell to develop and market computer-networking technologies for their machines. Acquisitions that year included Digital Research Inc. for $136 million and a five-percent stake in AT&T Corp.'s UNIX System Laboratories. Novell and UNIX also founded Univel, a joint venture that developed UNIX-based products. Noorda restructured Novell into three units: NetWare; general operations; and a division working on the development of extensive corporate networks that would later become known as intranets.

Lotus and Novell agreed to increase the compatibility of Netware and the Lotus Notes networking software in 1992. By then, Novell had become the world leader in computer networking. Its products included operating software, network management software, hardware, and services. Novell acquired UNIX System Laboratories from AT&T in 1993. Eventually, the UNIX operations were folded into Novell's Netware division. NetWare 4.0 was shipped that year. In 1994, Novell paid $1.4 billion in stock for Word-Perfect, a leading word processing software maker. The firm spent another $145 million on the spreadsheet operations of Borland International, which formed the basis for the Quattro Pro spreadsheet. Robert J. Frankenberg was named CEO, chairman, and president.

Taking a huge loss, Novell sold WordPerfect and Quattro Pro—both of which were struggling to compete with Microsoft's word processing and spreadsheet programs—to Corel Corp. for $186 million in 1996. The firm then refocused on its core network platform operations. Sun Microsystems Inc. licensed its Java platform for use with NetWare. Frankenberg was succeeded by John Young as chairman and Joseph Marengi as president. That year, Novell began focusing on developing technology for the Internet. To this end, it forged alliances with other firms and improved network connections with NetWare Embedded Systems Technology. Novell Inc. and Japan's Nippon Telegraph & Telephone Corp. launched a data networking service for Japanese companies. Eric Schmidt was appointed CEO in 1997. According to an August 2000 article in *The Economist,* he began working to "transform the company from a provider of traditional networking programs into a force in the promising 'net services' business: software for and delivered by the Internet."

In 1998, the firm acquired minority stakes in Evergreen Internet, GlobalCast Communications, NetPro Computing, and NetVision. The following year, computer security software maker Network Associates Inc. (NAI) agreed to work with Novell on technology to shield NetWare users from the increasing number of computer viruses. Novell, Sun, and CMGI established a joint venture in 2000. The new firm began working on ways to enhance Internet performance and increase a Web site's ability to gather information on visitors and use it to deliver customized content. In an effort to cuts costs, the firm laid off 900 workers. It also began beefing up its service offerings. To this end, Novell agreed to pay $266 million for Cambridge Technology Partners in March of 2001. When the deal is finalized, Cambridge CEO Jack Messman will take the reins at Novell.

FURTHER READING:

Berinato, Scott; and John S. McCright. "Mea Culpas, Closed Windows—Cover Story: Novell Admits Its Failures and Missed Opportunities As It Radically Reinvents Itself—Again." *PC Week.* January 17, 2000.

Fox, Pimm. "Novell's Tragic Tale." *Computerworld.* September 25, 2000.

Langley, Nick. "Novell's Reinvention Pains." *Computer Weekly.* January 11, 2001.

"Novell Inc." In *Notable Corporate Chronologies.* Farmington Hills, MI: Gale Group, 1999.

"Novell—Promises, Promises." *The Economist.* August 26, 2000.

Rooney, Paula. "Microsoft, Novell Eye Services Too." *Computer Reseller News.* June 18, 2001.

SEE ALSO: Compaq Computer Corp.; Hewlett-Packard Co.; IBM Inc.; Linux; Local Area Network (LAN); Lotus Development Corp.; Microsoft Corp.; Noorda, Raymond J.; UNIX

NOYCE, ROBERT

Robert Noyce was one of the giants of 20th century high-tech science and the multi-billion dollar business it spawned. Along with 15 other patents, he was a co-inventor of the integrated circuit, a device former National Science Foundation Director Erich Bloch called "the key invention of the 20th century." In addition to his contributions to computer technology, Noyce co-founded two of the most influential companies in the computer industry, Fairchild Semiconductor and Intel. Those companies in large measure established the region around Palo Alto and San Jose, California—now universally known as Silicon Valley—as the premier area for computer research, development, and manufacture; and earned Noyce the nickname "the Mayor of Silicon Valley." For the last decade of his life, Noyce was an outspoken advocate of the American microprocessor and computer industry and actively lobbied in Washington for measures that would protect American companies from the threat of unfair Japanese competition. He died in 1990.

EARLY LIFE

Robert Norton Noyce was born in Burlington Iowa on December 12, 1927. He grew up, the son of a Congregationalist minister, in nearby Grinnell, Iowa. As a boy he tinkered with machines and chemistry; in later life he identified his origins as the roots of his inventiveness. "In a small town," he told writer Tom Wolfe, "when something breaks down, you don't wait around for a new part, because it's not coming. You make it yourself." In 1948, while Noyce was studying at Grinnell College, his physics teacher, Grant Gale, obtained two of the first transistors in the world, and began teaching the first college class in solid state electronics anywhere. Noyce was captivated by the subject, and went on to do Ph.D. work on it at the Massachusetts Institute of Technology (MIT).

With degree in hand in 1953, Noyce went to work for vacuum tube maker Philco Corp. for three years. He finally left to join Shockley Semiconductor Laboratory in Mountain View, California, where William Shockley, one of the inventors of the transistor, was pursuing cutting-edge research on four-layer diodes. Although Noyce acknowledged Shockley as the ''guru, after whom the disciples. . .followed,'' the Nobel Prize winner was both difficult to work with and had different ideas than Noyce and others about the most promising directions for research.

In 1957, Noyce and seven colleagues, left Shockley's company. With the assistance of venture capitalist Arthur Rock and funding from the Fairchild Camera and Instrument Company, they founded a new company, Fairchild Semiconductor. The ''Gang of Eight'' set up shop in an old warehouse in Mountain View, down the road from Shockley's lab. It was a time of growing interest in transistors for consumer goods; government interest in research was driven by the Soviet's launch of *Sputnik*. In that climate, Fairchild was poised for great things. One of Noyce's first projects was to develop a simple means around the complicated wiring together of individual transistors. Noyce's idea was to put all the transistors onto a single piece of silicon without any wires. The result was the first silicon integrated circuit in mid-1959. It came just months after Texas Instruments' Jack Kilby invented one. After a protracted patent battle, the two men were recognized as co-inventors. The integrated circuit was a key technology that made possible other inventions ranging from the pocket calculator to the onboard computers used by NASA in their moon shots.

INTEL TAKES SHAPE

Noyce was named Fairchild's General Manager in 1959, and under his leadership the firm's sales rose from less than $10,000 a year to over $130 billion in 1968. By then, Noyce was ready to form his own company. With Gordon Moore, another Shockley defector, and venture capitalist Arthur Rock, Noyce founded Intel Corporation, the firm that almost single-handedly made possible the personal computer revolution of the 1980s and 1990s. In the early 1970s, working on the relatively neglected area of computer memory, Noyce, Moore, and Intel developed a string of innovations: the 1103 memory chip; the 4004 CPU chip, considered the world's first microprocessor; the 8080, the first 8-bit microprocessor; the 8086, a 16-bit microprocessor.

It was also at Intel that a genius for business that equaled his genius for electronics came into full flow-

er. Already developed at Fairchild, he established a company culture he called a ''meritocracy,'' in which there was virtually no traditional hierarchy, no executive parking spots, and no isolated offices. Researchers were given nearly complete autonomy over their projects. At Intel Noyce established the stock option, rather than profit-sharing, as a means of fostering a spirit of innovation among employees. Perhaps because of his roots in the Congregational faith, Noyce insisted on completely ethical business practices at Intel. Of this achievement Tom Wolfe has written: ''Noyce managed to create an ethical universe within an inherently amoral setting: the American business corporation in the second half of the twentieth century.''

PURSUING BROADER GOALS

During the 1980s, Noyce turned to lobbying, urging Washington to take steps to protect the American computer industry from unfair foreign competition, especially from Japan, which was closing its market to American computer products while dumping its goods below cost in the United States. Noyce helped found the Semiconductor Industry Association and served as its first president. In 1988 he agreed to move to Austin Texas to head Semtech, a research consortium of fourteen semiconductor companies established to narrow the gap between the semiconductor manufacturing technology in the U.S.A. and Japan. He continued to work at forging partnerships between the government and the computer industry, activities that were controversial and of only limited success in his lifetime. By April 1990 he had begun to withdraw from running Semtech's day-to-day operations.

RECOGNITION OF ACHIEVEMENTS

Robert Noyce won every major honor in his field, short of the Nobel Prize. He received the AEA Medal of Achievement in 1974, the IEEE Medal of Honor in 1978, the I.E.E. Faraday Medal in 1979, the National Medal of Science in 1980, and the National Medal of Technology in 1987. He was a co-recipient of the AFIPS Harry Goode Award for leadership in computer science, the Ballantine Medal of the Franklin Institute, the Cledo Brunetti Award of the IEEE for inventing the integrated circuit, and the National Academy of Engineering's first Charles Stark Draper Prize. He was inducted into the National Inventors Hall of Fame in 1983 and the U.S. Business Hall of Fame in 1989.

Robert Noyce married Elizabeth Bottomley in 1953. They had four children together, and were divorced in 1974. Later in 1974 Noyce married Ann Bowers. Active all his life, Noyce was an avid swimmer, skier, hang glider, and pilot. He died suddenly of a heart attack on June 3, 1990 at his home in Austin Texas.

FURTHER READING:

Kehoe, Louise. ''Natural Leader With a National Purpose.'' *Financial Times* (London), June 12, 1990.

Ladendorf, Kirk. ''Electronics Legend Robert Noyce Dies.'' *Austin American-Statesman,* June 4, 1990.

Lydon, Jim, and Richard McCausland. ''Industry Mourns Death Of Robert Noyce, 62.'' *Electronic News,* June 11, 1990.

Richards, Evelyn. ''In Noyce's Passing, An Era Also Ends; Electronics Pioneer Symbolized A Swashbuckling, Innovative Age.'' *Washington Post,* June 5, 1990.

Sprackland, Teri. ''Robert N. Noyce: 1927-1990.'' *Electronic Business Buyer,* June 25, 1990.

Wolfe, Tom. ''The Tinkerings of Robert Noyce.'' *Esquire,* December 1983.

SEE ALSO: Intel; Moore, Gordon

O

OFFICE OF ELECTRONIC GOVERNMENT

While businesses raced to embrace the Digital Age and use its myriad innovations to develop winning business strategies, governments increasingly considered how to utilize information technology, and particularly the Internet, to better fulfill their traditional roles for citizens as well as to develop new services particular to the social, economic, and political realities of the 21st century. As more and more Americans spend greater proportions of their time online, and as they come to expect information and services to be available at the click of a mouse, governments, to be effective and responsive to their constituents, faced mounting pressures to overhaul and streamline their systems and processes to include information technologies, Internet-based services, and Web-based interfaces. The U.S. federal government thus spent the late 1990s and early 2000s devising new strategies to provide Americans with the information they need at their computers, and to implement tools whereby routine civic tasks—from paying taxes to applying for grants to checking visa information—could be conducted from anywhere with an Internet connection.

Originally called the Office of Electronic Commerce, the U.S. Office of Electronic Government is the main federal body devoted to using the Internet to promote electronic-based information and services to U.S. citizens. Operating under the General Services Administration, the Office of Electronic Government provides a general framework for various governmental departments and agencies to communicate with and provide services to citizens, businesses, contrac-

tors, as well as government employees and other government entities.

According to the Office, the concept underlying e-government was to move government away from a passive orientation toward citizens in favor of a more proactive approach, whereby government agencies come to citizens online with the full range of information and service offerings to which citizens are entitled. In this way, Americans can derive the fullest and most satisfying level of service from the government and most effectively take advantage of the democratic process.

Three separate teams comprise the Office of Electronic Government. The Electronic Government Strategy and Development Division coordinates the activities of various federal agencies and departments with the aim of identifying methods by which the shift to electronic government may proceed and implementing complementary strategies and policies related to the role of electronic communications in governmental services. The Electronic Business Technologies Division focuses on the technical aspects of implementing e-government solutions on a cross-agency basis. Specifically, this division helps foster alliances between agencies and departments designed to further electronic access to and interaction between federal agencies and their constituencies. Finally, the Electronic Acquisition Systems Division is charged with the development, operation, and maintenance of governmental acquisition policies, practices, tools, and information.

Several pieces of federal legislation in the late 1990s furthered the goals and principles of the Office of Electronic Government. For instance, the Government Paperwork Elimination Act of 1998 (GPEA) mandated that federal agencies offer online services and transactions as an alternative to their paper counterparts by October 2003. Meanwhile, the Electronic Signatures in Global and National Commerce Act of 1999 (E-SIGN) furthered the cause of electronic transactions in general by ruling that electronic signatures are as legally binding as traditional written signatures, and that electronic transactions may not be legally discriminated against.

The Office of Electronic Government strove to live up to the following core goals and principles: interoperability between government agencies and with industry partners; provision of citizen-oriented services as opposed to department-centered template services; development of user-friendly online portals that allow citizens to quickly and easily find the information they seek; strong security measures to ensure the integrity of information passed between citizens and the government; overhauling of paper-based processes to take advantage of the efficiency of electronic communications; and further promotion of electronic information-sharing via inter-agency governmental leadership.

FURTHER READING:

U.S. Government Services Administration. Office of Electronic Government. "eGov Home Page." Washington, D.C., 2001. Available at egov.gov.

OMIDYAR, PIERRE

Pierre Omidyar is the founder and chairman of eBay.com, the world's largest online auction site, with more than 22 million registered users and roughly 8,000 product categories. As chairman, Omidyar is responsible for planning the company's future direction and growth, as well as developing its business model and the Internet site itself. He holds a 27 percent stake in eBay.

After earning an undergraduate degree in computer science from Tufts University, Omidyar cofounded eShop, an online shopping forerunner eventually bought out by Microsoft Corp. He also worked as a software developer for Apple Computer's Claris and communications software maker General Magic Inc. The idea for eBay.com emerged in 1995 when Omidyar's girlfriend Pamela, an avid collector of Pez candy dispensers, expressed her desire to interact with other collectors in their area. Recognizing that the Internet could help make this possible, the 31- year-old Omidyar created Auction Web, a rudimentary online auction site which simply allowed sellers to post

items for sale by describing the merchandise, setting a minimum bid, and choosing the length of the auction, which could range anywhere from three to ten days. Buyers could then bid on an object, and the highest bidder at the end of the auction was able to purchase the object for the bid price. Payment and delivery were handled by the buyer and seller. At the time, the site offered no search engine, no guarantees of any type regarding the merchandise sold, and no dispute resolution services. Omidyar's marketing efforts consisted of simply listing Auction Web on a "What's Cool" site operated by the National Center for Supercomputing Applications.

The following year, as site traffic grew well beyond his expectations, Omidyar quit his job at General Magic and began focusing on Auction Web full time. Omidyar worked on improving the technology, while his partner, Jeff Skoll, drew up a business plan. Auction Web began charging a small fee, including a commission based on the final price, for each item listed for sale. With overhead costs at a minimum since the entire auctioning process was automated, Omidyar's business became profitable very quickly, setting it apart from other Internet ventures. By the middle of 1996, the site had roughly 5,000 users who expressed their likes and dislikes about Auction Web on message boards. Their main complaint had to do with the anonymity of the process, which made it easy for sellers to mislead buyers about an object. Buyers also had no recourse once they paid for an object, even if they never received it from the seller. Based on this user feedback, Omidyar created the Feedback Forum, which allowed buyers and sellers to rate one another.

In September 1997, Omidyar changed his site's named to eBay. Revenues for that year neared $6 million, and traffic continued to grow exponentially. Realizing that he needed help managing what was becoming one of the most highly trafficked sites on the World Wide Web, Omidyar sold a 22 percent stake in eBay to Benchmark Capital for $4.5 million. Benchmark began recruiting an experienced management team, eventually hiring Margaret Whitman as CEO. To prepare the firm for its initial public offering, she began increasing its advertising efforts. For example, Whitman oversaw eBay's $12 million, three-year marketing agreement with America Online Inc. (AOL), who agreed to list Ebay as the preferred provider of person-to-person auction services. On September 24th, Omidyar and Whitman took eBay public, watching its shares jump from $18 apiece to $50 apiece in a matter of minutes. Within two months, share prices reached $100. The number of registered users climbed by the end of 1998 to 1.2 million. Sales soared 724 percent to $47.4 million.

In 1999, Whitman and Omidyar began expanding eBay by launching sites in the United Kingdom and Canada. They also spearheaded efforts to begin selling more expensive merchandise on site. To this end, they launched several regional sites, which they believed would facilitate trading of larger items, such as vehicles and musical instruments, that were difficult and expensive to ship. By year's end, the number of registered users reached ten million, with daily visitors averaging nearly two million. eBay listed more than three million items for sale. Despite competition from the likes of Yahoo! and Amazon.com, who launched their own auction sites, eBay continued to thrive in late 2000 and early 2001. According to a May 2001 article in *BusinessWeek Online*, this was because "in the world of Pez dispensers, critical mass counts. If you want to sell something, you want to go to the place where you'll find the most buyers. Because eBay built its storefront first, it quickly achieved critical mass. Even when Yahoo! offered sellers commission-free auctions and Amazon offered buyers quality guarantees on merchandise purchased through its auctions, the crowds failed to come. eBay had already won the war."

FURTHER READING:

Banks, Brian. "The Silicon Billionaire." *Canadian Business,* July 30, 1999.

eBay Inc. "Company Overview." San Jose, CA: eBay Inc., 2001. Available from pages.ebay.com.

Jaffe, Sam. "Online Extra: eBay: From Pez to Profits." *BusinessWeek Online,* May 14, 2001. Available from www.businessweek.com.

Lee, Jeanne. "Why eBay is Flying." *Fortune,* December 7, 1998.

Roth, Daniel. "Meg Muscles eBay Uptown." *Fortune,* July 5,1999.

SEE ALSO: Auction Sites; eBay Inc.; Whitman, Margaret

OPEN SYSTEMS

Database management systems, operating systems, solutions used to manage the performance and operation of computer networks, and a host of other software programs are key elements in the world of information technology. Without them, e-commerce would not be possible. These critical systems and applications are developed by large, powerful companies like Microsoft, as well as by the cooperative efforts of developers, users, and enthusiasts with like interests and concerns. In the latter scenario, the resulting systems are said to be open, because the source code (the instructions that serve as their foundations) on which they are built is not proprietary or controlled by a central organization; it is freely available to developers and end-users, including companies seeking to build custom e-commerce solutions. In addition to critical system software, the Internet and World Wide Web have been called open systems because of their development and control is distributed among millions of users.

Both approaches have inherent advantages and disadvantages. In May 2001, Craig Mundie, Microsoft's senior vice president of advanced strategies, denounced open-systems development. According to *CIO,* during a speech at New York University's Stern School of Business, Mundie argued: "The open source development model leads to a strong possibility of 'forking' a code base, resulting in the development of multiple incompatible versions of programs, weakened interoperability, product instability, and hindering business' ability to strategically plan for the future. Furthermore, it has inherent security risks and can force intellectual property into the public domain." Mundie's comments angered members of the open source community who were quick to point out that innovative open systems were being used successfully by many software developers.

It has been argued that open systems further competition because the technology behind them is not proprietary. More parties are then able to develop applications and components for them. This can work to the system's benefit because more perspectives contribute to its development. When more developers are able to provide input about a system, it becomes easier to fix flaws and bugs that hinder performance; roll out improvements; increase the speed of system evolution; and combine an application's components in new and exciting ways not intended by the original developer.

In the early 2000s, the Open Source Initiative (OSI) was a non-profit organization that offered an open source software certification mark and program to developers. Through its program, OSI managed and promoted the Open Source Definition (OSD) for the public good. The OSD set forth specific criteria that true open source software needed to meet, including the availability of a program's source code and the absence of restrictions pertaining to free redistribution. The OSD sought to present and clarify what the software community as a whole defined as open source, since the term was being used rather widely and in different contexts.

One example of open source software is the freely distributed and cooperatively developed operating system called Linux, which in the early 2000s was a popular, stable platform for running networks, including Web servers, e-mail servers, and domain name servers. Like many open systems, Linux is universal and functions on many different platforms, including Macintosh and IBM-PCs. Compared to more expensive operating systems, Linux was an economical alternative for cost-conscious companies that needed to quickly create Web-based applications or support programs used for e-commerce. Linux is very similar to UNIX—another open system that is vital to e-commerce. Like Linux, UNIX is used to run many Web servers and computer workstations. More specifically, it is a popular system to use for processing Web-based transactions. Behind the system's popularity are characteristics like scalability, dependability, manageability, security, and availability. UNIX was created for use by researchers and scientists during the 1970s, but collaboratively evolved into a powerful business tool. In 2001, UNIX became the foundation for Macintosh's OS X operating system.

FURTHER READING:

Heller, Martha. "Does the Open-Source Movement Hurt Innovation?" *CIO,* May 17, 2001. Available from comment.cio.com.

Liebmann, Lenny. "Network Management Goes Open Source." *Communications News,* April 2001.

Patrizio, Andy. "Unix: Not Just for Geeks Anymore." *InformationWeek,* March 5, 2001.

SEE ALSO: Linux; UNIX

OPRAH.COM

Oprah.com, launched by world renowned talk show host Oprah Winfrey in June 1997, operates as part of the Oxygen Media Group's online division. It is the official Web site of The Oprah Winfrey Show and *O, The Oprah Magazine.* The site also offers information on Oprah's Book Club and Oprah's Angel Network and vows to help women "Live Their Best Life" by giving advice on relationships, food, mind and body, and lifestyles. Web surfers visiting Oprah.com—the site averages more than 155 million hits per month and 3,000 e-mails per day—can subscribe to Winfrey's magazine, see post-show discussions via streaming video, write in an online journal, chat with other online Oprah fans, and even e-mail Oprah Winfrey herself.

The Oprah Winfrey Show, which debuted in 1986, gained unprecedented popularity within a few years of its first airing and quickly became the most successful and highest-rated talk show in all of television. In 1995, Winfrey teamed up with America Online (AOL) to provide her online viewers with Oprah

Online, an AOL site dedicated to information about her show. Two years later, ABC Internet Group and Winfrey's company, Harpo Productions, created Oprah.com to provide Web surfers information on the show, its guests, and a variety of other topics including its famed book club and the Angel Network. The site also allowed those who could not watch the show during the day access to information about its topics and provided an easy way for viewers to communication with the show's staff.

In 1998, Winfrey formed Oxygen Media LLC, a company dedicated to providing entertainment and information to modern women. Oxygen Media included Harpo Group LLC, GBL LLC, and Carsey-Werner-Mandabach LLC. The media group eventually included a cable network and several online properties including Thriveonline, Moms Online, Girls On, and ka-Ching. Oprah.com joined the Oxygen.com group of Web sites in August 1999.

Oprah.com's popularity continued to grow as more women began using the Internet. According to Forrester Research, 29 percent of all American women—compared to 39 percent of American men—were using the Internet on a regular basis in 1999. By 2005, the firm predicted that more than 71.2 million women would be online. Forrester also predicted that the average annual growth rate over the next five years for women would be 19 percent—compared to 13 percent for men. As more women went online, researchers found that sites most often patronized by women were those relating to health and quality-of-life issues. Oprah.com was able to use the success of the popular television show to tap into the increasing number of female Web surfers, turning the Web site into the one of the most popular online destinations for women. In fact, Winfrey herself encouraged women to become Web savvy by promoting the Oxygen production "Oprah Goes Online" on Oprah.com. The 12-part series detailed the steps she and friend Gayle King took in learning how to use the Internet themselves.

Oprah.com, primarily known for its informative Web content, slowly entered the arena of e-commerce when Winfrey began using Oprah.com to promote *O, The Oprah Magazine.* By late 2000, visitors to the site were able to subscribe to the magazine and hear messages from Winfrey in specialized sections of the Web site that included Here We Go, What I Know for Sure, and Oprah's Cuts, which featured excerpts from magazine interviews. The Oprah's Book Club section of the site also was popular. It was rated as one of the top 10 places to find literary information on the Web by Galaxy.com, a vertical Internet directory. While visitors were not able to purchase book club selections directly from Oprah.com, many used the information on the site to make purchases elsewhere.

Oprah.com also featured the O List, a myriad of Winfrey's favorite products including everything from vases to bath salts to tin plates. The list included links to the product's Web site or information on how and where the listing could be purchased.

In June 2000, Oprah.com was rated the top TV show Web site by PC Data. Winfrey was contracted through the 2003-2004 television season, securing the Web site's position as a leading online destination for women, which like Winfrey's daytime show continued to work toward her vision of empowering women across the globe.

FURTHER READING:

"Data Zone: Top TV Show Web Sites." *Electronic Media.* August 7, 2000.

Donahue, Dick, and Daisy Maryles. "Oprah Yet Again." *Publishers Weekly.* October 18, 1999.

Greenberg, Paul A. "Gender Gap Narrows As Women Take to the Net." *E-Commerce Times.* November 9, 1999. Available from www.ecommercetimes.com.

"Need an Oprah Fix? Now She's on Your PC." *BusinessWeek Online.* November 5, 1998. Available from www.businessweek.com.

"The Oprah Winfrey Show Fact Sheet." Chicago, IL: Oprah.com, 2001. Available from www.oprah.com.

Schneider, Mica. "Go to Oxygen.com If You Can Never Get Enough Oprah." *BusinessWeek Online.* November 24,1999. Available from www.businessweek.com.

"Top Ten Literature Web Sites Announced." *PR Newswire.* September 29, 2000.

SEE ALSO: Women and the Internet

OPTICAL SWITCHING

The Internet structural backbone's total carrying capacity in the early 2000s was expected to fulfill only a minuscule portion of tomorrow's requirements. With Internet traffic accelerating exponentially and fiber-optic networks facilitating cheaper and faster transmissions, optical switching was the grand prize for telecommunications firms and Internet operators seeking to keep the bandwidth capabilities of the Internet commensurate with growing demand.

The specific purpose of the switches is to route transmissions in the telecommunications network from one point to another. Optical switches send data packets along their route to one destination or another without stopping to convert their signals into electrons, thereby saving time and taking full advantage of the fiber-optic network. Optical switches, in other words, never even touch the transmission itself; they just direct it on its way. Optical switching was slated to replace electronic switching, the traditional means of transmitting telecommunications signals. In the network configuration most widely used in fiber optics in the early 2000s, fiber-optic transmissions were routed through electronic switches, which impeded the capabilities afforded by fiber optics since the signals required conversion into electrons and then back into photons, thereby slowing the speed of the transmission. Optical switches promise to lower the cost of telecommunications, boost transmission speeds, and enhance the quality of signals.

The primary impetus for the development of optical switching was increasing demand for network capacity. While, on the one hand, the Internet provided unprecedented access to a wealth of information very quickly, it conversely created a shortage of patience as users came to expect faster and faster connection speeds. As more and more people accessed the Internet through the 1990s and early 2000s, the demand for faster connections only grew. Businesses, especially, demanded greater network capacity to facilitate quick and efficient transaction speeds and thereby generate sales and maintain customers. To eliminate the bottlenecks that cause connection delays, Internet operators and telecommunications firms increasingly turned to optical switching to fulfill the promise of fiber-optic telecommunications. The technology for optical switching was developing at an astonishing rate. According to *Scientific American,* the speed of optical fiber transmissions, measured in bits per second, doubles every nine months, twice the rate of improvement for computer chips popularized by Moore's Law.

The fiber itself is a tiny glass core surrounded by a layer of "cladding," both designed with a specific degree of refraction, the degree to which it bends light. The fiber receives the transmission from a laser or light-emitting diode. As the photons travel through the fiber, the signal is amplified by fibers infused with erbium, restoring the signal to its original strength at high speed. Moreover, this amplification system, developed in the 1990s, can amplify the wavelengths of multiple signals simultaneously. Dense wavelength division multiplexing (DWDM), as this process is known, was a key breakthrough for optical switching, because it enables the transmission of large numbers of signals down a single fiber without compromising speed or creating bottlenecks, greatly reducing telecommunications costs and boosting speed and clarity.

Analysts expected that the Internet of the near future will utilize optical switching as the basis for the creation of seamless integrated networks that will transmit all traffic over the same fiber connection and provide alternate routes for traffic to traverse when one channel breaks down. The net result, enthusiasts insist, will be a faster, more convenient Internet.

FURTHER READING:

Alpert, Bill. "Seeing the Light." *Barron's,* December 4, 2000.

Cope, James. "''et There Be [Network] Light." *Computer World,* May 22, 2000.

"Fiat Lux." *The Economist,* February 5, 2000.

Rendleman, John. "Infrastructure—Innovators and Influencers 2001: Optical Switching's Evangelist." *Information Week,* January 1, 2001.

Stix, Gary. "The Triumph of the Light." *Scientific American,* January, 2001.

SEE ALSO: Fiber Optics; Moore's Law; Next Generation Internet Initiative (NGI); Photonics

ORACLE CORP.

Oracle Corp. is second only to Microsoft Corp. among the world's leading software companies. Best known for its database systems, Oracle became a major e-commerce player in the late 1990s when it unveiled Oracle 8i, a version of its mainstay database program that allows all of a firm's database functions to be handled on the World Wide Web. In 2001, Oracle 9i helped more than 8,500 firms across the globe manage their data on a variety of operating systems.

EARLY HISTORY

In 1977, computer programmers Lawrence J. Ellison and Robert N. Miner co-founded a software firm, named Oracle Systems Corp., in Belmont, California. With their combined experience designing specialized database programs for governmental organizations, the men convinced the Central Intelligence Agency (CIA) to award them a $50,000 contract to develop a customized database program. Ellison and Miner also began developing and marketing database management systems (DBMS) software for business clients. Ellison, as president and CEO, headed up sales and marketing efforts while Miner oversaw software development. Well known venture capitalist Donald L. Lucas served as chairman of the board.

While working on the CIA project, Ellison became interested in IBM's efforts to develop a relational database that would allow computer users to retrieve corporate data from a variety of sources using Structured Query Language (SQL). Believing SQL would emerge as a standard language in the database industry, Ellison and Miner began working on developing a similar program for minicomputers. In 1978, the fledgling firm unveiled Oracle RDBMS, the world's first relational database using SQL. One year later, Oracle began shipping RDBMS, beating IBM to the market by nearly two years. With 24 employees and a customer base of 75, the company reported annual revenues of nearly $2.5 million in 1982. Approximately 25 percent of those revenues were earmarked for research and development. That year, international expansion efforts resulted in the founding of Oracle Denmark.

In 1983, Oracle developed the first portable RDBMS, which allowed firms to run their DBMS on various machines including mainframes, workstations, and personal computers. The product boosted annual sales to more than $5 million. By the mid-1980s, Oracle had become known for both innovative technology and competitive advertising. Ellison and Miner took their company public in 1986. By that time, sales had reached a record $55.4 million and Oracle was recognized as one of the world's fastest-growing software companies. The company's rapid growth came in large part from its ability to develop applications that worked across the previously incompatible computer systems of large corporations. New product launches included a distributed DBMS. Based on SQL-Star software, the system granted users the same kind of access to data stored on a network they would have if the data were housed in a single computer.

By 1987, the number of software companies using Oracle products as a foundation for their applications had grown five-fold. As a result, the firm created a value-added reseller (VAR) alliance program as a means of fostering cooperative selling and merchandising relationships with other software makers. At the same time, Oracle also became the relational DBMS of choice for most major computer manufacturers, and the firm continued to develop software compatible with an increasing number of hardware brands. Sales exceeded $100 million. With more than 4,500 end-users spanning 55 countries, Oracle ranked as the largest database management software company in the world.

New products in 1988 included the Oracle Transaction Process Subsystem, a software package designed to speed processing of financial transactions. This new program allowed the firm to target banks and other financial institutions. Further diversification came with the launch of a line of accounting programs, including a database designed to work with the Lotus 1-2-3 spreadsheet program. The company also unveiled a line of computer-aided systems engineering (CASE) application development tools, including CASE Dictionary and CASE Designer products, and its first version of a DBMS program for Macintosh systems. That year, Oracle established a new subsidiary called Oracle Complex Systems Corp. to offer systems integration services to its clients. Services like these eventually came to account for half of the firm's revenues.

SLOWING GROWTH

Diversification efforts continued in 1989 when Oracle established Oracle Data Publishing, a subsidiary focusing on creating and marketing reference material and other information electronically. That year, Oracle was included for the first time on Standard & Poor's 500 index. Believing its intense growth pace would continue, Oracle sought $100 million in public capital. In 1990, when the firm experienced its first quarter of poor earnings, stock prices dropped from $25.38 to $17.50 in a single day. Several shareholders filed suit against the firm, alleging that management had issued misleading earnings forecasts. In the wake of this negative publicity, Oracle made public its intent to audit operations and reshuffle management. Larry Ellison assumed the additional post of chairman, while Lucas remained a director. When the internal audit results were made public, prompting the firm to restate earnings for the first three quarters of 1990, Oracle's stock plummeted to $11.62 per share. To protect itself from hostile overtures, the firm's board implemented a poison pill, or stockholder rights plan, that would make takeover attempts much more expensive. Oracle also scaled back its annual growth rate targets from 50 percent to 25 percent and eliminated 10 percent of its employees. The milestone achievement in 1991 of reaching $1 billion in sales was marred by Oracle's first ever annual loss, which totaled $12.4 million.

FOCUSING ON THE INTERNET

Oracle and Hewlett Packard began working on an interactive TV system for Pacific Telesis in 1995. That year, Oracle established Oracle Store, a Web site that allowed the firm to electronically delivery its products to clients. The firm released Oracle Express Server 6.0 in 1996. This Web-enabled server supported the Windows NT operating system and offered complete online data analysis via both the Web and corporate intranets. Oracle also began working on its network computer, a simplified and less expensive machine that facilitated easier access to the Internet, which many analysts believe prompted industry giants like Intel and Microsoft to focus on developing desktop systems that were much simpler to manage.

In 1998, Oracle began to restructure itself around its Internet operations. According to *BusinessWeek*

Online columnist Sam Jaffe, "Back then, some experts argued that the database software market Oracle dominates would quickly erode as companies found cheaper and simpler ways of managing their data on the Web. Instead the opposite happened—after CEO Larry Ellison ordered an 'Internetization' of his company." The firm eventually released Oracle 8i, a program allowing firms to manage all of their database functions on the Web.

Oracle also began using its e-business products to streamline its own operations. It merged its order fulfillment and shipping networks with its sales network to manage customer relations from a single source. A Web-based expense reporting system allowed the accounts payable department to cut its staff by 25 percent and deposit paychecks into employee bank accounts more quickly. Oracle's e-mail system was restructured to run on two servers and four databases, rather than 97 servers and 120 databases. As the firm began to cut its costs and improve its operating margin (from 21 percent in 1999 to 30 percent in 2000), Oracle began using improved performance as a marketing tool for its Web-based database products. However, several analysts asserted that things like layoffs had more to do with the higher margins than the technology itself.

In 2000, Oracle continued to develop new Internet-based technology. In May, the firm launched its E-Business Suite. According to *Forbes* writer Elizabeth Corcoran, "Instead of selling separate packages for sales force automation, accounting, employee benefits and so on, Oracle ties together 70 'modules' in a package and juices them up with Internet technologies." Also launched that year, the Oracle 9i software database management system included an application server allowing users to run e-commerce applications related to their databases. Thanks to this new technology, Oracle managed to outperform many of its competitors through the end of 2000, although the technology sector's slowdown finally seemed to catch up with the firm in March of 2001, when it announced that database software sales were sluggish and application server sales were slipping.

FURTHER READING:

Corcoran, Elizabeth. "Oracle: Walking the Talk." *Forbes.* January 8, 2001.

Cox, John. "Oracle Eats Its Own E-business Dog Food." *Network World.* July 17, 2000.

Doyle, T.C. "The Oracle Economy: Warning Lights are Flashing—The Company Must Outline What the Opportunity for Integrators Will Be." *VARbusiness.* April 2, 2001.

Jaffe, Sam. "Oracle: A B2B Rebirth That Few Foretold." *BusinessWeek Online.* April 6, 2000. Available from www.businessweek.com/technology.

"Oracle Corp." In *Notable Corporate Chronologies.* Farmington Hills, MI: Gale Research, 1999.

Slywotzky, Adrian. ''Four Lessons From Larry: Ellison Was Late in Reshaping Oracle for the Net. But When He Did It, He Did It Fast. Here's How.'' *Fortune.* March 5, 2001.

Tebbe, Mark. ''We May Not All Buy NCs, But We Can Thank Ellison for Manageable PCs.'' *InfoWorld.* June 23, 1997.

SEE ALSO: Database Management; Ellison, Lawrence J. (Larry)

ORDER FULFILLMENT

Success in the realm of e-commerce requires more than an appealing Web site and a compelling advertising campaign. Attracting online customers is important, but delivering an enjoyable, hassle-free buying experience is another key factor. Online fulfillment is a cornerstone of e-commerce, encompassing all of the steps involved in purchasing a product, from order placement and billing to packaging, shipping, and sometimes beyond.

A DIFFERENT GAME

Companies sell their products in different ways. Some provide wholesale products to other businesses or distributors for re-sale. Others sell directly to consumers, and some use a combination of both approaches. E-commerce spending is expected to exceed $3 trillion by 2003, according to *Warehousing Management,* and the potential for additional revenue has lured companies in all of these categories to the Web.

In the process, those attempting to sell directly to consumers quickly discovered that online order fulfillment differs in many ways from traditional fulfillment models used for brick-and-mortar stores. Rather than shipping relatively small numbers of large orders to retail chains or distributors, high volumes of smaller orders for individual consumers must be processed. This presents a new set of requirements for retailers, such as providing customers with real-time information about available products in inventory. Once a product is ordered, successful companies provide shipping and order confirmations, notices about problems, and other real-time, up-to-the-minute details. As explained in *World Trade,* ''Today's customers want to know a lot about their order: whether it's in stock, when it was shipped, where it is, and how soon they'll get it. Statistics say that Internet customers typically check on their order seven times before they receive it.''

Having the ability to offer information of this nature to consumers is easier said than done. To do so,

companies not only need to make sure all of their systems—including accounting and shipping—are able to handle high volumes of consumer orders efficiently, they also must make sure the systems are integrated. As explained in *InfoWorld,* ''Retail success hinges on what happens behind that fabulous Web site: logistics and fulfillment, payment systems, systems and policies to handle returns, customer service, and, running through it all, integration. Without these the site won't scale, and customers who once loved the Web store will quickly turn fickle and point their browsers elsewhere.''

Integration allows data from one order to be shared instantly, in real-time between multiple areas of the organization, including the billing, shipping, marketing, and customer service departments. If systems aren't connected, the movement of data and the fulfillment process slow down.

HOW THE FULFILLMENT PROCESS WORKS

The way fulfillment happens differs from company to company, but many aspects of the process are similar among successful e-tailers. Fulfillment begins after marketing efforts bring potential customers to a company's Web site. At this very early stage, companies take steps to make sure products are easy to find and order. Some e-tailers offer chats with customer service representatives or lists of frequently-asked questions to make this process unfold smoothly.

When consumers select products for purchase online, they often place them into a virtual shopping cart—technology that keeps track of items consumers are interested in until they are done shopping. When items are added to a shopping cart, the Web site may automatically check a company's inventory for availability. Otherwise, out-of-stock items may not even appear on the Web site.

Immediately before a consumer actually submits an online order, shipping and freight charges are often calculated and displayed. If the charges are excessive, this may cause the order to be abandoned. After a customer provides their name, address, and payment information during the order submission, the data is shared with appropriate areas throughout the company almost instantly. If a credit card is used, the number is verified before payment is authorized. The customer's name, street and e-mail addresses might be sent to the marketing department for use in future campaigns, to customer service in case the customer contacts the company with questions or concerns, and to the shipping and receiving department.

Next, the company's warehouse is notified about the new order. If a company has several warehouses or distribution centers in different regions of the country, the order is sent to the one closest to the consumer, taking inventory and workload issues into account. When an order is received on the Web, workers might be notified on handheld devices via a wireless computer network and directed to perform different tasks in order to pack, label and prepare items for shipment. In the early 2000s, companies relied on warehouse management software (WMS), overhead scanners, conveyor belt systems, wireless computer networks, wearable computers, hand-held bar code scanners and portable printers to streamline operations and automate the movement of goods through their warehouses. The way such technologies were used was complex and varied depending on the warehouse or distribution center. However, in general they eliminated the need for human involvement for tasks like checking incoming shipments against paper purchase orders and figuring out where incoming shipments need to go in a warehouse (to inventory or to another dock for immediate delivery).

Eventually, the packaged product makes its way to the loading dock, where a carrier like United Parcel Service (UPS) or Federal Express (FexEx) handles delivery. Those retailers with regional or national networks of physical stores are able to use them as a strategic advantage, whereby goods ordered online are available for pickup at nearby retail locations. This saves consumers money on shipping, and also makes it easier for them to return unsatisfactory products. In the early 2000s, one national convenience store chain was considering contracting with different pure-plays (retailers who sell exclusively online) so its stores could be utilized as locations for online order pickups.

At some point in the process, an e-mail confirmation is sent to the consumer, providing details about the order (product descriptions, model numbers, quantities, colors or sizes) and outlining how the package is being delivered. Information about the company's return policy may be included in the e-mail. A tracking number also may be provided so the consumer can check on the delivery status of their order and stay informed about the date and time it will be delivered. The entire process—from Web order to the shipping dock—can happen in a matter of minutes or hours if an efficient system is in place. But the fulfillment process doesn't always end at the dock. If customers order groceries or large items like appliances, which require them to be home for delivery or setup, a company may enable communication between drivers from its own fleet and the customer.

Online fulfillment allows companies to tie manufacturing more closely to actual demand, thereby reducing storage space and financial resources associated with large inventories. If a company doesn't manufacture its own products but resells goods from other manufacturers (such as a sporting goods e-tailer), an effective high-speed fulfillment network will allow it to see inventory and supply information from one or more trading partners, giving them the ability to spot supply shortages before they cause problems. Additionally, by using special software, companies can forecast demand and make necessary adjustments for seasonal or cyclical fluctuations.

HOW COMPANIES MANAGE FULFILLMENT

The generalized fulfillment process outlined above reveals the many steps and technical systems involved in delivering a positive customer experience. Often, this is too difficult or costly for companies to handle independently. In order to focus on what they do best—developing and marketing new products, for example—retailers often turn to third parties to handle the fulfillment process on their behalf. Because they focus exclusively on fulfillment, third parties often are able to perform this function more effectively and efficiently. According to *Logistics & Distribution Report,* a large number of *Fortune* 500 companies had outsourced transportation, inventory and warehouse management by the late 1990s. In 1999, third-party logistics contracts grew by 16.5 percent, with total revenues of $46 billion. Growth rates of 15 to 20 percent were expected through 2003.

When a third-party fulfillment provider is used, a company usually continues to manage its own Web site, but everything that happens after an online order is submitted is handled by the third party. Third-party fulfillment companies come in all shapes and sizes and vary in the services they offer. Most offer the ability to process orders, manage inventories in a warehouse and ship products, but some provide customer service via phone or e-mail, printing, e-commerce services, assembly, promotional fulfillment, and more. All are invisible to consumers, meaning that when they ship goods on behalf of a retail client, packages normally carry the client's logo.

Transportation & Distribution divided third-party fulfillment companies into three categories—physical infrastructure providers; technology providers; and integrators, which offer the services of both physical infrastructure and technology providers.

Physical infrastructure providers store and manage inventories for their clients, distribute products for them and provide value-added services, including customer support and the handling of returned merchandise. Technology providers, unlike physical infrastructure providers, don't warehouse products or handle shipments on behalf of clients. Instead, they provide the technical systems that are used to link trading partners together, including the processing of credit card information.

TRANSPORTATION COMPANIES GET INVOLVED

Leading transportation companies like United Parcel Service and FedEx began to play more involved roles in e-commerce during the early 2000s. Going beyond the delivery of packages, each company established business units focusing on the fulfillment aspect of e-commerce. UPS created a subsidiary called e-Ventures to identify, test, and launch new e-commerce-related businesses within the company. The first such business to emerge from e-Ventures was UPS e-Logistics, a business unit that offered clients "turnkey supply chain management solutions," by taking advantage of its transportation and warehouse networks. The services it offered included inventory management, shipping and delivery, warehousing, order fulfillment (pick, pack and ship), management reporting, customer care and telephone support, and returns management. UPS previously offered similar services to large corporate customers like Nike.com.

In May 2000, FedEx Logistics announced that its FedEx Supply Chain Services, a third party provider of supply chain solutions, had created FedEx eLogistics—a new division focusing on providing e-commerce logistics solutions to businesses. According to Doug Witt, then vice president and general manager of new division, FedEx Supply Chain Services helped customers to decrease cycle times, improve the management of returns, and lower fulfillment costs.

FULFILLMENT PROBLEMS

E-commerce moves at a fast pace. Marketing, sales, ordering, packaging and shipment all can happen in a manner of minutes or hours. Fulfillment problems arise when a breakdown or bottleneck occurs at some point in the process. Before the Internet, companies could often hide inefficient fulfillment systems, but with e-commerce this is not possible. Among the reasons e-tailers experience problems with order fulfillment are a lack of integration and poor forecasting.

When a company's Web site is not integrated to its other back-end systems, such as accounting or inventory, fulfillment happens slowly. In such a situation, orders come in quickly via a company's Web site and then sit for days or weeks waiting to be manually re-entered by someone into another system. The chance for human error also becomes a problem because product codes, prices, shipping addresses and more can be accidentally altered. When companies do a poor job of forecasting, they often fail to deliver on the promises of product availability and fast shipping made in advertisements. The failure to look ahead and

plan for seasonal or cyclical spikes and dips can lead to embarrassing inventory shortages and inadequate warehouse staffing.

FURTHER READING:

Aichlmayr, Mary. "From Data to Delivery: Finding Fulfillment in e-business." *Transportation & Distribution.* November 2000.

Arntzen, Bruce. "Fulfillment Partners in the Internet-driven Supply Chain." *Transportation & Distribution.* November 2000.

Burnson, Patrick. "The Logistics of e-fulfillment." *Logistics Management & Distribution.* September 2000.

Christensen, Doug. "Delivering on the Promise of 'E'." *World Trade.* December 2000.

"Deliverance." *Chain Store Age.* August, 2000.

Enslow, Beth. "Internet Fulfillment: The Next Supply Chain Frontier." Descartes Systems Group. Available from enslow.ASCET.com.

"FedEx Logistics Forms New eLogistics Division." FedEx. May 3, 2000. Available from www.fedex.com/us/about. November 2000.

Richardson, Helen. "Streamlining Fulfillment with Automation." *Transportation & Distribution.* January 2001.

Scheraga, Dan. "The Nightmare Before Christmas." *Chain Store Age.* March 2000.

"UPS e-Ventures." United Parcel Service of America, Inc. March 15, 2001. Available from www.eventures.ups.com.

SEE ALSO: FedEx Corp.; Fulfillment Problems; Shipping and Shipment Tracking; Supply Chain Management

OUTSOURCING

In the 1990s and into the beginning of the twenty-first century, technological advancements continued to develop at breakneck pace. This was especially true of the Internet technologies used during e-commerce. Keeping up with all these developments and making solid, informed decisions about them became difficult or impossible for many companies, who needed to focus most of their resources on core business competencies to be successful. For this reason, it was common for organizations to outsource, or have other vendors handle, different aspects of their e-commerce initiatives.

Even leading international companies with large departments devoted to information technology (IT) often find it more cost-effective to outsource certain aspects of e-commerce rather than develop the expertise themselves, which can require hiring scarce workers and investing large sums to train and retain them. Accordingly, it's not surprising that a survey from CommerceNet found nearly 75 percent of e-commerce firms outsourced parts of their work in early 2001, or had plans to do so. Eighty-seven percent of the companies surveyed viewed outsourcing as an effective way to scale their business offerings based on fluctuating revenue streams.

OUTSOURCING EXAMPLES

While it's possible for a company to outsource virtually any kind of service, in the early 2000s several were especially common in the e-commerce arena. Among them were IT management; logistics and order fulfillment; Internet video production, management, and distribution; customer relationship management; and Web site development and hosting. The ease and cost efficiency of handling different aspects of e-commerce in-house was easier and more cost-effective for some companies than it was for others, so companies outsourced services differently.

Many companies looked to outside parties to handle online order fulfillment (filling and shipping orders they received via the Internet) instead of building or renting their own warehouse operations, which required special expertise for e-commerce. This freed them to focus on core competencies like creating new products and services, and marketing. *Logistics & Distribution Report* indicated that many *Fortune* 500 companies were outsourcing transportation, warehouse management, and inventory management by the late 1990s. In 1999, third-party logistics contracts grew by 16.5 percent, and revenues totaled $46 billion. According to the publication, growth rates were expected to reach 15 to 20 percent by 2003.

When companies rely on third-party fulfillment providers, they normally manage the front end of e-commerce (the content and appearance of their Web site) and leave the rest to the third party. In other words, the third party receives orders from customers, manages the inventory of available products in its warehouse, and coordinates shipping. Some also provide value-added extras like customer service.

Another example of outsourcing involves application service providers (APSs), third parties who manage business applications for companies so they can focus more on their core business. These applications often involve things like payroll, billing, and customer service. The software systems offered by the ASP are sometimes Web-based, so that client companies do not have to host the software and devote resources to maintaining and updating them. Although ASPs held the potential to simplify things for client companies, they also moved long-held control over internal systems and data to outside parties, which made some organizations uncomfortable.

THE FUTURE OF OUTSOURCING

According to a March 2001 survey conducted by Merril Lynch, chief information officers in the United States and Europe were planning to scale back IT spending on outsourcing, among other areas of IT. However, despite this indication of possible cutbacks, the market for outsourcing was substantial. *IT Outsourcing Market Forecast,* a study from market research firm Input, projected that the information technology outsourcing market would grow 22 percent annually between 1998 and 2003, reaching $110 billion.

However, as with any kind of business practice, the use of outsourcing as an approach will vary depending on the service involved. For example, the future of outsourcing looked especially positive in the area of customer relationship management (CRM)—database systems companies use to maintain details about their customers, including their contact information and preferences for products and services. A July 2001 Harte-Hanks survey found more than 80 percent of companies in North American were outsourcing the task of building and maintaining their CRM systems. On the other hand, *Frontline Solutions* cited results from an Aberdeen Group survey that indicated outsourcing business-to-business software applications was not as promising. Although more and more software applications were available from ASPs, Aberdeen's survey of the Oracle Applications Users Group found that less than five percent were using ASPs, and 82 percent were not planning a strategy involving them.

FURTHER READING:

Chow, Elsie. "Outsourcing E-commerce Fulfillment." *Warehousing Management,* December 2000.

"CommerceNet: Most E-commerce Firms Outsource Work." *Nua Internet Surveys,* April 30, 2001. Available from www.nua.ie.

"CyberAtlas: U.S. Firms Prefer to Outsource CRM." *Nua Internet Surveys,* July 9, 2001. Available from www.nua.ie.

"E-marketplaces Remain Erratic." *Frontline Solutions,* May 2001.

"Input: Outsourcing Worth USD110 billion by 2003." *Nua Internet Surveys,* October 6, 1999. Available from www.nua.ie.

King, Julia. "E-commerce Solution: Let Someone Else Sell Your Product." *Computerworld,* November 13, 2000.

SEE ALSO: Application Service Provider (ASP); E-commerce Consultants; E-commerce Solutions

P

PACKARD, DAVID

David Packard, along with fellow Stanford University graduate William Hewlett, founded California-based Hewlett-Packard Co. (HP) in 1939. Due in large part to their revolutionary management practices, Packard's and Hewlett's brainchild grew from a small testing-device manufacturer into the world's second largest computer company, behind IBM Corp., with nearly 85,000 employees and annual revenues in excess of $48 billion.

Packard was born in Pueblo, Colorado, in 1912. He studied radio engineering at Stanford University, where he met Hewlett. General Electric Co. hired Packard as an engineer in 1936, but two years later, Packard resigned and returned to Stanford to pursue a graduate fellowship. That year, with $538 in capital, he and Hewlett started a business in Packard's one-car garage. Stanford professor Frederick Terman advised the partners to market a resistance capacity audio oscillator—a sound equipment tester—that Hewlett had created as a graduate student. Packard and Hewlett named their first major product the HP 200A. The fledgling partnership's first major order came when Walt Disney requested eight of the new oscillators for the production of *Fantasia*. In January of 1939, Packard and Hewlett officially named their business Hewlett-Packard Co. The order of their names had been decided by a coin toss, which Packard lost.

When HP incorporated in 1947, Packard was appointed president. It was during the late 1940s, that Packard and Hewlett, who was serving as vice president, began putting in place the management practices that would later earn them recognition as the pioneers of Silicon Valley. According to *Computer Reseller News* columnist Jeff Bliss, ''The best talent at Eastern institutions such as the Massachusetts Institute of Technology and Bell Labs took notice, and the Western migration of the country's technological brain trust began. The environment awaiting these scientists, teachers, and engineers could not have been more conducive to encouraging technology.'' These practices—which eventually became known as the ''HP Way''—included an Open Door Policy that was created to help facilitate frequent, comfortable, and candid communication between employees and management. Employees worked in open cubicles, while the offices inhabited by managers had no doors. Packard and Hewlett also frequently walked through their facility, making themselves as accessible as possible to employees.

Packard took HP public in November of 1957. He also created a set of written objectives for HP, believing that a tangible mission would help ensure all employees were working toward the same goals. The following year, Packard oversaw HP's first acquisition, a maker of graphics recorders. In addition, he steered the firm's initial international growth efforts, which included the establishment of a manufacturing plant in Germany and a European headquarters office in Geneva, Switzerland, in 1959. By the end of the decade, Packard and Hewlett had put in place a highly decentralized structure that would endure for the next forty years. Each of HP's autonomous divisions oversaw its own research and development, manufacturing, and advertising activities. To help the firm retain its entrepreneurial climate despite rapid growth, Packard and Hewlett also decreed that each time a division's employee count exceeded 1,500, the division would be divided into two separate entities.

Hewlett replaced Packard as president in 1964. Packard spent the next three years serving as chairman and CEO. He left HP in 1969 to serve the Nixon administration as Secretary of Defense. After returning to the firm in 1971, Packard was reappointed HP's chairman. Although he had resigned as Secretary of Defense, Packard continue his governmental work throughout his career. From 1975 to 1982, he was a member of the science and technology committee of the U.S.- U.S.S.R. Trade and Economic Council. In 1985, Ronald Reagan named him chairman of the Blue Ribbon Commission on Defense Management. He also served on the President's Council of Advisors on Science and Technology between 1990 and 1992.

One year after Packard's return to HP, the firm launched the world's first scientific pocket calculator, the HP 35. HP also began its foray into computers when it unveiled the HP 3000 minicomputer. By that time, the firm had become one of the first to eliminate time clocks, to grant employees a flexible work schedule, and to add profit sharing to compensation packages. HP created its first personal computer, the HP-85, in 1980, and its first desktop mainframe machine, the HP 9000, in 1982. Two years later, HP created its most successful product ever, the LaserJet printer. While Packard was not at the helm of operations when these blockbuster products were shipped to market, he did help to create an atmosphere that fostered the development of new technology.

In 1990, after earnings dipped nearly 11 percent, Packard decided to take a more active role in HP's daily operations. Roughly 3,000 employees were laid off. In 1991, earnings rebounded, reaching $755 million on revenues of $14.4 billion. Two years later, Packard retired as chairman. He served HP as chairman emeritus until his death in 1996.

FURTHER READING:

Akin, David. ''Hewlett Helped Define Silicon Valley Success.'' *National Post,* January 13, 2001.

Bliss, Jeff. ''William Hewlett.'' *Computer Reseller News,* November 16, 1997.

Hewlett-Packard Co. ''David Packard.'' Palo Alto, CA: Hewlett-Packard Co., 2001 Available from www.hp.com.

''Hewlett-Packard Co.'' In *Notable Corporate Chronologies.* Farmington Hills, MI: Gale Research, 1999.

O'Hanlon, Charlene. ''High-Tech Visionary—David Packard.'' *Computer Reseller News,* November 13, 2000.

SEE   Hewlett, William R.; Hewlett-Packard Co.
ALSO:

PALM INC.

Founded in 1992 by Jeff Hawkins and Donna Dubinsky, Santa Clara, California-based Palm Inc. is a leader in the handheld computing industry. In the early 2000s, the company produced five different lines of handheld computers, also known as personal digital assistants (PDAs), for consumers and businesspeople: the Palm m100, Palm III, Palm V, Palm m500, and Palm VII. Although thousands of different software programs were available for these PDAs from different independent developers, Palm's devices came with pre-installed programs for productivity and managing personal information. These included a calculator, to-do list, memo pad, expense manager, date and address books, games, and more. Users also enjoyed a backlit screen for operating in dark conditions, the ability to send information from their device to other PDA users via an infrared beam, and a cradle that allowed them to synchronize data on their PDA with desktop software on their personal computer (PC) or a corporate network. This synchronization was possible through technology known as HotSync, developed by Hawkins.

Palm has an expansive global reach, selling products in more than 35 countries. According to a July 2001 market analysis and forecast from International Data Corp, Palm held 55.9 percent of the global market for personal companion handheld devices. In the area of handheld operating systems, its global market share totaled 71.8 percent.

Skokie, Illinois-based U.S. Robotics Corp. acquired Palm Computing Inc. in 1995 and made it a subsidiary. At the time, Palm created software—including applications for handwriting recognition and file transfer—for PDAs manufactured by other companies, including Tandy Corp.'s Zoomer PDA. However, soon after it became a part of U.S. Robotics, Palm unveiled its own PDAs. The pen-based Pilot 1000 and Pilot 5000 were released in March of 1996, and were powered by Palm's own operating system, Palm OS. Critics pointed out that Palm's first PDAs were lacking in communications capabilities and didn't include keyboard functionality. However, the Pilot 1000 received *PC Computing's* MVP Usability Achievement of the Year Award.

The company had an eventful year in 1997, with revenues totaling approximately $114 million. In March, U.S. Robotics introduced Network HotSync technology that enabled users to connect to computer networks or their computer desktops using an optional snap-on modem. In May, Palm became a subsidiary of 3Com Corp. when U.S. Robotics was acquired by 3Com. According to *CNET News.com,* the deal, which involved $6.6 billion in stock and resulted in a new company with revenues of $5 billion, was "the largest U.S. data networking merger" at that time. 3Com Chairman and CEO Eric Benhamou retained his role with the new organization, and U.S. Robotics Chairman and CEO Casey Cowell was named vice chairman. The year ended on a positive note when the company received awards for its products from *InformationWeek* and *Newsweek*. Finally, Palm announced that it would license its Palm OS platform to other manufacturers.

In 1998, revenues increased to approximately $272 million. That year, the company released the Palm III handheld. Palm co-founders Jeff Hawkins and Donna Dubinski also left the company that year. According to *Fortune,* the two departed "over frustration that 3Com wouldn't spin off the handheld starlet." After leaving, Hawkins and Dubinsky started Handspring, which would evolve into one of Palm's top competitors. Handspring's first handheld product, the Visor, used the Palm OS. Slightly after one year of operations, Handspring had captured 21 percent of the market. Subsequently, Palm's market share shrank from 83 percent to 63 percent, according to *Fortune.*

Approximately 3,500 loyal developers were creating applications for the Palm OS by the end of 1998. Palm's products remained popular and were being adopted in a variety of new markets including healthcare, where doctors used the devices to capture information from patients; and the financial sector, where traders were testing an application that allowed them to view desktop data while on the trading floor. In December, the company won its second MVP Award from *PC Computing.* However, competition was heating up from Microsoft, which had introduced its Windows CE platform for handheld computers the previous year. A number of manufacturers, including Casio Computer Co., Hewlett-Packard Co., and Compaq Computer Corp., were selling devices powered by Windows CE.

Despite Microsoft's presence in the marketplace, things continued to go well for Palm in 1999. That year, revenues totaled approximately $563 million. The company introduced a bevy of new PDAs, including the Palm IIIx and Palm V (February), Palm VII (May), Palm IIIe (July), and the Palm Vx and Palm IIIe Special Edition (October). It also cemented a number of partnerships with companies like Sun Microsystems, TRG, Computer Associates International Inc., and mobile phone manufacturer Nokia. In the May 1999 issue of *Upside,* 3Com Chairman and CEO Eric Benhamou described the company's core focus as, "The Internet is just a set of technologies that has made this possible. . . So 3Com is about connecting people to information, and we do it in more ways across more networks than anyone else. We do

it for large businesses, small businesses, ISPs, consumers; we do it across wires, across wireless networks; we do it locally; we do it remotely; but the common theme is connectivity."

The Palm VII was especially noteworthy because it allowed users to access the World Wide Web and corporate networks via a wireless connection. Along with the new device, Palm created new technology as part of its Palm.net Web service. Known as "Web clipping," the technology allowed Palm VII users to visit participating Web sites and access the most relevant information from them. (Palm devices were not suitable for viewing full-featured Web pages.) Many leading sites took measures to make their content accessible in this format. Among them were ABCNEWS.com, Amazon.com, ESPN.com, E*TRADE, Ticketmaster, Travelocity, UPS, and The Weather Channel. The new Palm VII also had wireless messaging capabilities. However, to take advantage of these features, users were required to subscribe to Palm.net wireless Internet service.

Around the time it unveiled the Palm VII, Palm was a handheld product market leader. According to IDC, in May 1999 the company held 73 percent of the U.S. market and more than 68 percent of the global market for such devices. In addition to its dominant position, in June 1999 Palm's developer base, which totaled about 3,500 just six months earlier, mushroomed to more than 13,500. Finally, ending the year on a high note, the PalmPilot received *Business Week*'s Design of the Decade award in the gold category.

Carl Yankowski was named Palm's CEO in December 1999. He was brought in by 3Com CEO Eric Benhamou to improve morale after the departure of the firm's co-founders and manage the company's transition from a hardware focus to a software focus, particularly by licensing Palm OS to other companies. Prior to joining Palm, Yankowski, who graduated from MIT, held positions with several leading companies including Sony, Reebok, and Polaroid.

In 2000, Palm's revenues reached approximately $1.1 billion. Several noteworthy developments occurred during the year. First, the company introduced several new models of handheld computers. It unveiled the Palm IIIc and Palm IIIxe in February, followed by the enhanced wireless Palm VIIx and a new version of the Palm m100 in July. The company's developer base also continued to grow at a rapid pace, reaching 41,000 developers in March; 65,000 in April; and 100,000 in September. In March of 2000, Palm Inc. filed its initial public offering (IPO) and became an independent company traded on the NASDAQ stock exchange. The spin-off from 3Com was officially completed that July, at which time Palm was named to the S&P 500. In addition to going public, other significant events for Palm during 2000 included the acquisition of two companies—AnyDay.com in May and Actual Software in June. Palm also formed Palm Computing K.K., a Japanese subsidiary, to roll out Japanese versions of its products.

A variety of new applications for Palm's handhelds emerged in 2000. Most gleaned their usefulness from the wireless Internet connectivity made possible by the Palm VII. For example, in January 2000 advertising agency ORB Digital provided its clients with Palm VII devices so they could track the results of their Internet advertising campaigns in real time from virtually any location. By using the agency's ORBit Express 2000 software, users could view a variety of information about their ads, including click-through rates and impressions. Around the same time, a company called Vindigo introduced a free downloadable program that provided users with reviews and directions to New York City restaurants, shopping venues, and movies. Finally, Britannica.com offered Palm VII users access to the content on its Web site through a free program called Britannica Traveler. In addition to manually searching for content, users also could automatically obtain information about their surroundings by taking advantage of the Palm VII's geographical positioning capabilities, which interfaced with Britannica's database.

In 2000, Palm also began to venture into the enterprise market. It introduced HotSync Server software that allowed companies and organizations to manage handheld computers at the network level. Instead of synchronizing devices to an individual PC, users were able to do so with a server, either within the organization at any number of terminals, from PCs remotely connected to the company's network, or via a wireless connection. In fall 2001, Microsoft also was attempting to enter this market.

In 2001, Palm's developer base reached 140,000 and the company's products continued to find new markets as it drew in revenues of approximately $1.6 billion. New product introductions included the Palm m105, m500, and m505. However, Palm was forced to lay off workers due to the worsening economy and declining market share, which slipped from 75.9 percent in April 2000 to 63 percent in April 2001, according to *Business 2.0.*

In mid-2001 *Network World* indicated that "next-generation handheld computers" were on the horizon for 2002. Powered by advanced microprocessors, these new devices would have the ability to more effectively process images, sound, and video. According to the publication, Palm was to license part of its operating system to computer chip manufacturers. The decision was viewed as a good one in light of the developments taking place with advanced chips, and was one sign that Pam would remain a dominant force in a highly competitive industry.

FURTHER READING:

"3Com Acquires U.S. Robotics." *CNET News.com,* February 26, 1997.

Cox, John. "Palm Bolsters Processing Power." *Network World,* July 30, 2001.

Doler, Kathleen. "Interview: Eric Benhamou, Chairman and CEO of 3Com Corp." *Upside,* May 1999.

Lashinsky, Adam. "Is Handspring Really the Second Coming of Palm?" *Fortune,* May 15, 2000.

Moore, John Frederick. "Handheld Pioneer Must Now Fight Serious Fiscal Battles, After a Botched Product Transition and April Sales Gains by Pocket PC Rivals." *Business 2.0.,* June 6, 2001.

Palm Inc. "Company Information." Santa Clara, California: Palm Inc. November 5, 2001. Available from www.palm.com.

Simons, John. "Has Palm Lost Its Grip?" *Fortune,* May 28, 2001.

SEE ALSO: Personal Digital Assistant (PDA)

PARTNERSHIPS AND ALLIANCES

Businesses continually form strategic alliances and partnerships with other firms, many times competitors, for a variety of reasons such as growing product and service offerings, gaining access to new markets, and working together on new product developments. The motivation behind alliances and partnerships in the e-commerce arena includes gaining access to cutting-edge technology, building content offerings on a Web site, and attracting more online visitors. In fact, many of the leading e-commerce players owe their dominant positions to successful alliances and partnerships.

Yahoo! is the world's busiest Internet portal, with more than 100 million visitors every month. The reason for the site's intense level of traffic, according to *Advertising Age*, is co-founder Jerry Yang's efforts to create a "destination where Web surfers could get whatever they wanted from the site's personalized content, e-commerce offerings, special promotions, and other interactive data." Yang did this by continually forging alliances with companies as a means of offering new products and technology to users. For example, Yahoo! diversified into Internet access services a few years after its inception by teaming up with AT&T Corp. to offer Internet access through AT&T's WorldNet Service. A 1999 alliance with Motorola Inc. allowed Yahoo! to expand into wireless Internet service. Another deal with TIBCO Software Inc. allowed the firm to launch Corporate My Yahoo!

in its first attempt to target corporate clients. In November of that year, Northpoint Communications and Yahoo! began jointly promoting broadband services such as digital subscriber line (DSL) to residential and business Internet users. Kmart Corp., SOFTBANK Venture Capital, and Yahoo! worked together to launch BlueLight.com, a free Internet access service, in December. The following year, Yahoo! partnered with growing online search engine operator Google Inc., agreeing to make Google.com its default search results provider.

Internet service provider (ISP) Earthlink used alliances and partnerships in an effort to reach its goal of becoming the largest independent ISP. For example, in August of 1995 the company greatly expanded its service area via a deal with UUNET Technologies. According to the terms of the agreement, Earthlink was able to use UUNET dial-up access numbers to offer service in nearly 100 U.S. cities. In February of 1998, the firm combined its ISP services with those of Sprint Corp. As a result, Earthlink strengthened its position in the ISP market and gained access to Sprint's extensive base of customers. The firm also convinced Apple Computer to use Earthlink software as the default Internet access application on its newly launched iMac computer. In similar deals, both Packard Bell and NEC Ready Computers made Earthlink the default ISP on their computers in late 1998, just in time for the upcoming holiday season. These partnerships—the most successful in Earthlink's history—secured more member sign-ups than any other marketing promotion to date. A similar alliance with U.S. computer retailer CompUSA made Earthlink the chain's official ISP, giving Earthlink access to CompUSA's customer base and inclusion in CompUSA advertisements.

With more than 1 million customers by the start of 1999, Earthlink continued to pursue alliances aimed at growth. In 2000, Sprint allowed the company to use its DSL network to offer high-speed Internet access to customers for the first time. In addition, Earthlink and UUNET jointly launched nationwide DSL access to consumers, and both Micron Millenna and Phoenix Technologies added Earthlink software to their new computers. Continuing to diversify its services, Earthlink partnered with Hughes Network Systems in November 2000 to offer high-speed satellite broadband services to those in rural areas. The following month, rival America Online (AOL) agreed to permit Earthlink to use AOL and Time Warner cable lines to offer additional high-speed services to its members.

Internet retailing giant Amazon.com also relied heavily on partnerships and alliances to reach a dominant position in the world of e-commerce. Hoping to fuel growth, one of the firm's first moves was the creation of its "associates" program in July of 1996. This program allowed individual Web site owners and operators to partner with Amazon by including links to Amazon on their site. Associates received a commission each time a Web surfer who clicked on the Amazon link actually purchased a book. In 1997, Amazon created alliances with AOL and Yahoo Inc., both of which resulted in Amazon's promotion on these high-traffic sites. By the following year, the associates program had reached 30,000 members, and it continued to grow rapidly throughout the remainder of the decade. According to *Fortune* columnist Eric Nee, Amazon "helped gain dominance and bolster its brand name by signing up 200,000 'associate' Web sites that refer customers to Amazon in return for a share of the revenues."

Ameritrade, the fourth-largest Internet-based brokerage in the United States, also used alliances to grow its service offerings in the late 1990s. The firm expanded its reach in 1997 by convincing AOL to include links on AOL.com to Ameritrade's Accutrade and Ceres sites. The firm struck a similar deal with Microsoft, which agreed to furnish users of the Microsoft Investor program with online access to both financial services. Additional alliances that year included deals with Yahoo! Finance, Excite Business & Investing, and Infoseek Personal Finance. Thanks to a partnership with Data Broadcasting, Ameritrade was able to offer stock quotes via the Internet for the first time in 1998. An additional partnership with PostX allowed Ameritrade to also make trade confirmations online. Along with reaching out to U.S. partners, the company also began pursuing deals with international partners, including France-based discount broker Cortal and Deutsche Bank AG.

Adobe Systems Inc., a leader in Web authoring tools and other Internet publishing technology, got its first big break in the mid-1980s when Apple Computer Inc. agreed to use Adobe's PostScript printer language with its LaserWriter printer. As part of the partnership, Apple purchased a 19-percent stake in Adobe. Via a similar deal, Texas Instruments Inc. began using PostScript in its IBM-compatible PCs in 1986. In 2000, well after Adobe had successfully transformed itself from a desktop publisher into an Internet publishing tools vendor, the firm began seeking strategic alliances as a means of staying abreast of cutting-edge Internet publishing technology. For example, in the second half of 2000, Adobe integrated its GoLive software with WebTrends Corp.'s Web tracking technology. As a result, clients creating Web sites with GoLive were able to monitor things like site traffic.

Discount travel site Priceline.com is an example of an e-commerce venture that simply would be unable to function without alliances and partnerships.

To begin operating its name-your-price site, the dot-com had to convince major airlines to agree to sell their extra tickets on Priceline.com. Although the site offered airlines a way to fill some of the 500,000 seats left empty each day, at first many airlines proved reluctant to partner with an Internet upstart. Initially, only TWA and America West signed deals with Priceline. It wasn't until the firm recruited an experienced management team that Delta Airlines signed on. Eventually, Northwest and Continental followed suit. Additional alliances with United Airlines, American Airlines, and US Airways allowed Priceline to increase its offerings in November of 1999. Deals with A&P, ShopRite, Stop Shop, D'Agostino's, Key-Food, and other grocery stores formed the basis for a name-your-price online grocery service called Priceline WebHouse Club, established in 2000. Diversification into new product areas is dependent upon alliances with businesses willing to participate in an online name-your-price venture.

Some companies form alliances and partnerships in an effort to impact an entire industry. For example, IBM Corp. and Nokia Corp., the world's largest cell-phone manufacturer, forged an alliance to hasten the growth of the wireless Internet in 1999. The two companies agreed to work together to develop enterprise wireless application protocol (WAP) solutions that would allow customers to immediately begin extending e-business beyond the PC to a variety of mobile devices. With cellular phone markets nearing saturation in many nations, Nokia had started looking to the Internet as a way to ensure future sales, believing that wireless devices would replace PCs as the most popular method for accessing the Internet. IBM also was hoping to bolster its foothold in what looked to be a promising new market. Alliances and partnerships likely will continue to play an important role for e-commerce firms, impacting the performance of individual businesses, as well as the development of various industries.

FURTHER READING:

"Adobe and Allaire Join to Simplify Development of E-Business; ColdFusion Extension for GoLive is First of Many Joint Development Efforts." *Canadian Corporate News.* August 28, 2000.

"Adobe and WebTrends Form Alliance to Provide E-Business Intelligence for Adobe Web Applications." *Canadian Corporate News.* August 29, 2000.

Crum, Rex. "Nokia Keeps on Keeping on." *Upside Today.* September 19, 2001. Available from www.upside.com.

"Earthlink, DirectPC in Two-Way Satellite Internet Deal." *Newsbytes.* November 18, 2000.

"Earthlink History." Atlanta, GA: Earthlink Inc., 2000. Available from www.earthlink.com.

Elkind, Peter. "The Hype Is Really, Really Big, at Priceline." *Fortune.* September 6, 1999.

Elkin, Tobi. "Jerry Yang." *Advertising Age.* April 17, 2000.

Fox, Justin. "Nokia's Secret Code." *Fortune.* May 1, 2000.

Hazleton, Lesley. "Jeff Bezos: How He Built a Billion-Dollar Net Worth Before His Company Even Turned a Profit." *Success.* July 1998.

"History." Omaha, NE: Ameritrade Holding Corp., 2001. Available from www.amtd.com.

Nee, Eric. "Microsoft Gets Ready to Play a New Game." *Fortune.* April 26, 1999.

SEE ALSO: Adobe Systems Inc.; Amazon.com; Ameritrade Holding Corp.; Co-opetition; Earthlink; Priceline.com; Yahoo!

PAYMENT OPTIONS AND SERVICES, ONLINE

As online shopping grew in popularity throughout the late 1990s and early into the 21st century, so did the number of methods by which shoppers could make online payments. Some methods were quickly adopted by electronic merchants and their customers, while other methods, due to issues surrounding security and ease of use for both payers and payees, were rather short-lived. By 2001, along with more traditional credit card payments—which accounted for roughly 50 percent of all online payments—options for online shoppers included making online payments via electronic withdrawals from a checking account or from a prepaid debit card.

CREDIT CARD PAYMENT

After selecting products or services they wish to purchase, the majority of online shoppers opt to make payment via credit card. They begin an online credit card transaction by completing a merchant commerce application. To ease consumer concerns regarding the risks involved in transmitting credit card numbers via the Internet, most merchants use secure electronic transaction (SET) or Secure Sockets Layer (SSL) technology, which encrypts personal information sent over the World Wide Web.

An online merchant who receives a completed commerce application sends it to an acquiring bank, which then sends a request for credit card authorization to an acquiring processor, a firm that supplies credit card processing, billing, reporting, and settlement services. The acquiring processor transmits the request to the card-issuing bank, the bank that actually issued the credit card to the customer, which responds with either an approval or denial code that the acquiring processor then relays to the merchant. Thanks to

Real Time Online Processing technology, this entire process usually takes less than 15 seconds. Although a shopper's credit card account is not actually charged at the time of purchase, the card-issuing bank does put a hold on the account for the transaction amount. Typically, credit card transactions are settled at the end of each business day, at which time the shoppers's credit card is charged. The card-issuing bank sends the fund to the acquiring bank which deposits those funds into the merchant's bank account.

For online merchants, one downfall of the credit card payment method is the higher fees credit card companies tend to charge for online transactions. In a traditional retail transaction, the merchant typically makes contact with both the credit card and the consumer, reducing the likelihood of fraud. Because online transactions are completed without the customer or the credit card present, both merchants and credit card companies are more susceptible to chargebacks, which occur when a card holder disputes a charge appearing on his or her credit card statement. If a chargeback is issued after the claim is investigated, the credit card company must withdraw the payment from the merchant and return it to the shopper's account. To combat this, many merchants use address verification service (AVS) technology to verify the first four numbers of a U.S.-based street address and zip code supplied to the online merchant by the consumer at the time of purchase. Shoppers who provide a billing address that does not match their credit card billing address are prevented from completing their purchase. In 2001, 40 of the top 50 Visa and MasterCard credit card issuers in the U.S. used Merchant Express LLC's FraudScreenNet. To improve a merchant's ability to pinpoint fraud, the software application goes beyond simply verifying addresses, by also scrutinizing each shopper's email address, shipping method history, product purchasing pattern, payment method history, work and telephone number patterns, and typical purchasing frequency and time.

DIGITAL CASH

Another downfall of the credit card payment method is that it excludes anyone without a credit card. To allow individuals without credit cards to make purchases online, many firms began devising online cash payment systems. A prime example of a digital cash payment method provider is InternetCash, which was founded in March of 2000. InternetCash users purchase a cash card at a retail outlet, such as a convenience store. Using a credit card reader, the retailer who sells the cash card sends notice to InternetCash that the card has been purchased. The next time the InternetCash cardholder goes online, he or she logs onto the InternetCash Web site, activates the account, and selects a password. From that point for-

ward, the shopper can use the money in the InternetCash account to purchase goods and services from any merchant that accepts InternetCash. To be equipped to accept InternetCash payments, merchants simply install software that operates in the same fashion that credit card payment processing applications work. For shoppers, one major benefit of using InternetCash to pay for online purchases is the anonymity it offers. According to *PC World* writer Karen Bannan, ''Merchants benefit as well. They not only increase their potential buying audience, but they also gain the ability to offer inexpensive items ($10 and under) that are not profitable when handled via credit card transactions. May e-cash vendors charge merchants lower fees than credit card companies do and have a simpler sign-up process.''

Some digital cash firms have even gone so far as to attempt to create a new form of online currency. For example, Beenz.com, founded in March of 1998, was based on a system that allowed users to accrue points by doing things like completing surveys, registering at Web sites, and spending a certain amount of money at a particular online store. Users who had accumulated enough ''beenz'' could redeem them for merchandise. Using a similar tactic, Robert Levitan, co-founder of leading women's Internet hub iVillage.com, created Flooz.com in September of 1999. According to an August 2001 article in *American Banker*, the firm sold ''a digital currency that was meant primarily for online gift certificates. A consumer could charge, say, $50 worth of flooz on a credit card, e-mail it to a friend, and let the friend use the flooz (which could not be turned back into cash) to buy things online from merchants that accepted it.'' The article points out that while both firms ''must have had visions that consumers would be as eager to collect their products as housewives of yore were to amass S&H Green Stamps, they systems they set up did not mesh well with the existing payment systems.'' As a result, by mid-2001, Flooz.com and Beenz.com had halted operations.

DIGITAL WALLETS

Like the digital cash firms that attempted to create an alternate currency for the Internet, digital wallet services proved particularly short-lived. Companies like American Express Co. and Wells Fargo & Co. ventured into digital wallet technology in late 1999 and early 2000, only to discontinue those offerings in 2001. Essentially, a digital wallet allows online shoppers to save in a single place all of the address and payment information they'd need to supply an online merchant with before making a purchase. The impetus behind the technology was that increasing convenience and reducing the amount of time shoppers spent filling out lengthy forms would encourage online shopping. However, consumers failed to embrace the idea for a variety of reasons. Some analysts claim the technology was poorly marketed by the sites that adopted it. Some point to the fact that consumers were uncomfortable with the idea of storing so much personal information in a single place. Others cite the inconvenience of having to download the technology, particularly since sites like retailing giant Amazon.com saved each shopper's information automatically anyway.

ELECTRONIC CHECKS

Electronic checks offer another method of online payment. Fidesic Corp., founded as CheckSpace Inc. in February of 2000, allows small businesses to make and receive payments via email. In short, Fidesic clients may present bills and make payments to other Fidesic clients via a simple email message. Using the bank account and routing data provided by its clients, Fidesic is able to transfer money between its clients' accounts. Clients are also able to download transaction data to spreadsheets like Excel and Quicken. To make money, the upstart charges 95 cents per transaction. As stated in a March 2001 issue of *Oregon Business*, digital checks offer a variety of benefits to companies, particularly smaller businesses. "For the average small business, say analysts at Internet research firm Gomez, the 50 percent reduction in the labor required to process payments would drop the total cost of payments nearly $600 per month. Cash flow also could benefit by speedier receipt of money owed. And there's not discounting the convenience of not having to stand in line at the bank or post office."

Operating with technology similar to that used by Fidesic, Achex, Inc. has offered electronic check payment services to consumers since its inception in mid-2000. Online shoppers making purchases at BlueLight.com, Bizland, Yakpak, and Netgrocer.com can use Achex Online Checks to submit payment electronically. Funds are then debited via an electronic clearinghouse operated by Achex from the shopper's checking account and deposited into the merchant's account; although both shoppers and merchants receive instant notification that payment has been made, the process of transferring funds typically takes two to three days. Like most other online payment methods, this electronic checking service is free to shoppers. Achex makes money by charging online merchants a small per-transaction fee. In July of 2001, First Data Corp. bought Achex, and a few months later, merged it into MoneyZap, its peer-to-peer (P2P) online payment service arm, which operates as a subsidiary of Western Union.

PEER-TO-PEER PAYMENT

Other than credit card transactions, the most popular online payment option is the peer-to-peer (P2P) option by which individuals can send one another payment via a third party. PayPal is the leader in this category, boasting the largest Internet-based payment network in the world with roughly 8 million customers. Founded in November of 1999, PayPal began to attract attention from the millions of users buying and selling merchandise on auction site eBay. By March of 2000, when PayPal merged with online banker X.com, the firm was signing up nearly 15,000 new clients a day.

To sign up for online payment services, PayPal customers are required to key their name, daytime phone number, home address, and email address into an online form. Users can opt to charge purchases to a credit card, or they can provide PayPal with the account information necessary to allow PayPal to withdraw funds from a bank account. Once their account is activated, PayPal members can send funds to any other PayPal account holder via an automated email message with the subject line, "You've Got Cash!" Compared to the 2.9 percent monthly fee typically charged by credit card firms, along with an additional charge of 30 cents per transaction, PayPal simply charges 1.9 percent of each transaction completed for e-businesses bringing in more than $100 per month.

In June of 2000 PayPal diversified into payments between businesses and consumers (B2C). The firm also began allowing clients to conduct transactions via cell phones. P2P customers exceeded 3 million in August. When PayPal began focusing on business-to-business (B2B) payments, the value of transactions conducted via the firm multiplied, prompting the launch of fraud protection services, similar to that offered by credit card companies. As part of its new Cybersource Fraud Scan, the firm also established a member information guide, to allow buyers to verify that sellers had been reviewed by the firm.

By the year's end PayPal had secured 4 million P2P customers and conducted nearly 50 percent of the transactions competed on eBay, more than conducted by eBay's own payment service, Billpoint Inc. International expansion efforts included allowing Internet users outside the U.S. open PayPal accounts. By March of 2001, PayPal offered e-mail based payment services in 26 countries. To help shoppers more easily find merchants that supported PayPal transactions, the firm compiled a listing of 5,600 "PayPal Shops," which it posted on its Web site. Hoping to entice more customers to abandon their credit cards in favor of P2P online services, PayPal began paying interest on funds deposited into a PayPal account.

Although PayPal was the first firm to gain critical mass in the online payment arena, a P2P payment competitor emerged in March of 2001. Banking and insurance behemoth Citigroup joined forces with Microsoft Corp. to offer its c2it online payment service on Microsoft's MSN.com Internet gateway. With a daily visitor rate of roughly 7 million, MSN.com hoped it would quickly attract a large base of c2it clients.

In 2001, Gartner Group predicted that debit cards, such as those offered by InternetCash, would be the payment method used by roughly 30 percent of all online purchases by 2003. With roughly 10 million individuals online without credit cards, the potential for alternative online payment methods certainly seems promising.

FURTHER READING:

Arar, Yardena. ''The Check's in the E-Mail Really.'' *PC World,* December 2000.

Bannan, Karen J. ''No Credit? No Problem! Digital Cash Made Easy.'' *PC World,* February 2001.

Capachin, Jeanne. ''Digital Wallets: Their Potential Exceeds Their Performance.'' *American Banker,* August 17, 2001.

''Dreams of a Cashless Society.'' *The Economist,* May 5, 2001.

Ernst, Steve. ''Now, the Check Is in the E-mail.'' *Puget Sound Business Journal,* October 6, 2000.

Kuykendall, Lavonne. ''Amex Says E-Wallet Proved Too Awkward.'' *American Banker,* June 22, 2001.

Monson, Megan. ''The Check's In the E-Mail.'' *Oregon Business,* March 2001.

''Paying By E-mail.'' *Forbes,* September 11, 2000.

''The Tech Scene: Don't Spend Your Last Flooz on Web Money.'' *American Banker,* August 15, 2001.

Tillett, Scott L. ''Merchants Grapple With Payment Options.'' *InternetWeek,* May 22, 2000.

SEE ALSO: Acquiring Bank; Authentication; Authorization and Authorization Code; Card-Issuing Bank; Charge-back; Cryptography, Public and Private Key; Digital Cash; Digital Certificate; Digital Signature; Digital Wallet Technololgy; Encryption; Electronic Payment; Fraud, Internet; Merchant Discount; Pay Pal; Pay-Per-Play; Pay-Per-View; Peer-to-Peer Technology; Transaction Issues

---

Pal offered at no charge. By supplying funds from a credit card, bank account, or PayPal money market account, consumers were able to send and request money from one another through the service. For a fee, businesses could take advantage of premium services including the ability to accept unlimited credit card payments on their Web sites. PayPal also enabled wireless Internet devices like personal digital assistants (PDAs) and mobile phones to function as digital wallets.

In its first year of operation, PayPal achieved a great deal of success. More than 5 million users were registered with the service by the end of 2000, accounting for more than $1 billion in payments. According to the company, at that time its transactions accounted for more than 10 percent of all Internet traffic in the area of financial services, and more than two thirds of them generated fees. By April of 2001 the company had registered an additional 2 million users and had doubled the total value of its transactions ($2 billion).

PayPal was a popular means of settling transactions on the Internet in the early 2000s, and the company received accolades from the likes of *Fortune Small Business, Red Herring,* and *Forbes.* However, according to the Gartner Group, the company was also scrutinized by the Better Business Bureau because of consumers who said the company failed to respond when they had complaints. The Gartner Group further indicated that vendors like PayPal are not covered by the regulations pertaining to banks, and urged parties to exercise caution when doing business them.

FURTHER READING:

Goldsborough, Reid. ''Buying and Selling on the Internet Without Cash.'' *Link-up,* May/June 2001.

PayPal. ''About PayPal.'' PayPal, May 30, 2001. Available from www.paypal.com.

''PayPal's Stumbles Demonstrate the Risk of Person-toPerson E-Payments.'' GartnerGroup Inc., January 29, 2001. Available from www3.gartner.com.

SEE ALSO: Payment Options and Services, Online

PAYPAL

PayPal is an Internet-based payment service that offers increased security for online transactions. PayPal is used, for example, at auction sites like eBay and at many other e-commerce Web sites. In the early 2000s, consumers could use many of the services Pay-

PAY-PER-PLAY

When Web-based proprietors charge visitors ''by the session'' to play an online game, access a software application, or view streaming video content, the scenario is referred to as pay-per-play. Pay-per-play scenarios usually involve micropayments— online transactions for low-priced items on the Internet that range from a few cents to as much as $10.00. In the mid-to-late 1990s, when the Web was still a relatively new environment for the public, some video game companies discovered that consumers wouldn't pay monthly subscriptions to access Web-based games. This caused a movement to hourly charges for playing games. By the 2000s, although many online games were available for free at various Web sites (supported by advertising revenue instead of time-based fees), many also were available on a pay-per-play basis. The approach also was being used for other types of software.

In order to have a quality experience, users wishing to access software or video via the Web must have adequate Internet connection speeds, or enough bandwidth to receive large chunks of data. Poor bandwidth was a roadblock in the mid-1990s when the Web first became popular with consumers. In 1995, Wave Systems was one company that unsuccessfully tried to deliver pay-per-play software to consumers with wireless radio frequency modems. As Internet connection speeds increased this approach became more realistic. Unlike audio and video, software applications are used incrementally, or in bursts. After accessing the initial information required to begin the software session, users access other pieces of the software as needed, depending on the tasks they are performing. This makes software especially suitable for distribution over networks like the Internet.

Into Networks was one company providing pay-per-play software in the early 2000s. The company housed software programs from companies like Disney Interactive, Hasbro Interactive, Macmillan USA, and Simon & Schuster Interactive on special servers, to which users with broadband connections linked for access. These servers were located with different Internet service providers (the entities to which consumers subscribe in order to connect to the Internet), and at other locations across the Internet. For users, the company's technology eliminated installation problems one might experience if software were installed locally, reduced long download times, and provided a way to try programs before buying them. It eliminated the problem of lost or damaged CD-ROMS, and was more economical for users who only needed to use applications a few times. For software publishers and marketers, it provided access to new users, extended the lifecycle of products, provided new sources of revenue, and offered a means to test new titles.

Implementing pay-per-play technology posed some challenges for companies in the early 2000s, namely in the areas of structuring licensing fees, adapting for use over the Internet applications that weren't originally designed for that purpose, and resolving issues surrounding the operating systems (such as Windows, Macintosh, Linux, and Unix) that were employed by computer users worldwide. Despite these challenges, the future of the pay-per-play approach looked very positive in the early 2000s. Microsoft CEO Steve Ballmer predicted that as broadband applications became widely adopted, packaged software would vanish in lieu of online access to applications. Additionally, *InfoWorld,* indicated that from 2000 to 2003 IBM planned to invest at least $4 billion to establish itself as a leader in fee-based, on-demand computer services. IBM planned to focus on its own applications, and to build the infrastructure other software companies would use to offer their products.

FURTHER READING:

Bannan, Karen J. ''Pay-Per-Play: Let The Games Begin— Again.'' *Inter@ctive Week,* February 2, 1999. Available from www.www.zdnet.com.

Frame, Greg. ''Games and Software: Flowing Streams.'' *StreamingMedia,* October 12, 2000. Available from www.intonet.com.

Ryan, Michael E. ''Pay-per-Play Web Games.'' *PC Magazine,* April 22, 1997. Available from www.zdnet.com.

Preston, Robert. ''Personalization Requires Better Cross-Pollination.'' *InternetWeek,* June 1, 2001. Available from www.internetweek.com.

Vizard, Michael, Brian Fonseca, and Ed Scannell. ''IBM Readies Apps on Tap—Vendors Adapting to Evolving Utility Model.'' *InfoWorld,* December 18, 2000.

SEE ALSO: Micropayments; Payment Options and Services, Online

PAY-PER-VIEW

The concept of pay-per-view, or paying a fee to watch or obtain specific content, became popular through cable television during the 1990s. By 2000, the pay-per-view cable and satellite industry was securing $1.5 billion per year by charging customers to view certain movies and special events. Believing the Internet would prove a lucrative sales channel for pay-per-view events and content, many firms began utilizing the World Wide Web to broadcast movies and television shows, as well as content, on a pay-per-view basis.

The development of streaming media in the late 1990s allowed radio, television, and movies to be heard and viewed on the Internet. This technology, coupled with faster Internet connections including digital subscriber lines and cable modems, allowed Web surfers to use personal computers to view what had traditionally been available only through regular and cable television. Cable station Showtime Networks launched its foray into pay-per-view on the Internet in 1999. That year it launched its first event online—a boxing match between Mike Tyson and Orlin Norris. In July of 2001, television network CBS teamed up with RealNetworks Inc., a leading Internet media delivery firm, to offer reality television show *Big Brother 2* on a pay-per-view basis. Online viewers had different payment options including a $9.95 per month option that included RealNetwork's Gold-Pass service. This service allowed the viewer access to the show, along with broadcasts of sporting events including professional basketball and baseball games.

Other examples of entertainment companies utilizing pay-per-view include Hollywood.com and CinemaNow. The duo launched a movie site in June 2001 which streamed independent films and allowed Web surfers who paid $2.99 to have access to a movie for 48 hours. At roughly the same time, Intertainer.com began offering older television shows such as the *Beverly Hillbillies* on a pay-per-view basis.

The ability to broadcast movies online on a pay-per-view basis sparked the advent of video on demand (VOD). While still in its infancy in 2001, VOD was expected to eventually replace traditional pay-per-view cable movies. VOD allows a viewer to rewind, fast-forward, pause, start, and stop a movie at will. A VOD movie begins at the time of payment, rather than at a scheduled time, and typically can be viewed for 24 hours on either a personal computer or through television. Companies including Sony Pictures Entertainment, Blockbuster Video, AOL Time Warner's Road Runner cable service, and Intertainer invested in technology which would allow VOD to become available to Web surfers utilizing pay-per-view billing methods.

Content-based Web sites unrelated to the movie and television industries also use pay-per-view methods. News sites including the *Wall Street Journal*, for example, charge users to view portions of its online content. *USA Today* also charges its online readers to access its articles; a customer can view one article for $1.50, view up to ten articles a day for $4.95, or pay $14.95 per month to access up to 100 articles. Web portal Yahoo! offers buying guides and product ratings from Consumer Reports. The reports costs $2.95 each, and users can view them for 30 days. Similarly, California-based Ebrary offers books and journals on a pay-per-view basis, charging 15 to 25 cents per page.

Whether selling entertainment or information, many dot.com firms utilize a pay-per-view system. While some critics question the long-term viability of selling content via the Internet, an August 2001 *EContent* article claimed that ''the Internet will be very much like cable TV. At first, many analysts said cable TV would never catch on, that people would never pay for content. The same will happen with the Internet, particularly as better content goes up for sale.''

FURTHER READING:

Graham, Jefferson. ''Video on Demand Has Come into View.'' *USA Today,* June 15, 2001. Available from www.usatoday.com.

Hillebrand, Mary. ''Showtime Brings Pay-Per-View Boxing Online.'' *E-Commerce Times,* October 18, 1999. Available from www.ecommercetimes.com.

Macaluso, Nora. ''Yahoo! to Offer Consumer Reports Content.'' *E-Commerce Times,* June 4, 2001. Available from www.ecommercetimes.com.

Mahoney, Michael. ''Internet Pay-Per-View Movie Site Unveiled—Does it Matter?'' *E-Commerce Times,* June 1, 2001. Available from www.ecommercetimes.com.

McGarvey, Robert. ''Pay-Per-View's Payback: Cashing In on Content.'' *EContent,* August 2001, 31.

Naraine, Ryan. '''Big Brother 2' Goes Pay-Per-View Online.'' *InternetNews,* July 6, 2001. Available from www.internetnews.com.

SEE ALSO: Payment Options and Services, Online; Pay-Per-Play; RealNetworks; Streaming Media

PEER-TO-PEER TECHNOLOGY (P2P)

Broadly speaking, peer-to-peer (P2P) technology employs a network to put individuals in direct contact with each other in some form. A simple telephone call to a friend, then, could be considered a form of P2P. In contemporary parlance, however, P2P refers almost exclusively to computer-based systems of sharing information directly with others via the Internet. Peer-to-peer technology has its roots in locally-based hardware arrangements in which each individual system shares certain identical features and capabilities. In the Internet Age, however, P2P refers usually to specific applications rather than hardware arrangements.

The peer-to-peer philosophy and network architecture eliminate the direct top-down relationship between clients and their servers in favor of linking each connected individual as a peer, eschewing the centrality of traditional networks by placing the focal points at each individual computer. Users in a P2P network can pool their resources, sharing each other's files, storage systems, and applications, thereby paving the way for extensive collaboration and efficient information sharing.

Perhaps the most well known example of peer-to-peer technology in the late 1990s and early 2000s was the Napster music file-sharing system, consisting of a distributed network of millions of personal computers, whereby users could search for and download songs directly over the Internet for free. While Napster itself generated a flood of controversy due to allegations of copyright infringement and record companies' fears that such technology would undermine their position in the music business, the technology itself raised many eyebrows in corporate America.

Another major thorn in the side of copyright owners in the early 2000s was Freenet. Created by Ian Clarke, Freenet went Napster one better in that there was no central network for authorities to focus on. Most P2P applications in the early 2000s, including Napster, still required a central server or directory. Freenet consisted of encrypted, anonymous files in the manner of Napster, and was designed ostensibly to protect individual privacy on the Internet by ensuring open access to all files and absolute anonymity, while simultaneously shielding the distribution of shared files from scrutiny. Copyright holders screamed that the system would destroy the integrity of their copyrights by making their work freely and anonymously available to any and all Internet users. But the ability to bypass the need for central networks and the maintenance and administration that accompanies them was particularly attractive to companies seeking to modernize their corporate organizations for the Internet Age. In spring 2001, Intel gave Clarke and his startup firm, Uprizer, $4 million to develop a decentralized distributed networking system for commercial applications.

In July 2000, Napster turned itself into a secure membership-based service with the help of the media conglomerate Bertelsmann. In so doing, Napster created a scheme for copy protection that limits what can be done with the downloaded files. For example, only the PC used in the download is able to play the songs downloaded through Napster. While such moves by what had once been an extremely threatening P2P service were a breath of fresh air to copyright holders, these kinds of restrictions embedded into P2P technology worried some observers interested in the future of P2P applications, insisting that they will inhibit P2P's potential. Others, however, see the field as diverse enough to incorporate a number of eventual niches.

Investment in P2P business applications was pouring in by the early 2000s. *Business Week,* in a special industrial/technology edition in the spring of 2001, reported that roughly $300 billion in venture capital had been funneled into about 150 P2P startups. P2P companies generate their revenue by selling software packages that consumers can then use to communicate-and collaborate—directly with one another, bypassing central servers. Peers in these distributed networks, according to *Business Week,* bypass central computing points altogether, so power devolves to the distributed, individual computer nodes, in what proponents herald as a more democratic form of computer networking.

In a sense, P2P brings to life the distribution of power for which the Internet was originally designed, in that it allows computers to communicate directly with each other without going through any intermediary channels. However, *Business Week* noted that the difference between early Internet designs and the P2P of the early 2000s lay in the vastly superior power of contemporary PCs. Napster, for instance, instead of storing music files on a central server, simply provided means for users to access other members' hard drives where the music files were actually stored. In short, P2P put the largely untapped potential of today's powerful PCs to work. Most computers—particularly those used at home but also in office settings—harbor much more power than is ever actually used.

Security, of course, is a major concern for businesses looking to implement P2P networks. Since P2P allows users direct access to others' hard drives, the protection of corporate data gave pause to executives who saw P2P as the ultimate way to generate efficiency and encourage employee collaboration. The different layers of access that often accompany corporate intranets and extranets would necessarily have to be extended to the P2P systems to afford access to company computers. The idea of installing yet another hierarchy of access controls is unappealing to systems managers who already have several of those to maintain.

Another obvious security concern was the heightened need to safeguard against malicious or careless P2P users uploading viruses directly onto others' computers. In 2001 the first P2P virus appeared as a requested media file on the Gnutella file-sharing system, which infected the users' computers upon download. Corporate systems operators were especially wary of such possibilities to compromise data or cripple crucial systems in a corporate network. And, of course, the larger and more integrated the P2P network, including overlapping and intermingling P2P systems, the more likely that such viruses could potentially spin out of control.

FURTHER READING:

Ante, Spencer E., Amy Borus, and Robert D. Hof. "In Search of the Net's Next Big Thing." *Business Week,* March 26, 2001.

Biggs, Maggie. "P-to-P Promises to Streamline Business Processes." *InfoWorld,* April 2, 2001.

"Going Straight." *Economist,* April 7, 2001.

Savage, Marcia. "Looking Beyond the P2P Buzz." *Computer Reseller News,* February 19, 2001.

Scannell, Ed. "Startup to Create Applications Based on Freenet." *InfoWorld,* April 16, 2001.

Winblad, Ann. "Life on the Edge." *Forbes,* February 19, 2001.

Vance, Ashlee. "First Virus Infects Peer-to-Peer Communications Systems." *InfoWorld,* March 5, 2001.

SEE
ALSO: Napster

PEOPLESOFT INC.

Pleasanton, California-based PeopleSoft Inc. is a leading developer of enterprise software. Its offerings connect companies and their employees with business partners and customers. In 2001, the company's products included PeopleSoft Customer Relationship Management, PeopleSoft Financial Management, PeopleSoft Supply Chain Management, and People-Soft Human Resources Management. In addition to different customer service options and consulting services, the company offered learning opportunities via on-demand classes and live Webcasts through its PeopleSoft University. It also offered products on a hosted basis, via the PeopleSoft eCenter. In the early 2000s some of the world's leading organizations were PeopleSoft customers, including Visa U.S.A. Inc., Pepsi-Cola Co., Quaker Oats Co., Amazon.com, and AOL Time Warner Inc. Government agencies and educational institutions also used the company's products.

EARLY HISTORY

PeopleSoft's roots go back to 1987, when Ken Morris and David Duffield founded the company. Although Morris eventually parted ways with People-Soft, Duffield remained with the company as its leader. He became popular for maintaining a culture where people were valued, soft drinks were on the house, and pets were welcome. After graduating from Cornell University with an MBA and an undergraduate degree in electrical engineering, Duffield worked as a systems engineer and marketing representative for IBM. He then co-founded Information Associates, a company that developed systems for higher education, and established Integral Systems, a firm that developed accounting and human resources software. According to the company, as chairman of PeopleSoft Duffield was "the driving force behind the company's vision, product, market direction, and commitment to services."

Morris and Duffield established PeopleSoft to develop business software exclusively for client-server environments. At the time, this was a somewhat progressive approach because mainframe computer applications were more commonplace. Many enterprises were faced with the challenge of moving from one environment to the other, and PeopleSoft's products found a niche. The company unveiled PeopleSoft Human Resources Management Systems in 1988. Over time, the company's dominance in this business segment would grow until it attained market share of 50 percent.

EXPANSION BEGINS

International expansion first occurred in 1990 when an office was established in Canada. Three years later, the firm had established operations on five continents and opened offices in Africa, Asia, Central America, Europe, South America, and the Pacific Rim. PeopleSoft's products and services continued to find new markets. In 1992, its fifth year of operation, the company went public. Shares were offered for $4.25 each. Additionally, the firm introduced People-Soft Financials (accounts payable, accounts receivable, asset management) which would become a strong seller. In 1993, PeopleSoft announced its plans to release two new applications: PeopleSoft Distribution, for materials management (purchasing, inventory management, billing, and processing orders); and PeopleSoft Student Information System, which was targeted at schools for managing information about students.

GROWING PAINS

In 1994, *Fortune* named PeopleSoft the nation's fastest growing software company. The company's revenues increased from $6 million in 1990 to $113 million. New products were unveiled, including People-Soft Financials for the Public in 1994, and applications for the education, manufacturing, healthcare, financial services, and government sectors the following year.

In 1995, PeopleSoft ventured into the manufacturing arena. It established PeopleSoft Manufacturing Inc. (PMI) as a separate company to shelter the larger organization from the risks associated with the new venture. Some industry analysts criticized the company's entry into the manufacturing market as too late. Some PeopleSoft customers who were using the company's human resources and accounting software were unable to wait for a manufacturing application and pursued other options.

PMI—which actually included PeopleSoft Manufacturing Inc. and PeopleMan LP—was formally acquired by PeopleSoft in 1996 along with Red Pepper, a manufacturing and supply chain software developer. For the remainder of the 1990s and into the 2000s, the company would live up to the accolades for fast growth it received from *Fortune*. PeopleSoft began acquiring companies at a rate of 1-2 per year through 2001, including Salerno Manufacturing Systems, Campus Solutions, and TeamOne in 1997; TriMark Technologies and Intrepid Systems in 1998; Distinction Software in 1999; Vantive and Advance Planning Solutions in 2000; and SkillsVillage in 2001.

NEW DIRECTIONS AND STRATEGIES

PeopleSoft continued to branch out in new directions into the late 1990s. In 1998, the company announced that it would create a new business unit devoted to outsourcing services. Specifically, the unit would handle the outsourcing of business processes and technology. After seeing revenues increase approximately 80 percent in 1997, PeopleSoft secured lucrative deals with both Boeing and General Motors. Additionally, its manufacturing product was adopted by companies like 3Com and Hewlett-Packard.

In 1999, PeopleSoft announced that it would alter its strategy of selling enterprise resource planning (ERP) products directly to larger companies and make an effort to reach emerging smaller and medium-sized firms through resellers. The company planned to do so in secondary markets; at that time, its core U.S. markets were Atlanta, Chicago, New York, and San Francisco. In the last half of 1999, PeopleSoft's customers began to enjoy more applications from third-party vendors that were able to integrate with PeopleSoft products. This "open integration" approach was the result of efforts the company began in 1998, and promised to make the PeopleSoft's ERP products more attractive to customers.

Several big things happened at PeopleSoft toward the end of 1999. In October, the company made a huge acquisition when it acquired Vantive Corp., a manufacturer of customer relationship management software, for $433 million. Finally, in September Craig Conway was named PeopleSoft's CEO, assuming responsibility for day-to-day operations from Duffield. After one year on the job, Conway commented on the impact he had made on the firm in *Computerworld*. "It's a very, very different company," he said. "We've retooled our management team and business processes, so we're a better-run company. And I think the company's morale and confidence is at an all-time high. . .I think I added an ingredient of intensity and accountability and competition to the corporate culture."

In 2000, PeopleSoft ventured into yet another new arena—professional services automation. It introduced its PeopleSoft PSA product, which helped companies match employees with projects based on their skills. PSA also was useful for managing other aspects associated with projects including billing, scheduling, and proposals. Finally, PeopleSoft became an application services provider (ASP) by offering its applications on a hosted basis via its eCenter.

Just as it had done in the 1980s by offering client-server-based solutions, PeopleSoft began focusing its efforts on a new model in the early 2000s. At that time, companies were interested in the potential business advantages offered by the Internet, especially in the area of transactions. In keeping with this focus, PeopleSoft channeled the lion's share of its resources into creating a "new pure Internet platform for the collaborative enterprise." Over the course of two years, the company devoted 2,000 developers and $500 million to the creation of PeopleSoft 8. The new platform made analytical and relationship data more pervasive and easily accessible for a company's employees.

Late in 2001, PeopleSoft introduced Enterprise Performance Management, a suite of software that included tools for modeling customer behavior. The software enabled companies to "pull data from PeopleSoft's operational CRM applications in real time and use that information to segment, profile, and model customer populations—critical for generating lists for e-mail marketing campaigns," according to *InformationWeek*.

FURTHER READING:

PeopleSoft Inc. "Company Information." Pleasanton, California: PeopleSoft Inc. November 6, 2001. Available from www.peoplesoft.com.

"PeopleSoft Inc." *Hoovers Online*, November 6, 2001. Available from www.hoovers.com.

Songini, Marc L. "CEO: PeopleSoft Has Changed for the Better." *Computerworld*, September 18, 2000.

Southwick, Karen. "Going for the Jugular." *Upside*, November 1995.

Whiting, Rick. "PeopleSoft Joins Knowledge Race." *InformationWeek*, September 3, 2001.

SEE ALSO: Application Service Provider (ASP); Customer Relationship Management (CRM); Enterprise Application Integration (EAI); Enterprise Resource Planning (ERP)

PEROT SYSTEMS CORP.

Perot Systems Corp. is a technology services and consulting firm based in Dallas, Texas. The company offers systems management, systems integration, customer relationship management, and e-commerce services to its enterprise clients, most of which operate in the financial services, healthcare, and manufacturing industries. Sales in 2000 exceeded $1 billion, and employees totaled roughly 7,500.

Texas billionaire Ross Perot founded Perot Systems in 1988 to compete with Electronic Data Systems Corp. (EDS), the computer services firm he founded in 1962 and eventually sold to General Motors Corp. for $2.8 billion. At the time, that price was more than had ever been paid for a computer services company. When General Motors took control of EDS in June of 1984, Perot was named to the General Motors board of directors. Several bitter disputes over the direction of EDS eventually prompted Perot to resign his post and establish his second technology services business.

Perot Systems remained a relatively small player in the late 1980s and early 1990s. In 1992, after he decided to run for the presidency of the United States, Perot recruited Morton H. Meyerson, who had served as EDS' president and CEO from 1979 to 1985, to take the helm at Perot Systems. Meyerson had been ranked as ''The Best CEO in the Computer Services Industry,'' by the *Wall Street Transcript* for three consecutive years in the early 1980s. It was under Meyerson's leadership that Perot Systems forged its 25-year agreement with Swiss Bank Corp. in 1995. The contract eventually accounted for nearly 25 percent of Perot Systems' total revenues. According to the terms of the deal, estimated to be worth $250 million each year, Perot oversaw the network maintenance and software installation of the information technology (IT) operations of Swiss Bank's investment banking arm, SBC Warburg. Due in part to the new contract, sales in 1996 neared the $600 million mark, compared to $342 million in 1995. Earnings also grew nearly twofold, reaching $20 million.

In the mid-1990s, Perot Services expanded its product and service offerings by acquiring several software and consulting businesses. In July of 1996, SportsTrac Inc. hired Perot Systems to develop an Internet database of high school athletes that could be used by college recruiters. The firm also diversified its new management team, hiring James A. Cannavino, a former IBM Corp. executive, and James A. Champy, a consultant who played an integral role in the reengineering trend that had swept through the business world in the mid-1990s. Cannavino replaced Meyerson as CEO in September of 1996. According to a November 1996 article in *BusinessWeek Online,* Cannavino spent his first few months at the helm ''zeroing in on key industries, such as financial services, health care, and energy, and developing functional expertise in areas that cross industry boundaries, such

as logistics management. At the same time, Cannavino has made sure that Perot is up to speed in all the new software technologies, including those used for the Internet and intranet setups. Perot is now investing in software startups to get new technology early.'' For example, the firm paid $9 million for the assets of Nets Inc., a business-to-business (B2B) e-commerce system developer that had run out of money, in May of 1997.

Two months later, Cannavino made the sudden decision to resign as president and CEO after less than one year at the helm. Perot himself stepped in as interim CEO. When Meyerson resigned as chairman in January of 1998, Perot took over that role as well. He put in place several cost cutting measures that allowed the firm to boost profits from a tenuous $11.2 million in 1997 to $40.5 million in 1998. The firm completed its initial public offering (IPO) in February of 1999, initially listing its shares for $16 apiece. By then, Perot Systems was using the technology and expertise it had acquired when it purchased Nets Inc. to build B2B exchanges on the Internet for clients such as industrial supply distributor W.W. Grainger. Like most other IT service firms, Perot Systems saw its share price soar to a high of $85 shortly after its IPO before plummeting to roughly $20 per share later in the year.

Perot Systems purchased Health Systems Design Corp. in 2000, gaining access to Diamond, a healthcare payment software application. Sales that year exceeded $1 billion for the first time. A 2001 reorganization refocused the firm on three core industries: financial services, healthcare, and manufacturing. Operations in other industries were grouped together in an emerging industries unit. Perot Systems also condensed its services into three main groupings: business consulting, software engineering and integration, and technology infrastructure services. As part of the overhaul, the firm laid off 200 employees, roughly 2.5 percent of its workforce, and took a $48 million charge.

New product releases that year included iQom, an Internet-based application that helps organizations reduce their energy costs by monitoring, collecting, and analyzing information regarding the use and management of things like electricity. Wyndham Hotels & Resorts hired Perot Systems to use iQom for a five-year period. In May, La Quinta Inns Inc. contracted Perot Systems to improve its central reservations, financial management, sales management, and e-mail systems. The firm also secured a 10-year contract, worth an estimated $600 million, from Catholic Healthcare West to streamline its information systems. In addition, Burger King Corp., the second-largest fast food chain in the world, outsourced its global network management, enterprise systems management, data center management, and help desk support to Perot Systems. Acquisitions that year included Covation, a software services provider for the health-care industry, and Advanced Receivables Strategy Inc., a provider of hospital revenue management services and technology.

FURTHER READING:

Ackerman, Elise. "Ross Perot Is All Business Now. Really." *U.S. News & World Report.* April 19, 1999.

"Burger Kings Taps Perot." *InformationWeek.* September 10, 2001.

Hildebrand, Carol. "The Odd Couple." *CIO.* May 15, 1996.

Judge, Paul. "Perot Systems Snatches the Brains of Manzi's Nets Inc." *BusinessWeek Online.* June 5, 1997. Available from www.businessweek.com.

"Perot: E-Commerce Pioneer?" *Fortune.* March 15, 1999.

"Perot Systems Launches iQom(TM) Energy Services Solution." *PR Newswire.* March 23, 2001.

"Perot Systems Refines Operating Structure and Streamlines Operations." *PR Newswire.* January 10, 2001.

Zellner, Wendy. "Gearing Up at Perot Systems." *BusinessWeek Online.* November 11, 1996. Available from www.businessweek.com.

———. "It's Simple, See: Ross Perot Is Back in Business." *BusinessWeek Online.* November 11, 1997. Available from www.businessweek.com.

SEE ALSO: E-commerce Consultants; E-commerce Solutions

PERSONAL COMPUTER (PC), INTRODUCTION OF THE

No single person or institution can be credited with the advent of the personal computer (PC). Rather, the rise of the PC is due to the work of multiple individuals, government entities, and businesses. While Apple Computer Inc. and Microsoft Corp. played pivotal roles in developing PC operating systems, the microprocessors developed by Intel Corp. proved equally important, as did the actual PC launched by IBM Corp. in 1981.

EARLY DEVELOPMENTS IN THE COMPUTER INDUSTRY

Many developments took place in the computer industry before work truly began on the machines that became known as personal computers. For example, in conjunction with Harvard University, IBM created the Automatic Sequence Controlled Calculator, the first large-scale device that could process lengthy cal-culations, in 1944. More than eight feet tall, the five-ton machine, known as Mark I, housed nearly 500 miles of wire and 765,000 parts. Some industry experts consider Mark I the world's first computer. In 1951, Ken Olsen, who went on to found Digital Equipment Corp., and Jay Forrester developed the first real-time computer, the Whirlwind, at the Massachusetts Institute of Technology (MIT). That year, the U.S. Bureau of Census began using the UNIVAC I computer to hold data. In 1952, IBM launched a computer designed for scientific calculations, the IBM 701. The vacuum tubes used in the 701 were smaller and easier to replace than the switches used in earlier machines. Remington-Rand developed the world's first high-speed printer for the UNIVAC in 1953. IBM employee John Backus created the FORTRAN programming language the following year. Japan developed its first computers when NEC Corp. created NEC-1101 and NEC-1102 in the mid-1950s. The IBM 705 machine, launched at roughly the same time, was one of the world's first general purpose business computers. Its success helped to oust Remington-Rand, maker of the UNIVAC, from its first place spot in the new computer market.

Digital Equipment Corp. released the PDP-1, the world's first minicomputer, in 1960. Four years later, IBM introduced the System/360, which used software and peripheral equipment compatible with each of the firm's computer models. This interchangeability was a new concept in the computer industry. Firms like Digital Equipment and IBM continued developing computer technology throughout the 1960s. In 1966, analysis and measurements instrument maker Hewlett-Packard Co. developed its first computer, the HP 2116A. Gordon Moore and Robert Noyce left Fairchild Semiconductor to established Intel Corp., which would become another major computer technology innovator, in 1968.

The development of the first personal computers resulted from the convergence of several types of technology. One of the earliest breakthroughs came in 1969 when Intel developed a four-bit central processing unit (CPU) that was able to follow instructions to perform simple data processing functions. Five years earlier, Dartmouth College mathematics professor Thomas Kurtz, and John G. Kemeny, chairman of the mathematics department there, had developed the BASIC (Beginner's All-Purpose Symbolic Instruction Code) computer programming language to allow their students to write programs that could be tested on the GE-225, a computer system developed by General Electric Corp. Because Kemeny and Kurtz did not copyright or patent BASIC, other individuals were free to use it as they saw fit.

One of the best known players in PC history, Bill Gates used BASIC to make his first major mark on the PC industry in February of 1975. The 19-year-old Harvard University student worked with 21-one-year-old Honeywell employee Paul Allen to create a new version of BASIC to run the Altair 8800, considered one of the world's first personal computers. The Altair had been developed the previous year and was powered by the Intel 8088, which was the world's first general purpose microprocessor. A few months later, Gates and Allen established Microsoft Corp. The Altair 8800 was released, with 1KB of memory, to the general public for $375. By 1977, Microsoft had become the largest U.S. distributor of microcomputer languages.

In 1976, computer programmers Steve Jobs and Steve Wozniak founded Apple Computer Corp. to market their new Apple I computer, which was essentially a computer circuit board with no keyboard, case, sound, or graphics. The following year, Apple released the Apple II, the first PC to offer color graphics capacity. The Apple II also included a keyboard, power supply, case, and 4KB of memory. Sales at Apple reached $1 million that year, fueled by the popularity of the new machine, and Apple became one of the fastest growing companies in the United States. Apple's employees replaced their typewriters with PCs in 1979.

Throughout the 1970s, IBM continued to develop new computer systems, including the 370, its most powerful computer system to date, and the 5120, its least expensive computer system to date. The firm also created the Displaywriter word processing system and started offering 24-hour telephone assistance to customers having technical problems.

THE RISE OF THE PC

IBM Corp. chose Intel's 8088 chip for its new personal computer line in 1980. That year, IBM asked Microsoft to develop four languages, as well as an operating system, for its new PCs. Microsoft released Softcard, which allowed Microsoft BASIC to operate on Apple II machines. Apple Computer released the Apple III, its most advanced machine to date. Boasting a new operating system, a built-in disk controller, and four peripheral slots, the Apple III was priced at $3,495, nearly double the price of its predecessors.

In August of 1981 IBM began selling its landmark PC, which was powered by Microsoft's new operating system, known as MS-DOS. The machine was IBM's smallest and least expensive computer system to date, and it is credited for helping to launch the PC revolution. Although other firms, like Hewlett-Packard, actually had beaten IBM to market with their own PCs, IBM's dominance in the business machines market gave it a considerable edge as most IBM business machine clients simply replaced those machines

with IBM computers. To sell its PCs, IBM began authorizing retailers like Sears, Roebuck & Co. and Computerland. The firm also expanded its sales channels to include manufacturers who integrated IBM products into their systems. Within several months of IBM's launch of its first PC, more than 50 microcomputer manufacturers had licensed MS-DOS from Microsoft. That year, Apple Computer completed its initial public offering (IPO), selling 4.6 million shares at $22 apiece. The IPO was the largest in U.S. corporate history since Ford Motor Co. had first listed its shares in 1956. With more than 1,000 employees, a network of 800 distributors in the United States and Canada, and an another 1,000 distributors overseas, Apple had the largest worldwide presence in the computer industry.

In 1982, Apple became the first PC company to secure $1 billion in annual sales. By that time, more than 100 companies had started manufacturing PCs, including Compaq Computer Corp., which focused its efforts on developing a machine similar to IBM's PC. In January of 1983, Compaq released its first PC. The upstart's sales reached $111 million that year, setting a record for the highest first-year sales of any U.S. business. Apple shipped its blockbuster Macintosh machine in 1984, after first advertising it on television during the SuperBowl. Initial versions of the Macintosh retailed at $2,495, while the more powerful Macintosh 512K sold for $3,195. In November of that year, Microsoft introduced its Windows operating system, which was based on the MS-DOS operating system and offered users a graphical user interface (GUI), similar to the one offered by Apple machines. The firm marketed the new platform to the 200 microcomputer manufacturers already licensing MS-DOS. Within a single month, Microsoft sold more than 500,000 copies of Windows. The company also began developing software, including a version of its recently launched Microsoft Word program, for Apple's Macintosh computer. IBM's dealer outlets across the globe reached 10,000, as the firm's sales soared to $46 billion.

By the end of 1985, Microsoft had started distributing Windows to retailers for sale to consumers. It also headed up an alliance with IBM's competitors—including Compaq, Hewlett-Packard, Texas Instruments, and Digital Equipment—in an effort to weaken IBM's monopoly on PC standards development. In response, IBM began to work with Microsoft's competitors on software programs. Despite its increasingly rocky relationship with IBM and the fact that several problems had emerged with the earliest version of Windows, Microsoft convinced IBM to use an upgraded version of Windows on its next line of PCs. By then, more than 30 million PCs had been sold in the United States.

Microsoft conducted its IPO in March of 1986, offering its shares at $21 each and raising $61 million in fresh capital. When Microsoft shares began trading at $85 the following year, the firm's 31-year-old founder, Bill Gates, became the PC industry's first billionaire. Microsoft released a third version of Microsoft Word, which quickly became the firm's best selling product. By 1987, Apple had extended its reach to 80 countries and released the next generation of Macintosh PCs. To compete with Microsoft's increasingly popular software offerings, Apple also founded Claris, an independent software manufacturer.

After several decades of considerable growth, IBM's sales began to decline in the mid-1980s in the face of stiff competition from rivals like Compaq, which was named to the *Fortune* 500 list in 1986. In fact, many manufacturers of IBM "clones" were able to outsell IBM in the retail PC market. Ironically, the PC revolution that IBM had played a major role in sparking eventually hindered the computing giant's success. Used to selling large-scale systems to businesses, IBM was not prepared to target the fastest growing segment of the booming PC market: individual consumers.

STRUGGLE FOR CONTROL IN THE PC INDUSTRY

Compaq's sales exceeded $1 billion in 1987. That year, Packard Bell introduced its first PC. The following year, Apple filed suit against Microsoft, alleging that the firm had used the appearance of the Macintosh operating system as the basis for its Windows program. Apple's lawyers requested that Microsoft either pay royalties or simply stop selling Windows. By then, Microsoft had grown into the leading U.S. maker of PC software, and by the end of the decade more than 2 million copies of Windows 3.0 had been sold. In 1989, PC sales throughout the world exceeded 100 million, and the number of U.S. computer users reached 50 million. The increased speed offered by Intel's 386 and 486 microprocessors helped to fuel the PC's growth, as did the decision by firms like Packard Bell to market PCs via discount chains, electronics centers, and other mass retail outlets.

Revenues exceeded $1 billion at Microsoft for the first time in 1990. Tension between Microsoft and IBM worsened, resulting in a price war between Microsoft's DOS 5.0 and IBM's competitor to DOS, OS/2. In 1991, in what was viewed by many analysts as a plan to wrest market share back from Microsoft, IBM and Apple forged an alliance to develop a new operating system that would not only make computers easier to use, but also facilitate compatibility between

IBM and Apple machines. By then, roughly 90 percent of worldwide PCs used the MS-DOS platform, and Apple had broadened its litigation against Microsoft. In 1992, Microsoft won the case against Apple after a judge decided that the appearance of the Macintosh operating system was not protected by Apple's copyrights. Therefore, Microsoft's Windows platform, though very similar to Macintosh in appearance, was not in violation of copyright law. Apple unsuccessfully appealed the decision. Meanwhile, another PC upstart, Dell Computer Corp., had made the *Fortune* 500 list, just eight years after its inception. By the end of 1993, Dell had become the world's fifth-largest PC maker with sales of more than $2 billion. The worldwide PC industry continued to grow at a rapid pace, and PCs themselves continued to increase in speed and capacity.

FURTHER READING:

"Apple Computer, Inc." In *Notable Corporate Chronologies.* Farmington Hills, MI: Gale Group, 1999.

"Compaq Computer Corp." In *Notable Corporate Chronologies.* Farmington Hills, MI: Gale Research, 1999.

Gantz, John. "This Year's News: Good Computers, Cheap." *Computerworld.* April 27, 1998.

"The Global PC Market: Facing the Eastern Challenge." *Computer Industry Report.* May 30, 1996.

Hudson, Daniel P. "A Brief History of the Development of BASIC." Available from www.phys.uu.nl.

"IBM Corp." In *Notable Corporate Chronologies.* Farmington Hills, MI: Gale Group, 1999.

"Microsoft Corp." In *Notable Corporate Chronologies.* Farmington Hills, MI: Gale Group, 1999.

Polsson, Ken. "Chronology of Personal Computers," 2001. Available from www.islandnet.com.

SEE ALSO: Allen, Paul; Apple Computer Inc.; BASIC; Compaq Computer Corp.; Dell Computer; Digital Equipment Corp.; FORTRAN; Gates, William (Bill); Hewlett-Packard Co.; IBM Inc.; Intel; Jobs, Steve; Microprocessor; Microsoft Corp.; Wozniak, Stephen G.

PERSONAL DIGITAL ASSISTANT (PDA)

Personal Digital Assistants (PDAs) are handheld or pocket computers capable of a wide range of functions. At their most basic level, they serve as electronic address books and to-do lists. However, the capabilities of PDAs have evolved considerably since their introduction in the late 1980s to include wireless access to phone, fax, e-mail, the Internet and other subscription-based data services. Users are able to download information (including books, games, spreadsheets, and word processing documents) from desktop computers or the Internet to their PDAs and beam text messages or business information to other PDA users. Information can also be entered directly into PDAs by using a pen-like stylus—most PDAs are able to convert handwritten characters into type—or via small, portable keyboards.

Because immediate access to information is important to both consumers and retailers, PDAs' wireless properties make them especially valuable tools in the world of e-commerce. PDAs link to the Internet by using a communication standard known as wireless application protocol (WAP), in which a special computer language allows information to be displayed on small screens via a cellular connection. According to *Nua Internet Surveys,* The Strategis Group predicted the number of individuals subscribing to mobile data services would climb from 5 million in 2000 to 172 million in 2007. Also according to *Nua Internet Surveys,* Cahners In-Stat Group predicted wireless Internet access device sales would achieve triple-digit growth from 2000 to 2004, eventually surpassing desk-top computers as the most popular means of accessing the Internet.

According to *The Detroit News,* documents filed with the Securities and Exchange Commission by PDA manufacturer Handspring Inc. indicated sales of handheld computers would exceed $35 million by 2003. According to *Federal Computer Week,* IDC projected demand for PDAs to grow at a compound annual rate of 28.8 percent between 2000 and 2005.

In the early 2000s, it became possible for consumers with credit cards to purchase goods through wireless devices. Kbkids.com, Amazon.com, and Barnes & Noble.com were among the first retailers to begin offering shopping services to consumers in this manner. Wireless shopping portals also began to emerge, through which consumers could access products from a number of different retailers by downloading a single site onto their PDA or wireless phone.

According to *InformationWeek,* in the early 2000s Andersen Consulting developed prototype technology enabling PDAs and other wireless devices to function like synthetic currency. Known as Mobile Micropayments, the technology enables consumers to receive special offers from merchants in their immediate location via their wireless device. For example, a consumer who walks past a vending machine might be presented with a range of selections on the display of his or her PDA, which could be purchased immediately. Mobile Micropayments used Qpass Inc. to handle billing and payment in a manner very similar to automatic payment systems used on toll roads. The technology can be used to pay for everything from fast food to cab fares. In late 2000, Andersen Consulting expected an increasing number of devices—including printers, cash registers and vending machines—would be able to seamlessly communicate with other wireless devices in their immediate vicinity.

PDAs also are important to the corporate e-commerce sector. For example, salespeople are able to use them to access company databases for sales figures or inventory information, to conduct research, and to process orders. In *Pharmaceutical Executive,* Josh Weinstein, president of Torre Lazur PR Healthcare Public Relations, explained: "Executives' connections to their workplaces are driven more and more by the Internet and wireless applications. Web-linked corporate e-mail seems to be the most developed, and it is common for traveling pharmaceutical executives to log on daily. More workgroup projects develop from such e-mail sessions than from the urgent voicemail messages or pages executives receive when office fires need to be extinguished."

PDAs also are valuable to securities brokers, who are able to use them in the trading process. In a *Planet IT* article by Talila Baron, Ron Valeggia, senior vice president and CIO of New York-based Quick & Reilly Inc., commented that the use of PDAs would increase tremendously due to their small size and convenience. Quick & Reilly's brokers already were using wireless phones to trade in mid-2000.

In 1989, Atari introduced the Atari Portfolio, one of the very first handheld computers. Apple Computer also became an early PDA pioneer when it introduced the Apple Newton in 1993. In 1996 U.S. Robotics, which eventually was acquired by 3Com, introduced its PalmPilot model, which eventually became a strong market leader. The introduction was a catalyst for the widespread adoption of PDAs by consumers. In the early 2000s, manufacturers of PDAs included Palm Inc., Handspring, Microsoft, Compaq, Symbian, Motorola, Hewlett-Packard, Fujitsu, Norand, Sharp, Psion, and Sony.

FURTHER READING:

Jerome, Marty. "How WAP Works." *ZDNet,* February 6, 2001. Available from www.zdnet.com.

Morrison, Kara G. "Handheld Computers are, well, Handy." *The Detroit News,* April 29, 2000. Available from detnews.com.

Nelson, Matthew G. "Innovation: A Remote Control for E-commerce." *InformationWeek,* October 30, 2000.

"Strategis Group: Mobile Data to Take Off in the U.S." *NUA Internet Surveys,* January 30, 2001. Available from www.nua.ie.

Zbar, Jeffery D. "E-commerce Eyes Potential of Communication Devices." *Advertising Age,* March 6, 2000.

SEE ALSO: Motorola, Inc.; Nokia Corp.; Palm, Inc.

PERSONALIZATION

Personalization enables more intimate relationships between companies and their customers and is an effective tool for building brand loyalty. In it simplest form, personalization can involve Web site visitors creating personal profiles that outline the kinds of features or information they want to see. This usually requires the visitor to fill out an online questionnaire or survey. By providing a host of details during the initial visit, successive visits to the site become more meaningful and valuable, at least in theory. Yahoo!'s My Yahoo!, which it introduced in 1996, is an example of this approach. By registering on Yahoo!'s site, visitors were able to customize the content (including information about weather, TV program lineups, news, sports, and stocks) and advertising displayed.

Lands' End was another company that successfully used personalization during the early 2000s. The company's My Personal Shopper asked visitors a series of questions in order to understand their clothing preferences, after which the site was able to better recommend possible selections. This involved looking at a series of ensembles and choosing the degree to which one was preferred over the other. By filling out a simple questionnaire, consumers also could take advantage of My Virtual Model, which used information like hair style and color, face and eye shapes, skin tones, weight, height, and silhouette to create virtual models which could display clothing selections prior to purchase.

In addition to retail applications, personalization technology also was valuable to corporate users within companies. As information technology plays an increasingly dominant role in the business world and the amount of information workers rely on to do their jobs grows, manageability can become a problem. In late 2000 Goodyear Tire & Rubber Co. turned to personalization as a solution to the demand for information, which employees often needed in specific formats. Portal technology from Computer Associates International Inc. allowed users to access and arrange many different kinds of corporate information from a single interface based on their needs and requirements.

Personalization goes beyond users willingly customizing the content and features they'd like to see or use at a given Web site. It also involves e-tailers using sophisticated predictive techniques to profile visitors based on factors like the Web sites they just came from, the kinds of products they put into their online ''shopping carts,'' information about past purchases, and more. These profiles are then used to present highly targeted special offers to customers.

In the early 2000s, Edina, Minnesota-based Net Perceptions was one company offering solutions to companies like Kmart and J.C. Penney in this area. In 2000, it helped Guitar Center, a leading national retailer of music products, and subsidiary Musician's Friend to increase catalog and e-commerce sales by 60 percent. The company's technology enabled targeted recommendations based on ''insight into the individual's personal product and music tastes combined with established business rules that leverage knowledge about product relationships, profit margins, overstock conditions and more.''

Companies often rely on special software programs to personalize their Web sites. These applications normally correspond to a site's content, the manner in which ads are generated, and product offerings. Artificial intelligence, mathematical algorithms, and elements like business rules serve as the basis of many such programs. However, by the early 2000s personalization had become a sophisticated endeavor for many retailers, and off-the-shelf software alone wasn't enough to meet the needs of all users. Some required custom applications and strategies. This was due to the fact that companies, their customers, and product or service offerings varied considerably—even within the same industry. What represented meaningful personalization for one company often was not meaningful for another.

Although the technology exists to recommend purchases based on a customer's past history or items placed into a shopping cart, such methods by themselves do little to deliver the kinds of meaningful experiences that are possible when data from other sources is added to the equation. The most effective techniques rely on predictive analysis techniques that draw information from many different sources as a basis for recommendations. In *InternetWeek,* Robert Preston criticized companies for a lack of sophistication in the area of personalization, explaining that ''sophisticated personalization isn't a single, simple product. It's a process—a complex combination of software, networking and best practices that revolves around data gathering, sharing, and mining. It requires multiple departments to swap data and link systems. It entails analyzing information from multiple outside sources.''

Successful companies were using personalization more and more in the early 2000s. *eMarketer* found that the number of online retailers in the United States offering interactive tools or personalization increased from 36 percent at the end of 2000 to 56 percent in mid-2001. At that time, almost all companies were offering an online newsletter to their customers at the time of checkout that could be customized in respect to frequency or content. Customers were very receptive to personalization features. In mid-2001, research from Cyber Dialogue revealed that customers were more likely to shop at and register with sites offering the technology. The research also indicated that consumers who take advantage of personalization are likely to spend more than those who don't. Therefore, because of its value to companies and consumers alike, its likely that personalization will continue to play an important role in e-commerce.

FURTHER READING:

"Cyber Dialogue: Personalization Appeals to Customers." *Nua Internet Surveys,* May 14, 2001. Available from www.nua.ie.

"eMarketer: More Personalization on Retail Sites." *Nua Internet Surveys,* June 12, 2001. Available from www.nua.ie.

Kemp, Ted. "Personalization Isn't A Product." *InternetWeek,* May 31, 2001. Available from www.internetweek.com.

Manber, Udi, Ash Patel, and John Robison. "Experience with Personalization on Yahoo!" *Communications of the ACM,* August 2000.

Preston, Robert. "Personalization Requires Better Cross-Pollination." *InternetWeek,* June 1, 2001. Available from www.internetweek.com.

Sullivan, Jennifer L. "The Challenges and Rewards of Personalizing Customer Interactions." *Customer Inter@Ction Solutions,* April 2001.

Vinas, Tonya. "Manufacturers Are Tapping Into Personalization Technology To Increase The Value Of Information." *Industry Week,* November 20, 2000.

Waltner, Charles. "CRM Makes Shopping Online Personal." *InformationWeek,* January 29, 2001.

SEE ALSO: Mass Customization; Profiling

PHOTONICS

By the 21st century, photonics was on the cusp of unseating electronics as the optimal and revolutionary science underlying cutting-edge telecommunications and computing technology. The primary thrust of photonics research in the 1990s and early 2000s was toward the fiber-optic networking for use in telecommunications, particularly to accommodate rapidly escalating demand for Internet bandwidth. In these and other industries, photonics was poised as the next-generation technology that would transform the speed, clarity, and manner in which data is transmitted and stored, and, in the process, create a vibrant market in its own right.

The greatest immediate value of photonics applications in telecommunications is in their ability to dramatically expand carrying capacity. As the research and market behind photonics mature, analysts generally expected telecommunications operations in the near future to phase electronics out completely in favor of photonics. For the time being, however, most telecommunications systems that employ photonics technology operate as hybrids of photonics and electronics, whereby photonics strengthens and supports electronics where the latter is at its weakest and most sluggish.

Photonics is the science of generating and harnessing light and other radiant energy sources to provide power to technology. At the base of photonics communications is the optical fiber, a miniscule, lightweight, durable conduit for light signals. Photons, the unit of measure of this energy, are uncharged particles of light. As a result, photons are unaffected by electromagnetic forces, thereby enhancing the flexibility of the medium. Unlike electrons, the driving force behind electronics, photons do not require any copper wires or other barriers to keep them from interacting with one another; crossing and mingling photons have no adverse interactions whatsoever, where clashing electronics results in signal confusion and noise. Electronic chips, meanwhile, may have tremendous carrying capacity, but only a limited number of wires can actually connect with it to transport the electronically beamed transmission. As a result, electronic systems increasingly harbor more information than they have the capacity to transmit, resulting in transmission bottlenecks, whereby the traffic literally clogs up as signals filter through the limited space available to pass through.

Photonic systems greatly expand the amount of bandwidth available; photonic transmissions are measured in trillion hertz (terahertz), compared with less than 10 billion hertz (gigahertz) used to measure electronics. Moreover, photonic systems were doubling their carrying capacity roughly every nine months, although this acceleration was necessary to keep pace with rapidly growing Internet traffic. Generally, photons are transmitted through fiber-optic cables, although it is possible to send photons beaming in any direction, which allows for a number of interconnected data channels to work in harmony. The information travels on independent wavelengths of light. Fiber amplifiers, doped with erbium, renew the strength of the original signal, which inevitably weakens as it travels over miles of optical fiber. The potential for materials-cost savings with photonics thus presents a particularly attractive alternative to electronics for telecommunications companies. The materials photonics systems do incorporate include lasers, fiber optics, optical and electro-optical instruments, and advanced hardware and software, all of which work in concert to transmit, relay, detect, amplify, and store light carrying information in some form.

Photonics research dates back to the early 1950s, when the primary means of generating photonic power was through harnessing light from the sun and from mercury arc lamps, both of which proved unsuccessful. Experiments with laser technologies in the 1960s also disappointed, as the relatively high generation of heat in photonics, coupled with the lack of adequate materials, rendered photonics applications impractical. However, as laser technology improved, particularly by bringing the temperature down to room level, photonics research picked up again. As scientists developed optical fibers and semiconductor lasers in the 1970s, telecommunications specialists began to covet the possibilities of high-speed data transmission that photonics could bring about.

Where photons suffer by comparison to electrons is in their malleability. Because electrons have a charge, simply applying a voltage makes them easy to manipulate. As a result, routing electrons toward a specific destination or containing them to provide fuel for storage is relatively simple. Not so with photons. Absent any charge, they are difficult to control, as they tend to scatter in random directions when they are routed around a corner. So while sending photons long distances, say from New York to Seattle, is simple and much faster and more efficient than sending electrons, having some of the photonic signals stop at local neighborhoods along the way or routed to another destination such as Dallas, is relatively difficult, and thus must be converted to electrons before they make the turn.

To correct for this disadvantage, scientists were hard at work developing systems designed to squash the wavelength of light as tightly as possible. Using these waveguides, the flow of photons through integrated optical circuits is brought as much as possible under control, making it simpler to route signals in different directions without compromising the integrity of the original signal.

Generally, all-optical networks were beyond the reach of network operators in the early 2000s, though that was changing quickly as optical switching technology matured and became more affordable, promising an all-optical network in the near future. In the meantime, however, photonic transmissions require nonoptical means of instilling information onto lightwaves, and so most photonic circuits and switches still rely heavily on electronics. Pending the development of all-optical networks, operators generally implement hybrid systems incorporating photonics and electronics to create optoelectronic systems. As long as that's the case, the true promise of photonics won't be realized, simply because the conversion between photonics and electronics that the technology currently requires takes time, slowing down the transmission.

Moreover, as photonic technology matures, it puts greater strain on the more limited electronic systems, and electronics find it harder and harder to keep up. Meanwhile, however, the existing bottlenecks that arise as a result of the conversion back and forth between electrons and photons were greatly alleviated by the development of dense wavelength-division multiplexing (DWDM), which dramatically increases the amount of signal that can a single fiber can carry by pumping several laser pulses simultaneously down a single optical fiber.

While DWDM can squeeze many signals onto a single fiber, there was a limit to just how many lightwaves a single fiber could support, simply because the shrinking of the wavelength required by DWDM can only go down as far as the wavelength of visible light. Therefore, electronic switches and conversions remain necessary until the time when photonic switches ripen into maturity, and simply laying more optical fiber becomes an optimal solution, since it will no longer run against the bottlenecks created by the conversion to electronics. Scientists pinned much of their hopes for future photonics development on the perfected photonic crystal, a chip that will transmit and bend light, making it turn corners with minimal compromise of the original light signal. Though the technology to bend lightwaves exists, the photonic chip remains a goal rather than a reality.

It's not only speed that will be improved at the user end via the widespread adoption of photonic networks. With the boosted bandwidth available via all-optical networks and, eventually, photonic microprocessors, the Internet will likely open the floodgates for other technologies that have been stalled at the gates for years, particularly holography and instant video transmissions akin to voice phone calls. Without creating tremendous bottlenecks, Internet shoppers may one day be able to view clear three-dimensional images of the car they're thinking of purchasing and talk to friends and business associates with a video picture accompanying their voice, all of which will be interactive with other computer operations such as file and software downloads, transactions, and so on. Viewing entire films over the Web, in perfect clarity and without gaps or choppiness, will become a feature available to the average Internet user without tying up Internet traffic for others.

FURTHER READING:

Brown, Chappell. ''Bell Labs: Riding a Photonics Wave.'' *Electronic Engineering Times,* January 31, 2000.

————. ''Electronics, Photonics Vie for Optical-Net Switching.'' *Electronic Engineering Times,* August 14, 2000.

Fairley, Peter. ''The Microphotonics Revolution.'' *Technology Review,* July, 2000.

''Fiat Lux.'' *Economist,* February 5, 2000.

Hecht, Jeff. "Hot Fibre Optics." *Electronics Times,* February 28, 2000.

Johnson, R. Colin. "Device Turns Photons On and Off—New Optical Switching Method Comes to Light." *Electronic Engineering Times,* March 27, 2000.

Salamone, Salvatore. "An Awful Lot of Vendors and Providers Are Seeing the Light, and It's Coming from Photonic Switches." *tele.com,* May 1, 2000.

Weinberg, Neil. "Hooked on Photonics." *Forbes,* November 29, 1999.

SEE ALSO: Bandwidth; Fiber Optics; Next Generation Internet Initiative (NGI); Optical Switching

PLATFORMS

A platform consists of the software and/or hardware that allows a computer system to run. Two of the most well-known personal computer (PC) platforms are DOS and Windows, both manufactured by Microsoft Corp. They typically run on microprocessors, such as the Pentium, developed by Intel Corp. Apple Computer Co.'s Macintosh system is another major PC platform, and UNIX is a well known platform for networking systems.

In terms of e-commerce, platforms are what allow businesses to conduct business electronically. They include technology that allows online merchants to showcase their wares online, accept payment, keep track of customers, provide customer support, and complete many other tasks that brick-and-mortar establishments perform manually. An example of a highly successful e-commerce platform is the one built and used by online retailing titan Amazon.com. In fact, the platform worked so well for Amazon that traditional retailers struggling to move into e-commerce, such as Toys 'R' Us and Borders, gave up on developing their own technology and opted to let Amazon's e-commerce platform power their Web sites.

Initially, e-commerce platforms mainly focused on allowing e-merchants to publish their catalogs electronically and handle online transactions. Eventually, however, the platforms grew beyond these basic business-to-consumer (B2C) functions to include the content management, personalization, and back-end business management features desired by firms engaged in both B2C and business-to-business (B2B) commerce. As a growing number of companies began handling all types of business operations online, many traditional firms began developing e-commerce platforms. For example, IBM Corp. created the WebSphere platform, and Microsoft Corp. developed its

BizTalk platform. They competed with startups like Blue Martini Software Inc., founded in 1998; InterWorld Corp., founded in 1995; and Germany's Intershop Communications, which developed Enfinity, ranked the top e-commerce platform by Forrester Research Inc.'s eBusiness TechRankings.

FURTHER READING:

Meister, Frank. "E-Commerce Platforms Mature." *InformationWeek.* October 23, 2000. Available from www.informationweek.com.

"Platform." In *Ecommerce Webopedia.* Darien, CT: Internet.com, 2001. Available from e- comm.webopedia.com.

SEE ALSO: Apple Computer Inc.; IBM Inc.; Linux; Microsoft Windows; UNIX

PORTALS, WEB

A Web portal, also known as a gateway, presents itself as a starting point for Internet users when they first connect to the Web. Portals have evolved from simple search engines to sites offerings a wide range of services. The leading portals in terms of traffic include America Online's AOL.com, Yahoo!, and Microsoft Network (MSN).

All of the leading portals offer an integrated package of services that includes a search engine, news, chat, e-mail, calendars, personalization, content, music downloads, video streaming, and electronic commerce. These services are designed to give portals "stickiness," which means that users will stay there longer and keep coming back to the site. Where portals once acted as a gateway to the larger interconnected world of the Internet, portals are more interested in having users stay within their sites as much as possible. Their strategy is to be a destination, not just a starting point.

PORTALS EVOLVED FROM SEARCH ENGINES, 1996-1998

Three Internet search engines—Yahoo!, Lycos, and Excite—all went public in April 1996 and began the process of transforming themselves into Internet portals. Yahoo!, for example, rolled out many new features and services that were designed to add stickiness. These included a personalization feature called My Yahoo!, and Yahoo! Finance, which included investment research, market summaries, and financial news as well as links to stock quotes, company profiles, and similar information. Yahoo!'s strategy was to become a media company, not just a tool for searching the Internet.

Following its initial public offering (IPO), Excite launched a redesigned Web site and added a menu of defined-content categories on its opening page. The new Excite also included reviews and ratings of some 60,000 Web sites. Before the end of 1996 Excite had added a broad array of information and services to encourage Web users to make it their default home page. The site included City.Net, an information service covering major U.S. and international cities, along with news, reviews, directories, and other resources.

After it went public, Lycos redesigned its graphic interface to look like an Internet portal. While it continued to upgrade its search engine, it added features such a city guide to 400 cities. It also established a Club Lycos that created online communities and provided users with merchant discounts. Lycos, following its transformation into Terra Lycos in 2000, became a dominant international portal with 98 million registered users in 41 countries by mid-2001, making it the third most popular online network in the world.

Not all search engines were able to make the transition to portal. InfoSeek, another search engine, also went public in 1996. It developed into an Internet portal when the Walt Disney Co. acquired part ownership for $472 million in 1998. In 1999 Disney purchased the rest of InfoSeek and launched the Go.com portal. Go.com included content from the full range of Disney properties, including news from ABC, sports from ESPN, and children's and family-oriented content from Disney programs. By 2000, however, it was clear that Go.com would not be able to compete with the leading Internet portals. After Disney sustained more than $1 billion in losses from Go.com and other Internet properties, the company announced plans to close Go.com in 2001.

As Web demographics changed, interest in portals grew more intense. By 1998 Internet users had become more reflective of the general population. Portals were seen as a way to meet the broader range of needs that such an audience would seek to satisfy on the Internet. As part of their strategy to reach this new Internet audience, portals became more interested in adding content, and content providers wanted to leverage their content over the Internet. It was such considerations that led a content provider such as Disney to become interested in executing a portal strategy by acquiring a major search engine like InfoSeek and launching its own portal. Similarly, in 1998 NBC spent $38 million to acquire a 19 percent interest in Internet portal Snap!, which was owned by CNET. NBC subsequently combined Snap! with other properties to launch its own portal, NBCi, in 1999.

In 1998 Netscape's portal, Netcenter, was a hot property whose long-term strategy was to reach the corporate IT (information technology) market. It planned to become a trading platform for business customers and add virtual trading communities in such areas as finance and travel. However, the launch of Netcenter 2.0 in mid-1998 added several consumer-friendly features, including new content channels, a consumer-oriented search feature, e-mail, and browsing services. Before the end of the year, Netscape was acquired by America Online in a $4.2 billion stock-for-stock transaction.

Traffic at Netcenter lagged behind that of other portals. In January 2000 Netcenter had 347,000 unique visitors, compared to 37 million for Yahoo!, 26.2 million for AOL.com, 15.6 million for Go.com, 13.8 million for Lycos, and 9.9 million for AltaVista. America Online was completing its merger with Time Warner when it announced it would recast Netcenter as a business professional's portal. In addition to adding AOL features to Netcenter, such as instant messaging and e-mail services, AOL planned to integrate content from Time Warner into the site.

PORTALS CAPTURE A SHARE OF ELECTRONIC COMMERCE, 1998-2001

In 1998 the major portals were laying the groundwork for adding electronic commerce capabilities to their sites. Yahoo!, for example, acquired software developer ViaWeb Inc. to support business transactions at its site. Many larger corporations, including Office Depot, CitiCorp, and Barnes and Noble, began paying portals for space on their sites. Excite, for example, was charging Office Depot $1 million per year for space on the Excite Web site. Barnes and Noble entered into a five-year, $40 million agreement with America Online to become the featured bookseller on AOL.com. CitiCorp began marketing home-based banking services at Netcenter.

As portals became the default starting point for Internet users, they replaced what were known as online services. Both AOL and The Microsoft Network (MSN), for example, realized they would be more successful if they were positioned as Internet portals rather than simply as online services or Internet service providers (ISPs). Online services that were unable to develop into portals, such as CompuServe and Prodigy, pursued other strategies.

By 1999 the leading portals—Yahoo!, Lycos, Excite, AOL, and others—were among the most prominent of Internet companies. They enjoyed high stock valuations and financial backing from blue-chip companies. More than 20 major brick-and-mortar companies announced plans to develop their own portals. One problem facing the Internet portals was their inability to distinguish themselves from one another. Most portals offered the same features and functions, even to the point of using identical language to structure their content into channels. As a result, as many as 22 million Internet users—more than half the market in 1999—said they had no loyalty to any of the portals, according to research firms Media Metrix and IDC.

Toward the end of 1999 the leading portals added shopping capabilities and other services for the holiday shopping season. AltaVista launched a network of online services that included Shopping.com. Lycos launched LycosShop, which included product reviews and information and links to selected retailers. Lycos also acquired the gaming site Gamesville.com and financial site Quote.com. Excite@Home, formed when Excite was acquired by high-speed Internet access provider At Home, acquired online greeting card company Blue Mountain Arts. Yahoo!, meanwhile, bought GeoCities to enhance its community-building and Internet publishing efforts. It also acquired Broadcast.com to offer more streaming media to users and more rich media options to advertisers.

Many consumer portals began courting the business-to-business (B2B) market during 2000. Yahoo! had already introduced Corporate My Yahoo! in 1999, which featured personalization tools and allowed the integration of corporate content. In 2000 Yahoo! launched its B2B Marketplace, a central site where buyers and sellers could compare prices from different B2B communities across the Web. B2B Marketplace was designed as a portal leading to other vertical trading communities, also known as vortals, rather than as a large trading community of its own.

America Online's B2B initiatives in 2000 included positioning Netcenter as a portal for business professionals. In Fall 2000 AOL unveiled its new Netscape Netbusiness service, which was designed to help small businesses build Web-based storefronts and engage in business-to-business e-commerce. AOL and PurchasePro, a marketplace developer, formed an alliance to develop Netscape Netbusiness. Netscape Netbusiness was organized in three sections: My Industry, My Business, and My Life. It included e-mail, a business version of Netscape Instant Messenger, industry-specific news, market research, expert opinions, maps and directions to member businesses, and community tools for sharing information. Hewlett-Packard agreed to link its HP Business Store to Netbusiness, while Monster.com agreed to develop a recruitment industry marketplace for Netbusiness.

According to a study by Booz-Allen & Hamilton, portals were more successful in attracting eyeballs than were entertainment or financial sites in 2000. Nearly 98 percent of all U.S. Internet users visited a portal during 2000, compared to 80 percent visiting an entertainment site and 43 percent visiting a financial Web site. The study found that users spent 49 percent of their time using portals as a search engine or gateway. The rest of their time at portals was spent using other portal options, including telecommunications and Internet services (17 percent), news and information (10 percent), online communities (6 percent), directories and classified ads (4 percent), entertainment (4 percent), financial services (3 percent), and shopping (2 percent).

During 2000 Web portals appeared to be turning those eyeballs into electronic commerce and enticing their visitors to portal-affiliated shopping sites. According to June 2000 ratings compiled by Nielsen/NetRatings, Yahoo! Shopping was the Web's top portal shopping site with 5.8 million unique home-based users, or 7 percent of all Internet users. AOL's Shopping Channel had more than 3.4 million unique visitors, while AltaVista's shopping area drew 2.6 million unique users. MSN's shopping center ranked fourth with 1.2 million unique shoppers.

When it came to online shopping, portals offered visitors specialized search engines and the ability to comparison shop. Portals also attracted more small retailers through their storefront business models first made popular by Yahoo! Shopping. Portals also offered auction sites that attracted many small businesses. These developments reduced the cost of selling online for smaller businesses and made it more attractive for them to sell online.

The portals' e-commerce strategies seemed to pay off during the 2000 holiday shopping season, when the leading portals experienced higher growth rates in holiday sales than stand-alone online retailers. American Online reported an 84 percent increase in holiday sales from $2.5 billion in 1999, while Yahoo! and Lycos both said that the e-commerce activity generated by their shopping services doubled from the previous year. By comparison, e-tailers had an average growth rate of 40 percent for the holiday season, according to the Yankee Group. Yankee also reported that 57 percent of online consumers began their online shopping trips at a portal or a portal-based mall. While portals enjoyed higher growth rates than stand-alone retailers, specialty brand name e-tailers were still considered to be the leaders in online shopping.

FURTHER READING:

Carr, Dave. ''Portals in Pinstripes.'' *Internet World,* September 15, 1999.

Enos, Lori, and Elizabeth Blakey. ''Portals Turn Eyeballs into E-Commerce.'' *E-Commerce Times,* July 20, 2000. Available from www.ecommercetimes.com.

Evans, Daniel S. ''Web Portals.'' *PC Magazine,* November 21, 2000.

Graziano, Claudia, and Jim Kerstetter. ''A Portal to Profits.'' *PC Week,* July 6, 1998.

Ince, John F. ''Portals: Who Gets the Bigger Slice?'' *Upside,* March 2001. Available from www.upside.com

Jacso, Peter. "Portals, Vortals, and Mere Mortals." *Computers in Libraries,* Febraury 2001.

Kerstetter, Jim. "Will Portals Pay Off?" *PC Week,* August 31, 1998.

Lidsky, David. "Home on the Web." *PC Magazine,* September 1, 1998.

Mahoney, Michael. "Report: Portals Gaining on Stand-Alone E-tailers." *E-Commerce Times,* January 15, 2001. Available from www.ecommercetimes.com.

Ott, Karalynn. "Consumer Portals Step up B-to-B Features." *B to B,* April 2, 2001.

Regan, Keith. "Do Portals Still Matter to E-Commerce?" *E-Commerce Times,* March 23, 2001. Available from www.ecommercetimes.com.

Rupley, Sebastian. "Big Portals Do B2B." *PC Magazine,* May 23, 2000.

Swartz, Jon. "Internet Portals Find International Markets Tough to Tame." *E-Commerce Times,* March 1, 2001. Available from www.ecommercetimes.com.

SEE ALSO: Advertising, Online; AltaVista; AOL Time Warner; Excite@Home; Microsoft Network (MSN); Netscape Communications; Terra Lycos; Vortals; Walt Disney Co.; Yahoo!

PRETTY GOOD PRIVACY (PGP)

Pretty Good Privacy (PGP), one of the leading data encryption protocols, was launched in 1991 by cryptographer Philip Zimmerman, who founded Pretty Good Privacy Inc. around his encryption algorithm in 1996. PGP was designed to protect the civil liberties of those communicating over the Internet by utilizing a mathematical code, or algorithm, to scramble information in such a way that only authorized parties could decode it. Not only was PGP widely used in e-mail transactions in the United States and other relatively stable countries for the purpose of securing day-to-day communications, it was also employed in highly sensitive areas, such as Sarajevo, Kosovo, and Guatemala, for the protection of data from hostile governmental or police forces. In a way, such uses fulfilled the original intentions of Zimmerman and PGP: to safeguard information from governmental intrusion.

Since World War II, the U.S. government, particularly the National Security Agency (NSA), has been at the forefront in developing encryption schemes, primarily to safeguard sensitive government- and security-related information, including secrets procured by U.S. spies. As private cryptographers pursued their own encryption schemes for use in the private sector, however, the U.S. government protested, and fought for years to keep advanced encryption algorithms under wraps. Zimmerman was among the cryptographers leading the fight against the NSA to open up the field of cryptography to the public. Zimmerman began work on what would become PGP in 1984, and spent the late 1980s perfecting his mathematical algorithm.

The U.S. government didn't take kindly to PGP at first. Zimmerman spent the early 1990s locking horns with the United States Department of Justice to open up the field of e-mail encryption, as part of a broader effort by cryptographers to force the government to open the doors to greater use and trade of encryption tools and schemes. In 1993 the Justice Department began investigating Zimmerman for violation of export restrictions on encryption technologies. After much bitter fighting, the government backed off three years later, signaling a shifting mood in the government toward a realization that encryption schemes were going to proliferate and were in fact important for the development of e-commerce.

The first personal-security software designed for the personal computer, PGP employed 56-bit encryption, which was at the time the strongest encryption available to the private sector. PGP not only boasted message encryption capability, but also featured digital signatures and data compression. PGP utilizes public-key cryptography, in which a private key, or source code for encrypting messages, is held by the PGP user, and a public key is openly available for anyone who wishes to send an encrypted message to that user. To broadcast the public key, the user simply sends it to one of PGP's servers. To send a message to a PGP user, one encrypts it with that user's public key; then, using the unique private key, the user decrypts the message to read it. Only when the public key interacts with the private key through the use of a password will the message unlock. PGP was available as freeware to noncommercial users, while the program itself usually had to be installed on individual computers, although it was increasingly accessible on a central PGP server.

Zimmerman sold the rights to PGP in 1997 to Network Associates, Inc., which he then joined as a consultant, and continued to play a role in PGP's development. Following NAI's acquisition, PGP Inc. was renamed PGP Security and branched out into constructing enterprise applications around the code, which the company continued to revise and release to the public as freeware. By the early 2000s, however, Zimmerman was concerned that the future of PGP as a freeware program may be limited, his concern sparked particularly by NAI's decision in 2001 to withhold the source code of its latest PGP version 7.0.3 from the public; the source code of all previous versions were freely available. For its part, NAI insisted it had no plans to discontinue its PGP freeware. At any rate, Zimmerman chose to leave NAI in February 2001 to join a rival firm, the Irish company Hush, convinced that NAI wouldn't continue to develop PGP in the manner Zimmerman most desired.

FURTHER READING:

Dugan, Sean. "E-Business Innovators: Phil Zimmermann-Security." *InfoWorld,* October 9, 2000.

Fisher, Dennis. "PGP Creator Phil Zimmerman Moves On." *eWeek,* March 5, 2001.

Gantenbein, Douglas. "For Your Eyes Only." *Business Week,* April 23, 2001.

Messmer, Ellen. "E-mail Encryption Guru Focuses on PGP's Future." *Network World,* February 26, 2001.

Verton, Dan. "PGP Investor Resigns from Network Associates." *Computer World,* February 26, 2001.

Weil, Nancy. "U.S. Grants PGP Encryption Export License." *Network World,* December 20, 1999.

SEE ALSO: Advanced Encryption Standard (AES); Cryptography, Private and Public Key; Data Encryption Standard (DES); Digital Signature; Encryption

PRICELINE.COM

From a consumer's point-of-view, it was a great concept, one that truly seemed to leverage the power of the Internet for the benefit of the consumer. The concept was deceptively simple: Let the consumer decide how much he or she would be willing to pay for an item, then find a business willing to match it. From a business point-of-view, though, there were many questions. How many airline companies, for example, would really consent to providing tickets on a name-your-price basis to consumers? And if it worked for airline tickets, could the concept be successfully applied to other goods and services?

These were some of the questions that Jay Walker and his company, Walker Digital, believed they could answer when they established the pioneering name-your-price Internet business, Priceline.com. When Priceline.com opened its Web site in April 1998, it was limited to offering airline tickets. Travelers could book tickets through Priceline.com by listing their points of departure and arrival and their travel dates (but without specifying a time of day), and then naming the price they were willing to pay for the tickets. Participating airlines, which Priceline.com refused to identify at first, had supplied Priceline.com with a database of unpublished fares, which Priceline.com searched each time a ticket request was made. If tickets were available at the requested price, Priceline.com would issue them within an hour for domestic travel and within 24 hours for an international ticket. Buyers were notified by e-mail, first to acknowledge their request and then to confirm whether the tickets had been issued. The tickets were non-refundable and non-transferable, and flyers had no control over the time of day they would be flying.

Although Priceline.com claimed to have the participation of several major airlines in its program, the company refused to identify them, honoring the airlines' desire to have consumers pay higher prices by ordering through other sources. It was reported that Continental, U.S. Airways, and American Airlines were not involved and that Northwest Airlines and Alaska Airlines were in discussion with Priceline.com. It later became known that Delta Airlines was a major investor in Priceline.com. Airlines were willing to participate in Priceline.com's program, because they felt that Priceline.com was offering tickets that otherwise would have gone unsold. The airlines did not perceive the Priceline.com model to be a threat to the published fare system, but rather as a complement to it. On its first day of business, Priceline.com claimed to have 621,000 visitors and requests for $575,000 worth of tickets. However, the company did not say how many ticket requests were actually filled.

EXPANDS NAME-YOUR-PRICE CONCEPT TO OTHER GOODS AND SERVICES

During 1998 Priceline.com expanded its business model to let consumers name their price for hotel rooms and, on a limited basis, automobiles. Consumers who successfully bid on a car paid $25 to Priceline.com for each completed sale, with dealers kicking in another $75 to Priceline.com. Later in the year Pricline.com began offering hotel rooms from more than 1,000 participating hotels on a name-your-price basis to consumers. While consumers could not pick a specific hotel, they could specify a two, three, four, or five-star rating for their hotel along with a specific city, an area within the city, and the nights they wanted to stay. Matches were confirmed within an hour, and a non-refundable and unchangeable reservation was issued.

In August 1998 Priceline.com was granted a patent on its business model. The model was developed in 1995 by Walker Digital, whose business was to generate patentable business ideas and sell them to other companies. According to *Inc.* magazine, "Priceline.com's patent covers 'bilateral buyer-driven commerce,' in which a consumer names the price at which he or she is willing to buy a product, lists acceptable substitutes for that product, guarantees the intention to buy with a credit card, and then transfers to a 'controller' the authority to conclude the transaction. The controller then alerts sellers, who may accept the offer and charge the buyer's card.'' While Priceline.com was hoping to generate revenue by licensing its patented business model to other Internet firms, many remained skeptical whether such ''business model'' patents were enforceable and whether the courts would uphold them.

By the end of 1998 Priceline.com was selling 1,000 airline tickets a day. Its aggressive radio and newspaper advertising strategy (later expanded to include television) featured the actor William Shatner as a spokesperson and resulted in the company having name recognition among at least a quarter of the U.S. adult population, or some 50 million people, according to a study by Opinion Research Corp., which listed the top five Internet ''megabrands'' as America Online, Netscape, Yahoo!, Amazon.com, and Priceline.com.

GOES PUBLIC IN 1999 AND FURTHER EXPANDS ITS BUSINESS MODEL

Priceline.com's initial public offering (IPO) on March 30, 1999, was one of the hottest Internet IPO's of the year. The company raised about $115 million from the initial sale of shares at $16 each. By April 18 the stock had reached nearly $60 a share. When the company announced on April 26 that more than 1 million customers had tried Priceline.com in its first year, the stock rose to $121 a share. *Forbes* noted that Jay Walker's initial $25 million investment in the company was now worth $4.3 billion.

During 1999 Priceline.com expanded its business model to include mortgages and automobiles. It created a new automobile unit and hired Maryann Keller, a veteran auto analyst, to be in charge. Her mission was to take the company's automobile business, which was available only in New York, nationwide. Later in the year AutoNation Inc., the world's largest car retailer, agreed to a three-month test in the Tampa, Florida area, whereby it would submit bids to try and sell cars to consumers who had named a price for a specific vehicle on Priceline.com.

Priceline.com first offered mortgages through an alliance with LendingTree Inc., which would forward mortgage requests to 22 lenders in its network. Priceline.com and LendingTree subsequently added home refinancing and home equity loans. Later in 1999 the company expanded its mortgage business by establishing a joint venture with Alliance Capital Partners of Jacksonville, Florida, called Pricelinemortgage. The companies claimed their online mortgage application process would save consumers up to $1,000 in closing costs.

Meanwhile, more major airlines were signing up and providing seats to Priceline.com, including Continental and Northwest. The company claimed that it had improved its matching rate on reasonable bids from 11.2 percent in 1998 to more than 42 percent in 1999. Priceline.com made money on each transaction by purchasing tickets from the airlines at prices lower than consumers were willing to pay for them. Those tickets were selected by Priceline.com from a private fare database to which the airlines had contributed a portion of their ticket inventory.

As a public company Priceline.com reported losses of $17.2 million in its first quarter of 1999 and $14.3 million in its second quarter. Second quarter revenue reached $111.6 million, nearly double the company's first quarter revenue. A secondary offering of stock and convertible debt raised some $500 million in new capital in 1999. As part of the offering Delta Airlines sold 1.5 million of its Priceline.com shares, which were worth about $145 million. Although the company did not expect to turn a profit anytime soon, its stock remained popular with investors. Its services were also a hit with consumers. A single-week sales record of 50,000 tickets prompted Priceline.com to announce that it had captured more than two percent of all leisure airline ticket sales in the United States. By the end of the year United Airlines, US Airways, and American Airlines had joined Delta, Continental, Northwest, TWA, and America West as participating airlines.

CUTBACKS AND FALLING STOCK PRICES MARK 2000

Prior to the start of 2000 Priceline.com announced it would begin offering groceries on a name-your-price basis through a new venture called Web-House Club. The new service was introduced in the New York City area in November 1999, with some 600 stores participating. Customers could name their price for groceries and other non-food items, but they could not specify specific brand names. If their prices were accepted, customers would be quickly notified by e-mail, their credit cards charged, and they could print out a voucher that would be accepted by a nearby store. Participating retailers hoped the new service would boost store traffic and increase the average size of each consumer's market basket. Priceline.com planned to roll out the service nationally over the course of the coming year, with Philadelphia and the Baltimore-Washington, D.C. markets getting the service next. Although WebHouse Club had a specific financial relation to Priceline.com, it was set up as a separate privately held company and its revenue figures were not consolidated with those of Priceline.com.

One of the first indications that 2000 might be a difficult year for Priceline.com also came toward the end of 1999, when Microsoft Corp. announced it would offer reverse auctions for hotel rooms on its travel site, Expedia. After Microsoft offered its Hotel Price Matcher service for about a month, Priceline.com brought a lawsuit against Microsoft to defend its patent on buyer-driven commerce. The news caused Priceline.com's stock to fall to just one-third of its previous high.

At the beginning of 2000 Priceline.com launched several new services. The company announced it would add domestic and long-distance telephone service for business and residential customers through an agreement with Net2Phone, a provider of IP (Internet protocol) telephony. After an initial test period, Priceline Long Distance was launched in May 2000 with three service providers: Net2Phone, Deltathree.com, and ZeroPlus.com. The service allowed consumers to bid on prepaid phone cards for long-distance service.

Priceline.com also began to offer deals on car rentals, with National Car Rental System Inc. and Budget Rent-A-Car Corp. participating. The Hertz Corp. and Alamo Rent A Car LLC joined the program in mid-2000. An agreement with NextCard Inc. resulted in the creation of a co-branded Priceline.com credit card, which allowed customers to name their own terms for a co-branded Visa or MasterCard credit card. In addition the company expanded its new car sales service to 13 additional states, making it available in 26 states. Ford Motor Co. also agreed to a Florida market test, whereby customers could submit a bid for a car through Ford's Web site that would be distributed to Ford dealerships in the customer's area. By May the auto service was available in 48 states, competing directly with sites such as CarsDirect.com, Autobytel.com, and Autoweb.com.

Another new venture was Perfect YardSale, formed by Priceline.com and an Atlanta, Georgia-based company of the same name. Perfect YardSale would use the Internet to match buyers and sellers of secondhand goods. Perfect YardSale would generate revenue from fees collected from sellers for listing their goods and for successful sales.

Priceline.com found the early results from WebHouse Club encouraging. In the New York metropolitan area it had achieved two percent market penetration in the first three months and hoped to achieve three to five percent. WebHouse Club had 150,000 active members and sold more than 5 million grocery items in its first three months. In April Safeway grocery stores joined the service, followed by Kroger in June.

Rising gasoline prices in early 2000 made Priceline.com's announcement that it would offer gasoline on a name-your-price basis seem well-timed. To obtain their gas, consumers picked the grade of gas, at least three gas stations from a list, and a price. They would then be notified if any stations accepted their bid. Consumers would receive a refund if the pump price dropped below their bid price before they purchased their gas. Offered through WebHouse Club, the name-your-price gasoline service appeared to have garnered little support from the petroleum industry when it launched on May 20, 2000. Priceline.com hoped that the major oil companies and refiners would subsidize part of the savings to attract new customers, but none were willing to participate in the program. As a result, Priceline.com subsidized the consumer discount from different sources, including fees from paying retail partners, revenue from paid advertising on its Web site, and third-party sponsors. Priceline.com formed partnerships with about 5,000 independent gasoline marketers. The service was also available through about 25,000 outlets that accepted the US Bank Voyager Fleet Card, the debit card that also administered Priceline.com's gasoline card.

FIRST OF MANY PROBLEMS

Slumping sales of airline tickets caused Priceline.com to announce its third quarter revenue would be down $20 to $25 million from the second quarter and well under analysts' expectations. The announcement in September 2000 caused the company's stock to lose 42 percent of its value in one day, reaching a 52-week low around $10 a share. By the beginning of November the firm's stock was trading for less than $5 a share, and the company announced it would lay off 16 percent of its workforce, or about 90 workers. Another 48 workers were let go at the beginning of December. Around this time Priceline.com began to experience a series of executive departures, including its chief financial officer Heidi Miller and the head of its automotive unit Maryann Keller. Company founder Jay Walker vacated his position as vice chairman at the end of 2000 to spend more time focusing on the business challenges facing the firm.

At the beginning of October 2000 Priceline.com announced that it would shutter its WebHouse Club affiliate, through which the company offered name-your-price groceries and gasoline. At the time of the announcement WebHouse Club had been operating for 11 months and had about 2 million grocery and gasoline customers, with some 7,200 grocery stores and 6,000 gas stations participating. The reason given for the closing was that the company was unable to raise enough capital for the coming year to complete its business plan and start turning a profit.

Other problems facing Priceline.com in the final quarter of 2000 included the advent of a competing airline ticket service, Hotwired.com, which was backed by a Texas investment group and six major airlines: America West, American, Continental,

Northwest, United, and US Airways. Unlike the Priceline.com model, though, Hotwired asked consumers to indicate when and where they wanted to travel and let the airlines submit bids for the tickets. Consumers would then have 30 minutes to purchase the lowest quoted ticket. Priceline.com was also falling prey to growing consumer complaints about its service. The Connecticut Better Business Bureau received so many complaints that it suspended Priceline.com's membership for about three months, reinstating the firm toward the end of December 2000.

In spite of these problems, Priceline.com remained optimistic. The company's revenue for all of 2000 rose more than 150 percent to $1.24 billion, compared to $482.4 million in 1999. With these trends under way, the firm hoped to begin generating profits in the early 2000s.

FURTHER READING:

''Be Your Own Barcode.'' *Time,* July 10, 2000.

''Beam It Up.'' *Business Week,* May 10, 1999.

''The Birth of Priceline.'' *Supermarket News,* February 14, 2000.

Elkind, Peter. ''The Hype is Big, Really Big, at Priceline.'' *Fortune,* September 6, 1999.

''Grant, Elaine. ''The Priceline Effect.'' *Travel Agent,* August 2, 1999.

''It Was My Idea.'' *The Economist* (U.S.), August 15, 1998.

Machan, Dyan. ''An Edison for a New Age?'' *Forbes,* May 17, 1999.

Nelson, Brett. ''Mogul.com.'' *Forbes,* May 3, 1999.

''A Net Monopoly No Longer?'' *Business Week,* September 27, 1999.

''Priceline's Bid for the Big Time.'' *Business Week,* January 18, 1999.

Rosner, Hillary. ''Jay Walker: Priceline Founder and Vice Chairman.'' *MC Technology Marketing Intelligence,* January 1999.

''Want a Car? Name Your Price.'' *InternetWeek* July 13, 1998.

''Wired for the Bottom Line.'' *Newsweek,* September 20, 1999.

''Zipping onto the I-Way.'' *Business Week,* July 19, 1999.

SEE ALSO: Auction sites; Business-to-Consumer (B2B) E-Commerce

PRICING

Although the pricing of products and services may appear to be simple at face value, there actually are many different dimensions to pricing in the business world. Pricing is a major component of any business strategy, online or otherwise, and companies take a variety of strategic approaches to pricing depending on their particular goals. The objectives of pricing can include everything from gaining market share, eliminating competitors, and reinforcing the position of a brand's image to simply selling high volumes of a product or service.

Generally, consumers seek to buy more when prices are lower and less when prices are higher. However, things are rarely that simple. Emotions and status also play critical roles in the pricing process, and shrewd marketers are able to tap into the minds of buyers and charge more money for so-called luxury items or status symbols. They also employ different pricing tactics, including odd-number pricing (selling an item for $19.95 as opposed to $20.00), in their attempts to sell goods and services.

In the physical world, the majority of sales transactions occur in face-to-face situations. Although some negotiating may take place, prices for goods and services are often fixed for consumers, and sellers possess a great deal of control. Consumers make purchases with relatively limited capabilities for quickly comparing prices from other sellers. Such is not the case on the Internet, where new sets of variables affect pricing. Online, both individual and business consumers are able to quickly find pricing information for similar or identical items from many different sellers in a matter of seconds. Additionally, individuals can use different tools, including software programs called intelligent agents (also known as shopping bots), to search the Internet for the best price and report back results. In some cases, intelligent agents also negotiate terms and prices on behalf of users, taking the search process a step further. Chat rooms and online communities also work to quickly spread the word about where the best deals can be found online.

THE POWER OF COMPARISON

On the Internet, there are several different tools customers can use to comparison shop for just about any kind of product or service, all within a matter of seconds or minutes. Among the Web's largest comparison shopping sites in the early 2000s was mySimon. The company's service was powered by intelligent agent technology created by one of the company's founders. According to mySimon, ''by using the power of next-generation intelligent agent and advanced parallel search technologies, mySimon automatically combs Web merchants' sites for product and price information and presents it so that it is easy to read and sort. mySimon's proprietary Virtual Learning Agent (VLA) technology takes a unique approach to create mass quantities of intelligent agents that mimic human behavior and can be 'trained' to extract specific information from any merchant Web site.''

At mySimon.com, consumers could shop for products in many categories from more than 2,000 different sellers, and then make actual purchases at a seller's Web site. In addition to listing prices for new items sold by leading e-tailers, search results could include products listed in online classified ads and online auctions. Details about the availability of items and the merchants who sold them also were available. In late 2000, mySimon announced expanded capabilities that gave more power to consumers and extended the Internet's reach to the physical retail world. The company made it possible for consumers to access mySimon from a variety of wireless devices including personal digital assistants (PDAs), wireless phones, and radio-modem-powered handheld devices from eLink.

Another company that gave consumers the ability to comparison shop was NexTag—an online marketplace where both companies and individuals consumers went to buy and sell both new, used, and reconditioned items. As with mySimon, NexTag allowed visitors to search for an item in one of several different categories. However, buyers also could ''choose from name brand retailers, small stores, or individual sellers and between new or used versions of the same item.'' The prices listed on the site included sellers' taxes and shipping costs, and reviews from other users were available to assist shoppers in the decision-making process.

Sites like mySimon and NexTag helped to create a challenging atmosphere for companies engaging in e-commerce. One of the ways companies sought to gain an advantage in a marketplace where competing on price alone became difficult was to focus more on the buying experience they delivered to customers, including the aesthetic appeal of their Web sites and site personalization options. Focusing on hard-to-compare items and services was another strategy used by online sellers. While the prices of some items (including stocks, cameras, and books) can be compared quite easily, others (such as houses, even within similar price ranges and geographic areas) are harder to compare side-by-side. In general, the more variables involved with a product or service purchase, the harder it is for consumers to engage in comparison shopping, and the more room companies have to levy higher prices.

Online, traditional seller-established pricing is similar to its counterpart in the offline world in that every product or service has an associated market range within which businesses must stay when they set prices. Some ranges are wider than other, allowing for varying degrees of markups. The trick for many retailers is finding the highest price the market will bear without affecting demand. This can be accomplished more easily online because feedback on the Internet is both immediate and measurable. Conducting analyses into consumer reactions to pricing is also much cheaper online. Companies don't have to wait weeks or months to analyze sales reports or have retail staff physically adjust prices on store shelves. E-commerce allows them to monitor sales and make price adjustments electronically. Companies must be careful how they test prices, however, because consumer dissatisfaction can result when identical items are sold for different prices to different customers. This is one potential pitfall for e-commerce companies, especially those that take a dynamic approach to pricing.

DYNAMIC PRICING

Although traditional pricing schemes are used online, e-commerce allows for exciting scenarios not found offline. One unique advantage the Internet offers is the ability to customize prices to individual consumers or business customers based on their purchase histories. This price segmentation approach is made possible through the power of databases. Based on customer data, companies are able to offer better deals to their best customers, or to strategically price items that are similar to those purchased in the past.

In many ways, the Internet shifts the balance of price-setting power. As *Business Horizons* explained, ''The Net enables customers to become both price takers and price makers, and for firms to gain both buying advantages (by buying at good prices from their suppliers) and earn commissions on customer trades (by allowing and facilitating customers to trade with each other). IT, and in particular the Web, have made variable pricing an option for many firms, which now have the opportunity to change and disseminate prices as often as desired. Prices can be set with a single transaction or multiple interactions.''

Variable, dynamic pricing is a key characteristic of e-commerce pricing, allowing for prices that change or fluctuate due to different variables, conditions, and situations. Being able to manage dynamic pricing strategies is a key ability for companies wishing to succeed in the world of e-commerce, according to professors at the University of California-Irvine Graduate School of Management. The forces of supply and demand are leading variables that dictate pricing. They cause some e-tailers to continually analyze supply and demand information and adjust prices accordingly. When demand for products or services increases, savvy e-tailers respond quickly by increasing their prices. Likewise, when demand begins to fall they adjust prices downward to stimulate more purchases.

In mid-2001, *InfoWorld* announced that IBM, Compaq, Hewlett-Packard, and Dell were all looking into dynamic pricing approaches for their e-commerce operations. Different factors were involved in each company's strategy. For Dell, the price of computer memory chips and processors was an influencing factor, while IBM's approach involved product life cycle and demand. Hewlett-Packard referred to its approach as ''contextual pricing,'' as the number of total items being purchased as part of special promotions would affect what customers paid overall. As a consultant pointed out in the article, dynamic pricing must be handled carefully. Such approaches have been known to cause problems for companies if consumers feel as though they have not received a fair deal.

Some dynamic pricing scenarios are value-based, involving situations in which customers pay what they think a product or service is worth. Priceline.com is an excellent example of value-based pricing. From airline tickets, rental cars, and hotel rooms to long distance phone service, new automobiles, and even mortgages, buyers used Priceline.com to get deals they might not have ben able to obtain through traditional means. At Priceline.com, consumers were able to make offers for different goods and services in one of four categories (travel, personal finance, automotive, and telecommunications), which they guaranteed with a credit card. The company then attempted to find sellers willing to honor the offer. In order to make things work, buyers were required to allow a degree of flexibility concerning things like brand names, features, and time frames.

Although the concept behind Priceline.com was popular with consumers, its success has been somewhat limited for a number of reasons. After its initial launch, Priceline.com founded a licensee called Web-House and attempted to apply the name-your-price model to other product categories like groceries and gasoline. However, the new endeavor failed because of customer service problems, which attracted considerable media attention. The company's stock price suffered badly, several key executives left the organization, the Connecticut Better Business Bureau removed Priceline.com as a member in good standing, and it was investigated by that state's attorney general. Priceline.com later was reinstated as a member of the Connecticut Better Business Bureau after it improved its customer service and named consumer advocate and former New York State Attorney General Robert Abrams as an advisor. This goes to show that low pricing alone isn't always enough to guarantee success; customer service also is a critical facet of e-commerce.

Are one pair of blue jeans worth $46,532? They were to Levi Strauss & Co., which purchased a rare vintage pair for that price on online auction site eBay. Online auctions are another form of dynamic, value-based pricing. Founded in 1995, consumers and business across the world congregate on eBay to buy and sell just about every imaginable kind of product and service. In late 2001, 29.7 million users were registered on eBay. Additionally, Media Metrix ranked the auction as the Internet's most popular shopping site, in terms of total user minutes. On eBay, users had the ability to buy items at fixed prices, as well as via a traditional auction format. In 2000 alone, more than $5 billion worth of merchandise was traded on the site.

eBay wasn't the only online auction in the early 2000s. More specialized, business-oriented auctions involving high-priced items also existed. Additionally, reverse auctions also were an option. These involved buyers indicating what they were looking for and how much they were willing to pay. Auctions like these were useful to companies that needed to get rid of excess inventories. Instead of selling off such inventories at deep discounts to third party re-sellers, auctions provided them with a way to leverage the real value of their inventories by reaching interested parties directly in a cost-effective way.

One example of a specialized online business auction was IronPlanet, where interested parties bought and sold used heavy equipment. Unlike eBay, IronPlanet's auctions were not continuous; it held events at specific dates and times. In mid-2001, one of IronPlanet's auctions involved 37 pieces of equipment being sold for more than $1.8 million. Including the sales from that auction, IronPlanet had sold more than $17.4 million worth of used equipment since its first auction in April 2000.

FURTHER READING:

Fischer, Frank. ''Using the Web to Sell Surplus Inventory.'' *Office.com,* July 20, 2000. Available from www.office.com.

mySimon. ''mySimon Company Information.'' mySimon, September 3, 2001. Available from www.mysimon.com.

Pitt, Leyland F., Pierre Berthon, and Richard T. Watson. ''Pricing Strategy and the Net.'' *Business Horizons,* March/April 2001.

Regan, Keith. ''Harnessing the Power of Online Pricing.'' *E-Commerce Times,* March 22, 2001. Available from www.ecommercetimes.com.

Vigoroso. ''Study: Winning at E-Commerce Requires Evolved Management Style.'' *E-Commerce Times,* July 20, 2001. Available from www.ecommercetimes.com.

SEE ALSO: Commoditization; MySimon; Product Review Services; Shopping Bots

PRIVACY: ISSUES, POLICIES, STATEMENTS

Few Internet-related issues have generated as much controversy, conflict, and concern as privacy. The debate encompasses freedom of expression, security of intellectual property, marketers' abilities to gather information about consumers on the Web, workplace productivity, and rights of Internet users. Governments, industry, and citizen-advocacy groups are struggling to define workable privacy guidelines and enforcement procedures that will satisfy all parties in the rapidly changing universe of the commercial Internet. As data-collection technologies such as cookies, Web-crawlers, and Web cameras proliferate, the issue becomes more pressing.

Activity on the Internet in the early 2000s continued to increase rapidly, and with it, the rate of personal data collection, commercial transactions, and surveillance of Web users. Americans thus have grown more concerned about safeguarding their privacy online. A 2000 Pew Internet & American Life Project survey reported that 86 percent of the 1,017 Internet users polled wanted legal requirements mandating that Internet companies gain explicit permission to collect personal data online. Furthermore, 54 percent felt that tracking users' movements online constituted an invasion of personal privacy.

Many groups have motives for collecting and storing users' personal information online. Governmental and law-enforcement officials contend that access to such information spurs rapid identification of criminals, helping to combat credit fraud, terrorism, and illegal immigration. Businesses have a seemingly insatiable appetite for minute details about the identities and personal habits of online consumers. This information enables them to tailor promotions and advertising in hopes of generating sales and increased profits. Individual Web users appreciate the ease and efficiency provided by personalized Web sites, which store credit card information for future purchases, remember passwords, and modify Web pages automatically to cater to their interests.

But commercial and governmental organizations can compromise the privacy of online users. For example, Toysmart.com, an online toy retailer, contained a privacy statement guaranteeing that it would not make its customer list available to outside organizations. But when its operation failed amid the dot-com shakeout, Toysmart.com attempted to sell its customer database to a third party. In another retail example, in the year 2000, the online bookseller Amazon.com faced a U.S. Federal Trade Commission (FTC) probe and two privacy-invasion lawsuits charging it improperly handled the personal information stored in its online database. Meanwhile, government data was called into question when Image Data Inc. entered into a $1.5 million contract in 1997 with the U.S. Secret Service to digitize drivers' licenses and other personal data in order to create a national identity database for governmental use. A three-state pilot program was launched, only to be halted after widespread media coverage revealed the program's existence. Government surveillance was again at stake in July 2000, when it was disclosed that the Federal Bureau of Investigation (FBI) was using an Internet monitoring system called Carnivore, which it installed in Internet service providers' sites to monitor their traffic. Carnivore became the object of a Freedom of Information Act (FOIA) suit brought against the FBI by the Electronic Privacy Information Center (EPIC). By January 2001, the FBI had complied in part with the FOIA request to release documents regarding the information Carnivore had gathered.

METHODS OF ONLINE SURVEILLANCE

Commercial Web sites' early collection of user data generally consisted only of how many hits a particular site received. No method of information gathering existed to build profiles of typical users who frequently visited the site—the very information that helps marketers tailor advertisements and promotions for specific target audiences. But as Internet software and technology became more sophisticated, online information-gathering techniques grew more powerful and precise. Since the mid-1990s traffic-logging systems have routinely provided details about the brand of browser, version number, and available plug-ins that an individual uses, as well as identify sites previously visited and recreating searches the user conducted on a search engine. Web servers record the Internet address of each computer that visits a site, though this does not reveal the personal characteristics of the actual person operating that computer.

Web sites can also identify visitors via "cookies"—small text files that the Web site writes to a user's hard drive. Cookies contain the name of their proprietary Web site and a unique identifier they assign to a user's computer, which is written to the cookie file the first time a person visits the site. On subsequent visits, the Web site reads the cookie and recognizes the user's computer. Only the originating site can read the cookie, which may also store user passwords. Most browsers contain a feature that permits users to disable cookies.

Banner ads are another online information-gathering device. They are controlled by network advertisers, third-party companies that function as intermediaries between advertisers and Web-site companies. Banner ads place and read cookies, just like Web sites. Network advertisers can track users' surfing habits across the Web by placing banner ads on thousands of different Web pages.

Cookies and banner ads can only generate aggregate user profiles, based on the computers used for browsing rather than individual humans users. To collect more user-specific data, some companies permit users to customize their sites. Often they give users an incentive for registering, such as offering access to restricted content, in the hopes of gathering more detailed information about visitors. This helps online merchants fine-tune their profiles of individual users. When users enter personal data required for site registration or online purchases, the company gains access to that information.

E-COMMERCE AND PRIVACY

Most e-commerce Web sites monitor the movements of online visitors and consumers. Often companies sell or release customer information to third parties to promote additional products or to support direct-marketing campaigns. Online marketing generates spam, or ''junk'' e-mail, in the form of unsolicited advertisements and promotions. Studies indicate that many Americans consider these practices an unwarranted invasion of their privacy. Forrester Research estimated that $12.2 billion in e-commerce revenue was lost to privacy concerns in 2000, up from $2.8 billion in 1999.

Internet users can block monitoring of their online behavior in various ways. Two simple examples are giving false information when personal data is requested and encrypting their own e-mail. Software is also available to prevent online tracking and block spam. But despite Americans' nervousness about online surveillance, only 10 percent of Internet users have set their browsers to reject cookies, according to a 2000 Pew Internet Survey.

WORKPLACE PRIVACY

Employees constitute another group whose Internet use has come under increasing scrutiny. Workplace surveillance pits employers' financial interests, the protection of corporate intellectual property, workplace productivity, and security against the privacy rights of employees.

International Data Corporation (IDC) attributes 30 to 40 percent of all lost worker productivity to personal Web surfing on company time; this costs U.S. companies about $54 billion annually. According to the American Management Association, in 2000 nearly 75 percent of all major U.S. companies monitored employee communications, including telephone calls, e-mail, and Internet connections; this represented nearly twice the percentage that did so in 1997.

Frequently the supervision of employee behavior falls to the information technology (IT) department, though increasingly U.S. firms also hire CPOs—Chief Privacy Officers. Many companies use monitoring software that scans not only Web-site URLs, but the actual content of Web pages, to determine whether employees' online activity is linked to their workplace duties.

CHILDREN AND PRIVACY

The law views children as less capable of making well-reasoned judgments than adults, and there's a common understanding that children need special legal protections from harm and exploitation. Children are particularly vulnerable to manipulation by online marketers and more likely than adults to surrender personal or family information on the Web. In 1998, an FTC survey of 212 child-oriented Web sites concluded that although 89 percent of the sites collected personal data, 46 percent failed to notify users of that fact. In part to remedy such situations, Congress passed the Children's Online Privacy Protection Act (COPPA) in 1998. COPPA, which took effect in 2000, prohibits organizations from gathering personal information online from children under age 13, unless their parents give ''verifiable'' consent before the information is collected or shared with third parties. Web-site operators must also post their privacy policies online and notify parents of the types of information that they collect.

It was unclear whether COPPA was effective. In 2001 the FTC cited survey data revealing that 91 percent of children's Web sites contained privacy policies, compared with only 24 percent in 1998. However, a report the same year by the University of Pennsylvania's Annenberg Public Policy Center stated fewer than half of the 167 children's sites surveyed complied with COPPA guidelines.

LEGAL DIMENSIONS OF ONLINE PRIVACY

U.S. law governing online privacy is in a state of enormous flux. The Constitution contains no explicit right to privacy, though the Fourth Amendment protects Americans from illegal searches and seizure of personal records. Supreme Court decisions have created a variety of privacy rights, based on the Fourth Amendment and on the Fourteenth, which restricts the government from compelling individuals to disclose certain personal information. However, these rights apply to government actions, not the private sector. Hence, the U.S. lacks all-encompassing, federal data-privacy laws similar to those of the European Union (EU), as well as clear legal remedies for breaches of electronic-data privacy.

The Supreme Court has ruled that the Fourth Amendment protection of privacy holds where an individual has a ''reasonable expectation'' of privacy. However, since anyone can access the Internet, a Web user cannot have a ''reasonable expectation'' that his or her activities will be considered private, except if they occur on a limited network or when that user transmits information to a discrete Internet address. Thus data exchanged on electronic bulletin boards and chat rooms does not merit protection. In addition, any e-mail taken if a computer is seized is not protected.

One legal solution proposed to enhance privacy protection was the granting of intellectual property status to personal data. In other words, individuals would hold property rights to their personal data. However, this generates First Amendment concerns; in general, ''data,'' or basic facts that are not part of a creative work, is not subject to ownership. Thus it is difficult to prevent Web sites from gathering and storing users' personal information.

The FTC, the chief governmental agency responsible for regulating personal data, has preferred to promote user control over personal data, rather than ownership rights to it. It has encouraged e-marketers to develop and post privacy statements that guarantee the security of personal data gathered online. But public-interest privacy advocates argue that this strategy will fail because few Web users even read privacy policies, many sites do not follow their own policies, and few policies guarantee enforcement. Noncompliant Web sites can be charged with engaging in deceptive trade practices, but the responsibility for forcing compliance rests with private citizens, who must lodge the suits to get results.

U.S. ONLINE PRIVACY-PROTECTION LEGISLATION

A series of existing laws addresses the privacy dilemmas spawned by the Internet, with dozens of new bills proposed in each Congressional session.

Title III of the 1968 Omnibus Crime Control and Safe Streets Act, also called the Federal Wiretap Statute, represents one of the first legislative attempts to protect the privacy of individuals' communications. It levies criminal and civil penalties for the intentional and unauthorized interception or disclosure of private communications, but it extended only to aural, not electronic, communications. In 1986, the Electronic Communication Privacy Act (ECPA) added electronic communications to those already protected by the Wiretap Statute. The Stored Communications Act, which safeguards electronic data stored after transmission, followed in the same year.

However, the ECPA allows governmental officials with a valid court order to trace private communications. Judges must approve requests for such court orders if prosecutors can verify that the data is relevant to ongoing criminal investigations. Furthermore, the statute doesn't protect users' identifications, only the content of their communications.

Congress asked the FTC to assess the privacy risks associated with computer databases in 1995. Partly as a result of FTC findings, a series of subsequent laws were passed, each addressing a separate facet of online privacy.

The 1996 Health Insurance Portability and Accountability Act (HIPAA) requires that safeguards be instituted to protect patients' medical records, which health-care organizations are increasingly storing and transmitting online. The Health and Human Services (HHS) Department drafted attendant regulatory protections in 1999. They grant patients the right to review and obtain copies of their medical records; require patients' consent before health information is released; and allow patients to restrict the use of their medical information.

Individuals' online financial information is protected under the Fair Credit Reporting Act (FCRA) of 1997. It gives consumers control over their credit histories, requires employers to notify employees in advance if they are to be subject to workplace misconduct investigations, and obligates them to inform employees of the results of such investigations. Proposed changes to FCRA would require online companies to notify individuals about data-sharing arrangements with third parties and to permit them to opt out of such arrangements.

The Gramm-Leach-Bliley Act of 1999 further targeted the security of personal financial data. It mandated that financial institutions reveal to consumers what personal information they share with third parties and that they notify their customers annually about how personal data is gathered and protected.

By 2000, there was growing bipartisan support in Congress for Internet privacy. Many relevant bills were submitted to congressional sessions in the late 1990s and in 2000. The 107th Congress introduced nearly 50 bills in its first four months alone. Among them were bills proposing the establishment of a federal privacy commission, the protection of social security numbers online, and the prohibition of any future governmental attempts to establish a uniform national identification standard.

Proponents of stronger privacy-protection legislation cite a 2000 FTC report to Congress, which revealed that only 20 percent of the most heavily visited Web sites had implemented comprehensive ''fair information practices'' regarding online data-gathering. The report concluded that industry self-regulation alone had failed to guarantee sufficient protection for user privacy and personal data, and that more comprehensive legislation would be needed, in tandem with self-regulation, to accomplish that goal.

GLOBAL PRIVACY STANDARDS

Many industrialized countries possess far more stringent legislative rules protecting online users' privacy than exist in the U.S. The emerging global standard at the beginning of the 21st century was the European Commission's Directive on Data Protection, which took effect in 1998. It restricts all unauthorized transmission of personal data of EU citizens to any countries lacking legal standards that guarantee a similar level of online privacy protection. Since the directive's adoption, many other countries began drafting similar rules, among them Argentina, Australia, Canada, Switzerland, and New Zealand. Some countries also created governmental privacy directors or agencies to oversee Internet privacy.

For U.S. companies to exchange Internet users' personal data with EU members, they must participate in the Safe Harbor data-sharing agreement, which was devised by the EU and the U.S. Department of Commerce. The agreement, which became operational in November 2000, holds American businesses to implement data and privacy protection standards equivalent to those in the EU directive. Once a company complies with the Safe Harbor program, EU regulators can sue them only for breach of their own policies, not the standards of the EU Directive.

INDUSTRY SELF-REGULATION

Unlike the EU, the United States has relied primarily on industry self-regulation to ensure that Internet users receive an adequate level of privacy protection. Proponents of self-regulation argue that the breakneck speed of Internet growth, and its many successes, mandates against sweeping regulations that might stifle future development. U.S. businesses argue that self-regulation encourages industry to safeguard user privacy in order to boost consumers' confidence in the security of e-commerce transactions. In essence, business leaders believe that market forces will punish companies that breach privacy, causing them to lose business, while rewarding with increased sales those that protect privacy.

In the spirit of self-regulation, many e-businesses post privacy policies on their Web sites and permit opt-out avenues for users who don't wish to submit personal information online. When companies violate their own privacy policies, breach of contract suits and actions for deceptive business practices or false advertising can be brought against them. But this arrangement provides no penalties for failure to have a privacy policy, and such policies rarely cover the actions of third parties, such as network advertisers, who might acquire personal data online.

Detractors of self-regulation claim it can't be enforced. Thus it operates on the principle of *caveat emptor* (''let the buyer beware''), placing on consumers the responsibility of determining whether an online marketer is trustworthy and has the best interests of the consumer in mind.

FURTHER READING:

Anderson, Teresa. ''Congressional Legislation.'' *Security Management,* March 2001.

Cohen, Sacha. ''Thought Cop.'' *InfoWorld,* February 26, 2001.

Coyle, Karen. ''Protecting Privacy.'' *Library Journal,* Winter 2001.

DiSabatino, Jennifer. ''FTC OKs Self-Regulation to Protect Children's Privacy.'' *Computerworld,* February 12, 2001.

''First Privacy Bill Filed In 107th Congress.'' *Electronic Privacy Litigation Reporter,* February 5, 2001.

Frisone, Deborah. ''Privacy: Is Big Browser watching? Privacy in the Internet Age.'' *Commercial Law Bulletin,* November/December 2000, 8.

Fox, Susannah, et al. ''Trust and Privacy Online: Why Americans Want to Rewrite the Rules.'' Washington: Pew Internet & American Life Project, August 20, 2000. Available from www.pewinternet.org/reports.

Hetcher, Steven. ''The FTC as Internet Privacy Norm Entrepreneur.'' *Vanderbilt Law Review,* November 2000, 2041.

Kelly, Shan. ''Is Someone Watching You?'' *Information World Review,* January 2001, 18.

Kemper, Cynthia. ''Surveillance Software: Big Brother.'' *Communication World,* December 2000/January 2001.

Knopf, Allegra. ''Privacy and the Internet: Welcome to the Orwellian World.'' *Florida Journal of Law and Public Policy,* Fall 1999.

McCullagh, Declan. ''Smile for the U.S. Secret Service.'' *Wired News,* September 7, 1999. Available from www.wired.com.

Rombel, Adam. ''Privacy and Security in a Wired World.'' *Global Finance,* January 2001.

———. ''The Privacy Law Debate: Navigating the Privacy Law Divide.'' *Global Finance,* January 2001.

Thibodeau, Patrick. ''Europe's Privacy Laws May Become Global Standard.'' *Computerworld,* March 12, 2001.

Tillett, L. Scott. ''Pressure Builds For Privacy Laws.'' *Internetweek,* June 5, 2000.

Trombly, Maria. ''FTC Seeks Input on Revisions to Credit Card Data Privacy Guidelines.'' *Computerworld,* January 1, 2001.

U.S. Department of Health and Human Services. ''HHS Fact Sheet: Protecting the Privacy of Patients' Health Information.'' Washington: GPO, April 23, 2001. Available from aspe.hhs.gov.

U.S. Federal Trade Commission. ''FTC, Self-Regulation and Privacy Online: A Report to Congress.'' Washington: GPO, July 1999. Available from www.ftc.gov.

———. ''Privacy Online: Fair Information Practices in the Electronic Marketplace.'' Washington: GPO, May 2000. Available from www.ftc.gov/reports.

SEE ALSO: e-Government Web Privacy Coalition; Electronic Frontier Foundation; Electronic Privacy Information Center (EPIC); Encryption; European Commission's Directive on Data Protection; Legal Issues; Pretty Good Privacy (PGP); Safe Harbor Privacy Framework

PRODUCT MANAGEMENT

Product management has played an important role in business strategy since the early 1930s. A product manager's job description can vary from organization to organization, but it typically includes overseeing many aspects of a product's life cycle, ranging from product creation and development to marketing and selling of the product. The advent of e-business during the 1990s added yet another facet to product management, as the Web created a new, global marketing and selling channel for both consumer retailers and business-to-business (B2B) enterprises. Traditional retailers including Levi Strauss & Co. and cataloger Lands' End Inc., along with technology-based firms like IBM Corp. were forced to change their product management strategies in order to compete in the changing marketplace. Dot.com start-ups like Amazon.com Inc. and Datek Online Brokerage Services LLC also placed strong emphasis on product management in order to stake their claim in the online arena.

EARLY HISTORY

The concept of product management was created in the early 1930s by Proctor & Gamble. At the time, the company's Ivory soap was a top seller. Its Camay soap, on the other hand, was not performing as well. Proctor & Gamble executives appointed a brand manager to focus specifically on the Camay line in hopes of reviving the product. This management approach proved successful and soon other consumer packaged goods firms began using a similar strategy to manage their products.

As product management began to take hold in many business organizations, the concept gained popularity among business colleges and became part of the curriculum of marketing classes. During the 1960s, Harvard Business School professor N. Borden created the four P's of marketing: product, which involved the creation and development of a product; place, the markets in which the product would be sold; price, how much the product would sell for; and promotion, how the product would be marketed and sold. Borden's marketing theory soon became a standard in business classes throughout the United States. Soon thereafter, three additional P's were added to that concept: people, process, and provision of customer service. While product management has traditionally encompassed all of these P's, changing technology and evolving market conditions leave it subject to constant change within an organization.

IMPACT OF THE INTERNET

Up until the 1990s, product managers relied on traditional marketing and sales channels such as television ads and retail outlets to promote their product or brand. As the Internet became a more common tool used by enterprises for advertising and selling in the late 1990s, product managers were forced to reposition their products to compete on the Web. Product management also started to become interchangeable with brand management, as establishing a strong, recognizable brand name became increasingly important. An August 2001 *BusinessWeek Online* article claimed that ''for companies in almost every industry, brands are important in a way they never were before. Why? For one thing, customers for everything from soda pop to software now have a staggering number of choices. And the Net can bring the full array to any computer screen with a click of the mouse.''

Lands' End Inc. is one catalog apparel company who successfully adapted its product management strategies to the Internet. Launched in 1995, LandsEnd.com started out selling 100 items. To promote its products online, the firm used both print and television advertising and also launched innovative technology on its site to draw in customers. Lands' End Live, for example, provided online shoppers with real-time personal assistance twenty-four hours a day, seven days a week. Shop With a Friend enabled people in different locations to shop online together. Outfits Online allowed an online customer to coordinate outfits with 4,750 different items on the LandsEnd.com Web site. Another feature included Your Personal Model, which allowed a user to create a three-dimensional model of their body shape. The tool would then suggest clothing that was appropriate for that body type. By 2000, LandsEnd.com included all Lands' End catalog products and was visited by 38 million Web surfers. Due in large part to its successful product management, Landsend.com grew into the leading online apparel site with $218 million in sales in fiscal 2001.

Levis.com, launched by fashion retailer Levi Strauss in 1996, is another example of a traditional retailer utilizing the Web as part of its product management strategy. While the site never took off as a sales channel, it did become an effective marketing tool for the company. Levis.com was originally launched as an informative company Web site; however, the site became a sales outlet for over 120 clothing items in 3,000 different styles in 1998. Levi Strauss' share of the denim jeans market slipped from 30 percent in 1990 to 17 percent in 1998. The firm saw the Internet as a potentially lucrative sales and marketing channel for its products and believed its online efforts might bolster Levi Strauss' faltering image. The company's move into online sales arena did not fare well, however, because of several product management-related issues. For example, Levi Strauss' transition from selling large quantities of merchandise to retail outlets to shipping specific items to individual online consumers did not go smoothly. The firm faced product distribution problems both in its retail and online channels due to major cuts in workforce. When sales continued to falter in the late 1990s, the advertising budget for Levis.com was slashed, leaving it unable to compete with its online competitors. As a result, Levi Strauss shifted the site's focus from selling to marketing Levi's products. Along with promoting the Levi's brand image, the site also encouraged Web surfers to purchase Levi's apparel from its retailer's Web sites. Used as a marketing tool, Levis.com included information on men's, women's, and children's Levi's apparel. The site also featured company commercials, information on fashion, and the firm's Original Spin program, which allowed consumers to order customized jeans at certain Levi Strauss stores. While unsuccessful as a sales channel, Levis.com played an important role in Levi Strauss' product management strategy as a marketing outlet for its products.

Hardware and information technology services giant IBM was also forced to adopt a new product management culture. As technology advanced at breakneck speed in the 1990s, IBM not only had to develop cutting edge products and services, but also market and manage them effectively as well. In the early 1990s, the company's different product groups were disorganized and had no clear marketing objective, leaving consumers confused about IBM's product line. As a result, the firm turned to advertising firm Ogilvy & Mather Worldwide Inc. to bring all of IBM's products under a single brand image. The move to unify IBM's products and services proved successful, especially during the dot.com boom of the late 1990s. The company also weathered the subsequent dot.com fallout successfully because of the popular brand image it had established over the past several years. In fact, other technology firms, including software company SAP AG, began to follow suit, adopting IBM's branding strategy. The chairman of Ogilvy & Mather claimed in the aforementioned *Business Week* article that, "once an enterprise understands what the brand is all about, it gives direction to the whole enterprise. You know what products you're supposed to make and not make. You know how you're supposed to answer your telephone. You know how you're supposed to package things. It gives a set of principles to an entire enterprise."

Along with traditional retailers, dot.com startups also used product management to reposition their brands. For example, Amazon.com, which began selling books online in 1995, eventually forged partnerships with leading Internet players such as America Online Inc. and Yahoo! Inc. as part of its overall branding campaign. A key component deals such as these was Amazon.com's promotion on high traffic Web sites. In 1999, Amazon.com began to diversify its product holdings; to manage these products, the firm organized them into online "stores" including Software, Video Games, Gift Ideas, and Tools and Hardware. By 2001, the company advertised its offerings as the Earth's Biggest Selection of products including books, e-cards, online auctions, CDs, videos, DVDs, toys and games, kitchenware, and electronics. Having established its brand, by successfully managing its various products, Amazon.com had secured millions of customers in over 220 countries.

Another dot.com start-up that fared well was Datek Online, an online trading site launched in 1996 by Jeffrey Citron and Peter Stern. Considered a pioneer in the online trading industry, the firm quickly grew to become one of the largest online traders with over 640,000 customer accounts and nearly 100,000 trades per day. A significant factor in Datek's success its product and brand management. From the start, Citron and Stern diligently worked to establish Datek's brand throughout the online industry. The company lured day traders with a low commission fee of $9.99 per trade and also developed innovative products and services to attract industry attention. It was the first online brokerage to offer free real-time streaming quotes and was also among the first to offer real-time account portfolio updates and account balance information to its customers. In July 1999, the firm became the first to offer extended hours trading sessions, which enabled members to trade NASDAQ securities from 8 a.m. to 8 p.m. Roughly one year later, Datek became the first to offer decimal-based online trading, a dramatic change from the traditional fractional system. By managing its innovative products successfully, Datek secured its position as a leader among online trading firms.

According to Linda Gorchels, author of *The Product Manager's Handbook*, a product manager's job is to "oversee all aspects of a product/service line to create and deliver superior customer satisfaction while simultaneously providing long-term value for the company." Regardless of industry, this job will continue to hold a significant role in an enterprise's business strategy as the Web continues to evolve into a popular marketing and selling channel, and the global marketplace continues to become increasingly competitive.

FURTHER READING:

Abend, Jules. ''Lands' End Uses Internet to Expand Sales, Personalize Customer Service.'' *Bobbin,* June 1999, 10.

Bell, James. ''Brand Management for the Next Millennium.'' *Journal of Business Strategy,* March-April, 1998.

Benezra, Karen. ''Branding the Web.'' *Chief Executive,* January 2001.

''The Best Global Brands.'' *BusinessWeek Online,* August 6, 2001. Available from www.businessweek.com.

Brady, Diane, and Robert D. Hof. ''Is Amazon Out of its Depth?'' *BusinessWeek Online,* August 6, 2001. Available from www.businessweek.com.

Breen, Brant. ''Building Stronger Internet Identities.'' *Marketing,* September 16, 1999.

Datek Online Brokerage Services LLC. ''About Datek.'' Iselin, NJ: Datek Online Holdings Corp., 2001. Available from datek.com.

Gorchels, Linda. *The Product Manager's Handbook,* Chicago: NTC Business Books, 1996.

Greenberg, Paul A. ''Levi's to Bow Out of E-Commerce.'' *E-Commerce Times,* October 29, 1999. Available from www.ecommercetimes.com.

Hastings, Hunter. ''Big-Spending Dot.coms Need to Learn Brand Management's Five 'Reversals.''' *Brandweek,* March 20, 2000.

SEE ALSO: Advertising, Online; Brand Building

PRODUCT REVIEW SERVICES

As the number of consumers shopping on the Web has increased, so has the number of online services available to these shoppers. For example, Shopping bots such as MySimon.com, Dealtime.com, and Shopping.com help consumers find the best deals on products. Site evaluation services like Bizrate.com and Gomez.com steer shoppers to reputable online merchants. BBB Online, the electronic arm of the Better Business Bureau, also looks after online shoppers, providing dispute resolution services when needed and issuing ''seals'' to online merchants whose business practices meet Better Business Bureau criteria. Shoppers seeking information about products themselves have a variety of online options as well, including expert product review compiler Consumer Search and consumer review sites ConsumerReview.com, Deja.com, and Epinions.com.

ONLINE PRODUCT REVIEWS BY EXPERTS

In the late 1990s, expert reviews of all kinds of products became available on specialized Web sites. For example, Point.com began reviewing cellular telephones, as well as the cellular telephone service plans available in various geographic areas. Imaging-Resource.com reviewed digital cameras. Publications like *PC World* put their product reviews online. Even *Consumer Reports* began publishing its reviews on the Web for a fee. Wanting to offer shoppers a single, comprehensive source of product information, Derek Drew and Carl Hamann created New York-based ConsumerSearch.com in May of 2000. According to Drew, he had been contemplating creating such a site since the early 1990s when he found himself reading three different computer magazines in an effort to make a decision about which desktop publishing system would best serve his interests at the time.

Doing the work for consumers, ConsumerSearch culls publications like *Consumer Digest, Consumer Reports,* and *PC World* for several reviews of a single product. ConsumerSearch's writers, several from leading publications likes *The New York Times>, PC Magazine,* and *Consumer Reports,* then compile a Full Story report which analyzes what the various experts said about the product. Summaries are offered in a Fast Answers section. The site also posts links to the original reviews, offers a description of each of the major reviews, and ranks the reviews. After they have finished perusing the site's content, shoppers who identify a product they wish to purchase can link directly to various retailers selling the product, and ConsumerSearch earns a commission off each product sold via one of these links. The firm also makes money through advertising.

ONLINE PRODUCT REVIEWS BY CONSUMERS

Competing with sites like ConsumerSearch are a wide range of sites that use product reviews written by consumers. According to a January 2001 article of *PC World,* ''the difference between an expert site and one that uses consumer reviews can be the difference between a well-written opinion full of facts and a vague endorsement or a flaming condemnation of a product.'' To increase the credibility of its consumer product reviews, one consumer product review site, Epinions.com, allows users to rate reviewers; it also labels the reviews of writers who earn the ''trusted reviewer'' distinction. Reviews by those who have proven untrustworthy can be blocked via filtering software. Epinions.com also stands out because it pays it writers a nominal fee, one to three cents each time their reviews are read.

Brisbane, California-based Epinions.com was founded in May of 1999 by executives from Yahoo!,

Netscape Communications Corp., and @Home. August Capital and Benchmark Capital gave the startup roughly $8 million in venture capital. A preview of the product evaluation site was launched that September, which prompted Goldman Sachs, Dell Computer Corp., and Bowman Capital to issue another $25 million in funding. Epinions spent the rest of the year forging alliances with portals like Lycos, Inc. and Excite@Home, both of whom agreed to add Epinions' reviews to their shopping channels. Microsoft Corp.'s MSN network began using Epinions' reviews at its eShop in July of 2000. The success of these partnerships prompted the site to create its Content Partner Program, which allowed Web sites to incorporate the reviews into their existing content for a syndication fee.

During its first full year of operation, Epinions won several awards, including being named Best Product Advice Web Site by Yahoo! Internet Life. Its reviews database includes more than 200,000 products and services and more than 1 million reviews. The site also houses buying guides, product definitions, and how-to guides. Along with selling its reviews to other Web sites, the firm makes money by sending shoppers who had decided on a product to online merchants like Amazon.com and Travelocity.

Another online product review site based on consumer input is ConsumerReview.com. The site was first created in 1996 as Mtbreview.com, a site for mountain biking devotees that included reviews of bikes, seats, handlebars, and related biking accessories. Eventually, the site expanded into a hub that now encompasses 18 product specific sites, one of which is the original mountain biking site. Other sites include AudioReview.com and SailingReview.com, ''where enthusiasts of different activities can get news and information and product reviews,'' writes *CNET News.com* columnist Troy Wolverton. ''These amateur experts provide detailed reviews—without the expense of hiring an editorial staff.'' The site makes money by licensing its content to shopping portals such as Yahoo! and AltaVista, selling advertising on its site, and allowing users to click through to various online merchants, who paid a fee for each product purchased by a shopper coming from ConsumerReview. In July of 2001, ConsumerReview and auction giant eBay reached an agreement whereby ConsumerReview will provide product reviews to eBay and provide links to eBay from several of its sites.

Product review site Deja.com got its start in 1995 as Dejanews.com, a site that allowed Internet users to access postings from newsgroup service Usenet. During its first five years of operation, Deja underwent two major overhauls. According to a June 2000 article in *BusinessWeek Online*, ''In May 1999, it shortened its name and relaunched as a site where consumers could swap opinions on thousands of products and services, from VCRs to veterinarians. In March, Deja molted again, this time into what it calls a 'precision buying service,' where consumer reviews are bolstered by expert opinions, related magazine articles, and numerical ratings.''

The firm's planned 1999 initial public offering (IPO) never panned out, mainly because non-cash advertising agreements accounted for nearly one-fourth of its revenues, a fact which concerned investors, particularly those already growing leery of dot.com startups. Deja withdrew its (IPO) application in June of 2000. The troubled firm eventually reduced its staff from 140 to a mere 20 employees.

Like many dot.coms, several of the leading product review sites, including deja.com and epinions, were forced to cut costs in 2001 as investors began demanding profitability. In January of 2001, epinions laid off 27 percent of its workforce. Deja continued its downsizing efforts, cutting another 10 percent of its staff before being acquired by Google Inc. in February of 2001. Less fortunate product review sites, such as Productopia.com and Brandwise.com, declared bankruptcy.

While the need for online services such as product reviewing will likely continue to grow as the rate of online shopping increases, the viability of the online product review site business model, as with most other e-commerce models, has yet to be proven.

FURTHER READING:

''ConsumerReview Proves Content Is Still King.'' *Silicon Valley Business Ink,* January 25, 2001. Available from www.siliconvalleybusinessink.com.

ConsumerSearch, Inc. ''About ConsumerSearch.'' New York: ConsumerSearch, Inc., 2001. Available from www.consumersearch.com.

Epinions.com. ''Epinions Timeline.'' Brisbane, CA: Epinions.com, 2001. Available from www.epinions.com.

''A Glitch in Deja's Latest Incarnation.'' *BusinessWeek Online,* June 8, 2000. Available from www.businessweek.com

Keizer, Gregg, and David Bock. ''How to Pick the Best Products, Shop for the Best Prices, and Close the Deal—All Online.'' *PC World,* January 2001.

Schoenberger, Chana R. ''The Opiners.'' *Forbes.* September 4, 2000. Available from www.forbes.com.

Turner, Rob. ''Consumer Reports: Are the New Online Communities Your Best Source of Consumer-Product Advice?'' *Money,* January 1, 2000.

SEE ALSO: BBBOnline; BizRate.com; Gomez Advisors

PROFILING

Online profiling generated heated opinions for both pro and con as e-commerce achieved prominence in the late 1990s and early 2000s. A method by which online businesses trace browsing and shopping habits of Internet users and compile detailed information files for future marketing purposes, online profiling was seen at one and the same time as an invaluable marketing tool and an affront to Internet users' expectation of privacy.

The most obvious and overt way in which personal data is collected electronically is via online forms, which are often required when making a purchase or downloading software. Items such as names, e-mail addresses, and so on are stored in the site owner's database for future reference. Usually, such companies maintain privacy policies, available to customers, that spell out exactly what will and will not be done with accumulated information.

Other methods of online profiling are far more covert, however. One of the main profiling vehicles employed in the 1990s and early 2000s worked in concert with the banner advertisement. Many companies operate their Web sites via the click-through model. In these cases, the Web site garners some or all of its revenue by selling space on their pages to other companies, who advertise on the pages with banner ads—large graphics that promote the company and provide a link to its Web site. Embedded in many banner ads are ''cookies,'' coded identifiers that are shot into the Web surfer's hard drive and which allow the owner of the banner ad to track subsequent movement on the Web for the purposes of building comprehensive profiles of individuals. Cookies record the universal resource locator (URL) addresses that the Web user visits, and profilers infer from these online movements some general characteristics about the customer. For instance, if a cookie records visitations to several Web sites relating to children's clothing and education, the profiler may conclude that the user is a parent; repeated visits to online bookstores and literary sites would lead the profiler to conclude that the user is an avid reader. After compiling such information, the profiler either uses this information to target specific advertisements to the customer or sells the profile to other companies—in this example, to bookstores and children's outlets.

In these cases, individuals are almost entirely unaware that any profiling is occurring, and privacy advocates charge that this practice, even when used benignly, represents a potentially dangerous breach of individual privacy. In the late 1990s, privacy and consumer groups began to organize against these prac-

tices. For instance, in 1999 consumers brought a class-action lawsuit against Seattle-based RealNetworks, claiming that the company failed to notify customers who had downloaded its free music-listening software program that it was tracking their listening habits. RealNetworks settled the lawsuit by fixing the software to eliminate its ability to profile users and by issuing an apology.

Advertisers insist that online profiling is a cornerstone of their business, and they put a pro-consumer spin on the practice, arguing that profiling ensures that they can target advertisements in such a manner as to most benefit customers by ensuring that they can acquire what they want when they want. In this way, they hold, the consumer society is made even more efficient, since advertising spending goes to its optimal location. By improving the shopping experience, moreover, e-commerce players hold that profiling ensures continued growth in e-commerce to the advantage of all businesses and the economy as a whole.

So, for instance, online retailers can notify select customers of upcoming sales in product areas of particular interest to those customers. Additionally, companies might be more able to sell off older inventory by targeting specific customers with special reduced prices. The logic behind these kinds of arguments holds that the more information in circulation, the better for all involved.

Beyond simply compiling information, online profilers have launched a new industry in the sale of accumulated information to other companies. By virtue of implementing the systems to conduct profiling, the profiler essentially becomes the owner of that information and may choose to profit from it directly or by selling it to interested parties. The individuals profiled, however, have no control over what happens to the information compiled on them. To hedge against a rising backlash toward the practice of online profiling, many companies choose to provide opt-out features, allowing users to prohibit the use of their information after registering for a software download or filling out an online subscription.

According to the Washington, D.C.-based Electronic Privacy Information Center, online profiling is largely invisible to the public. That is, most individual shoppers and Web surfers are unaware of how much and what kind of information about them is being compiled and analyzed. This is one of the primary alarms for privacy advocacy groups; if individuals remain in the dark about online profiling, they are in a poor position to decide for themselves whether engaging in Internet-based shopping and other activities is worth the price they have to pay in lost privacy.

A 1999 report by the Pew Internet and American Life Project found that fully 86 percent of Internet users worried that businesses, governments, or other entities could acquire information about them or their families without their knowledge or permission. These fears, especially prevalent in the United States where the expectation and valuing of privacy run especially high, meant that businesses wishing to continue utilizing this practice had to tread lightly and not give off the impression to customers of any sort of dishonest or underhanded profiling. The same study, however, revealed that only 10 percent of all online users had disabled cookies in their Web browser, while 56 percent of users weren't even aware of the existence of cookies or what they do.

In 2000, the U.S. Federal Trade Commission (FTC) issued a report on online profiling calling for the practice to be informed by five "core fair information practice principles": notice, choice, access, security, and enforcement. In other words:

- Web sites should be bound to disclose their profiling practices.

- Consumers should be given the chance to opt out of the practice or at least have a say in how the information is used.

- Once information is collected, profiled individuals should have access to their profile.

- The profile should be secured from unauthorized viewers.

- Enforcement mechanisms should be in place to ensure that Web sites meet their own requirements regarding their profiling practices.

The most ominous possibilities of online profiling remain a part of privacy advocates' critiques of the practice. Such critics fear that profiling conjures visions of Big Brother forever monitoring individuals' behavior. Relatedly, critics worried that such information in the hands of governments, corporations, or other entities could potentially be used for ill purposes. For instance, critics point out that profiling could be used to identify political beliefs, sexual orientation or tastes, medical information, religious affiliation, or other behaviors. Critics worry that, unless kept in check, such practices could lead to widespread discrimination or otherwise undermine democracy and civil liberties.

FURTHER READING:

Berners-Lee, Tim, and Mark Fischetti. *Weaving the Web: The Original Design and Ultimate Destiny of the World Wide Web by its Inventor.* San Francisco, CA: HarperCollins, 1999.

Bayan, Ruby. "Privacy Means Knowing Your Cookies." *Linkup,* January/February, 2001.

Cantos, Lisa, et al. "FTC Releases Online Profiling Report." *Intellectual Property & Technology Law Journal,* October, 2000.

Tanaka, Jennifer. "Getting Personal." *Newsweek,* November 22, 1999.

Thibodeau, Patrick. "Online Profiling." *Computerworld,* September 18, 2000.

SEE ALSO: Affiliate Model; Banner Ads; DoubleClick Inc.; Electronic Privacy Information Center (EPIC); Privacy: Issues, Policies, Statements; Weblining

PROGRAMMING LANGUAGE

In order for computers to accept commands from humans and perform tasks vital to productivity and e-commerce, a means of communication must exist. Programming languages provide this necessary link between man and machine. Because they are quite simple compared to human language, rarely containing more than few hundred distinct words, programming languages must contain very specific instructions. There are more than 2,000 different programming languages in existence, although most programs are written in one of several popular languages, like BASIC, COBOL, C++, or Java. Programming languages have different strengths and weaknesses. Depending on the kind of program being written, the computer it will run on, the experience of the programmer, and the way in which the program will be used, the suitability of one programming language over another will vary.

At the most basic level, computer hardware is controlled through machine language, consisting of numbers (mainly zeros and ones). Immediately above machine languages are assembly languages, which use mnemonic names instead of numbers to represent instructions. This level of language is the lowest a programmer is likely to see. Special programs known as assemblers take assembly code and translate it into the machine language used by a computer's hardware. Although they aren't numeric, assembly languages have several disadvantages, including the fact that they are hard to understand and often are very specific to a certain machine's central processing unit (CPU). Each kind of CPU has its own form of assembly language. In the early 2000s, programs usually were not written directly in assembly language. Rather, it was used by experienced programmers to work on critical parts of computer programs.

When people refer to programming languages, they normally mean one of many different kinds of high-level languages or fourth-generation languages that reside above the level of assembly language. Unlike machine and assembly languages, high-level languages resemble human grammar and syntax more closely, and are often portable to different operating systems and machines. Three programming languages were instrumental in opening the lines of communication between programmers and computers. FORTRAN, COBOL, and ALGOL were created around the 1950s and many variations of these languages were still in use during the early 2000s.

Once a program is written in a high-level language, a program called a compiler or an interpreter is used to convert it to a computer's specific machine language, much like an assembler converts assembly code into machine language. As explained by Daniel Appleman in his book *How Computer Programming Works,* ''A compiler translates an entire program into machine language. Once translated, a program can execute by itself. An interpreter reads your program source code and performs the operations specified without actually translating the code into machine language. The interpreter program executes the program you create, so your program always requires the interpreter.''

HISTORY OF PROGRAMMING LANGUAGES

According to *Computer Languages,* Konrad Zuse created the very first high-level language in 1945. During World War II, Zuse, who had previously constructed several basic, general purpose computers in his parent's apartment, fled Berlin for the Bavarian Alps, where he lived as a refugee. The programming language Zuse created translated from German as ''The Plan Calculus.'' In theory, this computer language could be applied to a variety of different computer problems. Unlike the computers that existed at the time, Zuse's program relied not on decimals, but on binary notation.

Zuse's programming language was never adopted for widespread use on actual computers. FORTRAN and COBOL were the first high-level programming languages to make an impact on the field of computer science. Along with assembly language, these two high-level languages have led to or influenced the development of many modern programming languages, including Java, C++, and BASIC.

FORTRAN (FORmula TRANslating), released in 1957 after a three-year developmental period, is well suited for math, science, and engineering programs because of its ability to perform numeric computations. The language was developed in New York by IBM's John Backus. At the time, IBM was trying to make computer's more user-friendly in an effort to increase sales. FORTRAN achieved this goal, because it was easy to learn in a short period of time and required no previous computer knowledge. It eliminated the need for engineers, scientists, and other users to rely on assembly programmers in order to

communicate with computers. Although FORTRAN is often referred to as a language of the past, computer science students were still taught the language in the early 2000s for historical reasons, and because FORTRAN code still exists in some applications.

COBOL (COmputer Business Oriented Language), was released in April of 1959 and has been updated several times since then. Shortly after the introduction of FORTRAN, users from different fields, including academia and manufacturing, convened at the University of Pennsylvania to discuss the need for a standardized business language that could be used on a wide variety of computers. The eventual result was COBOL, a programming language well suited for creating business applications. COBOL's strength is in processing data, and in its simplicity. Because the language is readable and easy to understand, it is difficult to hide malicious or destructive computer code within a COBOL program, and is easy to spot programming errors.

In the early 2000s, COBOL was a frequently discussed topic in e-commerce circles. Many companies sought to allow customers to access data on mainframe computers running COBOL programs. Finding ways to enable COBOL to interface with hypertext markup language (HTML), which is used to create pages on the World Wide Web, became important.

FURTHER READING:

Appleman, Daniel. *How Computer Programming Works.* Berkeley: Apress. 2000.

Computer Languages. Alexandria: Time-Life Books. 1986.

Hansen, Augie. *C Programming.* New York: Addison-Wesley Publishing Publishing Co., Inc. 1989.

Radcliff, Deborah. ''Moving COBOL to the Web—Safely.'' *Computerworld,* May 1, 2000.

''Programming Language.'' *Ecommerce Webopedia,* March 12, 2001. Available from www.e-comm.webopedia.com.

''Programming Language.'' *Techencyclopedia,* March 12, 2001. Available from www.techweb.com.

SEE ALSO: BASIC; C; COBOL; FORTRAN; HTML; Java

PROMOTING THE WEB SITE

The Web represents a new marketing channel. Promoting the Web site is about giving people specific, tangible reasons to visit your Web site. These include service-oriented reasons, such as being able to track order status, review purchase history, and receive e-mail reminders, among others. Price-related reasons for visiting an e-commerce site include discounted merchandise and special sales.

A site's content can also give people a reason to visit. In addition to product descriptions, an e-commerce site can include editorial stories, tips, recipes, how-to advice, and similar items that indirectly promote a business's products and services.

There are many specific ways to promote an e-commerce Web site. Some ways, such as offline advertising, involve millions of dollars. Others can be done at little or no cost. In addition to online and offline advertising, Web sites are promoted through e-mail marketing, promotions and incentives, viral marketing, search engine listings, reciprocal links from other sites, and affiliate programs, among other ways.

According to a 2001 report by the Yankee Group, traffic to a Web site remains driven primarily by offline methods. Instead of developing integrated marketing plans that incorporated both online and offline media, companies were typically listing their Web sites only in traditional marketing materials.

Web marketers are interested in how Internet users discovered the Web sites that they visited. According to a survey by Forrester Research, the most popular ways that Internet surfers found Web sites in 2000 were

- by using search engines (80 percent)
- by linking from another site (59 percent)
- via viral marketing (56 percent)
- by watching television (48 percent)
- by guessing the URL (22 percent)
- and through radio (19 percent).

Since respondents could list more than one method through which they found Web sites, the totals added up to more than 100 percent. All of these methods suggest ways that Web sites can be effectively promoted to increase traffic.

BUILDING TRAFFIC AND SALES

Increasing sales at a Web site is a two-step process that involves driving traffic to the site and, more importantly, converting a percentage of visitors into customers. E-commerce sites must develop strategies to attract the maximum number of buyers to their Web sites and also entice them to return to the site often.

There are a wide range of marketing activities that companies can engage in to drive traffic to their Web sites. Once marketing efforts have driven a high number of visitors to an e-commerce Web site, the site itself must convince them that the company is serious about meeting their needs and providing a sufficient level of service. In other words, building traffic is only half of promoting the Web site. The other half of the equation involves promoting the site to people who are already there and converting them into repeat customers.

OFF-SITE PROMOTIONS

Offline advertising in print and broadcast media is probably the most expensive way to build name recognition and drive traffic to an e-commerce Web site. The online job recruitment site Monster.com spent about $45 million on branding in 1999, with about 65 percent of the budget going to television advertising. The company's ads ran more than 500,000 times during 1999, including its first Super Bowl ad. Immediately after the Super Bowl ad appeared, traffic at Monster.com increased by 450 percent. The results encouraged the company to spend more on TV advertising and brand building. Monster.com spent an estimated $250 million around the world to build the company's brand in 2001.

Online brokerages spent heavily on print and television advertising to gain brand recognition. In 1997 Ameritrade launched a $20 million national advertising campaign that focused on Ameritrade's online trading fee of $8. Heavy advertising expenditures helped increase the number of new accounts at Ameritrade and boosted revenue, but they also resulted in much higher quarterly losses. Ameritrade justified its strategy of pursuing market share by noting that online accounts were relatively cheap to acquire through advertising and marketing.

Priceline.com adopted an aggressive radio and newspaper advertising strategy that later expanded to include television. It featured the actor William Shatner as a spokesperson and resulted in the company having name recognition among at least a quarter of the U.S. adult population, or some 50 million people, according to a study by Opinion Research Corp.

PROMOTING THE WEB SITE ONLINE

According to a report from Jupiter Media Metrix, the top 25 new Web sites of 2000 achieved their ranking through word-of-mouth, direct marketing, traffic-sharing, sweepstakes, and promotions. Without the help of brand-name backers, many of these new Web sites asked visitors to register at their site in order to build a database. The Web sites would then market to their databases of visitors and extend their online reach. Again, the challenge for these sites was to convert visitors into customers.

After debuting in March 2000, discount online marketplace Half.com grew more than 500 percent in terms of traffic, from 1.3 million unique visitors to 8.2 million in December. It was the top ranked new e-commerce firm of 2000 in terms of traffic growth, according to Jupiter Media Metrix. Half.com was the most advertised new site of 2000 with nearly 800 million online ad impressions. It was owned by auction giant eBay and thus enjoyed big-brand affiliation.

Ad swaps can help reduce the cost of online advertising. It's common practice to swap ads with other sites. Instead of paying for an ad, a Web site puts up a banner ad on its site for free and places its ad at the other site for free.

SEARCH ENGINE OPTIMIZATION

Web sites can improve their traffic by optimizing their placement with search engines. Search engine optimization is the process by which companies can improve a Web site to achieve higher search engine rankings. Search engine optimization can be a cheap and effective marketing tool for promoting a Web site.

According to research published by www.searchengines.com, a search engine optimization resource, some 55 percent of all e-commerce transactions originate with a search listing. By optimizing key elements of a Web site, the site can improve its rankings on searches within its category. Web sites that appear on the first page of a search result are likely to attract more traffic than Web sites that appear further down on the search results.

There are several aspects to optimizing a Web site for better search engine placements. They include elements internal to the Web site, such as HTML tags, meta tags, ALT tags, URL names, and more. External elements that affect a site's ranking include link popularity, click popularity, and themes. The major search engines, such as Yahoo! and AltaVista, have their own submission procedures, which must be followed in order for a Web site to show up on their search results.

OTHER WAYS TO PROMOTE A WEB SITE

E-MAIL NEWSLETTERS. These are regarded as one of the most effective and low-cost ways to promote a Web site and generate leads. Through a weekly newsletter, companies can communicate with existing and potential customers on a regular basis. Often, these newsletters are forwarded to friends and colleagues, thereby increasing the Web site's reach to a wider audience of potential customers.

EVENT MARKETING. Large companies hold events that are designed to generate enthusiasm about their products and services, including Web site promotion. Company representatives also talk with the media, visit customers, work trade shows, and speak at conferences to build enthusiasm for their company, its brand, and its products and services.

AFFILIATE PROGRAMS. These programs let other sites drive traffic to a specific site. Programs for associates or affiliates are designed to make it easy for others to link to the designated site and to receive a commission on sales they generate. The simplest way to set up such a program is to put up a link to a simple sign-up form on the Web site. It's a good way to acquire new customers. The cost in commissions is usually no more than the cost of acquiring new customers by other means. Affiliate programs also make a Web site's content more valuable to visitors by offering them links to other products and services that are likely to be of interest. In addition to acquiring new customers, affiliates gain additional revenue from the traffic, leads, and sales they generate for other affiliates. Linkshare (www.linkshare.com) is an online information center for affiliate programs through which Web sites can join a variety of programs in different categories.

PUBLIC RELATIONS. Web sites can be promoted very cheaply through a steady stream of news releases. News releases announcing new products, services, and features can be sent to local and national media. Once these news releases appear in the media, they become not just a business promotion but actual news.

PARTNERING. Web sites that affiliate with established, brand-name companies enjoy higher visibility than stand-alone sites. E-commerce Web sites can build relationships with well-known trade magazines and media companies to gain more exposure and promotion.

USE ONLINE PROMOTIONS TO DRIVE REVENUE

Sweepstakes generate a large database of potential customers. It is effective to build a large database of people who are interested in your products or services, and then market to them on a regular basis. Price incentives work in term of attracting first-time customers. These can include a free trial offer, free shipping, or a 30-day money-back guarantee. For repeat buyers, loyalty programs work well but may be expensive. Price incentives based on the size of a purchase also work with repeat customers.

PROMOTIONS AT THE WEB SITE: SERVICE AND CONTENT

On-site service brings back customers. Web sites can increase repeat traffic by adding a range of services that make it easier for customers to place orders, develop a feeling of trust, and create a meaningful relationship. Web sites can publish their corporate contact information and provide detailed information on each product. By disclosing privacy and security policies (which may rarely be read) Web sites create a feeling of trust and reassure visitors.

In terms of services, e-commerce sites can provide order tracking and let customers review their purchase history. Many e-commerce sites offer reminder services that allow visitors to set up reminder e-mails for important birthdays, anniversaries, and holidays. Many sites also offer an opt-in mailing list and send out a regular e-mail newsletter. Online help and video chat are not always expensive to add, and they again serve to reassure visitors, even if they are only available periodically in real time.

Web sites can provide links to the Web sites of manufacturers or partners while keeping customers within their site. E-commerce sites create a better impression on their visitors if they are selective about the links, logos, and banner ads they display. A confusing array of those items can alienate visitors and leave a bad impression.

All of these elements serve to promote the Web site to visitors who are already there and help to convert them first into customers, and then into repeat customers.

CONTENT KEEPS PEOPLE COMING BACK

If it is true that people go online to find answers and assistance, in both their personal and professional lives, then e-commerce sites that provide relevant content will fare better than sites that do not. Major online retailers that sell items such as books, music CDs, and consumer electronics, offer a wide range of relevant content, including product descriptions and reviews, that help consumers make purchase decisions. For business-to-business sites the notion of relevant content can include items such as case histories that demonstrate how a firm's products and services can be used to solve problems and create solutions. Adding relevant content that addresses the broader needs and concerns of potential customers to an e-commerce or corporate Web site involves extending online efforts beyond merchandising and transaction processing.

Relevant content that is presented at an e-commerce site may result in orders being placed online or offline. Since potential customers form opinions online, a company's Web site can be seen as the natural starting point in making purchase decisions. To the extent that a Web site can provide relevant content to help customers make decisions, the site will generate orders that may be placed through any channel.

VIRAL MARKETING AND COMMUNITY-BUILDING

In addition to strong content and value, some of the common factors among sites that have quickly built communities of repeat visitors include positive word-of-mouth, positive media exposure, and the fulfillment of an untapped audience segment. The most loyal audience of visitors is one that feels empowered. Giving them a sense of involvement and even ownership has been a key element in developing a loyal following.

Creating an online community within a Web site is an effective way to encourage users to visit more often, stay longer, and become repeat customers. Depending on the type of Web site, online communities can be structured in different ways and offer different features. In business-to-business e-commerce, online marketplaces have created community programs through bulletin boards, live chat sessions, distance learning, Webcasts, streaming video, collaborative work tools, user profiles, industry newsletters, and expert advice.

The principal function of an online community is to provide information through interaction. This keeps visitors returning to the Web site and creates a relationship with them. Over time visitors become more comfortable with the site and how to conduct business there. In some cases successful online communities turn individuals into evangelists who spread the word to others about the site and its products and services.

Viral marketing is simply word-of-mouth. Community-building is one way to generate positive word-of-mouth comments and draw visitors to a Web site, but there are many other viral marketing techniques being used to promote Web sites. These include interactive online advertising games, specialized e-mail campaigns, and product samples. The key to a successful viral marketing program is to identify and target opinion leaders among an identified group of users. Once the opinion leaders have been identified, a compelling message must be delivered. In order for them to tell others about your Web site, they must have had a positive experience with it. Then when they do tell others about a Web site, people are likely to trust them because their opinion is respected.

Through viral marketing, companies can build personalization and loyalty programs around their Web sites. Viral marketing is especially effective when marketing to passionate consumers, such as Harley-Davidson motorcycle owners. Web sites that have built a community of users with common needs often gain visitors when friends and relatives recommend it to one another.

Online interactive games are used in some viral marketing programs. The idea is to get Web users to challenge their friends to play the game, thereby gaining more traffic for the site where the game is played. Major companies including IBM, Nike, Ford Motor Co., and General Motors have begun to include games in their online advertising as a way to draw traffic to their Web sites. People are typically notified of the games through e-mail marketing programs. According to *E-Commerce Times,* Ford Motor reported that 40 percent of those who received an e-mail clicked through to play an online game, and those people forwarded the game to an average of three friends each. Other fields for which viral marketing has been recommended include entertainment industry products, such as movies, records, books, and television shows.

IT DOESN'T HAVE TO BE EXPENSIVE

There are many ways to promote Web sites for free, such as posting to newsgroups and mailing lists, soliciting links from other sites, banner exchanges, newsletter ad swaps, free classified ads, and free-for-all link pages. According to Paul Lang of ''Sell it on the Web'' (www.sellitontheweb.com), the most effective ways to promote an e-commerce Web site are to publish a weekly e-mail newsletter, submit to major search engines and directories, post to discussion lists, and buy keywords at GoTo.com. Moderately effective ways to promote an e-commerce Web site include writing articles for other Web sites and newsletters and exchanging links with other Web sites. Lang has obtained poor results from promoting Web sites through classified ads, free-for-all links pages, submitting to minor search engines, and banner ad exchanges.

The key to successfully promoting a Web site is to provide reasons to visit the Web site. Simply listing the Web site in an ad, without including a reason to visit the site, is a missed opportunity. It is important not only to mention the site across all media, but also to include at least one reason to visit the site. Special promotions, such as the opportunity to win a free trip, a contest, or a sweepstakes, are good options that draw visitors. Special editorial content that provides in-depth information about topics potential customers are interested in is another draw. Such content not only brings in visitors, it establishes a relationship with them and keeps them coming back.

FURTHER READING:

Abel, Amee. ''It's All in the Positioning.'' *Sm@rt Reseller.* July 26, 1999.

''Affiliate Information Center.'' 2001. Available from www.linkshare.com.

Bank, Vince. ''Give Reasons to Visit Your Web Site,'' *DM News.* December 4, 2000.

Berkowitz, David. ''A Rewarding Conversation with BountySystems,'' *eMarketer.* September 10, 2001. Available from www.emarketer.com.

Ceolin, David. ''Quality Content Helps Drive Sales,'' *DM News.* February 19, 2001.

Chiem, Phat X. ''Net Marketplaces Weigh the Value of Community Programs in E-Commerce,'' *B to B.* April 2, 2001.

Daniels, Jim. ''Step-by-Step to Your Own Profitable Web Business.'' *Sell it on the Web.* December 20, 2000. Available from sellitontheweb.com/ezine.

Hirsh, Lou. ''Tell a Friend: Viral Marketing Packs Clout Online.'' *E-Commerce Times.* October 31, 2001. Available from www.ecommercetimes.com

Lang, Paul. ''Top Tips for a Successful E-Commerce Web Site.'' *Sell It on the Web.* April 24, 1999. Available from sellitontheweb.com

Macaluso, Nora. ''Report: Executives Give the Web a lsquo;Thumbs Down.''' *E-Commerce Times.* September 5, 2001. Available from www.ecommercetimes.com

Robson, Kathleen Look. ''Incentives and Promotions.'' *B to B Hands-On Newsletter.* June 21, 2001. Available from www.btobonline.com

Saliba, Clare. ''Report: Online Ads Drive New Site Growth.'' *E-Commerce Times.* February 9, 2001. Available from www.ecommercetimes.com

Sernovitz, Andy. ''Internet Marketing on a Budget.'' *DM News.* January 29, 2001.

Shapiro, Yelena, and Etelka Lehoczky. ''Search Engine Optimization.'' November 9, 2001. Available from www.searchengines.com

Shaw, Russell. ''Enhanced Site Encourages Collaboration.''*B to B.* April 2, 2001.

Thomases, Hollis. ''Growing Online Loyalty Organically.'' *DM News.* February 5, 2001.

SEE ALSO: Advertising, Online; Brand Building; E-Mail Marketing; Marketing, Internet

Q

QWEST COMMUNICATIONS INTERNATIONAL

Qwest was one of the first companies to build a fiber-optic network for high-speed data communications that forms the backbone of the Internet and provides a key element of electronic commerce. After completing construction of its 18,500-mile national fiber-optic network in 1999, Qwest added 4,300 route miles in Canada and Mexico and continued to build fiber-optic rings in Europe. As of 2001 the company had more than 100,000 miles of fiber capacity and planned to have 12,500 miles installed in Europe by year-end 2001.

Qwest's national fiber-optic network enables it to provide advanced communication services—including data, multimedia, and Internet-based services—on a national and international basis principally to large and mid-size business and government customers. Nationally, the company also offers local and long-distance telephone service.

In 2000 Qwest completed the acquisition of US West, a regional Bell operating company (RBOC). The acquisition gave Qwest 25 million US West local phone customers in 14 western states. Within this 14-state region Qwest offers wireless services, local telecommunications, and related services, and directory services to consumers, businesses, and government entities. Under federal regulations, Qwest was not able to offer long-distance service within the states served by US West. By opening its network to local exchange telephone competitors within the 14-state area and conforming to other federal requirements, Qwest hoped to begin offering long-distance services to customers within the 14-state area.

Qwest's Web hosting services are offered under its CyberCenter program. In March 2000 Qwest entered into an agreement with IBM to open 28 CyberCenters, which would host applications, services, and network infrastructures. The first facility under the agreement was opened in Dallas, Texas, in February 2001. At the time Qwest operated a total of 15 U.S. CyberCenters. Internationally, Qwest created a joint venture with KPN, called KPNQwest, to open 18 CyberCenters in Europe. The first center in Europe opened in mid-2000.

ORIGINATES AS SUBSIDIARY OF SOUTHERN PACIFIC, 1988-1995

Qwest Communications International originated as SP Telecom, a subsidiary of the giant railroad company Southern Pacific Transportation Co. SP Telecom was established in San Francisco in 1988 to construct telecommunications lines along Southern Pacific's 15,000 miles of railroad right-of-way. Later in 1988 Southern Pacific was acquired by reclusive Denver billionaire Philip Anschutz, who reorganized SP Telecom as a subsidiary of Anschtutz Corp. In 1992 Anschutz negotiated an easement agreement with Southern Pacific to lay fiber-optic cable along 11,700 miles of its tracks. By 1993 the privately held SP Telecom had annual revenue of more than $50 million and 410 employees. During the early 1990s SP Telecom built fiber-optic linkups for other carriers, sold space on its fiber-optic network, and introduced commercial products.

CHANGES NAME TO QWEST COMMUNICATIONS CORP., 1995-1996

In 1995 SP Telecom changed its named to Qwest Communications Corp. and moved to Anschutz's home city of Denver after it acquired the Dallas-based firm Qwest Communications Corp. Around this time Anschutz sold his interest in Southern Pacific to the Union Pacific Corp. for about $1.6 billion worth of stock, making him Union Pacific's largest shareholder.

Qwest reached an agreement with CSX Transportation Inc. to use its rail corridors to install a high-speed, high-volume, fiber-optic network in May 1995. CSX owned 19,000 miles of track in 20 eastern states. The agreement with CSX enabled Qwest to build a fiber-optic network from coast to coast. Later in 1995 Qwest gained permission to link several Mexican cities, including Mexico City, Monterrey, and Guadalajara, with about 5,000 miles of fiber-optic cable. This network was then linked to U.S. long distance carriers at the U.S.-Mexican border. To generate revenue Qwest negotiated with other long distance providers to buy or lease part of its fiber-optic network.

GOES PUBLIC AS QWEST COMMUNICATIONS INTERNATIONAL, INC., 1997

The company went public as Qwest Communications International, Inc. in 1997. Its initial public offering (IPO) on June 23, 1997, raised $297 million on the sale of 13.5 million shares. Only 14 percent of the company was offered to the public; the rest was held by Philip Anschutz, who became the new company's chairman. Anschutz hired Joesph Nacchio from AT&T to become Qwest's new president and CEO. In its first year as a public company Qwest reported revenue of $697 million.

At the time it went public, Qwest had already negotiated for nearly 90 percent of the rights-of-way it needed to complete its national fiber-optic network. Qwest believed that a ground-based network would be more reliable for the transmission of data than satellite-based networks. The company expected that demand for high-speed networks that could transmit data as well as audio and video would explode over the next five years. Demand would also be fueled by the regional Bell operating companies (RBOCs), who would be able to offer long-distance services under deregulation.

Qwest reached agreements with three companies to lease about half of the capacity of Qwest's network for an investment of about $1 billion. They were Frontier Corp., the fifth-largest long-distance carrier

in the United States; WorldCom Inc., the fourth-largest long-distance carrier and the largest Internet access provider with its acquisition of UUNet; and GTE Corp., the largest non-Bell local telephone company. Later in 1997 Qwest acquired Colorado's largest ISP, SuperNet Inc., for $20 million. Qwest also launched the first advertising campaign for its fiber-optic telecommunications network with the tagline, "Ride the light."

EXPANDS LONG-DISTANCE AND INTERNET SERVICES THROUGH ACQUISITIONS, 1998-1999

In March 1998 Qwest announced it would acquire long-distance carrier LCI International Inc. for $4.4 billion. The deal created the fourth-largest long-distance carrier in the United States behind AT&T, MCI Worldcom, and Sprint Corp. The combined companies had about 5,800 employees and revenue of $2.3 billion. The acquisition gave Qwest 2 million long-distance customers and a well-established sales force.

Qwest activated the portion of its fiber network that connected Los Angeles, San Francisco, and New York, giving the company more than 5,400 route-miles of its network in service in April. The company also joined with Cisco Systems Inc. and Nortel to create a new IP backbone network called Internet2 for use by the academic community. Qwest donated $500 million worth of bandwidth to the project.

Expanding into Europe, Qwest acquired EUNet, a European ISP based in Amsterdam with about 60,000 customers, for $154 million. In mid-1998 Qwest announced it would offer long-distance service in Europe. To head its international operations, Qwest snared John McMaster, another AT&T executive. The company planned to build a fiber-optic network in Europe with Dutch telecommunications company KPN.

Qwest began building 10 CyberCenters around the United States to offer a range of Web-hosting and multimedia applications to Internet customers. Four centers opened in 1998 in Los Angeles, New York, San Francisco, and Washington, D.C., with six centers slated for 1999. To boost its CyberCenter program, Qwest acquired Icon CMT, which provided Web hosting and related services, for $185 million.

In December 1998 Microsoft invested $200 million in Qwest, taking a 1.3 percent minority interest in the company. In exchange Qwest would use the Microsoft Windows NT Server OS as the basis of its electronic commerce and other services to be introduced in 1999, including Q-Commerce-Retail, an online storefront service, and the Qwest Business Partner Program, which offered a wide range of Internet services.

In early 1999, Qwest introduced its first Internet services for consumers and small businesses. Qwest introduced DSL service for businesses in 13 markets through Rhythms NetConnections and Covad Communications. Qwest also announced it would offer paging, conferencing, and faxing services from its Web site. In a move to increase its bandwidth, America Online Inc. selected Qwest to provide it with national Internet connectivity services in a deal valued at $13 million.

Qwest gained additional financing with a $1 billion revolving credit facility from a consortium of banks and financial institutions led by Bank of America. In addition, Bell South Corp. agreed to purchase a 10 percent interest in Qwest for $3.5 billion. The funds enabled Qwest to reduce the debt it took on for international expansion and helped the company finance construction of its fiber-optic network. Qwest completed its national fiber-optic network with 18,500 route miles in September 1999. In December it added 4,300 route miles in Canada and Mexico. Qwest's 1999 revenue was $3.92 billion, with net income of $458 million, compared to 1998 revenue of $2.2 billion.

SWALLOWED US WEST IN HOSTILE TAKEOVER, 1999-2000

In mid-1999 Qwest announced hostile takeover bids for US West, a RBOC with local phone customers in 14 Western states, and Frontier Communications, the fifth-largest U.S. long-distance carrier. At the time, US West was already the subject of a $52 billion takeover proposal from Global Crossing Ltd., a Bermuda-based company that was building an undersea fiber-optic network. Wall Street reacted to the announcement by driving Qwest's stock down more than 20 percent. At first, US West rejected Qwest's bid, but following some negotiations Qwest and US West reached an agreement whereby Qwest would acquire US West for an amount estimated between $35 and $80 billion, according to various sources. Qwest's acquisition of US West also had the effect of diluting Bell South's interest in the new company from 10 percent to about 3.5 percent. Qwest subsequently withdrew its offer for Frontier, and Frontier agreed to be acquired by Global Crossing for $10.9 billion.

Qwest's acquisition of US West had to pass several regulatory hurdles, including approval from the U.S. Department of Justice, the Federal Trade Commission, the Federal Communications Commission, and public service commissions in seven of the 14 states served by US West. By July 2000 the merger with US West had received the necessary approvals. In many cases state approval was gained by agreeing to negotiate new service quality standards. The new

company dropped the US West name and continued using the Qwest name. Altogether, the merged companies had about 70,000 employees worldwide. Later in the year Qwest announced it would streamline its workforce by cutting about 11,000 employee positions and 1,800 contractor positions by the end of 2001.

With the acquisition of US West complete, Qwest announced it would make quality of service its top priority for the local telephone customers it had gained. Other announced goals included doubling its DSL users from 250,000 to 500,000; doubling the number of wireless users from 800,000 to 1.6 million; and doubling its Web-hosting space, all by the end of 2001. The company also planned to improve access to its network in order to be able to re-enter the long-distance market again in the 14 western states formerly served by US West.

PROFITS DISAPPEAR FOLLOWING THE MERGER, 2000-2001

Following the acquisition of US West, Qwest remained focused on higher-growth markets, including Web hosting, wireless, DSL, and broadband services. For the fourth quarter of 2000 revenue from Internet and data services increased by 40 percent over the previous year, while wireless revenue grew by 90 percent. The company's DSL customer base expanded by more than 130 percent to more than 255,000 subscribers. In September 2000 the company began a national rollout of its DSL service, moving into markets controlled by other RBOCs. At the end of the year president Afshin Mohebbi reiterated the company's mission to become the premier broadband Internet communications company in the world. During the year CEO Joseph Nacchio added the title of chairman, succeeding Philip Anschultz.

Qwest's financial picture for 2000 and 2001 was clouded by one-time charges and non-operating expenses. For the year 2000 Qwest reported revenue of $16.6 billion, well short of the $19 billion the company projected. Operating income was positive at $1.8 billion, but various expenses resulted in the company reporting a net loss of $81 million for the year.

For the first two quarters of 2001, Qwest had quarterly income of approximately $5 billion each quarter and positive operating income of $637 million in the first quarter and $135 million in the second. Non-operating and other expenses resulted in net losses of $46 million in the first quarter and a staggering $3.3 billion in the second. After the first two quarters Qwest claimed it was on track to reach its 2001 revenue target of $21 billion and $8.5 billion in earnings before interest, taxes, depreciation, and amortization (EBITDA). Deteriorating economic conditions in the third quarter forced Qwest to reduce its 2001 revenue estimate to $20.5 billion while announcing it would cut 4,000 jobs from its workforce of 66,000.

FURTHER READING:

Aun, Fred. "Qwest Communications." *Sm@rt Partner,* May 7, 2001.

Bryer, Amy. "Qwest Leads in Two Separate Categories." *Denver Business Journal,* October 20, 2000.

Carter, Wayne. "QWEST + LCI = IXC Powerhouse?" *Telephony,* March 16, 1998.

Goldblatt, Henry. "Wild, Wild Qwest." *Fortune,* June 8, 1998.

Kohn, Bernie. "In Search of Qwest's Bottom Line." *The Washington Post,* January 28, 2001.

"Phil Anschutz: The Power That Be." *Inter@ctive Week,* May 1, 2000.

Sullivan, Bruce. "Qwest Bolts from the Pack." *Communications Today,* December 22, 2000.

SEE ALSO: AT&T Corp.; Fiber Optics; Telephony

R

REALNETWORKS INC.

Headquartered in Seattle, Washington, RealNetworks Inc. offers Internet media delivery software and services. Its products allow computer users to send, receive, and view streaming media, including movie and video clips and audio programming, such as Internet radio broadcasts. In the early 2000s, RealNetworks offered several widely used software products including different versions of RealJukebox, which allowed users to record CD- and near-CD-quality versions of their own music onto PCs, and RealPlayer for playing streaming media via the Internet. In addition to offering products to individual users, RealNetworks also provided its products and services on an enterprise basis to large companies, schools, and government agencies for a variety of purposes including marketing, corporate communications, distance learning and training, investor relations, and customer service. According to *Hoover's Online,* more than half of RealNetworks' revenue comes from licensing fees consumers pay to receive premium versions of the company's software; basic versions are offered free of charge. RealNetworks CEO Robert Glaser holds a 35-percent stake in the firm.

EARLY DEVELOPMENT, 1994-1996

RealNetworks was founded in February 1994 under the name Progressive Networks by Rob Glaser, a former Microsoft executive. At Microsoft, Glaser worked in the area of applications and networking before becoming vice president of multimedia content

and consumer systems. In high school, he demonstrated an early interest in media by wiring the school's radio station to the cafeteria, gym, and several other locations. As president and CEO of Progressive Networks, Glaser introduced RealAudio at the annual convention of the National Association of Broadcasters in April of 1995, and the commercial version of RealAudio 1.0 was released that July.

According to RealNetworks' 1997 annual report, the firm spent much of 1995 getting operations established. Efforts were focused on activities like recruiting staff, obtaining funding, research and development, establishing brand awareness, and working to create a market for streaming media products and services. That year, the RealPlayer began distribution with Netscape's Web browser, Apple Computer's Internet Connection Kit, and Microsoft's Internet Explorer, and ABC News added live RealAudio content to its RadioNet Web site. By the end of October, the company announced the development of RealAudio System 2.0, which supported mono-quality music and audio for those with 28.8 modems. Additionally, the company secured $5.7 million in financing from venture capital firm Accel Partners.

In 1996, Progressive Networks continued to focus on research and development. The firm developed sales channels in the United States and abroad, and began establishing its administration. In February, Progressive named Bruce Jacobsen as the company's president and chief operating officer (COO). Jacobsen, who earned degrees from both Yale and Stanford, had previously served as COO of DreamWorks Interactive, a partnership between Dreamworks SKG and Microsoft. Glaser remained as chairman and CEO. Developments continued to un-

627

fold during 1996 when a premium version of the RealAudio Player was introduced in August and an additional $17.9 million in external financing was obtained in December from several investors.

OFFERINGS EXPAND TO INCLUDE VIDEO, 1997

In 1997, Progressive introduced RealVideo, which it touted as the Web's "first feature-complete, cross-platform video broadcast solution." Announced in February and commercially released in June, the software included "destination buttons" that allowed users to easily access programming from the likes of MSNBC, ABCNews.com, CBS/Sportsline, and Fox News. *Computer Reseller News* explained that the new RealPlayer, equipped with RealVideo, relied on a process known as dynamic streaming. The publication explained that the new version of RealPlayer "detects congested Internet traffic and adjusts the video-frame rate for continuous uninterrupted Web video." In addition to individual users, leading companies like Boeing Co. also began using the streaming video application to deliver training and corporate content to employees.

In August of 1997, Progressive partnered with MCI to create RealNetwork, which allowed multimedia content to be delivered more reliably and efficiently based on a user's geographic location. In September Progressive Networks changed its name to RealNetworks Inc. and announced that it had filed for its initial public offering (IPO). On the first day of trading, shares increased almost 50 percent, resulting in a market capitalization of $600 million. By October, more than 1 million people had downloaded RealPlayer 5.0, which included a variety of audio and video enhancements including near-CD-quality sound for those using 28.8 or greater modems. RealNetworks' revenues soared 134 percent in 1997 to $32.7 million, with a net loss of $11.2 million.

RAPID GROWTH AND DEVELOPMENT, 1998-2001

By 1998, more than 20 million RealPlayers had been downloaded and more than 150,000 Web sites used the firm's software to offer streaming content. Early in 1998, RealNetworks rolled out Mobile Daily Briefing, an Internet site that provided audio content to portable devices. In February, it acquired competitor Vivo Software Inc., which developed applications that Web developers used to create streaming digital media. The acquisition, which was completed in late March, increased RealNetworks' market share and added a base of talented individuals who could further develop RealNetworks' product line. It also was in

1998 that RealNetworks formed an alliance with Internet advertising firm 24/7 media to create an advertising network of Web sites offering rich media content. Prior to forming the alliance, RealNetworks had conducted an analysis of Web sites that included rich media ads and found them to have higher response (click-through) rates than traditional ads. The new network presented broader rich media opportunities to advertisers.

In November of 1998, Microsoft announced that it would sell the minority stake it held in RealNetworks. Glaser cited growth in the streaming media market, and the fact that Microsoft was an emerging competitor, as reasons for the move. Glaser eventually claimed that Microsoft added code to its Windows operating system that caused operating problems for RealPlayer, and tension developed between the two companies. Also in November, RealNetworks shipped RealSystem G2, which included 3D technology and search tools for finding multimedia content, along with many other enhancements. Revenues for the year reached $66.4 million.

Several developments unfolded at RealNetworks in 1999. The company introduced its free RealJukebox, which allowed users to record near-CD-quality versions of their own music onto PCs, and RealJukebox Plus, a premium version of the free product which the company heralded as "the first complete digital music system with CD-quality recording and playback." After the beta version of RealJukebox was launched in May 1999, RealJukebox quickly became a hit with computer users. Media Metrix placed the number of unique users at 2.2 million after only one month. In September, RealNetworks named Thomas Frank as the company's COO. Two months later, it announced the formation of the Real.com Network, which provided users with a single source for locating and accessing a wide variety of streaming media. RealNetworks also unveiled RealPlayer 7, which performed better than its predecessors and included better navigation capabilities. Seven days after it was introduced, a record-breaking 3 million copies of the new player had been downloaded. On a sour note, RealNetworks was hit with two class-action lawsuits in 1999. The company was accused of violating user privacy by collecting information about their listening habits without consent. However, good news came in the form of healthy net revenues, which soared 98 percent over the previous year, reaching $131.2 million.

Venturing into the new millennium, RealNetworks acquired Netzip Inc. in 2000. Netzip developed software for managing the downloading of files via the Internet. The acquisition improved RealNetworks' ability to deliver its products to customers throughout the world. In 2000, the company also introduced

Real.com Games, a site for downloading computer games from leading developers, and unveiled nine international editions of RealJukebox and RealPlayer 7. Adoption of RealNetworks' products continued to soar. Media Metrix indicated that approximately 29 million people used RealPlayer during March. Additionally, the number of unique registered RealPlayer users exceeded 115 million. RealNetworks introduced RealPlayer GoldPass in 2000, which it described as "the first all-in-one media subscription service on the Internet combining premium audio and video content, value-added software and games, and advanced services for consumers." Subscribers to the service would surpass the 150,000 mark by the end of January 2001. Besides introducing improved product offerings in RealVideo 8 and RealAudio 8, the company ended 2000 on a positive note as net revenues increased 84 percent over 1999, reaching $241.5 million.

In February 2001, Larry Jacobson was named RealNetworks' president and COO and assumed responsibility for the firm's daily operations. A graduate of Harvard Business School, prior to joining RealNetworks Jacobson served as president and COO of Ticketmaster Corp. and president of FOX Television Network. The company introduced RealArcade, which expanded the existing gaming offerings on the Real.com Games Web site. RealNetworks also joined with AOL Time Warner, EMI Group, and Bertelsmann to create a separate, independent company known as MusicNet to offer a subscription-based online music service. As high-speed Internet connections became more commonplace and the processing speed of the average PC increased, the market for streaming digital media looked promising, boding well for the future of RealNetworks.

FURTHER READING:

Dreyfuss, Joel. "RealJukebox is Real Hip." *Fortune,* June 7, 1999.

Lenatti, Chuck. "Multimedia Gets Real." *Upside,* August 1999.

Mardesich, Jodi. "Can Microsoft Kill the Video Star?" *Fortune,* October 26, 1998.

"Progressive Networks Announces RealVideo." Seattle, Washington: RealNetworks Inc. February 10, 1997. Available from www.realnetworks.com.

RealNetworks Inc. "Company Information." Seattle, Washington: RealNetworks Inc., November 12, 2001. Available from www.realnetworks.com.

Williamson, Debra Aho. "RealNetworks Transforms into Web Media Company." *Advertising Age,* July 17, 2000.

SEE ALSO: Glaser, Robert; Streaming Media

REAL-TIME TRANSACTION

When the World Wide Web began to take off as a commercial marketplace, many of the first corporate Web sites were little more than static pages providing company information or product and service promotions. Because these sites essentially were electronic brochures, they sometimes were referred to as brochureware. By the early 2000s, e-commerce—and many supporting Internet-related technologies—had evolved beyond this early stage. Consumers and businesses were engaging in many forms of online transactions that happened immediately, in real-time. The speed at which information traveled across the Internet, along with its widespread availability and integration with other systems, caused significant improvements for both consumers and businesses.

One simple example of a real-time transaction is an online credit card purchase of an e-book. Unlike traditional mail orders involving paper checks, order forms, postal services, and parcel shippers, someone ordering an e-book receives the goods immediately in the form of a downloadable file after their order is placed, and the seller receives immediate payment. These kinds of credit card transactions are validated almost immediately after an online order has been placed to prevent fraud. A more involved example could extend to the many different areas of an organization that are affected by a transaction. If the above scenario involved an online order for a paper book that had to be shipped to the buyer, information about the order might be instantly sent to the seller's accounting system for billing; to its customer service department in the event of problems or questions; to the warehouse for packing and shipping; and to the marketing department for use in targeted promotions based on the kind of book purchased. Successful e-tailers integrate their many different systems so that this process happens seamlessly in real-time.

Real-time transactions also extend to the business-to-business arena where manufacturers and suppliers integrate their systems online. In this situation, a manufacturer's computer might automatically order supplies when inventory reaches a certain level, keeping its real-time production levels in line with those of the supplier. Real-time transactions also have implications for customer service. For example, when packages are sent from one party to another, the receiving party often wants to know the status of their delivery. In the early 2000s, parcel/express carriers allowed customers to track shipments via the Web in a number of different ways. By entering tracking numbers into a Web site, customers could receive instant e-mail replies as to the status and location of their package in transit. Companies also could check the location of goods being shipped to them by truck or rail, and in some cases could check the temperature of cars moving perishable goods.

FURTHER READING:

Copacino, William C. ''The E-synchronized Supply Chain.'' April, 2000. *Logistics Management & Distribution Report,*

Neel, Dan. ''Wireless Tracking of Shipments Readied.'' *Info-World.com,* September 2, 2000. Available from www2.infoworld.com.

''Real Time.'' *Ecommerce Webopedia,*. May 29, 2001. Available from e-comm.webopedia.com.

SEE ALSO: Electronic Payment

RECURRING PAYMENT TRANSACTIONS

When consumers or businesses are billed regularly for services like Internet access, resulting in an automatic transfer of funds, a recurring billing transaction occurs. Recurring transactions can involve checking accounts or credit card accounts as the source from which funds are obtained. According to *Credit Card Management,* Visa indicated a 39-percent increase in recurring transactions during fiscal year 2000, totaling approximately $23 billion. The magazine indicated that recurring payments were a high-growth market in the early 2000s, especially among businesses like apartment management companies, cable TV providers, and health clubs. Additionally, a study from MasterCard revealed that ''36 percent of customers with recurring bills—for such services as cable, utilities, telecommunications, and insurance—would readily switch to a merchant or service provider who offered them a credit card payment method for their recurring bills.''

Recurring payments benefit the parties engaged in transactions in different ways. For companies engaging in e-commerce, they represent a measured flow of revenue, allowing merchants to foresee when and how much money they will receive from customers. For the banks that actually issue credit cards to consumers or business users, they represent an increase in interchange income (a merchant's bank pays a credit-card-issuing bank interchange fees for every transaction). Finally, recurring transactions represent convenience for consumers, who don't have to mail checks or money orders to pay bills.

Credit card companies were doing different things to encourage companies to promote recurring payments with their customers during the early 2000s.

Visa was testing a service that updated credit card information for merchants in the event that customers' cards were upgraded (for example, from gold to platinum status) or changed by an issuing bank. This helped to prevent charge-backs if consumers failed to provide the updated information to merchants. Additionally, MasterCard International's Service Industries Incentive Program, tailored to the telecommunications, utility, insurance, and cable TV industries, provided a host of benefits and incentives to merchants who promoted recurring transactions.

FURTHER READING:

''The Challenge of Recurring Payments.'' *Credit Card Management,* July 1999.

Lucas, Peter. ''New Markets for the New Century.'' *Credit Card Management,* December 2000.

''Service Industries Incentive Program for Recurring Payments.'' MasterCard International Inc., June 5, 2001. Available from www.mastercard.com.

SEE ALSO: Acquiring Bank; Card-Issuing Bank; Charge-backs; Electronic Payment; Payment Options and Services, Online; Transaction Issues

RESOLUTION

The term resolution is used to describe the quality or sharpness of images that are displayed on computer monitors or printed onto pages. Generally speaking, low-resolution images are of a lesser quality than high-resolution images. Resolution is expressed differently, depending on whether an image appears on-screen or in print.

The resolution of computer monitors is expressed in elements called pixels. Displayed as a set of red, green, and blue dots, pixels are the smallest pieces on a screen that can be manipulated. For example, the brightness or color of a pixel can be adjusted. Pixels normally are expressed in the form of two numbers (such as 640 x 480). When multiplied, these numbers reveal the total number of pixels a screen can display (such as 300,000). The value 640 corresponds to the number of pixels a screen can display across an individual horizontal line, of which there are a total of 480.

The earliest computer monitors were not capable of displaying the color images that are so important to Web pages and e-commerce. Instead, they were monochromatic and displayed text characters in green or orange. During the 1980s and early 1990s IBM developed display technologies like the Color Graphics

Adapter (CGA), Enhanced Graphics Adapter (EGA), Video Graphics Array (VGA), and Extended Graphics Array (XGA) that allowed monitors to display greater numbers of colors and pixels. In the early 2000s, the Ultra Extended Graphics Array (UXGA) standard was supported by most computer monitors. In tandem with enough video memory and the right graphics card, UXGA made it possible to achieve resolutions of 1600 x 1200 pixels and display 16.6 million colors. Around the same time, flat-panel displays and rear-projection monitors were evolving, holding the potential to improve the quality of images users saw on-screen.

When the term resolution is used to describe the quality of a printed image, it is expressed in dots-per-inch (DPI), or the number of dots a printer can fit into one linear inch. A printer capable of printing 600 DPI can produce 360,000 dots in every square inch. The resolution of an image on-screen may not correspond with its resolution in printed form, since each depends on the equipment on which it is viewed or printed. However, the resolution of a printed or viewed image generally will improve if its size is reduced, or become poorer if its size is enlarged. This corresponds with the concentration of pixels or dots.

FURTHER READING:

Chinnock, Chris. ''New Screen Designs are Leading to More Attractive Images.'' *Electronic Design,* October 2, 2000.

''Pixels and Resolution.'' *The PC Guide,* April 17, 2001. Available from www.pcguide.com.

''Resolution.'' *Ecommerce Webopedia,*. May 25, 2001. Available from e-comm.webopedia.com.

''Resolution.'' *Tech Encyclopedia,*. May 25, 2001. Available from www.techweb.com.

Tyson, Jeff. ''How Computer Monitors Work.'' *How Stuff Works,* May 30, 2001. Available from www.howstuffworks.com.

RESTRUCTURING

Many traditional brick-and-mortar enterprises have found it necessary to adopt some sort of e-business strategy as the Internet becomes an increasingly powerful venue for exchanging information, as well as for buying and selling products and services. According to market research firm International Data Corp. (IDC), Internet commerce is expected to reach $5 trillion by 2005, with over one billion Internet users across the globe. These figures, coupled with increased competition, have forced many firms to integrate e-business initiatives into traditional business models. Most of the time, this transformation involves some level of restructuring as business methods are changed to adapt to new technologies.

At the start of the new millennium, many dot.com startups and technology-based companies were undergoing major restructuring efforts as well. Low stock prices, difficulty securing investment capital, increased competition, and a weakening U.S. economy were forcing Internet-based firms who experienced great success in the mid-to-late 1990s to restructure operations to remain competitive.

BRICKS-AND-MORTAR TO CLICKS-AND-MORTAR

Many traditional brick-and-mortar enterprises have adopted—or are in the process of adopting—an e-business strategy that will transform them into a click-and-mortar entity. Whether simply creating a company World Wide Web site or developing a plan to provide products and services via the Internet, an enterprise entering the e-business world is faced with changing business models. Adapting to new technology, integrating the new e-business strategy into current operations, and handling new customer relationships, can all result in the restructuring of company operations. According to a May 2000 *Software Magazine* article, for established companies, ''e-business is a new and very different challenge. It cuts to the core of their operations and threatens to disrupt their currently successful and carefully crafted business models.''

Office Depot, General Mills Inc., and Victoria's Secret are examples of traditional enterprises that restructured operations as part of e-business initiatives. Office Depot's online business, developed in 1996, has recorded profits each year. Under the leadership of Monica Luechtefeld, the company has become the second largest e-tailer behind Amazon.com with online sales in 2000 reaching $850 million. The firm integrated its Web and store operations, allowing customers to purchase items online and either have them delivered or have them packaged and available for pickup at customer service centers in nearby stores. The Office Depot Web site also allows customers to check inventory at each of its stores. By restructuring both its inventory and distribution operations, adding additional warehouse space and trucks, the firm was able to offer its online customers over twice as many products on the Web than it could stock in its retail locations. The firm also restructured customer service operations at the retail level, which enabled store employees to handle increased business from online customers.

General Mills Inc. also restructured certain aspects of its traditional business as part of its Internet strategy. In the past, the firm conducted its market research by sending its researchers out into the field. In 2001, nearly 60 percent of the company's research was done online. The firm also revamped its purchasing and trucking operations by using Transora, a business-to-business electronic marketplace, to make many of its purchases. It shared trucking services through an online network in order to cut shipping costs. In a joint venture with a California-based research firm, General Mills also began selling market research services via the Web to consumer packaged-goods companies, securing such customers as Nestle and PepsiCo.

Victoria's Secret, a subsidiary of Intimate Brands, was restructured internally when a new division, VictoriasSecret.com, was created as an e-business segment of the firm. The company's marketing and distribution channels were also revamped as part of its push to gain an Internet presence. In 1999, Victoria's Secret offered the industry's first live streaming media fashion show, which logged over 500 million hits in ten weeks. The firm's customer tracking system was also updated to allow the company to record an individual's purchasing history. By integrating its catalog, Web site, and retail outlets, its Web operations secured profits in 2000.

RESTRUCTURING AMONG DOT.COM STARTUPS AND TECHNOLOGY-BASED FIRMS

While many traditional companies focused on restructuring to join the e-business world, dot.com firms and technology-based companies found themselves having to restructure to remain competitive in the markets they once controlled. Faced with a slowing North American economy, faltering stock prices, and increased competition, many in the dot.com industry were scrambling to remain afloat at the start of the 21st century.

Software e-tailer Beyond.com, for example, was one of the first to sell consumer software on the Internet in the mid-1990s. By 2000, however, its stock price had declined dramatically and the firm announced major restructuring efforts. It cut its workforce by 20 percent, replaced top management, and announced plans to shift its focus from retail customers to business customers. Theglobe.com, a leading interactive entertainment and game Web site, also restructured operations. It spun off various holdings and slashed its employee base by 40 percent as part of its reorganization plan.

Exodus Communications, a leading Web hosting firm, was also forced to retool. In order to cut costs, it reduced its workforce by 15 percent and slowed spending. In April 2001, three top executives resigned after losses were posted, leaving the company without key leadership during its shift from providing traditional hosting services to also offering equipment maintenance services and solutions for content distribution and caching, security, performance measuring and monitoring, and networking.

Computer manufacturer Dell Computer Corp. was forced to cut costs as fierce competition caused personal computer prices to fall. The firm reduced its workforce by four percent and slowed spending. Dell restructured its inventory operations, allowing suppliers to access company inventory levels via the Web. Using the new system, inventory was replaced on an as-needed basis which led to a decrease in overstocking. The effort saved $50 million in 2000.

With Carly Fiorina at the helm, Hewlett-Packard also underwent a major restructuring in order to keep pace with those in the technology industry. Fiorina divided the firm into four major groups including computer products, imaging products, consumer sales, and corporate sales. Its marketing division was also restructured to reflect the firm's new focus on providing information tools, infrastructure assistance, and e-services. After the restructuring, H-P released several new products that were key to its vision to become a leading computer supplier for dot.com companies.

As Internet growth is predicted to rise, e-business strategies will, no doubt, continue to become more commonplace among traditional brick-and-mortar firms. The ability to restructure and revamp old business models in both traditional and dot.com firms will be key to successful adaptation. A March 2001 *BusinessWeek Online* article stated, "over the coming decade, the biggest gains will come from restructuring the way work is done within companies." Erik Brynjolfsson, an economist from the Massachusetts Institute of Technology stated in the article, "most of the Net's benefits will come in changes to business practices and organization. What really matters is when companies and markets reorganize."

FURTHER READING:

"25 Leaders for a Dangerous Time." *BusinessWeek Online,* May 14, 2001. Available from www.businessweek.com.

E-Business Systems Integration Center. "E-Business Strategy." Falls Church, VA: E-Business Systems Integration Center, 2000. Available from sic.nvgc.vt.edu.

Hayes, Ian S. "Hype, Reality, and Vision." *Software Magazine,* May 5, 2000. Available from www.softwaremag.com.

Hazelwood, Sara. "Beyond.hope? Online Pioneer Not Giving Up." *The Business Journal,* January 21, 2000.

Hof, Robert D., and Michael Mandel. "Rethinking the Internet." *BusinessWeek Online,* March 26, 2001. Available from www.businessweek.com.

Mahoney, Michael. "Running Lean and Mean to Survive in E-Business." *E-Commerce Times,* March 2, 2001. Available from www.ecommercetimes.com.

Volpe, Nicole. "New Strategy For No.1 Dell: Be Ruthless." *PlanetIT,* May 3, 2001. Available from www.planetit.com.

SEE ALSO: Mergers and Acquisitions; Shakeout, Dot-com

RESULTS RANKING

Search engines are one of the most popular and widely used tools on the Web. When Internet surfers wish to locate something on the Web, they are more likely to use a search engine than any other method. After a user enters a search, most search engines utilize some formula for returning results that correspond with the user's search. The end result of this process is a results ranking, in which those Web sites that relate to the search are listed in a particular order determined by the search-engine. This issue has become tremendously important for Internet users and online businesses alike, because studies show that users are overwhelmingly more likely to visit those sites that appear early in the results ranking rather than those further down in the list.

Results ranking is the practice of listing search returns in order of their relevance to the search term or terms, with those most closely matching the search listed first. In other words, while a particular search term may result in thousands of site listings, those that most closely match the intentions of the user are featured prominently at the top. Of course, there are different methods of determining what the user may be looking for or find relevant, which amounts to the difference in the results rankings between search engines. According to *Online,* the practice of relevancy searching (also known as statistical or fuzzy searching) is one of the competitive grounds on which search engines work to distinguish themselves.

The criteria by which relevancy is determined are many. For instance, search engines may determine relevancy by

- identifying the number of times the search term appears on a Web page
- the location of the terms within the document (for instance, a site on which the term appears in the title would be tanked higher than one on which the term appears buried in a paragraph)
- whether all or only some of the search terms are matched
- whether an exact phrase or merely all the words in a search phrase are found
- the number of times the terms appear relative to the length of the document, and a host of other measures.

Most sophisticated search engines determine relevancy not by any one of these criteria, but by some mixture of several of them. The particular weight given to each individual factor and the relationship between these factors constitute the ranking algorithm. Ranking algorithms, then, are the bread and butter of search-engine firms, and as a result are kept highly secret.

Search results are generally listed with only limited information about those specific documents—usually the Universal Resource Locator (URL), the document title, and a brief summary often pulled from the document text—so users rely heavily on the relevancy listing to determine how useful they might find the page to be. Sometimes results lists feature confidence rankings as well. A confidence ranking is similar to a relevance ranking, but adds a measure of confidence for the relevance of individual pages. For instance, again using a complex algorithm to determine relevance, a confidence ranking may list for each site a percentage of confidence, where a higher percentage indicates a more useful site.

E-commerce firms need to take results ranking into account when they design their Web sites. For instance, companies are more likely to be listed higher in the results ranking for searches for their products and services if the facts of who they are and what they do are clearly and prominently stated on their Web sites. Importantly, however, simply having a Web site isn't always enough to get one's site listed in a results ranking. Most search-engines are built on Web directories compiled by way of individuals visiting sites and deciding if those sites warrant inclusion in the database. Some search engines, such as Yahoo!, offer users a link through which they can apply to have their own site reviewed for possible database inclusion. While other search engines work not via human-compiled databases but via simple search-engine robots that will find and list most any site on the Web, a great deal of effort goes into getting one's site placed near the top of a results ranking.

There exists a tension, however, between the efforts of companies and others to take advantage of search-engine strategies to make themselves more prominent in results rankings on the one hand, and the need for search engines to maintain the integrity of their tools on the other. If companies employ savvy Web optimization firms to devise a working search-engine strategy, search engines need to avoid the appearance of favoritism, or at the least keep their search engines valuable to users as a whole. As a result, ranking algorithms tend to be under constant scrutiny and modification.

FURTHER READING:

Brandt, D. Scott. "Relevancy and Searching the Internet." *Computers in Libraries,* September, 1996.

Courtois, Martin P., and Michael W. Berry. "Results Ranking in Web Search Engines." *Online,* May/June, 1999.

Joven, Ellen. "Topping The Charts." *Financial Planning,* May 01, 1999.

SEE ALSO: Search Engine Strategy; URL (Uniform Resource Locator)

RICKETTS, JOSEPH

Joseph Ricketts is the founder and chairman of Ameritrade Corp., the fourth-largest Internet-based brokerage in the U.S. In addition to using the World Wide Web, Ameritrade clients may also complete trades via telephone and fax. After CEO Thomas Lewis resigned suddenly in August of 2000—in the wake of the dot.com fallout—Ricketts took over as interim CEO until March 2001, when Merrill Lynch executive Joseph Moglia accepted the top spot at Ameritrade. As chairman, Ricketts continues to oversee the development of Ameritrade's business plan. He owns roughly 65 percent of the firm.

After completing his undergraduate degree in economics at Omaha, Nebraska-based Creighton University, Ricketts launched his financial services career, which included stints at Dun & Bradstreet as a branch manager, and at Dean Witter. In 1975, after several regulations in the investment industry had been loosened, Ricketts co-founded First Omaha Securities—later named Accutrade—as a discount brokerage. Seven years later, Ricketts took over as chairman and CEO of Accutrade. He established AmeriTrade as a clearing broker in 1983, and he merged the firm's discount and clearing brokerage operations into TransTerra Co., a new holding company, in 1987. Accutrade introduced technology that allowed trading to take place via touch-tone telephones the following year.

Ricketts oversaw the acquisition of K. Aufhauser & Co., Inc. in 1995. Aufhauser became the first brokerage company to offer Internet-based trading when it launched WealthWeb in August of 1994. Ricketts also spearheaded the purchase of Internet-based trader All American Brokers Inc., the creation of Ceres Securities, and the launch of trading services on portable communication devices, such as cellular phones. Accutrade released Accutrade for Windows, an application serving individual investors engaged in online trading, in January of 1996. Ten months later, Ricketts changed the name of his firm from TransTerra to Ameritrade Holding Corp.

Ameritrade conducted its initial public offering in March of 1997. Ricketts convinced America On-line (AOL) to include a direct link to both Accutrade and Ceres on its site. Similarly, Microsoft Corp. agreed to allow Ricketts to provide users of the Microsoft Investor program with online access to both financial services. In October, Ameritrade Holding consolidated its online services into a single firm, named Ameritrade Inc., which offered Internet-based trades at a flat fee of $8 each. Additional strategic alliances forged by the year's end included deals with Yahoo! Finance, Excite Business & Investing, and Infoseek Personal Finance.

In conjunction with Data Broadcasting, Ameritrade began offering stock quotes via the Internet in 1998. A joint venture with PostX allowed Ameritrade to make trade confirmations electronically. Along with broadening his firm's reach via agreements with domestic partners, Ricketts also began forging deals with international partners, such as France-based discount broker Cortal and Deutsche Bank AG. In March of 1999, Thomas K. Lewis, Jr. was appointed co-CEO. With Lewis and Ricketts both at the helm, Ameritrade completed the acquisition of online brokerage R.J. Forbes Group, Inc. and introduced the Online Investor Index to track the transactions completed by online investors. Eventually, Ricketts handed over full managerial control to Lewis. However, the abrupt departure of Lewis in August of 2000 prompted Ricketts to take the reins at Ameritrade until a new leader was put in place. While Ricketts served as interim CEO, Ameritrade completed the $40 million purchase of TradeCast Ltd. early in 2001. The addition of TradeCast's business-to-business operations prompted the eventual reorganization of Ameritrade into two units serving different clients: individual investors and institutional investors. In March, Joseph Moglia took over as CEO, while Ricketts remained chairman.

FURTHER READING:

Ameritrade Holding Corp. "History." Omaha, NE: Ameritrade Holding Corp., 2001. Available from www.amtd.com.

"Ameritrade's Ricketts Sees Rebound as Markets Revert to Norm." *Futures World News,* June 8, 2001.

Ring, Niamh. "Ameritrade Revamps Structure and Lineup." *American Banker,* June 28, 2001.

SEE ALSO: Ameritrade Holding Corp.; Brokerage Model; Investing, Online

RSA DATA SECURITY

RSA Data Security pioneered and marketed the technology that makes it possible to communicate and transfer information and documents securely on the Internet and establish and authenticate the identity of virtual trading partners—developments essential to the widespread acceptance of electronic commerce. The technology could also be used to prevent snoopers from eavesdropping on cell phone calls and other digital communications. RSA's technology, called public-key encryption, was an advance of light-years over previous schemes to make computers, computer networks, and computer data tamper-proof. In fact, RSA encryption products almost proved too successful. As the digital age dawned, the company found itself squaring off with two of the most powerful and secretive agencies of the U.S. government, the National Security Agency (NSA) and the Federal Bureau of Investigation (FBI). The government claimed RSA's encryption techniques made it possible for spies and criminals to plan and act without fear of detection by intelligence or law enforcement agencies. Undeterred, in the middle 1990s RSA joined forces with another maker of electronic security products, and developed a fully-integrated line of security products for businesses and other organizations.

RSA's security systems are based on a mathematical theory for public-key encryption, which encodes data using formulas called algorithms. Public-key encryption represented a huge step beyond earlier encryption systems, which relied on a single "key" to encode and decode data. Everyone who wanted to send or receive information using this encryption system had to possess the secret key. Having to spread the secret around, however, was the weak link in a "single key" system. The more people who knew the secret, the more likely that it would eventually be found out by outsiders.

RSA's encryption products use two keys. If John Doe wants to receive encrypted files or e-mail, he has a public key and a private key, each one a number one hundred or more digits long, linked by the encryption algorithm. Doe can give the public key to anyone who wants to send him coded information. It can remain public knowledge, because it cannot be used to decode messages encrypted for Doe. For that, the private key is needed, and only Doe posesses it. An important application of public-key encryption in the realm of e-commerce is the transmission of credit card information securely to online merchants.

Alternately, John Doe can use the his private key to encode a document, such as a contract, and send it to someone who knows his public key. Using the public key, the recipient can open the encrypted message. The fact that Doe's key opens it guarantees that is came from Doe. In addition Doe could send two versions of a document, one scrambled and one unscrambled. If they match when opened, it guarantees that the documents have not been tampered with en route.

Thus RSA encryption systems not only hide data from prying eyes, they can be used to authenticate the identity of a sender and to verify the integrity of transmitted data.

Public-key encryption was invented as a viable computer technology in 1977 by three scientists at the Massachusetts Institute of Technology. They founded RSA Data Security in 1982 to market their invention. Unfortunately, the math done by their encryption software was far too memory-intensive for most computers in the 1980s. In 1986 RSA was on the verge of bankruptcy, and Jim Bidzos was brought in as CEO. Under Bidzos the company's fortunes turned around. Lotus adopted an RSA encryption system in 1987 for its Lotus Notes software. Two years later, Digital Equipment Corp., then was strongly committed to developing computer networks, joined a strategic alliance with RSA. The firm got an important endorsement in 1989 when its technology was adopted by the technical committee of a then little-known computer network with about a half million users, known as the Internet. The computer community, public and private alike, was clearly anxious to find a reliable, standard security solution for protecting its communications and networks. By 1991, RSA seemed to be the default winner. Nearly all major American computer companies, including Motorola, Apple, Novell, and Microsoft, were incorporating RSA software in their products—even the U.S. Department of Defense licensed the firm's encryption software.

The Defense Department adoption took on an ironic dimension shortly afterward. In July 1990 the National Security Agency (NSA), a large, highly secretive government intelligence agency that specializes in intercepting and decoding the encrypted communications of foreign governments, came out in opposition to a plan to endorse RSA as the standard for the entire government. NSA interest in RSA technology dated from the early 1980s when it used its behind-the-scenes influence to block the system's adoption by the Department of Commerce. In 1990 the NSA opposed RSA's system precisely because it was so effective—its codes were virtually uncrackable. The NSA feared that once the technology spread overseas, the agency would no longer be able to read coded communications. The FBI also denounced RSA products on the grounds that they would make monitoring the phones and e-mail of criminals and terrorists virtually impossible.

In April 1993 the government countered with a solution of its own: the Clipper chip. The Clipper chip created a third key with which gave the government access to any encrypted information. The implications for privacy played right into the hands of RSA's Bidzos, a promotional master who publicly called for the computer industry to boycott products with Big Brother inside. He argued that forcing a compromised system on the American computer industry would ultimately only succeed in giving the edge in encryption research and sales to foreign countries. Those nations, he argues, would simply reject out of hand any system that gave the U.S. government unlimited access. RSA cannily organized conferences on the encryption question that drew the computer industry together into a united front against government efforts to impose its system. At one conference, held in January 1994, a group of leading hardware, software, and telecommunications firms jointly defied the government and unilaterally rejected the Clipper chip in favor of RSA's system. By the middle of 1994, RSA has sold more than four million copies of its software.

By 1996, the computer industry was in agreement that the lack of a universally accepted structure of secure payment was the main roadblock to the acceptance of e-commerce. Nonetheless, by that time the widespread licensing of RSA by all major American computer firms had made it the de facto industry standard anyway. Bidzos continued to defy government. He challenged federal technology export restrictions by establishing an RSA subsidiary in Japan to manufacture encryption chips that RSA was prohibited from exporting. He formed another subsidiary in the People's Republic of China to produce 40-bit encryption technology, despite claims by the government that the Chinese would use the technology—whose export was federally-approved in any case—to develop much more powerful systems of their own.

There was widespread speculation that RSA would follow the trend among upstart Internet firms and go public with a stock offering in 1996. Instead Bidzos negotiated the firm's purchase by Securities Dynamics Technologies, Inc., a Massachusetts firm that produced computer security devices such as smart cards. The purchase price reflected how bright RSA's future was seen to be—at about $200 million in stock, it exceeded more than fifteen-fold RSA's 1995 sales. The two companies combined their two product lines into an integrated line of computer and electronic security software and devices. In 1999, Se-curity Dynamics changed its name to RSA Security Inc.

In 1998, RSA sponsored a contest which offered a prize of $10,000 to whomever was able to crack a code encrypted in DES—Data Encryption Standard—the standard finally adopted by the government and one used by numerous financial institutions for transmitting funds electronically. The prize was won by a two-man team, a computer privacy activist and a hacker who decoded the code in 56 hours. The contest showed the weakness of the government standard compared with RSA's. Ironically, the contest data was encrypted in a form of DES much more powerful than the encryption technology permitted for export.

FURTHER READING:

Blankenhorn, Dana. ''Building the Tools for Web Commerce.'' *Interactive Age,* February 13, 1995.

Clark, Don. ''Bay Firm's Scrambler To Guard U.S. Computers.'' *San Francisco Chronicle,* February 15, 1990.

———. ''Bidzos Is Holding the Key To Guard Internet Secrets.'' *Wall Street Journal,* April 17, 1996.

———. ''RSA Picked To Provide Computer Lock.'' *San Francisco Chronicle,* February 1, 1989.

Gelfond, Susan. ''Confounding Computer Crooks With Clever Cryptography.'' *Business Week,* April 17, 1989.

Markoff, John. ''Industry Defies U.S. on Data Encryption.'' *New York Times,* January 14, 1994.

———. ''Profit and Ego in Data Secrecy.'' *New York Times,* June 28, 1994.

———. ''U.S. Data Code Is Unscrambled In 56 Hours.'' *New York Times,* July 17, 1998.

Mintz, John. ''Chipping Away at Privacy?; Encryption Device Widens Debate Over Rights of U.S. to Eavesdrop.'' *Washington Post,* May 30, 1993.

O'Reilly, Richard. ''Firm Offers Key to Computer Security.'' *Chicago Sun-Times,* March 25, 1986.

Stipp, David. ''Techno-Hero Or Public Enemy?'' *Fortune Magazine,* November 11, 1996.

SEE ALSO: Advanced Encryption Standard (AES); Cryptography, Public and Private Key; Data Encryption Standard (DES); Encryption

S

SAFE HARBOR PRIVACY FRAMEWORK

Regulations governing consumer privacy on the Internet have been much stronger in the European Union (EU) than in the United States. On October 28, 1998, the EU adopted the European Community Directive on Data Protection 95/46/EC, which established minimum standards for the protection of users' personal data and privacy on the Internet. The Directive requires all EU members to generate and enforce comprehensive legislation to comply with those standards.

Article 25 of the EU Directive prohibits any EU country from transferring personal data via the Internet to, or receiving data from, countries deemed to lack ''adequate'' Internet privacy protection. The U.S. is among those countries, since it has no national data-privacy laws that meet the EU standards. Instead of laws, the U.S. government permitted American companies to address privacy issues through self-regulation, which many EU officials regard as too lax to adequately safeguard individuals who use the Web.

To meet EU concerns, the U.S. Department of Commerce (DOC) drew up the Safe Harbor Privacy Principles in conjunction with the EU. The DOC designated a series of ''safe harbor'' principles intended to meet the standard of ''adequate privacy protection'' required by the EU Directive. In July 2000, the European Commission approved those principles and the Safe Harbor program went into effect in November of that year.

Participation in the Safe Harbor Program is voluntary, but the DOC asserts that it eliminates the necessity of prior approval in order for companies to conduct electronic data transfers. Participating organizations must publicly announce their Safe Harbor compliance in writing to the DOC each year. In addition, they must include a similar statement in their published privacy policy statements. The DOC makes the list of all self-certified organizations available to the public. In exchange for Safe Harbor certification, U.S. companies are shielded from prosecution under the EU data-protection laws.

The Safe Harbor program encompasses seven principles. All compliant organizations must agree to:

- Notify Internet users about the type of data collected at the Web site, the manner in which it is collected, for what purpose, and whether it will be disclosed to third parties. They must also inform users of options for limiting the use and disclosure of that information.

- Provide individuals with the chance to opt out of having their personal data collected or disseminated to third parties.

- Guarantee that data will be transferred only to other Safe-Harbor compliant parties.

- Facilitate individuals' access to their personal data and provide a means for them to correct inaccurate information.

- Undertake ''reasonable precautions'' to secure the data from loss, alteration, or unauthorized access or disclosure.

- Utilize the data only for purposes that have been disclosed to the individuals.

- Put in place enforcement mechanisms that will ensure compliance. These include providing accessible, affordable, and independent venues through which individuals can lodge complaints for breach of Safe Harbor principles and through which justifiable damages can be awarded, and a system to verify that the company has in fact implemented the Safe Harbor principles.

American companies can adopt a variety of strategies to participate in Safe Harbor. These include joining a self-regulatory program that meets Safe Harbor guidelines or implementing their own organizational, self-regulatory privacy policies that meet those same guidelines. Any organization that violates the Safe Harbor principles may be held in violation of state or federal unfair and deceptive trade practices law.

Another option may permit American companies to bypass the Safe Harbor program altogether by negotiating ''model contracts'' with either an EU-country's data-protection authority or with an individual whose personal data will be transferred electronically. These contracts would verify that company practices conform with the EU's data-protection laws. As of 2001, such contracts were under negotiation by EU data-protection authorities and the U.S. DOC. Members of the American business community, however, warned that the standards enshrined in such contract might prove more stringent than the Safe Harbor principles.

Safe Harbor has struggled to get off the ground and major U.S. corporations have been slow to embrace the program. In February 2001, only 21 U.S. companies had signed on, prominent among them Hewlett-Packard Co. In addition, financial-services companies, such as insurers and banks, argued that they need not participate in the Safe Harbor program, because the online privacy protections contained in the Gramm-Leach-Bliley Act of 1999 assure their compliance with the EU Directive.

FURTHER READING:

''EU Privacy Safe Harbor.'' *Business Insurance,* November 6, 2000.

Gillin, Donna. ''Safe Harbor Principles for the European Privacy Directives are Finalized.'' *Marketing Research,* Winter 2000.

Goldstein, Heather, et. al. ''Safe Harbor Privacy Pact Implemented Between Europe and the United States.'' *Intellectual Property & Technology Law Journal,* February 2001, 27.

Johnson, Mark. ''As Seen from Europe: A Very Public War Over Privacy.'' *Global Finance,* January 2001, 30.

Thibodeau, Patrick. ''Big Companies Shy Away from Safe Harbor Accord.'' *Computerworld,* February 19, 2001, 12.

SEE ALSO: European Commission's Directive on Data Privacy; Privacy: Issues, Policies, Statements

SAPIENT CORP.

Internet services consultancy Sapient Corp. operates offices throughout the U.S., as well as in Canada, England, Germany, Italy, India, and Japan. Sales in 2000 exceeded the $500 million mark, and employees totaled roughly 2,300, as Sapient became the first Internet services firm to make the Standard & Poor's 500-stock index. That year, a survey conducted by Forrester Research Inc. ranked Sapient as the top e-commerce integrator—a firm that develops and implements e-commerce solutions—in the U.S.

In 1991, Jerry Greenberg and Stuart Moore cofounded Sapient Corp. in Cambridge, Massachusetts, to offer client-server integration services. Greenberg and Moore funded initial operations with $40,000 of their personal savings. When that capital began to dwindle, they ran up a $70,000 tab on their credit cards. The partners set their fledgling firm apart from rivals by not only finding technology-based solutions to solve problems or increase efficiency, but also by handling the implementation of these solutions. Sapient also set prices and deadlines prior to finalizing contracts and based employee compensation on client satisfaction, practices unlike any other consultancy at the time.

Sapient's innovative approach to technology-based consulting began to pay off in the mid-1990s. Both revenues and earnings more than doubled from 1994 to 1995. Offices in San Francisco and New York allowed the firm to extend its geographic reach. In April 1996, Sapient completed its initial public offering (IPO), generating $33 million in fresh capital, which was poured into expansion efforts. It was during the two years following the IPO, after management recognized that many Sapient clients were growing interested in e-commerce applications, that Sapient began its push into e-business integration services. The purchase of Studio Archetype, a World Wide Web integration firm, boosted Sapient's e-commerce services arsenal, which eventually became the most comprehensive in the industry. Earnings of $9.4 million in 1998 grew more than threefold to $30.3 million in 1999; over the same time period, revenues jumped 68 percent, from $165 million to $277 million. The firm acquired E-Lab LLC in October of 1999. That year, new offices opened in Texas, Colorado, Washington, D.C., and Italy. Major projects included the launch of Nordstromshoes.com, the largest virtual shoe shop on the Web; the relaunch of Adobe Systems Inc.'s Web site; and the development and launch of iWon.com, an Internet gateway that used frequent cash giveaways to draw traffic to its site.

Sapient added broadband and media applications developer Human Code Inc. to its mix in August of

2000. By then, according to a November 2000 article in *Computer Reseller News*, the firm had transformed itself from "a nine-year-old consulting and integration company grounded in client/server computing into one of the foremost Web integrators on the scene." The firm played an integral role in the development of an online real estate service in the U.K. and Internet portal India.com that year. However, despite Sapient's leading position in the worldwide e-commerce arena, the economic slowdown in North America began to take a toll on Sapient's earnings in the first quarter of 2001. As a result, the firm launched several cost-cutting measures, which included laying off 720 employees—roughly 20 percent of its workforce—closing down an office in Sydney, Australia, and consolidating its U.S. operations by merging multiples office in a single city into one main unit.

FURTHER READING:

Mulqueen, John T. "Young Company Flourishes." *Communications Week*, June 17, 1996.

Rosa, Jerry. "Eleven: Jerry Greenberg—The Stalwart." *Computer Reseller News*, November 13, 2000.

———. "The Right Move—Sapient Makes the Leap from Integrator to Web Innovator." *Computer Reseller News*, April 17, 2000.

Whitford, David. "The Two-Headed Manager: Sapient Co-CEOs Jerry Greenberg and Stuart Moore Have (Almost) Nothing in Common. That Helps Explain Why Their Relationship Works." *Fortune*, January 24, 2000.

SEE ALSO: Greenberg, Jerry; Integration; Moore, J. Stuart

SCALABILITY

Most average computer users have worked with word processing software applications that allowed them to select lines or blocks of text and increase or decrease the text's type size. This action is a very basic example of scalability, whereby the size of something can be changed (increased or decreased) according to need. In the case of e-commerce, the term scalability usually corresponds to the hardware, software, and network infrastructures used to keep Web sites and related systems up and running. Having scalable systems and applications is important for companies because it means that valuable resources and investments won't be lost when it is necessary to make changes to them.

From a technological standpoint, scalability can involve very simple actions like adding memory to a PC or server (computers used to host Web sites), increasing the number of nodes on a computer network, or adding new or more sophisticated features to an e-commerce Web site. However, it often involves a company's entire e-commerce architecture, which consists of many different technology elements. During e-commerce, companies rely on databases to store and present information about products (including prices, sizes, colors, and options), customers (including names, addresses, preferences, and credit card numbers), content that appears on dynamic Web pages, and more. Servers are another important piece of the puzzle. Finally, networks of workstation computers for staff, connected by miles of cabling and network hardware components, also play central roles. In an ideal world, it would be possible for a company to add, replace, or take away different pieces from this constellation without negatively impacting the entire system.

Unfortunately, such is not always the case. When companies find themselves in a position to grow, there are often hurdles that must be overcome first. Among these hurdles are old "legacy" systems that are still very important to the company's operations, but which were not designed for e-commerce. Although there are ways to connect legacy systems to e-commerce software, high volumes of transactions can present problems. Rather than establishing individual patches for many legacy systems, one possible solution to a challenge like this would be to replicate essential data from all legacy systems involved in e-commerce and place it into a special database called a data warehouse, which is compatible with the Web and e-commerce. This warehouse could then be scaled more easily, depending on the company's needs.

Two keys to scalability are size and replication. For example, a software application can be divided into different smaller sections or tiers, each corresponding to a different function or area of e-commerce. One tier might be devoted to a program's user interface while another deals exclusively with the data being accessed. *Computerworld* explained that successful e-commerce applications keep these tiers separated and require little interaction between them. This allows each layer to be more easily modified without affecting other system areas. If necessary, more memory or processing power can be devoted to one level of an application, but not to others. Replication also is key. When companies create a component for one area of their e-commerce operation, such as programming instructions that deal with accepting special promotional discounts, a good strategy is to then re-use this code in other applications or areas of the site, rather than re-creating it from scratch every time.

Besides technology, human systems can also be rendered scalable. Because the e-commerce business environment is dynamic and unpredictable, it requires e-companies to respond quickly to factors like volatile stock market conditions, pressure from investors and customers, new technologies, and competitive forces. A workforce that is truly scalable is one where many employees work remotely, instead of in the same physical location. Armed with laptops and telecommunications capabilities, such a workforce is able to grow (or shrink) as needed with less regard for other factors. Unlike companies where everyone works at the same physical location, the size requirements of buildings cease to be an issue in this scenario.

Rather than investing heavily in their own e-commerce systems, many companies opted to outsource different functions in the early 2000s. Application service providers (ASPs) were an attractive option. These third parties provided software applications on their own equipment and then charged customers for using it. As part of the arrangement, they assumed the responsibilities and risks involved. This was a cost-effective option for companies that needed to increase or decrease in size very quickly. In this scenario, the ASP makes the hardware and software investments, and the company is able to pay only for what it uses. One trend was that e-commerce software packages began including many essential e-commerce components, such as application servers, Web servers, and middleware (which allows different systems to communicate with one another). Along with choosing ASPs, more companies also were turning to third parties for Web site hosting. Although this did not decrease the need for scalability, Jupiter Media Metrix found that many executives underestimated scalability's importance. By doing so, they increased their chances of future problems, as well as additional costs.

FURTHER READING:

Desal, Gautam; Eric Sanchez, and Joe Fenner. "App Servers Meet E-commerce." *InformationWeek,* February 26, 2001.

Kurnit, Scott. "Scalability: Are You Fast Enough?" *Chief Executive,* February 2001.

Saliba, Clare. "Report: E-Biz Neglects External Web Hosting Options." *E-Commerce Times,* August 15, 2001. Available from www.ecommercetimes.com.

SEE ALSO: Outsourcing

SCENARIO PLANNING

Throughout most of the 20th century, business moved at a relatively slow pace. By the early 2000s, however, the business climate had changed significantly. The widespread adoption of the Internet and other communication devices allowed information to travel more quickly, and enabled consumers and companies to do business with one another across the globe. Along with the brisker pace came greater complexity. Combinations of many different factors impacted the success or failure of a company or industry in a short period of time. Among these factors were pressure from investors, the demands of customers, the impact of new technologies, domestic and international government regulations, legal issues, the environment, and even the cost of shipping products. In this more complex, uncertain environment, it became increasingly difficult for corporate executives to make important decisions and position their companies for success.

While it is not possible for executives to totally predict what impact factors such as these will have, it is possible for them to develop simulations or scenarios that paint pictures of what future conditions might be like if certain things were to happen. This approach is known as scenario planning. The purpose of scenario planning is to identify several different stories about, or visions of, how large-scale forces will have an impact over time. It is not used to predict specific future events. It is in this regard that scenario planning differs from other kinds of forecasting or trend analyses that companies use to assist them in the decision-making process. Instead of forecasting only one version of how things might evolve or develop, scenario planning involves painting several different pictures and takes into consideration the fact that the future is uncertain and can't be predicted.

Because of its large-scale focus, scenario planning often is used to study issues surrounding entire industries or nations. However, the approach also can be used to focus on smaller issues that are important to specific companies or organizations. Among those who have used scenario planning are the United States Postal Service, Levi Strauss, National City Corp., General Electric, Ericsson Inc., British Airways, IBM, Motorola, AT&T, United Distillers, Royal Dutch/Shell, and numerous retailers.

HOW SCENARIO PLANNING WORKS

Generally speaking, the process of scenario planning begins with leading executives at a company, who first identify a certain issue or focal point. For example, an e-commerce company may try to decide whether to expand the scope of its offerings new arenas. Before doing so, it may want to determine the likely long-term impact of different conditions and variables before significant resources are invested. Based on this central issue or focal point, different social, economic, political, and technological forces are taken into consideration. When considered along with current conditions, some of them may be quite easy to foresee or estimate, while others are more difficult. Those forces that are both uncertain and critical to the central issue or focal point serve as the basis for exploration in each scenario or story, several of which are developed. Each scenario shows a different possible end result based on how the different factors play out.

Darwin magazine provided an excellent real-world example of how one company used scenario planning. In 1996, National City Corp. was faced with several business challenges, including figuring out what role the Internet would play in the banking world, increasing competition for market share, and the need to increase earnings. The bank was about to invest $40 million in a new customer information system. However, there were many unanswered questions about the direction in which the company was headed. Jon Gorney, who was in charge of information systems at National City, needed answers before making such a big investment.

Gorney hired Northeast Consulting Resources Inc. (NCRI) to conduct a three-day scenario planning workshop at the cost of $500,000. His staff interviewed 50 executives from each of the bank's divisions to obtain information, including their visions of the bank's strategic direction and how they used technology. After many interviews, three different visions emerged. One vision (which was consistent with industry trends) saw the bank heading in a direction where many of its different services were tailored to meet the needs of individual customers. A second vision saw the bank focusing on the development of its financial products, instead of its customers. Finally, a third vision saw the bank launching a second online-only bank that would compete with its physical banks.

After these three visions of the future were developed, 150 events (both internal and external) were identified which could impact each vision. During the workshop, these events were ranked by executives from different National City banks, based on how likely each one was to occur. Later, different groups investigated how the different scenarios would be impacted by the events that had been ranked. After a great deal of debate and discussion, the ultimate decision was left to National City's chairman and chief executive officer, who opted for the customer-focused vision. Scenario planning helped the information technology and banking professionals to understand one another. It also helped everyone to share and agree on a common vision, and made Gorney more comfortable about spending $40 million.

THE HISTORY OF SCENARIO PLANNING

Scenario planning was originally developed during the Cold War years as a way of considering what might happen in the event of a nuclear war. The approach caught on in the corporate world in the planning department at Royal Dutch/Shell. There, Pierre Wack and Ed Newland led a department consisting of managers from several different countries and disciplines to develop the new approach, which helped Shell respond to the oil crisis of 1973. Peter Schwartz, chairman and co-founder of the Global Business Network (GBN), was responsible for scenario planning while working at Royal Dutch/Shell from 1982 to 1986. He too was instrumental in the approach's development. Along with Jay Ogilvy, Lawrence Wilkinson, Stewart Brand, and Napier Collyns, Schwartz eventually formed GBN. According to GBN, the organization is "a community of individuals and organizations committed to thinking broadly and collaboratively about the future and to pioneering tools for organizational learning, planning, and innovation." Companies from many different industries pay handsomely to receive scenario-planning consultancy from GBN. Among them are American Express, Lucent Technologies, Nokia, Campbell Soup, Disney, Nissan, Rubbermaid, Procter & Gamble, and Sun Microsystems.

THE FUTURE OF SCENARIO PLANNING

Although scenario planning has been around for many years, and interest in it has fluctuated, the approach holds a great deal of potential in a business world where changing market conditions and consumer preferences can spell disaster for e-tailers and other organizations. In *Serious Play,* Michael Schrage indicated that global business is being transformed by the exploration of new ideas through simulation and modeling, explaining that "Tomorrow's innovators will invest more in playing with prototypes, modeling marketplaces, and simulating scenarios because that will become the best way to create new value and profitably deliver it to customers."

FURTHER READING:

Baldock, Robert. *Destination Z.* West Sussex, England: John Wiley & Sons, Ltd. 1999.

Epstein, H. "Scenario Planning: Managing for the Future." *The Futurist,* August-September 1998.

Levinson, Meredith. "Don't Stop Thinking About Tomorrow." *Darwin,* January 1, 2000. Available from www.darwinmagazine.com.

———. "The Pros and Cons of Scenario Planning." *Darwin,* January 1, 2000. Available from www.darwinmagazine.com.

"A Perfect Day: Peter Schwartz Helps Companies to Think About the Future." *The Economist,* August 22, 1998.

Schrage, Michael. *Serious Play*. Boston: Harvard Business School Press. 2000.

Wilkinson, Lawrence. "How to Build Scenarios." *Wired,* 1998. Available from www.wired.com.

SEE
ALSO: Simulation Software

SCIENT CORP.

Scient Corp. is an Internet services consultant with offices in North America, Europe, and Asia. Like other upstart competitors who survived the dot.com fallout of 2000, it continues to reduce its reliance on newer dot.coms in favor of pursuing accounts with larger, better established clients looking to use e-business tools to improve operations. The firm is also working to change its reputation from one as a World Wide Web site designer and builder, to an integrator of new technology with existing business systems. Extensive layoffs and mounting losses prompted Scient to agree to merge with iXL Enterprises in 2001.

Scient was founded in late 1997 by Eric Greenberg, who had also founded Internet and e-commerce consultancy Viant, which mainly targeted industry leaders like Compaq Computer Corp., in February of 1996. After being ousted by Viant's board in June of 1997, due to Greenberg's deteriorating relationship with Viant CEO Robert Gett, Greenberg decided to use his $1.7 million severance package to establish a competitor to Viant. Benchmark Capital, Sequoia Capital, and Stanford University contributed another $20.5 million in capital for the new venture. Recognizing that experience and name recognition would lend his new business credibility with potential clients, Greenberg recruited seasoned executives for his management team. He lured CEO Robert Howe—known for shaping IBM Global Services into a top information technology (IT) consultancy and overseeing the development of the industry-leading firm's online financial services offerings—away from IBM by offering him an 11.7 percent stake in Scient. Other executives came from Anderson Consulting, EDS Corp., Bank of America, AT&T Corp., and other industry powerhouses. Greenberg balanced his traditional management team with young programmers and designers from the most respected technology and business schools in the U.S.

Heavy marketing of the company's slogan, "It takes courage to be legendary," proved lucrative for the firm when Scient landed several accounts, including dot.com upstarts like furniture e-tailer Living.com, PlanetRx Inc., and ePhysician, within a few months of its inception. The firm also hosted presentations such as "Lead or Get Crushed," to stress to potential customers the importance of being among the first to embrace new e-business technology and to warn business managers that their failure to develop an e-business strategy quickly might jeopardize their jobs. According to Scient chief marketing officer Christopher Lochhead, as quoted in a June 1999 *Computer Reseller News* article, "If it's worth doing, it's worth doing wrong fast." Although some industry analysts criticized Scient for using fear tactics to solicit business, speed was seen by many technology experts at the time, even those without a vested interest in selling e-business products and services, as the key to e-business success.

In 1999, Wineshopper.com hired Scient to create the wholesale wine database it needed for its online wine venture. In addition to securing business from fledgling Internet ventures like Wineshopper, the firm also helped to launch sites such as Chase Online for Chase Manhattan Corp. Domestic and international expansion efforts began in earnest with the creation of offices in Chicago, Texas, Singapore, and London. In May, Howe took the firm public at $10 a share, and by the year's end, shares were trading at ten times that amount, despite the fact that Scient had posted a $12 million loss on sales of $21 million. With Scient's market capitalization at a whopping 20 times anticipated yearly sales, Greenberg became a billionaire. In roughly two years, his firm had completely constructed a total of 15 e-businesses and had offered e-business integration services to another 85 companies.

In December of 1999, Texas Pacific Group hired Scient to create Hotwire, a Web site sponsored by six major airlines who wanted to compete with Priceline.com in offering inexpensive airline tickets to travelers. The site, hotwire.com, was launched in September of 2000. While 20 of Scient's consultant were working on the project, the Internet consultancy industry dramatically shifted gears in the wake of the dot.com meltdown. When dot.com startups began disappearing in the spring of 2000, larger companies no longer faced looming competition from these smaller, more technologically savvy firms. As a result, issues such as quality and added value replaced speed to market as the primary focus. According to a February 2001 issue of *Fast Company*, "Hotwire wanted to get to market quickly, because every week that lingered, after all, was one more week for priceline.com to win new customers. But speed wasn't the only priority, or even the most important one." It was more important that Scient ensure the site worked impeccably since it would likely attract high traffic volumes and media attention from the start.

The early months of 2000 proved to be the golden age for Scient. Sales grew more than sevenfold to $156 million, and employees totaled 1,180. The firm achieved profitability, and stock prices peaked at $133 per share. By May, however, as dot.coms found it increasingly difficult to secure funding, Scient and other Internet consultancies started to feel the effects of the technology industry's downturn. In August, competitors like iXL, Viant, and Marchfirst Inc. announced layoffs. Scient watched its stock prices plunge to roughly $10 per share. Many of the Web sites Scient had helped to build—Living.com, environmental news hub Verde Media, and jewelry e-tailer Miadora.com—shuttered operations. Realizing that the portion of its revenues that had come from dot.com startups—nearly 50 percent—had disappeared, Scient announced in December that its quarterly sales would fall by nearly 30 percent.

In 2001, the office in Austin, Texas, was closed, and headquarters moved from San Francisco to New York. Scient laid off 675 employees, nearly half of its workforce. According to a July 2001 article in *The Financial Times*, ''the small-scale Internet consultancies, which shot to prominence by building Web sites during the dot.com bubble, are fighting for survival in the wake of the technology slowdown and resurgence of larger, more established consultancies, who have made up for lost time in the e-business market.'' Recognizing that it needed to strengthen its ability to secure larger accounts, particularly when faced with increased competition from formidable competitors, Scient agreed to merge with rival iXL Enterprises Inc. in July. Howe will take over as chairman of the newly merged company, while iXL head Chris Formant will serve as CEO. Scient and iXL expect to finalize the deal in early 2002.

FURTHER READING:

Clancy, Heather. ''Web Innovators—Scient: Web Players Need to Be Risk Takers.'' *Computer Reseller News,* June 21, 1999.

Greenmeier, Larry. ''Scient and IXL Bet on Success with Merger.'' *InformationWeek,* August 6, 2001.

Hersch, Warren S. ''Robert Howe: Scient—He Has Set Out to Prove There Is a Huge Opportunity in E-Commerce.'' *Computer Reseller News,* November 9, 1998.

Jastrow, David. ''Moving at Web Speed—E-business Integrator Scient: It Is Better to Rush to the Net Than Wait.'' *Computer Reseller News,* September 20, 1999.

King, Ralph. ''The Talented Mr. Greenberg.'' *Business 2.0,* May 2001. Available from www.ecompany.com.

Mearian, Lucas. ''IBM Throws Egghead.com a $20M Lifeline.'' *Computer World,* March 12, 2001.

SEE ALSO: E-commerce Consultants; E-commerce Solutions

SEARCH ENGINE STRATEGY

Most people find what they're looking for on the World Wide Web by using search engines like Yahoo!, Alta Vista, or Google. According to *InformationWeek,* aside from checking e-mail, searching for information with search engines was the second most popular Internet activity in the early 2000s. Because of this, companies develop and implement strategies to make sure people are able to consistently find their sites during a search. These strategies oftentimes are included in a much broader Web site or Internet marketing plan. Different companies have different objectives, but the main goal is to obtain good placement in search results.

TYPES OF SEARCH ENGINES

In the early 2000s, more than 1,000 different search engines were in existence, although most Web masters focused their efforts on getting good placement in the leading 10. This, however, was easier said than done. *InfoWorld* explained that the process was more art than science, requiring continuous adjustments and tweaking, along with regularly submitting pages to different engines for good or excellent results. The reason for this is that every search engine works differently. Not only are there different types of search engines—those that use spiders to obtain results, directory-based engines, and link-based engines—but engines within each category are unique. They each have different rules and procedures companies need to follow in order to register their site with the engine.

SPIDER-BASED SEARCH ENGINES. Many leading search engines use a form of software program called spiders or crawlers to find information on the Internet and store it for search results in giant databases or indexes. Some spiders record every word on a Web site for their respective indexes, while others only report certain keywords listed in title tags or meta tags.

Although they usually aren't visible to someone using a Web browser, meta tags are special codes that provide keywords or Web site descriptions to spiders. Keywords and how they are placed, either within actual Web site content or in meta tags, are very important to online marketers. The majority of consumers reach e-commerce sites through search engines, and the right keywords increase the odds a company's site will be included in search results.

Companies need to choose the keywords that describe their sites to spider-based search engines carefully, and continually monitor their effectiveness.

Search engines often change their criteria for listing different sites, and keywords that cause a site to be listed first in a search one day may not work at all the next. Companies often monitor search engine results to see what keywords cause top listings in categories that are important to them.

In addition to carefully choosing keywords, companies also monitor keyword density, or the number of times a keyword is used on a particular page. Keyword spamming, in which keywords are overused in an attempt to guarantee top placement, can be dangerous. Some search engines will not list pages that overuse keywords. *Marketing News* explained that a keyword density of three to seven percent was normally acceptable to search engines in the early 2000s. Corporate Web masters often try to figure out the techniques used by different search engines to elude spammers, creating a never-ending game of cat-and-mouse.

Sometimes, information listed in meta tags is incorrect or misleading, which causes spiders to deliver inaccurate descriptions of Web sites to indexes. Companies have been known to deliberately misuse keywords in a tactic called cyber-stuffing. In this approach, a company includes trademarks or brand names from its competitors within the keywords used to describe its site to search engines. This is a sneaky way for one company to direct traffic away from a competitor's site and to its own. In the early 2000s, this was a hot legal topic involving the infringement of trademark laws.

Because spiders are unable to index pictures or read text that is contained within graphics, relying too heavily on such elements was a consideration for online marketers. Home pages containing only a large graphic risked being passed by. An emerging content description language called extensible markup language (XML), similar in some respects to hypertext markup language (HTML), was emerging in the early 2000s. An XML standard known as synchronized multimedia integration language will allow spiders to recognize multimedia elements on Web sites, like pictures and streaming video.

DIRECTORY-BASED SEARCH ENGINES. While some sites use spiders to provide results to searchers, others—like Yahoo!—use human editors. This means that a company cannot rely on technology and keywords to obtain excellent placement, but must provide content the editors will find appealing and valuable to searchers. Some directory-based engines charge a fee for a site to be reviewed for potential listing. In the early 2000s, more leading search engines were relying on human editors in combination with findings obtained with spiders. LookSmart, Lycos, AltaVista, MSN, Excite and AOL Search relied on providers of directory data to make their search results more meaningful.

LINK-BASED SEARCH ENGINES. One other kind of search engine provides results based on hypertext links between sites. Rather than basing results on keywords or the preferences of human editors, sites are ranked based on the quality and quantity of other Web sites linked to them. In this case, links serve as referrals. The emergence of this kind of search engine called for companies to develop link-building strategies. By finding out which sites are listed in results for a certain product category in a link-based engine, a company could then contact the sites' owners—assuming they aren't competitors—and ask them for a link. This often involves reciprocal linking, where each company agrees to include links to the other's site.

Besides focusing on keywords, providing compelling content and monitoring links, online marketers rely on other ways of getting noticed. In late 2000, some used special software programs or third-party search engine specialists to maximize results for them. Search engine specialists handle the tedious, never ending tasks of staying current with the requirements of different search engines and tracking a company's placement. This trend was expected to take off in the early 2000s, according to research from IDC and Netbooster, which found that 70 percent of site owners had plans to use a specialist by 2002. Additionally, some companies pay for special or enhanced listings in different search engines.

FURTHER READING:

Briones, Maricris. "Found On the Information Superhighway." *Marketing News,* June 21, 1999.

Coopee, Todd. "Simple Service Brings Surfers to Your Site." *InfoWorld,* August 14, 2000.

Greenberg, Karl. "Spiders Weave a Tangled Web." *Brandweek,* September 11, 2000.

Kahaner, Larry. "Content Matters Most in Search Engine Placement." *InformationWeek,* June 12, 2000.

McLuhan, Robert. "Search for a Top Ranking." *Marketing 47,* October 19, 2000.

Retsky, Maxine. "Cyberstuffing—A Dangerous Strategy." *Marketing News,* January 3, 2000.

Schwartz, Matthew. "Search Engines." *Computerworld,* May 8, 2000.

Sherman, Chris. "Search Engine Strategies 2000." *Information Today,* October 2000.

SEE ALSO: Results Ranking

SECURE ELECTRONIC TRANSACTION (SET)

A protocol designed to ensure the security and integrity of online communications and purchases, Secure Electronic Transaction (SET) uses digital certificates, issued to merchants and other businesses and customers, to perform a series of security checks verifying that the identity of a customer or sender of information is valid. SET provides the basic framework within which many of the various components of securing digital transactions function. Digital certificates, digital signatures, and digital wallets all function according to the SET protocol.

There are several components for the SET protocol.

- The Cardholder Application, also referred to as a digital wallet, is held by an online consumer and packages a digital signature and credit card information that ensures his or her identity and safeguards his or her financial information through a complex encryption system.

- The Merchant Server component is the verification product held by the merchant to process the online card payment.

- The Payment Gateway component is held by an acquiring bank or other trusted third party that accepts and processes the merchant's verification and the customer's payment information and filters them to their appropriate financial institutions.

- The Certificate Authority component, usually run by a financial institution, is the trusted agent that issues the digital certificates and is responsible for ensuring that all users of digital certificates are in fact secure and trustworthy customers.

Once a security product for any of these components has passed the SET Compliance Testing, it bears the SET Mark, ensuring all users that it meets the SET standards.

SET is an open standard available to anyone engaged in electronic commerce. MasterCard International and Visa International, recognizing that security was the key to the widespread use of credit cards for e-commerce, developed the SET protocol, which was launched on February 1, 1996. The first version of the SET Specification was published in May 1997. In December of that year, the credit-card giants and other major players in the e-commerce world, including Microsoft, Netscape, and IBM, set up a company called SET Secure Electronic Transaction LLC (SETCo) to maintain and implement the SET specification, administer compliance testing, and foster the increased global adoption of the SET standard.

Following the great fanfare that accompanied its launch, the adoption of the SET protocol proved greatly disappointing, and the standard was passed over by rival protocols such as the Secure Sockets Layer (SSL) encryption scheme. The primary obstacle to SET's widespread adoption in the United States and Europe in the late 1990s was the lack of feeling, among bankers and merchants, that fraud and security breaches posed so substantial a threat as to make the turn toward SET worthwhile. SET's procedures were viewed as too cumbersome to implement relative to comparative security protocols, and even though SET was ultimately the strongest technology for securing online payments, businesses tended toward the less sophisticated models as a means of establishing for themselves an online presence. As Barbara Smiley, research director at Newton, Massachusetts-based Meridien Research Inc., told *Computer World* in 1999, "for most people, SET is a nuclear warhead for a problem that may only need a cruise missile." SET was widely seen as too inflexible for what merchants widely saw as only a mild threat of online-payments fraud.

By the 2000s, however, reports of credit-card fraud and abuse rekindled interest in the SET protocol, and companies and card suppliers began integrating SET into their transactions systems. One factor helping the resurgence of the SET standard in the early 2000s was the switch from client-side digital wallets to server-side wallets, allowing for far greater flexibility in their use and for data storage. And as more and more consumers opt to use debit cards, rather than credit cards, for their online purchases, the demand for tighter security will only escalate. In credit-card transactions, the payment is actually drawn from a line of credit provided by the card issuer, while, for debit-card payments, it is the consumer's own money that is directly involved. Therefore, nervous customers will require the strongest possible security protocol for their online payments.

FURTHER READING:

"SET Secure Electronic Transaction LLC." Purchase, NY: SET Secure Electronic Transaction LLC, 2001. Available from www.setco.org.

Larsen, Amy K. "It Pays to Be Secure." *Information Week,* May 31, 1999.

Marlin, Steve, "SET Making Slow Progress in Banking Arena." *Bank Systems & Technology,* August, 1999.

Morgan, Cynthia. "Dead Set Against SET?" *Computer World,* March 29, 1999.

Murphy, Patricia A. "Fighting Internet Card Fraud." *Credit Card Management,* July, 2000.

Rolfe, Richard. ''Debit Cards on the Internet.'' *Credit Card Management,* November, 1999.

Visa International. ''Visa—Electronic Commerce: SET.'' Foster City, CA: Visa International, 2000. Available from www.visa.com.

SEE   Acquiring Bank; Certificate Authority; Cryptography;
ALSO: Digital Certificate; Digital Signature; Digital Wallet;
        Electronic Payment; Encryption; Transaction Issues

SEPTEMBER 11, 2001 TERRORIST ATTACKS: IMPACT ON E-COMMERCE

In the wake of the September 11, 2001 terrorist attacks on the World Trade Center in New York and the Pentagon in Washington, D.C., it was common for social and political commentators to proclaim that ''everything has changed.'' While the geopolitical and domestic landscape transformed in accordance with this pronouncement, the business world weighed up the implications of this changed environment for the future of e-commerce. Situating the terrorist attacks in the midst of a global economy heading into recession and an Internet economy still dusting itself off from the dot.com shakeout of 2000, analysts saw several different short-term and long-term scenarios for e-commerce. The very novelty of the situation—an attack on U.S. soil, the subsequent anthrax attacks and the fear and uncertainty they created— contributed to the problem facing analysts in trying to sketch out a clear forecast for the impact of the attacks. Since these kinds of horrors had never before visited the American public, it was difficult to gauge exactly how people would react.

IMMEDIATE EFFECTS

The immediate impact of the terrorist attacks on e-commerce was profound, if only for the technical ramifications. Due to the veritable phone-line blockout in New York, along with the sharply increased phone and Internet usage throughout the country in the hours after the attacks, Web and Internet traffic worked slowly for a while, causing slow download times and thus curtailed sales opportunities.

According to the comparison-shopping site BizRate.com, online retailing sales fell to 85 percent of their normal volume in the immediate aftermath of the attacks, and analysts and companies alike lowered their estimates for overall annual growth for 2001. Online retail sales the day before the attacks totaled $92.4 million; by September 17, sales were down to $82.5 million—a respectable total, considering the gravity of the situation and the broader fears about re-

cession that the attacks helped fuel. The biggest culprit, according to most analysts, wasn't e-commerce in particular, but simply damaged consumer confidence in general. The attacks certainly had a dramatic impact on an economy already in a precarious situation, seriously damaging the airline, tourism, and insurance industries and carrying consequences throughout the economy.

Online revenue for the month of September fell 15 percent from the month before, although that was largely due to the downfall of the largest e-commerce sector: the travel industry. On the other hand, Nielsen/NetRatings and Harris Interactive reported that online retail sales in September 2001 totaled $4.7 billion, compared with $3.1 billion the previous September. BizRate.com figures indicated that, overall, consumers hadn't lost their taste for e-commerce, and online shopping performed relatively well over the 2001 holiday season, particularly in light of continuingly poor economic news. With heightened tensions throughout society and bolstered security at travel locations—particularly at airports—consumers were far less likely to feel comfortable hauling around large packages, and thus relied more heavily on home shopping via the Internet and delivery straight to the house. Broader fears of large, public places, such as central shopping districts in major cities and elsewhere, were also expected to have a positive net effect of e-commerce. With consumers more hesitant to leave the security of their homes, and with shopping resources still at their disposal via the Internet, many business analysts expected e-commerce to undergo a resurgence.

TRANSFORMING E-COMMERCE

Many analysts looked to the Internet as a source of hope in a difficult economic and social climate. As companies tried to cut costs to maintain profit margins, those firms that had invested heavily in successful e-commerce infrastructures were in a particularly good position, since the Internet afforded companies the ability to trim inventory and other costs while generating new revenue streams.

According to *Business Week,* the attacks bolstered the new, post-shakeout mood of Internet commerce and initiatives. Plans for e-commerce operations were more than ever calculated specifically with a profit-based focus, rather than simply to build a brand online. E-commerce schemes were evaluated and pursued in accordance with their ability to generate short-term cost savings and profits. AMR Research Inc. predicted that, in the year following the attacks, investment in e-commerce initiatives would rise 9 percent, below the pace of the previous few years but still relatively healthy, particularly in light of the receding economy. That projection was below the 11 percent that was forecast shortly before September 11. AMR reported that the most common initiatives being funded included supply-chain management projects, customer-service schemes, and Internet-based product-development programs.

On the other hand, one of the Internet's key advantages in the world of commerce proved a handicap in the immediate wake of September 11. A central feature of e-commerce is that it diminishes the importance of geography, so that physical distance and international borders are rendered less prohibitive in the shopping and trading processes. However, following the terrorist attacks, borders were fortified and tightened, severely slowing international trade and rendering it more costly. The dramatically heightened fears over international terrorism following September 11 were expected to have a lasting impact on security measures at borders, so that e-commerce that trades in physical products (rather than digital products) requiring international shipping will be hampered both by slower delivery times and higher delivery costs. In turn, though, this trend played into the hands of larger firms with their own production and storage facilities abroad, diminishing the need for international shipping.

As the economy reeled and the e-commerce world was shaken up, the time seemed right to many investors and analysts for e-commerce firms to take the time to re-evaluate their e-business practices in the hope of finding a winning strategy into which companies could put more of their faith. As a result, firms were expected to closely examine their existing Web business practices and take the time to implement quality systems as the climate straightened itself out. Companies seemed more willing to accept changes to their fundamental business practices, particularly in the realm of e-commerce.

E-COMMERCE VS. SECURITY?

The heightened concern for security also threatened to renew the recently cooled battle between commercial interests and governments over computer encryption. Encryption is among the primary means by which companies are able to utilize an open network like the Internet to conduct secure and private transactions. In the late 1990s, the U.S. government finally bowed to pressure from businesses demanding the free dissemination of strong encryption schemes designed to fortify electronic transmissions from hackers or other cybercriminals, thereby protecting consumers and business information. Governments had long resisted the proliferation of strong encryption, fearing that it would compromise the efforts of intelligence agencies to conduct investigations into crime and international espionage and terrorism. In

the wake of September 11, governments began making moves to put greater checks on encryption schemes, fearing that international terrorist networks could use state-of-the-art encryption to transmit plans across electronic networks. As governments assumed greater powers for monitoring electronic communications, encryption was likely to find its way back into contested territory. Business analysts feared that the mandated use of weakened encryption schemes could have severe consequences for e-commerce, given that consumer and business fears over the security of their transactions was perhaps the primary impediment to the growth of e-commerce in the 1990s and early 2000s.

One prominent call was for all encryption schemes to come with a backdoor through which authorized government agencies could pass. U.S. Senator Judd Gregg of New Hampshire proposed such legislation, insisting that encryption software makers ''should understand that as a matter of citizenship, they have an obligation'' to allow government the means to crack into any encryption code deemed necessary by a court order. This means that vendors must build all codes in a way that allows government to break through them. However, these key-escrow systems, as they're called, generated controversy, since the keys given to governments to unlock the encryption codes, while kept securely hidden, could potentially be compromised, leading to a security nightmare. Alternatively, civil liberties groups worried that governments with such keys could potentially abuse their powers.

FURTHER READING:

Gibbs, Mark. ''The New Battleground.'' *Network World,* October 29, 2001.

Godwin, Mike. ''Just Say No—Will Strong Encryption Be a Casualty of War?'' *The American Lawyer,* November 2001.

Heun, Christopher T. ''Online Shopping Returns to Normal—Almost.'' *InformationWeek,* October 1, 2001.

Mangi, Naween A. ''The After Math.'' *Business Week,* November 5, 2001.

Rocks, David, Andrew Park, Aixa M. Pascual, Darnell Little, and Jeanette Brown. ''The Net As a Lifeline.'' *Business Week,* October 29, 2001.

Stoughton, Stephanie.''Dot-Bomb or Dot-Boon?'' *The Boston Globe,* October 22, 2001.

Tedechi, Bob. ''In Aftermath of Sept. 11 Attacks, Direct Mailers Try to Adjust and Online Mailers Try to Take Advantage.'' *The New York Times,* October 29, 2001.

Yasin, Rutrell. ''Encryption Debate Revived—Proposed Bans Could Thwart E-commerce, Though Major Shifts Unlikely.'' *InternetWeek,* October 1, 2001.

SEE ALSO: Computer Crime; Cryptography, Public- and Private-Key; Encryption; Computer Security; Privacy; Viruses

SERVICE LEVEL AGREEMENT (SLA)

Service Level Agreements (SLAs) are written contracts between a service provider and its client guaranteeing a certain minimal level of service. For instance, Internet service providers (ISPs) may devise SLAs guaranteeing continuous, high-quality Internet access to their subscribers, while applications service providers (ASPs) may offer SLAs to secure the efficient operation of high-tech business applications to corporations. SLAs set the parameters for technical support, access levels, business services, recovery protocols, and other standards of service. Usually, this quality of service is secured with the threat of substantial financial penalties levied against the carrier for allowing service to lapse below that minimal level by, say, failing to quickly address and remedy service outages.

The technical requirements of conducting business in the Information Age are such that many corporations chose to outsource portions of their information systems to the management and care of application service providers (ASPs). However, there was obviously a great deal of risk involved in such movements; for instance, by contracting with an ASP, companies give up day-to-day control of their own systems, thus losing control over whether those systems will be run correctly or in accordance with their best interests. Communication between companies, moreover, is more complicated than communication within companies, and thus problems that arise with systems and applications maintained by an ASP risk not being addressed in the time or fashion the company might prefer. In such cases, SLAs are a method of alleviating fears, providing a mechanism of assuring businesses that their strategic and technical objectives will be met.

In the early 2000s, SLAs were characterized by their increasing toughness. The ability to point to a stringent SLA agreement was a selling point in itself for network providers as consumers were less willing to stomach even short-term lapses in service. As a result, many SLAs levied heavy penalties for even brief service outages, forcing providers to beef up their systems and to prioritize their chain of responses to system problems. SLA penalty clauses serve a dual function. On the one hand, they provide an incentive to the provider to make sure that certain standards of service are maintained via the threat of financial vulnerability. On the other hand, in the event that the provider fails to meet its requirements, they ensure compensation so as to mitigate the losses incurred by the client.

Carriers were thus turning SLAs into more than simple prerequisites to attracting customers, but into valuable marketing tools. With a strong SLA to sell itself, a carrier is able to charge higher fees for its guaranteed service levels. Moreover, carriers can use the SLA as a springboard for differentiating themselves from competitors by offering different levels of performance for different services, at varying costs, thereby expanding the customers' options. SLAs thus provide a combination of carrot and stick incentive for carriers to institute the best possible service.

ISPs spent the early 2000s trying to trump each other's SLAs by rolling out newer, tougher service guarantees. For instance, in winter 2001 Cable & Wireless rolled out a new SLA promising its subscribers no more than 55 milliseconds of round-trip latency, topping AT&T's earlier guarantee of no more that 60 milliseconds of latency. For the average user, such differences aren't likely to amount to much, but for businesses tiny increments such as these are often worth investigating against their costs. ISPs usually bind themselves to their SLAs by offering one-day service credits when the conditions of the SLA aren't met. Other conditions included in SLAs often include financial penalties for each minute that service is curtailed.

Some analysts claim, however, that SLAs aren't quite the panacea that they seem to be, since enterprises that contract with carriers usually have little recourse in the event the carrier reneges on its service guarantees. As a result, such arguments run, SLAs are more likely to act as a general expectation of service quality than as an iron-clad promise. Moreover, the guarantees embedded in SLAs aren't particularly objective; each carrier devises its own measurement criteria, so that outside of obvious violations such as prolonged outages, the degree to which the carrier lives up to its SLA requirements is generally quantified by the carrier itself. To remedy this problem, SLA-verification tools were rolled out in the early 2000s and were turning into a healthy industry in their own right. Such tools usually came in the form of software designed to measure certain elements common to SLAs.

Another complication of SLAs is that a single operator often doesn't control the entire service delivery path. In such cases, the lack of enforcement assurance for SLAs could render them functionally inoperative. For instance, a company may contract with an outside host for it's e-commerce Web site, and that host may institute a comprehensive SLA of its own guaranteeing a certain level of service. But if, as is often the case, the company accesses that site by way of another provider, the SLA with the Web host is rendered virtually meaningless. What was emerging in the early 2000s, then, was a business environment characterized by layers of SLA agreements.

The negotiations between providers and clients during the course of drawing up an SLA draws attention to those issues that are covered and opens a dialogue about just what is expected, thereby improving the chances that those service levels will be addressed. The provider, in this way, comes to understand which services are of the highest priority to the client. Finally, a provider is more likely to pay close attention to areas of service that are likely to be measured to ensure that the SLA requirements are met.

Ultimately, however, SLAs are a natural outgrowth of an industry environment that, while increasingly necessary, is extremely unstable and provokes a great deal of uncertainty and hesitation in the business world. Thus, the future of SLAs in the early 2000s was uncertain. While they were becoming increasingly common, the basic reasons for SLAs were a condition of the immaturity of the telecommunications firms, ISPs, and ASPs in handling their services for subscribers and enterprise clients. As the sophistication and reliability of these services develop, the uncertainty underlying the SLA contract will likely disappear. The survival of SLAs, according to analysts, was most likely to be found in their ability to evolve into a value-added vehicle for communicating with clients and differentiating providers from their competitors.

FURTHER READING:

Boyd, Jade. ''Carrier Beefs Up SLAs.'' *InternetWeek,* February 19, 2001.

Lee, John. ''Service Guarantee.'' *Wireless Review,* March 15, 2001.

Liebmann, Lenny. ''Service Level Agreements Expect Uptime.'' *InternetWeek,* September 25, 2000.

Mears, Jennifer. ''SLA Picture Clearing Up for ASP Users.'' *Network World,* January 15, 2001.

Shand, Dawne. ''Service-Level Agreements.'' *Computerworld,* January 22, 2001.

Sturm, Rick. ''The Truth About Service-Level Management.'' *Insurance & Technology,* July 2000.

Turek, Norbert. ''A Safety Net for Your Web Site.'' *InformationWeek,* October 16, 2000.

SEE ALSO: Application Service Provider (ASP); Outsourcing

SHAKE-OUT, DOT-COM

For several years in the late 1990s, e-commerce companies, which quickly came to be known as ''dot-coms,'' could hardly avoid having money thrown at them by investors looking to cash in on what was widely touted as the financial windfall of the New Economy. Vigorous investment sent the stock valuations of dot-coms sky high, far outpacing what would be expected of firms based on their fundamentals. But the ever-climbing stock markets seemed to confirm to many investors that the Internet era had pushed the economy into a new phase where traditional business logic and investment patterns were obsolete. Dot-coms were widely seen as being among the hallmarks of this new era in business, and many players rushed onto the scene in an exuberant bid to grab a piece of the lucrative action.

Sober-minded analysts, however, recognized that the good times couldn't last, and that the market was due for a correction. A number of factors led to the collapse. In addition to the much-discussed precarious structure of the pure-play, dot-com business model of the late 1990s, market analysts insisted that the high-flying tech market was significantly overheated and due for a fall. With competitive pressures growing out of proportion with any market demand and extremely weak financials, skittish investors began fleeing the dot-com crowd as quickly as they had joined them, and the stage for the e-commerce shakeout was set. That correction finally came in 2000; in March the technology markets plummeted, and for the rest of the year, once proud and seemingly invincible dot-coms struggled to survive. Hundreds of firms closed their virtual doors in 2000, taking tens of thousands of jobs with them. One leading dot-com benchmark, the Goldman Sachs Internet Index, finished 2000 about 67 percent below its level at the start of the year. Merrill Lynch estimated in late 2000 that three out of every four public dot-coms would shut down within five years.

THE BUILDUP

An inherent difficulty—though it certainly wasn't always perceived as such—for dot-coms was that most relied overwhelmingly, if not exclusively, on investor dollars to stay afloat. That is, they often had little viable means of self-sustaining income and were thus dependent on the whims of the stock market and the attractiveness of their ideas in the venture capital markets. According to some analysts, this exacerbated the shakeout when it finally came, due to herd-like investment behavior.

On the financing side of the equation, in addition to the stock markets, dot-coms had been overwhelmingly propped up with copious amounts of venture capital. The mid- and late 1990s saw venture capital spending skyrocket largely so as to take advantage of the new crop of promising technology and Internet-based firms. With the economy strong and plenty of cash to go around, venture capitalists were quick to throw money at many different dot-coms at a time, the logic holding that one big success would easily pay for all the failures. As a result, scores of dot-coms hit the market with little preparation but plenty of seed money. Since simply announcing oneself as a new dot-com was often enough to secure significant financial backing, the Internet was bursting at the seams with e-commerce firms, many of which didn't even have a viable product, much less a plan for long-term profitability.

Since capital flowed so freely to e-commerce players in the late 1990s, they were able to engage in extremely unorthodox pricing practices, undercutting competitors by wide margins in order to draw in customers but without actually making money on their sales, and frequently even selling their products below cost. As long as investors remained confident in the possibilities of e-commerce, companies could get away with this. Investors who continued to put money behind companies engaged in this strategy were convinced that, given the uniqueness of e-commerce, the financial shortcomings of such plans would pay off in the long run by the hegemony of the e-commerce model. When that failed to materialize, investors rushed out of the market.

In addition, the strategy followed by many dot-coms called for rapid growth at all costs in order to stake a claim on the market; they felt they needed to grab the market's attention first, and then institute a viable market plan. As a result, companies spent vast sums of money on television advertising and other means of getting their names in the public spotlight. The shakeout stopped this trend in its tracks, as companies had to overhaul their strategies completely and show investors they actually knew how to make money. The bulk of dot-coms, however, were unable to accomplish this to investors' satisfaction, and soon perished.

For workers, dot-coms offered a work environment markedly different from that in most traditional corporate offices. Casual, flexible, and on the cutting edge of business practices at the time, dot-coms lured many skilled information-technology workers looking to circumvent the standard corporate profile. And, of course, workers were drawn to the stock options, one of the main vehicles by which dot-coms attracted workers. In the midst of the booming stock markets, largely fueled by e-commerce companies, stock options often displaced salary and benefits packages as the chief priorities for prospective workers. When the stock market ultimately proved still beholden to the traditional business cycle in the early 2000s, stock options were no longer seen as the optimal path to employee wealth, and IT workers again placed their priorities on more tangible and predictable means of compensation.

Without their own inventories, warehouses, or distribution centers, dot-coms ran into a great deal of trouble with regard to fulfillment and delivery, about which they received no shortage of complaints. One major firm that did manage to survive the shakeout was Amazon.com, which spent a great deal on its own warehouses in the late 1990s and earned high marks for customer service, generating tremendous repeat business. As a result, the company demonstrated it could make money and remained attractive to investors. A 2000 study by Jupiter Communications found that only 41 percent of individuals who made a purchase online were satisfied with the service they received from dot-coms.

Meanwhile, as more traditional bricks-and-mortar companies began catching up to the dot-coms in establishing their own online storefronts and other Internet operations, their more stable capital flows and economies of scale forced the comparative attractiveness of e-commerce start-ups to diminish rapidly. The shakeout was postponed slightly simply because traditional retailers were reluctant to delve too deeply into e-commerce without a clear strategy for integrating it into their existing operations. In other words, bricks-and-mortar firms were wary of cannibalizing their own operations. Once those companies began to wake up from the shock inflicted by their dot-com rivals and develop their own brick-and-click strategies, it was only a matter of time before their greater leverage and long-term growth strategies starved out their online competition. When the brick-and-click sites became operational, there was a strong tendency for consumers to maintain their loyalty to conventional brands online.

Other warning signs were certainly in place. In 1999 Jupiter Communications reported that only 6 percent of all e-commerce sales represented new business, meaning that most of the online shopping was performed at the expense of catalogs and retail stores. In other words, e-commerce didn't represent so much a boon for new business as a medium for increased channel conflict. As the tension between this factor and the unsound e-commerce business plans increased, the cracks in the e-commerce facade began to show. By the end of that year, e-commerce players were pouring money into fancy advertisement schemes designed to push themselves ahead of the competition over the crucial holiday season, sensing that their fields weren't strong enough to support four or more companies striving for the same few dollars.

THE SHAKEOUT COMMENCES

As the 1990s drew to a close, it was increasingly clear to analysts that the e-commerce world was becoming dangerously overcrowded, with sectors struggling to support more players than the market could reasonably maintain. The beauty products, consumer electronics, pets, and other consumer-goods sectors all featured upwards of 10 companies—all of them with large piles of capital backing—competing for what were actually exceptionally small and unproven markets. Other sectors, including those trafficking in Web content, enjoyed fantastic initial public offerings only to go belly up as market realities caught up.

For example, in 1999, there were over a dozen variations on the pets e-commerce theme, and while some enjoyed the support of major pet-supply chains like PETsMART and Petco Animal, few of them could boast anything close to a sound business strategy. For instance, *Business Week* reported in March 2000, just as the shakeout was beginning, that market leader Pets.com was collecting only about 43 cents in consumer sales for every dollar it spent on supplies, and that was before other major expenditures such as advertising and distribution. The online operation at PETsMART, meanwhile, collected only 62 cents for each dollar spent on supplies. This scene was repeated in dozens of market sectors, leaving it to investors and consumers to separate the wheat from the chaff. For most market sectors, those e-commerce players that weren't ranked first or second were extremely hard-pressed to stay afloat, and as brick-and-mortar firms caught up with dot-coms in e-commerce strategy, that factor grew more pronounced.

One clear sign that consolidation was in the cards for the dot-com industry was the surprise announcement in January 2000 that America Online, the largest property on the Internet, would merge with the media giant Time Warner. This, perhaps more than any major business realignment, signaled that the exclusively Internet-based business wasn't destined to displace the traditional bricks-and-mortar firm; rather, the future of e-commerce was likely to witness a blurring line between the two. When, a few months later, the bottom began to fall out of the Internet economy and the well of venture capital suddenly ran dry, e-commerce players scrambled to make themselves attractive to potential suitors. The survival method thus shifted from the reliance on stratospheric market capitalization to absorption into a deep-pocketed traditional business. Suddenly, dot-coms found that profitability was for the first time a major factor in the evaluation of their firms.

Other companies, convinced that the B2C (business-to-consumer) model was a dead end, quickly transformed themselves to take advantage of the B2B (business-to-business) market. However, while the shakeout in the latter sector wasn't as pronounced or as dramatic as that in the B2C field, B2B soon found that it, too, fell prey to the backlash against e-commerce. Particularly in the realm of business-to-business exchanges, it was simply a matter of too many businesses and too little differentiation, leading inevitably toward consolidation. As a result, B2B exchanges en masse either scrambled for particular niches or sought out a buyer. According to *Computerworld,* more than half of the 900 B2B e-marketplaces in existence in mid-2000 were defunct by the end of that year.

MATURITY AND OTHER SURVIVAL STRATEGIES

The e-commerce explosion was largely predicated on the notion that, somehow, e-commerce companies, particularly pure-plays, were a qualitatively new kind of business, and thus needn't follow any of the traditional business strategies or market logic. Alongside this ethos, according to critics, came a heavy dose of arrogance. Perhaps typifying this characteristic was the online retailer Buy.com, one of the brashest of the pure-plays and the second-largest e-commerce retailer after Amazon.com. Led by its flamboyant chief Scott Blum, Buy.com eschewed nearly every type of traditional business sense and styled itself as a daring alternative.

The company built its business by selling computers, books, electronics, and other goods well below cost, undercutting competitors' prices. However, this strategy clearly wasn't designed with an eye toward profits, and the company held out hope that it could generate money via advertising. Moreover, Buy.com chose to cut costs by maintaining no inventory, rather choosing to outsource its entire order-fulfillment operation to logistics companies. This model couldn't be farther from traditional business sense, but the New Economy hype carried enough weight on Wall Street to lift Buy.com's stock sky high with the help of heavyweight bankers such as Japan's Softbank.

The strategy seemed to work for a while, as the company amassed $125 million in sales in its first year, making it one of the fastest-growing companies ever. The company spent great sums purchasing other Web domain names with ''buy'' themes, such as ''buymusic.com'' and ''buycars.com.'' However, before long the company began to lose consumer confidence; its poor order handling, delivery, and consumer outreach —sparked in no small measure by its refusal to maintain any inventory—spawned dozens of Web sites devoted to bashing Buy.com.

Blum shortly after brought in a CEO to run day-to-day operations, and the firm, its future in doubt in the thick of the shakeout, began to change its character from the brashness of its early days to a more mature-and traditional-model. In other words, the firm took pains to map out for investors just how it planned to achieve profitability—in this case, by subtly raising its prices from their drastically low levels—and relied less for its revenues on flashiness and irreverence.

In Buy.com's story were several lessons for e-commerce firms. In particular, those pure-play dot-coms without access to durable distribution and fulfillment operations, lacking a solid and dependable customer base, and with little brand recognition were hard pressed to survive, unless they managed to make themselves attractive enough for acquisition.

THE AFTERMATH

For some companies, however, the dot-com bust was an ironic twist on the market euphoria that preceded it. That is, where in the late 1990s a simple —dot-com— appended to a company name could send valuations sky high, in the early 2000s that same company could be grossly undervalued for the same reason. According to *Business Week,* hidden among the New Economy rubble at the end of 2000 were doubtless a number of dot-coms unfairly neglected by the market; such firms would eventually arise out of the shakeout with a durable business plan and thinner competition for cash, in the process reaping ground-floor investors enormous rewards. Thus, the dot-com shakeout produced, alongside its layoffs and shattered fortunes, a number of bargains.

The shakeout didn't mean, however, that consumers and businesses gave up on the idea of buying and selling online. Rather, the shakeout was the natural process of any new growth industry, which inevitably undergoes consolidation as consumers and investors learn to distinguish the wheat from the chaff. Where the e-commerce shakeout proved so dramatic was in the tremendous hype many of the failed dot-coms had received, the enormous sums of money that were made and lost in just a few years, and the short-lived notion that e-commerce wasn't bound to the traditional laws of economics or business sense. But the shakeout did little to dissuade companies from conducting business online, nor consumers from shopping in cyberspace. As companies increasingly integrate their online storefronts into their bricks-and-mortar operations, creating a seamless and complementary whole, and as more and more individuals attain Internet access, the number of e-customers is only expected to grow.

FURTHER READING:

Chen, Christine Y. "All I Want for Christmas is a Pulse." *Fortune,* November 27, 2000.

"Dot-com Shakeout Dims IT Outlook." *InternetWeek,* November 27, 2000.

Dugan, Sean M. "Nasdaq Fluctuations Say it's Time to Cull a Few Dot-coms from the Herd of Bulls." *InfoWorld,* April 24, 2000.

Foust, Dean. "Some Dot-Com Jewels Will Shine Again." *Business Week,* December 25, 2000.

Gomolski, Barb. "The Five Success Factors Needed to Survive the Dot-com Shakeout." *InfoWorld,* November 20, 2000.

Green, Heather. "Shakeout E-tailers." *Business Week,* May 15, 2000.

—— Byrnes, Nanette, Alster, Norm, and Arlene Weintraub. "The Dot-Coms are Falling to Earth." *Business Week,* April 17, 2000.

Harper, Doug. "E-commerce Shakeout." *Industrial Distribution,* July, 2000.

Kadet, Gary. "B2B Shakeout." *Computerworld,* April 23, 2001.

Lay, Philip. "Get Ready for the Shakeout." *InformationWeek,* June 12, 2000.

Weintraub, Arlene, and Robert D. Hof. "For Online Pet Stores, It's Dog-Eat-Dog." *Business Week,* March 6, 2000.

SEE ALSO: New Economy; Startups; Volatility

SHIPPING AND SHIPMENT TRACKING

Since the earliest days of commerce, manufacturers and retailers have relied on shipping companies—including parcel/express shippers like FedEx and United Parcel Service;less-than-truckload shippers (LTLs); and railway shippers—to move goods throughout the nation. Traditionally, the process of shipping goods was relatively straightforward. Wholesale and retail orders were taken manually via mail, fax, phone, or in person, and a shipment hopefully followed within a reasonable period of time. Until technology allowed for the tracking of shipments, the shipping process often was characterized by a certain amount of mystery. As *Logistics Management & Distribution Report* explained: "Within memory of many logistics managers, transportation was often described as a 'black hole.' Freight went into the system, and managers hoped it would emerge at the other end intact and something close to on time."

In the mid-to-late 1990s, e-commerce changed the nature of shipping. Information about individual shipments became almost as important as the shipments themselves. Knowing everything from the whereabouts of a shipment in transit to details about its temperature became increasingly important. Companies also gained the ability to reroute shipments in transit as needed, depending on fluctuations in inventory or other factors. The importance of information changed the relationships between companies and shippers, and shippers quickly discovered that being technologically enabled for e-commerce was a requirement for doing business.

Besides an increased emphasis on information, e-commerce also changed the kinds of shipments made by companies. Rather than making fewer larger shipments, companies began making smaller, more frequent ones. As reported in *Transportation & Distribution,* in Morgan Stanley Dean Witter's Freight Transportation and Logistics Industry Report, 65 percent of respondents indicated they would increase their use of parcel/express carriers because of e-commerce. Fifty-seven percent planned on using more national or regional LTLs, and 53 percent expected to rely more on local couriers or trucking operations. These indications were good news for parcel shippers, LTLs, and others specializing in smaller shipments.

Along with greater utilization, parcel/express carriers like United Parcel Service, FedEx, and DHL Worldwide Express began to become more involved with the e-commerce efforts of their customers. Going beyond the delivery of packages, each company established business units focusing on the fulfillment aspect of e-commerce. UPS created a subsidiary called e-Ventures to identify, test, and launch new e-commerce-related businesses within the company. The first such business to emerge from e-Ventures was UPS e-Logistics, a business unit that offered clients "turnkey supply chain management solutions" by taking advantage of its transportation and warehouse networks. The services it offered included inventory management, shipping and delivery, warehousing, order fulfillment (pick, pack and ship), management reporting, customer care and telephone support, and returns management. UPS previously offered similar services to large corporate customers like Nike.com.

In March 2001, Mail Boxes Etc. announced that it would be acquired by, and become a subsidiary of, UPS. Among other strategic advantages, the acquisition would enable the two companies to better serve businesses and consumers engaging in e-commerce. UPS and MBE already had been working together for more than 20 years in various endeavors, including the shipment and return of goods sold over the Internet.

In May 2000, FedEx Logistics announced that its FedEx Supply Chain Services, a third party provider of supply chain solutions, had created FedEx eLogistics—a new division focusing on providing e-commerce logistics solutions to businesses. According to Doug Witt, then vice president and general manager of the new division, FedEx Supply Chain Services helped customers to decrease cycle times, improve the management of returns, and lower fulfillment costs.

Like UPS and FedEx, DHL Worldwide Express had a logistics unit offering product handling and distribution services (inventory management, storage, repair and return, and pick and pack) in the early

2000s. However, the company also had several other offerings related to e-commerce. DHL International operated a special Web site devoted exclusively to e-commerce called DHL Masterclass. The site was designed to help both small and medium-sized companies expand traditional operations to the Internet. It included tips and information on logistics and fulfillment, customer relationship management, supply chain management, selling chain management, e-business strategy, and more.

DHL Worldwide Express also offered Web Shipping, an Internet-based service especially for those with international needs. Customers were able to schedule pickups, complete export documentation, prepare and print airbills, estimate shipping charges, track shipments, and determine which shipments were dutiable, all from one Web site address. Additionally, with the exception of duty and taxes, DHL's Worldwide Priority Express service allowed customers to obtain shipping quotes that contained all charges involved, including pickup, air transit, clearance through international customs, and delivery.

In the early 2000s, DHL Airways Inc., the U.S. division of DHL Worldwide Express, also had plans to create a new service that would remove much of this frustration and mystery by allowing shippers to determine charges made by foreign customs authorities before shipments are made. While taking international orders online is relatively simple, shipping and delivery can be another story because of taxes, tariffs, government-imposed duties, and other fees that, historically, couldn't be determined until shipments were already delivered.

Like parcel/express carriers, LTLs also were playing more involved roles in the affairs of their customers. Roadway, one of North America's largest LTLs, created a special program to help companies manage returned goods during the holiday season and following special promotions. It also allows customers to access a wide variety of real-time information and services on a special, password-protected section of its Web site. In mid-2000, Roadway began offering electronic bill presentment and payment on the site, including real-time access to invoices and payment history information. Other features on the site included quick access to pricing and tariff information, the creation of special reports, calculation of transit times, problem resolution, and more.

TRACKING & TRACING

Of the many different aspects of the shipping process, shipment tracking was of the greatest concern to consumers and companies alike in the early 2000s. The Morgan Stanley Dean Witter report revealed that the section of a transportation company's

Web site devoted to real-time tracking and tracing were the most important to companies (9.4 on a scale of one to 10).

In the early 2000s, parcel/express carriers allowed customers to track shipments through the Internet in a variety of ways. One approach involved the use of e-mail, whereby customers entered anywhere from one to 25 different tracking numbers into the body of an e-mail message, sent it to the shipping company at a specific address, and received responses within minutes regarding the whereabouts of each one. In addition to this approach, UPS also allowed customers to import tracking numbers from spreadsheet programs and receive results via e-mail messages or saved to a data file. DHL Worldwide Express allowed customers to track packages using the text messaging capabilities of their mobile phones. After entering an airway bill number, DHL responded with information about shipment status in as little as 60 seconds. Customers with wireless Internet access also could access a DHL Web site to track packages.

LTLs like Roadway also offered customers the ability to track packages via e-mail as they moved through different stages of the delivery process. Some offerings were more sophisticated than others. Roadway offered customers a remote control feature that allowed real-time freight information to be displayed in a Web browser window on a customer's desktop computer. Consolidated Freightways (CF) enabled shippers to embed CF shipment tracking capabilities on their own Web sites. ABF Freight System Inc. had a predictive tracking system that notified shippers if a shipment appeared to be falling behind schedule so alternate arrangements, like re-routing, could be made if necessary.

To actually keep track of millions of individual packages, shippers relied on a variety of different technologies. In late 2000, FedEx equipped package handlers at its distribution hubs and its drivers with wearable computers and handheld scanners that were connected to a national wireless computer system. These devices were able to perform a variety of functions, including the ability to record digital signatures from customers who accepted shipments, notifying workers if they attempted to place packages onto the wrong vehicle, and updating FedEx's location database regarding the whereabouts of individuals packages. At the time, packages were scanned at different stages of the delivery process, known as routing events. *InfoWorld* indicated that the number of scans FedEx made to individual packages—then about six times each—would double with the new technology it introduced, making more information available in the company's location database.

LTLs used similar handheld scanning technologies and wireless computer networks so drivers and dock workers could track shipments as they moved from point to point. Additionally, both semi cabs and trailers were sometimes outfitted with devices that allowed them to be pinpointed via satellite. In addition to showing the whereabouts of cabs and trailers, sensors on trucks also could reveal when doors are opened; when trailers are empty, full, or hooked to different cabs; the temperature of perishable shipments like fruits or vegetables; and more.

The rail industry also was making it easier for customers to track shipments online. Individual railroads had similar means of tracking shipments for customers, including the ability to track individual railcars with Wireless Application Protocol (WAP)-enabled cellular phones. However, according to Morgan Stanley Dean Witter's Freight Transportation and Logistics Industry Report, 21 percent of respondents planned on scaling back their use of railroads as a shipping method. In response to customer complaints about the difficulty of tracking information on multiple railroad sites, the rail industry came together in a unified effort to develop Steelroads, a Web site that provides one interface for setting up shipments involving more than one railroad. In addition to allowing customers to access information about routes and payment, customers could track and trace shipments by entering car initials and numbers. The site expected to offer easier means of shipment tracking as it evolved.

Finally, one company was making it simpler for shippers to handle all modes of transportation from one Web site, including rail, marine, air, and ground transport. Arzoon allowed customers to inquire about rates, place orders, track shipments, and obtain information reports, with the ultimate goal of reducing cost, increasing efficiency, and customer service.

FURTHER READING:

DHL Worldwide Express. ''DHL Launches E-commerce Web Site to Help Companies Develop E-business Presence.'' DHL Worldwide Express, May 24, 2000. Available from www.dhl-usa.com.

''FedEx and VisualWorks Deliver On-Time!'' *Planet IT,* March 12, 2001. Available from www.eoenabled.com.

''Full Speed Ahead on the Electronic Highway.'' *Logistics Management & Distribution Report,* April 2000.

Hickey, Kathleen. ''Road Trip.'' *Trafic World,* January 29, 2001.

''Internet Use Will Change Freight Patterns.'' *Transportation & Distribution,* January 2001.

King, Julia. ''Shipping Firms Exploit IT to Deliver E-commerce Goods.'' *Computerworld,* August 2, 1999.

Luczak, Marybeth. ''Moving Goods, Not Paperwork.'' *Railway Age,* November 2000.

Milligan, Brian. ''High-tech Tools: Boon for Shippers & Carriers.'' *Purchasing,* August 12, 1999.

Neel, Dan. ''Wireless Tracking of Shipments Readied.'' *Info-World.com,* September 2, 2000. Available from www2.infoworld.com.

SEE ALSO: Channel Conflict/Harmony; Fulfillment Problems; Order Fulfillment; Supply Chain Management

SHOPPING BOTS

Shopping bots are price comparison sites on the World Wide Web that automatically search the inventory of several different online merchants to find the lowest prices for consumers. Typically, these sites rank products by price and allow shoppers to link directly to an online merchant's site to actually make a purchase. Many shopping bots also include links to product reviews from evaluation sites like Gomez.com and Bizrate.com.

One of the most popular shopping bots, mySimon.com, culls the offerings of more than 2,000 e-tailers using its Virtual Learning Agent software, for which a patent is pending. Users can either search for a specific product by keyword or browse several product categories including apparel, books, consumer electronics, movies, and wireless products. Searches result in a listing of products that can be sorted by various criteria including price, merchant ratings, and manufacturers. To change the way information is sorted, shoppers can simply click on a different category heading. Shoppers who reach a decision about which item they wish to purchase begin the transaction by clicking the ''buy'' button located beside each product. They then are routed to the Web site selling the item, where they can complete their purchase. mySimon.com offers its shopping bot service free to users. The site makes money via banner bar advertising. For a fee, merchants wishing to increase their visibility on the mySimon.com site can join the company's Building OnLine Demand (BOLD) program. The icons of BOLD members appear larger in the search results offerings than the icons for merchants who are not members.

Another leading shopping bot, PriceSCAN offers a wider selection of products than mySimon.com because it includes offers from merchants without Web sites. The site's databases are changed frequently as new information—pulled from catalogs, print advertisements, and faxes from the merchants themselves—is added daily. The bot relies solely on banner bar advertising as a source of revenue.

Unlike mySimon.com and PriceSCAN, some shopping bots require payment from each merchant they list. This practice does not always work to the benefit of the consumer, as those online merchants offering the best deals may not have paid for a listing on a certain bot. According to the November 2000 issue of *Searcher,* ''the reality is that most shopping bots make money by collecting listing fees from the merchants who sell through them. Merchants who pay more get higher rankings from the bots, and sometimes they can shut out competitors altogether. For example, the entire category of 'Books' on the Lycos shopping site searches only the Barnes and Noble site with absolutely no way to compare prices.'' Similarly, both Excite Shopping and DealTime only search the inventories of merchants who pay for a listing, limiting the options offered to shoppers using the sites. The Yahoo! shopping bot limits its searches to leading online merchants, appealing to online shoppers who prefer to use only the most recognized electronic merchants.

Some shopping bots specialize in certain types of merchandise. For example, IQShopping searches the inventories of online home electronics and video game vendors, as well as traditional brick and mortar retailers selling the same wares. BookFinder.com searches Amazon, Antiqbook, Barnes and Noble, Bibliofind, and other online book retailers—a combined database of roughly 15 million books—to find the cheapest book prices for shoppers. CNET's shopping bot focuses on computers and other types of consumer electronics, including wireless devices. One of the earliest shopping bots, Price Watch has allowed shoppers to search for computers and computer parts since 1995. Its Price Watch Info-Link system posts the prices offered by online retailers in real time.

Despite the obvious benefits of using a shopping bot to compare prices on a wide range of products, even the top shopping bots found themselves fighting to stay afloat in 2000 and 2001. Many saw their sales plummet as their main revenue source, banner bar advertisements, became something many struggling dotcom startups could no longer afford. Also, when the economy worsened many traditional firms tightened their marketing budgets, eliminating online advertising dollars. Other bots suffered when customers who used their service to find a low price ended up being dissatisfied with the customer service offered by the merchant selling the product. Although typical shopping bots have no control over customers' shopping experiences once they launch an online purchasing transaction, many customers associate the bot with the negative experience.

According to a July 2001 article in *E-Commerce Times,* bots will remain a part of the e-commerce landscape only if they make several changes, such as increasing consumer awareness via advertising, increasing their level of user friendliness by cleaning up page design and clarifying search procedures, and offering more information on the return policies of merchants.

FURTHER READING:

Greenberg, Paul A. "The Bottom Line on Online Shopping Bots." *E-Commerce Times.* July 13, 2001. Available from www.ecommercetimes.com.

McDermott, Irene E. "Shopping Bots: Santa's Electronic Elves." *Searcher.* November, 2000.

Pack, Thomas. "Intelligent Shopping Agents." *Link-Up.* March, 2001.

Turner, Rob. "Shopping on the Internet: Eight Rules You Can't Afford to Ignore." *Money.* December 1, 1999.

SEE ALSO: Bizrate.com; Intelligent Agents; mySimon.com; Spiders

SHOPPING CART

An electronic shopping cart serves the same purpose as a traditional metal shopping cart in a grocery or department store. It allows shoppers to select potential purchases and set them aside until they are ready to pay for their merchandise. While checkout procedures take place at a cash register in a bricks-and-mortar establishment, at an online store payment is most typically made via a real-time credit card transaction, and merchandise is then shipped to the address specified by the shopper. Along with providing the checkout path, most online shopping-cart programs handle multiple functions, such as allowing shoppers to confirm which items they have chosen to purchase; displaying information about whether or not these products are immediately available; asking shoppers to select the quantity of each product being purchased; displaying individual product prices, shipping costs, sales tax, and the total bill; and accepting and confirming contact, billing, and shipping information. These programs typically also include buttons that allow shoppers to continue shopping and remove items from their cart.

Shopping carts have been used by Web-based businesses since the mid-1990s. Some companies, such as online retailing giant Amazon.com, develop their own shopping cart programs. Some purchase shopping cart technology from a specialized vendor, such as VirtualCart, for integration into their own e-store. Others simply use an e-commerce solutions provider like One World Hosting to not only host their online business, but also to supply various applications, such as shopping carts, that are necessary for conducting e-commerce. In fact, One World Hosting offers its e-commerce clients two shopping cart options: the PayPal shopping cart and the Alacart system, which is available in three service levels. Alacart's Silver cart is set up to allow for the transmission of purchase information to a business via e-mail. The business can then handle the purchase transaction in whatever offline manner it chooses. Companies with 25 products or less might opt for Alacart Gold if they wish to allow customers to pay for purchases online with real-time credit card processing. Companies with a wide range of products—up to 1,000—can select Alacart Platinum.

Early online shopping carts were often criticized for being cumbersome and difficult to use. According to the August 1998 issue of *PC Week,* "Visibility is the first problem. Sites should not hide their shopping carts on separate pages. This design makes shoppers either delay all analysis and reconciliation to the end of their visit or flip back and forth between item pages and the shopping cart. Why should you have to wonder whether you already put the item in the cart or what your total bill will be?" In December of 1999, Apex Interactive Inc. developed a new shopping cart that addressed these concerns with a drag-and-drop program that allowed shoppers to drag images of products they wish to purchase into a shopping cart window that was displayed on the same screen. The shopping cart window remained open while customers continued shopping, and each item selected for purchase, as well as its price, was displayed. Each time a new product was placed into or removed from the cart, prices were recalculated and the total bill was adjusted.

One of the most important developments in shopping cart technology came in 1997 when Amazon.com developed its one-click method. According to *Electronic Business* writer Marc Brown, Amazon.com developed the technology in an effort to reduce the number of sales lost to customers frustrated with online checkout processes that included completing lengthy personal information forms. "Amazon.com captures the buying impulse immediately by storing this information in a database, assigning the customer a unique I.D., and storing the I.D. in a cookie on the customer's computer. The next time the customer visits, the I.D. is automatically read and used to locate the customer's record." From that point on, an Amazon.com customer is able to make a purchase simply by clicking on the "Buy Now" icon located next to each product. The online book e-tailer secured a patent for its one-click process in October of 1999 and immediately sued competitor Barnes & Noble.com for using similar shopping cart technology. In December, a U.S. District Court Judge ordered Barnes & Noble.com to stop using its single-click checkout method until a verdict was reached. Barnes & Noble.com appealed the ruling, and in March of

2001 the U.S. Court of Appeals lifted the injunction, citing concerns with the legitimacy of Amazon.com's patent.

Despite advances in shopping cart technology, a study conducted by e-commerce consultant Creative Good in late 2000 indicated that 43 percent of online shoppers planning to make a purchase at a Web site ended up failing to complete the transaction for reasons ranging from slow page load time and confusion regarding the checkout process to being unable to locate the product they wanted. More than 40 percent of the frustrated online shoppers actually had placed items in their shopping cart before they opted to leave the site. In those cases, the top three reasons for aborting the transaction were complicated account creation procedures, unclear error messages, and vague distinctions between paths for new and returning customers.

Along with a high number of abandoned shopping carts, online merchants also have found themselves dealing with hacking problems related to their shopping carts. In some cases, hackers have been able to use the HTML editing features available on most browsers to change the price of a product before buying it. In 2001, nearly one-third of all shopping cart applications were unable to prevent this type of price-switching activity, and the Internet Fraud Council estimated that fraud took place in 11 percent of all online purchases. Despite these problems with shopping carts, however, the number of online stores continues to rise, as does the number of online shoppers. Because shopping cart technology is key to e-commerce, advances that increase security and decrease lost sales will likely emerge in the near future.

FURTHER READING:

Brown, Marc E. "'One-Click Shopping' Still Risky to Implement." *Electronic Business.* May 2001.

Catchings, Bill. "Online Shopping Sites Need More Smarts in Their Carts." *PC Week.* August 31, 1998.

Enos, Lori. "Report: E-Holiday Glitches Could Cost $15B." *E-Commerce Times.* October 17, 2000. Available from www.ecommercetimes.com.

"e-Shoplifters Are Hacking into Online Stores and Altering Prices, Reports Interactive Week." *PR Newswire.* March 5, 2001.

Kelsey, Dick. "Barnes & Noble.com Wins Round in 1-Click Case." *Newsbytes.* February 14, 2001.

Mullins, Robert. "Technology to Make e-Shopping Easier." *The Business Journal-Milwaukee.* December 31, 1999.

Thumlert, Kurt. "Abandoned Shopping Carts: Enigma or Sloppy E-Commerce?" *E-Commerce Times.* June 27, 2001. Available from www.ecommerce.internet.com.

SEE ALSO: Amazon.com; Storefront Builders

SIMULATION SOFTWARE

Companies that engage in e-commerce rely on software for a variety of things, from ensuring security, operating servers, and managing customer relationships to providing visitors with online shopping carts and payment systems. By definition, software consists of instructions that tell computers what to do. Although it's customary to view hardware and software as separate and distinct elements that work in tandem to make a computers operate, the two are actually enmeshed together at many different levels. Software normally is placed in one of two different categories: system software and applications. Applications are software programs that users apply to various tasks, ranging from enjoyment to productivity. One particularly useful kind of application allows companies to generate simulations—models or pictures of what might happen in different situations.

In the past, simulation software was used almost exclusively in the fields of industrial engineering and statistics. In the 1960s, conducting simulations on large mainframe computers was a difficult task. However, by the early 2000s business professionals in many different industries were using simulation software to model different business scenarios and solve problems. For the most successful companies, this form of software had become a necessary tool for doing business because the global business climate was complicated and uncertain. A number of factors—including pressure from investors, the demands of customers, the impact of new technologies, domestic and international government regulations, legal issues, the environment, and even the cost of shipping products—made it difficult for corporate executives to make important decisions and position their companies for success.

By allowing companies to experiment with new ideas in artificial environments without taking any risks, simulation software evolved into a powerful tool for making more efficient, effective decisions, and for allocating resources in the most optimal ways. As *Darwin* magazine explained: "Simulation software doesn't draw conclusions for the user, but it reduces the time an executive needs to glean valuable insights from reams of data. Using it maximizes both a computer's remarkable ability to crunch through thousands of figures and details as well as the human capacity for generating insights and making decisions."

Many companies perform simulations or create models using spreadsheet programs like Microsoft Excel. When VisiCalc, the first spreadsheet program for desktop computers, was introduced in 1979, it changed the financial world. Banks and other companies were able to save hours of work by automating certain financial tasks, and it became possible to conduct a virtually unlimited number of "what if" scenarios simply by plugging in different sets of numbers. This approach was especially valuable to investors, legitimate and otherwise.

The simulations created by spreadsheets often are one component of the overall decision-making process. For example, at oil company Royal Dutch/Shell, they became an important part of an approach called scenario planning. The purpose of scenario planning is to identify several different stories about, or visions of, how large-scale forces will have an impact over time. Peter Schwartz, one of the pioneers of scenario planning, used spreadsheets to add a quantitative complement to the narrow scenarios his department created at Royal Dutch/Shell, thus making them more appealing and convincing to the company's management.

In addition to using spreadsheets alone, companies also rely on other types of software programs that focus specifically on simulation. Many of these applications work with spreadsheet programs. In the early 2000s, leading companies used software products that helped them analyze decisions. Working in tandem with spreadsheet applications like Microsoft Excel, these programs created diagrams, decision trees, and other graphical representations of data from the spreadsheet. These could include sequences of choices and possible events in chronological order. Software products like these also were able to help users evaluate the potential risks involved in a decision and see which variables were the most important or influential. In addition to decision tree analysis, these applications relied on other techniques to provide simulations. Among them were various forecasting methods, including a mathematical technique known as linear programming, which involves allocating resources optimally in order to meet objectives; and Monte Carlo simulation, which is useful for modeling random events.

Although simulation software can be applied to many different e-commerce situations, one particularly prominent application involves the management of company supply chains. Supply chains can include all of the different parties or entities that are involved (including suppliers, distributors, and production facilities) in the process of taking parts or raw goods and turning them into finished products. Simulation software can be used to emulate changes or fluctuations in any given number of variables (like supply and demand) so that companies can see how changes in some variables impact the conditions of others. This allows them to better prepare themselves, increase the supply chain's efficiency, and find the optimal balance between customer satisfaction and cost savings.

Another critical application of simulation software is in a company's warehouse. Many companies that achieved success in the world of brick-and-mortar commerce quickly discovered that that e-commerce was a different game. Rather than shipping relatively small numbers of large orders to retail chains or distributors, high volumes of smaller orders for individual consumers must be processed. This presents a new set of requirements for retailers, such as providing customers with real-time information about available products in inventory. This also changes the way products get moved behind the scenes in a company's warehouse.

In the early 2000s, companies relied on a complex array of warehouse management software (WMS), overhead scanners, conveyor belt systems, wireless computer networks, wearable computers, hand-held bar code scanners, and portable printers to streamline operations and automate the movement of goods through their warehouses, many of which had become very sophisticated operations. Some e-tailers used simulation software to generate models or simulations of their existing warehouses, based on the conditions different variables. For example, software can be used to emulate what would happen if an e-tailer were faced with a sudden influx of orders, a shortage in warehouse workers, or both. Software also can be used to figure out optimal ways to configure the physical layout of a warehouse, based on how goods and people move through it.

As explained in *Warehousing Management,* "Computer simulation models can represent all the detail of a warehousing facility, such as operating strategies, docking areas, conveyors, picking and storage, just to name a few. When a model is executed in the computer, simulated time advances the model just as the warehouse would actually operate. The model automatically collects statistics on bottlenecks, equipment utilization, inventory and throughput, and generates reports for analysis and optimization."

As computers continue to play central roles in everyday business processes and the business world becomes more complex, simulation software likely will continue to be an essential tool for successful companies. According to Michael Schrage, author of *Serious Play: How the World's Best Companies Simulate to Innovate,* simulation technology will play an increasing role in the corporate world during the early 2000s, becoming as commonplace as spreadsheets or e-mail.

FURTHER READING:

Bowden, Royce. "The Spectrum of Simulation Software." *IIE Solutions,* May 1998.

Duffy, Daintry. "Let's Pretend." *Darwin,* October 2000. Available from www.darwinmagazine.com.

Hickey, Kathleen. "Decisions, Decisions." *Traffic World,* October 25, 1999.

Rohrer, Matt. "Simulating Success." *Warehousing Management,* August 2000.

Schrage, Michael. *Serious Play: How the World's Best Companies Simulate to Innovate.* Boston: Harvard Business School Press. 2000.

Wyland, Brad. "Simulating the Supply Chain." *IIE Solutions,* January 2000.

SEE ALSO: Scenario Planning; Supply Chain Management

SITE EVALUATION SERVICES

The rise of e-commerce in the late 1990s brought with it many issues related to the security of online transactions, the accountability of online merchants, and the reliability of Internet sites. As a result, many organizations began offering site evaluation services. In some cases, site assessment is conducted for the benefit of customers considering purchasing goods or services from an e-merchant. For example, the Consumer Reports e-Rating service, launched in 1999, evaluates the customer service, ease of use, return policies, privacy, and product offerings of various Web sites. In other instances, a business operating an Internet site may contract an outside evaluation team, such as SurveySite or Cyberfirm, to provide feedback regarding the site's performance. Some companies offer site evaluation services that serve both consumers and businesses. Three of the most well known Internet site evaluators are Gomez, Inc., BizRate.com, and BBBOnLine, Inc.

Founded in 1997 as Gomez Advisors, Gomez Inc. is a leading Internet research firm that serves both consumers and e-business ventures. Using its "Internet Scorecard," the firm has evaluated more than 6,000 e-commerce sites, in terms of both performance and quality, across a wide variety of industries. The Internet Scorecard rankings, which are posted on the firm's Web site, consist of roughly 150 different criteria points, grouped in categories such as ease of use, customer confidence, on-site resources, relationship services, and overall cost. Each category covers different criteria; for example, ease of use includes overall site functionality, the actual process of completing a purchase, and site navigation. The firm also offers real-time World Wide Web site and transaction performance measurement and diagnostic services via its GomezNetworks arm. An Internet Quality Measurement (IQM) program helps clients evaluate online offerings and compare them against those of competitors; measure and monitor online performance against others in the same industry; and develop online strategies.

Initially, Gomez focused solely on evaluating online brokers, which it did by actually conducting business at various brokerage Web sites. In 1999, however, Gomez began expanding into other industries. Declaring itself the "E-Commerce Authority," the company began compiling scorecards for the Web sites of airlines, apparel retailers, consumer electronics and computer retailers, drug stores, furniture stores, grocery delivery services, hotels, loan and insurance brokers, pet stores, sporting goods vendors, and toy stores. Eventually, Marketwatch.com and America Online began making Gomez scorecards available on their sites. In 2000, Gomez also developed a Merchant Certification program for online merchants in over 25 industries. Merchants who met eight different requirements, including providing online access to customer support and publishing privacy policies, received a Gomez PASS seal to post on their Web site. Merchants who met more stringent criteria earned a PASS PLUS seal. Within a few months, more than 2,000 online merchants had posted Gomez PASS seals on their sites.

Unlike Gomez, rival BizRate uses data from actual shoppers, rather than staff, to create Internet site ratings. BizRate gathers information from consumers who conduct business at the site of a participating e-tailer, which displays a "BizRate Customer Certified" seal. Once an online shopper makes a purchase from such a site, a BizRate questionnaire is presented to the shopper. When a questionnaire is completed, BizRate dumps the data into existing information about the e-store, a practice that allows overall ratings to change over time. The benefits of such a system are twofold. Web surfers visiting BizRate can view ratings—which cover customer support, live phone support, on-time delivery, site performance, order ease, product information, product pricing, order tracking, and privacy policies—before making purchases. At the same time, the online vendors can use the information to better meet customer demands. BizRate also sells highly customized and detailed monthly data reports, based on the information gathered, to online retailers for $20,000 per year.

In June of 1996, at the age of 27, Farhad Mohit founded BizRate to help consumers find trustworthy and competent vendors in an increasingly complex online marketplace. Mohit wanted to provide objective evaluations of Web sites for shoppers who wanted information about an online business before making an online purchase. By 2001, BizRate.com had grown into one of the busiest retail hubs on the Internet, second only to online giant Amazon.com. More than 7 million different Web surfers visit BizRate each month. Along with evaluating online businesses for consumers, the site also allows users to search for items they would like to purchase and then link directly to the e-tailers selling the merchandise.

BizRate ratings are listed on such well known sites as Consumer Reports Online, Microsoft Network, Alta Vista, and CNET.

A third major site evaluator, BBBOnLine, Inc., has operated as the Better Business Bureau of the Internet since its founding in 1996. Browsers visiting BBBOnLine can search for information on specific e-tail sites, file complaints about e-tailers, and request dispute resolution assistance. To let consumers know which businesses meet its standards for fair and ethical online business practices, BBBOnline offers two Web site seals.

Since April 1997, the BBBOnLine Reliability Seal has identified companies that are members of their local business bureau, meet specific criteria regarding truth in advertising, and follow customer service principles similar to those used by traditional Better Business Bureau members. The BBBOnLine Privacy Seal, created in March of 1999, is granted to online businesses that collect, use, and protect the personal information of online customers in a manner approved by the Better Business Bureau. To qualify for the seal, a site must publish a privacy statement that clearly explains what information is being gathered, how it may be used in the future, and if customers may do something to prevent that use. The site must also allow BBBOnLine to conduct a review of its security procedures to determine if they are adequate. By March of 2001, nearly 9,500 Web sites—including eToys, CDNow, eBay, and Travelocity—had posted the Reliability Seal, and the Privacy Seal had been granted to nearly 800 firms, including AT&T Corp., Hewlett-Packard Co., and New York Times Co.

As e-commerce continues to grow, the need for services like site evaluation will likely climb as well. While some analysts argue that once consumers are comfortable with online shopping they will no longer turn to firms like BizRate and Gomez, others point out that new businesses emerge in the online world every day, a fact that seems to favor the future of online ratings firms.

FURTHER READING:

BBBOnLine, Inc. "About BBBOnline." Arlington, VA: BBBOnLine, Inc., 2001. Available from bbbonline.org.

Bennefield, Robin M. "BBB Online: A Seal with Teeth." *U.S. News & World Report,* March 3, 1997.

BizRate.com. "About BizRate.com." Los Angeles, CA: BizRate.com, 2001. Available from www.bizrate.com.

"BizRate.com Becomes Second to Amazon as the Most Popular Retail Site on the Web." *Business Wire,* February 15, 2001.

Gomez Inc. "About Gomez." Waltham, MA: Gomez Inc., 2001. Available from www.gomezadvisors.com.

Greenberg, Paul A. "Consumer Reports Takes E-Tailer Rankings Online." *E-Commerce Times,* October 1, 1999. Available from www.ecommercetimes.com.

Haley, Colin C. "Gomez Advisors to Make National Push." *InternetNews,* February 21, 2000. Available from www.internetnews.com.

Smith, Geoffrey. "How Good Are the Gomez Ratings?" *BusinessWeek Online,* October 25, 1999. Available from www.businessweek.com.

————. "There's Good Reason for the Buzz about BitRate." *Businessweek Online,* November 26, 1999. Available from www.businessweek.com.

Weintraub, Arlene. "E-Commerce Crusader." *Businessweek Online,* June 5, 2000. Available from www.businessweek.com.

SEE ALSO: Bizrate.com; Computer Security; Fraud, Internet; Gomez Inc.; Privacy: Issues, Policies, Statements

SITE RESPONSE TIME

The speed at which individuals connect to the Internet has increased significantly since the World Wide Web became popular in public circles. Early on, when the processing and dial-up modem speeds of computers were relatively slow, it was accepted that most tasks—including the time required to access a Web site—would take a certain amount of time, especially if the site included a large number of graphic elements. As faster technology came onto the scene and e-commerce and Internet adoption evolved, users were less tolerant of slow Web site response times. If pages took more than eight seconds to download, chances were good that users would direct their browsers elsewhere. Although the average site response time was approximately 17 seconds in mid-2001, this "eight-second rule" was something of a standard for Internet marketers, for whom such lost visitors represented lost revenue.

Web site response times can be affected by a number of different factors. A leading factor is the performance of the servers on which sites reside and operate. When a user attempts to download a site, that user's Web browser (software applications like Microsoft Internet Explorer or Netscape Navigator which are used for viewing Web pages) requests the site from the server, on which there may be several different sites. The server must acknowledge this request and then serve up the requested Web page. In the early 2000s, there were different software tools hosts could use to monitor the performance of their servers and Web sites, as well as applications that improved site response times in different ways. Other such factors include the amount of traffic on the Internet at any given time, as well as issues involving Internet service providers, which provide many individual consumer and business users with access to the Internet's backbone. The heavy use of graphics and multimedia elements also played a role in the download speed of many Web sites.

The economic impact of poor Web site response times is very real. Zona Research issued a report 1999 that placed lost U.S. e-commerce sales due to "user bailout behaviors" and unacceptable download speeds in the vicinity of $4.35 billion. In mid-2001, using information from Keynote Systems, Zona issued additional figures that placed the cost of slow-loading Web sites at $25 billion, indicating that bad connections caused the abandonment of up to half of all online transactions. The report also revealed that poor site response times were common to modem users and those with high-speed access. According to Zona, heavy use of graphic elements was causing many consumer Web site download times to increase as much as 20 percent.

FURTHER READING:

"Computer User: Slow Sites Costing Online Retailers." *Nua Internet Surveys,* May 8, 2001. Available from www.nua.ie/ surveys.

"The Economic Impacts of Unacceptable Web Site Download Speeds." Zona Research Inc., 1999. Available from www.zonaresearch.com.

"Increasing Web Site Profits With Improved Response Time." Trio Networks, August 7, 2001. Trio Networks. Available from www.trionetworks.com.

SEE ALSO: Web Site Usability Issues

SMARTMONEY.COM

SmartMoney.com, the online incarnation of *SmartMoney* magazine, is a comprehensive set of resources for individual private investors. It includes tools to aid in making investment decisions and tracking investments, as well as regularly updated information from the financial markets and daily news, analysis, and feature articles. SmartMoney.com gives intensive coverage to the most popular investment instruments, stocks, bonds, and mutual funds. The site is especially famous for its "Map of the Market," a graphical representation of approximately 600 different stocks, that offers investors an instant overview of market activity. The site also includes SmartMoney University, a set of interactive courses on a variety of investment topics, including strategic investment, investing for retirement, debt management, setting up and maintaining a college fund, and short-term investment. About 98 percent of the site is produced in-house by a staff of nearly 100 writers, editors, and designers. SmartMoney.com has been the recipient of numerous awards for design and content.

SmartMoney.com was the brainchild of Steven Schwartz, a former front-page editor of the *Wall Street Journal.* In 1992, with joint financing from Dow Jones & Company and the Hearst Corporation, Schwartz founded and took over the editorship of *SmartMoney* magazine. The magazine quickly became one of the most respected in the nation. It was named "Magazine of the Year" by *Advertising Age* and later won two National Magazine Awards.

Schwartz launched the online version of his magazine in September 1997 after two years of preparation. The Web site, also parented by Dow Jones and Hearst, was originally known as SmartMoney Interactive, positioning it clearly as a partner site to Dow Jones Interactive. From the start, the site was far more than just an advertisement for *SmartMoney* or an archive of its old articles. The site was staffed by 27 of its own technical, production, and editorial workers. Most of its content was produced independently of the magazine; it featured articles and analysis not available in *SmartMoney*—as many as ten original pieces every day. However, the soul of SmartMoney Interactive was to be found in elements that were impossible for any publication to duplicate, such as its regularly updated market charting functions and 30 interactive personal finance worksheets for calculating investment plans for retirement, college and the like.

When it was first launched, SmartMoney Interactive charged its users a fee. Regular subscribers paid $49.95 per year; *Wall Street Journal* and *SmartMoney* magazine subscribers paid $29.95 a year. Subscribers to the *Journal*'s online version, Wall Street Journal Interactive, could access SmartMoney.com free of charge. It became a free site, supporting itself primarily through advertising revenues, in summer 1999 and at the same time it changed its name to SmartMoney.com. Once access was free, the number of visitors to SmartMoney grew fourfold and the amount of time spent at the site every day for the average visitor doubled to forty minutes. Although most of the site was free, it continued to charge for some premium services, such as real-time market updates.

SmartMoney's site is one of the most comprehensive collections of investment information on the Web. Its securities section includes entire sections devoted to stocks, mutual funds, and bonds. Each section features news and analysis, historical information. Aimed at the personal investor, the SmartMoney site offers valuable tips on various aspects of personal finance: setting up a college fund for one's children, selecting the right insurance policy, purchasing an automobile and real estate, finding a job, making financial plans for marriage and divorce, and saving money on taxes. There is a searchable archive of two years worth of articles from *SmartMoney,* as well as from Dow Jones News and various newswire services. Selected articles from the current issue of *SmartMoney* are available to all Smart-Money.com users; they can purchase books and investment-related paraphernalia at the SmartMart.

SmartMoney.com's great innovation is the use it makes of the medium of the Internet. The site incorporates a variety of unique features that would be difficult, if not impossible, to realize outside the computer's virtual realm. SmartMoney's Tools page combines continual updates with an interactive capability that enables investors to plan an investment portfolio and monitor its performance. The "Stock Sifter" makes it possible to screen more than 7,000 different stock offerings by personal criteria that are determined by the individual investor. Investors use the "Your Portfolio" page to set up and track the performance of as many as 50 different portfolios, each with up to fifty stocks; a for-pay version called Screener allows investors to use formulas devised by the Web site's own experts. Another for-pay page provides real-time, instantaneous updates of prices from the stock markets. Subscribers can even set up a SmartMoney account, which will automatically receive and pay household bills electronically. Smart-Money's online calculators enable consumers to figure the costs of car lease agreements, mortgages, retirement accounts, compound interest, as well as various taxes including capital gains, estate taxes, home sales tax, and the "marriage penalty." In late 2001, the site introduced a "Bush Tax Cut Calculator" with which tax payers could estimate their savings over time under the new tax law.

In 1999, SmartMoney.com introduced Smart-Money University, a series of online tutorials that take investors, from beginners to old pros, through the fundamentals of investing and on into more specialized areas. The first course, "Investing 101," begins with interactive lectures on how investment works. From there the student moves on to a comparison of risk and reward in investment, a six-part class on the forces that affect the stock market, how to choose a mutual fund, the workings of the bond market, specialized investment forms such as certificates of deposit and money market funds, and finally the tax issues investors must consider. The second course, "Taking Action," is designed to prepare a potential investor for the dive into the action by teaching the basics of asset allocation, putting the first portfolio together, and finding a broker. "Strategic Investing" introduces the student to the ins and outs of selecting stocks, bonds, and mutual funds. The course "Retirement 401(k)" describes the investment accounts issues related to investing for one's retirement. "College Planning" tackles the same questions sending one's children to college. "Short-Term Investing" discusses strategies and risks connected with the short-term. The final course is entitled, perhaps ominously, "Debt Man-

agement." It is made up of individual tutorials on mortgage refinancing, debt consolidation, the pros and cons of borrowing from one's 401(k) account, and dealing with credit cards. Anyone who makes it through all of the lectures in SmartMoney University should find him or herself with a solid grounding in the language and concepts of investment.

Of all its features, SmartMoney.com was most famous for its stock market maps. SmartMoney's "Map of the Market" went online in early 1999 and was an immediate hit. The map breaks down the stock of some 600 companies into industrial sectors, represented as squares whose relative size on the map is proportional to the size in the market. Within the industry squares, companies are also represented proportional to their size, and are colored green or red to indicate whether the stock is up or down. As one moves the cursor from square to square and company to company on the map, charts, news, quotes, earnings estimates, analysts' recommendations, and other current information about companies pop up automatically. Updating of information on the map is constant. The map's graphic presentation provides a unique and understandable view of the forces at work in the market at any given time.

The Map of the Market quickly became one of the most popular features on SmartMoney.com. Other maps were later developed for the site, including historical maps and maps of specific market sectors such as technology, health care, the Internet, telecommunications, energy, consumer, and utilities sectors. An expanded Market Map 1000, which tracked 1000 U.S. and foreign companies, was introduced, along with real time, for-pay versions of all of the maps. In March 2000, SmartMoney.com released MapStation, a software package that enabled investors to create customized maps of their own which tracked the performance of their personal portfolios, broken down into sector and company. MapStation could also be set up to give instant on-screen alerts when a stock hit a certain price. MapStation was offered by Smart-Money.com as a free download or CD-ROM. The price of a subscription to the update service illustrated better than any graph the value of up-to-the-minute stock market information to the serious investor—for $49.95 one got real-time updates; for $9.95 the information was delayed 15 minutes.

SmartMoney innovations were adopted by other Web sites. In June 2001, Standard & Poor's Com-Stock Web site licensed SmartMoney's mapping technology. But Web sites that did not specialize in investment and financial also showed interest in SmartMoney. In summer 2001 the Smithsonian Institution unveiled a virtual exhibit titled "HistoryWired: A Few of Our Favorite Things," on the museum's Web site. It offered a tour of the Smithsonian's storage areas, including many items that are rarely on display at the museum because of space limitations. SmartMoney donated its MapStation technology, which was used to create the exhibit behind its Map of the Market, to the Smithsonian. It was one of the first times the software was used for a non-financial purpose, something SmartMoney's research and development department hoped would catch on.

In the course of establishing its presence on the Internet, SmartMoney.com established a number of important strategic alliances with other Web companies. In early 1998 it made a deal with Bridge Information Systems, a company that generated data about national and international financial markets. Under the agreement, Bridge's real-time and historical data was made available to SmartMoney.com. Later in 1998, it made deals to establish its presence on such popular Web sites as Lycos, Yahoo!, NetZero, Priceline.com, and America Online. So successful was the site that in October 1999 Hearst and Dow Jones jointly invested an additional $30 million in the SmartMoney venture to fund an expansion of staff, news coverage and editorial features. By the end of 2000, SmartMoney's technology unit was licensing its Web applications to other about 70 companies, among them financial leaders such as Fidelity, American Express, and J.P. Morgan.

SmartMoney.com won numerous awards for its site design and content. It won the Investment Company Institute/American University award for online personal finance journalism three years running, from 1998 until 2000. In 1999 it received both the *I.D.* magazine Gold Medal in Interactive Design and the Industrial Design Excellence Award from the Industrial Designers Society of America. In 2000 the American Association of Individual Investors (AAII) named it the most comprehensive Web site in seven different areas: Comprehensive Sites, Retirement Planning, Personal Finance/ Financial Planning, Portfolio Tracking, Financial News & Analysis, Mutual Funds Data, and Stock Data. It received a 2001 National Magazine award for Best Interactive Design.

FURTHER READING:

"Bridge Announces Agreement With SmartMoney Interactive." *Business Wire,* April 15, 1998.

Cardona, Mercedes M. "Smartmoney.com Adds to Winning Debut Campaign." *Advertising Age,* February 28, 2000.

Cullen, Terri. "Online Investing." *Wall Street Journal,* June 14, 1999.

"Dow Jones Sees Midsummer Launch For SmartMoney Interactive." *Dow Jones Interactive,* May 5, 1997.

Oldenburg, Doug. "Consummate Consumer; SmartMoney U." *Washington Post,* July 28, 1999.

O'Leary, Mick. "Something for Nothing from Dow Jones." *Information Today,* October 1999.

"SmartMoney.Com Unveils New Investor Learning Center." *PR Newswire,* July 26, 1999.

Synder, Beth. "Hearst and Dow Jones launch SmartMoney Interactive." *Advertising Age,* September 1, 1997.

"Wall Street Journal Unveils SmartMoney site." *Milwaukee Journal Sentinel,* September 8, 1997.

Zarem, Jane E. "10 Leading Edge Innovators Source." *Folio,* Summer 2000.

SEE ALSO: Investing, Online

SOFTWARE

Years ago, computers were huge expensive machines used mainly by large companies and universities. Since then, they have become useful everyday tools people use to share, store, and analyze information. While computers have affected the world in a very broad way, their impact in the business sector has been especially significant. Desktop computers, large mainframes, and the servers used to host Web sites are key elements in the world of e-commerce. However, contemporary computers would be useless without software.

E-commerce Web sites rely on many different kinds of software programs. Software makes it possible for e-tailers to ensure security, operate servers, manage customer relationships, allow customers to use online shopping carts and payment systems, and more. These many different pieces of software must be integrated so they work together seamlessly. This is often easier said than done. Each company needs to choose the right software programs and the right people to make them work together. In many ways, software serves as the glue that connects consumers with a company's core operations, from billing and payment to the shipping and storage.

Software itself has no physical properties like a computer's metal and plastic hardware components. Software consists of instructions that tell computers what to do. Although it's customary to view hardware and software as separate and distinct elements that work in tandem to make a computer operate, the two are actually enmeshed together at many different levels. As Paul E. Ceruzzi explained in *A History of Modern Computing,* "A computer system is like an onion, with many distinct layers of software over a hardware core. Even at the center—the level of the central processor—there is no clear distinction: computer chips carrying 'microcode' direct other chips to perform the processor's most basic operations."

Software normally is placed in one of two different categories: system software and applications. System software includes things like operating systems and drivers that deal with computer functions at a low level. Operating systems like Microsoft Windows, DOS, UNIX, or Linux, direct the basic functions of a computer. They provide a link between a user and the machine. Drivers are programs that support devices like printers or scanners, which are connected to the computer. Applications are software programs that users apply to various tasks, ranging from enjoyment to productivity. Applications function at a higher level than system software. Among the different kinds of applications are video games, word processing programs, spreadsheets, graphic arts programs, financial programs, and Web browsers.

Software programs are normally written in one of many different kinds of high-level programming languages like C or C++. High-level languages are much closer to actual human language than machine language, through which computer hardware accepts commands. High-level languages eventually get translated to machine language, which is numeric (consisting mainly of zeros and ones).

According to the Software History Center, contrary to popular belief, hundreds of successful software companies existed before Bill Gates and Paul Allen started Microsoft, which was the world's leading software company in the early 2000s. The industry's origin dates back to 1944 when Grace Murray Hopper and Howard Aiken wrote a program for an electromechanical computer known as the Harvard Mark I. At that time, programs consisted of sequences of holes punched on paper tape. Later, for the Harvard Mark III, Aiken developed a way for programs to be written using a keyboard. Code was written in mathematical notation and was stored on magnetic tape instead of paper tape.

FURTHER READING:

Ceruzzi, Paul E. *A History of Modern Computing.* Cambridge: The MIT Press. 1998.

Millman, Howard. "Committed to Their E-commerce Software." *Computerworld,* August 21, 2000.

"Software." *Ecommerce Webopedia,* March 29, 2001. Available from www.e-comm.webopedia.com.

"System Software." *TechEncyclopedia,* April 10, 2001. Available from www.techweb.com/encyclopedia.

"Welcome to the Software History Center." The Software History Center, April 16, 2001. Available from www.softwarehistory.org.

SEE ALSO: Linux; Microsoft Windows; Personal Computer, Introduction of; Programming Language; UNIX

SOFTWARE HOSTING

The pace of technological evolution is particularly quick in the Information Age. After purchasing new computer systems, consumers soon find them outdated. The same is true for corporate enterprises that invest large sums to purchase and implement new hardware and software solutions, only to find that continual upgrades and modifications are necessary. For reasons like these, in the early 2000s many companies were turning to application service providers (ASPs) for hosted software solutions. ASPs are third-party organizations that host software programs at one or more of their own facilities, and on their own equipment. They charge clients to use these applications remotely, either via the Internet or some other form of network access.

By using hosted software solutions from ASPs, companies—especially small and medium-sized companies with limited financial means—found a sound alternative to purchasing and implementing applications on their own. This was very important, because in addition to the licensing and product fees associated with software, companies often need to spend additional monies integrating new applications with existing ones, buying special equipment like servers, performing regular maintenance and upgrades, and so on. Depending on the situation, most of these issues are normally handled by ASPs, leaving client companies free to focus on their core business competencies.

Although integration with existing systems and compromised security were leading drawbacks, ASPs were growing in popularity because they provided companies with turnkey solutions that enabled them to avoid hassles and enter new markets quickly. They also provided scalability, which was very important for e-commerce companies in an era of constantly fluctuating market conditions. Hosted solutions can be easily scaled up or down, depending on a company's size or situation.

Virtually any software application can be offered on a hosted basis, and those related to e-commerce were especially popular. A February 2001 report from Zona Research, commissioned by the ASP Industry Consortium, found that among those using ASPs, communications, financial/accounting, and e-commerce were the three most popular uses. Other uses included human resources, customer relationship management, project management, education and training, and sales force automation.

The arrangements between clients and ASPs were very diverse in the early 2000s, much like the e-commerce industry itself. While some companies purchased a small number of hosted software applications, others looked to ASPs for total information technology solutions. Furthermore, different fee schedules and payment models existed, ranging from monthly subscription arrangements to ones involving charges per user or per transaction. Some agreements included the simple provision of a hosted application, while more sophisticated arrangements also included customer service and technical support as part of the deal.

In addition to a myriad of arrangements, diversity flourished within the ASP industry itself in terms of the range of ASP models employed. In addition to those companies that offered hosted software as one additional distribution method, "pure-play" ASPs licensed software from many different companies and then offered it as suite of programs for clients. Additionally, some ASPs were quite general, while others offered experience and applications specific to a particular industry. One common thread was that most new software companies were involved with software hosting in some way. According to some industry analysts, beginning in 2000, many venture capitalists were reluctant to or would not provide funding for new software companies that didn't at least offer hosting as an option.

One organization using hosted software in the early 2000s was the Salvation Army, a leading evangelical and social services provider known for its sound fiscal management. The Salvation Army's southern territory, which includes 2,314 centers of operation in 15 states, was able to realize a number of concrete benefits by using hosted applications from ASP ManagedOps Inc. instead of purchasing a new accounting system outright. The hosted solution met the Salvation Army's needs by connecting 1,000 geographically distributed users and enabling them to quickly consolidate financial data. At the same time, it saved them the expense of hiring 50 information-technology professionals to operate the new system.

The outlook for ASPs and software hosting was very bright in the early 2000s. July 2001 research findings from the Aberdeen Group, which included most of the aforementioned categories in which hosted software is used, projected global ASP revenues would increase from $3 billion to approximately $16 billion by 2005. Findings from IDC Research, released about the same time, projected ASP revenues would climb to $24 billion by 2005, with the United States representing the largest market. Wireless technology was an emerging area for ASPs. *Information-Week* presented figures from International Data Corp. that estimated spending on wireless access to ASPs would climb to $732 million by 2004. Another sign that ASPs are here to say was the formation of a trade association. With more than 700 members in 30 different countries, the ASP Industry Consortium was a

"global advocacy group promoting the application service provider industry by sponsoring research and articulating the strategic and measurable benefits of this delivery model."

FURTHER READING:

Cross, Margaret Ann. "Taking a Closer Look." *Internet Health Care Magazine,* July/August 2001.

"Looking for an ASP." *Modern Materials Handling,* January 2001.

"Organizational Information." ASP Industry Consortium. Available from www.allaboutasp.org.

Schmerken, Ivy. "Everybody Wants to Be an ASP." *Informationweek,* April 24, 2000.

SEE ALSO: Application Service Provider (ASP)

SPAM

Spam, the electronic version of junk mail, stirred enormous controversy and heated opinions as the Internet economy developed in the late 1990s and early 2000s. Following a visit or a transaction on a given Internet site, a user may find his or her mailbox filled with electronic announcements offering everything from cheap airline tickets to limited-offer retail sales, from faster Internet access to online pornography. While the absence of postage costs creates an almost unbearable temptation for firms to send spam, the amount of bandwidth it consumes on commercial networks and in users' mailboxes raised the ire of many Internet users and providers. According to *Forbes,* estimates place spam at up to 30 percent of all e-mail traffic.

Spam solicitors employ sophisticated search programs to locate Internet addresses not only from their own e-mail lists and that of aligned companies, but also from standard online directories. Customers routinely wind up on a spammer's list when registering for a software download or entering information at the point of online purchase. Mainstream sites increasingly allow users to opt out of having their e-mail addresses shared with others or used for the site's own promotions, but these options often remain buried in the fine print.

Overwhelmingly the most common response to unsolicited commercial e-mail is to hit the delete button, just as the bulk of unsolicited traditional mail winds up in the wastebasket. Nonetheless, spam still causes some problems for the consumer. Unsolicited commercial e-mail consumes space on computer hard drives, and lengthy download times can be costly for those Internet users who pay for Internet access by the minute. Internet service providers, to attract customers and to keep them happy, increasingly offer spam-filtering services that eliminate the spam on their servers before the customer downloads his or her e-mail. In addition, most of the major e-mail programs, such as Netscape Messenger and Microsoft Outlook, came packaged with options to sort through incoming mail and separate spam into its own folder-or in the trash. But these programs, too, cost money to develop and implement and maintain. Thus, short of eliminating spam altogether, there is little way of preventing spam senders' cost savings from being shifted to someone else—either the recipient or the operator of the recipient's mail server.

Because of all these problems and annoyances, spam has long been a dirty word on the Internet, and many Internet privacy groups, Internet service providers (ISPs), consumer groups, and even legislators, have taken strides to clamp down on spam mail. Privacy groups such as Green Brook, New Jersey-based Junkbusters, and anti-spam groups led by the Coalition Against Unsolicited Commercial Email (CAUCE) took up the fight against spam in the late 1990s. When the U.S. Congress first began debating in 2000 bills designed to limit the proliferation of spam, 16 states already had some form of anti-spam laws on their books, even as these laws varied greatly and were difficult to coordinate across state lines.

While Internet user groups and legislators increased their pressure on purveyors of spam in the early 2000s, spam supporters protested that the penalization of spam would result in severely hindered marketing opportunities. Since it entails such low costs, even the very few sales generated by spam make the bulk e-mails worthwhile, and thus companies remain attracted to it. In some cases, companies prefer to fight the negative publicity generated from spam by cleaning up their unsolicited e-mail, taking great pains to distinguish their spam as responsible and customer friendly by the measured tone and the ability, within the e-mail, for the recipient to opt out of the spammer's list. Spam activists, however, believe the most responsible measure marketers can take before soliciting via e-mail, however, is to obtain the recipient's permission before sending the e-mail, at which point it would no longer be considered spam.

FURTHER READING:

Armstrong, Larry. "Making Mincemeat Out of Unwanted Email." *Business Week,* December 18, 2000.

Blakely, Kiri. "Spam Warfare." *Forbes,* September 18, 2000.

Borrus, Amy, and John Carey. "Angry About Junk e-Mail? Congress Is Listening." *Business Week,* April 23, 2001.

Goldsborough, Reid. "Be Smart When Sending Email to the Masses." *Link-up,* November/December 2000.

Johnston, Margret. "Cracking Down on Spam." *InfoWorld,* July 24, 2000.

Philbrick, Charles L., and Matthew Z. Hammoudeh. "Lawmakers Search for Ingredients to Make Spam Less Appetizing." *Intellectual Property & Technology Law Journal,* October 2000.

Wildstrom, Stephen H. "It's Time to Can the Spam." *Business Week,* March 12, 2001, 24.

SEE ALSO: Netiquette; Privacy: Issues, Policies, Statements

SPEED-TO-MARKET

The hallmark characteristic of the Internet since its expansion into the personal and commercial realms is speed: instantaneous communication via e-mail, chat rooms, and instant messaging. In business those who were among the first to establish a quality presence on the Web were usually the ones who won and kept customers. As the Internet has grown, new Web-based collaborative applications have been developed that enable businesses, both electronic and traditional, to cut the time and cost of developing products and getting them to market. They not only give firms a natural competitive advantage; more and more customers actively seek out partner-firms who are committed to getting products to market faster. At the same time, they foster—even require—a degree of collaboration between co-workers and businesses hitherto rare. In the view of some experts, these tools are just the beginning of a revolution in how companies develop, design, and market their products.

The new electronic tools have been called Product Lifecycle Management (PLM) or Collaborative Commerce. They are designed to accelerate the movement of products to market using Web-based systems that form virtual workplaces. Collaboration is the key. The systems make it possible to share, manipulate, communicate and cooperate on data within and across organizations. They make every aspect of a project available to everyone working on it, such as members of teams working together on a particular design, or between a manufacturing business and its contractors, or for suppliers providing "in-time" service to retailers. They can be applied to virtually all phases of business: project management, product design, supply chain management and materials sourcing, and inventory control. They can be used by traditional as well as e-businesses.

One way a collaborative PML technology might increase a product's speed to market is to streamline a company's design process. The design phase in a complex project involves collaboration among numerous members of a company, as well as with staff of a contracting organization or suppliers. PML software places the work in one virtual space, rather than chopping it up into parts and distributing them to isolated, individual workstations. All engineers and marketing people have access to the same, most current information. Contracting firms are able to monitor a project's progress. The savings in time and money have a sizable impact on the costs of the final product. Forrester Research Inc. estimates that the design phase can determine as much as 70 to 80 percent of a product's cost over its life cycle.

Such systems offer a plethora of advantages to companies that implement them:

- Project data is always accessible. Everyone involved, even members of different companies or organizations participating in the project, have immediate access to plans. Team members no longer lack a crucial design element just because it is stored away in the computer—or head—of a worker who is out of the office. PML technology enables companies to build a comprehensive vault of data from the beginning of a project to its end, outlasting the presence of individual workers.

- Project data is always complete and up-to-date. Engineers, for example no longer waste time working on designs that have been made obsolete by other parts of the design process. Clients can track product specifications and offer timely input that reaches everyone. Some PML systems also permit the history of changes in a design to be tracked.

- Communication time is reduced. Suppliers can track inventory levels at their clients sites and take an active role in assuring that levels are always sufficient. Unanswered e-mail or phone calls no loner result in costly delays. Planners can sometimes hold real-time meetings in the virtual space of a PML system.

Studies show that the PML systems are extremely effective, in particular with complex systems. A study of manufacturers who used the technology by Sextant Research showed that tool changes were cut by 80 percent, inventory of finished goods by 60 percent, floor space taken up by raw materials by 25 percent, and unplanned weekend overtime by 75 percent. They also speed the movement of a product to market. Profits on a mobile phone, for example, can be boosted by as much as 50 percent if it hits the market a month ahead of schedule. Hence companies that utilize PML are extremely attractive to customers. Some analysts believe that PML may soon become a prerequisite to doing business in sectors like manufacturing.

A study by AMR Research predicted revenues in the PLM market would increase from \$1.2 billion in 2000 to about \$8 billion by 2005. Seventy-two percent of manufacturing executives surveyed by Forrester Research were convinced it would be critical to their success in the immediate future. As a result, a number of software and database manufacturers are diving into the area, including giants such as SAP AG and Oracle Corporation as well as smaller, more specialized firms like Alventive Inc., NexPrise Inc., Parametric.

Despite the undoubted benefits, there are also challenges to be met by users. Data security is critical to new product planning and marketing strategies, particularly so when they are done on networks that permit access from multiple organizations. The PML systems themselves will have to evolve in flexible frameworks that permit easy exchange of information between multiple computer systems. Another challenge will be getting engineers—used to working autonomously and without outside interference—to accept input from outside. On a broader scale, companies will be forced to implement significant changes to many internal processes, such as product design and inventory management.

FURTHER READING:

Adshead, Antony. ''The E-Supply Chain Is Only As Strong As Its Weakest Link.'' *Computer Weekly,* November 2, 2000.

Moore, Stephen. ''Web Based Design Capabilities Speed Product to Market.'' *Modern Plastics,* August 2001.

Quinn, Francis J. ''The Limited Inc.: Building a Seamless World-Class Supply Chain.'' *Supply Chain Yearbook,* 2000.

Salcedo, Simon, and Ann Grackin. ''The e-Value Chain.'' *Supply Chain Management Review,* Winter 2000.

Stackpole. Beth. ''Innovation In The Fast Lane—Web Used to Speed Products to Market.'' *eWeek,* July 16, 2001.

SEE ALSO: Product Management; Supply Chain Management

SPIDERS

When search engines (like Yahoo or Alta Vista, for example) are used to find information on the Internet, the results one receives normally come from giant indexes or databases, instead of from the actual Internet in real time. Because the Internet changes constantly, a search engine's index must be continually updated. Spiders are the tools used for accomplishing this critical task. They work in tandem with indexes and search software to comb the Web for information.

Without spiders, it would be difficult to find new Web sites, or current content on existing ones. Also called crawlers, ants, or wanderers, spiders technically are a member of the bot family—software programs that operate unattended, usually on the Internet. Therefore, spiders often are referred to as bots. However, it's important to know that spiders are not the same as intelligent agents—another kind of bot that has a wider range of capabilities, including interactivity.

Spiders travel from server to server, visiting different areas of the Internet—normally sites on the World Wide Web but also File Transfer Protocol (FTP) sites and Gopher archives. This process, known as discovery, can be performed blindly or in a more directed manner. When done blindly, a spider attempts to visit every possible Internet Protocol (IP) address—unique numbers assigned to every machine on the Internet. This approach takes longer than a directed approach, which involves searching registered domain names, or the names used to identify a site (such as Intel.com). Both approaches have advantages and drawbacks. Large search engines often employ many spiders at once, working in parallel on many different machines or servers to archive the online world in one database. After spiders report back to search engines with new information, it often takes additional time before the information is updated in the engine's index and made available for end-users to see in search results.

Some spiders record every word on a Web site for their respective indexes, while others only report certain keywords listed in meta tags. Although they usually aren't visible to someone using a Web browser, meta tags are special codes that provide keywords or Web site descriptions to spiders. Sometimes, the information listed in meta tags is incorrect or misleading, which causes spiders to deliver inaccurate descriptions of Web sites to indexes. In any case, the issue of keywords and how they are placed, either within actual Web site content or in meta tags, is important to online marketers. The majority of consumers reach e-commerce sites through search engines, and the right keywords increase the odds a company's site will be included in search results.

While spiders are critical elements of the online world, they also were a source of aggravation and controversy in the early 2000s. On the technical side, spiders sometimes slow down the performance of Web servers—the computers or applications that host Web sites—by visiting them over and over in a short period of time, sometimes as often as 100 times in a single minute. An example of this type of behavior includes spiders that search for up-to-the-minute news, or product or stock-market information. For companies without strong technical systems, spiders that exhibit this kind of behavior can cause major problems.

Another concern centered around how information collected by spiders was gathered, redistributed to other parties, and ultimately used. Part of this concern, which created related legal issues, involved security, because spiders sometimes uncover information a site's owner considers private or off-limits to the public. Another issue was misrepresentation, especially for distributors who risked having old, incorrect information about product availability or inventory displayed on other Web sites.

Because of these concerns, Web site administrators took measures to deny spiders access to their Web sites, or to certain areas within them. Administrators post specific rules about what spiders are allowed to access on their sites in an exclusion file called robots.txt, which spiders normally find and read. These rules can also be seen by the naked eye if one adds robots.txt to the end of a site's address or uniform resource locator (URL). By looking at an access log, site administrators are able to determine which spiders have visited their sites and what information they recorded. In this situation, spiders can be identified individually by name, which are given to them by their creators. This gives administrators the ability to exclude certain bots from visiting in the future, should they present a problem.

FURTHER READING:

Baljko, Shah. "Web Crawling: Sticky Issue For Distributors." *Planet IT,* November 1, 2000. Available from www.PlanetIT.com.

Champlin, Leslie. "E-firms Lure Search Spiders to Their Corner of the Web." *The Business Journal of Kansas City,* March 31, 2000. Available from www.kansascity.bcentral.com.

"Crawler." *Tech Encyclopedia,* February 1, 2001. Available from www.techweb.com/encyclopedia.

"How Search Engines Work." *Search Engine Watch,* February 1, 2001. Available from www.searchenginewatch.com.

Pallmann, David. *Programming Bots, Spiders, and Intelligent Agents in Microsoft Visual C++.* Redmond, Washington: Microsoft Press. 1999.

"Spider." *Ecommerce Webopedia,* February 1, 2001. Available from e-comm.webopedia.com.

"Spider." *Netlingo,* January 31, 2001. Available from www.netlingo.com/inframes.

"SpiderSpotting." *Search Engine Watch,* February 1, 2001. Available from searchenginewatch.internet.com.

"What's a Bot?" *Internet.com,* February 6, 2001. Available from www.bots.internet.com.

SEE ALSO: Intelligent Agents; Results Ranking; Search Engine Strategy; Webcrawler

STARTUPS

"Startups," in popular parlance, are generally understood to be companies conceived and developed as Internet-based enterprises, and they were all the rage in the economic world as well as in the popular imagination of the late 1990s. Startups were characterized by novel business models and a heavy reliance on venture capital, although that picture was changing in the early 2000s. The 2000 dot-com crash, followed by an economic slowdown, proved that despite much New Economy rhetoric the rules of business hadn't qualitatively changed with the development of information technology and the Internet business. While no analysts were proclaiming the end of Internet startups, it was clear that the era of easy money and public acclaim was at an end, and with established brick-and-mortar companies setting up their online storefronts and IT infrastructure, dot-com startups would have to work harder to succeed in the 2000s.

Most dot-com startups began with an idea, usually involving some novel concept of how to use the Internet in a way that would get people's attention. Once the idea was established, the startup set out to procure funding to bring that idea to life. For the typical startup, the development process involved a series of funding stages through which the business moved until it reached a seeming maturity that made it attractive to the public and to investors.

Angel investors are those wealthy individuals and organizations devoted to providing fledgling entrepreneurs with early-stage seed money to get an idea to its initial steps of development; in other words, to put a company on its feet so as to attract the next stage of venture capital funding. Angels throw their own money behind these startups in the hope of generating substantial returns when the company moves on to the venture financing stage or to an initial public offering (IPO). E-commerce "incubators" provide more comprehensive support to Internet startups than either angel investors or venture-capital firms. Like angel investors, incubators prop up startups that have yet to mature to the venture-capital stage. Unlike angels, however, incubators are actual businesses with expenses and revenues, not to mention physical resources such as ample office space and technical personnel employed to help the startup develop its business plan, products and services, and infrastructure. The goal—very much in keeping with the dot-com craze of the late 1990s—was to speed firms to market by accelerating the development process. In exchange for the incubator's resources and guidance, a startup will typically provide the incubator with equity in the new company.

Venture capital (VC) firms provide seed money to firms in the later pre-initial public offering (IPO) stages of development. VC companies pool the funds of institutions or wealthy individuals, which are then invested in companies in a manner determined by the VC managers. These companies tend to be less risky and aggressive in their investment behavior than angels or incubators, but usually guide their firms right up to the IPO stage. A startup may use the proceeds of the IPO to cash out the VC firm, or the firm may choose to stay on board and even forge a place in the company's management.

Each of these financing stages is likely to result in some degree of lost control over the management and development process, as angels, incubators, and VC firms attempt to protect their investments by maintaining a hand in the startup's early growth. Some financiers are more hands-on than others. One strategy for providers of seed funding was to simply throw money at as many firms as possible in the hope that one success would pay for the failures, thus limiting the resources they could devote to each firm. While this kind of funding is most likely to keep outside management at arm's length, it also failed to provide much of the added value offered in the guidance by more involved financial benefactors.

In the mid- to late 1990s, thanks in large part to the soaring stock market and the hype surrounding the dot-com business model, securing funding was a relatively easy task for Internet startups. Indeed, money was thrown behind dot-coms at a staggering rate during this period, as investors rushed to cash in on what many felt was the financial windfall of an Internet revolution. Unfortunately for dot-com startups, such good times were not to last. Once the dot-com boom turned to bust in 2000, the well of venture capital dried up in a hurry as venture capitalists of all stripes reexamined their portfolios and investment strategies. In the 2000s, according to most analysts, startups were expected to have much more coherent and practical business models and strategies before seed providers would get behind them. Startups needed to readjust their strategies to achieve a greater balance between raising capital and generating revenue. In other words, the market for dot-com startups was maturing, and competitive pressures were likely to occur earlier in the development process than in the relatively indiscriminate late-1990s.

Another novel aspect of the dot-com startup was the relation between the company and its employees. More than in most businesses, employees at dot-com startups tended to have a direct financial stake—in the form of stock options or other incentives—in the company's performance. This trend was particularly pronounced in the late 1990s, when the soaring stock market made such arrangements a particularly effective strategy for winning skilled talent to these risky new ventures. This tended to give such companies a more collaborative, but potentially more combative, atmosphere, which startup managers had to negotiate if the company were to develop as smoothly as its capital providers wished.

According to *Forbes,* startups were much more convoluted and dispersed enterprises than businesses of old. With such a premium placed on getting to market quickly with large sums of cash, the slow process of building skills and capabilities in-house was more often forsaken in favor of large-scale outsourcing of core business practices. There was no shortage of firms available to fulfill all manner of startups' needs, from designing an e-commerce-ready Web site to assembling a marketing team. In such an environment, the business was centered largely on an idea, a relatively small handful of core personnel, and access to cash, while the work was largely performed elsewhere.

Internet startups faced additional challenges in establishing their firms as viable competitors, including the building of logistics operations and distribution expertise, designing user-friendly and secure Web sites, generating customer awareness and trust, implementing effective customer-relations management, and devising efficient order-fulfillment and payment-procurement practices. Since startups generally lacked the economies of scale of their more established competitors, the allocation of resources toward these ends needed to be that much more efficient and successful, and those practices that not only fulfilled these purposes but also added value were most likely to gain a competitive edge.

FURTHER READING:

"Always Consult Your Employees—Even If You Don't Want To." *Fortune,* December 6, 1999.

Corcoran, Elizabeth. "Insta-Firms: Just Add Dollar." *Forbes,* April 17, 2000.

Finkelstein, Sydney. "Internet Startups: So Why Can't They Win?" *Journal of Business Strategy,* July/August, 2001.

Gill Roberts, Jennifer. "Restarting the Venture Economy." *Electronic Business,* July, 2001.

Hamilton, Andrea, and Maryann Jones Thompson. "High Noon." *Industry Standard,* May 22, 2000.

"Not All VCs are Created Equal." *MIT Sloan Management Review,* Summer, 2001.

Robb, Drew. "Getting a New Business Off the Ground." *Network World,* September 3, 2001.

SEE ALSO: Angel Investors; Business Models; Dot-com; Economies of Scale; Financing, Securing; Incubators, E-Commerce; New Economy; Shake-Out, Dot-com

STEMMING

In the English language, the root or underlying form of a word is called a stem. Stems serve as the basis for different variations of a word. For example, the word sell has the variants seller, selling, and sellable. The term stemming refers to the ability of Internet search engines to search for all of a word's possible variants to return more comprehensive search results. Therefore, someone searching for information about selling on the Internet could simply type in sell (or one of its variants, like seller) and the engine would return results with all possible variants of the word sell. This is obviously a great help for consumers and business professionals who conduct Internet research related to e-commerce.

Some Internet search engines, as well as the search tools and information retrieval systems on databases and other computer systems, allow users to enable or disable stemming. The manner by which this is achieved varies depending on how a search tool operates. On some applications it might involve checking a box or placing a character like the plus sign next to a word to enable the function. Conversely, a minus sign after a word, or some other character, might be used to disable the function. Stemming also can be used selectively, meaning that if someone were looking for information about selling apples, stemming could be enabled for the word selling, but not for the word apple. Therefore, irrelevant variations of the word apple, such as applet and applecart, would be excluded from the search results.

Stemming often is used as an alternative to wildcards. Wildcards are symbols that can be substituted for a character or value during an information search. By including a dollar sign after the keyword sell (sell$), a search engine might look for Internet resources containing different variations of that word (sell, selling, and seller), working in a similar fashion to stemming.

FURTHER READING:

"Stem Classes." The Center for Intelligent Information Retrieval. July 20, 2001. Available from ciir.cs.umass.edu/cgi-bin/stemming.

SEE ALSO: Search Engine Strategy

STOREFRONT BUILDERS

There are many different elements that e-commerce companies must have in place before they can conduct business successfully. First and foremost, they need to determine exactly how they will profit in the marketplace. This requires a solid business model. Additionally, successful e-tailers must map out strategic plans with goals, objectives, and tactics related to their specific business ideas. With these solid foundations in place, companies must then develop a presence in the electronic world. Although bricks and mortar are not involved, e-commerce requires online retailers to build storefronts nonetheless, albeit virtual ones. Storefront building software applications are the tools used to accomplish this critical task.

Storefront-building software allows companies engaging in e-commerce to showcase the products and services they sell on their Web sites by creating individual Web pages for them. These pages may contain visual images of products, as well as important text-based information about them including price, size, weight, color, and so on. They may be static, meaning that changes and modifications must be done at the actual page level, or dynamic, meaning that changes to page content are made in a database, from which Web pages are built on-the-fly, or as people request them. In either case, the software will provide the e-tailer with some form of interface for inputting or modifying new or existing data that eventually translates to the pages visitors see. In theory, these solutions make it relatively easy for e-commerce companies to keep the information about their offerings current.

Additionally, storefront builders usually include shopping-cart functionality. Like their counterparts in the physical world, virtual shopping carts are software tools that enable customers to keep track of items they wish to purchase. They also allow for a virtual checkout process to occur, whereby consumers are given the option to make final decisions about which products they do and do not wish to buy, and to go ahead and make purchases via credit card, an Internet payment provider, or other means. This component of the storefront builder also might include e-mail confirmations sent to customers, letting them know their order has been received.

Storefront-builder applications vary in terms of their flexibility and range of capabilities. Some allow e-commerce companies more options than others. Certain applications offer very limited Web page layouts and place limitations on how and where products are described and displayed, while others are more versatile and flexible. Beyond the ability to simply post items for sale onto Web sites, some storefront builders make it possible for e-commerce sites to recommend related products that a customer might be interested in, based on what they purchase or put into their shopping carts. Other features include the ability

to offer specific items or entire merchandise categories at sale prices, calculate sales taxes, list shipping charges with one or more parcel carriers, and so on.

In the early 2000s, there were many different ways that e-commerce companies set up shop. Some enterprises, especially very large ones with staff dedicated to information technology, often purchased their own e-commerce equipment, including servers (computers used to host Web sites, e-mail, and various forms of content), workstation computers, and other infrastructure elements. Not only did these pieces require heavy financial investments, they also required specialized resources to monitor and maintain. The same was true for e-commerce software. Licensing fees, upgrades, and troubleshooting were costs of doing business. Because of this, some companies chose to outsource different aspects of e-commerce, including storefront builders.

Hosted storefront builders involve the renting of an from an application service provider (ASP). ASPs are software companies that run software programs on their own equipment and charge customers a fee for using it. They assume all of the responsibilities for keeping these software programs current and operational. This can be a cheaper and simpler option for small or medium-sized e-commerce companies, or those who need to begin operations quickly. The alternative to using an ASP is for companies to buy storefront solutions ''off-the-shelf'' and then install and maintain them internally on their own servers. Choosing the best option was an important decision for many enterprises, and depended on the company, its situation, and its goals.

EXAMPLES OF STOREFRONT BUILDERS

One example of a storefront-builder solution for small and medium-sized companies in the early 2000s was SME Commerce, an application from Vancouver, British Columbia-based e-commerce software developer 5click. SME Commerce was a hosted solution that allowed users to handle a variety of e-commerce-related Web site functions through one interface tool. It was scalable, meaning that functions could be added or removed based on a company's needs. Companies used template-based tools to build and design product catalogs, eliminating the need for programming skills. SME Commerce's features included a shopping cart function, the ability to display images of products with descriptions in either English or French, shipping and tax calculations on both domestic and international orders, inventory management, traffic and accounting reports, a product search tool, and the ability to accept credit card payments. Companies were charged extra for some options, including listing more than 3,000 products or accessing customer support after the first three months. Among the kinds of companies using SME Commerce were a bicycle retailer, a seafood company, and a software retailer.

Actinic was another company offering storefront building solutions in the early 2000s. Although its Actinic Business product had many features that were identical or similar to 5click's SME Commerce, including design templates, Actinic Business was not offered on a hosted basis. Companies purchased this solution from Actinic and then installed it on their own servers, or on a server operated by a different host or Internet service provider. The company argued that, compared to hosted software, this approach offered more control, stability, and security to e-commerce companies.

In addition to providing features that were essential for selling products and services to consumers, like a shopping cart and credit card processing capabilities, Actinic Business also supported business-to-business e-commerce. In this regard, it offered features like inventory monitoring, customer account management, and customized pricing schedules. An independent review of the application praised it for its detailed stock monitoring features, reports, and warning features. Additionally, Actinic Business offered a great deal of flexibility for companies seeking an international customer base. This solution supported more than 30 different currencies and was able to calculate taxes for many different areas throughout the world.

Lesman Instrument Co., a distributor of process control products, used Actinic Business as an e-commerce solution to effectively deal with a customer base that was growing and spread across a wide geographic area. By making the company's catalog of more than 16,000 products available online at its Web site, www.ReadyShip.com, Actinic Business provided Lesman Instrument with an e-commerce solution that was easy to use and alleviated pressure on its sales force. It also offered Lesman Instrument's customers more flexibility and convenience, giving them the ability to customize certain configurable products. After launching the ReadyShip site, Lesman Instrument added e-commerce features to its corporate Web site, and again used Actinic Business.

Microsoft's Commerce Server 2000 was a storefront solution that was useful to large enterprises engaging in both business-to-consumer and business-to-business e-commerce. Commerce Server 2000 provided companies with one scalable package that was able to perform a vast array of different functions, including the ability to manage products and services, process financial transactions, profile customers, and manage targeted marketing campaigns. Companies were able to rely on the application's analytical capabilities to create detailed reports that provided different views of their e-commerce efforts.

Starbucks Coffee Co. is one large company that used Microsoft Commerce Server 2000 as its e-commerce solution in the early 2000s. With revenues of $2.2 billion in 2000 and more than 3,500 stores located throughout the world, a company like Starbucks requires and elaborate storefront solution; simply posting available products on a Web site is not sufficient. Starbucks initially went online in 1998 and soon experienced traffic in excess of 1 million hits each day. In 2001, Starbucks decided to upgrade to Microsoft Commerce Server 2000 from an older Microsoft product. At that time, the company had several different business goals, including making the site more effective for customers, more controllable for employees, and certain technical goals.

Starbucks' staff managed the company's Web site by using an application called the Business Desk. This was located on a special server and was accessible only to authorized staff responsible for managing promotions, making catalog updates, running reports, and so on. Microsoft's Commerce Server 2000 supported some very elaborate e-commerce features for Starbucks. One feature was personalization. This enabled customers to save basic personal information, including name, address, and credit card numbers, at the site so the information did not have to be re-entered at a later time. It also allowed them to build and save address books containing the addresses of people to whom they wished to send coffee-related gifts. Another feature was Starbucks' Gift and Taste Matcher, which recommend products based on different criteria provided by customers. Finally, custom programming enabled Commerce Server 2000 to give Starkbucks the ability to offer several different kinds of discounts, including ones for employees, shipping charges, special offers, and those tied specifically to certain promotions that required a special code to be entered.

FURTHER READING:

Kemp, Ted. "Small, Midsize Businesses Gear Up." *Internet-Week*, September 4, 2000.

"What is Storefront Software?" *Shortcutt.com*, August 13, 2001. Available from www.shortcutt.com.

SEE ALSO: Application Service Provider (ASP); E-commerce Solutions

STRATEGY, ONLINE

Businesses use online strategies to plan their Internet-based activities. Quite often, online strategies are designed to work in conjunction with other business strategies not related to the Internet. For example, traditional retailers like department store chain J.C. Penney, clothing chain The Gap, and book giant Barnes & Noble developed online strategies in the late 1990s, hoping to supplement existing revenues with online sales. In addition, leading software firms like Microsoft Corp. and Oracle Corp. sketched out their strategies for developing a leading presence on the Web by offering suites of Internet-related technology and services in addition to their more traditional products. An online strategy can also form the core of a company's business plan, as is the case with dot.com upstarts of all kinds such as Amazon, CDNow, and Ebay.

AMERICA ONLINE INC.

America Online founder Steven Case is considered by many industry experts one of the most successful online strategists. Case's early online efforts began in 1985 when he and partner Jim Kimsey established Quantum Computer Services, Inc. to offer Q-Link, a modem-based online service, to Commodore personal computer (PC) users. Case decided to extend the service to owners of PCs made by Tandy Corp. and other companies in 1987. The following year, Case offered online services to owners of IBM-compatible PCs; owners of Macintosh machines were targeted for the first time in 1989. One of the first in the industry to recognize the potential mass market for interactive online services and content, Case created America Online (AOL), a nationwide online network that included games, e-mail, and real-time chat capabilities.

In the early 1990s, Case devised a strategy designed to turn AOL into an online powerhouse. His plans called for consolidating operations to focus on IBM-compatible and Macintosh computer markets and growing the firm's subscriber base through aggressive marketing efforts such as giving AOL software to PC owners for free. The firm also began to grow its content by forging alliances with media firms. For example, to strengthen its position in the Midwestern U.S., AOL partnered with Tribune Co., publisher of the *Chicago Tribune*, to develop an online local news and information service for residents of the greater Chicago area. In 1993, AOL reached similar content deals with Knight-Ridder and CNN.

Case incorporated the development of an AOL version for the emerging Windows platform into his online strategy in 1994. When analysts began to predict the World Wide Web would render online services like AOL obsolete, Case began work on an Internet gateway, dubbed AOL.com, that would allow users to link directly to the Internet from AOL.

To broaden the firm's reach, Case expanded into international markets for the first time in 1995 by offering online services in Germany. With subscribers totaling three million, AOL moved into Canada, France, and the United Kingdom the following year. In perhaps one of his most important moves, Case played an integral role in negotiations with Microsoft, which culminated in AOL's decision to include Microsoft's Internet Explorer browser in its software, and Microsoft's decision to include AOL software on its landmark Windows 95 platform. In keeping with his growth strategy, Case reached similar cross marketing deals with AT&T, Apple, Sun Microsystems, Hewlett-Packard, and Netscape Communications. He also recruited Robert Pittman as president, chief operating officer, and head of AOL's e-commerce strategy. To develop the e-commerce potential of AOL, Pittman began working to convince online retailing giants like Amazon.com to sell their wares on AOL. Sales reached $1 billion for the first time in 1997, and subscribers exceeded ten million. AOL expanded its reach into Asia by offering services in Japan that year.

Case believed the reason for AOL's success was its simplicity. To reach as many users as possible, Case devoted considerable efforts to making AOL technology as easy to use as possible. He stated, in the October 1996 issue of *Forbes*, "If you want to reach a mainstream audience, you have to make it more plug and play. One-stop shopping. One disk to install. One price to pay. One customer service number to call."

The major flaw in Case's strategy that year was his underestimation of the technology AOL would need to handle its massive growth spurts. For example, when AOL launched a $19.95 per month flat fee program, with no limits on usage, it was unable to support the resulting surge in traffic. Users trying to log on to the service encountered busy signals more often than not, and the problems became so widespread that representatives from 36 state attorneys general offices eventually met to discuss the problem. Case responded by funneling $350 million into increasing AOL's system capacity and hiring 600 new customer service representatives. To counter the negative publicity and retain clients threatening to leave, the firm also issued refunds to those frequently unable to access their accounts.

Hoping the bulk of his troubles were behind him, Case retained his strategy of offering a user friendly and increasingly comprehensive online service to a growing number of subscribers. Continuing to grow AOL's services, as well as its subscriber base, Case oversaw two major acquisitions in 1998: instant messaging firm ICQ and rival CompuServe Inc. In 1999, AOL purchased browser software maker Netscape Communications. According to *BusinessWeek Online* writer Catherine Yang, Case's tenacity served him well. "More than any other leader in e-business, the

41-year-old chairman of America Online Inc. is responsible for bringing the Internet revolution to the masses.''

After recognizing that an increasing number of Web surfers were using things like cell phones and broadband technology, rather than PCs, to access the Internet, AOL began offering online access to wireless consumers via AOL Mobile Messenger in 2000. In 2001, Case's growth strategy culminated in the completion one of the largest mergers in media industry history—the $183 billion union of AOL and Time Warner Inc. to form AOL Time Warner Inc.

ADOBE SYSTEMS INC.

Adobe Systems Inc., one of the largest PC software companies in the U.S., used successful business strategies to emerge in the mid-1980s as a major force in desktop publishing and in the late-1990s as a leader in Web authoring tools and other Internet publishing technology. Its first move toward an online strategy came in 1994 when Adobe approached Aldus Corp., maker of PageMaker, the leading desktop publishing program for both Macintosh and Windows operating systems. Adobe was hoping to acquire a desktop publishing application for its PostScript printing language, and the $450 million merger with Aldus accomplished that goal; it also secured Adobe's position as a leading PC software manufacturer among giants like Microsoft, Novell, and Lotus. More importantly, however, the deal also positioned Adobe as a market leader in design and illustration software, image editing, and electronic document technology—areas that would prove essential to its emergence as a leader in Web publishing.

The firm began developing its online strategy in earnest in 1996 when it acquired Web tools manufacturers Ceneca Communications and converted the popular PDF into a Web format. Adobe began focusing the majority of its efforts on Internet publishing that year, developing Web versions of its most popular applications. Although sales reached nearly $1 billion in 1997, an economic downturn in Asia hurt profits in 1998, prompting Adobe to reduce management staff by ten percent and dump additional resources into creating new products, particularly those that would help strengthen the firm's foothold in the booming Web authoring tools market. Roughly one-fourth of sales, more than $207 million, was allocated to research and development. Adobe also pursued strategic acquisitions. For example, the firm bought GoLive Systems Inc., a maker of Web development and design tools, in early 1999. The purchase proved fruitful as Adobe later used GoLive technology to power LiveMotion, an award-winning graphics and animation manipulation software package for both beginning and expert Web page designers.

Believing that electronic books, particularly educational and professional publications, would become a key online market, Adobe included in its online strategy plans to develop software and hardware for displaying such books, as well as technology for protecting authors and publishers from the illegal distribution of copyrighted material, a key concern of publishers looking to transact business online. In 1999, Adobe developed PDF Merchant, allowing publishers to prevent individuals from downloading PDF files until they purchased the right to do so. Web Buy, an Acrobat ''plug-in'' program, could be attached to purchased files to impede unauthorized distribution to non-paying recipients. To further develop its e-books holdings, Adobe purchased display software manufacturer Glassbook Inc. in August 2000. Adobe Content Server, a program permitting book merchants to sell e-books in a secure format online, was launched the following year in tandem with the Adobe Acrobat e-Book Reader, a product based upon the Glassbook Reader. Along with granting users electronic access to books, with both text and graphics in PDF, the new application also offered searching, marking, annotating, and other interactive capabilities.

With strategic partnerships a key component of its strategy to remain abreast of the latest developments in Internet publishing technology, Adobe continually sought relationships with other top players. For example, in the second half of 2000, Adobe integrated its GoLive software with WebTrends Corp.'s web tracking technology to allow clients creating Web sites with GoLive the ability to monitor things like site traffic. The firm reached a similar technology integration agreement, at roughly the same time, with e-commerce software and services provider Allaire Corp.

Reflecting the success of Adobe's online strategy was the percentage of revenues in 2001 accounted for by Internet publishing products: more than 50 percent. In addition, Adobe's presence on the Internet had become widespread. According to *Forbes* columnist Elizabeth Corcoran, ''Pull up the Bridgestone/Firestone Web site to learn about defective tires and it tells you to use Adobe's free Acrobat Reader to see a graphical interpretation of the hieroglyphics on your tires' sidewalls. On ESPN's extreme sports site teeth-gritting images have been tweaked with Adobe tools. At Barnes & Noble on the Web you will find e-books viewable with readers from Microsoft and Adobe.'' In fact, more than 90 percent of all Web sites make use of Adobe's Photoshop software, while nearly three-fourths of all Web pages are designed with Adobe Illustrator.

COMPUWARE INC.

Like many technology industry players in 1997, software and computer services provider Compuware Corp. revisited its strategic plan in an effort to prepare for the future. The firm had recently acquired NuMega Technologies, Inc., one of the world's largest manufacturers of error detection and debugging software for Windows and Java systems. Because the mainframe computers Compuware's software applications were designed for had lost ground to Internet-based networks, the firm decided to reinvent itself as a Y2K troubleshooter. Essential to Compuware's strategy was the goal of retaining as many Y2K customers as possible after the millennium by offering them e-commerce services and solutions.

To set its new online strategy in motion, Compuware published *Millennium*, a newsletter about the effects the year 2000 would have on the computer industry, in an effort to position itself as an authority on the impending Y2K transition. In 1998, Compuware published *Millennium* online for the first time. To boost its e-commerce offerings, Compuware acquired CACI Products Co. in 1999. The firm integrated CACI's application capacity planning tools into its existing EcoSystems suite, enhancing its clients' ability to manage the performance of their e-commerce applications. Compuware was ultimately successful in its efforts to become a leading Y2K consultant for companies operating mainframe systems; however, a shortcoming in the firm's online strategy soon emerged. Compuware had simply overestimated how many clients would be looking to move into e-commerce early in 2000. The firm had also sorely underestimated the amount of time and level of complexity involved in training its Y2K specialists to work as e-commerce consultants. The resulting failure to meet earnings forecasts prompted stock prices to plummet that year.

Despite these setbacks, Compuware continued to work toward becoming a leading e-commerce service provider. In 2000, the firm added to its online strategy the creation of Digital Development Centers (DDCs) to offer full-scale e-commerce services to clients wishing to undertake e-business ventures. That year, two acquisitions—Montreal, Quebec-based Nomex, Inc., a provider of Web design and development services, and Kansas City-based Internet consulting services provider BlairLake, Inc.—were converted into Compuware's first DDCs. A third DDC was opened in Farmington Hills, Michigan, at the firm's headquarters complex, shortly thereafter. Other acquisitions that year included Optima, an e-business performance measuring software developer.

Along with making acquisitions, the firm's online strategy also called for the development of new e-commerce technology. One of Compuware's most

successful new products, Application Expert, was developed in response to growing demand by e-business operators, particularly those with increasing traffic, for Web site performance management tools. Application Expert allowed clients to pinpoint problems, as well as their causes, and also recommended solutions. *Network Computing* magazine named Compuware's Application Expert 2.1 the recipient of the Editor's Choice Award in 2001. Also that year, the firm unveiled a version of its Abend-AID fault diagnosis program designed specifically for e-business applications and upgraded its EcoPredictor to include the ability to use simulation to predict potential network bottlenecks. Like most players engaged in Internet-related operations, Compuware will likely revise its online strategy many times as the e-commerce landscape continues to evolve.

FURTHER READING:

''At the Epicenter of the Revolution.'' *BusinessWeek Online,* September 16, 1999. Available from www.businessweek.com.

Byrne, John A. ''Commentary: Is This Baby Built for Cyberspace?'' *BusinessWeek Online,* January 24, 2000. Available from www.businessweek.com.

Corcoran, Elizabeth. ''Go Forth and Publish.'' *Forbes,* October 2, 2000.

DeLong, Bradford J. ''Why the Valley Is Here to Stay.'' *Fortune,* May 29, 2000.

Koprowski, Gene. ''AOL CEO Steve Case.'' *Forbes,* October 17, 1996.

Simons, John. ''Steve Case Wants to Get America Online.'' *U.S. News & World Report,* March 25, 1996.

''A Theory of Case.'' *The Economist,* January 15, 2000.

Vogelstein, Fred. ''The Talented Mr. Case.'' *U.S. News & World Report,* January 24, 2000.

SEE ALSO: Brand Building; Product Management

STREAMING MEDIA

As a method of transmitting information, the Internet provides a wealth of opportunities. It wasn't long after the opening of the Internet to the general public that broadcasters and other media companies began considering how to distribute their content over the new medium and capitalize on the fresh business channels. Streaming media emerged as one of the primary methods by which these organizations broadcast their content in real time, requiring no massive and time-consuming downloads. By the early 2000s, most major media companies offered streaming media to supplement their other channels on television and radio. Television and radio broadcasters, in addition to making select features and archives available for streaming download, increasingly sought to provide live transmission of their content over the Internet, a process known as Webcasting.

ATTRACTIVE BUSINESS OPPORTUNITIES, BUT CHALLENGES ABOUND

As the Internet emerged as a central aspect of daily life in the United States, Americans spent greater proportions of their time online and, in so doing, increasingly accessed news and entertainment while plugged into the Internet. According to a report by Somerville, New Jersey-based Edison Media Research and the New York-based Arbitron Company, as of January 2001 about 61.3 million individuals—or 44 percent of all U.S. Internet consumers—had streamed Internet audio or video. Over 30 million Americans, moreover, accessed streaming media at least once a month. *American Demographics* reported that the demographic makeup of the average ''streamie'' was particularly attractive to advertisers, with approximately 46 percent receiving an annual income of at least $50,000.

Generating revenue from streaming media, however, poses problems akin to those of Internet content providers. Several options exist for purveyors of streaming media. Perhaps the most common revenue scheme was to fill the Web site from which the streaming media was accessed with advertising, bringing in money from other companies trying to catch the eye of its media customers. Pay-per-access was another, though less popular method, whereby customers agreed to pay a small fee for each individual access of a streaming media package. More commonly, companies provided subscription-based access privileges, which often combined access to streaming media with other value-added services and products.

As a model for making money, streaming media was likely to integrate elements of traditional broadcasting. For instance, Jupiter Media Metrix predicted in 2001 that streaming-audio advertisement revenue would reach $1.4 billion by 2004, meaning that streaming-audio networks will increasingly incorporate commercial slots into their programming. The 15- or 30-second commercial spots common on streaming radio and music stations in the early 2000s frequently accompanied and referenced onscreen graphics and banner ads for a multimedia advertisement scheme. The greatest factor behind the hesitance of advertisers to warmly embrace streaming-media marketing in the early 2000s was the fragmented nature of the audience. While Jupiter Research reported

in 2001 that streaming audio was beginning to hit critical mass, there was little coherence across the audience base, while streaming video, thanks to lingering bandwidth limitations among the Internet populace, was still confined to a relatively small segment of Internet users.

TECHNICAL ISSUES

Since the development of streaming media in the mid-1990s, both the compression qualities offered by software vendors and the bandwidth capabilities of the Internet have improved dramatically, resulting in greatly enhanced streaming-audio and -video quality. To stream audio or video content, it must first be converted to a digital format and compressed, or pared down in size so as to fit comfortably within limited storage space and to be transmitted without excessive delays. Usually, the content is streamed from a distributed network of servers rather than from a central point, since this method avoids clogging the server and allows for easier transmission to a number of users.

Bandwidth was a major concern to streaming-media providers. While broadband was the favored mode of streaming media, relatively few consumers had actually made the switch to broadband by the early 2000s. As a result, streaming media remained plagued by bandwidth bottlenecks at the receiving end of the transmission, often creating excessive delays and pauses in the transmission, and sometimes leading to its complete loss. The most frequent complaints lodged against streaming media, in fact, involved the choppiness of many of the broadcasts, in which the audio is momentarily scrambled or otherwise inaudible, or punctuated with skips and indecipherable noise or scrambled pictures. Producers and providers of streaming-media packages were thus encouraged to provide separate downloads catering to varying connection speeds.

The streaming-media software, stored on the user's desktop, connects with a server and accesses a streaming-media packet. Encoding software converts the media into compressed digital format, which can then be sent streaming to a media server. Because of bandwidth constraints, compression formats common for other types of media delivery are far too limited for streaming. Thus, a number of proprietary compression formats popped up in the late 1990s promising optimal streaming capabilities for specific streaming needs. The software player generally receives the stream and buffers several seconds of data at a time on the user's hard drive. Thus, these short media packets are played without interruption directly from the user's hard drive while further packets are downloading, leading to a continuous stream. This buffering helps alleviate some of the transmission glitches stemming from network clogging. In this way, lengthy downloads before the actual access of the media packages are altogether eliminated, allowing for immediate access as well as live Webcasting. Interruptions in the stream occur when, due to bandwidth or other technical shortcomings, the succeeding downloads take longer to complete than the downloaded packets take to play.

CONTENTIOUS MARKET, BUT A BRIGHT FUTURE

By the late 1990s, a handful of products emerged to dominate the market for streaming-media players, namely Microsoft's Windows Media, RealNetworks's RealAudio and RealVideo, and QuickTime. However, no clear standard emerged, and streaming media purveyors were obliged to gear their products to one or another software program, thereby fracturing the market and inhibiting the growth of streaming media. Gradually, streaming media solutions were manufactured for compatibility with more than one of these products, but the bitter rivalry between the software companies persisted.

Outside of traditional broadcasting and its attendant advertising, streaming media offered myriad other applications as well. While all uses of streaming media faced the same problems of distribution, it was finding its way into distance-learning programs, internal company training and communications, inter-business conferencing, and even the distribution of amateur films.

FURTHER READING:

Beardi, Cara. "Media Stream Hits Resistance." *Advertising Age,* February 26, 2001.

Hohenberger, Anne. "Road to NAB Multimedia: New Media on the Hunt for Revenue." *Broadcasting & Cable,* April 9, 2001.

Lam, Karen. "Stream Dreams." *American Demographics,* April 2001.

Luff, John. "Streaming Media Products: Moving from Software to Hardware." *Broadcast Engineering,* March 2001.

Mara, Janis. "Streaming Media Creating New Avenues for Advertising." *Adweek,* March 5, 2001.

Wonnacott, Laura. "When You Go Live on the Web, Take These Tips from a Real Survivor." *InfoWorld,* March 19, 2001.

Zimmerman, Christine. "Eye on Video Quality—Time Still Isn't Right For Streaming." *Internet Week,* January 8, 2001.

SEE ALSO: Bandwidth; Broadband Technology; Glaser, Robert; RealNetworks

SUBSCRIPTION MODEL

Subscription models are specific kinds of business models—tools used to describe how companies generate revenue. Business models describe how products, information, and other important elements flow, and what a company's role is during commerce. In the corporate world, there are many different ways to profit in the marketplace. Some companies sell products and services directly to consumers, some sell to other businesses, and some do both. Other companies simply are intermediaries that enable transactions between other parties, be they businesses or consumers. Because of this, there are a wide variety of different business models, from the simple and straightforward to the intricate. Companies, even those within the same industry, sometimes rely on very different business models. It is also common for a company to rely on a combination of different business models.

Although business models identify the general ways companies turn a profit, by themselves they do not necessarily map out a company's overall strategy. Specialized business models called marketing plans are used for that purpose. Marketing plans identify the specific situation a company finds itself in within a particular marketplace, the differentiating factors that set a company apart from the competition, and the individual marketing tactics used to accomplish strategic objectives.

At the heart of business models are different levels within supply chains or value chains. These chains outline the activities involved in creating value from the supply side of economics, where raw materials are used to manufacture a product, to the demand side when finished products or components are marketed and shipped to re-sellers or end-users. Companies review and analyze different steps in value chains to create optimal and effective business models, which may focus on one or more specific points within a chain.

BUSINESS MODELS AND THE INTERNET

Business models used in the offline corporate world may or may not translate to the Internet and e-commerce. Some, including the subscription model, have translated relatively well. Others that have been successful include mail-order models, advertising models, free-trial models, and direct-marketing models. The opposite also is true; some business models are unique to the Internet and have no real use outside of that environment. Internet-specific models focus heavily on the movement of electronic information and include digital delivery models and freeware models.

Online business models vary in their suitability for different enterprises. By themselves they are not enough to guarantee success in the physical or online worlds. As Jeffrey F. Rayport explains, ''Every e-commerce business is either viable or not viable. . .Business models themselves do not offer solutions; rather, how each business is run determines its success. So the success of e-commerce businesses will hinge largely on the art of management even as it is enabled by the science of technology.''

SUBSCRIPTION-BASED APPROACHES

Like its counterpart in the offline world, the subscription model applies to companies that charge subscribers a fee, normally to view text or graphical information. This model also has made inroads in the area of digital music sales. Jupiter Communications reported that subscription models would dominate this category by 2005, accounting for $980 million, compared with $531 million in downloads of individual songs. Subscription models also can apply to companies providing services rather than information. Many companies using subscription models also sell products or services offline as well.

Of the main challenges companies face when using a subscription-based approach is marketing to a much smaller niche audience that is willing to pay regular fees, as opposed to a much larger audience that might use services at no charge. In the latter scenario, the company would need to evaluate the potentially significant revenue it could make from online advertising, which also can be very unpredictable, and compare it to the more stable, steady, predictable revenue it could glean from a subscription-based approach. Marketing to a mass audience using a subscription model, while possible, was very difficult for many companies in the early 2000s.

In the category of online information, consumers initially were reluctant to pay subscription fees, even though they gladly paid for subscriptions to magazines and newspapers. Many leading newspapers tried to charge users to view content online, but eventually offered articles at no charge. Those companies that have succeeded by using a subscription-based model have done so by providing consumers with specialized or value-added information for which there is a strong demand. One example in the early 2000s was the451.com. The business community has access to a great deal of free news every day. However, making sense of it all and gleaning truly objective viewpoints can be a challenge. The451.com provided business subscribers with news analysis and commentary regarding the technology, communications, and media industries via several different channels, including the Internet and wireless services.

One company that has been able to successfully employ a subscription-based approach with a very large audience is MyFamily.com Inc. It accomplished this with its Web site Ancestry.com, where consumers with an interest in genealogy could search for information in thousands of free and subscription-only databases, which the company expected to contain more than one billion searchable records by the end of 2000. The site had more than 200,000 paid subscribers by July 2000, a significant increase from 92,000 paid subscribers only a year before.

According to MyFamily.com CEO Greg Ballard, ''subscription-based models can not only work on the Internet, but thrive with compelling content.'' Ancestry.com's databases were popular because they saved genealogists money and time compared to traditional research methods, which often involve travel or long waiting periods to receive information by mail from foreign countries or government offices. The company drove subscription growth through promotion on popular Web portal sites like Lycos, AOL, and Excite, which led to favorable rankings from several independent raters. For example, Media Metrix ranked My-Family.com Inc.'s four Web sites, which also included RootsWeb.com, MyFamily.com, and FamilyHistory.com, among the 10 fastest growing.

Providing a unique twist on traditional subscription models was Questia. By subscribing to its research service, college students were able to obtain unlimited access to an online library of scholarly journals and books, rather than having to seek out the print versions in their schools' libraries. In addition to offering text and visual information, students were able to use value-added tools like writing and search tools that helped them to better focus their research efforts. Questia planned to have more than 250,000 digital books in its library by 2004.

Unlike many companies using subscription models, Esoft applied the approach to services instead of information. Traditionally, this company sold Internet connectivity equipment to small and medium-sized businesses in 37 countries. However, in June 2000 it shifted its business model away from more expensive one-time sales to a subscription-based approach that generated more revenue per customer over time through established service contracts. Esoft also provided additional services on a subscription basis, including anti-virus protection and Internet usage reports. At the time of its announcement, eSoft cited information from Forrester Research indicating small and medium-sized enterprises, many of which prefer to outsource information technology services rather than handle them in-house, were forecast to spend $2.2 billion on subscription-based applications by 2002.

For companies in eSoft's situation, switching to a business model that relies heavily on subscriptions can be difficult in the short term. Microsoft was facing this challenge in the early 2000s when it was preparing to offer its popular Microsoft Office software via the Internet on a subscription basis. Companies risk losing higher revenues from products or services they sell off-the-shelf while they build up a large base of subscribers paying lower fees. One possible soultion is to continue using both methods, where people who purchase products on a one-time basis have an incentive to purchase the subscription-based version as well.

FURTHER READING:

''About Questia.'' Questia. May 2, 2001. Available from www.questia.com.

''Ancestry.com Fact Sheet.'' MyFamily.com Inc. May 2, 2001. Available from www.myfamilyinc.com.

Bambury, Paul. ''A Taxonomy of Internet Commerce.'' *FirstMonday,* 1998. Available from www.firstmonday.dk.

Donahue, Sean. ''Lock in your online subs.'' *Business 2.0.,* January 12, 2001. Available from www.business2.co.uk.

''eSoft Accelerating Transition To Subscription-Based Business Model.'' ESoft Inc. June 19, 2000. Available from www.esoft.com/press

McDowell, Dagen. ''Dear Dagen: Business Models Explained.'' *TheStreet.com,* September 13, 1999. Available from www.thestreet.com.

Rayport, Jeffrey F. ''The Truth About Internet Business Models.'' *Strategy+Business,* Third Quarter, 1999. Available from www.strategy-business.com.

''The451.com Bets On Content For Play.'' *Forbes,* April 5, 2000. Available from www.forbes.com.

Timmers, Paul. ''Business Models for Electronic Markets.'' *Electronic Markets,* April, 1998. Available from www.electronicmarkets.org.

SEE
ALSO: Business Models

SUN MICROSYSTEMS, INC.

Sun Microsystems, Inc. is a leading supplier of enterprise network computing products, including workstations, servers, software, microprocessors, and a full range of services and support. Through its software, hardware, and service offerings, the company is well positioned for the open, networked world of the Internet. Sun spent more than a decade working on the network capabilities of its servers, workstations, and operating systems. Its vision was captured by chairman and CEO Scott McNealy's trademarked statement, ''The network is the computer.''

As of 2001 the company had 40 percent of the high-end UNIX server market for systems costing more than $1 million. Sun's Solaris operating system is the industry's leading version of UNIX with more than 12,000 applications. UNIX was originally developed by AT&T in the 1960s and has undergone extensive refinements over time.

Throughout its history, Sun has resisted the Windows-Intel (Wintel) revolution. By focusing its efforts on optimizing Solaris for its UltraSparc RISC chips, Sun has been able to provide its customers with a continuous line of backward compatibility and scaleability. As a result, Sun's customers could start out small and then scale up their systems as they became larger enterprises.

Sun is also known as the creator of Java, the first universal software platform. The company introduced Java in 1995. Java technology allowed developers to write applications just once for use on any computer. The next year Sun licensed Java technology to all major hardware and software companies.

Sun competes primarily in the enterprise computing market. At first the company dominated the technical workstation market and led in unit shipments. More recently it has been focused on network-driven, UNIX- and Java-based system solutions for enterprise networks and electronic commerce.

HISTORY

The original Sun workstation was called the SPARCstation. It was designed by Andreas Bechtolsheim while he was a graduate student at Stanford University. Bechtolsheim's project captured the interest of two experienced computer engineers, Vinod Khosla and Scott McNealy. The three men, along with UNIX guru William Joy, formed Sun Microsystems, Inc. in 1982. In 1986 the company went public.

Sun achieved success in the 1980s by providing technical workstations principally to financial institutions and telecommunications companies. Its network file sharing (NFS) technology was introduced in 1984 and licensed free to the computer industry. In 1986 NFS technology for the personal computer brought network computing to PC users.

Sun's alliance with AT&T to develop a UNIX system for business computing began in 1987. Sun became the leader in the workstation market, with revenue reaching $1 billion in 1988, making Sun the fastest growing computer company with a direct sales force in history.

In the early 1990s the company began to address the wider commercial market of enterprise computing. It introduced two families of servers for networked enterprises in 1992 and 1993. In 1993 the company shipped its one millionth system and joined the Fortune 500. Sun's week-long Enterprise Computing Summit marked the coming of age of enterprise computing in 1994.

In 1995 Sun introduced Java, the first universal software platform. In 1996 Sun licensed Java to all major hardware and software companies. Java 2, the next generation of Java technology, was introduced in 1998. It delivered more speed and flexibility. In 1998 and 1999 Sun acquired several smaller companies that were developing Java applications, Internet connectivity, and software. Sun hoped that Java would become a universal Internet operating system and an alternative to proprietary operating systems such as Microsoft's Windows NT. Java technology running on Sun's network-based operating system allowed a Web browser to download small applications from the server to the desktop, where they would run locally.

In 1998 the Sun-Netscape alliance was formed when America Online acquired Netscape Communications. The Sun-Netscape alliance, which later became iPlanet E-Commerce Solutions, promoted Internet server software to start-up Internet companies. iPlanet products also made it easy for companies to make the transition to electronic commerce. The iPlanet Web Server was introduced at the beginning of 2000; it brought the former Netscape product up-to-date with Java technology and could run on Linux and Windows NT as well as Solaris. In 2001 Sun announced that iPlanet would become a division of Sun in 2002.

In the late 1990s Sun expanded its software product line as part of its strategy to become an independent software vendor. It acquired application server vendor NetDynamics and network software developer I-Planet, Inc. in 1998 and Forte Software for $540 million in 1999. In 1999 Sun also acquired the Star Companies for $60 million and StarOffice GmbH for $14 million, primarily for their office productivity software.

Major acquisitions in 2000 included software developer Innosoft, which Sun acquired for $42 million. Sun planned to incorporate Innosoft's messaging and directory services technology into its iPlanet Directory Server 5.0, due February 2001. Sun acquired Trustbase, the United Kingdom-based parent company of JCP, for $21 million. Its secure public key infrastructure enabling technology was used in business-to-business e-commerce.

NEW INITIATIVES, 2000-2001

In March 2000 Sun announced its iForce initiative, a group of products and services designed especially for Internet start-up companies to help them get up and running quicker and more efficiently. More than 40 partners pledged their support of the iForce initiative. Sun planned to invest $300 million in its iForce partners, which included Oracle, Inktomi, and Open Market.

Sun's chief scientist and co-founder William Joy announced in early 2001 that Sun planned to develop a foundational technology for peer-to-peer (P2P) communications called Juxtapose, or Jxta. The company intended to provide a simple code layer that would enable other vendors to build applications using P2P technology that could interact with each other. In a networked enterprise computing environment, P2P technology offered the possibility of sharing information without storing it in a central repository. Instead, P2P technology employed a crawler that searched for information on the hard drives of all the networked computers in the enterprise.

PEER-TO-PEER TECHNOLOGY. As part of its P2P initiative, Sun acquired InfraSearch, also known as Gonesilent.com. InfraSearch developed search technology for P2P communications and offered users real-time P2P information sharing. It appeared that Sun did not intend to join any other industry coalitions working on P2P technology. Research firm The Gartner Group projected that by 2003 some 30 percent of companies would have experimented with data-centered P2P applications for content distribution, and that by 2005 half of all current server-based content-management vendors would offer data-centered P2P technology.

STORAGE TECHNOLOGY. In 1998 Sun redefined data storage for networked computers by introducing an intelligent storage network architecture that delivered reliability, expandability, and cross-platform information sharing. The company significantly expanded its presence in the open storage market with the 1997 acquisition of Encore Computer Corporation's storage business. By 2000 Sun had captured about 10 percent of the storage hardware market and was the fourth-largest supplier in that market. At the end of 2000 Sun announced it would acquire HighGround Systems, a key developer of storage management technology, for about $400 million. Much of HighGround's development strategy was based on the Windows NT operating system, although under Sun it was expected that HighGround would make its storage resource management software work on the Solaris operating system as well. The 2001 acquisition of LSC, a Minnesota-based producer of file systems and data storage software, for $74 million further strengthened Sun's presence in this market.

E-TRAINING. Sun was also involved in online training through its Sun Educational Services division. In

2001 the company acquired Isopia, which developed E-learning software, for an undisclosed amount. Isopia's integrated learning-management system was a Java-based software package that managed and delivered course content over the Web. Businesses were expected to spend more than $23 billion on online training by 2004.

STRONG REVENUE GROWTH, 2000-2001

Sun enjoyed exceptionally strong revenue and income growth in its fiscal 2000, ending June 30. Overall revenue grew from $11.73 billion in fiscal 1999 to $15.72 billion in fiscal 2000. Net income increased from $1.03 billion in fiscal 1999 to $1.85 billion in fiscal 2000. For its fourth quarter in fiscal 2000 Sun's quarterly revenue surpassed the $5 billion mark for the first time. Pointing to widespread customer acceptance of Sun's products and services, Scott McNealy noted that Sun was the "undisputed number one" open system server provider.

Sun extended its product line with the acquisition of Cobalt Networks, which made low-end server appliances that ran on Linux, an open-source operating system considered a competitor to Sun's Solaris system. The $2 billion acquisition in fiscal 2001 was one of Sun's largest, and its first involving Linux. Following the acquisition, Cobalt became the server appliance business unit of Sun's network service provider organization.

A cooling of the Internet economy as well as a general economic slowdown cut into Sun's revenue growth in fiscal 2001. While the company's revenue increased to $18.25 billion, its net income dropped to $1.45 billion. Still, McNealy reported that "we continued to take share from our principal competitors." Throughout fiscal 2001 Sun continued to improve its product quality, enhance its software business, and make numerous additions to its hardware line. In software the company made key developments in its iPlanet product line and Java technologies. It expanded solutions for managing open storage networks. Sun's Solaris 8 platform won several awards as the best mission-critical server operating system. New hardware introductions included the Sun Blade 1000 line of workstations, Netra servers, the Sun StorEdge T3 arrays, Sun Cobalt appliances, and the Sun Fire midrange servers. A new high-end Sun Fire enterprise server was scheduled for delivery in the first half of fiscal 2002, as were additional UltraSPARC III technology-based products. With its focus on supporting the Internet and intranets, Sun remained a premier supplier of e-commerce enabling hardware and software solutions.

FURTHER READING:

Darrow, Barbara, and Mark Hachman. "Sun, Cobalt Deal Puts Linux in Spotlight." *TechWeb,* September 20, 2000.

Dragan, Rich. "The Scalable Solaris 8." *PC Magazine,* April 4, 2000.

Garvey, Martin J. "Strong Network Focus Makes Sun's Future Bright." *InformationWeek,* November 15, 1999.

Goodridge, Elisabeth. "Sun Shines More Brightly in E-Learning with Isopia Buy." *InformationWeek,* June 25, 2001.

Kleinbard, David. "Sun Benefits from Internet Growth." *InformationWeek,* July 26, 1999.

Kovar, Joseph F. "Keeping Current by Storing up Investments." *Computer Reseller News,* February 12, 2001.

Nelson, Matthew G., and Martin J. Garvey. "Sun Targets Net Startups with iForce Initiative." *InformationWeek,* March 13, 2000.

Petreley, Nicholas. "The Open Source." *InfoWorld,* October 2, 2000.

Rogers, Amy. "Sun's Share of AOL-Netscape Deal." *Computer Reseller News,* December 7, 1998.

Sun Microsystems, Inc. "Sun Microsystems Home Page." Sun Microsystems, Inc., September 17, 2001. Available from www.sun.com

Taft, Darryl K. "Sun Deal Bolsters P2P Technology." *Computer Reseller News,* March 12, 2001.

Vijayan, Jaikumar. "Sun Still Mines Gold from Unix Focus." *Computerworld,* January 31, 2000.

SEE ALSO: Netscape Communications; Peer-to-Peer Technology (P2P)

SUPPLY CHAIN MANAGEMENT

Supply chain management is the practice of using the Web and other information technologies to coordinate and keep track of supplies as they move through a business's supply networks. The simultaneous goals of supply chain management are to quickly meet customer demand—by, for instance, fulfilling their orders in a timely fashion and offering them accurate projections—and to minimize costs by reducing inventories and making supply chains optimally efficient. In an age of increased outsourcing and larger webs of business relationships in the global economy, supply chains have become particularly complex, making them increasingly difficult for individual firms to control. The proliferation of electronic business relationships, in the forms of extranets and online business-to-business exchanges, made supply chain management both tempting and technically feasible. Supply chain management was thus a quickly emerging, if still problematic, element of business-to-business e-commerce in the late 1990s and early 2000s.

Electronic management of business supply chains coordinates all business partners in the supply chain over electronic networks and gives all parties an up-to-the-minute overview of all available inventories. Technically, supply chain management ''Web-enables'' existing enterprise resource planning (ERP) systems, which include everything from product catalogs to order files to inventory databases. Companies take their back-end databases and other systems and integrate them into a Web portal shared across the entire supply chain network. In this way, companies can feed all essential information across the entire supply chain. Most such systems closely detail all components as they move through the system—including the quantity and precise time of parts shipped through the supply chain. In this way, suppliers can log onto secure Web sites and determine exactly how many components to send to the factory, and the companies are aware of exactly what they need to complete projected orders in the most efficient fashion.

Supply chain management systems can take many forms. The most basic route is to simply coordinate existing databases over supply networks using extranets. More sophisticated systems, however, are the specialty of a new breed of service providers that specialize in software and systems management geared specifically toward supply chain management. These companies, such as the Santa Barbara, California-based SupplySolution Inc., one of the most prominent names in the field, simply contract with companies to receive their inventory data and organize it for optimal management across networks.

The layers of potentially useful information are many. By implementing comprehensive databases of components and integrating them into the supply chain management system, companies have the opportunity to cut costs at almost every corner. For instance, by detailing all the components that go into a completed product, firms can monitor each individual component to determine its optimal production and shipping level, determine which components are moving below peak efficiency, and coordinate their entire supply lines to bring them into equilibrium at the greatest level of efficiency. From there, the savings can spread through their operations, as, for instance, firms that have successfully cut down inventories can cease renting warehouse space to store excess components.

Supply chain management, in addition, provides all companies connected in a supply partnership with the greatest level of transparency. That is, all orders and requests are readily accessible to all connected parties, which not only facilitates the transaction process by providing all companies with information, but also increases accountability, as all companies are made aware of each movement through the supply chain and can spot shortcomings. In this way, business partnerships are forced to become more honest, and there is less room for laziness or skimming off the top.

There was a defensive logic to building supply chain management systems as well. By the mid-2000s, e-commerce was expected to reach some $6.8 trillion, and there was concern that existing supply chains would be unable to accommodate such volume. In order to fully take advantage of e-business opportunities, businesses will feel pressured to upgrade their internal and external systems architecture to keep their supply chains in pace with e-commerce as a whole. And evidence into the early 2000s lent credence to the view that existing supply chains were a drag on e-commerce. While companies were competent at taking orders online, order fulfillment left a great deal to be desired. The convenience of e-commerce adds pressure for more sophisticated supply chains as well. Since sales procured over the Internet are more difficult to project, companies are harder pressed to order adequate supplies far in advance.

One of the barriers to supply chain management is that, for the system to live up to its potential, all connected parties need to operate on a common platform. The investment into new systems is substantial enough, and becomes more complex when all players need to coordinate those investments and convert their existing systems to compatibility with the new platform.

A number of dangers lurk in adopting supply chain management. For instance, companies may be reluctant to align themselves too closely to any particular firm if it means closing off their options to shop for supplies elsewhere. Since setting up an efficient and worthwhile supply chain management system calls for a major investment, companies need to be sure that those firms with whom they establish such a relationship are solid and will prove compatible partners over the long term. Relatedly, companies may be uneasy about tying their own strategies too closely to those of other companies since such an arrangement could impede the firms' autonomy and limit their ability to shift direction should the need arise. Businesses also need to be wary of overextending the supply chain management relationship with those firms that also act as competitors in other fields or that may one day become competitors. Sharing intimate company details could give such a competitor an unfair advantage.

FURTHER READING:

Greengard, Samuel. ''New Connections.'' *Industry Week,* August 13, 2001.

Lundegaard, Karen. ''Bumpy Ride.'' *Wall Street Journal,* May 21, 2001.

Mahoney, Chris. ''Global Supply Chains.'' *Executive Excellence,* August, 2001.

SEE   Business-to-Business (B2B) E-commerce; Channel
ALSO: Transparency; Enterprise Resource Planning (ERPs);
Fulfillment Problems; Intranets and Extranets; Order
Fulfillment; Shipping and Shipment Tracking

SYSTEMS ANALYSIS

During the normal course of doing business, companies engaging in e-commerce are faced with a wide variety of challenges or problems. These vary depending on many factors, including the way a company is structured to profit in the marketplace, the industry in which it operates, legal requirements for tracking or reporting information, and more. A process called systems analysis is used to create new solutions to these challenges, or to improve solutions that already are in place. Solutions normally involve the use of information systems or software applications, which are developed with specific issues or challenges in mind.

Information systems themselves can vary in form and type, and involve various elements like databases, software applications, and computer hardware. Among the different kinds of information systems are transaction processing systems (TPS), which involve the movement of data as it relates to things like payment or inventory; management information systems (MIS), which include databases that managers rely on to evaluate and organize operations; decision support systems (DSS), which are similar to MIS but focus more heavily on supporting a user's actual decision; and office automation systems (OAS), which allow employees to manipulate and distribute data with productivity tools like word processors, e-mail, electronic scheduling, and spreadsheet programs.

Systems like MIS and DSS, which helped e-commerce executives make faster or better-informed decisions, were especially valuable in the early 2000s. At that time, the pace of Internet business was very quick. Combinations of different conditions—including the impact of new technologies, customer demands, government regulations, legal issues, and pressure from investors—changed frequently and could impact the success or failure of a company or industry in a short period of time. TPS systems were another example of critical e-commerce systems. The ability to engage in fast, secure transactions and integrate them with many different areas of an enterprise (including accounting and inventory) was central to its success.

Professionals generally known as systems analysts are responsible for understanding what a company's business challenges are, how they change over time, and how these issues translate to or affect systems. More specifically, systems analysts evaluate data input, flow, processing, storage, and output as related to business challenges. To accomplish this, analysts work with an organization's management team as well as those who currently or eventually will use the solution or application and engage in information gathering and problem solving. As explained in the *Journal of Systems Management,* ''With this information, the systems analyst, working with other MIS personnel, defines the requirements which are used to modify an existing system, or to develop a new system. The systems analyst identifies and evaluates alternative solutions, makes formal presentations, and assists in directing the coding, testing, training, conversions, and maintenance of the proposed system.''

HOW SYSTEMS ANALYSIS WORKS

Ideally, system analysis begins by developing an outline or map of the organization and how it functions. According to the *Journal of Systems Management,* ''A Map lets management see how functions are performed and an Analyst see what to do first and where to go afterward. A Map may suggest where productivity improvements might be made and even where an analysis could begin. For example, there may be duplication of effort, or effort not tied to the rest of the business or even similar effort under split management leadership.''

After developing a clear picture of a business and the situation in which it operates, analysts draft and present project proposals prior to the beginning of the systems analysis process. Because e-commerce can involve many different business or operating units, especially within a large organization, system projects often require the ultimate approval of a committee, rather than just one person. Included in a good proposal are several different elements, including a detailed description or explanation of the business problem or situation; an explanation of why the problem is important to the organization; several possible solutions; how computerized information systems might be used as a part of a solution; and a list of the individuals who have an interest in or knowledge about the problem or situation.

There are six problem-solving steps involved in producing a new computer information system, collectively known as the systems development life cycle (SDLC). Each step or phase involves different tasks, which may take place over several phases. Additionally, it may be necessary to revert to a previous phase during the analysis process. Although the following is a representative overview of the systems analysis process used by many organizations, much like the general title of systems analyst, the SLDC process may vary from company to company. The first step in SDLC is preliminary investigation, in which the problem is defined and investigated. Next, characteristics of an existing system are evaluated, along with the requirements of the proposed system. A general systems design is then developed, followed by the creation of the new system. System installation, which involves replacing an existing system with the new one, then occurs. Finally, systems evaluation and monitoring take place, with the ultimate goal of enhancing performance and increasing functionality.

FEASIBILITY

One potential problem with any system is that it may become more cumbersome than the problem it is trying to solve, in terms of the amount of resources required to properly maintain and develop it. A system may lead to the development of new problems that, when considered in sum, make its ultimate development a bad idea. Systems analysts often conduct feasibility studies to review factors like the problem or situation itself; costs versus benefits; the needs of users; and the resources required to provide a solution. Depending on the situation, this information may be collected in a number of different ways, including interviews with managers, customers, users, and other employees; questionnaires; monitoring or observing users of existing systems; collecting and reviewing different manuals, reports, and documents; and sometimes simulation or modeling of existing systems. The ultimate goal is to determine which solutions are worth pursuing, and of those, which hold the most potential for the organization.

FURTHER READING:

Bauer, Michael W. ''The Very Beginning of Analysis and Development: The Map.'' *Journal of Systems Management,* December 1992.

Farah, Badie N. *Business Information Systems: Development and Implementation* 2nd ed. Needham Heights, MA: Simon and Schuster, 1996.

Kendall, Kenneth E. and Julie E. Kendall. *Systems Analysis And Design.* 1999. Upper Saddle River, New Jersey: Prentice Hall.

Misic, Mark. ''The Skills Needed by Today's Systems Analysts.'' *Journal of Systems Management,*. May/June 1996.

Schuptheis, Robert, and Mary Sumner. *Management Information System.* 4th ed. Chicago: Richard D. Irwin, 1998.

Stair, Ralph M. *Principles of Information Systems: A Managerial Approach.* 2nd ed. Boston: Boyd and Fraser Publishing Company, 1996.

''System Analysis & Design.'' *Techencyclopedia,* May 7, 2001. Available from www.techweb.com.

''Systems Analyst.'' *Ecommerce Webopedia,* May 9, 2001. Available from e-comm.webopedia.com.

Zwass, Valdimir. *Foundations of Information Systems.* Chicago: Richard D. Irwin, 1998.

T

TALENT, RECRUITING AND RETAINING

The novel business practices, environments, and structures—not to mention the new range of desired skills—that characterize e-commerce have created a range of challenges and concerns for companies in their attempts to recruit and retain talented employees. To attract and retain the best available workers, professionals, and executives, firms need to pinpoint the appropriate combination of attractive salaries, enticing financial and other incentives, challenging and engaging projects, a healthy and inviting atmosphere, and meshing of personalities.

The challenge of drawing and maintaining quality talent extends to all levels of the e-commerce organization, from technical employees to chief financial officers. Since, for all such personnel, the novelty of e-commerce presents many risks—alongside potentially dramatic rewards—companies worked to devise strategies designed to highlight the opportunities and benefits of their way of doing business. According to *InfoWorld,* most businesses looking for e-commerce and information technology (IT) talent focus on three primary groups: technical professionals, creative professionals, and business strategists. Technical professionals, for instance, are most likely to be skilled in architectural issues like supply-chain management systems or user interfaces. Creative professionals are those who specialize in innovative technological and commercial strategies and applications. Business strategists tend to concentrate on turning the creative possibilities and technical capabilities into a practical and profitable business strategy.

E-commerce firms have a number of methods for seeking out talented individuals, including Web-based employment sites, local newspapers, applications, internal employee referrals, college-campus recruitment efforts, and others. Moreover, firms may choose to maintain their own recruitment staff, sending out employees with the specific task of locating and attracting skilled workers, or they may choose to outsource such responsibilities to recruitment specialists.

Companies seek out personnel with a range of knowledge and skills in such areas as Web-site development, information-technology architecture, electronic customer-management applications and customer-relations systems, supply-chain management systems, intranets and extranets, and much more. Since the work of skilled e-commerce and IT workers and managers often coincides with that of management and IT consultants, many e-commerce companies partner with consulting firms, particularly in the initial phases of the business—the startup and seed periods, for instance. This gives e-businesses a leg up in devising their e-commerce strategies with experienced personnel to help guide the development process. In addition, it provides companies with an idea of what kind of skills to look for when embarking on their own recruitment ventures.

Recruiters in the 1990s and early 2000s had to contend with the tightest job market in decades, and thus competition for talent was heavy. Even as the economy slowed in the early 2000s, positions were abundant for skilled workers who could help companies stake a claim to the still-emerging global e-commerce market.

But the practices of recruitment and retention were fraught with difficulties. Particularly after the dot-com bust of the early 2000s, companies, executives, and employees were far more wary of e-commerce firms—particularly pure-plays—that seemed too good to be true. In the late 1990s, as e-commerce soared and dot-coms' stock valuations went through the roof, e-commerce firms had a relatively easy time of attracting hot talent by such means as highlighting the novel and relaxed work environment, the opportunity to be at the forefront of the dominant new business and technological trends, and the lure of stock options, which often carried as much weight as basic salary in the stock-market boom of the day. By the early 2000s, however, talent was far more likely to be skeptical and attempt to separate the wheat from the chaff. Suddenly, once-hip and attractive business models were deemed questionable and suspect, forcing e-commerce companies to alter their recruitment and retention strategies to suit their new, more difficult environment.

Even the image a company projects is an important consideration in any recruitment strategy. Firms need to ask themselves what kind of talent they hope to attract, and then consider what kind of company image will be likely to draw such candidates. Does the firm promote its fun atmosphere or its placement at the cutting-edge of technological development? Is it a serious, business-like environment? Is it internally competitive or collaborative, or some mixture of the two? These are among the features an employee will try to identify, and the image a company projects can greatly influence the type of employees that are drawn to it. Thus, while it's important to project an image that will give a company a competitive edge in the recruitment wars, it's also paramount that they not stray too far from the truth, or the talent may prove a poor fit.

The qualities that companies seek out, particularly in their senior management, altered as well as the Internet economy matured. Whereas in the late 1990s boom younger personnel with fantastic unorthodox ideas were all the rage, by the early 2000s companies were once again seeking out seasoned management teams; experience, rather than novelty and excessive optimism, were again in vogue. In a recession-oriented business environment, companies increasingly sought out managers with a knack for focusing on the bottom line and delivering a firm to profitability, whereas in the boom days there was little such concern, and companies saw growth possibilities as virtually without limit.

Demographic considerations were also expected to play a prominent role in companies' recruitment and retention strategies. While, in the early 2000s, the World War II generation of leadership was mostly retired and the baby boomers assumed the responsibility of spearheading corporate America, it was increasingly clear that, as the economy expands well into the 21st century, there simply weren't enough members of Generation X to take the place of the baby boomers. Analysts hold that this will intensify cross-border competition, as companies seek out the top talent from around the globe to help the firms succeed in an increasingly integrated international economy.

According to the *InternetWeek's,* "Transformation of The Enterprise" survey, about 76 percent of 300 information-technology managers insisted that e-commerce and other Internet-related endeavors increased their workload, and, while 44 percent reported increasing their IT staff to accommodate such projects, nearly two-thirds nonetheless still felt they were short on skilled IT talent. Forrester Research, meanwhile, reported that 58 percent of polled business executives rate the recruitment of skilled IT staff as the primary obstacle to implementing e-commerce strategies.

This combination of skills shortage and heightened demand for e-commerce know-how resulted in dramatically escalating payrolls, according to the survey; the mean salary increase reported by the 300 IT managers was a hefty 17.2 percent. RHI Consulting's 2000 Salary Guide listed average salaries for various e-commerce specialists, reporting that Web developers could expect to earn an annual salary between $48,750 and $71,250; an Internet programmer earned from $50,000 to $72,250; and e-commerce specialists raked in between $53,000 and $82,500. And, as *InfoWorld* pointed out, chief executives that signed on with pre-initial public offering (IPO) firms could potentially earn far in excess of these figures, even before stock options. Thus, companies looked to make their recruitment and retention strategies as efficient as possible to minimize costs and avoid turnover. With such substantial investments at stake, firms could ill-afford haphazard or outdated strategies for drawing and keeping talent within their ranks.

Recruitment, of course, was only one part of the problem. Once companies collar the best IT talent they can get, the challenge was to keep them. The late-1990s dot-com frenzy was marked by rapid employment turnover, as hotshot IT workers jumped ship to follow the latest recruitment offers—and often the greatest prospects for stock options. Companies resort to all manner of activities to keep employees happy, including financial incentives; lenient policies on work hours, dress code, and other traditional business standards; office lunch parties and casual Fridays; flexibility related to workers' family and personal needs; and so on. Retention strategies frequently also include company-sponsored training programs to keep IT workers on top of the latest technological developments pertinent to their positions. This serves not only to keep the company in step with its competition, but provides the employees with continuing challenges and the opportunity to expand their range of skills.

FURTHER READING:

Connet, Mel, and Liz Bicknese. ''Basic Skills Back in Demand.'' *Financial Executive,* July/August, 2001.

Fisher, Susan E. ''Scoping for Hot Talent.'' *InfoWorld,* April 3, 2000.

Fryer, Brownyn. ''Who Wants to be a Millionaire?'' *Computerworld,* May 1, 2000.

Gallagher, Terry. ''The War for E-commerce Talent.'' *Consulting to Management,* May, 2000.

Howle, Amber. ''IT Skills Shortage Leads to Creative Recruitment Ideas.'' *Computer Reseller News,* December 6, 1999.

Villano, Matt. ''Fighting to Retain E-biz Talent: Dot-coms Fight Fear Factor of Mergers, Shakeouts.'' *eWeek,* October 9, 2000.

Wagner, Mitch. ''Casting A Wide Net For Web Talent.'' *InternetWeek,* October 30, 2000.

SEE ALSO: Workforce, E-commerce

TAXATION AND THE INTERNET

The commercial Internet, by the 21st century, had already substantially transformed business transactions, both in the United States and worldwide. In the early 21st century, similar changes were expected in the realm of taxation. Despite the financial downturn of the early 2000s and the collapse of many dot.com start-ups, projections for rapid growth and burgeoning e-commerce profits suggest that the financial stakes involved could be exceptionally high. Thus, the nature of taxation in e-commerce was the source of no small amount of debate.

The very nature of e-commerce complicates the issues surrounding taxation. The lack of physical connection between the parties in online transactions renders collection of taxes difficult. Many items sold online, such as music, videos, and software, can be downloaded directly from the Web, making the tracking of their dissemination problematic. Furthermore, such items are considered intangibles, which historically have been exempt from U.S. sales taxes. States usually tax income where it is earned, but the Internet often obscures the identity and location of individuals or businesses engaged in taxable activities. The development of anonymous e-currencies could facilitate tax evasion. Finally, the Internet aids the mobility of firms and workers, who can easily transfer to low-tax destinations or tax havens. Many large-scale, chain retailers have created independent, online businesses with a physical presence in just one state to avoid collecting sales taxes elsewhere.

Consistent data about the financial ramifications of e-commerce taxation are difficult to find. A University of Tennessee study estimated that states and localities could lose $10 billion in sales tax revenue to untaxed e-commerce by 2003. However, Forrester Research reported that in 1999 these jurisdictions experienced only $525 million in lost sales tax revenue. A University of Chicago economist concluded that if sales taxes were applied to e-commerce transactions, online purchasing could decrease by 24 percent.

U.S. E-TAX POLICIES: LEGAL AND CONSTITUTIONAL DIMENSIONS

The Constitution's Commerce Clause grants Congress the power ''to regulate commerce...among the several states.'' However, the formulation of state and local tax policy has traditionally been left to those jurisdictions. If the federal government preempts the states' ability to set their own tax policies, some argue it would violate the principles of federalism. Congress can regulate activities that ''substantially affect'' interstate commerce, but it cannot order states to enforce federal regulatory programs, since that infringes upon state sovereignty. A state's authority to regulate commerce within its borders is limited by the Due Process Clause of the 14th Amendment and the Commerce Clause. The latter gives states the jurisdiction to tax commercial sales only when sufficient contact between the buyer and seller exists within the state.

Generally, sales of intangible property are not taxed in the U.S. But technology now permits the conversion of many tangible goods, such as books and recordings, to digitized content that can be delivered entirely online. The taxable status of such content remains uncertain.

The Supreme Court established two important legal precedents for the e-taxation debate. In 1967, it ruled in *National Bellas Hess v. Illinois* that a state could only tax commercial transactions when the seller maintained a physical presence, or ''nexus''—an office, a warehouse, of a sales agent—in that state. Requiring out-of-state vendors to cope with the complexity of various state and local sales tax systems constituted a barrier to interstate commerce. In 1992, the Court reinforced this decision in *Quill Corp. v. North Dakota,* which involved state sales taxation and out-of-state mail-order vendors. It reiterated the nexus requirement, but noted that Congress could pass laws requiring remote vendors to charge state sales taxes on all sales, if Congress provided national guidelines to simplify state sales tax collection.

This constitutional and legal framework affects e-commerce taxation in several ways. Since consumers can purchase goods and services online from e-vendors located anywhere in the U.S., questions of whether the federal or state government is the appropriate authority to generate tax regulations come to the forefront. The parallels between catalog sales and e-commerce transactions led officials to apply the *Bellas Hess* and *Quill* rulings to online sales taxation. However, the Internet's lack of geographical borders and the difficulty of defining what constitutes a ''physical presence'' or ''substantial nexus'' between e-buyer and e-vendor complicate this practice.

To gain time to generate comprehensive e-taxation policies and to allow unfettered growth of e-commerce, Congress passed the Internet Tax Freedom Act (ITFA) in 1998. ITFA placed a three-year moratorium on the creation of ''discriminatory and multiple'' e-commerce taxes by states and localities. It also banned federal sales taxes of Internet transactions, promoted tax-free international e-commerce, and established an Advisory Commission on Electronic Commerce to develop national guidelines for e-taxation. But the Advisory Commission failed to offer any official recommendations to Congress and the matter remained inconclusive.

The federal government levies excise taxes on Internet service transactions such as airline ticket sales and on telecommunications. Internet access is taxed in nine states and downloaded information and software in 29. Most states levy corporate income taxes on profits generated from providing Internet access and from the online sale of goods and services. States usually ''source'' income from e-commerce sales of tangible property to the customer's state of residence, and income from the sale of intangible digital content to the vendor's home state. The federal government taxes income earned through e-commerce in the same manner as income earned via traditional channels.

Numerous e-commerce taxation schemes have been proposed, many as legislative bills submitted to Congress. Possible solutions include:

- permitting state and local e-sales taxes if states simplified and standardized their tax systems

- banning all e-commerce taxation

- instituting a national e-commerce sales tax

- creating a centralized, third-party collection system for state sales taxes, to be used by all online vendors

- establishing a national value-added tax (VAT) levied on all household consumption of goods and service, regardless of how they are sold.

ARGUMENTS FOR AND AGAINST E-COMMERCE TAXATION

Supporters of e-taxation argue that state and local governments, which rely on sales-tax revenues for one-third to one-half of their operating funds, will face serious income shortfalls if e-commerce remains untaxed. Sales-tax revenues pay for essential services such as schools, fire and police departments, public libraries, and health care. If budget needs can't be met, states will either shift the tax burden to other sources, such as telecommunications, energy, income, or property taxes, or simply cut services. And as online retailers drive traditional merchants out of business, property values and property taxes would decline, leading to greater revenue losses. Tax advocates also state that keeping e-commerce tax-free unfairly disadvantages traditional vendors who must pay sales taxes, while online retailers enjoy a competitive pricing edge.

In response to complaints that the thousands of separate U.S. tax jurisdictions create a taxation universe too complex for e-vendors to cope with, tax supporters counter that software could be developed that automatically identifies the applicable e-sales taxes for all taxable goods or services in each ZIP code. Tax proponents also claim that the Constitution guarantees states the right to collect tax revenues; thus legislation such as ITFA infringes on state sovereignty.

Finally, taxation proponents argue that tax-free e-commerce benefits the wealthy. Studies identify a growing gap in the percentage of higher-income versus lower-income households that utilize the Internet (the ''digital divide''). Since lower-income groups have less access to the Internet, they cannot avoid sales taxes by purchasing online.

In comparison, e-tax opponents claim that taxing e-commerce would smother its expansion and impede online innovations. This argument formed the main impetus behind the ITFA. Opponents also point out that the U.S. contains roughly 7,000 state and local sales-tax rates in 45 states and Washington, D.C. In addition, taxable items are classified differently in different jurisdictions. It would cost far too much for e-retailers to calculate, collect, and remit sales taxes under such conditions. Opponents also question why e-vendors located in one jurisdiction should subsidize goods and services located in another.

Anti-tax arguments propose that Internet taxes imperil America's international competitiveness, since domestic e-businesses would relocate to evade them. And e-sales taxes would hamper overall U.S. economic growth, since e-commerce was one of the mainsprings of the 1990s boom. Finally, they point out that sales tax revenues lost to e-commerce have been so small as to have little effect on state revenues.

INTERNATIONAL E-COMMERCE AND TAXATION

Discussion of e-commerce taxation in the global arena primarily concerns industrialized nations, where most e-businesses are based and where the vast majority of online transactions occur.

As of 2001, downloads of digital goods made in the EU were subject to value-added tax (VAT) rates of the supplier's home country, while physical goods ordered online were assessed at VAT rates of the country in which they were consumed. Goods and services purchased from EU vendors by non-EU customers were generally zero-rated. Non-EU retailers selling digital goods and services to EU purchasers were not subject to VAT, giving countries such as the U.S. and Canada a pricing advantage in international e-commerce. New legislation was under consideration by the European Commission (EC) and the Organization for Economic Cooperation and Development (OECD) in the early 2000s. It was intended to ensure that online services and digital goods sold to individuals would be taxed where they are consumed. Non-EU vendors would register for VAT in one EU state and account for VAT on items and services delivered to EU residents at that country's rate.

International authorities are concerned about the potential tax revenue losses that may accompany untaxed e-commerce. However, they have proceeded cautiously regarding international e-commerce taxes. As in the U.S., foreign governments and industries have been loath to retard the early expansion of e-commerce, and special taxes levied only on e-commerce have met widespread rejection.

FURTHER READING:

Asher, Mukul. "Globalization and Tax Systems." *ASEAN Economic Bulletin,* April 2001.

Burnes, Gary. "Borderline Cases." *Financial Management,* May 2001.

Golden-Mumane, Laura. "E-Commerce and Internet Taxation." *Searcher,* June 2000.

Goolsbee, Austan. "In a World Without Borders: The Impact of Taxes on Internet Commerce." *Quarterly Journal of Economics,* May 2000.

Hellerstein, Walter. "Deconstructing the Debate Over State Taxation of Electronic Commerce." *Harvard Journal of Law & Technology,* Summer 2000.

Huddleson, Joe. "Internet Taxation Issues Remain Unanswered." *Tax Adviser,* February 2001.

Lukas, Aaron. "Should Internet Sales Be Taxed?" *USA Today Magazine,* January 2001.

"The Other Tax Battleground of 2001: The Internet." *Business Week,* February 19, 2001.

Powell, David. "Internet Taxation and U.S. Intergovernmental Relations: From Quill to the Present." *Publius,* Winter-Spring 2000.

Weidenbaum, Murray. "The Fundamental Internet Tax Debate." *Washington Quarterly,* Winter 2001.

SEE ALSO: Digital Divide; Fraud, Internet; Internet Tax Freedom Act

TECHNOLOGY TRANSFER

One of the main ways in which the Internet and e-commerce provide value is through the transfer of information between different entities, be they consumers, businesses, non-profit organizations, government agencies, or entire industries. Networks like the Internet allow information to flow freely across the well-defined structures to which these entities normally conform. They foster collaboration, giving birth to new discoveries and ideas. When intellectual property or technology from one organization or industry is discovered by a party in a different field and used or applied in a novel or unintended way, the phenomenon is called technology transfer. Although technology and e-commerce often play important roles in the technology transfer process, the central foci normally are ideas and intellectual property, such as access to patented information. However, it also may involve cooperative research, exchanging professionals with different skills, sharing facilities, and providing access to services.

The success of technology transfer can be measured in different ways. On the very simple end, this may involve the improvement or enhancement of something that already exists, such as a product or manufacturing process. Reduced costs and improved organizational efficiency are other measurable benefits. However, initiatives resulting in new markets, products, or services frequently are the most lucrative and receive the most attention. These initiatives can be measured in terms of market share percentages or in monetary terms.

The human factor also plays a role in determining how successful technology transfer initiatives are. As *Industrial Management* explained, "Integrating the diverse organizational experiences and skills and focusing on serving customers with new, cutting-edge products appears a lot easier when technology transfer-related decision-making power is equitably shared, strong feelings of reciprocal interdependence exist, the level of decentralization is high, and team leaders understand the human interaction issues of the process. Failure to understand these central features of technology transfer results in sluggish development of new products."

Because technology transfer is a general phenomenon, it can happen in virtually any industry or field. Individual inventors and businesspeople, smaller and medium-sized businesses, and large corporations all engage in and benefit from technology transfer. Universities, where a great deal of basic-science and high-tech research takes place, are another important source of technology transfer. Some universities have departments devoted exclusively to this goal, staffed with individuals who facilitate the transfer of research ideas to real-world applications that benefit society. These technology transfer departments perform many roles, including that of record keeper, marketer, and negotiator. Universities receive royalties or flat fees for the patented technologies they market, although in many cases these amounts are small because new technologies are new and unproven, resulting in a risk for marketplace organizations.

The Internet and e-commerce played important roles in the facilitation of e-commerce. In the early 2000s, many different organizations established an online presence to promote transfer. One such organization was the Pantex Plant. Located in Texas, Pantex assembled and disassembled the United States' nuclear weapons, and was also involved in interim plutonium pit storage, high explosive research and development, and evaluating weapons. At its Web site, the organization indicated that it sought to share the knowledge gained from more than 40 years of such experience with American industry.

Like Pantex, many large corporations have information they wish to share with other parties. Scores of companies have patented ideas that are of no immediate use to them, and therefore go unused. Converting these into sources of revenue represented an area of great opportunity. In the early 2000s, several online marketplaces devoted to the exchange of intellectual property and ideas offered a solution. These sites functioned as third-party brokers or intermediaries. They charged people fees to belong to their service and search for intellectual property that was for sale, and in some cases received a percentage of or royalties from deals that resulted from the service. The IP Network, Patent & License Exchange, TechEx, and Yet2.com were among these exchanges. In theory, these intermediaries made it more convenient for buyers and sellers to find and access information about one another.

Founded by a member of the DuPont family and a former Polaroid executive, Yet2.com had a large number of sponsors including Procter & Gamble Co., Ford Motor Co., the Boeing Co., and Motorola Inc. The site involved all research and industry sectors and was valuable to scientists, researchers, and technology officers. In 2001, Yet2.com connected DuPont with technology researcher Batelle, resulting in an arrangement in which DuPont licensed its patented chemical synthesis technology to Batelle.

In the early 2000s a formal society was devoted to technology transfer. The Technology Transfer Society (T2S) was a ''not-for-profit professional organization dedicated to sharing methods, opportunities, and schools of thought with the technology transfer community. The T2S achieves its mission through programs, publications, forums, our annual conference, and other services designed to provide resources of information and contacts.'' In 2001, T2S had local chapters in several locations, including Washington D.C., Massachusetts, Alabama, California, Arkansas, Colorado, and West Virginia.

FURTHER READING:

Jassawalla, Avan R. and Hemant C. Sashittal. ''Practical Issues of Technology Transfer in High-tech Industrial Organizations.'' *Industrial Management,* November/December 1996.

''Making a Profit from Ideas.'' *The Financial Times.* July 3, 2001. Available from www.ft.com.

''University Technology Transfer—Questions and Answers.'' The Regents of the University of California. 2001. Available from www.ucop.edu.

''Who We Are.'' Technology Transfer Society. August 23, 2001. Available from www.t2s.org.

SEE ALSO: Intellectual Property

TELEPHONY

Telephony is the technology that allows telephones to work. When a telephone call is placed, sounds are converted into electrical signals, transmitted over telephone lines, and converted back into sounds. Early telephony was analog; a single pair of copper wires carried signals over short distances. As the number of telephone calls increased, telephone companies attempted to overcome the limitations of early analog telephony by devising a process known as frequency division multiplexing; this allowed a single pair of copper wires to handle more than one call by routing calls through different bits of the frequency spectrum in much the same way radio stations are assigned a specific frequency. Eventually, analog telephony was replaced by digital telephony, which uses a binary format. By digitizing speech into a binary code, in a manner similar to the digitization of music on CDs, telephone companies were able to reduce noise, increase capacity, and reduce costs.

Internet telephony, the use of Internet technology to make and receive phone calls, emerged in the mid 1990s. In February of 1995, Vocaltec Communications Ltd., which was founded six years prior, created its Internet Phone software application. Internet Phone allowed Internet surfers around the world, most of whom used a local phone connection to access the Internet, the ability to speak with other Internet Phone users at a much cheaper rate than offered by traditional long-distance providers. Soon thereafter, the Information Systems Group of Motorola Inc. began including a copy of Internet Phone with its 28.8 desktop modems. Eventually, personal computer (PC) owners were able to gain access to Internet telephony technology simply by purchasing a telephony board, which integrated modem, sound board, speaker phone, and voice-mail hardware and software. Many Internet telephony packages also included microphones and headphones.

The leading Internet telephony carrier, Net2Phone, Inc. was founded in 1996. The firm released the world's first PC-to-phone application that November. Within four months, more than 2 million Net2Phone calls had been completed. However, by most accounts, the industry was still in its infancy; in fact, Internet telephony accounted for less than half a percent of all telephone usage in 1997. By the year's end, Net2Phone had unveiled its phone-to-phone over IP (Internet Protocol) technology; it launched its Net2Fax service, a fax-to-fax over IP service, and Click2Talk, an e-commerce customer service solution that allowed online shopper to speak to customer service representatives, early in 1998. That year, Frost & Sullivan named Net2Phone the Internet Telephony Services leader. IDC dubbed the firm the IP Telephony Services leader in 1999.

Panasonic announced its intent to incorporate Net2Phone technology into its new cordless phones in 2000. As part of a similar alliance, software behemoth Microsoft Corp. added the technology to its MSN Messenger. In March of that year, Internet portal Yahoo! purchased a 5 percent stake of Net2Phone for $150 million. Telecommunications giant AT&T Corp. paid $1.4 billion for a 32 percent stake in Net2Phone in August. Minutes per day of use reached 8 million in December, compared to 1 million in July. Although sales grew to $72.4 million, the firm posted a loss of $118 million. Customers totaled 1 million.

Despite the many advances made in Internet telephony—particularly in transmission quality and reliability—in the late 1990s and early 2000s, voice over IP (VOIP) calls accounted for less than one percent of all voice traffic in 2001. According to a February 2001 issue of *Business Communications Review,* this is due, at least in part, to reluctance on the part of traditional telecommunications firms to enter the fledgling market. "While start-ups have forged into the market, the established carriers have moved much more slowly." MCI WorldCom's decision to begin testing VOIP services in mid-2000 may well prove to be a turning point if other telecommunications giants follow its lead. "If the major carriers were to join the fray, the analysts believe customers will accept the concept."

FURTHER READING:

"Analogue Telephony." London: Wilco Telephony Ltd., 2001. Available from www.wilco-telephony.co.uk.

"Equipment and Services: A Fast-Growing Market for a Fast-Moving Industry." *IEEE Computing Online.* 2001. Available from www.computer.org.

Korzeniowski, Paul. "VOIP—Still Only a Drop in the Bucket." *Business Communications Review.* February 2001.

Net2Phone, Inc. "Net2Phone Timeline." Newark, NJ: Net2Phone, Inc., 2001. Available from www.net2phone.com.

"Telephony." *Webopedia,* Darien, CT: Internet.com, 2001. Available from e-comm.webopedia.com.html.

TELIGENT, INC.

Teligent, Inc. is a Vienna, Virginia-based competitive local exchange carrier (CLEC) that uses its own high-frequency microwave and broadband SmartWave networks to offer local and long-distance phone services, Internet access, World Wide Web hosting, and similar services to small and mid-sized businesses. Domestically, Teligent serves 43 major cities; its international reach includes Argentina, Spain, France, and Germany. Like most other telecommunications upstarts in the early 2000s, Teligent struggled with mounting debt as intense competition and falling prices undercut profitability. When investors began dumping telecommunications stocks, the firm found itself unable to secure the additional capital it needed to maintain operations. As a result, in May 2001, Teligent filed for Chapter 11 bankruptcy protection.

Teligent was first known as Associated Communications, jointly owned by Telecom Ventures and Pittsburgh, Pennsylvania-based Associated Group, which had held licenses to offer broadband fixed wireless services in 31 U.S. markets since the beginning of the 1990s. The company secured the licenses free of charge, before the Federal Communications Commission began auctioning them to interested parties. Associated Group also owned stakes in a personal communications service provider and a mobile communications firm based in Mexico.

When the telecommunications industry was deregulated in 1996, allowing competition in the local telephone carrier market for the first time, Associated

Group decided to put its licenses to use. According to Peter Elstrom in a *BusinessWeek Online* article, the industry's deregulation came at the same time that "European countries, led by Britain, were opening up their markets to competition. The stakes were huge. Telecom revenues on both continents totaled nearly $300 billion, and the markets were growing about 10 percent each year." Believing they needed a seasoned executive to best capitalize on this growth, Associated Group used a $20 million sighing bonus and an 18 percent stake in Associated Communications to lure Alex Mandl away from his position as president and chief operating officer of AT&T Corp. In August 1996, Mandl began to oversee the new venture, which became known as Teligent, a wireless service provider that competed with the local exchange carriers.

In October 1997, Nippon Telegraph and Telephone (NTT), the largest telephone company in the world, invested $100 million in Teligent. Associated Group and Telecom Ventures fronted the firm another $60 million in capital. When Teligent completed its initial public offering (IPO) in November, Associated owned a 55 percent stake; NTT, a 12.5 percent stake; and Telecom Ventures, a 45 percent stake. The IPO raised $400 million. A private offering in February of 1998 secured another $250 million. Northern Telecom, which agreed to provide network hardware to Teligent, invested another $800 million in the firm. Throughout 1997 and 1998, Mandl worked on developing Teligent's infrastructure and securing authorization for the firm to operate as a CLEC.

Teligent began offering its services in Austin, Dallas, Houston, and San Antonio, Texas; Los Angeles, California; New York, New York; Tampa, Florida; and Washington, D.C. in October 1998. Teligent's 18 GHz frequency, lower than the 38 GHz frequency offered by competitors like WinStar Communications, allowed the firm's digital microwave networks broader coverage and increased capacity, two things Mandl believed would become increasingly important when his firm's networks started being used for things like video conferencing, data transfer, and Internet access. The technology also allowed the firm the flexibility to allocate bandwidth—the amount of data that moves along transmission lines or circuits at a given speed— based on customer demand. And rather than develop their own versions of the expensive cooper and fiber networks used by traditional local telephone services providers, Teligent instead placed antennas on the roofs of its customers, mainly small and mid-sized companies housed in office complexes, and transferred digital signals from a nearby site. A typical site cost roughly $260,000 and covered 30-square miles. Because Teligent's infrastructure was markedly less expensive than conventional fiber networks, which cost an estimated $300,000 for each mile completed, it was able to offer its services for roughly 75 percent of the price charged by competitors. Sales in 1998 reached $1 million.

Teligent offered its services in 40 markets by the end of 1999. Revenues that year surged to $31 million. Although losses totaled $539 million, stock climbed to a high of $97 per share in March of 2000. In October of that year, the firm paid $74 million for teleconferencing services provider Executive Conference, Inc. One month later, Dell Computer Corp. and Teligent forged an agreement to sell Dell personal computers, capable of handling high-speed Internet connections, to businesses already using Teligent for Internet access. Despite a 400 percent jump in revenues to $31 million, the firm's lack of profitability and $1 billion debt, which cost more than $100 million in interest each year, became increasingly important issues to shareholders. Losses for the year grew to $808 million. In an effort to placate investors, Teligent laid off roughly 800 employees and announced its intention to slow growth in the interest of generating earnings more quickly. By December, stock had plunged to roughly $3.50 per share. Customers totaled 35,500.

The problems plaguing Teligent were symptomatic of issues surrounding the telecommunications industry as a whole, according to an April 2001 *BusinessWeek Online* article. "Telecom just didn't turn out to be the fast-growth business executives had banked on. The number of bits transmitted and the number of minutes on the phone are rapidly rising, but severe prices drops have meant overall revenue growth is modest. Company after company has missed its financial targets, stocks have plunged, and burned investors have slammed capital markets shut." Although Teligent was growing more quickly than many of its competitors, revenue growth had fallen short of expectations, and shareholders began to bail out. In April 2001, long-distance firm IDT purchased a 54 percent stake in Teligent, prompting Mandl to tender his resignation. The firm laid off another 900 employees in May. However, these cost-cutting measures failed to satisfy potential investors. Unable to secure the $350 million in funding it needed, the firm declared bankruptcy that month. NASDAQ removed the firm from its National Market in June. Despite these blows, Teligent remained operational, planning to emerge from Chapter 11 a leaner, more competitive telecommunications player.

FURTHER READING:

Andrejczak, Matt. "Former AT&T Head Takes Teligent Public." *Baltimore Business Journal,* October 24, 1997.

Dix, Denise. "Teligent's Mandl Sizes Up a Tough Market." *Network World,* March 6, 2000.

Elstrom, Peter. "Telecom Meltdown." *BusinessWeek Online,* April 23, 2001. Available from www.businessweek.com.

Haynes, Peter. "Teligent's Test." *Forbes,* March 9, 1998.

Meyers, Jason. "Insurgent Intentions: Its Launch Target Met, Teligent Enters Price and Service Battle." *Telephony,* November 2, 1998.

Swartz, Nikki. "InTeligent Challenger." *Wireless Review,* March 31, 1999.

"Teligent Files for Chapter 11 Bankruptcy." *Fiber Optic News,* May 28, 2001.

"Teligent Scales Back Telecom Effort." *The Business Journal,* December 1, 2000.

"Turning to Chapter 11; Teligent Declares Bankruptcy." *Telephony,* May 28, 2001.

"Web Bill Breakthrough—Startup Teligent Providing Value-Added Service to Small and Midsize Companies." *InformationWeek,* November 2, 1998.

SEE   Mandl, Alex
ALSO:

TERRA LYCOS, INC.

Terra Lycos, Inc. was formed in October 2000 by the merger of Spain's Terra Networks, S.A. and the popular Internet portal and search engine, Lycos, Inc. Pittsburgh-based Lycos originated as an Internet search engine in 1995. Through partnerships and acquisitions it became an Internet portal operating several Web sites under different brands, from dating service Matchmaker to financial chat service Quote.com. Lycos expanded internationally by forming joint ventures in Asia, Japan, Latin America, and Europe. Following the acquisition of Lycos by Terra Networks, Terra Lycos had 98 million registered users in 41 countries in mid-2001, making it the third most popular online network in the world.

A LEADING INTERNET SEARCH ENGINE, 1995-1997

Lycos, Inc. was created in 1995 by CMG@ Ventures, which purchased the exclusive rights to Lycos Spider Technology from Carnegie Mellon University. Lycos was established as a subsidiary of CMG@Ventures, which later became CMGI Inc., to develop and market the technology. Lycos Spider Technology utilized software robots to scan the Internet and abstract the home pages that it found. Lycos built a catalog of more than 3.7 million Internet pages and had nearly 3.5 million hits a week. The name Lycos was derived from a Latin word for a special kind of spider that leaves its web to hunt.

Lycos went public in April 1996 and raised $40 million. It was one of four search engine companies that had their IPOs that year. Yahoo!, the best-known search engine, InfoSeek, and Excite.com also went public. Following their successful IPOs, other companies announced plans to go public or provide commercial searching products.

Throughout 1996 Lycos continued to upgrade its search engine by increasing its speed and making it possible to search for telephone numbers and e-mail addresses as well as individual sound, video, and other multimedia files. Lycos also added a city guide that featured 400 cities, and it established a Club Lycos for users that provided them with discounts with merchants. In addition Lycos redesigned its graphic interface to look like an Internet portal.

Lycos Europe was formed in May 1997 as a joint venture with German media conglomerate Bertelsmann AG. Later, when Lycos was acquired by Terra Networks in 2000, Bertelsmann pledged $1 billion to advertise and purchase services on Lycos. In the United States, Lycos signed a three-year agreement with Barnes & Noble that made BarnesandNoble.com the exclusive bookseller for Lycos. For fiscal 1997 ending July 31, Lycos had revenue of $22.3 million, up from $5.3 million in fiscal 1996.

PURSUED PORTAL STRATEGY, 1998-2000

In 1998 Lycos introduced e-mail and chat capabilities. It added content to its portal-like site through partnerships and acquisitions. It acquired Tripod Inc. for $58 million as part of its strategy to increase traffic and build online communities around targeted content. Tripod provided free Web pages to about one million users, with news and commentary tailored to young adults. Both Lycos and Tripod were among the top 10 most-visited sites on the Web. Following the acquisition, Lycos and Tripod would continue to operate under their own names as part of Lycos's multibranding strategy.

Other content partnerships were formed with Preview Travel, which became the exclusive multi-service provider of travel reservations on Lycos's Travel Web Guide and Travel Network, and CDNow, which became the exclusive retailer of music-related products on Lycos and Tripod sites. CDNow paid Lycos $18.5 million over three years to be featured on Lycos's Shopping Network and Entertainment Web Guides as well as on music-related search results pages, banner ads, and links. Other deals were struck with contact management site PlanetAll and career sites The Monster Board and Online Career Center. During 1998 Lycos introduced its free SafetyNet service, which filtered out objectionable content from Web site searches. Lycos also became the designated content provider for Juno Web, which had 5.5 million subscribers to its free e-mail service.

Lycos's $133 million stock purchase of WhoWhere Inc. was a major step in its portal strategy.

The acquisition included the popular WhoWhere Internet white pages; MailCity, a free electronic mail system; and Angelfire, a free Web page hosting service. MailCity had 9.3 million registered users, and Angelfire had 1.3 million users.

Lycos made another major acquisition in October 1998 when it purchased Wired Digital Inc.'s online products, which included the popular HotBot search engine, Wired News and HotWired news sites, and other content sites offering shopping, e-mail, chat, and travel services. Wired Digital was the last remaining piece of Wired Ventures Inc., which launched *Wired* magazine in 1993 and subsequently sold it to Conde Nast Publications in 1998.

Lycos's acquisitions of different brands and products were designed to make it a ''super site'' that offered a portfolio of products for a variety of users. Lycos was also developing a community of users by offering features such as chat and gaming. For fiscal 1998 ending July 31 Lycos reported revenue of $56 million but still posted a loss.

ENJOYED GROWTH AS AN INDEPENDENT PORTAL, 1999

At the beginning of 1999 Lycos was enjoying tremendous growth. Its audience reach had grown to 46.5 percent, only three percentage points behind Yahoo!. According to a Media Metrix report, Lycos attracted 26.3 million visitors monthly and was the fastest-growing Web portal. The company had recently launched its first national TV advertising campaign, which also included radio spots in 11 major cities and was estimated to cost $25 million. Lycos and the National Football League announced Lycos would create Superbowl.com, the official Web site for Super Bowl XXXIII, in 1999.

In early 1999 Lycos was one of the few remaining independent Internet portals. Walt Disney Co. owned a significant portion of Infoseek; Netscape was sold to AOL; Snap was 60 percent owned by NBC; and Excite was being absorbed by @Home. In early 1999 USA Networks, which also owned Ticketmaster and Home Shopping Network, and Lycos were negotiating a deal valued at $22 billion to merge and create USA/Lycos Interactive Networks Inc. However, CMGI Inc., Lycos's largest shareholder with a 22 percent interest in the company, opposed the combination. By May 1999 the deal was declared officially dead.

Meanwhile, Lycos's revenue continued to climb. According to figures released by Media Metrix Inc., Lycos surpassed Yahoo! for the first time in March 1999, when nearly 32 million people, or 51.8 percent of U.S. Internet users, visited Lycos, compared to 31.2 million visitors, or 50.8 percent, to Yahoo!. Lycos's visitors included those at the Tripod and Angelfire Web site hosting services, the WhoWhere Internet directory service, the Wired Digital news service, and the Lycos and HotBot Internet search sites, all of which were run as separate entities under the Lycos Network. To further develop its community of users, Lycos launched Lycos Clubs, which enabled members to create virtual clubhouses around shared interests.

Other initiatives in 1999 included the Open Directory, a guide to the Web that was operated by some 8,000 volunteers. Lycos Radio Network was introduced in April 1999, making Lycos the first portal to incorporate streaming audio and video. Bertelsmann, Lycos's international joint venture partner, invested $12 million for the expansion of Tripod Europe, which was the fastest growing online community in Europe. Meanwhile, Lycos's largest shareholder CMGI Inc. acquired AltaVista from Compaq Computer Corp. for $2.3 billion. For its fiscal year ending July 31, 1999, Lycos reported a net loss of $4.4 million on revenue of $40.6 million.

Later in 1999 Lycos established music.lycos.com, a comprehensive online music destination that offered MP3 search and hosting areas, legal MP3 downloads, 35 radio channels, music news, reviews, chat rooms, message boards, commerce, and an MP3 player download. The company acquired Internet Music Distribution Inc. for about $38 million in stock. Internet Music's music-playing software, Sonique, allowed users to download music files and play them on their personal computers.

To bolster its financial services and create a community of users interested in financial information, Lycos purchased Quote.com Inc. for about $78 million in stock. Quote.com provided stock quotes and other financial information. Lycos also expanded its gaming content with the purchase of Gamesville.com, which had 2.2 million registered users, for $207 million in stock.

Lycos expanded internationally in the final months of 1999. It formed a pan-Asian joint venture, Lycos Asia, with Singapore Telecom. Lycos Asia launched a site in Singapore and planned to go online in Malaysia and the Philippines. Other plans called for setting up customized versions of Lycos in 10 Asian cities. Lycos launched 12 country-specific sites in Latin America as well as two sites for Spanish speakers in the United States. The firm also launched a Japanese version of Tripod.

For the 1999 holiday shopping season, Lycos introduced the Lycos WebShopper, a new comparison-shopping tool, and added links to epinions.com and other sites that provided consumer and professional product reviews. Lycoshop, which featured listings from major retailers and comparative shopping services, was also launched. As a result, Lycos reported a 450 percent increase in the number of unique shoppers for the holiday season over the previous year. As of December 1999 Lycos claimed an audience of 29 million users.

TERRA LYCOS CREATED BY MERGER WITH SPAIN'S TERRA NETWORKS, 2000-2001

In May 2000 it was announced that Lycos would be acquired for $12.5 billion by Terra Networks. Wall Street jitters sent Lycos's stock down more than 20 percent. With support from CMGI, Lycos combined with Terra Networks to create Terra Lycos, Inc. in October 2000. Estimates of the merger value ranged between $5.3 and $6.5 billion.

Terra Networks had been established in December 1998 as Telefonica Interactiva by Spain's largest telephone company, Telefonica, S.A. Through acquisitions Telefonica Interactiva quickly became the top-ranked portal and Internet service provider (ISP) in Spain. Later in 1999 the company acquired ISPs and Internet portals in Brazil, Central America, Mexico, Argentina, Chile, and Peru. In November 1999 Telefonica Interactiva went public and changed its name to Terra Networks, S.A.

Bertelsmann also participated in the formation of Terra Lycos. The German media giant agreed to provide content to Terra Lycos and to purchase $1 billion worth of services and advertising over a five-year period. With operations in 54 countries, Bertelsmann was the third-largest media company in the world.

At the end of 2000 Terra Lycos was providing Internet access to more than 5 million customers worldwide. The company was the leading ISP in Spain, Chile, Peru, and Guatemala, offering both paid and free subscription services. Lycos Asia received permission from the Chinese government to operate a Web portal from Shanghai. Lycos Indonesia was launched in October 2000, and the launch of Lycos Thailand in December 2000 gave Terra Lycos an international presence in 41 countries. Terra Lycos acquired portals in France and Sweden and in 2001 launched Terra Caribe in the Dominican Republic, its 42nd country, and a portal in Russia.

Terra Lycos continued to add new content and services to its Web portal through acquisitions and partnerships. It acquired Matchmaker.com, a Texas-based online dating service, for $44 million. The company continued to strengthen its brand through a $20 million national advertising campaign and high-profile partnerships that included building Web sites for the 2000 Olympics in Sydney, Australia. In 2001 it acquired financial Web site Raging Bull from AltaVista.

Although Terra Lycos continued to make acquisitions in 2001 that were funded in part by a multibillion dollar rights offering, the company was forced to make some cutbacks as the economy slowed. Jobs were cut and revenue estimates were lowered. The company discontinued free Internet service in Brazil and planned to reduce its overall workforce by 15 percent. After first quarter revenues were lower than expected, Terra Lycos projected that it would return to a positive EBITDA (earnings before interest, taxes, depreciation, and amortization) in 2002. The company's stated goal was to become the first or second leading Internet destination in each of the countries in which it operated.

FURTHER READING:

Andrews, Whit. "In Every Way, Lycos/USA Is a Big Deal." *Internet World,* February 15, 1999.

———. "Portal Companies at a Crossroads." *Internet World,* June 14, 1999.

Charski, Mindy. "Opening a Worldwide Portal." *Inter@ctive Week,* May 22, 2000.

Davis, Robert J. *Speed Is Life: The CEO of Lycos Reveals His Secrets to Surviving and Thriving on Internet Time.* New York: Doubleday, 2001.

"Ex-Lycos Chief Executive Tells All in Book." *Knight-Ridder/ Tribune Business News,* May 21, 2001.

Gibney, Frank, Jr. "Ahem, Bob Davis Was Right." *Time,* May 28, 2001.

"The Internet—Portal Plays." *The Economist (US),* May 20, 2000.

"Lycos." *Washington Business Journal,* October 13, 2000.

Roth, Daniel. "The Revenge of the Search Engines." *Forbes,* March 9, 1998.

Taylor, Cathy. "Search for Tomorrow: Three Internet Search Engines Are Set to Start Selling Stock." *Mediaweek,* April 1, 1996.

"Terra Calypso." *Communications International,* May 2001.

"Terra Lycos Hits Terra Firma." *Communications Today,* May 14, 2001.

"Terra Lycos: Mano a Mano with Yahoo?" *Business Week,* January 8, 2001.

SEE ALSO: Portals, Web

THESTREET.COM INC.

TheStreet.com Inc. is an online financial news source with roughly 75,000 subscribers. Access to the site is free, although the firm does operate a subscription-based sister site, RealMoney.com, which offers more in-depth information for stock trading professionals. Sales grew 63 percent in 2000 to reach $23 million. However, TheStreet.com lost $62 million that year. In an effort to attain profitability, the firm launched a series of cost cutting measures, including a 20-percent reduction in workforce, in 2001.

TheStreet.com was founded in November of 1996 by James J. Cramer, a well known money manager and writer for *New York* magazine, and Martin Peretz, the editor-in-chief and chairman of *New Republic*. Andrew Drake was named president and CEO of the new Web site and Dave Kansas, a reporter for *The Wall Street Journal,* was hired as executive editor. For $12.95 per month, users were granted access to performance reports profiling Wall Street analysts, and other articles written by Cramer himself, as well as by Michael Lewis, the senior editor of *New Republic*. Subscribers also received a daily newsletter via e-mail that offered both news and commentary on current trading activity. Cramer and Peretz began marketing their service to the 1.5 million U.S. residents engaged in some form of electronic trading by the end of 1996. According to a Forrester Research report published shortly after TheStreet.com was launched, the number of U.S. households trading stocks electronically would double within a year and exceed 10 million by 2001. Cramer and Peretz believed that many of these individuals would be willing to pay for immediate market information, despite many predictions to the contrary.

By the end of 1997, the new company had signed up 15,000 subscribers. Growth brought with it bandwidth problems, prompting TheStreet.com to hire Seattle, Washington-based StarWave to oversee the management of its servers. The increased capacity allowed TheStreet.com to put an online system in place that allowed clients to track their mutual fund and stock portfolios in real time. In 1998, the site published roughly 30 articles per day. Content was organized into four major categories: Fund Watch, which covered mutual fund activity; Company Watch, which offered breaking news about various firms, as well as company profiles; Truth Serum, which dealt with the causes and effects of conditions in various industries; and Market Facts, which analyzed current market conditions. Most articles totaled 800 to 1,000 words, compared to the 1,500 to 2,000 words typical of articles in most businesses publications. While TheStreet's 18 writers were free to express their opinions about things like the activities of fund managers and the performance of stock, U.S. Securities and Exchange Commission (SEC) regulations prohibited the firm from making explicit buy and sell recommendations. Subscriptions accounted for roughly 70 percent of total sales, while advertising from Charles Schwab,

Ameritrade, Fidelity, and other brokerages accounted for the additional 30 percent. Despite continued growth, the firm lost $16.3 million in 1998.

The young company began gearing up for its initial public offering (IPO) in 1999. The New York Times Co. invested $15 million in TheStreet.com in February, and the two firms' Web sites began offering links to each other's online headlines. By then, subscribers had reached 37,000. In April, News Corp. invested $7.5 million in the firm. Goldman Sachs agreed to underwrite the IPO, which actually took place in May. TheStreet.com's share price of $19 jumped to $75 in the first day of trading. The New York Times Co. and TheStreet.com agreed to launch a joint online newsroom in November. Sales that year reached $14.3 million, and the firm posted a loss of $28.4 million.

The online personal finance arm of Microsoft Corp., MSN MoneyCentral, agreed to license content to TheStreet.com in February of 2000. That month, the firm decided to make its site available for free in an effort to gain a mass market. According to *Electronic Information Report,* TheStreet.com "completed a refocusing of its services in an effort to meet the needs of the entire gamut of investors. . .the change was an effort to accommodate the average retail investor who doesn't need the level of service professionals require and who doesn't want to pay a subscription fee for information." However, to meet the needs of its more active individual investors, as well as those of its professional clients, TheStreet.com eventually moved a portion of its more intensive stock analysis content to a new site, RealMoney.com, which charged a monthly fee of $20 or an annual fee of $200. RealMoney.com users were able to interact with the TheStreet.com's writers. A third site, TheStreetPros.com, was designed solely for industry professionals. Accordingly, subscription rates were double those of RealMoney.com.

Although sales in 2000 jumped to $23.3 million, losses mounted to $61.9 million. When investors began questioning the firm's ability to earn a profit, TheStreet.com decided to undertake several cost cutting moves. Roughly 40 employees—nearly 20 percent of its total workforce—were laid off, and the firm pulled out of its joint newsroom venture with the New York Times Co. Also, operations in the United Kingdom were halted. Management estimated that the cutbacks would save roughly $18 million per year. In addition, TheStreet.com acquired SmartPortfolio.com, an online publisher of financial newsletters, believing that SmartPorfolio's base of 10,000 paying subscribers would help TheStreet.com achieve critical mass, something many industry pundits viewed as crucial to profitability.

Cost cutting efforts continued into 2001, when TheStreet.com laid off another 20 percent of its workforce in April. The firm also began looking into ventures that were unrelated to the Internet. According to an August 2001 article in *The Financial Times,* "it may be surprising to discover that this proto-typical dotcom's latest business initiatives have nothing to do with the Internet at all. Among these is TheStreet-View, a daily bulletin for hedge fund managers, which is delivered to subscribers through fax machines. The Street's latest venture is even more 'old media.' In July, the company began broadcasting Real Money Talk with Jim Cramer, co-founder of the TheStreet, on radio stations in 14 U.S. markets." Some analysts believe that using the Internet as one of many distribution vehicles will likely emerge as a characteristic of the most successful online content providers.

FURTHER READING:

Bicknell, Craig. "The Street Storms the Street." *Wired News.* May 11, 1999. Available from www.wired.com.

Elkind, Peter. "Founders Feud at TheStreet.com." *Fortune.* April 26, 1999.

Grimes, Christopher. "Old Media Methods are Good Business for TheStreet.com." *The Financial Times.* August 29, 2001. Available from news.ft.com.

Hall, Eric. "Information Wants to Be Free? Not at TheStreet.com." *InfoWorld.* December 8, 1997.

Hammer, Ben. "TheStreet.com to Shut Down in U.K., Lay Off 20 Percent in U.S." *The Industry Standard.* November 16, 2000. Available from www.thestandard.com.

Li, Kenneth. "TheStreet.com Lays Off 20 Percent." *The Industry Standard.* April 4, 2001. Available from www.thestandard.com.

Luskin, Donald L. "Walk It Like You Talk It." *The Industry Standard.* June 14, 2001. Available from www.thestandard.com.

Stern, Gary M. "TheStreet.com: Gaining the Competitive Edge." *Link-Up.* February 1998.

Taylor, Cathy. "Takin' It to the Street." *MEDIAWEEK.* November 18, 1996.

SEE ALSO: Investing, Online; Motley Fool, Inc., The

THREE PROTOCOLS, THE

The World Wide Web is one of several utilities—including e-mail, File Transfer Protocol (FTP), Internet Relay Chat (IRC), Telnet, and Usenet—that form the Internet. At the heart of the Web is a system of many Web servers. While the term server is normally used to describe the computers that host Web sites, it also can refer to the software used to store Web pages. The World Wide Web Consortium (W3C) describes the Web as "the universe of network-accessible information, the embodiment of human knowledge." This statement describes the vision of the Web's creator, a computer scientist named Tim Berners-Lee, who developed three critical protocols that make it work.

WHY THE WEB WORKS

The three protocols Berners-Lee developed are Hypertext Markup Language (HTML), Uniform Resource Locator (URL), and Hypertext Transfer Protocol (HTTP). Protocols are formats or sets of rules that computers use when they communicate. Residing either in software or hardware, they ensure that each device understands exactly how information will be sent and received.

Locations on the World Wide Web, which commonly reside on individual servers, are known as Web sites. Web sites have individual addresses called URLs, which must be used to gain access. Much like a street address or telephone number is linked to a person or company, URLs are linked to Web sites. Originally, URLs were called Universal Document Identifiers (UDIs) or Uniform Resource Identifiers (URIs).

Upon visiting a Web site, visitors normally begin on the site's home page. This document serves as an index to other pages or documents within the site, which are written in a language called HTML—an authoring or presentation language (not a programming language) used for creating pages on the World Wide Web. The HTML language consists of special codes or tags that determine a page's visible appearance when read by a Web browser like Microsoft's Internet Explorer. In addition to defining the overall structure and layout of a Web page, HTML also is used to denote links to other Web pages, the placement of graphics or pictures on a page, and the appearance of text, including bold or italicized type and different fonts.

HTML documents, or Web pages, are connected together with hypertext links. This linking is made possible by HTTP, a protocol used by computers to transfer hypertext documents and other chunks of information over the Internet. HTTP relies on a client-server model, similar to other protocols used on computer networks. In this scenario, clients are programs like Web browsers that interact with Web servers to request and retrieve information. As explained in *HTTP Made Really Easy,* "An HTTP client opens a connection and sends a request message to an HTTP server; the server then returns a response message, usually containing the resource that was requested. After delivering the response, the server closes the connection (making HTTP a stateless protocol, i.e. not maintaining any connection information between transactions).''

Web pages are viewed through software applications called Web browsers. Microsoft's Internet Explorer and Netscape's Navigator were the two popular Web browsers during the 1990s and early 2000s. Web browsers are the essential link between end-users and a vast sea of static pictures, video, sounds and text. Said differently, they also enable buyers and sellers of goods and services to engage in electronic commerce.

HOW IT ALL HAPPENED

In 1980, shortly after graduating from Oxford University, Tim Berners-Lee held a temporary software consulting job at the European Particle Physics Laboratory (CERN). There, he experimented with programs, including one called Enquire, which stored information along with links. He developed Enquire as a way of helping himself remember connections between the many people and projects at CERN. After his temporary position ended, Berners-Lee eventually returned to CERN in a more permanent role in 1984. He had a vision of a ''global information space'' where information on computers throughout the world was linked together. Many of the researchers who worked with CERN were scattered throughout the world. CERN made them submit documents in a special format that was compatible with its own computer system. This caused a great deal of frustration, both for the researchers and the people who were employed at CERN. Consistent with his vision, Berners-Lee proposed creating a web of information that would be in a universal format all could share. This web could contain cross-links between relevant documents, such as research papers. Although the idea generated little initial interest at CERN, Berners-Lee's boss, Mike Sendall, gave him permission to explore his dream there. In response, he created a hypertext-editing program called WorldWideWeb in 1990. The program ran on a machine from NeXT, a computer company started by Apple co-founder Steve Jobs, and included the Web's three main elements—URLs, HTTP, and HTML—which Berners-Lee created.

The concept of hypertext existed long before Berners-Lee introduced HTTP and HTML. During the 1940s, the concept existed in the academic world. Also, during the 1980s, Apple Computer Programmer Bill Atkinson created a program called Hypercard. According to WC3, the program allowed users ''to construct a series of on-screen 'filing cards' that contained textual and graphical information. Users could navigate these by pressing on-screen buttons, taking

themselves on a tour of the information in the process. Hypercard set the scene for more applications based on the filing card idea.'' One limitation to programs like Hypercard was that they were limited to a person's computer system and couldn't be used to access information on other computers or networks in remote locations.

Berners-Lee introduced his WorldWideWeb program, along with the very first Web server (called info.cern.ch), to people in the field of high-energy physics. Later, he introduced WorldWideWeb to people introduced in hypertext and NeXT. At info.cern.ch, the specifications for URLs, HTML, and HTTP were published in order to encourage others to learn about and use them.

After Berner-Lee introduced his creation to the world, it began to take off. However, the browser he made for NeXT was not sufficient for the many people using IBM-PCs, Macintosh computers, and other systems. Development of various point-and-click browsers soon followed. According to *ibiblio*, ''Students at the Helsinki University of Technology wrote Erwise-a browser for Unix machines, and Pei Wei, a U.C. Berkeley student wrote Viola. Colleagues of Berners-Lee at CERN wrote a browser for Mac machines called Samba.'' In 1992, Dave Thompson and Joseph Hardin of the University of Illinois at Champaign-Urbana's National Center for Supercomputer Applications decided to develop the Mosaic Web browser. Lou Montulli was among the first people to create a text browser, when he released Lynx in March of 1993. That same year, Hewlett-Packard Labs' Dave Raggett created a browser called Arena. In November 1994, Marc Andreessen, who had worked as a programmer on Mosaic, and Jim Clark formed what would eventually become Netscape Communications. Microsoft released its Internet Explorer browser in August of 1995, and along with Netscape went on to dominate the market for Web browsers.

Since Berners-Lee effectively changed the world, the Web has evolved. For example, various versions of HTML, including HTML+, HTML 2, HTML 3.2, HTML 4, have been released. HTML is closely related to another language called Standard Generalized Markup Language (SGML). In the early 2000s a subset of SGML known as Extensible Markup Language (XML) led to the development of XHTML, a hybrid language that combines HTML with XML. XHTML has powerful implications for e-commerce because the language's XML component allows users to share information in a universal, standard way without making the kinds of special arrangements required Electronic Data Interchange (EDI), or the manner in which many large companies exchange electronic data with suppliers and other entities.

FURTHER READING:

''The ABC's of HTML.'' The National Center for Supercomputing Applications. February 11, 2001. Available from www.ncsa.uiuc.edu.

Baker, David W. ''A Guide to URLs.'' 1996. Available from www.netspace.org.

''A Beginner's Guide to HTML.'' The National Center for Supercomputing Applications. February 11, 2001. Available from www.ncsa.uiuc.edu.

Berners-Lee. ''The World Wide Web: A very short personal history.'' Available from www.w3.org.

Berners-Lee. ''The World Wide Web—past, present and future.'' July 17, 1996. Available from www.tec.uno.edu.

''HTML.'' *Ecommerce Webopedia.* February 10, 2001. Available from e-comm.webopedia.com.

''HTML.'' *Tech Encyclopedia.* February 10, 2001. Available from www.techweb.com.

SEE ALSO: Berners-Lee, Timothy; HTML; XML

TICKETMASTER

Those who attend major sporting events, plays, and concerts likely obtain their tickets through Los Angeles-based Ticketmaster, which sells tickets at physical locations, through call centers, and via ticketmaster.com. The world's leading ticket company, Ticketmaster sold more than 83 million tickets worldwide (totaling $3.2 billion) for its clients in 2000. Formerly known as Ticketmaster Corp., the company became known as Ticketmaster when it merged with Ticketmaster Online-CitySearch in 2001—which until that time had served as Ticketmaster Corp.'s exclusive agent for online sales. USA Networks Inc. holds a majority stake in Ticketmaster, which is a part of the TV network's interactive group.

Tickets aren't Ticketmaster's only game. In addition to its subsidiary TicketWeb, a provider of Internet-based box office services and software, the company also operates several other enterprises. These include Match.com, an online matchmaking service; Citysearch.com, which provides people with details about hundreds of different cities; Evite.com, an event planning, hosting, and management site for individuals and businesses; LiveDaily, a news and information hub for music fans; TM VISTA, a provider of event solutions for organizations; and ReserveAmerica, a provider of campground management and camping reservation solutions.

EARLY E-COMMERCE EFFORTS, 1994-1997

Founded by Fredric Rosen, Ticketmaster arguably is an e-commerce pioneer. In November of 1993 Microsoft co-founder Paul Allen paid more than $300 million for an 80 percent stake in the company when he saw its e-commerce potential. In the July 11, 1994 issue of *Fortune,* he explained: ''Ticketing just naturally seemed like something you'll want to do in this wired world.'' The company's e-commerce initiatives took shape in 1995, when the World Wide Web was still catching on with consumers. That year, ticketmaster.com began operation and Citysearch, which would later merge with Ticketmaster, was founded. By the end of 1996, Citysearch launched its Web site and Ticketmaster.com was doing online transactions throughout the United States.

By 1997, Ticketmaster was investing heavily in its e-commerce initiatives, even though they were not generating significant incremental returns. According to *InformationWeek,* in September 1997 the company's projected monthly Web sales were $4 million. However, they represented approximately two percent of Ticketmaster's revenue, which at the time was more than $2 billion. In May 1997, Home Shopping Network and Silver King Broadcasting, owned by USA Networks Chairman Barry Diller, agreed to acquire Ticketmaster. A main reason for the acquisition was the role Ticketmaster could play as television evolved into an interactive medium between marketers and consumers.

GROWTH AND EXPANSION, 1998 TO PRESENT

In 1998, e-commerce was catching on with consumers, especially in the area of online ticket sales. Consequently, Ticketmaster's online business began to take off. In June, *Computerworld* reported that the company reached $20 million in online sales (500,000 tickets) during the first quarter, up from $5.3 million the previous year. The company also began expanding its e-commerce operations on the international front. Already the leading provider of tickets in the United Kingdom, Ticketmaster enhanced its position there by offering online sales in mid-1998. By the year's end, Ticketmaster Online-CitySearch Inc., which was handling the e-commerce side of the ticket company's business, reported revenues of approximately $40 million, a 159 percent increase from the previous year.

Many developments unfolded at Ticketmaster Online-CitySearch in 1999. USA Networks, which then had become the company's majority stakeholder, began the year by announcing that it would merge Ticketmaster Online-CitySearch, Home Shopping Network, and Internet Shopping Network/First Auction with Lycos. However, the agreement eventually was terminated. Instead, Ticketmaster Online-CitySearch and Lycos ended up forming a relationship that allowed the two companies to benefit from cross-promotional opportunities. Ticketmaster Online-CitySearch also saw online ticket sales surge to $60 million during the first quarter, an increase of 275 percent from the same period the previous year.

In 1999, Ticketmaster Online-CitySearch ventured into the business of online matchmaking and auction services by acquiring CityAuction Inc., a "person-to-person online auction community;" online dating and matchmaking service Match.com; and auction/matchmaking service provider One & Only Network. Ticketmaster Online-CitySearch then formed a partnership with USA Networks Inc.'s Internet Shopping Network (ISN). The joint venture allowed consumers to access the person-to-person auction services of CityAuction or the business-to-consumer auction services of ISN's First Auction from either Web site. Finally, in September Ticketmaster Online-CitySearch partnered with Excite@Home, FairMarket Inc., and Microsoft Corp. to develop an online auction network capable of reaching more than 70 percent of all Internet users.

Also in 1999, Ticketmaster Online-CitySearch acquired the entertainment city guide section of MSN Sidewalk from Microsoft. Sidewalk included other services besides city guides—including yellow pages and buyer's guides—that weren't part of the deal. By November, Ticketmaster Online-CitySearch and Microsoft offered arts and entertainment information about approximately 3,000 U.S. locations via a new MSN Local Channel, and through the MSN Entertainment Channel and Microsoft WebTV Network. Ticketmaster Online-CitySearch also gained a direct link on MSN.com for ticket sales, and saw its Match.com subsidiary become MSN's featured personals service. Ending the year on a high note, USA Networks invested an additional $40 million in Ticketmaster Online-CitySearch, giving the company more capital for development and expansion. During the fourth quarter, overall revenue soared 168 percent over the previous year, and online ticket revenue jumped 262 percent. Annual revenues reached $105 million.

During 2000, Ticketmaster Online-CitySearch unveiled an electronic ticket service which allowed customers to buy and print Ticketmaster tickets from the comfort of their own homes. In addition to forging strategic and content-based agreements with several other companies—including ARTISTdirect Inc., Ask Jeeves, Yahoo!, and weather.com—the company also made several acquisitions. It acquired ticketing and visitor management firm 2b Technology Inc. in February; TicketWeb Inc. in May; and Essential Data

Control Systems' Fan Loyalty System (a loyalty/incentive program for sports fans) in July. Finally, near the end of the year Ticketmaster Online-CitySearch announced that it would acquire Ticketmaster Corp. and change its formal name to Ticketmaster. The merger, which became official in January 2001, combined the offline ticketing and reservation operations of Ticketmaster Corp. with the other firm's broad e-commerce offerings. At the time, the company indicated that "The new Ticketmaster will have a customer database of over 20 million, including more than 12 million active customers, processing over 80 million tickets annually, through 3,430 ticketing outlets, 16 call centers, in more than 80 cities and via eight primary websites."

It also was in 2000 that Ticketmaster Online-CitySearch moved into the mobile and wireless arena. In February, the company announced that it had formed a dedicated wireless group and a new strategic partner affiliate program that allowed wireless content providers to provider subscribers with Ticketmaster Online-CitySearch's content, including local information, reservation and ticket capabilities, and personals. Ticketmaster Online-CitySearch's Local Intelligence service provided users with recommendations, as well as the ability to make reservations at restaurants and buy tickets from their mobile devices. As part of its wireless strategy, Ticketmaster Online-CitySearch made several moves to bolster its position in this area, including alliances and arrangements with companies like Phone.com, NeoPoint Inc., Verizon Wireless, Nextel Communications, and Sprint. It also made its content and services available to MSN Mobile and AT&T Digital PocketNet customers.

Ticketmaster Online-CitySearch made several developments on the international front during 2000 by extending offerings to Japan, Iceland, and Brazil. The firm's reach also had become very pervasive. By covering more than 2000 ZIP codes, Ticketmaster Online-CitySearch's local information offerings reached more than 90 percent of the U.S. adult online population, according to Media Metrix's Measures Report, released in February. Financially, Ticketmaster Online-CitySearch saw its revenues increase approximately 110 percent in 2000, reaching $220.6 million.

In 2001, Ticketmaster Online-CitySearch's acquisition of Ticketmaster Corp. became official. Growth and expansion continued to occur. That January, the newly named Ticketmaster announced that it would acquire ReserveAmerica Holdings Inc., which at the time was the nation's leading campsite reservation company, allowing customers to make reservations at more than 150,000 campsites in 43 states. The acquisition allowed Ticktmaster to expand its reservation capabilities outside of the ticket business. Ticketmaster announced two more acquisitions during the spring. In March, it announced the acquisition of Evite.com, an online activity center where people planned a wide range of events from baby showers to weekend getaways. The acquisition extended Ticketmaster's capabilities by making its offerings more comprehensive. In addition to offering people the ability to buy tickets, make reservations, and find out more about cities via CitySearch, Ticketmaster customers were now able to plan their events in those cities.

The company also continued to expand internationally in 2001. In March, Ticketmaster subsidiary Match.com and MSN.co.uk, then the most visited Web site in the United Kingdom, formed an alliance that resulted in Match.com being featured as the main personals service on MSN.co.uk's Love and Relationship channel. In April, Ticketmaster announced that it would acquire Towne Ticket Centre. Based in Kelowna, British Columbia, the acquisition expanded Ticketmaster's presence in that Canadian province. The firm extended its reach in Norway as well by announcing the acquisition of Billettservice AS, the country's leading ticket company, in October.

Besides acquisitions, Ticketmaster continued to form strategic alliances with other companies, including ones between FlipDog.com and Citysearch, and Network Communications Inc. However, one of the leading alliances it formed in 2001 was with America Online (AOL). As part of the deal, Ticketmaster agreed to offer the ticket and movie information of AOL Moviefone on its local city guides. In return, it was able to distribute its tickets through AOL. Ticketmaster also was able to have Match.com offered on Netscape.com, CompuServe, AOL.com, and AOL, and have the site included as the main personals service on Love@AOL.

In the area of services, Citysearch began providing users with automobile pricing information from Edmunds.com Inc. Additionally, Ticketmaster saw the use of its ''Print My Own'' technology, which allowed users to print bar-coded tickets from their home or office computer upon purchase, begin to take off. The technology was adopted by several leading organizations during 2001 including the Rose Garden, Orlando Magic, Seattle Mariners, National Car Rental Center, and the Utah Starzz. Midway through 2001, Ticketmaster also re-launched its Match.com subsidiary with an upgrade that made it easier to use. The re-launch was made in June, due to strong growth; Jupiter Media Metrix had rated the site as the leading online dating and personals site that April. Despite the challenges faced by many dot.coms, the pervasiveness of Ticketmaster, as well as the scope of the services it offered, seemed to position it well for success in the early 2000s.

FURTHER READING:

Biotano, Margaret. ''Barry Diller's Dot-Com Nuptials.'' *Fortune,* March 5, 2001.

''Company Information.'' Los Angeles, California: Ticketmaster. November 15, 2001. Available from www.ticketmaster.com.

Kirkpatrick, David. ''Over the Horizon with Paul Allen.'' *Fortune,* July 11, 1994.

''Ticketmaster.'' *Hoover's Online,* November 19, 2001. Available from www.hoovers.com.

''Ticketmaster Online-Citysearch to Acquire Ticketmaster Corporation.'' Los Angeles, California: Ticketmaster. November 21, 2000. Available from www.ticketmaster.com.

SEE ALSO: Travelocity.com

TIME AND TIME ZONES

On the surface, the concept of time may seem relatively simple and straightforward. Anyone who interacts with other individuals or organizations relies heavily on time to manage daily activities. People constantly complain that they don't have enough of it and continually save it, waste it, and try to find more of it. Without clocks, time frames, and time zones, the fabric of organization and structure that holds the world together would quickly unravel. If the world did not share a similar definition of time, coordinating activities and making arrangements (such as the delivery of goods) would become extremely difficult, if not impossible.

Webster's College Dictionary defines time as ''the system of those sequential relations that any event has to any other, as past, present, or future; indefinite and continuous duration regarded as that in which events succeed one another.'' Time corresponds to measurable real-world phenomena. For example, the movement of the Earth around the Sun signifies one year, one revolution of the Earth around its axis signifies one day, and so on. However, because it can only be defined through measurement, time is not absolute according to Albert Einstein's Theory of Relativity. To confuse matters further, some scientists disagree as to whether time itself really exists.

U.S. cities relied on the Sun to set time until the late 19th century. At that time, the railroad industry spearheaded the development of time zones to prevent train collisions and to better manage their schedules. Because of factory production schedules, the Industrial Revolution also made it important for the public to have access to more precise time measurements, which allowed them to show up for work at specific points in time. Standard Time was developed in 1884 to create uniform time standard across the globe. This led to the creation of 24 different international time zones. In theory, these regions are spaced longitudinally at 15 degrees, causing time to vary by one hour in each successive zone from a meridian running through Greenwich, England. This is the basis of Universal Time or Greenwich Mean Time (GMT). Based on political factors and other issues, the exact points at which time zones end and begin can vary in certain areas of the world.

INTERNET TIME

With the advent of the Internet and e-commerce came the concept of Internet Time, which generally referred to the breakneck speed at which things happened on the Internet, including success, failure, new product development, funding from venture capitalists, initial public offerings (IPOs), and the desire to get rich quick. It refers to the frantic rush many dot.com companies felt, especially during the late 1990s. *InformationWeek* writer Chris Murphy dubbed Internet Time as "a volatile mix of extraordinary opportunity, irrational exuberance, and blind panic," and explained that Internet Time transformed business into a sporting event where the goal was to finish first before time ran off the clock. Seeming to confirm Einstein's claim that time frames are not absolute, some compared Internet time to dog years, claiming that things like product development cycles unfolded faster on the Internet than in the "real" world. This was attributed to a variety of different factors, including the speed of data transmission and computer processors.

The concept that being the first company to introduce a product or service to the marketplace would guarantee success, even if the introduction were premature due to poor development, was associated with Internet Time. Although some e-companies, including Amazon.com and Yahoo, achieved success by being first, such an action was not a guarantee for success. In the early 2000s, many dot.com companies failed and saw their stock values plummet. Successful executives recognized that a sound business model and flexible, scalable technology also were critical components for staying in business, not just being the first-to-market.

In *Technology Review,* Andrew Odlyzko, head of mathematics and cryptography research at AT&T Labs in Florham Park, N.J., argued that Internet Time was a myth, and that the Internet's impact on the world, while important, happened according to the same time frames as other inventions and developments throughout history. Odlyzko explained that predictions about how the Internet would quickly revolutionize different aspects of the world and render things like phone companies and classified ads obsolete had yet to occur by the early 2000s. "As a general historical rule, it takes about a decade for even the most compelling new product or service to be widely accepted," he said. "That's still true. Even such attractive technologies as music CDs and cell phones, which many of us now regard as indispensable, took more than 10 years to move from commercial introduction to widespread use. Today we are seeing similar rates of adoption for DVDs, as well as digital cable TV, personal digital assistants and other emerging technologies."

TECHNICAL TIMING

Besides the perception that time unfolded more quickly on the Internet, the technical aspect of time measurement and synchronization was important to e-commerce companies in the early 2000s. This was due to a growing reliance on the accurate movement of data across the many networks that comprise the Internet. When data is sent over the Internet, it travels in packets and passes through a variety of different devices during transmission, including computers, servers, and routers. In the early 2000s, Symmetricom, which was formed through a merger between Telecom Solutions and Hewlett-Packard's timing division, was a leading provider of synchronization equipment for networks. The company used "atomic clocks, quartz, and GPS technologies to time over 21,000 nodes, or central offices, in more than 1,000 telecommunications networks in over 70 countries around the globe."

E-COMMERCE AND TIME ZONES

The advent of e-commerce led to a variety of issues corresponding to doing business in multiple time zones. Some of these presented opportunities for criminals to engage in malicious business practices. As Europe's Interactive Media in Retail Group (IMRG) explained, "occasions will inevitably occur in e-commerce when goods are not owned by anyone (either inadvertently or deliberately) presenting opportunities for chaos and crime. Alternatively, goods may at the same time be owned by two parties. How many times in a minute could someone online sell a piece of software or intellectual property? Who would be responsible? Whose insurance/legal jurisdiction would apply?"

During e-commerce, positive and negative issues also arise involving intra-time-zone communication. This applies to business-to-business interactions, those between consumers and companies, and even virtual teams of employees who must communicate with one another over great distances. When the differences between time zones are great, people may be asleep in one zone while counterparts are working in another. Depending on the geographic differences involved, real-time communication via phone or satellite- or Web-based video conferencing is often limited to small windows of several hours.

Communicating between distant time zones often leads to asynchronous communication patterns in which people exchange messages via e-mail or electronic bulletin boards. On one hand, this can cause communication delays, and various date and time stamping issues can make it a challenge for people to sequentially piece together chains of correspondence should they need to do so. However, virtual teams communicating in this manner also are able to increase productivity by working around-the-clock. This is accomplished by passing the workload around—such as between London, San Francisco, and Hong Kong—every 24 hours.

With the growth in virtual teams and virtual offices, which consist of work groups whose members are geographically distributed, the role of time zones was an important one in the early 2000s. According to *Time*, a 2000 PricewaterhouseCoopers study involving 82 large multinational firms revealed that, although the majority still relied heavily on relocation, nearly one quarter permitted employees based at home to manage international operations. Many of the companies expected to adopt virtual approaches. One company that relied heavily on remote communication was Popeyes Chicken, the world's second-largest quick-service chicken restaurant chain. In 2001 Popeyes operated restaurants in 41 states and 17 foreign countries. Its employees were able to effectively deal with issues like chicken supply shortages in Alaska and the opening of new restaurants in remote locations like Iceland from the company's Atlanta headquarters.

TIME ZONE SOLUTIONS

By the early 2000s, several solutions to time zone issues had been proposed. They attempted to make the issue of time less confusing by creating one universal time for the entire world. This had benefits for e-commerce companies in the areas of delivery agreements, online transactions, customer service, and more. In January 2000, British Prime Minister Tony Blair announced an initiative led by Europe's IMRG to create Greenwich Electronic Time (GeT). Like GMT, GeT was based on the meridian running through Greenwich, England and relied on the worldwide network of atomic clocks responsible for keeping precise time. Swiss watchmaker Swatch also began making watches that displayed what it coined Internet time. Instead of dividing every day into 1,440 minutes, Swatch's concept divided days into 1,000 beats. Unlike GMT, Internet time was based on a meridian running through Biel, Switzerland, the home of Swatch's headquarters.

Finally, AppSense Technologies Ltd. was a company addressing the technical side of time zone issues in the early 2000s. It provided a solution for application service providers (ASPs) and companies who served users on distributed computer systems throughout the world. Its TimePortal supported multiple time zones, making it possible for users to see their local time on the desktop, instead of the system time of the remote server to which they were connected. The software allowed this through a simple dropdown menu that enabled distributed users to select their local time and save it in the form of a profile that was effective each time the user logged on. If necessary, time zones could be adjusted as users traveled between different time zones.

FURTHER READING:

Alexander, Steve. "Virtual Teams Going Global." *InfoWorld,* November 13, 2000.

"Background to GeT." Interactive Media in Retail Group. May 24, 2001. Available from www.get-time.org.

Baldwin, Marina. "Keeping Time with the Global Market." *World Trade,* December 1999.

"Greenwich Electronic Time (GeT) Project to Help Business Make the Most of Time for Global E-commerce." Interactive Media in Retail Group. January 1, 2000. Available from www.imrg.org.

Harmon, Amy. "Is It Time For No-Time-Zones Idea? Swatch Tries To Make Its 'Internet Time' Fly." *Chicago Tribune,*. March 15, 1999.

Hohenstein, Peter C. "Crossing E-commerce Borders Like a Diplomat." *Afp Exchange,* Fall 2000.

"In Control, 10 Time Zones Away." *Time,* April 9, 2001.

Kiser, Kim. "Working on World Time." *Training,* March 1999.

Demetrios, Matsakis. "It's About TIME." *GPS World,* February 2000.

Moschella, David. "Why it's Time for a New Way to Handle Time on the Net." *Computerworld,* April 5, 1999.

Murphy, Chris. "The End of Internet Time." *InformationWeek,* January 22, 2001.

Murphy, Kathleen. "Facing A Global Challenge." *Internet World,* June 21, 1999.

Odlyzko, Andrew. "The Myth of 'Internet Time.'" *Technology Review,* April, 2001.

O'Shea, Dan. "Buying time." *Upstart,* September 2000.

Parker, Dan. "It's About Time." *Traffic World,* January 17, 2001.

''The Riddle of Time.'' *Time,* December 27, 1999.

Solomon, Charlene. ''Sharing Information Across Borders and Time Zones.'' *Workforce,* March 1998.

SEE ALSO: Global Presence, Becoming a; Shipping and Shipment Tracking; Speed-to-Market

TIMESTAMPING

In the digital world, it is necessary to have a means for verifying the integrity and accuracy of documents and important records. Used in conjunction with digital certificates, which are issued by third party organizations to ensure the legitimacy of Web site operators, timestamping is used to prove and verify the date and time when a digital document or record was created. Simply typing dates and times onto digital records is not enough because they can be easily falsified (backdated, future-dated, or otherwise tampered with). This can have serious consequences. One example involves electronic records of a company's trade secrets. If these were ever stolen or misused, resulting in a court case, a timestamped digital record would be one way to prove ownership of the company's intellectual property (proprietary ideas resulting from the company's own creative processes). Timestamping is especially valuable in e-commerce, where companies exchange large amounts of digital information (invoices, confirmations, purchase orders, shipping records, inventory data, and other data) with consumers and other businesses that may need to be verified.

As with digital certificates, trusted third parties provide timestamping services. Reston, Virginia-based Surety.com was a leading digital notary service in the early 2000s. Created in 1994 by two scientists from Bellcore, the company's Digital Notary service provided timestamping and notary services for a wide range of digital items including database records, e-mail messages, business transactions, video clips, text documents, pictures, spreadsheets, and more. Surety.com's customers included companies in the manufacturing and financial sectors, as well as those focusing on the exchange of electronic documents. Bose Corp., a manufacturer of electronic sound systems, used Surety.com's timestamping service for a pilot program in its research department. The program involved securing intellectual property in Bose's archiving system. Previously, Bose researchers had to enter signed, dated, handwritten notes about their research into notebooks. The new system eliminated duplication of effort, since electronic information no longer had to be duplicated on paper.

Services like Surety.com's rely on formulas called algorithms to perform timestamping. More specifically, document owners use one-way hash functions (special types of algorithms) to convert the text in their digital documents or records into corresponding hash values. These hash values are unique to the original records or documents, much like fingerprints are unique to human beings. When timestamping is desired, hash values are sent to third parties like Surety.com who assign dates and times to them. Additionally, a widely witnessed system is used, meaning that the public is able to see that timestamping has occurred. This helps to ensure that all parties involved in the process are honest and legitimate.

In a widely witnessed system, the hash value from a submitted record is incorporated into a large summary hash chain that includes hash values from other users' timestamped records. Another one-way algorithm is then used to create a summary hash value. According to a Surety.com white paper, in addition to an assigned date and time, timestamped records are returned to record owners with details about the exact place in the summary chain their record resided when timestamping occurred. Also provided are hash values from other records in the chain, which is made publicly available. The white paper explains that ''the probability of being able to retrospectively substitute a false document's hash value and then produce the same summary hash value while still retaining the other chain hash values is far to the right of infinitesimal.'' Although every kind of security system has weak points, this method was perhaps one of the soundest available in the early 2000s, providing much needed security in an increasingly electronic age.

FURTHER READING:

Cox, Beth. ''A Body Guard for your Ideas.'' *Internet.com,* February 8, 2000. Available from ecommerce.internet.com.

''Secure Time/Date Stamping in a Public Key Infrastructure.'' Surety.com Inc. June 29, 2001. Available from www.surety.com.

''Surety.com.'' Surety.com Inc. June 30, 2001. Available from www.surety.com.

Trowbridge, Dave. ''Super Hash Serves Up Super Privacy on the Internet.'' *Computer Technology Review,* April 1995.

''What is Digital Timestamping?'' RSA Security Inc. June 30, 2001. Available from www.rsa.com.

SEE ALSO: Computer Crime; Cryptography, Public and Private Key; Digital Certificates; Privacy: Issues, Policies, Statements; Real-time Transaction

TRADE SHOWS

Trade shows related to the Internet, e-business, electronics, and computers grew in popularity throughout the 1990s. As certain shows—including the PC Expo, Internet World, and COMDEX— became known as the "who's who" trade shows of the e-business industry, technology-based companies began eyeing the trade show arena as a lucrative venue for securing customers. During the dot.com boom of the late 1990s, these companies scrambled to secure exhibition space at well known shows in order to launch cutting edge products and services. Also known as expositions or conventions, such shows often last three or more days, take place in large cities, and feature industry leading keynote speakers addressing hot topics and issues of concern to the exhibitors and attendees.

As trade shows became more elaborate in terms of duration and size during the late 1990s, show organizers, as well as exhibitors, began to seek out the help of professional exposition companies with trade show expertise. GES Exposition Services, for example, operates as a trade-show management company involved in planning and exhibit services. The $1.8 billion firm has been responsible for some of the largest trade shows in the industry including PC Expo, the Internet World shows, and the Consumer Electronics Show. The number of associations for trade show organizers and exhibitors also increased during this time period. Among the most popular in the industry are the Professional Convention Management Association (PCMA), the Trade Show Exhibitors Association (TSEA), the International Association for Exhibition Management (IAEM), the Exhibition Services & Contractors Association (ESCA), and the Computer Event Marketing Association (CEMA). All of these membership-based groups provide information to and act as a resource for companies that plan and stage trade shows.

According to industry magazine *Tradeshow Week,* the average computer and electronics trade show in 1999 had approximately 426 exhibiting companies and 20,178 professional attendees; each show also had roughly 158,857 square feet of exhibition space. The West Coast and Midwest were the most popular regions for trade shows that year, and the majority of shows were held in June. After growing at a rapid clip for several years, computer and electronic trade shows began to experience a decline in attendance and size as the American economy slowed and dot.com frenzy began to fizzle in 2000.

POPULAR INDUSTRY EVENTS

During the earliest years of the 21st century, the Internet became an increasingly popular tool used by enterprises for many facets of business. While the e-commerce tools of the late 1990s focused on using the Web for marketing and sales efforts, the e-business

tools of the 2000s broadened in scope to also handle things like procurement and other back-end business functions. Major trade shows began reflecting this trend, and instead of focusing solely on information technology (IT) or e-commerce tools, they began to incorporate both into events. In fact, CMP Media LLC canceled its 2001 eBusiness Conference & Expo in order to retool the show's focus. Instead, the company planned to hold the TechEnterprise Conference & Expo in December 2002, with a focus on the integration of technology and e-business.

Even as size and attendance at technology-based trade shows began to dwindle in the new millennium, many events continued to focus on both technology and e-business. In fact, some of these shows evolved into popular annual or seasonal events. Among the most well known are the Internet World shows, the International Consumer Electronic Show (CES), the COMDEX show, Seybold Seminars conferences and technology expositions, the Macworld Conference & Expo, the COMNET Conference & Expo, PC Expo, @d:tech, and the infamous DefCon conventions.

The Internet World shows are the largest trade show events in the e-business and Internet industries. Owned by Penton Media Inc., the Internet World conventions have experienced a decline in attendance over the past several years. In fact, according to a 2000 *B to B* magazine article, "the Internet industry's flagship event now faces competition from a slew of specialty e-commerce and b-to-b shows, as well as from traditional IT industry events such as COMDEX or PC Expo that increasingly focus on Internet technologies." During the Internet World Fall 2000 show, over 1,000 companies were on display in over 300,000 square feet of exhibition space at the Jacob K. Javits Convention Center in New York City. The event drew nearly 60,000 attendees interested in the show's Web content management, wireless, and streaming media conferences. Keynote speakers included executives from Intel Corp., America Online Inc. (AOL), Oracle Corp., CMGI Inc., and idealab!. Over 30,000 people are expected to attend the Internet World Fall 2001, which is postponed until December due the terrorist events of September 11, 2001. The show's keynote speakers will include Compaq Computer Corp.'s CEO Michael Capellas, AOL's co-chief operating officer Robert Pittman, and RealNetworks Inc.'s CEO Rob Glaser.

Sponsored by the Consumer Electronics Association, the first CES show took place in New York in 1967 with 200 exhibitors and 17,500 attendees. By 2001, the show had evolved to include 2,000 exhibitors; 126,730 attendees; and 1.2 million net square feet of exhibition space. Known as the world's largest annual trade show in the consumer technology industry, CES draws its audience from 110 countries around the world. It showcases products and services ranging from digital imaging to wireless communications to satellite systems. The January 2001 CES four-day show held in Las Vegas, Nevada, featured keynote speakers Bill Gates, of Microsoft Corp., and Intel's CEO Craig Barrett. During the event, Microsoft launched its new gaming system Xbox, and Intel introduced its Pocket Concert wireless digital music player.

The COMDEX show, produced by Key3Media Group Inc., is the largest annual IT trade show, attracting exhibitors and attendees from over 140 countries. In existence for over 20 years, COMDEX operates as global marketplace serving the IT industry. While attendance was down nearly 30 percent at the COMDEX Fall 2001 show in Las Vegas, some 2,000 exhibitors introduced approximately 390 new products at the event. The number of companies present at the 2001 show dropped by roughly 400, while the number of new products introduced rose by over 130. Bill Gates gave his annual keynote address, predicting that even while the economy was slowing, 2002 would be a year of growth for the technology industry. At the show, Microsoft touted its new book-sized tablet computer, claiming that the tablets would replace laptops within five years; a tablet PC has the same memory capacity as a laptop, but can recognize handwriting and connect wirelessly to the Internet. In 2002, the COMDEX Fall show will be held in Atlanta, Georgia, along with Key3Media Group's NetWorld+Interop event, a show that caters to the Internet protocol (IP) networking and telecommunications industries.

Key3Media Group also produces the Seybold Seminars conferences and technology events, which focus on media technology- and publishing-related products and services. The Seybold San Francisco 2001 show was sponsored by Apple Computer Inc. and Adobe Systems Inc., and included special sessions on convergence among devices such as Palm Pilots, cell phones, pagers, and laptop computers. The event also addressed the issue of digital rights management (DRM), a popular topic dealing with protection of the rights of copyright holders, and also focused on e-books and e-publishing. Key3Media Group produces a total of 40 e-business-related events in 17 countries across the globe. These events feature over 6,000 exhibiting companies and draw over one million attendees each year.

The Macworld Conference & Expo, put on by IT event management company IDG World Expo, is a semiannual event taking place each year in New York City in July and San Francisco in January. For nearly twenty years, Macworld has showcased the Macintosh (Mac) operating system and Apple Computer's hardware and software. The event draws thousands of Mac enthusiasts each year and is typically used to launch new Mac products. IDG also produces the COMNET Conference & Expo, a networking and communications trade show. Ivan Seidenberg, president and co-CEO of Verizon Communications; Wolfgang Kemna, CEO of SAP America Inc.; and Patrick Nettles, chairman of CIENA Corp., were slated to keynote the January 2002 four-day show, which will be held in Washington D.C. The themes of the event include such issues as enterprise networking security, optical networking, regulatory issues, and wireless infrastructure.

PC Expo, part of CMP Media LLC's Technology Exchange Week New York (TECHXNY) lineup, is a yearly trade show event focused on cutting edge technology in personal computing. Attendance at the show dropped in the early 2000s. Nevertheless, 500 exhibitors including Adobe Systems, Compaq, Hewlett Packard Co., Gateway Inc., IBM Corp., Intel, and Iomega Corp. introduced new products at the 19th annual show. Palm Inc.'s CEO Carl Yankowski delivered the leading keynote speech, signaling the shift in the show's focus from the personal computer to hand-held appliances, including wireless devices. Bill Gates and Andy Grove of Intel had been featured keynote speakers in the past.

@d:tech, a seasonal show known as the premier event for Internet marketing and advertising, also experienced a drop in exhibitors and attendance during its Spring 2001 show, when the number of exhibitors fell 26 percent to 102, and attendance decreased 32 percent to 2,500. During the Fall 2001 event, the number of exhibitors fell to 75. Keynote speakers for the event included executives from Yahoo! Inc. and DoubleClick Inc.

The controversial DefCon show is an annual event that started in the early 1990s. Held in Las Vegas, the yearly show draws over 4,000 computer hackers and those interested in computer security. While DefCon doesn't compare to other leading industry shows in size and scale, it does garner significant media and industry attention due to the rising interest in security issues relating to the Internet. According to research group Datamonitor, spending related to network security is expected to increase from $10.6 billion in 2001 to $22.3 billion in 2004. Although show organizers claim that the intent of the event is to improve Internet security, many in the industry believe the purpose of DefCon is to demonstrate techniques for stealing information from large companies. During the 2001 show, Dimitri Sklyarov, a Russian programmer employed by ElcomSoft Co., was arrested by the FBI for violating the Digital Millennium Copyright Act of 1998. At the time, Adobe Systems had developed e-book software that allowed publishers to distribute books electronically. These e-book were encrypted and did not allow the purchaser to copy and resell the book. Sklyarov was paid by his company to create Advanced eBook Processor, a program that removed Adobe System's encryption, thus allowing users to make unauthorized copies of the e-book. Adobe eventually dropped its complaint against ElcomSoft and Sklyarov due to negative publicity and pressure from the Electronic Frontier Foundation, but the FBI chose to indict the programmer and his company for trafficking in technology designed to circumvent the rights of a copyright owner and conspiracy charges.

Even as trade show growth slowed during the new millennium, exhibitions continued to play a significant role in the industry. According to an October 2000 *Business Week* article, "trade shows are indispensable for making contacts, nailing sales, and showing off a hot new product." Finding this to be true, many companies continued to include trade show exhibiting in yearly marketing budgets.

FURTHER READING:

Chapman, Ben. "The Trade Show Must Go On." *Sales & Marketing Management,* June 2001, 22.

Goode, S.E. "Are Trade Shows Really Worth It?" *CRM Daily.com,* January 15, 2001. Available from www.crmdaily.com.

Hilts, Paul. "Russian Hacker Indicted." *Publishers Weekly,* September 3, 2001, 14.

IDG World Expo. "About IDG World Expo." Framingham, MA: IDG World Expo, 2001. Available from www.idgworldexpo.com.

Keefe, Bob. "Scaled Down Comdex Opens As Gates Reports Record Windows XP Sales." *NewsFactor Network,* November 12, 2001. Available from www.newsfactor.com.

Key3Media Group Inc. "About Us." Los Angeles, CA: Key3Media Group Inc., 2001. Available from www.key3media.com.

Klein, Karen E. "Trade Secrets." *Business Week,* October 21, 2000.

Tradeshow Week Inc. "Tradeshow Trends." Los Angeles, CA: Tradeshow Week Inc., 2001. Available from www.tradeshowweek.com.

"The Wide, Open Spaces of PC Expo." *Business Week,* June 29, 2001. Available from www.businessweek.com.

Wrolstad, Jay. "Gadgets Galore at Consumer Electronics Show." *Wireless Newsfactor,* January 5, 2001. Available from www.wireless.news.factor.com.

TRANSACTION ISSUES

As companies embraced electronic commerce and worked to devise winning online business strateg-

ies they faced a number of key challenges. Among these, perhaps none were more pressing or problematic in the late 1990s and early 2000s than the issues related to online transactions. With problems ranging from implementing effective online ordering systems to securing electronic payments and customer information, from devising quick and efficient delivery and return operations to integrating transaction applications into the technological infrastructure, transaction issues were at the heart of the movement to electronic commerce.

Before the Electronic Age, paper-based documents validated and sealed with a written signature were the overwhelmingly dominant means of conducting commercial transactions for nearly a thousand years. The onset of electronic transactions disrupted established models for nearly every area of commerce, and businesses, facing tough competitive pressures, scrambled to find new models to adjust to a changed commercial environment. How does one validate an electronic document? At what point in an electronic transaction is it considered legally sent and received? What kind of infrastructure is required to record and store electronic transactions? What measures are required to protect sensitive information, such as credit-card numbers or company secrets?

ACCOMMODATING CUSTOMERS

Some of the major transaction issues that e-commerce firms needed to address at the start of the 21st century were revealed and prioritized in a report released by PricewaterhouseCoopers in 2000. Titled *Barriers to Online Purchasing 2000,* the report found that, of all the major barriers to online shopping, 79 percent of survey respondents listed credit card security as their greatest concern, while 77 percent most feared disclosure of their personal details, 48 percent reported that their lack of trust in online merchants most prevented them from shopping online, 40 percent were bewildered by Web storefronts, 21 percent were befuddled by the convoluted order processes, and 20 percent were simply fed up with the time it took to complete a transaction.

Clearly, security was among the preeminent transaction concerns, for obvious reasons. On the consumer side, the novel electronic shopping environment provides unique opportunities for convenience, comparison shopping, and speed, but through the 1990s and early 2000s, many consumers were wary of trusting companies—and even the Internet itself—with their personal and financial information out of fear that it could potentially fall into the wrong hands. In many cases, these fears were justified; electronic credit card theft was not unheard of in the early years of widespread e-commerce. Thus businesses had a clear incentive to fortify their transaction systems to ward off hackers and other cybercriminals. If customers weren't at ease making online purchases, then companies wouldn't be able to reap the full advantages inherent in e-commerce. Moreover, if firms earned a reputation for lax security measures, they could simply lose their customers to competitors. At the macro level, analysts placed great hope in the promise of e-commerce, and recognized that security concerns were holding back the potential national and international benefits that online business holds.

It was for these reasons that U.S. legislators finally relaxed restrictions on the proliferation of strong encryption schemes in the late 1990s. For years, governments were concerned about the widespread use of powerful encryption technologies, as it could render criminal investigations harder to conduct. At the close of the 20th century, however, the United States opted to allow wider international proliferation of encryption schemes as a way of fostering the development of e-commerce. Encryption was among the key methods of securing electronic transactions, scrambling and coding sensitive information in a manner that only authorized persons could decode and read. However, encryption schemes continually grow stronger in response to more sophisticated hacking technologies and methods, representing a sort of arms race between hackers and security designers.

There was a more immediate and pragmatic reason for companies to be on guard against potential criminals and untrustworthy customers. Credit card companies, highly aware themselves of the risks involved in e-commerce, charge online merchants much higher percentages than their brick-and-mortar counterparts for services such as credit authorization, verification, and payment. Moreover, charge-backs, or those occurrences where a credit card number comes up empty, are the sole responsibility of the online company, and constituted a conspicuously high expense for e-businesses in the 1990s and early 2000s.

TECHNICAL ASPECTS

For completing online transactions, some form of seal is required akin to the traditional signature. For that reason, digital signatures came to prominence in the late 1990s and early 2000s. Digital signatures are encrypted packets of information that validate the identity of an individual in cyberspace. The U.S. Electronic Signatures in Global and National Commerce Act (E-SIGN), signed into law by President Clinton with a digital signature in 2000, renders digital signatures as legally binding as traditional written signatures. Legally, electronic signatures not only verify the identity of the sender but also ensure the validity and authenticity of the document to which the signa-

ture is attached. Digital signatures utilize public key infrastructure (PKI), a mode of encryption whereby the signature owner maintains an exclusive private key that only he or she can use to view or alter the signature, and a public key that anyone can use to verify that the signature did indeed come from the private key's owner. Importantly, digital signatures cannot be taken out of their context; that is, they are bound to the document or order form to which they are attached and can't be copied and illicitly affixed to other documents.

Another major concern for e-businesses, both those devoted to consumers and those geared toward other businesses, was the development of Web-enabled transaction services and applications. Since the World Wide Web has emerged as the dominant Internet medium and the primary means by which customers shop online, there were growing pressures to implement transaction systems that could complete orders and payments right on the Web, thereby saving time and making online shopping a less cumbersome process. In this way, companies ease their transaction costs and processing time, while customers' shopping experience is rendered more pleasant and convenient.

A central element of smoothing online transaction issues was the development and implementation of eXtensible Markup Language (XML), a meta-language that allows programmers to closely define the meaning and format of data presented in electronic documents. Poised to emerge as the lingua franca of e-commerce, XML was the basis for most existing electronic procurement systems in the early 2000s. In the business-to-business realm, transaction networks have grown more convoluted and multifaceted, with businesses connected in ever more intricate Webs of relationships operating on different systems and platforms. As a result, companies were scrambling to devise increasingly flexible ordering, procurement, and other transaction systems that can readily respond to all systems employed in their business relationships. The development of XML, and the continued use of electronic data interchange (EDI), were key characteristics of this trend, but these were complemented by still-existing proprietary systems and industry-specific arrangements.

To fully take advantage of the Internet's capabilities, analysts point out that the future of online commerce will be characterized by instantaneous, real-time transactions. In such a system, electronic banking, the organizing and display of shipping information, confirmations, and other details pertinent to the transaction all take place at high speed so as to present all information to the customer in real time. Obviously, real-time transactions were a long way off in the early 2000s, as banks required days to clear online credit-card information and logistics required great coordination after the order was placed. Moreover, in a business setting, many important transactions require time for various levels of the organization to regroup and coordinate for that particular transaction; a transaction may require approval from certain segments of the organization, it may demand consultation, and so on. In the early 2000s, transaction-processing applications were generally very rigid, in that they required all details to be firmly in place before they processed the information in the transaction. According to *InformationWeek,* the potential of online commerce for real-time transactions could be achieved if those transaction-processing applications could be retooled for great flexibility and thus harness their capabilities for use earlier in the transaction process.

FURTHER READING:

Bernstein, Barbara. ''Slow Down Transactions.'' *Information-Week,* May 24, 1999.

Gantz, John. ''There's No Foolin' in E-commerce Transactions.'' *Computerworld,* April 2, 2001.

Radding, Alan. ''Overcome the Web-transaction Barrier.'' *InformationWeek,* December 13, 1999.

Sowinski, Lara L. ''Web-based Financial Settlement Comes of Age.'' *World Trade,* April 2001.

Waugh, Don. ''The Silver Bullet for E-commerce Security.'' *CMA Management,* July/August 2001.

SEE ALSO: Cryptography, Public and Private Key; Encryption; Fraud, Internet; Digital Cash; Digital Certificates; Digital Signatures; Real-time Transaction; XML

TRANSPARENCY

The term transparency is used to describe conditions under which information flows freely and important business information is readily disclosed so that it is obvious and easily understood. In the realm of e-commerce, the term transparency can be applied to different aspects of business, including the general concept of fair and honest business practices; pricing; and the degree to which companies can benefit by sharing data without compromising security.

In the area of pricing, transparency can refer to the very basic principle of honesty. If consumers order goods or services online, the listed prices for those goods and services should be all-inclusive. In other words, consumers should not find surcharges or extra fees added onto their credit card statements for purchases. Transparency is an important concept, because the consumer's fear of making purchases online

has serious consequences for companies engaged in e-commerce. Although the practice of buying goods and services online was widely accepted by mid-2001, a study conducted by Brigham Young University revealed that many individuals were still fearful of online shopping at that time. For those who were reluctant, the biggest fear factor involved revealing credit card numbers.

Pricing transparency also applies to the business-to-business sector, especially in the area of online marketplaces or exchanges. Online marketplaces are Web sites (both public and private) where corporate buyers can purchase goods and services from a wide variety of sellers. In the early 2000s, such marketplaces existed for many industries, including packaged goods, electronics, chemicals, and food and beverage. These venues gave companies the power to break long-established relationships with local suppliers and more easily seek out the best price, nationally or worldwide. In this scenario, transparency comes in the form of a supplier's price being visible to every other party (both buyers as well as competing sellers). Online marketplaces can lead to increased competition and more uniform prices, and, in some cases, lower prices. According to *E-Commerce Times,* a report from Morgan Stanley Dean Witter indicated transparency leads to specialization among suppliers seeking an advantage in an increasingly competitive marketplace, and predicted this would ''lead to more customization, more choice, and better service.''

E-commerce requires the disclosure of information from one entity to another (suppliers to manufacturers, manufacturers to distributors, customers to retailers, and so on). For example, Wal-Mart placed its entire supply chain online for all to see. This form of transparency creates value for trading partners in a supply chain, but also poses potential security risks. Companies that reveal too much data regarding prices and production can open themselves to pressure that may result in reduced profits. Additionally, partners in a supply chain need to be careful about the information they impart in order to prevent the violation of antitrust laws or the revelation of too much company intelligence to competitors.

Despite concerns about sharing details with outsiders, some companies have benefited significantly from this transparent approach, relying on end-users to help them develop new products and services. Microsoft relied on the input of more than 500,000 software engineers to test its Microsoft 2000 operating system. Their feedback was useful in working kinks out of the final product and making it better in many ways. Similarly, the Linux operating system (used as on many Web servers) also benefited from a collaborative developmental process.

FURTHER READING:

''Brigham Young University: Would-be Shoppers Still Worry on Security.'' Nua Internet Surveys. July 13, 2001. Available from www.nua.ie/surveys.

Enos, Lori. ''Study: U.S. Distributors Not Ready for the Net.'' June 8, 2001. Available from www.ecommercetimes.com.

Lee, Hau L. and Seungjin Whang. ''Sharing Information to Boost the Bottom Line.'' Stanford Graduate School of Business, 1999. Available from www.gsb.stanford.edu.

Prahalad, C.K., Venkatram Ramaswamy, and M.S. Krishnan. ''Customer Centricity.'' *Planet IT*. April 10, 2000. Available from www.planetit.com

SEE ALSO: Channel Transparency

TRAVELOCITY.COM

Travelocity.com is a leading online travel Web site where travelers can make airline, hotel, and car rental reservations, book cruises and vacation packages, find information about destinations, and access a range of other travel-related services. It was launched in March 1996 as a joint venture of Sabre Interactive and Worldview Systems Corp. Sabre Interactive was a business unit of American Airlines' parent company AMR Corp. Sabre's principal business was to develop and install computer systems for travel agents. Sabre was the leading travel reservation system used by travel agents. In 1995 Sabre offered an easySabre service through online services CompuServe and Prodigy, giving consumers access to the same booking information available to travel agents. For 1997 Sabre reported $1.8 billion in revenue and $200 million in net income.

Worldview was a partnership formed by publisher Random House and regional Bell operating company (RBOC) Ameritech. Worldview provided content for Travelocity.com, while Sabre booked the airline reservations. Travelocity's strategy at first was to offer compelling content, including hotel recommendations, restaurant reviews, entertainment listings, weather reports, video clips, photos, maps, news, chat forums, and other information about specific destinations. Travelocity's Web server was connected to Worldview's multiple databases by Kiva's Enterprise Server software, which processed user requests and pulled down real-time data from Worldview's databases, then displayed it on the Travelocity site. In February 1997 Sabre Interactive bought out Worldview's interest in Travelocity, with Worldview remaining as the site's featured provider of destination information.

TRAVELOCITY ENJOYS STEADY GROWTH

In the first three months 144,000 people registered at Travelocity.com, which reported 1.2 million visits during the period. At first the site sold airline tickets and provided destination information. It then added features such as vacation packages, car rentals, and hotel reservations. Through an agreement with Vicinity Corp., Travelocity users were able to access street maps of areas around specific U.S. sites. Before the end of 1996 Travelocity was chosen to be the travel content provider for Time Warner's experimental online service, Road Runner. During the year Travelocity refined its Web site to make it easier to use. By the end of the year it offered travel information for more than 200 destinations around the world and had more than 400,000 registered members. In October 1996, Microsoft launched a competing travel service, Expedia. Travelocity and Expedia would become the top two travel sites on the Internet. Another online travel competitor, Preview Travel, would be acquired by Travelocity at the end of 1999.

Travelocity enjoyed steady growth during its first two years in business. It provided reservations on more than 400 airlines, schedules for more than 700 airlines, reservations at 35,000 hotel locations, and access to 50 rental car companies. Registration was required to make a purchase over Travelocity, with tickets being delivered either to a local travel agent or through Travelocity's own travel agency, the Travelocity Service Center. To maintain the support of travel agents who utilized the Sabre reservation system, Sabre and Travelocity built 12,000 customized Web sites for travel agents to help them handle online bookings. It was important that Travelocity position itself as an ally, rather than as a competitor, to travel agents. Travelocity was created as the key element in Sabre's strategy to capture the biggest possible share of overall travel bookings, both on and off the Web. For 1997 the company handled more than $100 million in bookings, a sizeable percentage of the estimated $900 million booked in online travel reservations that year.

MERGER WITH PREVIEW TRAVEL CREATES A CATEGORY LEADER

Toward the end of 1998 Travelocity unveiled an upgraded Web site that reduced the number of screens required to book a flight from 13 to three. In the first half of 1999 it added personalization features and richer content. In a move that consolidated two of the top online travel services, Travelocity merged with Preview Travel in October 1999. The new company would be called Travelocity.com and would be headquartered in Fort Worth, Texas. In addition to creating a category leader in online travel services, the merger had the effect of making Travelocity a publicly traded company and giving it access to equity markets, because Preview Travel was a public company. The merger also separated Travelocity from its parent company, Sabre, which continued to be Travelocity's principal technology partner. Sabre also provided technology for other online travel services, including Priceline.com and Hotwire. Sabre retained a 70 percent ownership in Travelocity, while Preview's shareholders owned 30 percent. In addition, Sabre contributed $50 million in seed money.

The merger of Travelocity and Preview Travel created the third most-visited electronic commerce site in the world, behind Amazon.com and eBay. The new Travelocity had about 17 million registered members and 8 million monthly visitors. It was the preferred travel provider for all of the major portals, including America Online, Excite, Go Network, @Home, Lycos, Netscape, USA Today, and Yahoo!. According to Forrester Research, online travel purchases were projected to increase from about $8 billion in 1999 to $32 billion by 2004. Another research firm, PhoCusWright of Sherman, Connecticut, predicted that online travel purchases would reach $20 billion by 2001.

Prior to the merger both Travelocity and Preview Travel sustained losses in order to gain customers and build market share. For 1998 Travelocity reported a loss of $21 million, while Preview Travel lost $27 million. For all of 1999 Travelocity and Preview Travel had combined revenue of $90.9 million and a combined loss of $49.8 million. While the merger between Travelocity and Preview Travel was pending, Microsoft's Expedia went public with a successful initial public offering in November 1999. According to Media Metrix, Expedia had slightly more traffic than Travelocity during the 1999 holiday season.

As part of their strategy to gain market share, Travelocity and Preview Travel entered into an agreement with name-your-own-fare service Priceline.com. The three companies agreed to refer customers to each other's sites and collect referral fees when purchases were made. The arrangement gave Travelocity and Preview Travel access to Priceline.com's reverse auctions and enabled them to serve customers that were looking for the cheapest fares. Principal competitor Expedia countered by announcing its own plans for a name-your-own-price scheme for airline tickets.

The merger between Travelocity and Preview Travel was completed in March 2000, and in April the new Travelocity launched a $50 million advertising campaign to attract new customers. The print and TV campaign positioned Travelocity as the place where people could take control of their travel arrangements. The radio component of the ad campaign portrayed

Travelocity as the online site that listed 45,000 hotels, 700 airlines, and 50 car rental companies. According to Media Metrix, Travelocity had combined traffic of more than 8 million visitors in February 2000, making it the top online travel site in terms of traffic. Expedia had 5.3 million visitors, while Travelocity by itself had 5.1 million.

Travelocity completed its integration with Preview Travel by mid-2000 and introduced a redesigned Web site. New features included a group shopping tool, a message board, customer reviews, and wireless travel services as well as a redesigned home page. At the end of June Travelocity had 21.6 million registered members, up from 19.2 million at the end of the first quarter. In September Travelocity teamed with American Airlines Publishing to launch *Travelocity Magazine,* a bimonthly title with a controlled circulation of 250,000. The new magazine was a logical extension of the Travelocity brand and enhanced the company's position as a provider of tools for travelers who wanted to take control of their travel planning. In October Travelocity sold its 10 millionth airline ticket.

By the end of 2000 Travelocity supported Web sites in Canada, the United Kingdom, and Germany, with agreements in place to launch a site in Japan in 2001. Travelocity was first able to serve customers outside the United States in September 1997, when it altered its infrastructure to support global pricing and taxation. International customers were served by Travelocity's main site in the United States, with tickets delivered through Sabre's international network of more than 10,000 travel agents. In mid-1998 Travelocity established a customer service center in Cardiff, Wales, to support its United Kingdom customers. It partnered with a U.K. travel agency to provide local content for a Web site designed specifically for the United Kingdom. Travelocity Canada was established in April 1999, and a bilingual customer service center was opened in Ottawa. Travelocity then focused on Germany and launched Travelocity Germany. A mid-2000 agreement with Japan Airlines, All Nippon Airways, and 11 other international carriers resulted in the subsequent launch of Travelocity Japan in 2001.

For 2000 Travelocity's gross travel bookings reached $2.5 billion, more than twice that of 1999 and a significant percentage of the $11 billion spent in online travel during the year. At the beginning of 2001 Travelocity was the top-ranked online travel provider with 8.72 million visitors in January 2001, or 18 percent market share, according to Nielsen/NetRatings and Harris Interactive. The other top four online travel providers were Southwest Airlines, with 5.1 million visitors (14 percent market share); Expedia, with 4.8 million visitors (11 percent); Priceline.com (3.4 million visitors, 9 percent); and Delta Airlines (3.0 million visitors, 8 percent).

STRIVING FOR PROFITABILITY

Travelocity faced new competitive pressures from the airlines in 2001, including two new airlines-backed online ticketing services by Hotwire.com and Orbitz.com. In addition, the airlines capped commissions at $10 per ticket for all airline tickets sold online or offline, and some airlines—notably Northwest and KLM—eliminated commissions for tickets sold online. In March Travelocity also stopped booking flights on Southwest Airlines after the two companies experienced customer service problems. It also began charging $10 commissions on flights booked on Northwest and KLM.

Travelocity celebrated its fifth anniversary in March 2001 by launching new services, including a travel club (Travelocity Preferred Traveler) and Goodbuy, a negotiated fare service for 20 airlines and rooms at 2,500 hotels. A new feature, Option Finder, searched for alternate airports and departure dates. For the quarter ending March 2001, Travelocity reported a profit of $618,000 before special items and a positive cash flow. However, special items totaling $26.4 million resulted in a quarterly loss of $22.1 million, compared to $9 million for the same quarter in 2000. Travelocity's stock rallied on the news and increased more than 134 percent from January through the end of April. Travelocity's second quarter was also profitable on a pro forma basis, excluding the write-off of goodwill.

During the year Travelocity added new products and services. An investment in Viator added that company's database of sightseeing tours, attractions, and other destination activities in 33 countries to its offerings. A partnership with American Classic Voyages Co. enabled Travelocity to offer Hawaiian cruises. In July Travelocity launched its Bon Voyage e-mail service, which recommended activities, events, and personalized special offers to its members. A toll-free telephone service was also offered to provide customers with offline support. Internationally, Travelocity announced it would acquire Air Tickets Direct, a U.K.-based online travel agency with a dedicated call center for offline sales support. The company also entered into agreements with British Airways and Lufthansa, and it began offering the entire range of 73 European rail passes.

In the quarter ending September 30 memberships increased to 30.4 million, an increase of 1.7 million over the previous quarter. While the online travel industry was the best performing sector of the Internet economy for the first eight months of 2001, the terrorist attacks of September 11 had a dramatic impact on online travel providers. Online bookings dropped to only 30 to 40 percent of their previous levels. At the beginning of October Travelocity announced it would close its call center in Sacramento, California, and reduce its workforce by 19 percent, or 320 jobs. The company had about 1,700 employees before the cutbacks and planned to institute a hiring freeze. Given the uncertainty of the times, it remained to be seen if Travelocity could achieve profitability.

FURTHER READING:

Anderson, Karen M. "Gloves Are off in Fight Between Expedia and Travelocity." *Travel Agent,* January 10, 2000.

Biesada, Alexandra. "Travelocity.com." *Texas Monthly,* February 2001.

Bittle, Scott. "Travelocity Site Gets Lots of Bites." *Travel Weekly,* July 11, 1996.

Caulfield, Brian. "A Balancing Act for One Travel Site." *Internet World,* April 27, 1998.

Cone, Edward. "Travel Combo Taxies into Lead." *Inter@ctive Week,* October 18, 1999.

Cronin, Mary J. "The Travel Agents' Dilemma." *Fortune,* May 11, 1998.

Goetzi, David. "Travelocity Voyage Puts the Consumer in Charge." *Advertising Age,* April 17, 2000.

Goodridge, Elisabeth. "Travelocity Overcomes Barriers in Its Global Expansion." *InformationWeek,* December 11, 2000.

Maddox, Kate. "Traveling on the Web." *InformationWeek,* January 20, 1997.

McGee, William J. "Travelocity-Preview Merger Creates Online Powerhouse." *Travel Agent,* October 11, 1999.

Meehan, Michael. "Online Travel Deals Make for Strange Bedfellows at Sabre." *Computerworld,* August 14, 2000.

Schaal, Dennis. "Travelocity Tries Human Touch." *Travel Weekly,* August 30, 2001.

"Travelocity Redesigned." *Travel Agent,* July 3, 2000.

SEE ALSO: Ticketmaster

24/7 MEDIA INC.

24/7 Media Inc. is an advertising agency specializing in the Internet and interactive media. Headquartered in New York City, the company operates globally and offers a wide range of advertising, direct marketing, promotions and sponsorships, and technology services and solutions. Starting in 2000, the firm organized its business into three functional areas: 24/7 Network, 24/7 Mail, and 24/7 Technology Solutions.

The 24/7 Network is a global advertising network represented in 24 countries. It includes high-profile, high-traffic Web sites that 24/7 Media represents to advertisers, including more than 400 Web sites in the United States, 80 in Canada, more than 250 in Europe, and more than 30 in Latin America. Through an agreement with Chinadotcom Corp., 24/7 Media portrays more than 500 major Web sites in Asia. The 24/7 Network is organized into topical channels covering such areas as automotive, business/financial, career, college, entertainment, music, news/information, search engines, sports, and more.

The company's second principal line of business is e-mail marketing. 24/7 Mail provides a range of opt-in, e-mail, direct-marketing services. The company's database of more than 20 million e-mail addresses enables direct marketers to target their campaigns to consumers who have chosen to receive commercial messages via e-mail. Campaigns can be targeted using more than 260 pre-selected categories of user demographics and psychographics. Such valuable information can provide businesses with concrete factual data on consumer specifics, as well as insight into Web users' values and beliefs. In addition, 24/7 Mail aggregates and manages opt-in e-mail lists for more than 200 third-party Web sites. Consumers who choose to receive e-mail or other information through one of these Web sites are added to the company's database. 24/7 Mail also acts as a list broker and rents lists to supplement its managed lists. It can assist direct marketers by running campaigns and delivering HTML (hypertext markup language) banner ads and text links in e-mail editorial newsletters. 24/7 Mail can handle all aspects of a direct marketing e-mail campaign, including order fulfillment and the reporting and tracking of results.

Technology solutions offered by 24/7 Media include ad-serving systems offered under 24/7 Connect for Networks and 24/7 Connect for Advertisers and Publishers. These services were launched in the first quarter of 2000, and during the year 24/7 Media converted its entire 24/7 Network to the new technology. The distinguishing feature of 24/7 Connect was its ability to select an appropriate advertisement for a Web page at the same time that content was being delivered to that Web page from a third party. The selection of the appropriate ad was based on pre-selected targeting criteria. The company also offers e-mail technology solutions.

BEGAN OPERATIONS IN 1998

24/7 Media was formed in New York City by a merger of three companies involved in online advertising: Petry Interactive, Interactive Imaginations, and Katz Millennium Marketing. The formation of 24/7 Media was announced in December 1997, and the merger was completed in April 1998. David Moore, who was CEO of Petry Interactive, became 24/7

Media's CEO in February 1998. In its first year 24/7 Media raised $45.5 million through an initial public offering (IPO) in August 1998, with shares offered at $14 each. The company planned to grow through acquisitions and to challenge online advertising industry leader DoubleClick.

At its inception, 24/7 Media represented about 200 medium and large-sized Web sites with a staff of 30 sales representatives. By the end of 1998 the company was operating three ad networks and representing thousands of mostly small and medium-sized Web sites as well as 100 to 200 major Web sites. During the year it acquired the CliqNow network of 75 financial, college, and travel-related sites from K2 Design for $4 million in cash and stock. In another acquisition, 24/7 Media purchased Intelligent Interactions, which developed an ad-serving product called Adfinity, for $7.7 million in stock.

ENTERED E-MAIL MARKETING IN 1999

24/7 Media gained entry into e-mail marketing in March 1999 with the acquisition of Sift Inc. for $22 million. Sift was based in Sunnyvale, California, and had about 20 employees. It had an opt-in e-mail database of 3 million addresses and customers that included Cisco Systems, Dell Computer, and RealNetworks. The acquisition was consistent with 24/7 Media's avowed policy of not sending out unsolicited e-mail, since all of the addresses in Sift's database were for consumers who were interested in receiving commercial e-mail. Later in the year, 24/7 Media acquired a second e-mail marketing firm, ConsumerNet of Red Bank, New Jersey, for $52 million.

In order to provide a national sales force to focus on the convergence of television and the Internet in local markets, 24/7 Media entered into a three-year agreement with NBC Interactive Neighborhood during 1999. Under the agreement 24/7 Media established a sales force to sell ads on the Web sites of local NBC affiliates. The deal enabled NBC to offer combined Web and television advertising packages to local advertisers. The program began with six large NBC-owned affiliates in New York, Los Angeles, Chicago, Washington, Dallas, and San Diego, and eventually was expected to involve more than 100 NBC stations.

In 1999 and 2000, 24/7 Media continued to expand internationally. In July 1999 it acquired Click-Through Interactive, a Toronto, Canada-based advertising sales network that represented more than 65 premium Canadian Web sites. In August the company expanded its European operations to 12 countries with the addition of 24/7 Suomi in Finland. Later in the year the firm's German unit, 24/7 Deutschland, opened offices in Dusseldorf and Frankfurt, in addition to its existing office in Hamburg. In February 2000, 24/7 Media acquired the Australian ad network Sabela for about $70 million. In March it launched 24/7 Mail in the United Kingdom, offering opt-in e-mail marketing services to advertisers there. European e-mail service was rolled out to France, Germany, Holland, and Scandinavia later in the year, and in mid-2000 the company opened an office in Lausanne, Switzerland. Additional expansions were taking place in Latin America and Asia.

MORE ACQUISITIONS FOLLOWED BY DOWNTURN IN ONLINE ADVERTISING, 2000-2001

Major acquisitions in 2000 included Exactis.com Inc., a Denver-based e-mail marketing and communications firm, for $490 million in stock. Exactis reportedly sent out more than 10 million e-mail marketing messages a day and had highly scalable, precise e-mail delivery and advanced data mining systems. Following the acquisition 24/7 Mail had 23 million permission-based e-mail addresses under management. Another acquisition involved iPromotions, a market leader in incentive marketing programs. The acquisition added online sweepstakes, incentive offers, premiums, contests, and viral marketing programs to 24/7 Media's offerings. In August 2000 24/7 Media acquired Website Results for $95 million in stock. Through its proprietary technology, Website Results was able to deliver traffic to client Web sites. It accomplished this by performing queries on major Internet search engines and improving a site's positions within search results.

By the third quarter of 2000, the downturn in Internet advertising was apparent. The stock prices of the three largest ad networks—DoubleClick, 24/7 Media, and Engage—were all down approximately 90 percent from their 52-week highs. Although 24/7 Media had diversified into e-mail marketing, Internet banner ads still accounted for most of the firm's revenue. In November 24/7 Media laid off about 200 workers, followed by another 100 layoffs in January 2001, which brought the company's workforce to about 900. While it continued to maintain offices in Europe, Asia, and Latin America, 24/7 Media UK dropped about 25 percent of its client base to focus on top brands. The action marked a rethinking of the

firm's strategy to gain the greatest reach in favor of representing only the strongest Web publishers.

News of 24/7 Media's second round of layoffs sent the company's stock price below one dollar a share. The company announced it was evaluating strategic alternatives regarding its cash position and even took the drastic step of delaying the announcement of its fourth quarter results. When the company finally released its financial results for 2000, it reported revenue of $185.2 million, an increase of 106 percent over 1999. European operations posted revenue of $35.8 million, a 501-percent increase over 1999. The firm's three principal sources of revenue were its ad network (68 percent), e-mail (16 percent), and technology (16 percent). Overall, the company had a net loss of $677.1 million for 2000. With the downturn in Internet advertising and an overall economic slowdown, 24/7 Media reduced its revenue forecast for 2001. The company remained confident that the online advertising market would recover by the end of 2001. However, by April 2001 the firm's stock had traded below one dollar a share for 19 consecutive days, and it faced de-listing from the NASDAQ.

FURTHER READING:

24/7 Media Inc. Company information. 2001. Available from www.247media.com.

Beale, Matthew. "24/7 Expands European Operations." E-Commerce Times. August 13, 1999. Available from www.ecommercetimes.com.

Brookman, Faye, et al. "The Biggest Players." Crain's New York Business. November 30, 1998.

Clark, Philip B. "Working 24/7 Entails Global Reach." B to B. July 3, 2000.

"Crunch Leaves Alley Firms Few Choices." Crain's New York Business. February 26, 2001.

Fineberg, Seth. "Dot-Com Sea Change Forces Ad Networks to Rethink Strategies." Advertising Age. September 25, 2000.

Frook, John Evan. "U.S. Firms Dominate Worldwide Ad Networks." B to B. November 20, 2000.

Maddox, Kate. "Ad Networks Adjust to Slowdown." B to B. April 2, 2001.

Virzi, Anna Maria. "24/7 Media Adds Services with Purchase of E-Mail Marketing Firm." Internet World. March 15, 1999.

SEE ALSO: Advertising, Online; DoubleClick Inc.

U

UBIQUITY

Ubiquity refers to the ability of a company—and the products and services it sells—to establish a dominant presence among consumers. Although physical retail locations and traditional marketing initiatives support this end, the Internet and e-commerce do much to champion ubiquity for a company. The Internet makes it possible for consumers and companies to be in constant contact with one another, albeit electronically. Thus, consumers who wish to buy goods and services online can do so at any time, and from virtually any location.

Ubiquity means much more than being open for business around the clock in case consumers wish to do business. More specifically, the term is used to describe the degree to which a company has made inroads with customers in terms of product or service adoption. Microsoft, and the many software products it sells, is one example. The company's Windows operating system, Internet Explorer Web browser, and Microsoft Office suite of productivity software are so pervasive that almost every computer user relies on one of the company's products while engaging in e-commerce.

The disposable cameras sold by Eastman Kodak Co. are another example of ubiquity. By design, the cameras are convenient for consumers to buy and use in just about any location or situation. Capitalizing on this, Kodak rolled out a marketing initiative to sell the cameras and film in locations where consumers are likely to want them—including amusement parks and scenic locations—via refrigerated vending machines connected wirelessly to the Internet. Kodak worked with Dixie-Narco, the vending machine unit of appliance maker Maytag Corp., and Pennsylvania-based e-Vend.net to develop the program. E-Vend.net's Internet-based technology enabled the vending machines' inventories to be monitored remotely and made it possible for the machines to accept credit-card transactions and collect marketing data for Kodak.

In a company statement, Steve Hallowell, Kodak's general manager and vice president of cameras and sponsorships, explained why the initiative supported the ubiquity of its one-time-use cameras. "Pictures are what make people celebrate life's memories, but more than one third of these pictures are missed due to not having a camera on hand," he said. "Through e-Vend.net's state-of-the-art technology, we are now able to put film and cameras in the hands of consumers right where they're going to take pictures, fulfilling our continuing strategy of growing the market."

In addition to referring to the penetration of a company and its products in the marketplace, the term ubiquity also can apply to the use and meaning of terms. In the e-commerce arena, this has happened with the term "platform." Historically, this word was used to describe operating systems like Microsoft Windows, Macintosh OS, Unix, and Linux. Operating systems are the software applications computers use to function. In the early 2000s software vendors began to describe certain software solutions they offered to companies as platforms. Use of the term thus grew more widespread, and its meaning more common. This was especially true in the case of application servers, which allow software applications within a company to communicate with one another for e-commerce and other purposes, even though they may not have been designed to do so.

FURTHER READING:

Gilbert, Jennifer. "Visa Stamps Name All Over Cyberspace in Bid for Ubiquity." *Advertising Age,* May 3, 1999.

"Kodak, Maytag and e-Vend.net Ally for Vending Program; Will Put Film, One-Time-Use Cameras at 'Points of Picture' Nationwide." Eastman Kodak Co. January 11, 2001. Available from www.kodak.com.

Lake, David. "From Here to Ubiquity." *The Industry Standard,* June 11, 2001. Available from www.the standard.com.

SEE   Brand Building
ALSO:

UNCITRAL AND THE DRAFT MODEL LAW ON LEGAL ASPECTS OF EDI AND RELATED MEANS OF COMMUNICATION

In the old days, international trade relied exclusively on paper documents, and over the years an international consensual framework evolved to facilitate trade by this means. However, with the development of sophisticated information technology—and particularly the Internet—international commerce was forced to readjust itself to accommodate a new technological and economic environment. The growth of electronic data interchange (EDI) as a means of transmitting data—transaction specifications, contracts, order forms, legal documents, and so on—between companies across borders necessitated an international legal consensus. The United Nations Commission on International Trade Law (UNCITRAL) was charged with establishing such a framework.

WHAT IS UNCITRAL?

Based in Vienna, Austria, UNCITRAL is the primary United Nations organization devoted to international trade issues, with a mission to harmonize and unify the laws of international commerce. UNCITRAL coordinates and encourages cooperation between organizations operating in specific areas of international trade; prepares and encourages recognition of its model laws; and promotes universal interpretations and applications of international standards including its own model laws.

Established by the UN General Assembly in 1966, UNCITRAL's original purpose was to smooth out inconsistencies between national commercial and trade laws to facilitate a more unified global economy as a way for the United Nations to play a more active

role in this field. The commission is comprised of 36 member states chosen by the General Assembly for a term of six years to adequately represent all the world's regions and major economic and legal systems. Each of UNITRAL's three working groups performs the bulk of its work at annual sessions in New York and Vienna, where the commission members as well as non-member states and interested international organizations devise a framework for future policies through participatory sessions.

HISTORY

UNCITRAL launched its EDI working group to devise a Draft Model Law in 1991. UNITRAL began work on the topic the following year, before the onslaught of e-commerce, and thus limited its activities to electronic data interchange considerations. The first version of the Draft Model Law was produced in October 1994, at which point UNCITRAL began considering criticisms and shortcomings of that draft and devising draft guidelines for the eventual implementation of the model law. In the mid-1990s, as the Internet hit critical mass and other forms of electronic transactions achieved prominence, UNCITRAL realized that the original Draft Model Law wasn't significant enough to address the emerging international e-commerce environment.

In 1996 UNCITRAL completed work on a Model Law on Electronic Commerce to update international trade law so as to facilitate global e-commerce. The e-commerce Model Law augmented the Draft Law on EDI by including not only EDI but also electronic mail and other electronic, optical, and other non-paper exchanges in one seamless whole. UNCITRAL deliberately left the final structure of the Model Law on Electronic Commerce open-ended and flexible so as to remain a living and valuable document in light of future technological developments.

Through the mid- and late 1990s, UNCITRAL's EDI working group was devoted to smoothing the legal transition from paper-based transport documents—such as bills of lading—to their electronic format. International trade law regarding transport documents was often complex and convoluted, but many payment and transport schemes depend on the physical presentation of shipping documents, according to *Project & Trade Finance.* Bills of lading, moreover, are particularly useful in international maritime commerce to transfer ownership rights to merchandise while en route overseas.

However, the paper format for the extensive information and legal documentation involved in international commerce adds up to enormous costs per transaction. *Project & Trade Finance* reported the results of a European Commission Study from the mid-

1990s that found that up to 15 percent of international commercial transport costs can be attributed to documentation, while the simple acts of processing and correcting all such documents accounts for 10 percent of the finished products' total cost. Obviously, then, in addition to the enhanced overall efficiency of electronic documentation and its harmony with emerging e-commerce and information-technology infrastructures, companies were eager to adopt EDI as a way of limiting their basic operating costs.

THE DRAFT MODEL LAW

The Draft Model Law on Legal Aspects of EDI and Related Means of Communication rendered the use of EDI equally valid a means of data transmission as paper documents, particularly for the purpose of establishing contracts. The Draft Model Law is divided into three chapters.

- Chapter one sets forth the general provisions stating the breadth of the law's application, limiting it specifically to commercial law, and spelling out the definitions of the law's terms.

- Chapter two draws out the legal requirements of electronic communications in commercial law. This chapter prohibits the denial of legal effectiveness of electronic documents that meet the Draft Model Law's requirements; in other words, it bars parties from discriminating against electronic documents.

- Chapter three deals with the technicalities of electronic communications, such as when—from a legal standpoint—a message is deemed to have originated or been received, and from what physical location the message was sent and to where it was received.

To iron out any legal ambiguities over document reception using EDI, the Draft Model Law took special pains to resolve lingering uncertainties over the legal considerations stemming from when and where a document was received. Since electronic networks are more fluid, dispersed, and decentralized than physical data transmissions, the Draft Model Law expressly stated that a data transmission is considered legally received at the location of the recipient's business, or unless mutually agreed to the contrary, at the location within the business that is most directly related to the transmission's content. The transmission is, moreover, considered received as soon as the data enters the recipient's system. In the event that the message requires decryption or some other form of decoding, it is legally received once this process is complete.

The Draft Model Law was intended to prohibit organizations or jurisdictions from denying legal va-

lidity to documents or information transmitted electronically, and to harmonize the legal environment between physical and electronic media. In this way, international e-commerce and other forms of electronic data exchanges carry equally legal weight, and governments and companies couldn't discriminate unduly against specific media.

A number of key legal issues arose as commercial transactions moved to the electronic realm. Among the most pressing were the following questions: Are signatures or any other key aspects of transaction documents required to appear in writing? If not, what forms of electronic substitutes are legally binding? In legal proceedings, can electronic documents be used as evidence? Given the extensive legal dealings of firms engaged in international transactions, UNICTRAL saw addressing questions such as these as among the primary goals of the Draft Model Law.

Article 5 of the Draft Model Law specifically addresses these concerns, and is the heart of UNCITRAL's rules governing EDI and other electronic communications used in commercial transactions. The article reads as follows: "Where a rule of law requires information to be in writing or to be presented in writing, or provides for certain consequences if it is not, a data message satisfies that rule if the information contained therein is accessible so as to be usable for subsequent reference." The same article, however, also leaves room for exceptions, particularly in its allowance that certain national laws may trump this ruling in certain circumstances. In addition, the Draft Model Law's wording allowed room for the adoption of digital signature technologies as a legally valid means of authentication and verification of the documents' integrity.

Importantly, however, the Draft Model Law carried no legal weight on its own terms; rather, the rules contained therein grew teeth only as nations adopted them into their own trade laws. UNCITRAL's work is designed primarily to set an example of a collaborative framework that harmonizes existing and prospective national and technological capabilities and structures. UNCITRAL's work—and the Draft Model Law on Legal Aspects of EDI is no exception—has a track record of enjoying widespread adoption.

FURTHER READING:

Andersen, Mads Bryde. "The UNCITRAL Draft Model Law on EDI—Its History and Its Fate." *Lex Electronica—International Journal of Law,* Winter, 1995. Available from www.lex-electronica.org.

Heinrich, Gregor. "Harmonized Global Interchange? UNCITRAL's Draft Model Law for Electronic Interchange." *Web Journal of Current Legal Issues,* 1995. Available from webjcli.ncl.ac.uk.

Hill, Richard and Ian Walden. "The Draft UNCITRAL Model Law for Electronic Commerce: Issues and Solutions." *Computer Lawyer,* March, 1996.

"UN Tackles EDI on Shipping." *Project & Trade Finance,* May, 1996.

United Nations Commission on International Trade Law (UNCITRAL). "UNCITRAL." Vienna, Austria: United Nations Commission on International Trade Law (UNCITRAL), 2001.

Winship, Peter. "International Commercial Transactions: 1996." *Business Lawyer,* August, 1997.

SEE ALSO: Digital Signatures; Electronic Data Interchange (EDI); UN/EDIFACT

UN/EDIFACT

As both international and electronic commercial activity escalated dramatically in the closing decades of the 20th century and into the 2000s, businesses, governments, and international economic and trade organizations recognized the growing importance of standardizing the protocols used to transmit electronic data. If such protocols were inconsistent or competing within and across industries and international borders, the overall flow of international commerce could ebb, to the eventual detriment of all players. Thus, the 1980s and 1990s were marked by efforts to harmonize the various standards of electronic data transactions. To facilitate this process, the United Nations Economic Commission for Europe developed the United Nations rules for Electronic Data Interchange For Administration, Commerce, and Transport (UN/EDIFACT).

EDI

Electronic data interchange (EDI) systems provide a standardized method for conducting and tracking electronic transactions and business documents structured according to EDI syntax and design rules. Using EDIFACT, businesses are able to engage in transactions on a global basis, using a standard that renders business documents in a global language. EDIFACT aimed to standardize EDI programs used in commercial activities on a worldwide basis so as to ease the transition to both a global and electronic economy. By using EDIFACT, companies and organizations can transmit electronic data with each other regardless of the software or computer used to generate it.

The original impetus toward the development of electronic data interchange was to cut the costs and time spent on the myriad paper documents involved in transactions, including contracts, bills, manifests, letters of credit, and many others. By coalescing all these into a series of standardized electronic protocols, the time spent of each transaction; the costs of each transmission of data; and the propensity for documents to be lost, misfiled, or miscopied all decline considerably. EDI is in fact at the heart of such staples of the information economy as just-in-time manufacturing, supply chain management, and scores of other practices and processes central to the contemporary commercial environment.

THE DEVELOPMENT OF UN/EDIFACT

The Centre for the Facilitation of Administration, Commerce, and Trade (CEFACT) provides the 55 Economic Commission for Europe (ECE) members as well as non-ECE members and the private sector a formal say in the development of EDIFACT and other programs as they relate to worldwide trade protocols. CEFACT is the UN organization coordinating policies and technical development to facilitate trade and electronic business. Working with the International Standards Organization (ISO), CEFACT designed EDIFACT in 1986, and the protocol was formally adopted as a global standard in 1987. UN/EDIFACT is independent of any specific industry, country, or region.

The first organizations to adopt the standard, according to the *Journal of Commerce,* were those entities with the highest stake in international trade, particularly multinational corporations who were primarily concerned with conducting smooth, international, intra-firm transactions. Over time, the adoption of EDIFACT spread through these companies' supply chains and into their transactions with governmental, insurance, and banking organizations.

CEFACT in 1990 announced its official definition of UN/EDIFACT, which states that its rules for EDI "comprise a set of internationally agreed standards, directories and guidelines for the electronic interchange of structured data, and in particular that related to trade in goods and services between independent, computerized information systems."

EDI COMPETITION AND HARMONIZATION

The late 1990s were characterized by the movement toward harmonization between UN/EDIFACT and the established U.S. EDI standard, the American National Standard Institute's Accredited Standards Committee X12 (ASC X12). ANSI's X12/EDIFACT Alignment Plan, and the subsequent launching of the U.S. X12 Strategic Implementation Task Group, drove efforts to coalesce the two standards into one global standard, and by the late 1990s U.S. firms and governments increasingly adopted the EDIFACT standard. As part of the plan, according to ANSI ASC X12 Chair Kendra L. Martin, where X12 was incompatible with EDIFACT, X12 transaction sets were rewritten in the international syntax.

Up into the mid-1990s, however, ANSI and ASC were steadfast in their refusal to maintain their X12 standard independent of EDIFACT, opting instead for co-existence with the international standard, even allowing X12 users to continue developing new, specific standards based on the X12 design format and syntax. In other words, rather than simply migrate to the worldwide EDIFACT standard, ASC X12 plans centered on an "administrative alignment," in which ASC would modify X12 standards using EDIFACT's design rules, but remain independent and allow users to develop X12 freely within its established boundaries.

The reluctance of U.S. businesses and standards writers to adopt UN/EDIFACT was based on many reasons. First, critics of EDIFACT contended that it was less flexible in its methods of data definition than was X12. Beyond technical complaints, X12 support—as well as advocacy for convergence to EDIFACT—also drew on cultural and competitive rivalry. Developers and users of the older X12 resented the rapid rise of the upstart EDIFACT, and some U.S. organizations feared a competitive disadvantage stemming from the U.S. investment in converting to the international standard. For years, the convergence of X12 and EDIFACT was furthered by debate over which system would have to bend more.

Thus, by 1999, X12 was still the rule rather than the exception for U.S. companies. But efforts by leading companies to adopt EDIFACT were producing a ripple effect. For instance, General Motors, having adopted EDIFACT, ordered that its suppliers do likewise. U.S. standards organizations, led by ANSI, developed EDIFACT-friendly conversions that would allow companies to maintain their legacy applications while conducting international transactions using the EDIFACT standard. Outside the United States, EDIFACT was the overwhelming standard, although it often vied with local and regional EDI standards for preeminence.

THE FUTURE OF EDI AND EDIFACT

By the 2000s, Internet-based e-commerce, particularly commerce between businesses, was slowly leading to the replacement of EDI in favor of eXtensible Markup Language (XML), which was poised to become the lingua franca of e-commerce. But while the new standard created a great deal of excitement, and analysts tended to position XML as the basis for future electronic exchange, EDIFACT was still a hot issue in the early 21st century.

Few analysts were willing to pronounce the imminent death of EDIFACT, much less EDI. In fact, the most commonly envisioned scenario involved a layering of XML with the EDI structure, most likely with EDIFACT playing a major role in systematizing the two broad technologies into a seamless and compatible whole. In 2000, for instance, the European Commission called for the design, development, and installation of a bridge between EDIFACT and XML in which communications may be transmitted, received, and read in both formats.

While the development of the Internet as a commercial vehicle prompted some to declare that EDI's days were numbered, EDI transactions were generally Internet friendly. Moreover, until the Internet proves capable of handling the more intensive business-oriented data transmissions for which EDI was created, many firms may feel more comfortable sticking with their EDI systems rather than investing in a full-scale conversion.

On the other hand, for most small and medium-sized businesses, EDI technology can be prohibitively expensive. To remedy this problem, in the late 1990s and early 2000s CEFACT was developing Simpl-EDI and Object-Oriented EDI to upgrade the EDIFACT standards to incorporate the developments in information technology and the sophistication of user interfaces through the 1990s. Simpl-EDI is a less information-heavy version of EDI, in which messages are simplified to their most essential elements. Since most EDI systems were designed for larger businesses with more convoluted dealings, they function to incorporate higher degrees of complexity than was required by the average smaller business. Simpl-EDI, involving less complexity, was thus designed to present smaller firms with a cost-effective opportunity to employ EDI.

FURTHER READING:

Boleat, Mark. "The Internet vs. EDI: It's Not 'Either/Or.'" *Insurance & Technology,* May, 1998.

Kilbane, Doris. "International Groups Making Progress on X12/EDIFACT Interoperability." *Automatic I.D. News,* March, 1999.

———. "X12 Seeks Supporting Role in XML Standards Setting." *Frontline Solutions,* August 2000, 13.

Martin, Kendra L. "UN/EDIFACT in the United States Another Step Toward Global EDI." *EDI NEWS,* May 12, 1997.

Millman, Howard. "A Brief History of EDI." *InfoWorld,* April 6, 1998.

"United Nations Economic Commission for Europe." Geneva, Switzerland: United Nations Economic Commission for Europe, 2001. Available from www.unece.org.

Williams, Frances. "EDI Data Exchange Spreads its Wings." *Financial Times,* March 21, 1997.

Zuckerman, Amy. "EDIFACT Gaining in Acceptance." *Journal of Commerce,* November 10, 1999.

SEE ALSO: Electronic Data Interchange (EDI); XML

UNISYS CORP.

Blue Bell, Pennsylvania-based Unisys Corp. provides systems integration, network management, technology support, outsourcing, and consulting services to clients in communications, financial services, publishing and transportation industries, as well as to government agencies. Major competitors include IBM Corp. and Computer Sciences Corp. In the late 1990s, the firm shifted its focus away from commodity hardware operations and created the e@ctions Solutions division, which offers, among other things, Web-based services. With sales of $6.9 billion and 37,000 employees, Unisys is working toward of goal of deriving half of its revenues from e-business by the year 2002.

EARLY HISTORY

The foundation for Unisys Corp. was first laid in 1885 when William S. Burroughs invented the arithmometer, an adding machine that records numbers. The following year, Burroughs incorporated his business as American Arithmometer Co. He obtained a patent for his adding machine in 1892, and five years later, the Franklin Institute awarded him the John Scott Medal. The inventor and businessman succumbed to tuberculosis in 1898; however, his business remained operational, being reincorporated as Burroughs Adding Machine Co. in 1905. The company completed its first two purchases—Universal Adding Machine and Pike Adding Machine—three years later. A machine able to both add and subtract was unveiled in 1911. By 1915, Burroughs Adding sold more than 90 different data processing machines, mainly to accountants. Interchangeable parts allowed clients to customize the machines to suit their needs.

Growth continued in 1921 with the acquisition of Moon-Hopkins Billing Machine. Burroughs Adding Machine launched a direct multiplication billing machine and a portable adding machine mid-decade. By 1945, sales had neared the $100 million mark. To better reflect its broadening product line, the firm changed its name to Burroughs Corp. in 1953. Three years later, Burroughs unveiled its first commercial

electronic computer and purchased high-speed computer manufacturer ElectroData Corp. The firm diversified into automated office machines in 1958, developing an electronic bank bookkeeping machine known as the Sensitronic. One year later, the firm's president, John Coleman, reached an agreement with RCA to pool financial resources in an effort to better compete with industry leader IBM Corp. However, Coleman died before his plan was implemented. By the end of the decade, the firm had diversified into magnetic ink and automated check-sorting machinery. Sales neared $400 million.

Burroughs launched the B5000 mainframe computer, which used dual processors and virtual memory, in 1961. Six years later, the firm landed a U.S. Department of Defense contract to build the Illiac IV supercomputer. Cost cutting measures implemented in the mid-1960s were blamed for reliability problems with the B6500 computer. As a result, plans for the B8500 computer were shelved until engineers figured out how to fix the glitches. Burroughs completed the Illiac IV supercomputer in 1972. The $30 million purchase of Graphic Services in 1974 gave the firm entrance to the facsimile industry. The following year, Burroughs paid $8.8 million for automatic typewriters and computer equipment manufacturer Redactron. W. Michael Blumenthal, former Bendix chairman, joined Burroughs as executive vice president in 1979. He hired a new management team, discontinued adding machine and calculator operations, and funneled more resources into the firm's repair services. By the end of the decade, sales had reached nearly $3 billion. Blumenthal eventually took over as CEO.

Burroughs unveiled its A Series line in 1981; the technology would prove to be integral in the firm's future development of the ClearPath HMP System. To bolster its effectiveness against rival IBM in the mainframe industry, the company paid $85.2 million for Memorex and $9.6 million for System Development Corp. The purchases boosted sales by roughly $1 billion. In 1985, Burroughs and Sperry Corp. began merger negotiations. Sperry had been founded by Elmer Sperry in 1910 as Sperry Gyroscope Co., a manufacturer of navigational equipment. In 1955, Sperry merged with Remington Rand, maker of ENIAC, "the world's first large-scale, general-purpose computer" and UNIVAC, the ldquo;world's first business computer." Sperry's product launches in the 1960s included the 1100 computer series and the first multiprocessor computer, the 1108. In the 1970s, Sperry acquired RCA's computer operations and developed a cache memory disk subsystem. Its 2200 Series, shipped in 1986, would also play an instrumental role in the development of the ClearPath HMP system.

Both Burroughs and Sperry believed a merger would allow them to reduce costs and fund increased research and development, both of which were necessary to compete with IBM, which boasted revenues ten times those of both firms. Burroughs borrowed $2.5 billion to finance the merger, and the $4.8 billion deal was completed in 1986 when Burroughs and Sperry formed Unisys Corp., the second-largest computer firm in the U.S. Employees from both companies had agreed upon the name, which was essentially an acronym for ''United Information Systems.''

AFTER THE MERGER

Blumenthal was named CEO of the new firm. He closed several plants and laid off 24,000 employees. Earnings totaled $578 million in 1987. That year, Unisys sold off Sperry's marine operations and Burroughs's Memorex unit. Data Resources bought the firm's computer equipment and services arm. Integration continued as Unisys divested its South African marketing and sales unit for $28 million to Mercedes Information Technologies. The firm also paid $300 million for communications equipment maker Timeplex Inc. and $351 million for office workstations manufacturer Convergent Technologies.

In 1989, Unisys purchased File-Tek, Inc. to gain access to the company's Unix-based storage systems for the financial industry. Unisys also entered the small and mid-sized computer market, using AT&T Corp.'s new Unix operating system for its mainframe machines. The company posted a $639 million loss that year, which was due in large part to the increasing popularity of personal computers, which undercut mainframe computer sales. Unisys began manufacturing its own personal computers as a result. However, financial troubles continued in 1990 as mainframe computer demand took a sharp downturn. After the company posted losses of $436 million and suspended shareholder dividends, Blumenthal resigned. Unisys divested Timeplex for $207 million in 1991. The firm also slashed its workforce by 50 percent, which reduced losses for the year to $1.4 million. Public relations suffered when a federal judge found Unisys guilty of landing U.S. defense contracts via bribery and fined it roughly $190 million.

Hoping it legal and financial woes were a thing of the past, Unisys diversified into information technology (IT) services in 1992. Although it had worked to reduce its reliance on the mainframe industry, the firm did continue to make advances in that arena, including a mainframe machine using CMOS (complementary metal oxide semiconductor) technology, unveiled in 1993. The following year, Unisys landed a $127 million contract from one of the world's leading banks, the Savings Bank of the Russian Federal. Divestitures during 1995 included computer-aided design operations to Cadence Designs and aerospace

and defense operations to Loral for $862 million. The company also purchased European software vendor Topsystems International, folding it into a new software unit known as Usoft. A restructuring of operations into three business units allowed the firm to focus on its services arm. One unit, Information Services Group, offered consulting, outsourcing, and enterprise systems integration.

Layoffs continued in 1996 when the firm reduced its workforce by 20 percent. On a more positive note, Unisys launched its ClearPath 61000, a multiprocessing system for Pentium processors that allowed clients to integrate Unisys applications with UnixWare and Microsoft Corp.'s Windows NT. Despite several restructuring efforts, the firm remained burdened by $2.3 billion in debt, partly the result of its 1986 merger. In 1997, the firm named Robert Brusk its new chief financial officer and appointed former Arthur Anderson CEO Larry Wienbach as CEO. By then, services accounted for more than 60 percent of sales.

Cellular multiprocessing technology, which boosted the capabilities of Windows NT, was unveiled in 1998. In effort to reduce debt, Wienbach decided Unisys should take a one-time charge of $1.1 billion—related to the 1986 merger—which resulted in a fourth-quarter loss of $947 million. He also contracted Hewlett-Packard Co. to handle the firm's personal computer production, wanting to focus efforts on services. In May, Unisys secured a $600 million contract from Dell Computer Co. to provide IT services to Dell's corporate and government clients. Wienbach's efforts appeared to pay off according to a November 1999 *InformationWeek* article that described Unisys as ''a $7 billion former mainframe manufacturer whose big moneymaker has become sales and service of hardware with Intel processors running Windows NT.''

The firm established its e-business unit, known as e-@action Solutions, in 1999. By November, e-business sales accounted for 18 percent of total revenues, and Weinbach announced his goal of tripling that percentage over the next three years. In 2000, the firm distanced itself further from low-end hardware manufacturing via outsourcing and divestitures. In 2001, Unisys launched a new version of its ClearPath server, known as e-@ction Clear Path, which increased compatibility between applications running on Intel Corp. processors and those using proprietary Unisys platforms. Throughout the year, the firm continued to focus on its e-business services.

FURTHER READING:

Gerber, Cheryl. ''Unisys Does a Service 180.'' *Computerworld.* July 28, 1997.

Markowitz, Elliot. ''Even Behemoths Can Bend.'' *Computer Reseller News.* January 10, 2000, 14.

Ricadela, Aaron. ''Unisys Seeks to Turn Servers Into Mainframes.'' *InformationWeek.* November 1, 1999.

Royal, Weld. "Unisys Serves up Services." *Industry Week.* August 17, 1998.

Schaff, William. "The Prince of Unisys." *InformationWeek.* October 13, 1997.

"Unisys Corp." In *Notable Corporate Chronologies.* Farmington Hills, MI: Gale Research, 1999.

Unisys Corp. "Unisys: A History of Excellence." Blue Bell, PA: Unisys Corp., 2001. Available from www.unisys.com.

Vijayan, Jaikumar. "Unisys Pins Hopes On New Servers." *Computerworld.* April 23, 2001.

SEE ALSO: E-commerce Consultants; E-commerce Solutions; Integration

UNITED PARCEL SERVICE, INC. (UPS)

With sales of nearly $30 billion, profits of almost $3 billion, and roughly 360,000 employees, United Parcel Service (UPS) is the largest package shipper in the world. Since the early 1990s, the firm has spent roughly $1 billion per year on information technology. Considered the most technologically savvy of the world's largest shipping firms, UPS uses things like UPSnet, with more than 500,000 miles of communications lines, as well as a satellite that tracks hundreds of thousands of packages each day and connects roughly 1,300 UPS distribution plants in 46 different nations. In addition, the firm's expertise in logistics allows it do things like oversee the transport and delivery of 4.5 million vehicles to 6,000 North American automobile dealers each year; in 2000, the process cut delivery time by nearly one-quarter and reduced inventory, which saved Ford roughly $240 million. With a fleet of 152,000 delivery trucks, the firm handled about 70 percent of all U.S. ground shipping in 2001, as well 55 percent of e-commerce-related shipping worldwide.

EARLY HISTORY

Since most individuals did not own telephones in the early 1900s, telegraph messages were carried to homes by hand. In 1907, this fact prompted Jim Casey to establish a bicycle delivery service known as American Messenger Co. in Seattle, Washington, to deliver both telegraph messages and lunches. Six years later, Casey agreed to join forces with a rival business, Merchants Parcel Delivery, and he began focusing on delivering packages for retailers. The newly merged firm, which used the Merchants Parcel name, bought a Ford Model T to speed deliveries and broaden its range. By then, the U.S. Postal Service had started to deliver packages as well, creating increased competition for delivery services like Merchants Parcel. In 1918, three department stores in Seattle contracted Merchants Parcel to make deliveries to their customers on the same day they made their purchases, and the little company employed more than twenty delivery workers. Service to department stores accounted for the bulk of the firm's revenues over the next three decades. During this time, Merchants Parcel developed its consolidated delivery strategy, which called for organizing deliveries so that packages going to one area were all given to the same delivery person.

Moving outside of the Seattle area for the first time, Merchants Parcel acquired Oakland, California-based Motor Parcel Delivery in 1919. To better reflect its more diverse holdings, the firm then changed its named to United Parcel Service (UPS). The word "United" represented the firm's consolidated delivery strategy, which had allowed it to increase efficiency and cut costs. In the early 1920s, UPS began to offer parcel pickup and delivery services to any business in its service area for a flat fee. Expansion into Los Angeles, California—then the fastest growing city in the U.S.—took place in 1922. Three years later, UPS extended its reach to the Eastern Seaboard by launching service in New York City; Newark, New Jersey; and Greenwich, Connecticut. The firm diversified into air delivery services in 1929 via its new United Air Express division, which had convinced airlines to allow UPS packages on passenger planes. However, the air services were cancelled just a short while later due to the economic problems that led to the Great Depression.

Revenues continued to decline after the Depression ended as people purchased automobiles and began to pick up their own packages. In the early 1950s, UPS launched its delivery services in San Francisco and Chicago, and expanded its reach in New York. The firm also relaunched its air service as Blue Label air, completing air deliveries in two days or less. Realizing that the retail delivery market was shrinking, UPS gained permission to act as a "common carrier," an entity that could deliver packages for individuals, as well as businesses. The restrictions placed on both interstate and intrastate deliveries created another hurdle for UPS as the firm was forced to seek permission from each state government to deliver packages within each state, as well as across state lines.

Jim Casey retired in 1962; he was succeeded as CEO by George D. Smith. By the end of the decade, UPS was operating in 31 U.S. states, and sales had reached nearly $550 million. More than 22,000 drivers worked for the firm. The Blue Label air service was expanded in the early 1970s to cover Washington, Oregon, California, and 28 states in the eastern

U.S. Ground service in Germany began in 1976, marking the firm's first foray into Europe. To cuts costs, UPS began to use part-time employees to replace full-time package handlers. As a result, 17,000 workers went on strike. Although the strike was resolved that same year, relations between management and employees remained strained. By 1978, the Blue Label air service was offered in all 50 U.S. states.

The deregulation of the U.S. airline industry fueled the firm's growth in the early 1980s as UPS began purchasing planes of its own. For example, UPS paid $28 million for nine used 727 aircraft in 1981. Profits grew to roughly $190 million on sales of $4 billion that year as UPS shipped 1.5 billion packages. The following year, UPS launched its overnight air delivery service, undercutting the rates of rival Federal Express by roughly 50 percent. With 62,000 UPS trucks in operation, sales grew to $5.2 billion. UPS paid $208 million for an additional 13 cargo jets in 1984. Overnight air services were made available to every address in the 48 contiguous states and Puerto Rico in 1985, and International services were launched between a few states in the northeastern U.S. and six European countries. Sales exceeded $10 billion for the first time in 1987. Compared to the 57 percent share of the overnight package market held by Federal Express, UPS held only 15 percent. To strengthen its position against Federal Express, UPS spent $1.8 billion for 110 additional aircraft.

EARLY INFORMATION TECHNOLOGY EFFORTS

In 1986, to compete with technology developed by Federal Express, UPS launched efforts to automate door-to-door package tracking. The new technology took five years to put in place and cost roughly $1.5 billion. Throughout the late 1980s, ground shipping operations at UPS grew nearly 8 percent each year, and air shipping sales increased at an even higher rate. By 1988, sales had jumped to $11 billion; more than 2.2 billion packages were shipped that year. International sales accounted for 6 percent of annual revenues in 1989, compared to 2 percent the previous year; this growth in international activity stemmed from the addition of several countries to UPS shipping routes. The firm's tracking technology proved increasingly valuable as its reach extended across the globe.

UPS paid $11.3 million for a 9.5 percent stake in rival Mailboxes, Etc. in 1990. Service in Eastern Europe was broadened to include cities in Poland, Czechoslovakia, Hungary, Yugoslavia, Rumania, and the USSR. The firm ventured into the Japanese package delivery and air freight markets for the first time via a joint venture with Yamato Transport. Despite in-

ternational losses of $200 million, total revenues reached $13.6 billion. By 1991, the firm had increased its share of the overnight delivery market to 30 percent. The following year, UPS added to its international holdings with the purchase of Beemsterboer, a Dutch package delivery company, and Star Air Parcel Service an Austrian package carrier. Next-day air services were offered to nearly all addresses in the ten provinces of Canada. In 1994, UPS established UPS logistics to offer logistics management services to businesses; this unit would prove to be a cornerstone in the e-commerce efforts undertaken by UPS in the late 1990s. The firm made its largest purchase to date in 1995 when it bought SonicAir in an effort to move into the same-day delivery market.

MOVE TO THE INTERNET

UPS began allowing clients to track their packages on the Internet in 1995. After Federal Express announced its intent to retreat from the European market, UPS revealed its plans to invest $1.1 billion in its European operations over the next five years. J.C. Penney Co. awarded UPS a $1 billion contract to handle the delivery of its smaller products. The following year, Gateway 2000 hired UPS to ship more than half of its computer equipment; the contract was valued at $350 million. Although a highly publicized strike that year cost the firm roughly $200 million in 1997, sales exceeded $22 billion that year.

In 1998, the firm began working with online retailers to place UPS package shipment data on their Web sites so that shoppers could avoid the extra step of securing a tracking number from the retailer and then logging onto the UPS Web site. Also, UPS Capital was established to create new methods of securing payment, including electronic funds transfer, for delivered goods. UPS shipped more than 50 percent of all online holiday purchases that year.

On November 10, 1999, UPS conducted the largest initial public offering in U.S. business history, selling 109 million shares to investors for $5.5 billion. Sales that year grew 9 percent to $27.2 billion as the firm delivered roughly 13 million packages to 200 countries each day. Profits reached $2.3 billion. Also that year, the firm unveiled its Document Exchange Internet site, which allowed users to instantaneously transmit documents; UPS believed that nearly one-third of its documents would be transmitted via Document Exchange within two years. According to a May 2001 article in *Business 2.0,* the firm's attempts to upgrade its technology throughout the 1990s were extremely worthwhile. ''Begun a decade ago as a way of streamlining UPS's internal operations, the company's push into infotech fortuitously prepared it for the Internet age. When the Net came along, all UPS had to do was plug itself in.'' For example, the firm's expertise in logistics, as well as its information-technology savvy, allowed it to offer services well beyond simple delivery to Internet upstart Nike.com. UPS began stocking Nike shoes and athletic gear at its massive warehouse in Louisville, Kentucky, from where it shipped Nike.com orders. In addition, the firm's call center in San Antonio, Texas, began taking Nike.com customer service calls. Along with faster order fulfillment than it could have offered by itself, Nike.com also reduced its overhead expenses by allowing UPS to handle its logistics.

UPS created eVentures in February of 2000 to focus on various e-commerce initiatives, such as allowing clients to track all of the packages they are receiving, as well as those they are shipping, and the development of Web-based financial services by UPS Capital. Accordingly, UPS Capital began working with Princeton eCom and Bottomline Technologies shortly thereafter to create an electronic billing and payment service for Web-based business-to-business transactions. The firm was also determined to increase its electronic supply chain management services for business customers via e-Logistics, a new unit of eVentures. Logistics sales in 2000 surged 58 percent to exceed $1 billion for the first time as UPS began completing work on major projects it had secured from the likes of Ford Motor Co. and National Semiconductor Corp. According to a May 2001 article in *BusinessWeek Online,* UPS designed and constructed a National Semiconductor warehouse, based in Singapore, that uses ''a delivery process that is efficient and automated, almost to the point of magic.'' Once new products, such as computer chips, are manufactured and sent to the Singapore warehouse, ''it is UPS's computers that speed the box of chips to a loading dock, then to truck, to plane, and to truck once again. In just 12 hours, the chips will reach one of National's customers, a PC maker half a world away in Silicon Valley. Throughout the journey, electronic tags embedded in the chips will let the customer track the order with accuracy down to about three feet.'' Between 1999 and 2001, National Semiconductor estimates that using UPS logistics services cut its shipping and inventory management expenses by roughly 15 percent.

To combat a decline in business resulting from the North American economic downturn, the firm halted all hiring and reduced business travel allowances in 2001. In an effort to increase its logistics operations, UPS purchased Germany's Uni-Data. By 2007, UPS planned to increase its non-shipping business, particularly its logistics, freight forwarding, and e-business services, from seven percent of its revenues to 15 to 20 percent of annual sales.

FURTHER READING:

Barron, Kelly. ''Logistics in Brown.'' *Forbes,* January 10, 2000, 78.

Haddad, Charles. ''UPS vs. FedEx: Ground Wars.'' *BusinessWeek Online,* May 21, 2001. Available from www.businssweek.com.

Rynecki, David. ''Net Effects: Why E-Commerce Makes UPS a Complete Package, But Not FDX.'' *Fortune,* February 7, 2000. Available from www.fortune.com

Schonfeld, Erick. ''The Total Package.'' *Business 2.0,* May 2001. Available from www.ecompany.com.

Tsao, Amy. ''Can UPS Deliver in a Downturn?'' *BusinessWeek Online,* July 26, 2001. Available from www.businssweek.com.

''United Parcel Service, Inc.'' In *Notable Corporate Chronologies.* Farmington Hills, MI: Gale Group, 1999.

United Parcel Service, Inc. ''The UPS Story.'' Atlanta, GA: United Parcel Service, Inc., 2001.

SEE ALSO: FedEx; Fulfillment Problems; Order Fulfillment; Shipping and Shipment Tracking

UNIX

UNIX is a multi-tasking, multi-user operating system (programs responsible for running computers). It plays an important role in e-commerce because millions of Web servers (computers used to host Web sites) run on UNIX, along with many workstation computers. In *InformationWeek,* IBM indicated that UNIX was a cornerstone of e-businesses because ''most major Internet developments have been driven by UNIX architectures.'' In the same issue, Hewlett-Packard noted that the operating system is ideal for e-commerce because of features like security, scalability, manageability, and the fact that it's widely available. Because of its dependability, UNIX is frequently used for critical procedures like processing transactions on the Web. UNIX isn't as user-friendly as graphical operating systems like Windows. It relies on commands that can be puzzling to inexperienced users. However, during the early 2000s a graphical interface called Motif was available that made the system easier for more people to use on regular desktop computers.

UNIX was created by Ken Thompson and Dennis Ritchie, two researchers at AT&T's Bell Labs in Murray Hill, New Jersey. Thompson initially created the system in 1969 on an old PDP-7 minicomputer made by Digital Equipment Corp. He reportedly created UNIX over the course of one month in his spare time, after Bell pulled the plug on a seven-year project called Multics, which was attempting to create the first multi-tasking, multi-user operating system. Ritchie also contributed to the system's development, and by the mid-1970s UNIX was being used on many PDP computers. Thompson and Ritchie also invented the high-level programming language known as C, which they created to make UNIX capable of running on various different computer systems. UNIX was the first major program to be written in the C language.

In the beginning, many universities and governmental bodies used UNIX through a licensing agreement with Bell Labs, taking the source code and customizing the operating system for their own specific needs. Anti-trust regulations prevented Bell from marketing it as a regular product until the early 1980s, when the company was broken into separate units. After that time, AT&T began to push for one standard version of UNIX, releasing several versions during the 1980s. Since then, ownership of the UNIX code has changed hands several times. Novell acquired it in 1993, followed by The Santa Cruz Operation (SCO) in 1995. Many attempts have been made to create one standard version, but this has proved challenging because so many variations of UNIX are in use throughout the world. Two main dialects of UNIX existed in the early 2000s; AT&T's System V and Berkeley University's BSD4.x.

FURTHER READING:

Brandel, Mary. "Unix, Net: '60s Brainchildren." *Computerworld*, May 24, 1999.

Computer Languages. Alexandria, Virginia: Time-Life Books. 1986.

"PDP-7." *LinuxGuruz*, March 10, 1995. Available from www.linuxguruz.org.

Reimers, Barbara Depompa. "Unix: Reliable, Scalable, Available, indestructible." *InformationWeek*, October 25, 1999.

SEE ALSO: C; Programming Language; UNIX

URL (UNIFORM RESOURCE LOCATOR)

Uniform Resource Locators (URLs), also known as Uniform Resource Identifiers (URIs) or occasionally as Universal Resource Locators, are strings of letters, numbers, and special characters that constitute the addresses of documents, files, electronic mailboxes, images, and other resources in cyberspace. One of the hallmarks of Tim Berners-Lee's invention of the World Wide Web was the ability to make all information on the Internet accessible by a simple click of the mouse, rather than through the tedious process of logging on to various servers and following their own unique interfaces. URLs are the means by which that is accomplished.

The most common use of a URL is to designate an address on the World Wide Web. This address appears in the "Location:" or "Go to:" box of most Web browsers. URLs all follow a similar basic pattern. First, the URL string is prefixed by a code indicating the particular access method for the electronic resource. These schemes include the following.

- Hypertext Transfer Protocol (indicated by the prefix "http:"), the standard method for downloading documents and images on the Web.

- File Transfer Protocol ("ftp:"), used primarily for downloading files from one server to another.

- Electronic mailboxes ("mailto:"), for sending e-mail

- Gopher ("gopher:"), for accessing files on a Gopher server.

- Usenet News ("news:") for referencing Usenet newsgroups.

- The Telnet protocol ("telnet:") for connecting to a remote host's internal system.

- Wide Area Information Servers ("wais:") for accessing a WAIS database.

- Host-Specific File Names ("file:") for retrieving documents from a remote host using a chosen protocol.

- The Prospero Directory Service ("prospero:") for tapping into Prospero resources.

The next section of the string indicates the domain name of the server being accessed. The suffix of this section indicates either what kind of server it is or in what country it's located. For instance, the "com" suffix in the domain name "www.website.com" indicates that the particular file being accessed resides on a commercial server; the suffix "uk" indicates that the server is located in the United Kingdom. The list of such suffixes was growing in the early 2000s as regulators sought to accommodate the expansion of the Web.

Any information that appears after this string simply designates where in the server's hierarchical file structure the particular resource is located—that is, it spells out the path to the file. For instance, a URL —www.website.com/files/webpage.html" indicates that the resource is stored on the "website.com" server in a folder called "files," and that the file "webpage" is an HTML document.

This syntax was defined by the policy document RFC 1738 produced by the Network Working Group of the Internet Engineering Task Force. To locate an Internet resource, the URL must be matched exactly. URLs rendered with flaws will fail to turn up the desired resource. Certain characters are avoided entirely in URLs, since for various reasons they are deemed ''unsafe.'' Spaces, for instance, are always to be avoided, while characters such as angle brackets are discouraged because they are often used to mark out URLs in free text. That is, these characters are used to list URLs in documents, marking the beginning and end of the URL string. To avoid confusion over exactly what should be entered as a URL, these characters are discouraged.

FURTHER READING:

Berners-Lee, T., L. Masinter, M. McCahill, eds. ''RFC 1738.'' Internet Engineering Task Force, December 1994. Available from www.cis.ohio-state.edu.

The World Wide Web Consortium. ''Web Naming and Addressing Overview (URIs, URLs).'' Cambridge, MA: The World Wide Web Consortium, 1997. Available from www.w3.org.

SEE ALSO: Domain Name; ICANN

USER INTERFACE

For a long time, the ease with which humans and computers interacted was not a primary area of focus. The earliest computers relied on interfaces that by modern standards were very primitive and cumbersome. As computing became a part of life for more than just a handful of scientists, academics, and businesspeople, it became necessary to devise user interfaces that were not terribly difficult to understand and use. The field of human-computer interaction evolved, leading to systems that were much easier for the average person to operate.

In general, the term user interface can apply to the many different means humans have for interacting with computer systems, applications, and networks. These include everything from physical tools like monitors, mice, light pens, keyboards, and microphones (for voice recognition commands and audio input) to elements that appear on screen, such as basic text characters used for writing programs and issuing commands, help modules in software applications, search tools, and the graphical user interfaces (GUI) characteristic of the Macintosh and Windows operating systems. The term user interface even applies to the ways in which Web sites, wireless devices, and e-commerce applications are set up for interaction with customers.

The earliest user interfaces were limited to only a few buttons on a computer device or punch cards

that contained instructions. Text-based, on-screen interfaces, such as a list of menu choices, eventually became available. They evolved into the GUIs—containing toolbars, pointers, pop-up windows, virtual desktops, and icons—that were very pervasive across different computing platforms, systems, and devices in the early 2000s. Because GUIs rely heavily on visual elements, these interfaces became increasingly sophisticated and subjective, and were received and interpreted by a diverse population of computer users in different ways.

When users find a particular interface appealing and understandable, it becomes possible to take full advantage of all the capabilities the underlying system or application has to offer. Otherwise, a poor interface can limit the power and potential uses of the system or application. Although it was arguably easier to operate computers and operating systems in the early 2000s than it was at the beginning of the computer age, poorly designed user interfaces were an issue for many software programs. Making matters worse was the fact that bad interface precedents set by leading software companies were sometimes followed by other players throughout the industry. Isys Information Architects Inc. was one company specializing in information systems design during the early 2000s. According to Isys, among the leading roadblocks to effective interfaces were hard-to-understand terminology, improperly used metaphors and visual element design, unclear or incorrect error messages, and the misuse of color.

The degree to which a user finds an interface easy to understand and use not only affects the extent to which he or she can take advantage of what the system has to offer, it also may impact how often the user operates a system. For companies engaging in e-commerce, this can have serious implications. Even if a company has a product or service that consumers want, and at a price that is competitive, a frustrating or confusing online experience can kill a potentially lucrative sale. Therefore, it is necessary for e-commerce Web sites and their underlying systems to be well designed.

In the early 2000s, personal digital assistants (PDAs) like the Palm Pilot, and various kinds of handheld computers and wireless Internet-enabled phones were exploding in popularity. These devices held great promise for e-commerce. The development of user interfaces for these devices was an emerging area that presented a variety of challenges. Among them was the issue of getting modern wireless devices to not only communicate with older legacy systems (common at many companies), but to then present the data in a format that was easy to understand and navigate.

FURTHER READING:

''Interface Hall of Fame/Interface Hall of Shame.'' Isys Information Architects Inc. July 31, 2001. Available from www.iarchitect.com/.

Zetlin, Minda. ''The Web's Master Builders.'' *Computerworld,* January 22, 2001

SEE
ALSO: Web Site Design

UTILITY MODEL

Whether a company sells products or services to consumers, other businesses, or both, there are many different ways to approach the marketplace and make a profit. Business models are used to describe how companies go about this process. They spell out the main ways in which companies make profits by identifying a company's role during commerce and describing how products, information, and other important elements are structured. Just as there are many different industries and types of companies, there are many different kinds of business models. While some are simple, others are very complex. Even within the same industry, companies may rely on business models that are very different from one another, and some companies may use a combination of several different models.

General business models by themselves do not necessarily map out a company's specific strategy for success. Strategic marketing plans, which are a specialized type of business model, are used for that purpose. They identify the specific situation in which a company finds itself in a particular marketplace, the differentials that set a company apart from its competitors, the marketing tactics used to accomplish strategic objectives, and so on.

Business models involve different levels in what are known as supply/value chains. Value chains outline the activities involved in creating value from the supply side of economics, where raw materials are used to manufacture a product, to the demand side, when finished products or components are marketed and shipped to re-sellers or end-users. Companies review and analyze different steps in value chains to create optimal and effective business models.

Some long-established business models used in the physical world have been adopted on the Internet with varying degrees of success. Among these are mail-order models, advertising models, free-trial models, subscription models, and direct marketing models. Other business models are native to the Internet and e-commerce and focus heavily on the movement of electronic information. These include digital delivery models, information barter models, and freeware models.

Every business model has its own inherent strengths and weaknesses. Just as is the case in the physical world, online business models vary in their suitability for different enterprises. Business models themselves are not enough to guarantee success in the physical or online worlds. As Jeffrey F. Rayport explains, ''Every e-commerce business is either viable or not viable. They hardly qualify for the paint-by-number prescriptions that business people seem to expect. Business models themselves do not offer solutions; rather, how each business is run determines its success. So the success of e-commerce businesses will hinge largely on the art of management even as it is enabled by the science of technology.''

THE UTILITY MODEL

One Internet business model is the utility model. It is based on the concept of metered use, where people pay for services as they are used. Services that are based on a utility model may involve the use of micro-payments—online transactions of low value, ranging from several pennies to approximately $10.00. Micro-payments are commonly used to pay for downloads of newspaper articles, electronic books, music clips, or software, but could be used for virtually any low-priced item for sale on the Internet. Because the cost of accepting credit cards for small purchases is prohibitively expensive, some companies involved in e-commerce have turned to third-party vendors to manage the billing and collection of micro-payments. Such vendors normally receive a percentage of each transaction as compensation.

According to *Computerworld,* both Forrester Research and the Gartner Group expected person-to-person micro-payments to grow in popularity. *Communications International* also expected the concept of mobile commerce to take off, where mobile phones and wireless devices like personal digital assistants (PDAs) are used to make micro-payments. In the early 2000s, Andersen Consulting developed prototype technology called Mobile Micropayments that had many potential uses. According to *Information-Week,* the technology enabled consumers to receive special offers from merchants in their immediate location via their wireless device. For example, a consumer who walks past a vending machine might be presented with a range of selections on the display of his or her PDA, which could be purchased immediately.

Digital Goods was one company that relied on the utility model in the early 2000s. Through its Digigoods service, the company sold eBooks (books that can be downloaded off of the Internet and read on-screen or printed on a desktop printer), reports, and guides on a wide array of topics ranging from business and computer books to works of fiction. Many of the company's titles were from leading print publishers like Dun & Bradstreet, Simon & Schuster, and Harper Collins. Consumers were able to select titles of interest, and then download them to their computer for a fee.

Another company exemplifying the utility model was Fatbrain, owned by Barnes & Noble. In the early 2000s the company worked with new and established writers by allowing them to post their works online. When someone purchased the work, the writer spit the fee with Fatbrain on a 50/50 basis. Similarly, MP3.com provided downloadable music files to consumers. Just as an online bookstore might provide a sample chapter or excerpt to a potential purchaser for review, MP3.com allowed consumers to hear music before purchasing it. In addition to allowing artists to create their own Web pages with band information, the company handled the manufacturing and fulfillment of an artist's CD for a 50/50 split, similar to Fatbrain.

The utility model also has far reaching potential in the area of software. In this scenario, people are able to use software programs via the Web as they need them for small fees, instead of paying larger sums to purchase the entire applications and install them on their computers. According to *InfoWorld,* from 2000 to 2003 IBM planned to invest at least $4 billion to establish itself as a leader in on-demand computer services that rely on a usage fees. According to Rajeev Bharadwaj, CTO and founder of Mountain View, Calif.-based Ejasent, in order for such a model to work three elements were necessary, including ''a reliable, secure, and shared infrastructure; a flexible network to handle the up-and-down demands; and a pay-as-you-go financial model.'' IBM planned to do far more than offer its own software programs to users on a pay-as-you-go basis. Its intent was to provide the infrastructure other software companies need to offer their products according to this model.

In order for this model to work in the software industry, companies faced several challenges. One involved the programming languages in which applications were written. In some cases software companies would be required to rewrite programs altogether in order to make them work on the Internet. Additionally, companies would need to change the way their licensing fees are structured, from one-time fees to per-usage fees. Finally, there were technical considerations surrounding memory for storage and compatibility issues for users on different kinds of computing platforms, like Windows, Macintosh, or Linux.

The utility model appeared to have potential in the early 2000s. In addition to companies like Digigoods, Fatbrain, and MP3.com, and big plans from companies like IBM, computer industry leaders like HP and Sun Microsystems, as well as some companies in the telecommunications industry, were moving toward this business model for different types of services.

FURTHER READING:

Bambury, Paul. ''A Taxonomy of Internet Commerce.'' *First-Monday,* 1998. Available from www.firstmonday.dk.

Caulfield, Brian. ''The Technology's Here—But are Net Businesses Ready to Use It?'' *Internet World,* October 1, 2000.

Nelson, Matthew. ''Innovation: A Remote Control for E-commerce.'' *InformationWeek,* October 30, 2000.

Raffray, Nathalie. ''Who Will Get the Credit?'' *Communications International,* October, 2000.

Rappa, Michael. ''Business Models On The Web.'' April 9, 2001. Available from www.academic.uofs.edu.

Rayport, Jeffrey F. ''The Truth About Internet Business Models.'' *Strategy+Business,* Third Quarter, 1999. Available from www.strategy-business.com.

Short, Sharon Gwyn. ''Beyond Digital Wallets: Internet Payment Services as Ecommerce Boom or Bust?'' *EContent,* April/May, 2000.

Solomon, Melissa. ''Micropayments.'' *Computerworld,* May 1, 2000.

Timmers, Paul. ''Business Models for Electronic Markets.'' *Electronic Markets,* April, 1998. Available from www.electronicmarkets.org.

Vizard, Michael; Brian Fonseca, and Ed Scannell. ''IBM Readies Apps on Tap—Vendors Adapting to Evolving Utility Model.'' *InfoWorld,* December 18, 2000.

Weiner, Stuart E. ''Electronic Payments in the U.S. Economy: an Overview.'' *Government Finance Review,* April, 2000.

SEE
ALSO: Business Models

UUNET

UUNET, a subsidiary of telecommunications giant WorldCom, is a leading provider of Internet services and products primarily to business customers worldwide. It offers Internet access, Web hosting, remote access, and other services throughout the world to more than 70,000 businesses. The company also owns and operates a global network in thousands of cities.

UUNET's customers can choose from a range of Internet access options, including dial-up and remote access, dedicated access over DSL, ATM, frame relay, and high-bandwidth dedicated leased line connections. UUNET's Web hosting services include managed Web hosting on shared or dedicated Web servers as well as co-location at its WorldCom Hosting Centers. UUNET also provides businesses with virtual private networks (VPNs), security solutions, and Internet multicasting.

UUNET provides wholesale services to Internet service providers (ISPs), carriers, and others who use UUNET's Internet infrastructure as the basis for the Internet services they offer to their own customers. Among the leading Internet services for which UUNET has provided Internet backbone are America Online, the Microsoft Network (MSN), GTE, EarthLink, and CompuServe.

As of mid-2001, UUNET's IP (Internet protocol) network spanned more than 2,500 points of presence, making it one of the most widely deployed IP networks in the world. UUNET offered connectivity in more than 100 countries.

FIRST COMMERCIAL ISP

Founded in 1987, UUNET is recognized as the first commercial Internet service provider (ISP). In the early 1990s it introduced several innovative services, including the first commercial application-layer firewall services for IP networks in 1992, T-1 connections to the Internet in 1993, the first virtual private network (VPN) service and Web hosting services in 1994. In 1994 John Sidgmore became UUNET's CEO and president. He was formerly president and CEO of CSC Intelicom.

When Microsoft Corp. began preparing its Microsoft Network (MSN) to coincide with the release of Windows 95, UUNET provided the Internet backbone that would allow MSN users to have dial-up access to both MSN and the Internet. At the time UUNET had 25 points of presence and was building out its network. Microsoft also took a minority interest in UUNET, with the funds going toward UUNET's build-out. Microsoft also took a seat on UUNET's board of directors.

UUNET completed its initial public offering (IPO) in May 1995, offering shares at $14 and raising more than $50 million. By July UUNET's stock was trading in the $45 range. Although UUNET had not shown a profit, investors were betting on its potential for explosive revenue growth in the coming year. At the time of UUNET's IPO, Microsoft owned about 15 percent of the company. UUNET's revenue for 1995 was $94 million, compared to $12.4 million in the previous year, making it the leading ISP in the industry.

From the beginning UUNET was focused on the corporate market, which was expected to grow sooner and more quickly than the consumer market for Internet access. The corporate market gave UUNET higher revenue streams, bigger margins, and a more reliable customer base. UUNET also offered premium services, such as network management and security, for which it could charge more. UUNET's corporate clients included America Online and AT&T as well as Microsoft. UUNET's two principal services were leased-line connections for businesses under its AlterNet program and dial-up access through its AlterDial program. AlterDial was expected to have 130 points of presence by the end of 1995. In 1996 UUNET began offering more services related to electronic commerce, inlcuding end-to-end security, FTP (File Transport Protocol) hosting, and dedicated servers that companies could lease.

NEW OWNERS FOR UUNET, 1996

In 1996 MFS Communications Inc. acquired UUNET for $2 billion in stock, a 37 percent premium over market value. The acquisition made 40 of UUNET's 700 employees who owned UUNET stock millionaires. MFS Communications was based in Omaha, Nebraska, and offered local and long distance telephone service in New York and nationwide. It built fiber-optic cable connections to 7,400 buildings in key financial districts in the United States and Europe. Together, the two companies were able to offer end-to-end voice, data, and Internet services. Following the acquisition UUNET extended its AlterDial service to 92 international cities.

In mid-1996 GTE, then the largest local telephone service provider in the United States, became a UUNET customer when it introduced GTE Internet Solutions. GTE used UUNET's existing network to offer Internet access in 250 cities in 46 states. Later in 1996 UUNET became the first major commercial ISP to offer Web hosting services for Windows NT 4.0. UUNET first offered Web hosting services in 1994 using the Unix platform, and had more than 800 customers.

Web hosting was one service that ISPs could offer to distinguish themselves from their numerous competitors. In late 1996 UUNET began offering another service, ExtraLink, a package of extranet services that enabled companies to share information with customers and suppliers over a virtual private network (VPN). A related service, called ExtraLink Remote Access, allowed remote workers to access the corporate network without having to employ a large bank of modems.

For 1996 UUNET's revenues were estimated to be $216 million. Before the end of the year WorldCom Inc. acquired MFS Communications for approximately $12 billion in stock. Sidgmore remained CEO of UUNET and became vice chairman and chief operating officer (COO) of WorldCom.

WORLDCOM INVESTS IN UUNET, 1997-2001

With WorldCom as its parent company, UUNET was able to offer a pioneering service guarantee promising uptime of more than 99.9 percent for intranet and business-to-business services. The guarantee applied to sites that were connected to one another by the UUNET network. It covered more than 300 locations in the United States and 500 in Europe and Asia.

UUNET received $300 million from WorldCom to upgrade its Internet backbone in the United States and quadruple its capacity. Company officials estimated that the load on UUNET's backbone doubled every quarter, which meant the company needed to increase its capacity tenfold within a year and a hundredfold within two years. UUNET expected to have to spend about $300 million a year on network expansion for the next four or five years. UUNET's principal ISP customers were Microsoft, GTE, EarthLink, and America Online.

In 1997 UUNET began offering global Web hosting facilities to help multinational companies overcome the problem of narrow bandwidth between continents. During the year UUNET introduced IDSL connections, which offered high-speed Internet access over standard phone lines. IDSL provided small and medium-size businesses with direct connections to the Internet at a low cost.

Reliability became an issue for UUNET when two UUNET hubs—in Los Angeles and Tyson's Corner, Virginia—failed. To ensure the reliability of its customer's Internet connections, UUNET introduced a Shadow Support Program that provided a secondary T-1 or T-3 line to businesses. Network administrators could then redirect traffic if there was a line outage or other problem, thus avoiding an interruption of service.

UUNET expanded its global network to nearly 1,000 points of presence in 1997 with the acquisition of NLnet, the leading ISP in the Netherlands. NLnet's 45 points of presence there provided comprehensive local-dial access throughout the country. At the time the Netherlands was one of the top five countries for Internet usage on a per capita basis.

Other services introduced in 1997 included UUCasting, the first commercially available multicasting service to give Internet content providers a way to reach hundreds of thousands of users without having to invest in their own T-3 lines. Before the end of 1997 UUNET became the first ISP to offer OC-3 service, which provided users with 155Mbps direct access to UUNET's Internet backbone, the fastest speed then available and faster than anything being offered by other ISPs. OCDirect was only offered in the San Francisco Bay area, Washington, D.C., and New York City, mainly to ISP resellers, large Web-hosting services, and large corporate users.

In 1998 WorldCom reorganized into two main divisions to consolidate the acquisition of three other ISPs: ANS Communications Inc., CompuServe Network Services, and GridNet International. One division, UUNET WorldCom, emphasized packaged services, while WorldCom Advanced Networks provided Web hosting, intranet and extranet, VPN, and data security services. UUNET Worldcom was headed by Mark Spagnolo, UUNET's president and COO, while WorldCom Advanced Networks was headed by former CompuServe Network Services president Peter Van Kamp. Both reported to John Sidgmore, WorldCom's vice chairman and UUNET's CEO. Following the reorganization UUNET Worldcom had about 3,000 employees and Worldcom Advanced Networks about 1,700 employees. In November 1998 WorldCom completed its acquisition of MCI Corp. for $40 billion. John Sidgmore became vice chairman of MCI Worldcom and remained CEO of UUNET.

A mid-1999 survey of ISPs by *Data Communications* magazine revealed that UUNET was the largest, serving 178 of the 500 largest domains. UUNET was also ranked the best overall ISP and received the magazine's User's Choice Award. In 1999 UUNET increased the capacity of its national network backbone and quadrupled its network speed to stay ahead of increasing demand for Internet bandwidth. It also expanded its DSL service to include more than 1,000 points of presence in 850 cities. UUNET strengthened its presence in the Web hosting market by expanding Web hosting centers in San Jose, California, and Washington, D.C., and announcing plans to build seven others, giving UUNET a total of 15 data centers. The overall Web hosting market was projected to grow from $4.4 billion in 1999 to $14.4 billion in 2003, according to The Yankee Group. During the year UUNET also began offering a managed global VPN service called UUsecure, which included network design, construction, management, and monitoring.

In 2000 UUNET upgraded traffic between major hubs in its U.S. network to OC-192 (10 Gbps, or 10 billion bits of information per second) using Juniper Networks Inc.'s new M160 routers. The company also introduced turnkey Internet services to small businesses under its Business Essentials program. Under UUNET's ISP Program, a different set of turnkey Internet services was offered to small telecommunications companies and emerging Internet players that wanted to offer Internet access to their customers or expand their ISP offerings.

During 2000 UUNET invested heavily in building data centers, where application, Internet, and Web-hosting service providers could co-locate their services. The first two data centers of the $1.2 billion program were opened on the East Coast to service demand from New York City. UUNET also upgraded its VPN service to offer both dial-up access service for remote workers and dedicated lines for site-to-site networks. The new VPN service also added wider geographic availability, bandwidth prioritization, and improved service-level agreements (SLAs).

Internationally, UUNET expanded into Latin America by establishing a Latin American regional headquarters in Sao Paulo, Brazil. UUNET's parent company, WorldCom, held a controlling interest in Embratel, Brazil's former state-owned long-distance company. UUNET planned to take advantage of Embratel's infrastructure and presence in Brazil to enter the ISP market there, then expand throughout Latin America. At the time UUNET operated in 114 countries and served more than 70,000 businesses around the world.

Backed by the resources of parent company WorldCom, UUNET will likely continue to expand globally, develop new services, and upgrade existing services to maintain its leadership position as an ISP. Some new services may be developed internally, while others could come from acquisitions made by UUNET's parent company. When WorldCom acquired Intermedia for $6 billion in 2000, it added Intermedia's Web hosting subsidiary Digex to its group of companies. The demand for more speed and more bandwidth among Internet customers will put industry-leader UUNET in a strong position in the future.

FURTHER READING:

DeVeaux, Paul. "UUNet Announces ISP Program for Vertical Markets." *America's Network,* March 1, 2000.

Gerwig, Kate. "Uunet Plants Multicast Flag." *InternetWeek,* September 29, 1997.

Jones, Jennifer. "UUNET Goes Public with Policy for ISP Peering Agreements." *InfoWorld,* January 29, 2001.

LaPolla, Stephanie. "UUNet Props up Backbone with New Shadow Support." *PC Week,* June 2, 1997.

Perez, Juan Carlos. "UUNet Eyes Latin American Market." *InfoWorld,* September 18, 2000.

Rendleman, John. "UUNet Has the Essentials." *eWeek,* June 5, 2000.

Spangler, Todd. "Two Executives Get New Roles at Revamped Uunet." *InternetWorld,* May 11, 1998.

UUNET. "About Us." UUNET, September 19, 2001. Available from www.uu.net.

"UUNET Thinks Small." *ISP Business News,* May 29, 2000.

"UUNet's IPO Millionaires." *Forbes,* October 7, 1996.

Williams, David. "Top 25 ISPs." *Data Communications,* June 7, 1999.

SEE ALSO: Business-to-Business (B2B) E-commerce; Internet Service Provider (ISP)

V

VALUE CREATION

In order for customers to visit Web sites, make initial online purchases, and then develop into return customers, companies must provide them with good reasons for doing so. In general, value creation is the process companies use to make their Web sites destinations of choice, distinguished from and with advantages over other Web sites or retail channels. A company's ability to create value increases as its Web site evolves from static, advertising-focused Web pages to a site with more interactive capabilities, including online customer support or the ability to accept electronic orders for products and services.

The Association for Computing Machinery's journal, *Communications of the ACM,* revealed that as the World Wide Web becomes an increasingly important medium between producers and consumers, it affects many key channels in the supply chain, including order processing, advertising, and customer support. Therefore, from a big-picture standpoint, as products move along the many points between a manufacturer's assembly line and end-users—be they individual consumers, other businesses or re-sellers—there are many opportunities to create value online. In order for this to occur, information must be gathered, organized, selected, synthesized, and then distributed, as Jeffrey F. Rayport and John J. Sviokla explained in Don Tapscott's book *Creating Value in the Network Economy.*

A report studying best practices in value creation among European companies, issued by 3i Venturelab and summarized in *European Venture Capital Jour-* *nal,* identified three unique areas where value can be created during e-commerce: bringing many different groups or products together; delivering information to everyone involved in a way that is faster, richer or more meaningful than through other means; and creating alternatives to or simulations of the elements one would expect during an offline purchase, including the physical handling of products and the ability to talk to others.

Opportunities for creating value can be viewed from the standpoint of how companies interact with customers. According to *Across the Board,* Andersen Consulting identified that companies often attempt to create value by focusing on two specific kinds of interactions with customers: buyer-focused interactions and user-focused interactions. In a buyer-focused interaction, companies attempt to make the buying process more convenient or powerful for customers. On the other hand, user-focused interactions occur after a purchase takes place. Such interactions often involve things like online technical support, value-added information to enhance the use of a product or service, and notices about product updates.

In addition to buyer- and user-focused interactions, some companies create value based on the intentions of their customers. A company specializing in the sale of log homes could use this approach to make its Web site more meaningful for customers by listing current mortgage rates, providing links to different lenders, offering articles about choosing the right kind of log home, showcasing popular areas for building log homes, and so on. Thus, the site goes beyond mere details about a company's products or services and becomes a useful tool for customers who are seeking complementary information.

Another approach to creating value, called customer co-creation, involves customers contributing to the development or evolution of a company's product or service. According to a *Planet IT* article by C.K. Prahalad, Venkatram Ramaswamy, and M.S. Krishnan, "consumers are getting used to the idea of an active dialogue with providers of products and services. The emerging dialogue is not restricted to help-desk communication. Increasingly, the dialogue involves an active role in product design and testing." Microsoft used this approach by involving more than 500,000 software engineers in the testing process for Microsoft 2000 and using their feedback to make the final product better. Other examples of this type of interaction include the collaborative development of the Linux operating system—a software program used to control the basic operating functions of many Web servers.

The potential for value creation also exists when companies assist customers in the disposal of unwanted goods. For example, a company selling new office equipment might directly buy—or help a customer to sell—their old furnishings as an added service. In addition to benefiting consumers, this type of interaction also creates leasing, pricing, and promotion opportunities for companies on the sales side.

In the early 2000s, personalization and the formation of online communities were two other ways companies could create value on their Web sites, although the approaches had not been adopted on large scales. With personalization, customers' Web site experiences are customized, based on information the host company acquires about them. To accomplish this, some companies use software programs to conduct behavioral analyses of Web site visits, which reveal the most popular areas of their sites, such as pages with specific products or services. By keeping track of visitors' purchase histories, Web pages can be customized to include content or special offers that are more relevant to them. Companies also can go beyond basic personalization and engage in dynamic profiling, in which Web sites try to predict what a visitor is likely to buy. In this scenario, based on a visitor's history and the areas they are viewing during an actual visit, special software reconfigures Web pages to display items that visitor might purchase. Ultimately, the company's goal is to generate more return visits and purchases.

Finally, online communities were a channel through which value could be created. Online communities involve existing or potential users of a product or service providing support and information to one another, usually by posting messages, exchanging e-mail, or engaging in chat sessions. In addition to saving companies money in the area of customer service, online communities arguably provide a deeper,

more insightful level of support to customers. A variety of different consumer experiences often result from one product or service. Online communities allow end-users to share them with one another and exchange perspectives. Because value is so important to a Web site's success, the topic likely will remain a major focus for online marketers and the customers they serve.

FURTHER READING:

Bushrod, Lisa. "Report on E-commerce Value Creation." *European Venture Capital Journal,* November 1, 2000.

Chaudhury, Abhijit, Debasish Mallick, N. Rao, and H. Raghav. "Web Channels in E-commerce." *Communications of the ACM,* January 2001.

Garvey, Robert A. "How E-commerce Will Add Value." *Iron Age New Steel,* November 2000.

Kambil, Ajit, and Erik Eselius. "Where the Interaction Is." *Across the Board,* November/December 2000.

Nemes, Judith. "Inspiring Surfers To Browse, Browsers To Buy, And Buyers To Return." *Planet IT,* April 27, 2000. Available from www.PlanetIT.com.

Prahalad, C.K., Venkatram Ramaswamy, and M.S. Krishnan. "Customer Centricity." *Planet IT,* April 10, 2000. Available from www.planetit.com.

Tapscott, Don. *Creating Value in the Network Economy.* Boston: Harvard Business Review Publishing, 1999.

SEE ALSO: Community Model; Mass Customization; Personalization; Profiling

VIRTUAL COMMUNITIES

Virtual communities organize and bring together individuals, groups, and businesses in cyberspace around common interests or purposes. From identity- and interest-based communities to industry-based business-to-business exchanges, virtual communities proliferated in the late 1990s and early 2000s. Each community has its own character, rules, culture, interface, and features, depending on the purposes to which it is dedicated and the community it serves. Thus, it is difficult to articulate the make-up of a "typical" community, although virtual-community operators shared many of the same technical and logistic concerns common to the community model. In general, however, the manner in which a virtual community develops must be dictated by the organic needs of its members, not the other way around.

According to Howard Rheingold, former online host for one of the world's largest virtual communities, The WELL, and founder of his own company specializing in helping businesses build virtual communities, businesses looking to add value by providing a business or customer community on their Web sites would do well to first consider how the community will fit into their marketing schemes—in other words, to determine how the community will add value not only for the customers, but for the firm. Secondly, businesses need to amass and implement the appropriate technical infrastructure. Finally, businesses must decide on what Rheingold refers to as the ''social infrastructure,'' which includes the basic ground rules for the types of questions that will be addressed, the modes of etiquette that users must abide by, whether the community discussions will be moderated, and so on.

Each of these architectural and design issues has its own layer of considerations. For instance, communities need to determine what kinds of people they do and do not wish to attract, and what they're going to do to procure the desired audience. These kinds of issues can prove crucial down the line. For example, U.S. courts generally hold that virtual communities that host chat rooms are not liable for slanderous or libelous postings by their members provided that the chat room is unmoderated. But if a moderator is present in the online chat rooms, the virtual community can be held responsible.

While businesses tapped into the community model to gain a competitive edge and create value with the Internet, some commentators viewed the virtual community as one of the primary methods by which the Internet could deliver on its promise of democratizing not only information but social and political life in general. According to this view, online communities allow generally isolated or marginalized groups to find each other in cyberspace, share ideas and concerns, and begin to build institutions for effecting societal change.

According to *Online Community Report,* in the early 2000s online communities were facing a turning point in their business operations. Typically, a community will try to sustain itself via a combination of membership fees, e-commerce, and advertising. While a handful of communities enjoyed success with this model, the majority of communities were likely to shift their business models to stay afloat. Online advertising, for instance, was in poor shape throughout the e-commerce world, and companies were particularly reluctant to advertise on pages on which the content was generated by users, such as in community conferences. Moreover, it was difficult to generate subscriber fees substantial enough to make up the difference, because users are hard-pressed to pay too much simply to talk to others. Thus, for all but some of the largest and most established communities, the early 2000s were likely to see communities seeking out a tighter focus, trying to capture a niche in which they can generate revenues to cover costs.

There exist a plethora of tools frequently employed by virtual communities, including chat rooms, listservs, message boards, email, forums, and more. Some virtual communities, such as GeoCities, simply provide users with free home pages and let them build communities themselves from the ground up. In this case, users establish their own sites to draw traffic, and in the course of its growth the page adds links to other sites of interest, until a community of common interests emerges from the grass roots.

SOME PROMINENT VIRTUAL COMMUNITIES

One of the most popular of the Internet's online communities was The WELL, one of the oldest and most pioneering of communities. The WELL catered to an intellectual audience of educators, journalists, artists, activists, programmers, and others. To give its members a community feel, the WELL refuses to sell any information on its subscribers to marketers or conduct advertising inside membership areas on the Web site.

Born in 1985 as the Whole Earth 'Lectronic Link, the WELL emerged from a dialog between independent readers and writers of the *Whole Earth Review*. As the community grew, it was dominated by a literary and intellectual membership, though its specific focus expanded beyond the world of literature, initially drawing in counter-culture and computer enthusiasts and eventually opening its doors to thousands of topics of interest. In 1992, the WELL became one of the earliest commercial sites plugged into the Internet, and its Web site went online in 1994. In 1996 the community split in two, with the Whole Earth 'Lectronic Link splitting from the Internet access operations to concentrate on the full-service community model, developing its own forum software and becoming The WELL, LLC. In 1999, The WELL, LLC was acquired by Salon.com.

The hallmark of the community was its Conferences, numbering in the hundreds and devoted to wide-ranging topics, from the technical to the philosophical, from the social to the artistic. Conference hosts orientate new members and spur new lines of discussion. The WELL sees its core mission as providing space for rich conversation along with tools and services for building new, viable communities. Known mostly for its vigorous, often contentions intellectual discussions, the WELL particularly gave birth to many of the possibilities inherent in the Web for fueling intelligent discussion across worldwide networks.

The ezboard Web site went online in 1999, built only on a dial-up modem and a laptop computer, according to founder and chief executive Vanchau Nguyen, and grew into a hub of some 700,000 communities hosting 10.9 million users as of April 2001. ezboard provides its users with tools to personalize their online experience within the community so as to extract the greatest value out of their community experience. To generate extra revenue, ezboard instituted its Community-Supported Communities program, in which community users can make a small monthly contribution in return for boosted services. In this way, ezboard, with its large user base, was able to continue generating revenues despite declining advertising fees, and was further able to enhance communities where users voted with their dollars.

Founded in 1996, iVillage.com first emerged as a support community for parents. Over time, the community recognized that the shortfall in its revenues could be traced to advertisers' reluctance to market to such a broad demographic as "parents." Thus, iVillage decided to narrow its focus to women specifically, labeling itself the Woman's Network. From there, iVillage opened its community doors to topics of interests—family, parenting, career, relationships, legal advice, medical information, and more—specifically from women's perspective. The message boards are monitored by volunteers drawn from the community. In the early 2000s, iVillage merged with Women.com to form the largest online community devoted to women's issues. By 2001 the community boasted some 5 million members.

BlackVoices.com was among the most popular virtual communities for African Americans. The community featured a variety of chat rooms focusing on diverse topics of interest to the African-American community, along with extensive news coverage and other writings. Moreover, BlackVoices.com featured an online career center for the exchange of resumes, company-profile searches, job postings, and other employment-related services, as well as a shopping center specializing in products produced and sold by African-American entrepreneurs. In addition to its many online systems and features, the community sponsors monthly events in the physical world for members to meet face-to-face. Other African-American-oriented online communities, such as Net-Noir.com, focus primarily on African-American culture and lifestyles, and feature extensive content in the form of poetry and prose, events listings, streaming-media performances, and culture-based shopping venues.

FURTHER READING:

Andrews, Whit. "Who's Responsible? Host, Moderator, or Member?" *Internet World,* September 21, 1998.

Berst, Jesse. "What's Igniting Online Communities?" *ZDNet,* October 1, 1998. Available from www.zdnet.com.

"Care for the Community." *New Media Investor,* February 15, 2001.

Cashel, Jim. "Top Ten Trends for Online Communities." *Online Community Report,* July 2001. Available from www.OnlineCommunityReport.com.

Etzioni, Amitai. "E-Communities Build New Ties, But Ties That Bind." *New York Times,* February 10, 2000.

ezboard, Inc. "Welcome to ezboard." San Francisco, CA: ezboard, Inc., 2001. Available from www.ezboard.com.

Hafner, Katie. "The Epic Saga of The WELL." *Wired,* May 1997. Available from www.wired.com.

iVillage, Inc. "iVillage.com: The Women's Network—Busy Women Sharing Solutions and Advice." iVillage, Inc., 2001. Available from www.ivillage.com.

McKay, Jason. "Virtual Communities." *Black Enterprise,* October 2000.

Shapiro, Andrew L. "The Net that Binds: Using Cyberspace to Create Real Communities." *The Nation,* June 21, 1999.

Telleen, Steven L. "What it Means to Have Virtual Communities on an Intranet." *Internet World,* November 16, 1998.

The WELL LLC. "The WELL." San Francisco, CA: The WELL LLC, 2001. Available from www.well.com.

SEE ALSO: Community Model

VIRUSES

Viruses are computer programs, usually malicious but occasionally unintentional, that spread through networks replicating themselves on shared programs and corrupting the computers in their path. While viruses have existed for years, they have taken on a new prominence and danger in the Internet Age, when they can spread much faster and compromise more—and more important—systems. A vast industry arose to combat viruses, but it was largely engaged in an arms race in the early 2000s, as viruses continued to proliferate and mutate, growing more powerful and damaging.

Since computers and networking have become such a central component of economic and social activity, virus attacks, even relatively minor ones, have the potential to severely disrupt daily life. Out of that growing recognition, governments, corporations, and organizations, were coordinating efforts to prepare for and respond to computer viruses.

In a 2001 report titled *Virus Prevalence Survey,* the Reston, Virginia-based Internet security assurance firm ICSA.net reported that the number of companies that experienced major virus-related disasters increased more than 20 percent in 2000, while 40 percent of companies reported data losses from virus attacks. The report also noted that a typical company spent between $100,000 and $1 million on virus disasters and protection each year, and that figure was rising.

ICSA reported that the prevalence of virus attacks has increased from about 10 per 10,000 computers in 1996 to 91 per 10,000 in 2000, and analysts warned that the proportion would rise in the early 2000s. To make matters worse, each generation of viruses grows more sophisticated. In the early 2000s, virus hunters were challenged by new breeds of self-replicating and mutating viruses that change shape as they spread so as to avoid detection. Virus programmers increasingly incorporate encryption schemes into the programs so as to shield the source code, and metamorphic viruses include a mutation engine in their algorithms that enable them to alter slightly at each replication.

HOW VIRUSES WORK

To perform its function, a virus need only be able to replicate itself. Once a virus infects a computer—by e-mail, disk, or some other method—the program to which the virus is attached only has to be executed to trigger the virus into action. On top of mere replication, viruses may include a malicious payload, a mark that invites the user to perform an operation, such as opening an e-mail attachment. For example, the tag ''I LOVE YOU'' in the worm virus of the same name in 2000 constituted that virus's payload.

Viruses work in a variety of ways to disrupt a system, but the most common method was to simply overburden it by repeating the same messages over and over via rapid self-replications, eventually crashing the system. In addition, a computer virus may not take effect immediately. It can sit undetected in computer systems for months waiting for the right operation to trigger it into action. By that time, it may be quite difficult to retrace the steps of how a virus was lodged in a system to begin with.

TYPES OF VIRUSES

File infectors target data and executable files on a system's hard drive, and spread primarily by attaching themselves to such files as they spread through a system that uses shared programs. Since executable files are far less likely to be shared over diskettes or e-mail than are data files, according to *Security Management,* file infectors don't tend to be as successful at spreading outside of local networks.

Boot-sector infectors (BSIs) attack the master boot record the computer taps to start up. BSIs are among the most difficult virus programs to write, according to *Security Management,* and their claim on the virus population was declining since they don't tend to proliferate over networks and are spread primarily by diskette rather than by e-mail. Modern networking technology, then, was phasing out BSIs, although by the early 2000s they still constituted a significant threat.

Macro viruses attach themselves to those programs that alleviate computer users from performing repetitive tasks, and have grown more prominent in an environment of sophisticated personal computers with many automated macros. Macros are also frequently attached to data files, thus speeding the spread of macro viruses.

Worms were a particular subset of viruses that distinguish themselves by replicating across networks without ever directly attaching themselves to a host program, although the most widely publicized worm viruses were spread as e-mail attachments. Generally, worms invade an individual's computer through e-mail, and then use that individual's e-mail address list to send themselves to others. Worms are characterized by the speed with which they spread through systems; several major worms, such as Melissa and LoveLetter, spread globally before anti-virus players had even detected the problem, much less devised a disinfection program.

Trojan horses, as the Homeric name implies, distinguish themselves by deceit. They appear to the user as benign or beneficial, but instead—or in addition—perform unwanted and potentially destructive functions. Some Trojan horses directly attack files or programs, while others compromise security measures, most commonly by stealing passwords. Still other Trojan horses do no damage at all, but pretend to. These are joke or hoax programs that deceive the user into believing an infection has occurred.

FENDING OFF VIRUSES

By the early 2000s, virus attacks, or threats thereof, were so frequent that businesses were hard pressed to be prepared in advance for all potential attacks. Since predicting when or how a virus would occur was nearly impossible, most businesses, governments, and organizations devoted their efforts to detection, containment, and disinfection programs.

Scores of antivirus vendors specialize in software designed to detect incoming viruses and deflect them from their targets. Since viruses are constantly evolving, so are the programs designed to thwart them, and many organizations, particularly IT-intensive businesses, must make frequent online trips to those vendors' sites to acquire the latest virus patches and other updates. Once these fortifications are acquired, IT security personnel must allocate all the updates to their proper locations, which can be a tedious and time-consuming process.

Antivirus programs typically work by scanning all incoming information for known viruses by seeking out virus ''signatures,'' or tell-tale signs of previously detected viruses. Such signatures generally include known programming patterns and codes, as well as more overt characteristics such as file names or types of e-mail attachments. But by its nature, this method forces antivirus vendors to continually play catch-up with viruses, and vendors are judged not only by the success of their products in fortifying systems against viruses, but also by how proactive they are in anticipating new virus strains. At any rate, IT security staffs are compelled to continually download the latest signature updates. With dozens of vendors issuing such updates, the task of regularly allocating the fortifications to their proper locations was increasingly costly, provoking many analysts to begin calling for more effective and user-friendly methods.

To make such tasks more manageable, antivirus vendors increasingly designed products for the server level, rather than the computer level. Not only were server-level virus screens easier to implement, they were increasingly practical as viruses were spread over server-based vehicles like e-mail. In addition, this provided multiple layers of security so that if an antivirus program failed to stop a virus at one level, it might still be thwarted at another level.

The emerging generation of antivirus programs may render obsolete the daunting task of updating signatures at the desktop level. Increasingly sophisticated programs were aimed at identifying and thwarting viruses based not on comparing their characteristics to lists of previous viruses, but by seeking out malicious behavior. This would be a huge step in the virus-antivirus arms race, allowing antivirus vendors to stop playing catch-up with virus programmers.

One obstacle to virus detection and eradication, according to some analysts, was the propensity of firms to keep internal virus damage quiet so as to avoid compromise of their stock prices or to otherwise try to circumvent financial or competitive disadvantage. While such practices can save a business from short-term headaches, it could also prove an obstacle to broader virus response techniques, since information sharing is so essential in order to get a handle on viruses.

FURTHER READING:

Greiner, Lynn. "IT's Battleground: The Quest for Virus Protection." *Computing Canada,* August 4, 2000.

Harley, David. "Living with Viruses." *Security Management,* August 2000.

Messmer, Ellen. "Experts Predict More Mutating Viruses." *Network World,* October 30, 2000.

Montana, John C. "Viruses and the Law: Why the Law is Ineffective." *Information Management Journal,* October 2000.

Nevin, Tom. "Computer Virus—Know the Enemy." *African Business,* April 2001.

Rash, Wayne. "What To Do When The Usual Security Steps Aren't Enough." *InternetWeek,* August 20, 2001.

Scheier, Robert L. "Managing the Virus Threat." *Computerworld,* May 7, 2001.

Trembly, Ara C. "The 10 Most Unwanted: 2001's Most Popular Viruses." *National Underwriter,* August 20, 2001.

"Viruses Rise, Criminals Walk, Public Confidence Falls." *Security,* February 2001.

SEE ALSO: Computer Crime; Denial of Service Attack; National Information Infrastructure Protection Act of 1996; National Infrastructure Protection Center; Computer Security; Worms

VOLATILITY

Internet technology changed the world in many ways. By connecting millions of people and businesses together, it increased the pace at which information travels, and therefore the pace of people's lives. No longer was it necessary to wait for news about emerging industry trends or details about the performance or conditions surrounding a particular company. As the Internet became more pervasive, such information traveled quickly via e-mail and found its way onto Web sites in seconds or minutes. In addition to information traveling at a much faster pace, as the World Wide Web caught the attention of consumers and businesses it gave rise to e-commerce. Much like a gold rush, e-commerce caused a flurry of activity. New ways of doing business were rapidly conceived, developed, and executed. With the promise of great wealth, investors poured large amounts of money into new ventures, some of which failed miserably.

Along with new social and lifestyle challenges, the aforementioned factors caused unprecedented volatility in the stock market. Volatility is characterized by sudden, often drastic changes in stock prices. This phenomenon can cause the New York Stock Exchange and other major exchanges to suddenly drop by many points and bounce back quickly as stock trades are influenced by the rapid, instant exchange of information. In many ways, volatility changed the nature of the investment game for everyone involved.

In addition to causing a flurry of mergers among investment banks, which banded together to more effectively deal with market uncertainties, volatility also required investors to become more focused. Simply investing in the technology sector was no longer specific enough. As it became necessary for important investment decisions to be made faster, a more specific focus made this already difficult task somewhat simpler. Investment funds emerged which emphasized specific kinds of technology, such as data communication, networking, Internet Security, or business-to-business technology.

Many different factors can be attributed to volatility. The faster pace of business was one factor. In the new economy, a departure from time-honored investment standards took place. Shorter periods of time (months as opposed to years) transpired before companies made initial public offerings (IPOs), and venture capitalists began quickly devoting large sums of money to new, unproven ventures. The faster pace of business translated to heightened movement on the part of the investment community. According to *Venture Capital Journal,* an emphasis on speed "altered and compressed the very process of screening, analyzing and making investments." In order to capitalize on changing, volatile markets, capitalists were required to focus on effectively managing risk and being strategic about investment liquidity. They also were faced with the challenge of applying existing methods and strategies in a more fast-paced environment.

Related to the issue of speed was the information that traveled quickly throughout the investment world via chat rooms and other channels. Investment news, accurate or otherwise, had the power to cause interesting ripple effects within markets and specific industries. For example, bad news from a chipmaker like Intel might cause stock prices to fall for other companies within the technology sector, such as PC and server manufacturers. Also of importance was the kind of information that traveled, and when. In October of 2000, a new Securities and Exchange Commission regulation, called Regulation FD (fair disclosure), went into effect in an effort to deal with selective disclosure. Selective disclosure is an unfair practice that decreases the confidence of investors. It happens when nonpublic information about a company is released to only certain parties, such as securities analysts, instead of to the general public as a whole.

Over the years, many theories have been developed to explain stock market volatility. These have been used in attempts to predict future market activity. According to some theorists, psychological factors—such as the attitudes of investors and their different reactions and access to information—cause volatility. Other theories are rooted more heavily in the field of economics. In reality, no one theory will likely ever explain volatility. Rather, the numerous theories each explain different factors and conditions that contribute to this phenomenon.

According to *CMA Management,* capital market volatility "is directly related to a lack of proper new economy standards, standards that are needed to value both old and new economy companies and to measure their periodic performance. Until such standards are developed and adopted, the daily guessing—as it relates to our stock markets—will continue and volatility will reign supreme." The publication cited the example of General Motors, a long-established old economy company, and Cisco Systems, a company with roots in the new economy. In mid-2000, General Motors' market value totaled $90 billion, while Cisco's was more than $500 billion. This was so even though General Motors listed a significantly higher number of assets on its balance sheet. This variance was due to the different way value was calculated for each company.

FURTHER READING:

Brain, Marshall. "How Stocks and the Stock Market Work." *How Stuff Works,* August 11, 2001. Available from www.howstuffworks.com.

Conway, Brian. "Viewpoint: Speed Thrills—The Opportunities and Challenges of Investing at E-Speed." *Venture Capital Journal,* June 1, 2000.

Grimm, Dennis. "Reporting Value in the New Economy." *CMA Management,* July/August 2001.

SEE ALSO: Investing, Online; New Economy; Shake-out, Dot-com

VORTALS

Vortals, or vertical portals, funciton like portals in that they serve as Internet starting points. Unlike portals, which have a broad, general appeal, vortals serve narrow, well-defined interests. A vortal provides Internet users with a route to content that is relevant to their specific interest. Through a careful selection of content and links to other Web sites, vortals focus in on a particular slice of the Internet.

Vortals may or may not be involved in electronic commerce. Some vortals serve specific communities and social groups. Other vortals are focused on hobbies and special interests. These vortals may range in complexity from a simple list of links to compelling content of its own. Add-on services such as branded e-mail are also available on some non-commercial vortals.

E-COMMERCE VORTALS SERVE SPECIFIC INDUSTRIES

Commercially based vortals typically serve a particular industry. *B to B* magazine publishes an annual directory of U.S.-based business-to-business vertical portals. Among the industries served by vortals are advertising, agriculture, automotive, business, business services, chemicals, computers, construction, design, electronic components, energy, engineering, entertainment, event planning, finance, food, food service, government, health care, hospitality, HVAC (heating, ventilation, air conditioning, and refrigeration), industrial, instruments, life sciences, livestock, machinery and equipment, metals, office products, paper, printing, purchasing, retail, shipping, surplus equipment, telecommunications, and Web site development.

These industry-specific vortals offer various mixes of content and transaction applications. Vortals may include news, industry information, and links to other content sources. Some include job postings and training resources. In terms of transaction capabilities, they may provide e-commerce transactions and services. Some vortals facilitate e-commerce by providing procurement software for a specific industry.

Commercial vortals also follow different models of functionality, including auctions, marketplaces, information providers, and resources. An auction vortal unites buyers and sellers and provides a site to submit jobs or items to be bid on. A marketplace vortal matches buyers and sellers and allows them to conduct transactions in real time. Information providers and resources may or may not offer the capability to conduct transactions.

Business-to-business vortals have had difficulty in generating a sufficient volume of transactions. One reason given is that b-to-b transactions are typically much more complex than business-to-consumer transactions. While vortals can facilitate the matching of potential buyers and sellers, there are many additional steps that need to be taken before a b-to-b transaction can be successfully completed.

VERTICALNET OFFERS VORTAL SOLUTIONS

At the beginning of 2001 VerticalNet operated 58 vortals and electronic marketplaces for a variety of industries. VerticalNet was originally conceived as an online trade magazine publisher. It evolved into an operator of industry-specific Web sites that combined content with electronic commerce capabilities.

VerticalNet encountered difficulties in 2001 and laid off more than 400 workers in the first half of the year. The company sold its electronics marketplace to a consortium of information technology (IT) vendors that included Hewlett-Packard and IBM. In a move that marked a change in strategy, VerticalNet became the software provider to the electronics marketplace it sold. During 2001 VerticalNet subsequently entered into agreements with Computer Sciences Corp. and Microsoft to bolster its position as a software provider to e-commerce vortals.

VORTALS PROVIDE ADVERTISERS WITH WELL-DEFINED AUDIENCES

Vortals appeal to online advertisers, because they serve well-defined audiences. Vortal users also tend to be more action- or market-oriented than their portal counterparts. As a result, vortal ads typically cost two to three times more than ads placed on portals.

In the competition for online advertising dollars, portals have copied vortals to some extent by organizing their content around specific interests. Portals also offer advertisers a much broader reach than vortals. In 2000 Forrester Research estimated that the top three portals—Yahoo!, America Online (AOL), and the Microsoft Network (MSN)—accounted for 15 percent of all Internet traffic and 45 percent of all online advertising.

As vortals evolve, they will likely not remain committed to an advertising supported business model. They will generate revenue by membership or subscription fees, transaction fees, software licensing, and other sources.

OUTLOOK FOR B2B VORTALS

In 2001 *B to B* magazine noted several trends that it forecast would develop among business-to-business vortals. Among them, the magazine predicted that the number of portals and e-marketplaces would decline, with some consolidating and others going out of business. This prediction was supported by the low volume of transactions on many public vortals as well as questions about the long-term viability of an advertising-based business model for portals and vortals.

Also, private exchanges were projected to increase. They would be formed by partnerships between content providers, portals, and consortium exchanges. Companies reluctant to join a public marketplace would be more likely to conduct online transactions over a private exchange. Industry-leading vortals were projected to emerge, and regional vortals were expected to replace national vortals. Finally, corporate portals were projected to add industry content to their Web sites and become broader and deeper.

FURTHER READING:

Buss, Dale. "The Big Vortal Payoff." *Internet World,* April 15, 2000.

Derfler, Frank J., Jr. "E-Procurement & B2B Marketplaces." *PC Magazine,* July 1, 2000.

Griffin, Cynthia E. "Portals, Vortals, Oh My..." *Convenience Store News,* November 27, 2000.

Jacso, Peter. "Portals, Vortals, and Mere Mortals." *Computers in Libraries,* February 2001.

O'Leary, Mick. "Vortals on the Rise." *Online,* March 2000.

———. ''Vortals Target Business Info Needs.'' *Link-Up,* January-February 2001.

Ott, Karalynn. ''Special Report: Portal Directory.'' *B to B,* April 2, 2001.

———. ''Special Report: Trends to Track.'' *B to B,* April 2, 2001.

Rupely, Sebastian. ''Portals to Vortals.'' *PC Magazine,* June 27, 2000.

Rospigliosi, Asher. ''Vortals: Grouping Sites by Subject.'' *PC Magazine (UK),* November 1999.

''VerticalNet Takes Aim at E-Commerce.'' *InformationWeek,* February 12, 2001.

SEE ALSO: Business-to-Business (B2B) E-Commerce; Portals

WAGNER, TODD

Todd Wagner, along with partner Mark Cuban, founded Broadcast.com in 1995. Due in large part to Wagner's business experience, the Internet start-up grew to become a leading Internet broadcasting firm in just a few short years. Wagner left the company in 2000, shortly after Yahoo!'s $5.7 billion purchase of Broadcast.com. The following year, Wagner and Cuban—both anxious to team up again—announced that they were planning to create a movie production company.

Born and raised in Gary, Indiana, Wagner graduated with a degree in accounting from Indiana University and went on to the University of Virginia where he earned a law degree. By the age of 33, Wagner had worked as an attorney for Akin, Gump, Strauss, Hauer & Feld and as a partner for Hopkins & Sutter. By that time, Wagner realized that he was not well suited to a career in law. Disregarding the advice of Hopkins & Sutter's senior partner, who claimed he would never be successful as an entrepreneur, Wagner, along with Cuban, created Broadcast.com Inc. in 1995. The duo started the firm with three employees and one computer, and they worked from Cuban's house. In just three years, Wagner's drive to become successful, along with his business expertise, had secured Broadcast.com a leading position in the fledgling Internet-based audio and video programming industry. Under Wagner's tutelage, the firm also became known as a pioneer in using the Internet as a broadcasting medium via streaming media, a technology which allowed radio and television to be heard and viewed on the Internet.

Wagner secured private financing from the likes of Motorola Inc., Intel Corp., Yahoo!, and Premiere Radio Networks. He also led the company in a highly successful initial public offering, after which he and Cuban became overnight millionaires. As CEO of Broadcast.com, he spearheaded the firm's entrance into the global market by teaming up with Softbank Corp. to create Broadcast.com Japan. That year, over one million Web surfers logged on to the company's Web site to watch President Clinton's grand jury testimony.

By 1999, Broadcast.com had become an international firm with over 300 employees and more than 1,100 clients who used the firm's services to broadcast business events, including financial announcements and conferences. It also catered to hundreds of thousands of daily users who tuned in to over 370 radio stations and 30 television stations. The firm's leading position made it an attractive acquisition target, and in July, Wagner and his partner decided to sell Broadcast.com to Yahoo!. After the $5.7 billion deal was complete, Wagner headed up the new Yahoo! Broadcast division. In April of 2000, however, he turned down an offer to become Yahoo!'s chief operating officer. Instead, having left an indelible mark on the Internet broadcasting industry, Wagner left the firm to focus on philanthropic efforts.

FURTHER READING:

Brull, Steven V. "Can Broadcast.com Keep Making a Big Noise?" *BusinessWeek Online,* November 9, 1998. Available from www.businessweek.com.

Dunn, Ashley, and Joseph Menn. "Yahoo, Broadcast.com Merging in a $5.7 Billion Stock Deal." *Los Angeles Times,* April 1, 1999.

Goldstein, Alan. "Cuban, Wagner Want to Be in the Movie Biz." *Dallas Morning News,* May 30, 2001.

Todd R. Wagner Foundation. "Who We Are." Dallas, TX: Todd R. Wagner Foundation, 2001. Available from www.toddwagnerfoundation.com.

Webb, Cynthia D. "Todd R. Wagner." *Dallas Business Journal,* February 9, 2001.

SEE ALSO: Cuban, Mark; Streaming Media

WAITT, TED

Theodore (Ted) Waitt is the founder and CEO and Gateway, Inc., a direct seller of made-to-order personal computers (PCs). He is credited for parlaying a home-based business into a $10 billion mail-order PC powerhouse in just 15 years. Under Waitt's direction, Gateway was the first direct PC seller to offer its machines on the Internet and the first to offer its own Internet services along with its PCs.

The foundation for Gateway was first established in 1985 when, along with partner Mike Hammond, the 22-year-old Waitt abandoned his studies at the University of Iowa to create TIPC, a mail-order company selling peripheral computer equipment and software directly to Texas Instruments computer owners. With a $10,000 loan co-signed by Waitt's grandmother, operations launched in Sioux City, Iowa, in a farmhouse owned by Waitt's parents. In 1986, Waitt decided that the PC market would be more lucrative than peripherals, and he began assembling his own computers and selling customized versions to customers. The following year TIPC unveiled an IBM-compatible PC similar to the one sold by Texas Instruments. With a price tag of $1,995, however, it cost only half what the Texas Instruments machine cost.

Waitt changed his firm's name to Gateway 2000 in 1988, and he relocated headquarters from his family home to a 5,000-square-foot facility. Although employees were paid only $5.50 an hour, they were able to earn extra money via monthly bonuses based on profits. Sales jumped from $1.5 million to $12 million that year and to $70.6 million in 1989. Waitt moved his firm to South Dakota in 1990. He also hired six experienced computer industry executives to help him manage Gateway's explosive growth and a marketing manager to develop advertisements that focused on the firm's unlikely rural location. Sales that year grew more than threefold to $275 million.

Inc. magazine named Gateway the fastest growing private firm in the U.S. in 1991. That year, the company began selling its PCs to corporations. Sales exceeded $1 billion for the first time in 1992, and earnings reached $1.1 million, positioning Gateway

as the nation's top mail order computer maker. Finding itself unable to fulfill a flurry of orders at the end of the year, Gateway hired 200 new employees. Waitt launched Gateway's international expansion in 1993 by establishing a unit in Dublin, Ireland. Waitt also took his firm public, retaining an 85 percent stake, and funneled the $150 million raised into product line expansion efforts. By 1994, Gateway was selling printers, networking products, fax modems, and software along with its PCs.

When competitors began charging fees for technical support, Waitt decided to continue offering services free of charge and also to upgrade Gateway's support operations. International expansion continued into France, Germany, Japan, and the United Kingdom. Sales grew to $3.5 billion in 1995. Modeled after European showrooms, Waitt began opening Country Stores to allow consumers to inspect products before placing mail orders. The firm shortened it name to Gateway Inc. in 1998. Waitt spent considerable time in the late 1990s reshuffling his management team after outside evaluators determined that the firm's top 100 employees were lacking in several areas. To improve Gateway's ability to recruit industry leaders, Waitt also moved headquarters to San Francisco, California.

Gateway began offering Internet services via Gateway.net in 1999. Waitt relinquished the title of CEO to Jeff Weitzen in January of 2000, retaining the role of chairman. However, after earnings dropped 26 percent in 2000, Weitzen regained control of his firm early in 2001. He refocused Gateway on its direct sales operations and launched cost-cutting measures such as reducing Gateway's workforce by 12 percent.

FURTHER READING:

Brooker, Katrina. "I Built This Company, I Can Save It: Retired Gateway CEO Ted Waitt Shocked the Computer World When He Ousted His Successor and Seized Control." *Fortune,* April 30, 2001.

Colvin, Geoffrey. "The Truth Can Hurt—Get Used to It." *Fortune,* February 7, 2000.

Gateway Inc. "Theodore Waitt: Chairman and Chief Executive Officer." Sioux City, South Dakota: Gateway, Inc., 2001. Available from www.gateway.com.

Popovich, Ken. "Gateway's Outlook Still Grim." *eWeek,* March 12, 2001.

Sayer, Peter. "CEO Waitt to Shift Gateway's Focus." *Network World,* January 30, 2001.

SEE ALSO: Gateway, Inc.

WALKER, JAY

Jay Walker is the founder of Priceline.com, the World Wide Web site that allows customers to specify the price they are willing to pay for airline tickets, hotel rooms, and automobile rentals. When Priceline's performance began to falter in 2000 and 2001, as the dot.com industry as a whole fell apart, Walker resigned as vice chairman of Priceline.com and increased his efforts at Walker Digital, the technology-based business model developer he founded in 1995.

After earning his bachelor's degree from Cornell University in 1978, Walker began founding new businesses. Many of his upstarts failed, but he eventually found success with New Sub Services, an operation that allowed magazine subscribers to automatically renew their subscriptions each year via credit cards. By the mid-1990s, New Sub Services was pulling in $300 million in annual sales. Anxious to try his hand at something newer, Walker sold off roughly 33 percent of his shares in New Sub Services for $25 million, which he poured into Priceline.com, a discount airline tickets venture that launched operations in April 1998. At first, the name-your-price Web site struggled to keep pace with the deluge of orders it received. Its $15 million radio marketing campaign, featuring celebrity William Shatner, generated widespread interest in the new site. However, Walker was only able to convince TWA and America West to sell their extra tickets on Priceline.com, despite the fact he was proposing a way for airlines to fill the roughly 500,000 airlines seats left empty each day.

Because Priceline's initial offerings were so limited, only seven percent of those bidding for tickets on Priceline actually ended up purchasing tickets there. Walker found himself having to purchase tickets from other airlines in the same manner a travel agency would and sell them at discounted fares to Priceline bidders, a practice that cost the firm roughly $30 per ticket sold. Realizing he needed help, Walker began hiring experienced executives to run Priceline, retaining the role of vice chairman. Less apprehensive about forging an alliance with the startup once seasoned managers were overseeing operations, Delta Airlines signed on with Priceline, a move which eventually prompted Northwest and Continental to follow suit. Walker took his firm public in March 1999 in one of the most noteworthy dot.com initial public offerings of the year. Priceline stock jumped from its opening price of $16 per share to $69 per share by the day's end. In April, stock soared to $162. According to a May 1999 issue of *Forbes,* ''Walker's money-losing startup had been transformed overnight into a billion-dollar market phenomenon—and its founder

reborn as an Internet icon.'' Walker was also named the 53rd richest person in America by *Forbes.*

United Airlines, American Airlines, and US Airways all began selling their tickets on Priceline in November of 1999. The firm expanded into groceries early in 2000 via its Priceline WebHouse Club, which allowed shoppers to name their price for groceries, print out a sheet with approved prices, and take that sheet to their local grocery stores, including A&P, ShopRite, Stop & Shop, D'Agostino's, and KeyFood. By then, roughly three percent of all airline tickets in the U.S. were sold on Priceline.

Despite its growing customer base and increasingly diversified activities, Priceline was one of the Internet startups hit hardest by the dot-com fallout. By the end of 2000, its stock had plummeted 96 percent, relieving Walker of his billionaire status. Walker found himself the target of a class-action lawsuit that called into question his sale of 12 percent of his Priceline shares days before the firm announced it was shuttering its WebHouse Club operations. Walker resigned as vice chairman of Priceline in February of 2001.

FURTHER READING:

Dyan, Machan. ''An Edison for a New Age?'' *Forbes,* May 17, 1999.

Elkind, Peter. ''The Hype Is Really, Really Big, At Priceline.'' *Fortune,* September 6, 1999.

Loomis, Carol J. ''Priceline's Walker Loses Two and Wins One.'' *Fortune,* November 27, 2000.

Shillinglaw, James. ''The Web's New Guru.'' *Travel Agent,* November 29, 1999.

Stross, Randall E. ''Name Your Own Folly.'' *U.S. News and World Report,* October 16, 2000.

SEE
ALSO: Priceline.com

WALT DISNEY CO.

The Walt Disney Co.'s most successful Internet role was as a content provider. Since the mid-1990s the company has operated Web sites for kids and parents, including Family.com and the subscription-based Blast online. It developed other Web properties, including ESPN.com, ABC.com, ABCNews.com, and other Disney sites. In 1998 the company embarked on a strategy to create an Internet portal to compete with America Online and Yahoo!, among others. It acquired an interest in search engine InfoSeek in 1998 with an eye to transforming it into an

Internet portal. In 1999 Disney purchased the rest of InfoSeek and launched the Go.com portal. Go.com was renamed the Walt Disney Internet Group (WDIG) in 2000, a separate company that encompassed all of Disney's Internet ventures. With AOL gaining added muscle through its merger with Time Warner, it became clear that Go.com would not be able to compete with the leading Internet portals. After sustaining more than $1 billion in losses from Go.com and other Internet properties, Disney announced plans to close Go.com in 2001 and fold the WDIG back into the company. The company said it would focus on information and entertainment content rather than portals and electronic commerce.

DISNEY PUT ITS CONTENT ONLINE

The Walt Disney Co. launched its free, family-oriented Web site Family.com in 1996. The site had partnerships with more than 100 local parenting publications. It also offered a recipe library and a customized activities index for parents and their children. Parenting sites like Family.com attracted a large percentage of women, and thus advertisers were attracted to the site's demographics.

In 1997 Disney launched its Daily Blast site for kids. This subscription-based site charged $4.95 per month and was aimed at children age 12 and under. Its content included animated storybooks, downloadable games, and educational toys and puzzles. It also featured news and sports stories written by children. Disney's popular characters—including Mickey Mouse, Donald Duck, and Goofy—were also present at the site. Through an agreement with Microsoft Corp., users of the Microsoft Network (MSN) had free access to the Daily Blast site.

Other Internet sites operated by Disney at the time included Disney.com, where the company sold its merchandise, and sites affiliated with subsidiaries ABC-TV and ESPN. Disney also owned a majority interest in Starwave, based in Bellevue, Washington, which ran the family-oriented Family Planet site as well as ESPN SportsZone.

Disney.com was a popular site and consistently ranked high in popularity. As more people began to shop online in 1997, Disney.com reported a fivefold increase in online sales over 1996. The shopping site at Disney.com generated about as much revenue as three brick-and-mortar Disney stores, according to the company. In 1998 Disney and bookseller Barnesand-Noble.com teamed up to create Disney book boutiques that featured Disney titles and was available online at both companies' Web sites.

PORTAL STRATEGY FOR E-COMMERCE, 1998-2001

In 1998 Disney acquired a 43 percent interest in Internet search engine InfoSeek, with an option to purchase the rest of the company. At the time media companies in general were looking for ways to achieve a dominant presence on the Internet. NBC had just paid $38 million for a 19 percent interest in Snap!, an Internet portal owned by CNET. Later in the year America Online acquired Netscape Communications and its popular NetCenter portal. As part of its $472 million acquisition of InfoSeek, Disney paid $70 million in cash and turned over ownership of Starwave to InfoSeek. Disney would regain ownership of Starwave when it completed its purchase of all of InfoSeek in 1999. Disney also committed $165 million to provide promotional support for InfoSeek.

Disney's acquisition of InfoSeek was part of its strategy to distribute its content over all available media. Toward the end of 1998 Disney, InfoSeek, and Starwave introduced a new Internet portal, Go.com, in a beta version for consumers, followed by the official launch of the Go Network in January 1999. The home page of the Go Network resembled that of InfoSeek, but it was easily customizable. Content was organized into five major sections, which were accessible through page tabs: a sports area featuring ESPN.com; a news section featuring ABCNews.com; an entertainment area that included ABC.com and MrShowbiz.com; a family and kids area featuring Disney.com; and a personal finance section.

The launch of the Go Network in 1999 was supported by a national television advertising campaign that ran in 14 major markets. At the time of its launch, the Go Network had 20 million unique users, with 8 million of them registered. Following its launch the Go Network added Go Shop, an e-commerce site that featured more than 200 merchants, and Go Games, which offered a variety of individual and multiplayer games. In March 1999 Disney redesigned its Disney.com site, creating 12 content channels and merging its subscription-based Blast Online for kids into Disney.com. With about 80 percent of the new Disney.com content available for free, subscribers could join Club Blast for $5.95 per month or $39.95 per year and gain access to premium content, including the Disney BlastPad, a proprietary kid-safe instant messaging service that parents could control, and the Mouse House Jr., an area designed for children too young to read.

In mid-1999 Disney decided to acquire the remaining 57 percent of InfoSeek for $1.62 billion in stock. It created a new tracking stock company, Go.com, that incorporated InfoSeek, the Go Network, and Disney's Buena Vista Internet Group. When the purchase closed in November 1999, the transaction was valued at $2.15 billion.

DISNEY REVISES ITS INTERNET AND PORTAL STRATEGY, 2000-2001

By early 2000 it was clear that Go.com would not be able to compete with dominant portals such as America Online and Yahoo!. The company reported a loss of more than $1 billion in 1999 from its Internet properties. Adding to Disney's Internet losses was its venture into electronic commerce through a $45 million investment in Toysmart.com in 1999. As was the case with the Go Network, Toysmart.com ran into serious competition when Amazon.com formed an alliance with brick-and-click retailer Toys ''R'' Us. Toysmart.com officially went out of business in May 2000.

During 2000 Disney attempted to redesign the Go Network portal to concentrate it more on Disney's traditional family-and-fun content, building a self-contained search engine for all of Disney's Internet properties. In August Go.com was renamed the Walt Disney Internet Group (WDIG). Later in the year Compaq Computer Corp. became the WDIG's preferred technology provider through a $100 million agreement. The redesigned Go.com Web site was relaunched in September 2000. The new design featured Disney's individual Web sites more prominently. While it kept the InfoSeek search engine, the new Go.com site was designed as a place to find entertainment news and vacation information.

In January 2001 the WDIG and Walt Disney Parks and Resorts formed an online operation called Walt Disney Parks and Resorts Online that expanded Disney's presence on the Internet. In the face of a general economic slowdown and a slowdown in the Internet economy, Disney made deep cuts in its Internet operations in early 2001. The company announced plans to close down the Go Network and the Go.com Web site. In the interim Disney said it would operate a streamlined version of Go.com while it moved services and registered users to other sites. As part of the cutback Disney eliminated 400 jobs and folded the WDIG back into the company. All outstanding shares of WDIG common stock were converted into Disney common stock effective March 20, 2001. In had become clear that the tracking stock company was not providing enough revenue for additional investments or acquisitions or to retain employees. The management of WDIG would continue to be in charge of Disney's remaining Internet properties.

While Disney was not able to create an industry-leading portal, the company's other Internet properties remained leaders in their categories. Its experience with InfoSeek and Starwave enabled Disney to create a single, scalable platform for its Internet businesses. For the future, the company planned to continue to create and operate innovative, highly popular content sites. During 2001 the company was also involved in initiatives to bring online content to automobiles and wireless devices.

FURTHER READING:

Andrews, Whit. ''Infoseek, Despite Disney Money, Stumbles on Wall St. as It Charts New Course.'' *Internet World,* September 14, 1998.

''Disney Expands Online Presence.'' *Travel Weekly,* January 11, 2001.

Donahue, Ann. ''New Name, New Attitude.'' *Variety,* August 7, 2000.

Donohue, Steve. ''With InfoSeek Deal, Disney Joins the Gold Rush to Portals.'' *Electronic Media,* June 22, 1998.

Kerstetter, Jim. ''New Portal Player Set to Go.'' *PC Week,* December 7, 1998.

Lafayette, Jon. ''Disney's Internet Launch a Go.'' *Electronic Media,* January 18, 1999.

Machlis, Sharon. ''Disney to Launch Web Portal.'' *Computerworld,* June 22, 1998.

Mermigas, Diane. ''How Disney Is Creating Go.com out of Infoseek.'' *Electronic Media,* November 22, 1999.

Rose, Frank. ''Mickey Online.'' *Fortune,* September 28, 1998.

Tedesco, Richard. ''Disney Stakes Big 'Net Claim with Infoseek.'' *Broadcasting & Cable,* June 22, 1998.

———. ''Disney.com Redux.'' *Broadcasting & Cable,* March 29, 1999.

Wagner, Mitch. ''Disney Site Bucks Online Conventions.'' *Computerworld,* August 18, 1997.

SEE ALSO: Children and the Internet; Content Provider; Portals, Web

WEB SCRIPTING LANGUAGE

Web scripting languages are a form of high-level programming language. High-level programming languages are much closer to human language than machine language, through which computer hardware accepts commands. High-level programming languages, like C and C++, rely on programs called compilers or interpreters so they can be converted to machine language (mainly zeroes and ones). Programs written in scripting languages, called scripts, are not compiled ahead of time for specific computer systems like many high-level languages. Instead, the plain text that constitutes a script gets interpreted into computer commands while a program runs.

Scripts are used to add interactivity to otherwise static Web pages. They also can perform repetitive tasks like automatically filling out parts of Web-based forms, among other uses. *Encyclozine.com* described the capabilities of JavaScript, a popular Web scripting language: "Without any network transmission, an HTML page with embedded JavaScript can interpret the entered text and alert the user with a message dialog if the input is invalid. Or you can use JavaScript to perform an action (such as play an audio file, execute an applet, or communicate with a plug-in) in response to the user opening or exiting a page."

Scripting languages normally are interpreted by Web browsers like Microsoft Internet Explorer or Netscape Navigator. Web browsers interpret scripts along with Hypertext Markup language (HTML), the language in which Web pages are written. This can be done in one of two ways. In one scenario, programs written in scripting languages can run directly from a server. Otherwise, a script can be included with or directly in an HTML Web page that someone downloads to a computer. In either case, the Web browser is used to access the program.

In server-based situations, the Common Gateway Interface (CGI) allows users (clients) to run programs located on Web servers. CGI scripts are small programs written in a variety of different programming languages (including C, C++, and Perl) that run in real-time, which makes them ideal for such things as stock tickers, weather reports, or query results from a database that appear in the form of a Web page. In the 2000s, other methods—like Java servlets (Java programs that reside on Web servers) and Microsoft's Active Server Pages—began to replace CGI scripts.

JavaScript and Microsoft's Visual Basic Scripting Edition (VBScript) were two popular types of scripting languages in the early 2000s. JavaScript was created by Sun Microsystems and Netscape. It is based on the Java programming language, but was developed independently. JavaScript has the ability to interact with HTML code, enabling developers to create more interactive, appealing Web sites without having to learn a complicated programming language. JavaScript is used in Web browsers from both Netscape and Microsoft (Microsoft used its own version called Jscript). The language can be used for both client and server-based programs. Similar in many regards to JavaScript, Microsoft's Visual Basic Scripting Edition is based on the company's Visual Basic programming language. Among the benefits of Visual Basic Scripting Edition are its portability and speed. Not only is the language used by Web browsers, it also is used for other kinds of applications.

FURTHER READING:

Appleman, Daniel. *How Computer Programming Works.* Berkeley: Apress. 2000.

"CGI Script." *Techencyclopedia,* April 1, 2001. Available from www.techweb.com.

"JavaScript." *Ecommerce Webopedia,* April 1, 2001. Available from webopedia.internet.com.

"JavaScript Basics: Scripting Language." *DevX.com,* April 1, 2001. Available from www.projectcool.com.

Microsoft Corp. "Microsoft Windows Script Technologies." Redmond, WA: Microsoft Corp, April 1, 2001. Available from msdn.microsoft.com.

———. "Scripting Language." Redmond, WA: Microsoft Corp, April 1, 2001. Available from msdn.microsoft.com.

"Scripting Language." *Techencyclopedia,* March 12, 2001. Available from www.techweb.com.

"Web Design with CGI, CSS, HTML, Java, JavaScript, XHTML, XML, etc." *EncycloZine.* April 1, 2001. Available from www.encyclozine.com.

SEE ALSO: C; HTML; Java; Microsoft; Programming Languages; XML

WEB SITE BASICS

Through the late 1990s and early 2000s, the Internet transformed the way in which companies, organizations, and individuals interact with the world. Over that period, a new medium, the World Wide Web, gave birth to what became one of the most prominent means by which entities convey their personality, character, and features: the Web site. Increasingly, the Web site has emerged as a primary and central means by which information is transmitted. By the 21st century, it was the rare company—particularly if it were larger than a local small business—that did not maintain a Web site, and the field of business competition had likewise expanded to include Web strategies as well.

Over the course of just a decade, the conception of the Web page and Web site evolved considerably. The earliest Web sites were characterized by long strings of relatively undifferentiated text, separated by browser-length horizontal lines. Since such sites were primarily mere depositories of information, little attention was paid to aesthetic design or user-friendliness. Moreover, the mode of presentation was overwhelmingly informed by existing models of documentation in books and periodicals. It took designers a while to realize and implement the actual possibilities inherent in the interactive Web form of presentation.

By the 2000s, however, Web sites were among the most prominent means of communication, and the starting point for interacting with companies over the Internet. Business Web sites evolved quickly from the basic "brochure" sites—pages that simply established the company's presence in cyberspace but did little beyond explain the company's purpose, products, and services—to the myriad forms that graced the Web by the 21st century. Web sites all contain core elements, but on top of that basic infrastructure they take on personalities and forms of their own.

Ideally, business Web sites come to reflect in the most complementary manner possible the core strategic purposes of the company itself, and thus no small amount of research went into devising Web strategies that most fully took advantage of the Web's opportunities and added value to the company's operations. As competition—particularly Web-based competition—heated up, firms scrambled to find ways to generate the maximum amount of return on their Web efforts. One of the greatest challenges facing companies in the early 2000s was figuring out how to turn their Web sites into revenue generators. Venture capital firms, advertisers, and investors alike were all bringing pressure to bear on companies to transform their Web sites from simple business prerequisites to positive revenue streams. All demand a greater return on their investment into Web sites, and thus companies were under fire to enhance the per-page bottom line.

As a result, not only were Web sites growing more sophisticated in their design and implementation, but business strategies in the physical world increasingly pointed toward the Web. Television, print, radio, and billboard advertisements increasingly broadcast company Web sites so customers, clients, and investors can retrieve the most extensive information and interact with the company directly. Perhaps most importantly, however, the Web site has emerged as a key vehicle for buying and selling. The e-commerce boom of the 1990s and early 2000s was due largely—though not entirely—to the explosion of the World Wide Web.

WEB SITE ELEMENTS AND ORGANIZATION

Web sites exist for all sorts of purposes, but at their essential core is the conveyance of some kind of information in an interactive setting. Whether hawking goods and services, acting as an archive or resource for other data sources, offering content for free or for a price, or acting as a forum for like-minded users to exchange ideas, Web sites come to develop an organizational structure and logic of their own.

Web sites are almost always built around a central starting point known as the home page, from which the site extends in a linear, Web-like, or hierarchical fashion, depending on the specific goals of the site. The home page acts as the introduction and gateway to the site's offerings. The home page's Universal Resource Locator (URL) is the Web address that a company or organization uses to advertise its Web site. A general rule of thumb holds that all pages on a Web site should include a link back to the home page, so that, in the event that a user finds himself lost on a site, he can quickly and easily return to a convenient starting point.

Generally, the home page is the element of the Web site that designers will put the most thought and care into, since it is the first impression a user has of the site—and often of the company itself—and research suggests that Web users tend to be impatient with Web sites that don't load quickly or properly or that appear to be shoddily designed or laid out.

Particularly in the world of e-commerce, the hierarchical Web site model overwhelmingly dominates. Linear models are more useful where there is a logical sequence to a Web site's offerings, which is generally not the case with e-commerce sites. Similarly, the Web-like organizational scheme—in which pages are organized in a free-flowing manner with pages linked randomly throughout the text—can be useful for some types of information, but for the sake of their customers, businesses tend to require a more rigidly structured organizational scheme. Hierarchical organization schemes are easy for users to digest and navigate, since hierarchical models are so familiar in social life and users can easily construct a mental image of the site's layout.

In the hierarchical model, information is organized according to some logical scheme of importance. The most widely used hierarchical organization scheme employed on the Web is the home page-and-link scheme, in which users access the site through a centralized home page that contains a site overview and introduction and points users to all the different areas contained on the site. For instance, a company Web site may organize its site according to the different branches of its operations—products, services, and so on—and within each category the site narrows down to specifics: specific products, prices, etc.

This hierarchical organization frequently entails layers of menus and submenus stemming from the home page. For example, the home page of a large industrial firm may offer a link to ''Products and Services'' that carries users to a submenu that includes the categories of products and services the company offers. In addition, the home page may provide another link to ''Investor Relations,'' taking users to a submenu where they can choose to view ''Company History,'' ''Income Statements,'' ''Quarterly Reports,'' ''Letters to Shareholders,'' and so on. Larger companies with more extensive Web sites may include hundreds of submenus. But the larger and more hierarchical the site, the more conscious designers need to be of the ability for users to get lost. Thus, designers must implement a logical and helpful navigation scheme that allows users to quickly return to familiar territory if they stray in the wrong direction.

The layout of the pages themselves consists of a combination of text, colors, and graphics. There are myriad schemes for the layout of each of these elements, and overall design tools and techniques were growing more sophisticated by the month in the early 2000s. Again, companies must take a number of variables into consideration when devising their page layouts, including their own technical capabilities and those of their users, the particular message they're trying to convey, and so on.

Graphics include still pictures, background designs, logos, and animation. While good graphic design is essential to any professional-looking Web site, designers are still compelled to consider the balance between the most attractive possible site layout and the capabilities of their users. Graphics consume a relatively high amount of space on users' hard drives and in Internet transmissions, and thus an excessive use of graphics could cause the Web site to take an intolerably long time to download, particularly for users with low-end equipment.

At the least, most company and organizational Web sites include a graphic-based banner and logo at the top of their home pages to create an attractive first impression and provide a theme to the Web site. More advanced home pages veer toward an almost entirely graphics-based layout, including pop-up menus, moving text, and other features to grab the users' attention and provide the most user-friendly layout.

One of the primary ways in which Web pages differ from physical text documents—in addition to their ability to be infinitely copied—is their inclusion of hypertext links. Links give the Web its free-flowing quality, allowing users to leap instantaneously from one document to another, and from one site to another, by a simple click of the mouse. Web sites include links to other pages within and outside the site that the designer feels are conducive to the message the site is trying to convey. As such, there is as much planning and strategy to the inclusion and layout of hypertext links as to other elements of site design.

But since pages in a Web site are, for that reason, far more independent than ordinary text documents—that is, since pages are not automatically tied, from the user's experience, to a larger site or entire document—individual pages always need to reflect the broader context in which they're intended to be received. The most common way in which this context is conveyed is via headers and footers. Headers generally identify the document and its author or owner, while footers usually include links to other elements of the site or document, copyright information, the date of the page's most recent update, and links to a home page.

Depending on the size of a Web site and the frequency with which it is updated, many site designers opt to keep users posted of recently added or altered content by way of a link to all recent updates. Since Web users tend to have little patience if they can't find what they're looking for, it's important for sites—particularly larger, more detailed sites—to allow users a way to seek out only that information they want. Thus, to maintain users or clients inclined to visit the site regularly, it's helpful, and perhaps crucial, to devise a link to new material rather than compelling them to search through the site themselves in hopes of finding anything new.

THE BACKEND

A Web site is dependent on its "hidden" features: the backend equipment, systems, and programs that constitute the site's infrastructure and building blocks. There are several key elements of backend Web site components. At the ground level is the server software, the tools that are involved in actually hooking up a computer system to the Internet—that is, the software that turns a series of computer files into a Web site. Servers are generally built on the UNIX programming language. Most advanced Web sites also utilize databases, of which there are numerous varieties. Databases allow for quicker updating and organization of Web materials, and are generally a useful tool for constructing highly detailed Web content.

To place documents on the Web, pages, graphics, and all other sources referred to in the site's pages must be uploaded to the remote host computer that's connected to the Web. The host may be an Internet service provider (ISP), a Web hosting service, or even the company or organization itself, if it can afford the resources. Once a site is ready to go online, the company, organization, or individual must determine a URL for the site that hasn't already been taken by another site. Most companies try to make their URL as easy to remember—and as logically close to the company name—as possible. For example, a company known as My Company would likely try to register mycompany.com or my-company.com so as to create the least possible confusion in their customers' minds.

Hypertext Markup Language (HTML) is the traditional lingua franca of the World Wide Web. HTML consists of hundreds of tags that tell Web browsers how to read the information contained in the document, including the layout and font, the setting of hyperlinks, the referencing of graphics, and so on. By the 2000s, HTML was increasingly augmented by more advanced languages such as eXtensible markup language (XML) and eXtensible Hypertext Markup Language (XHTML), the latter of which was built ostensibly as a bridge between HTML and XML. XML was quickly emerging as the standard language for e-commerce, particularly in the business-to-business realm. XML is a metalanguage that allows programmers to more intricately define what the tags mean and how they interact with the data they define. While there are scores of other markup languages, the safest route for Web designers is to stick to the established standards—such as HTML, XHTML, XML, and Cascading Style Sheets (CSS)—that have been approved by the World Wide Web Consortium (W3C), the primary organization overseeing the World Wide Web's development. Designers can test their programming and Web authoring for compatibility with these standards at a number of free online validation sites.

FURTHER READING:

Lynch, Patrick J., and Sarah Horton. *Web Style Guide: Basic Design Principles for Creating Web Sites,* New Haven, CT: Yale University Press, 1999. Available from info.med.yale.edu/caim/manual.

Zeldman, Jeffrey. ''Web Publishing Secrets.'' *Macworld,* September 2001.

SEE ALSO: HTML; UNIX; URL; User Interface; Web Site Design and Setup; Web Site Usability Issues; World Wide Web; World Wide Web Consortium (W3C); XML

WEB SITE DESIGN AND SETUP

As many businesses found, to their dismay, in the early days of the World Wide Web in the mid-1990s, the design of a Web site can make or break a firm's attempts to establish a Web presence. Poor aesthetic design, weak technological backbones, inconsistent data integration, and illogical site organization and structure can discourage users and potential clients, causing them to give up on a site and take their business elsewhere. As competition for Web-based hegemony heated in the late 1990s and early 2000s, companies invested increasing time and money into the design and set-up of their Web sites—both the back-end architecture and the visual presentation of their information. The result was an ever-evolving Web of greater sophistication, enhanced aesthetic consideration, and more options for the average user.

In the early days of the Web, companies typically set up Web sites with little consideration to aesthetics or to efficient or user-friendly e-commerce architectures. Rather, the competitive pressures at the time spurred companies to simply get their sites out there to stake out a place on the Web. This process led to the phenomenon of the brochure site: a Web site that did little more than announce a firm's presence and explain their business, but with little capability of

handling e-commerce orders, customer service, or sophisticated interaction. Sites such as these were often built with generic brochure-ware, software set up as a basic template into which companies could enter their own information.

As e-commerce intensified, however, it became increasingly apparent that such a cookie-cutter and half-hearted approach to the Web wouldn't suffice. Firms began looking to the Web as more than just a prerequisite of doing business; they saw in their Web sites the potential for generating new revenue streams and adding value to their offerings. Through the late 1990s and early 2000s, Web site design and structure grew to reflect and propel larger business plans, integrating technical expertise and aesthetic design with sophisticated market research and broader company concerns, ranging from customer service and transaction issues to inventory management and procurement processes. Thus, corporate Web sites came to reflect the corporate culture and processes as a whole at the same time that the culture and processes were transformed to reflect the focus on Web-based e-commerce. In the process, Web sites were transformed from company-centered to customer-centered commercial outlets.

SITE LAYOUT

Since the human brain can only digest so much information in a single space before it becomes overwhelmed, and since large Web pages can take an impossibly long time to load, Web sites are intricately organized as a series of pages—often stretching into the hundreds—that interconnect in ways that have been thoroughly thought out by the designer to most accurately reflect the site's content and make the site as user-friendly as possible. A general rule of thumb holds that smaller, easily differentiated units of information are easier for users to sift through and use than are large, undifferentiated pieces. Through the late 1990s and early 2000s, e-commerce Web sites were shortened to limit the amount of scrolling a user had to do on a given page. Ideally, sites are organized so that all the information is presented to customers without their having to do anything. Obviously, this was not always possible, but design analysts generally agreed that the less a user has to hunt around to find what he or she wants, the more likely a purchase will result.

According to the *Web Style Guide: Basic Design Principles for Creating Web Sites* by Patrick J. Lynch and Sarah Horton, the organizational schemes of Web sites are ideally designed to limit the number of variables that the user must keep in short-term memory by way of intelligent site layout and a combination of textual content, graphic design, and layout schemes organized to complement the Web site's purpose—whether that purpose is to sell products, convey information, or provide tools by which users can find the information they want. "Most Web sites contain reference information that people seek in small units," Lynch and Horton wrote. "Users rarely read long contiguous passages of text from computer screens, and most people who are seeking a specific piece of information will be annoyed to have to scan long blocks of text to find what they are after."

Web sites are typically laid out in hierarchical organization schemes, and guide users through the site via a navigation path. That is, it points users toward various broad sectors of the site from the home page, and with each click the user gets closer to the precise information they want. The trick in devising this organization scheme is to make it obvious to the user without necessarily calling attention to itself. All things being equal, designers generally want to create navigation paths that allow users to get the information they want in as few clicks as possible while still maintaining a clear overall sense of logical navigation. A clear navigation path ensures that, no matter where users are on a site and no matter how many clicks from the home page they are, they still have a clear sense of where they are on the site, particularly in relation to the home page and the major subsections.

PAGE LAYOUT

Web documents contain a number of core elements. The first of these is a tag identifying the appropriate document type, marked by the DOCTYPE HTML tag. (XML has similar tags of its own, but in each case, the document starts off with a tag defining what kind of document follows.) This tag ensures that the Web browser understands the appropriate manner in which to render and interpret the document. This is followed by a header, in which the general color scheme is established and the title, appearing at the top of the browser, is set. Finally, the body of the document is established by the BODY tag in HTML. It is within the body that the Web page's information is conveyed. These are the essential elements that allow a Web browser to read a Web page. In addition to these, however, there are several general conventions that site designers tend to follow within the bodies of their documents.

Design consistency is important in order to create a common theme that users can identify as belonging to a particular company. In other words, consistent design parameters across a site help define the company's character on the World Wide Web. For example, wherever possible, designers are encouraged to use identical layout grids, color schemes, graphic themes, text fonts, and organization patterns. According to

Web Style Guide: Basic Design Principles for Creating Web Sites, designers need to make users comfortable with a site as quickly as possible, which requires users to be familiar with the site in only a few minutes; obviously, then, designers need to check their temptation to explore a wide range of design techniques within a single site. Headers, titles, footers, navigation links, and other common page elements thus need to appear in similar or identical fashion. Fast-loading graphics combined with comfortable color palettes are the most effective aesthetic combination.

Designers should also avoid what are known as "dead end" pages—those pages on which there are no links back to the home page or to another local page. Such dead ends give the impression of a poorly designed and unorganized site, and easily frustrate users. Sophisticated, consistent design that meets high standards and avoids sloppiness is crucial if users are to maintain confidence in the site.

MARKUP TOOLS

Various markup languages exist that designers use to render their information in Web-readable format. The chief among these is Hypertext Markup Language (HTML), a series of codes and tags that tells the Web browser how to interpret and present text data and links to other documents, files, and graphics on a Web site and elsewhere on the Internet. While this was the original standard markup language developed along with the World Wide Web itself, by the end of the 20th century, it was no longer the recommended markup methodology, according to the World Wide Web Consortium, the main body overseeing the Web's development.

In 2000, the chief recommended markup standard shifted to eXtensible Hypertext Markup Language (XHTML), conceived as a bridge between HTML and eXtensible Markup Language (XML), which was poised as the next-generation lingua franca of the Web, particularly for e-commerce. By the early 2000s, however, neither XHTML nor XML had been widely adopted, due largely to the great confusion these standards have caused for designers.

HTML tags focus primarily on the structure and layout of a document, while XML leaves presentation to style sheets, focusing instead on the definition and meaning of certain kinds of information, allowing for the flexible defining of terms and parameters for various types of data. It is for this reason that XML was touted as the future language of e-commerce, since XML deals specifically with giving meaning to information, allowing computer systems to intelligently apply Web-based information in meaningful ways in commercial transactions.

HOLISTIC BUSINESS WEB SITES

In the more mature e-commerce environment of the early 2000s, Web sites needed more than a pleasing look and convenient layout. As Web sites were positioned as integral aspects of firms' strategies, they were increasingly retooled to create a seamless overall network, integrating the Web site with the rest of the companies' information technology architectures. Thus, Web sites were increasingly built to work alongside company databases and systems designed to handle ordering, procurement, inventory management, payment processing, billing, customer relations, and intra-firm communications, among others. In this way, Web sites were beginning to reflect the broader promise of the World Wide Web and the Internet by creating value and harnessing the power of contemporary information technology to form more efficient business practices.

The last step in setting up a Web site is promotion. Depending on the size and stature of the business, site promotion can take many different forms. If a firm is well established, with several advertising means at its disposal, it can simply utilize its existing promotion channels to alert people to its Web site. Smaller and upstart firms need to establish links with sites already proven to draw traffic—particularly traffic from the firms' desired customer base—in the hopes of generating links to their new sites. Large and small businesses alike also invariably try to establish a presence on the major search engines, which often entails various applications or referrals. There were a range of search engine strategies, but the primary goal of any such strategy was to position a site to appear toward the top of user Internet searches.

CUSTOMER-CENTERED DESIGN

Ultimately, the customer is the most important element of the Web site, and thus design decisions need to reflect the customers' interests above all. Designers must be on the lookout to avoid too much or too little information, excessively long or convoluted registration or purchasing processes; an excessive or confusing dearth of advertisements; too many or too few clickable links; unobvious navigation schemes; a shortage of helpful tools such as search engines, site maps, help pages, or links back to a home page or other logical starting point; color schemes that strain the eye or render the text difficult to read; complex graphics that lower-end systems can't handle; and a host of other design sins.

Another important rule of effective Web-site design is that there is no such thing as static perfection. Rather, Web sites must constantly evolve to reflect and accommodate transforming business climates, improving technological capabilities, and, perhaps most importantly, shifting customer expectations. Effective corporate Web sites thus require constant updates and tweaking. If a site undergoes no substantial change for too long a period, customers may get the impression that the company isn't keeping pace with demands or technology, or that in some other way the company's site may not cater to their needs as well as that of the firm's competitors.

DESIGN RECOGNITION

As Web sites moved from simple information depositories to aesthetic creations and mediums for specific commercial activity and content, Web design evolved alongside a growing recognition of design achievements. By the early 2000s, the Web was littered with awards recognizing various criteria for excellent Web design. While some of these awards were amateur-driven—occasionally, the winners had no idea they won, not having heard of the award—and others functioned more as advertising and promotion schemes for the presenter, there were a number of prestigious awards that designers and businesses sought after. Recognition by the likes of the Webby Awards not only put a firm's name in good company—the winners were widely respected as quality Web sites and the awards themselves drew celebrity power from the Internet and business communities and from society at large—they brought much-needed recognition of and attention to the company's site, an endorsement that could give a Web site a competitive edge.

FURTHER READING:

"Design Matters." *Fortune,* Winter 2001.

Holzschlag, Molly E. "The Fear of X—What Web Designers Should Know About XML and XHTML." *PC Magazine,* August 1, 2001.

Lynch, Patrick J., and Sarah Horton. *Web Style Guide: Basic Design Principles for Creating Web Sites.* New Haven, CT: Yale University Press, 1999. Available from info.med.yale.edu/caim/manual.

Raskin, Jef. "The Humane Touch: Bad Design Can Be Costly." *Forbes,* May 28, 2001.

O'Donovan, Cheryl. "Dot Ugh." *Communication World,* June 2001.

Syers, Mandy. "ZDNet Developer: Build Your Own Web Site in Six Steps." *ZDNet,* 2001. Available from www.zdnet.com.

SEE ALSO: HTML (Hypertext Markup Language); Integration; Promoting the Website; Three Protocols, The; Search Engine Strategy; URL (Uniform Resource Locator); Web Awards; Web Site Basics; Web Site, Relaunching a; Web Site Usability Issues; World Wide Web Consortium (W3C); XML (Extensible Markup Language)

WEB SITE, RELAUNCHING A

The work to be done on a Web site usually doesn't end simply because the site goes live. Most sites of any complexity require ongoing maintenance; technological changes compel operators of Web sites to upgrade their pages in order to look current, offer new features, and maintain compatibility with new software and standards. By one estimate, major sites have tended to relaunch in some fashion every ten months or so, and with a few noteworthy exceptions, retail sites seem particularly susceptible to relaunching.

The main difference between a relaunch and more pedestrian maintenance sometimes boils down to how the maintenance cycle is organized. Usually a relaunch implies introducing a collection of changes and improvements, analogous to versions of software applications. Because applications are centralized on Web servers, however, it is easier to release small, incremental changes more frequently than is practical with traditional client/server software. As a result, some sites undergo constant retooling and revision, but never announce it as a relaunch, while others make a point of touting their new and improved wares. It may also be a matter of work organization, such as when a separate team of Web developers focuses on the new site, which becomes a clearly defined project in itself, as opposed to the staff who keep the existing site running.

Thus relaunching a site can be seen as a type of maintenance, albeit at the heavy end of the maintenance scale. Occasionally a Web site is relaunched because the old version was fundamentally flawed or ill-suited to the company's needs, but more often relaunches are closer to incremental improvements on an existing set of concepts and technical infrastructure. Thus relaunches are a way of life for major sites like IBM.com, which reached its eleventh version in 2001.

WHY RELAUNCH?

The exact reasons sites relaunch often stem from their individual histories, but there are three general motivators: enhancing technical features, creating a new or different brand image, and giving the site a fresh look. Often two or even all three of these factors are involved in a decision to relaunch or upgrade.

TECHNICAL UPGRADES. At one level, of course, all changes to a Web site have technical ramifications, but relaunches based on technical features are concerned with offering new functions, new applications, easier navigation, and so on. These upgrades have tended to take different forms as the Web has evolved. Many of the earliest relaunches by large corporations were migrating from the so-called brochureware of text- and image-based descriptive sites to more interactive models, many featuring personalization options that allowed users to create accounts and store personal preferences and information on the site. A further extension of this was the much celebrated (and sometimes later lamented) push toward e-commerce, enabling online transactions of all sorts. Behind the scenes, such revisions were sometimes related to the adoption of customer relationship management (CRM) systems and advanced application servers from vendors like BEA, IBM, Oracle, and Sun.

If the benefits of a technical upgrade are new front- and back-end capabilities, the drawback can be in a bumpy transition. Retooling a large site can be exceedingly complicated and may lead to unexpected problems, as was the case in a publicized failure during an ambitious relaunch of eBay.com in 1999. The company didn't devote adequate staffing to the project, and the result was costly downtime in which visitors could not use the site or all of its functions.

REBRANDING. Creating a new brand image—or significantly revising an existing one—is a weighty marketing decision, usually separate from any technical considerations. Companies face rebranding, for example, when they merge or are party to an acquisition, when their marketing results are substantially below potential, or when they adopt a new marketing or commerce strategy.

The risk is, of course, that the new brand image will alienate the market and cause the company to lose some of the equity it had established in its brand. When confronted with change, customers often adopt an agnostic, even wary stance, requiring the company to demonstrate to them again that its brand is worth their loyalty and high regard. For instance, long Flash animations on the home page—a trend of the late 1990s as the Flash language and higher-speed connections came into vogue—are widely considered annoyances that may drive some visitors away.

In situations like mergers and acquisitions, however, the company has little choice but to relaunch in order to reflect the new identity of the combined firm. Here the relaunch is most likely part of an integrated marketing program aimed at raising awareness of the new company and articulating its value new propositions to potential customers; Web content may be reinforced by advertising and publicity efforts.

STAYING CURRENT. Most, if not all, large sites have some form of program in place to keep the look and feel of the site fresh. Many have a specific technical infrastructure in place to do some of this on the fly, relatively speaking, rather than waiting for programmers to make each change on an individual basis. These sites automate the revision process by using content management systems and other architectures which allow site operators to quickly swap in new elements on pages.

When content shuffling isn't enough, companies opt for a larger revision or relaunch. This kind of approach has been especially visible among some of the so-called bricks-and-clicks retailers like J.C. Penney, Target, Rite Aid, and Wal-Mart, whose Web presence thus far has only been a small portion of their overall retail volume. They may, for instance, put a new face on the site for the Christmas holiday season, only to change it again in springtime. For these retailers the loss of brand equity is less of a concern, as their image is more keenly tied to their physical outlets. Clearly for many of these retailers changing the Web site is akin to the unending cycle of redecorating their stores and building new merchandise displays.

A few online retailers have avoided radical relaunches. The most prominent is Amazon.com, arguably the best-known retail site and one almost solely dependent on its online brand. Most of Amazon's changes have been subtle and gradual, and while its offerings have changed considerably over the years, it has largely stayed off the relaunch track.

FURTHER READING:

Krill, Paul. "A Bet on Technology." *InfoWorld,* September 17, 2001.

Maddox, Kate. "By Design: With Version 11, IBM.com Takes Care of the Customer." *B to B,* May 28, 2001.

Warren, Liz. "What's in a Name?" *Computer Weekly,* August 23, 2001.

SEE ALSO: Web Site Basics; Web Site Design and Set-up; Web Site Usability Issues

WEB SITE USABILITY ISSUES

No matter how sophisticated and well planned a Web site's design, it was ultimately the user's experience that counted most, particularly in e-commerce. If customers couldn't use a site's offerings, they couldn't make a purchase. Usability refers to the overall quality of a user's Web site experience. Did the page load quickly? Was she able to find everything she was looking for? Were all links "live"—that is, did they actually access other Web pages? Were all the more involved processes, such as order forms and shopping carts, functioning properly? Was the site's navigation scheme logical and easy to follow? In short, does the site do what it was intended to do, and could the user figure out how to use it?

In the tense commercial environment of the World Wide Web, customers are notoriously impatient, particularly when it comes to the usability of commercial sites. Since the great promise of the Web is its enormous convenience, particularly in terms of speed, customers learn relatively quickly what they want to find, and if it isn't readily available on one site, they'll simply seek it out elsewhere. As reported in *Fortune,* according to the research firm Keynote Systems, Web users grant a Web site an average of eight seconds of download time before clicking away to another site. Moreover, much research suggests that customers tend to be unforgiving of sites that fail to load quickly or provide an adequately usable environment, so sites that are too difficult for users to navigate or load may simply be written off altogether as customers develop loyalty to other, more user-friendly sites.

EFFECTS ON BUSINESS

The lack of optimal usability was hardly confined to a few unprofessional sites. Market researcher Forrester Research and Bradford, Massachusetts-based usability testing firm User Interface Engineering conducted a study in 2000 that found serious usability flaws on thirty leading e-commerce sites, including e-tailing giant Amazon.com. Forrester Research reported that 27 percent of all Web transactions were abandoned when users reached the payment Web page, while BizRate.com found that fully 75 percent of the respondents to their survey said they had abandoned their online shopping carts without completing a purchase. The main culprit for these lost revenue opportunities was a lack of usability on the Web site. According to a study by Redwood, California-based Zona Research, U.S. Web sites lost an estimated $25 billion in revenue due to slow Web site performance alone.

With such enormous sums at stake, companies were taking few chances. By the early 2000s, e-commerce firms were increasingly turning to consultants who specialize in Web site usability issues. In the process, they helped foster a hot site-testing industry. Particularly in the wake of the e-commerce shake-out of 2000, e-tailers sought to utilize their Web sites to generate as much revenue as possible, and thus could ill afford to lose customers due to easily avoidable flaws in their site design.

LOW-END USERS

A site's usability, first and foremost, must be measured in terms of the customers' capabilities, not those of the firm itself. As much as designers may wish to exploit the latest technologies, design techniques, and browser capabilities, conscientious and business-wise Web managers would do well to keep their entire range of customers in mind. Specifically, designers must remain cognizant of their lowest-end users—those users and potential customers with the least advanced browsing capabilities. It's extremely common for corporations to maintain cutting-edge technology, but more important is the technological capacities of the customers.

For example, a designer may wish to include fancy, intensive graphics and advanced search mechanisms to offer the best-looking and shopping-optimal site, but if a segment of the company's customers still operate on low-end browsers, they may be unable to utilize the site at all, in the process driving those customers away. If a corporation's customer demographics include a strong focus on lower-income groups or other demographics that are less likely to enjoy the latest broadband or other technologies, then the firm would be ill-advised to focus their Web sites too heavily on streaming media technologies or complicated graphic schemes, no matter how aesthetically pleasing or even how user-friendly such designs, in theory, may be.

COMPATIBILITY ACROSS SYSTEMS

Sites must be rendered equally useful across different platforms. That is, designers must be sure to cross-check their designs on various computers running different browsers. There were few more easily avoidable usability problems than this one. A site that was designed for a personal computer running Internet Explorer may function differently on a Macintosh using a Netscape browser. While there were efforts in the late 1990s and early 2000s toward greater compatibility between these different systems, designers were still encouraged to render their designs as neutral as possible. The most important precaution for designers to take, then, is to test their sites on all possible systems, correcting errors as they arise and making their sites as cross-compatible as possible. Another alternative was to maintain multiple ''mirror'' sites, in which a home page can point users toward sites tailored to different browsers via a click of the mouse.

MAKING WEB SITES HANDICAP ACCESSIBLE

While computer technology can be a highly empowering tool for those with disabilities, not all Web sites accommodated the needs of the disabled. By the early 2000s, there was growing awareness of the

kinds of practices that do and do not make for a quality Web experience for disabled users. For example, various forms of visual impairment, including some kinds of color blindness, can hamper a user's ability to make out everything on the site. Blind users, by the 2000s, were able to utilize Web pages with special software designed to create synthesized speech based on the text of the page and the alternate messages incorporated in the markup of the graphic references. Text-based alternate graphics and menus were thus steps companies could easily take to make their sites more accessible to the visually impaired.

CREATING OPTIMAL USABILITY

Among the most crucial steps in maintaining the usability of a Web site is providing a forum for—and attending to—user feedback. Often, this is as simple as establishing a ''Feedback'' link on the site, to which users can write their comments on what worked well and what was problematic to the site's Webmaster. Mike Ragunas, the chief technology officer for the Framingham, Massachusetts-based office-supply chain Staples.com, reported on *ZDNet* that ''customer feedback led us to streamline our registration process, to put our customers' virtual shopping cart on the screen at all times, and to display search results in an easy-to-read, bulleted list format. The upshot was a more user-friendly site with fewer barriers to purchase.'' In this way, companies not only render their sites more usable (and thus more likely to generate sales), but also potentially improve their overall relations with customers by actively seeking their input and incorporating it into the firm's operations.

In the near future, Web designers can expect a number of significant developments allowing for greater design freedom—along with enhanced responsibilities. As telecommunications systems improve and photonics and other improvements find their way into the Internet backbone, greater bandwidth will coincide with further penetration of Internet access to create a more seamless Web, requiring less concern of designers for lower-end users and their technological limitations. Not only will this allow for greater freedom of graphical layout and more complex design schemes, but designers will also be far freer to incorporate streaming media applications, which were expected to greatly enhance the Web's possibilities once its kinks were ironed out and its usability more universal.

LEADING THE USABILITY CHARGE

Jakob Nielsen, whose expertise in and efforts on behalf of Web site usability earned him the nickname ''Usability Pope,'' was a Sun Microsystems Distinguished Engineer until 1998, when he left to become a full-time writer and consultant, with a special focus on Web site usability and a goal of taking the haphazard World Wide Web of the early 2000s and establishing a more user-friendly order. He founded Nielsen Norman Group with former Apple Computer vice president Donald A. Norman to assist companies with their Internet interactions with customers. In the late 1990s and early 2000s, Nielsen spearheaded a new "discount usability engineering" movement devoted to building tools and processes for improving the usability of interfaces, including those used on the World Wide Web. In the process, he built a portfolio of 55 U.S. patents, most of which center on creating a more usable Internet.

According to *Econtent,* Nielsen feels one of the biggest mistakes companies make in setting up their Web sites is their failure to understand the online medium and what it entails. Simply taking print-oriented information and putting it on the Web makes for poor Web sites, according to Nielsen. Firms need to understand that their Web sites are not depositories of information; rather, they are online services. "I recommend," Nielsen remarked, "doing a field study of the audience to really discover their information needs and how they are ingrained in their everyday work, because what you should think of when you're developing online services is activity support or task support." According to Nielsen, "the Web can be made at least 2,000 percent more usable than it is now."

Nielsen wasn't the only one on a crusade to make the Web safe for the average user. The World Wide Web Consortium launched an initiative to incorporate usability issues into its broader guidance of the World Wide Web's development. The Web Accessibility Initiative (WAI) established guidelines, devised technologies and tools, and engaged in education and outreach to ensure that businesses, organizations, governments, and individuals incorporated Web practices that promoted the greatest overall accessibility on the Web.

FURTHER READING:

Fichter, Darlene. "Designing Usable Sites: A State of Mind." *Online,* January 2001.

Lynch, Patrick J., and Sarah Horton. *Web Style Guide: Basic Design Principles for Creating Web Sites.* New Haven, CT: Yale University Press, 1999. Available from info.med.yale.edu.

O'Donovan, Cheryl. "Dot Ugh." *Communication World,* June 2001.

Pack, Thomas. "Use It or Lose It: Jakob Nielsen Champions Content Usability." *Econtent,* June 2001.

Ragunas, Mike. "ZDNet Developer—Usability: Giving Your Web Site Tender Loving Care." *ZDNet,* 2001. Available from www.zdnet.com.

Raskin, Jef. "The Humane Touch: Bad Design Can Be Costly." *Forbes,* May 28, 2001.

Riedman, Patricia. "Latest Hot Trend Tests Usability of Web Sites." *Advertising Age,* October 2, 2000.

World Wide Web Consortium. "Web Accessibility Initiative (WAI) Homepage." Cambridge, MA: World Wide Web Consortium, September 2001. Available from www.w3.org.

Zeldman, Jeffrey. "Web Publishing Secrets." *Macworld,* September 2001.

SEE ALSO: HTML (Hypertext Markup Language); Web Site Basics; Web Site Design and Setup; Web Site, Relaunching a; World Wide Web Consortium (W3C)

WEBCRAWLER

Webcrawler was the Internet's first search engine that performed keyword searches in both the names and texts of pages on the World Wide Web. It won quick popularity and loyalty among surfers looking for information. Despite the fact that competitors like Yahoo!, AltaVista, Lycos, HotBot, Northern Light, and Infoseek have long overtaken Webcrawler in popularity and power, its name remains synonymous with search engines, and some, like Metacrawler, still pay homage to this pioneer.

During the Web's infancy, Webcrawler was born in January 1994. It was developed by Brian Pinkerton, a computer student at the University of Washington, to cope with the complexity of the Web. Finding one's way among first tens of thousands—soon to be millions—of individual Web pages was comparable to trying to find a book in a major library that had no indexing system or card catalog. Pinkerton's application, Webcrawler, could automatically scan individual sites on the Web, register their content, and create an index that surfers could query with keywords to find Web sites relevant to their interests.

The basic function of the program was something Pinkerton called its search engine. The search engine looked at a particular document somewhere on the Web, and used the various hyperlinks it found to lead it to other pages with similar content. It followed some of the links to new documents and repeated the process over and over. The search engine determined what general type of document it would visit as well as which individual documents it would visit. Pinkerton described Webcrawler as a "Web robot" that used the structure of the Internet itself to find documents on the Internet. In other words, it required no special, additional software; it searched for Web documents the same way a human user would—by following hyperlinks from one document to another until it found what it was looking for. Webcrawler just did it much faster. Pinkerton estimated, in the mid-1990s, that Webcrawler required about an eighth of a second to parse the query, contact the database server, perform the query, get the answer, format the results and return them to the query-maker.

Webcrawler's search engine performed two basic functions. First, it compiled an ongoing index of web addresses (URLs). Webcrawler retrieved and marked a document, analyzed the content of both its title and its full text, registered the relevant links it contained, and then stored the information in its database. When a user submitted a query in the form of one or more keywords, Webcrawler compared it with the information in its index and reported back any matches.

Faced with memory that could only store a fraction of the Web's total content, Pinkerton had to devise a criterion for which documents should be included in the index. The one he settled on was that the index should include documents from as many servers as possible. Webcrawler was written to ensure that new servers were visited before older ones were revisited. The protocol also guaranteed that the index would include at least one document from every server visited. That particular strategy gained Webcrawler an early reputation for broad coverage of the Web. During its first year, Webcrawler's index included about 50,000 documents—a number that would grow into the millions over the next few years—from some 9,000 servers. The index was updated every week.

Webcrawler's second function was searching the Internet in real time for sites that matched a given query. It was carried out using exactly the same process, following links from one page to another. However, it first searched its index for the criteria in the query and from there looked for new pages. Surfers themselves were not able to use the real-time function directly, but Webcrawler performed real-time searches, added the results to the index, and returned to the individual making the query.

For its first three months, Webcrawler was a desktop application rather than a Web-based service. It went live on the Internet on April 20, 1994 with pages indexed from about 6,000 servers. Its popularity grew rapidly. By October 1994, it was receiving 15,000 queries a day and had answered almost a quarter of a million in all. Only a month later, around the time Yahoo! was launching its search site, Webcrawler handled its millionth query, a search for "nuclear weapons design and research."

By the end of 1994, the service found two corporate sponsors and was starting to lure advertisers. In June 1995, it was acquired for $1 million by America Online, then just an upstart itself with less than one million subscribers. In April 1996, when Webcrawler

incorporated the human-edited GNN Select guide, its index was contained 500,000 entries. The service was processing about 3 million queries daily.

In November 1996 AOL sold Webcrawler to Excite, another online search engine for stock valued at about $19.8 million. The large purchase price was seen as evidence that search engines had been accepted as successful platforms for Web advertising. Why Excite, a search engine in its own (now defunct), would purchase Webcrawler, however, was not immediately apparent, and was even more puzzling in light of its purchase of the then-popular Magellan search engine only four months earlier. Webcrawler maintained its own staff within Excite until mid-1997; eventually the separate Webcrawler index was done away with as well. After that, Webcrawler continued to exist essentially as a separate brand name Web site, although its results were exactly the same as Excite's. Over the years, the Webcrawler Web site underwent various changes. In mid-2001, however, it eliminated all extraneous features—family pages, telephone directories, maps, etc.—in favor of a spare, clean, "pure" search site, in keeping with Webcrawler's slogan "It's that simple."

FURTHER READING:

Andrews, Whit. "Keep It Simple." *Internet World,* July 7, 1997.

Cleland, Kim. "Search Engine to Share Revenue with Content Firms." *Advertising Age,* June 16, 1997.

Pinkerton, Brian. "Finding What People Want: Experiences with the WebCrawler." 1994. Available from www.thinkpink.com/bp/WebCrawler/.

"Plans for WebCrawler." *Adweek,* February 23, 1998.

Sherman, Chris. "WebCrawler Gets Deportaled." *SearchDay,* July 3, 2001. Available from www.searchenginewatch.com.

Sullivan, Danny. "Excite Kills Magellan, WebCrawler Remains." *Search Engine Report,* June 4, 2001. Available from www.searchenginewatch.com.

SEE ALSO: Search Engine Strategy

WEBLINING (INTERNET REDLINING)

The Internet, particularly via e-commerce, takes one's personal information to unprecedented levels of common knowledge. On the one hand, companies argue that access to greater levels of information makes them more efficient and more able to meet the needs of their customers. On the other hand, privacy advocates caution about the Internet's ability to excessively invade personal privacy, with potentially ugly consequences. One such violation brought about by the dissemination of personal information is the practice of Weblining, or the use of the Internet by businesses to engage in ''redlining'' to unfairly discriminate against certain persons or groups.

Weblining sometimes involves a very blatant process of grading customers. For instance, a company's account listings may include ratings for individual customers that help the firm determine how much time, effort, or investment should be devoted to those customers. Such ratings are based on a number of factors, but the common denominator is that those are customers who, by various measures, are determined likely to generate a greater amount of money for the firm; because of this, such customers receive higher ratings. Once a lower rating pops up on an individual's account, for instance, the company employees may be less motivated to go out of their way to meet that customer's needs. Some companies—particularly banks''were quite open about such practices, according to *Business Week*. While this form of redlining raises serious ethical questions, the companies aren't necessarily doing anything illegal unless they actively discriminate in ways that violate existing discrimination laws.

The temptation for companies to engage in Weblining is significant. Obviously, companies want to devote their resources—marketing, paperwork, retention, and so on—to the most commercially viable segments of the population in which their products and services are likely to find an audience. The relationship, in this sense, doesn't assume that the customer is always right. Rather, the customer warrants attention according to some measure of the customer's worth.

Data collection and data selling grew into an industry in its own rite in the late 1990s and early 2000s. The speed, sophistication, and breadth of information available on the Internet created a situation in which thousands of databases stored information that could be used to generate extensive customer profiles and possibly to engage in Weblining practices. While companies have always actively monitored their customers to weed out those less conducive to profit making, the level of technology made available by the Internet allows companies the opportunity to create, according to *Business Week,* ''the equivalent of profit-and-loss statements on every customer.'' According to Forrester Research, nearly a quarter of all companies were beginning to micro-segment their customers by 2000, and the percentage was growing rapidly. Many companies see this as an effective management practice that engenders optimal efficiency and maximizes use of resources.

Redlining generally assumes that, for geographic—and, by implication, demographic—rather than individual reasons, a particular customer constitutes a greater risk or a potentially lower return to the firm, and thus the firm responds by placing greater restrictions on the company's dealings with that customer. Customers judged—rightly or wrongly—to represent more of a risk (or less likely to bring lucrative business to a firm) may be penalized in a number of ways. For instance, a firm may be less likely to give a low-rated customer the benefit of the doubt after a bounced check, may institute higher service fees, may offer their special deals only to their more highly valued customers, may perform service at lower levels of quality, and so on. On the Internet, redlining compounds the geographic discrimination with other forms of market segmentation based on electronically collected data.

Perhaps the most benign problem associated with Weblining is that it may proceed based on information that is derived out of context, irrelevant for the issues at hand, or that it otherwise generates baseless assumptions upon which companies act. But with such personal information filtered through several databases and sold from company to company, the meaning behind the original information often grows diluted, resulting in a general profile of customers that may have little relevance to a particular company, and perhaps even little resemblance to the individual. In the end, individuals are penalized for their predicted, rather than their actual, behavior.

Perhaps the most serious problem with Weblining, according to privacy and social activists, is that it's not only customer-related information that is stored and used to generate profiles. That is, companies collect more than credit histories and shopping habits. Individuals' race, ethnicity, sexual orientation, personal habits, Web-browsing practices, lifestyles, health status, political persuasion, and other private information can also be obtained rather easily. Critics warn that, in the wrong hands, such information could be used to discriminate based on factors that have nothing to do with potential value as a customer, but rather based on bigotry, malice, or social prejudice.

The late 1990s and early 2000s saw a string of lawsuits charging companies with using the Internet to redline neighborhoods and social groups. In 2000, Wells Fargo discontinued its online home mortgage operations after the Association of Community Organizations for Reform Now (ACORN), a leading housing advocacy organization, filed suit against the company claiming it violated the Fair Housing Act by using its online home-search system to steer individuals away from certain housing districts based on racial classifications and stereotypes about racial ''lifestyles.'' Although Wells Fargo claimed that it maintained no control over the ''Community Calculator'' service for which the company contracted, which used database information to generate profiles of neighborhoods and ''lifestyle indicators,'' the company decided the service's editorial content was at odds with Wells Fargo's practices, and the site was discontinued. That same year, Kozmo.com was slapped with a lawsuit for allegedly denying delivery service to residents in predominantly black neighborhoods in Washington, D.C., based not on individual information but on geographical location.

The end result of Weblining, as with redlining, is to force certain segments of the population to pay more—in one way or another—for the same service, or to close those segments off from services altogether. Weblining acts as a barrier to social mobility as well. As more and more economic activity shifts to cyberspace, Internet-based discrimination will have farther-reaching effects. Since Weblining typically victimizes underprivileged groups, to compound their difficulties puts them at an even greater disadvantage.

In effect, then, Weblining both proceeds on and contributes to social stereotypes. Since the information derived through databases necessarily only reveals a tiny proportion of relevant personal information, the interpretation of that data necessarily falls back on existing social assumptions about the tastes, means, and risks associated with social groups. But by acting on those assumptions and tailoring their products and services according to their expectations, companies effectively limit the choices available to those groups to what is expected by social stereotypes. Thus, Weblining segmentation can prove a self-fulfilling prophecy, and thereby limit the amount of social mobility and cultural interchange available to society.

FURTHER READING:

Marquess, Kate. ''Redline May Be Going Online.'' *ABA Journal,* August, 2000.

Stepanek, Marcia, et al. ''Weblining.'' *Business Week,* April 3, 2000.

SEE ALSO: Computer Ethics; Digital Divide; Privacy: Issues, Policies, Statements

WEBOPEDIA

Whether an Internet user is stumped for the meaning of a termor hung up on how many nibbles make up a bit, chances are online encyclopedia Webopedia has answers. One of several sites branded under the Internet.com technology portal and run by INT Media Group, Inc., Webopedia has never been a high-flying dot-com, but simply a stable reference source geared toward a general audience. Its award-winning material has been cited in a variety of mainstream and professional publications, and the site regularly appears in rankings of top Web references.

The Webopedia site sets out to define and elucidate practically every mainstream computer term and acronym that might be uttered in English. Beyond individual definitions, which can be retrieved using the site's search engine, it also classifies words into a hierarchy of categories, for example, by listing ADSL within an Internet access category, which is in turn part of a general networking category. Definitions often cite a variety of alternative and secondary meanings and contain ample cross-references to related words and categories. For many words, Webopedia also offers links to external sites with further information on the topic. The site also features such gratuities as a word of the day, special reference pages on popular themes, e-mail newsletters, and a form that allows users to suggest new words. For wireless users, Webopedia also offers a Wireless Application Protocol (WAP) version with features optimized for handheld devices at wap.webopedia.com.

While the 4,000-entry database includes foremost the whole litany of practical computer jargon and abbreviations that have entered the English lexicon over the last half-century or so, Webopedia occasionally delves into more esoteric matters through snippets on, among other things, the paperless office, computer literacy, Internet etiquette, foobar versus fubar, and geeks.

In addition to its main site, Webopedia also repackages portions of its content into sites for specialized audiences, including e-comm.webopedia.com for e-commerce information and applanet.webopedia.com for listings on application outsourcing. Webopedia content is likewise redistributed or linked by partners ranging from Lycos to Dell Computer.

Webopedia, based in Darien, Connecticut, was first offered in the mid-1990s by Mecklermedia Corporation and was affiliated from the start with Internet.com, an IT news portal. In 1998, Internet.com was spun off as a separate business and traded publicly, eventually adopting the name INT Media Group, Inc. In 2000 Webopedia's content was merged with that of ZD Webopedia, a nearly identical site produced by ZDNet, a technology portal that originated with Ziff Davis and was later reorganized as part of CNET Networks, Inc. The name Webopedia is thus a trademark of INT Media, although a handful of unrelated sites have used the name over time.

In addition to its Web content and electronic newsletters, INT Media Group operates trade shows for the IT professions and rents out opt-in e-mail lists of its subscribers to third-party marketers. The company also earns revenue from advertising on its sites and in its newsletters, as well as from various reports and subscription content it sells.

FURTHER READING:

Connelly, James. "38 Sites That Can Simplify Your Life." *Computerworld,* August 2, 1999.

Crouch, Cameron. "Tech Reference." *PC World,* August 2001.

Gottesman, Ben Z. "Technology." *PC Magazine,* March 21, 2001.

INT Media Group, Inc. "Webopedia: Online Computer Dictionary for Internet Terms and Technical Support." Darien, CT: INT Media Group, Inc., 2001. Available from www.webopedia.com/.

SEE
ALSO: Content Provider

WEBVAN GROUP, INC.

Webvan Group was an online grocery delivery service that operated between mid-1999 and mid-2001, when it ceased operations, shut down its World Wide Web site, and filed bankruptcy. During its short history, Webvan spent roughly $1.2 billion in capital, a fact which earned it the distinction of being one of the most costly failed Internet startups to date. Most analysts agree that the young business attempted to expand too rapidly into other goods without first ensuring its core grocery delivery operations were stable.

It was Louis Borders, the founder of the Borders bookstore chain, who established Webvan in 1999. Borders had started raising capital for his business, incorporated as Intelligent Systems for Retail, in December 1996. By April of 1999, Borders had amassed roughly $122 million in capital from Benchmark, Sequoia, and other venture capitalists. Visualizing a vast delivery service that handled all types of online orders, Borders decided to start with groceries. This decision posed problems for Webvan right from the start. According to *InfoWorld* writer Dylan Tweney, "Webvan, despite appearances, is more than just an online food vendor. It's a bold—and expensive—experiment in direct-to-consumer product distribution." Yet, as Tweney explained, the delivery of fresh food was much more difficult than the delivery of books or CDs. "You can't just pop a carton of eggs into a FedEx mailer. You need to make sure that groceries arrive quickly, intact, and at the right temperature. And you need to do it without big per-customer shipping charges, given the food industry's notoriously skinny margins."

Webvan's business plan called for the creation of automated distribution centers in each of its 26 target markets. The $30 million facilities—to be built by Bechtel Group by 2003—would be roughly 350,000 square feet. Webvan claimed that by automating much of the distribution process, labor costs for Webvan would be minimal. Each center would service customers up to 40 miles away. In June of 1999, Webvan launched operations in San Francisco; merchandise was delivered from a nearby distribution center in Oakland. Three months later, Borders convinced George Shaheen, CEO of Andersen Consulting, to leave his lucrative and secure post at Andersen to take over as president and CEO of Webvan. By then, Borders had secured a total of roughly $400 million in financing from a variety of funding sources

Webvan's Web site allowed customers to select the items they wished to purchase and place them into an electronic shopping cart, which displayed all of the items selected as well as the total cost of the items in the cart. To complete a purchase, shoppers were asked to select a 30-minute window in which the groceries would be delivered. Typically, the soonest an order could be delivered was the following day. To draw repeat business and to encourage larger orders, Webvan offered free delivery for orders over $50. Customers with questions about their orders could also call a toll-free customer service line.

Although losses totaled $144.5 million in the first six months of operation, sales reached $13.3 million. Compared to its rivals, Webvan's early results seemed quite promising. HomeGrocer.com's sales over nine months reached only $10.9 million, despite the fact that it was serving three markets in California and Oregon. Full-year sales at Streamline, which also served three markets, totaled $15.4 million. Also encouraging was Webvan's ability to attract customers quickly. In six months, Webvan managed to reach 47,000 customers in a single market, compared to the 110,000 clients secured by its largest competitor, Peapod, which had operations in eight markets.

Webvan's initial public offering, in November 1999, raised an additional $375 million in capital. By April 2000, Webvan was delivering roughly 20,000 grocery items, as well as flowers, books, office supplies, non-prescription pharmaceuticals, and pet supplies. Gomez Advisors ranked Webvan as the leading online delivery site among the 11 competitors it evaluated. Operations launched in Atlanta in May, and Webvan expanded its delivery service to include magazines and videos in June. Despite the firm's growth, its continued losses began to concern investors, and Webvan saw its stock prices tumble to $6 per share, compared to their high of $34. That month, the firm announced its intent to merge with Homegrocer.com in a stock swap valued at $1.2 billion. Although the merger, finalized by the end of 2000, was viewed as a positive step toward achieving profitability, investors began to question if the firm would be able to do so before its funding ran dry. Many pointed out that Webvan and Homegrocer had lost a combined total of $234 million in the first six months of 2000.

Rather than curb spending and focus its efforts on minimizing losses, Webvan launched new operations in Dallas, Texas, and Atlanta, Georgia. The firm also developed a new logo and branding strategy and redesigned its Web site, which was organized into eleven product categories: grocery, fresh market, household, pet shop, baby shop, kids stores, drugstore, books, CDs and videos, specialty shops, and electronics. The changes were designed to communicate Webvan's determination to become a leading force in online distribution of all kinds. However, many critics pointed out that the money and time would have been better spent on developing Webvan's original brand, which had yet to be fully developed. According to a July 2001 article in *The Industry Standard*, "Webvan was so intent on meeting its long-term goal of building a behemoth that could deliver anything to anyone anywhere that it lost sight of a more mundane task: pleasing grocery customers day after day. In the process, it jeopardized the shorter-term goal of being a modest but profitable online supermarket." Webvan was also criticized for switching HomeGrocer sites over to Webvan sites too quickly, which alienated many HomeGrocer customers.

Borders resigned from his firm in February of 2001, the same month that Webvan closed its Dallas warehouse and laid off 220 employees. Shaheen quit three months later. In July, Webvan ceased operating and filed for Chapter 11 bankruptcy protection. According to *U.S. News & World Report* writer Randall Stross, the idea behind Webvan was a good one and may have proved viable under different management. "The badly managed company is separable from the essential business concept—combining online ordering and home delivery." Webvan's story will likely become a case study for future Web-based delivery service ventures.

FURTHER READING:

Alsop, Stewart. "The Tragedy of Webvan." *Fortune,* August 13, 2001. Available from www.fortune.com.

Helft, Miguel. "What a Long, Strange Trip It's Been for Webvan." *The Industry Standard,* July 23, 2001. Available from www.theindustrystandard.com

Howell, Debbie. "The Grocer with a Business Plan That Delivers." *DSN Retailing Today,* May 8, 2000.

Khermouch, Gerry. "The End of E-Grocers? Not at All." *BusinessWeek Online,* July 16, 2001. Available from www.businessweekonline.com.

Stross, Randall E. "Requiem for Webvan." *U.S. News & World Report,* July 30, 2001.

Tice, Carol. "Webvan Shops for Time, Money to Fulfill Promise." *Puget Sound Business Journal,* July 28, 2000.

Tweney, Dylan. "Webvan Delivers Logistics Lesson to Online Vendors." *InfoWorld,* August 9, 1999.

Wilder, Clinton. "Webvan Bust Leaves a Big Hole." *InformationWeek,* July 30, 2001.

SEE ALSO: Business-to-Consumer (B2C) E-commerce

WETHERELL, DAVID

David Wetherell is the CEO and chairman of CMGI Inc., one of the world's largest Internet holding firms. Via one of the first Internet-based venture capital firms, a CMGI subsidiary entitled @Ventures, Wetherell began investing in Internet start-ups in 1995. By the beginning of 2000, he held stakes in more than 45 leading e-commerce and Internet technology firms, including search engine giant AltaVista Co. However, the dot-com fallout that year forced Wetherell to begin reducing his investments and divesting unprofitable ventures. Ranked 22nd among the technology industry's 100 richest persons, according to a list published in 2000 by *Forbes,* Wetherell dropped to 79th place in 2001.

In 1986, at the age of 32, Wetherell bought the College Marketing Group Inc., which was founded in 1968 as a marketer of educational publications. By the time Wetherell purchased the firm, it had refocused on selling the mailing lists it had accumulated through the years. Wetherell immediately began molding his new business into a database management firm. He acquired a printing and direct mail company, renamed SalesLink, in 1989. Five years later, Wetherell took his company—which had been renamed CMG Information Services Inc.—public, selling 1.2 million shares. By then, Wetherell was already interested in developing Internet-based firms. His first such business venture, a commercial World Wide Web browser named Book Link Technologies, allowed users to search for and purchase textbooks; it was launched with a $900,000 investment and later sold to America Online for $30 million in stock.

With the profits from the sale of Book Link, Wetherell created @Ventures, one of the first venture capital companies focused exclusively on Internet-based firms. Through @Ventures Wetherell paid $2 million for an 80 percent stake in search engine Lycos, which he took public in 1996. He also bought holdings in GeoCities Inc., ThingWorld.com, Silknet Software, Premiere Technology, and Vicinity Corp. In addition to these purchases, Wetherell created two majority-owned companies, Internet marketing solutions provider Engage Technologies and application service provider Navisite.

Both Intel Corp. and Microsoft Corp. made sizable investments in CMG in 1997. Wetherell invested in Ventro Corp., Speech Machines, Reel.com, Planet-All, Softway Systems, and KOZ.com the following year. He also launched online advertising network Adsmart and content provider Planet Direct, which eventually changed its name to MyWay.com. In 1998, Wetherell officially changed his firm's name to CMGI Inc. He sold Planet All to Amazon.com and Reel.com to Hollywood Entertainment, becoming the entertainment firm's largest stakeholder. Just a few months after Wetherell took GeoCities public, Yahoo! bought it for $3.9 billion in stock. Initial public offerings in 1999 included Critical Path, Silknet Software, and Ventro Corp., along with NaviSite and Engage. CMGI acquired Internet advertising firm Adforce that year. In June, Wetherell orchestrated his firm's largest deal to date—the $2.3 billion purchase of an 83 percent stake in search engine AltaVista for from Compaq Computer Corp.

After stock gains of 604 percent in 1998 and 940 percent in 1999, CMGI saw its share price plummet from $163.50 to roughly $10 with the dot-com fallout of 2000. Like many top CEOs in the dot-com industry, Wetherell was forced to cut costs and streamline operations. He folded the 17 operating companies of CMGI into six business units: search and portals, infrastructure and enabling technologies, Internet professional services, e-business and fulfillment, interactive marketing, and venture capital. Wetherell also canceled plans for AltaVista's initial public offering. Restructuring efforts continued into 2001 as Wetherell shuttered the AdForce unit in June. By then, CMGI had reduced its majority stakes in Internet firms from 42 to 15.

FURTHER READING:

CMGI Inc. ''Company History.'' Andover, MA: CMGI Inc., 2001. Available from www.cmgi.com.

Gilbert, Jennifer. ''Wethering the I-Storm: Wetherell's Vision Makes CMGI a Formidable Force.'' *Advertising Age,* November 1, 1999.

''Humbled Web Master: CMGI Chief David Wetherell Regroups After a Dizzying Year for Dotcoms.'' *Money,* January 1, 2001.

Long, Tim. ''David Wetherall—Wetherell Has Positioned Himself as the Largest Shareholder in Many of the Most Visited Web Sites.'' *Computer Reseller News,* November 16, 1998.

———. ''Dot-Com Determination—Chairman and CEO David Wetherell Plans to Make CMGI's Keiretsu Business Model Leaner-And Profitable.'' *Computer Reseller News,* September 11, 2000.

Willis, Clint. ''The 100 Highest Rollers.'' *Forbes.* April 2, 2001.

SEE ALSO: CMGI Inc.

WHITE PAPER

White papers are reports written by industry professionals and academics, all of whom are experts in their chosen field, on just about any imaginable topic. In the world of e-commerce, topics often include data management, computer programming, network security, customer service, business-to-business issues, the Internet economy, Web site development, directory services, naming and addressing, enterprise management, frame relay, performance engineering, remote access, routing and switching, voice/data convergence, and more. As part of the in-depth exploration of a subject, white papers may include case studies—real-world examples of how technology works in a business setting, as well as photographs, charts and graphs, and lists of resources (magazine articles, Web sites, other white papers, and the names of industry experts, companies, universities and associations).

White papers are important to companies engaging in e-commerce because they provide details to executives and IT professionals that can be useful when making important business decisions, such as whether to invest heavily in an emerging technology. White papers often provide examples of best practices or e-commerce methods that have proved successful for other companies. Some outline practices to avoid, and others describe what an organization's or expert's position is on a specific issue or hot topic.

In addition to providing useful information to end-users, white papers can be powerful marketing tools for those who write them. They serve as a way to position the author and his or her company as experts in their field, and may lead to lucrative consulting jobs or sales. Although some individual authors or consulting firms charge others to read their white papers, many offer them at no cost for publicity purposes.

White papers can be found on many Web sites. In the early 2000s, Microsoft offered its E-Commerce White Paper Series for free through its Web site. IBM, Sun Microsystems, and many other leading technology companies also offered free white papers on e-commerce. Additionally, white papers can be obtained at technology trade shows and seminars, university libraries, from numerous government agencies, and through online information services, many of which are available at public libraries. eFlash, a service from Lucent Worldwide Services, allowed individuals to subscribe to a service that provided e-mail notices when new white papers were posted on its Web site. While some white papers are available as Web pages, other are quite long and must be downloaded and read with special software, such as Adobe Acrobat Reader.

FURTHER READING:

Microsoft Corp. "E-commerce White Paper Series." Redmond, WA: Microsoft Corp., March 6, 2001. Available from www.microsoft.com/technet/ecommerce.

"White Paper." *Tech Encyclopedia,* March 6, 2001. Available from www.techweb.com/encyclopedia.

WHITMAN, MARGARET

Margaret Whitman is CEO of eBay.com, the world's leading online auction site, with more than 8,000 product categories and 22 million registered users. She joined eBay in March of 1998, to assist founder Pierre Omidyar in managing the growth of his booming business.

Omidyar came up with the idea for eBay.com after his girlfriend, a Pez candy dispenser collector, expressed her wish to contact similar collectors. In 1995, Omidyar created Auction Web, a World Wide Web site that allowed sellers to post items for sale and buyers to competitively bid on merchandise. Omidyar offered no guarantees for merchandise sold, and buyers and sellers were responsible for handling payment and delivery. The following year, as site traffic grew well beyond his expectations, Omidyar began focusing on Auction Web full time. Auction Web began charging a small fee for each item listed and also took a cut of the final price. Because the entire auctioning process was automated, overhead costs were minimal. As a result, Omidyar's business became profitable very quickly, unlike many other Internet ventures. In 1997, Omidyar changed the site's named to eBay. Revenues for that year neared $6 million, and traffic continued to grow exponentially. Recognizing that he needed help managing what was becoming one of the Web's most frequently visited sites, Omidyar sold a 22 percent stake in eBay to Benchmark Capital for $4.5 million. Benchmark recruited a seasoned executive, Margaret Whitman, as CEO. Whitman's wide ranging experience included running the preschool division of Hasbro Inc.; handling global marketing for Mr. Potato Head and Playskool brands; and serving as president and CEO of FTD, where she spearheaded the florist's Internet operations. The Harvard Business School graduate had also held management positions at Bain & Co., Procter & Gamble, Stride Rite Corp., and Walt Disney Co.

One of Whitman's first tasks at eBay was to increase advertising efforts. She oversaw the firm's three-year, $12 million marketing agreement with America Online Inc. (AOL), whereby AOL agreed to list eBay as the preferred provider of person-to-person auction services. Whitman also worked to grow the firm. The acquisitions of Kruse, Inc., a company that conducted auctions and performed appraisal services and auctioneer training for classic car auctions, and Butterfield and Butterfield Auctioneers Corp. were designed to position eBay as a big-ticket auction house. The purchase of alando.de.ag, Germany's leading online personal trading platform, marked eBay's first international venture. Omidyar and Whitman listed eBay publicly for $18 a share, a price that nearly tripled by the end of the day. eBay's registered users climbed to 1.2 million by the end of 1998, and sales soared 724 percent to $47.4 million.

In 1999, Whitman furthered international growth efforts by launching sites in the United Kingdom and Canada. She convinced Omidyar to begin guaranteeing purchases up to $200, move certain adult-oriented products to an "Adult Only" section, and prohibit the sale of firearms. To facilitate the trading of larger items—such as vehicles and musical instruments—that were difficult and costly to ship, Whitman masterminded the launch of several regional sites. By early 2000, the number of registered users on eBay reached ten million. Despite the launch of competing auction sites from Amazon.com, Lycos, and Yahoo!, eBay continued to grow in 2000. According to a May 2000 article in *BusinessWeek Online,* Whitman was able to fend off competitors because she "kept eBay growing fast by adding categories and 53 local sites . . . and remaining firmly in control of the fast-growing market for online auctions."

FURTHER READING:

Corcoran, Elizabeth. "The-Egang." *Forbes,* July 26, 1999.

eBay Inc. "Company Overview." San Jose, CA: eBay Inc. Available from pages.ebay.com/community.

Jaffe, Sam. "Online Extra: eBay: From Pez to Profits." *BusinessWeek Online,* May 14, 2001. Available from www.businessweek.com.

Kerstetter, Jim. "Meg Whitman." *BusinessWeek Online,* May 15, 2000. Available from www.businessweek.com.

Lee, Jeanne. "Why eBay is Flying." *Fortune,* December 7, 1998.

Roth, Daniel. "Meg Muscles eBay Uptown." *Fortune,* July 5, 1999.

SEE ALSO: eBay Inc.; Omidyar, Pierre

WIDE AREA NETWORK (WAN)

Wide Area Networks, or WANs, connect a geographically diverse group of computers within a state, country, or even across several states or countries. WANs typically are connected by telephone lines, other types of communication lines, or radio waves. Quite often, smaller local area networks (LANs) are linked together to form a WAN. This is accomplished via dedicated private lines, leased from telecommunications firms like Sprint and AT&T, or by Switched Multi-Megabit Data Services (SMDS) technology, developed in 1995 to eliminate the need for a leased line.

WAN technology has been refined over a period of several decades. It first emerged in the mid-twentieth century with the advent of networks like ARPAnet. Developed in 1969 by the Department of Defense, ARPAnet and several other networks eventually evolved into the Internet, the largest WAN in the world. The packet switching technology most commonly used with WANs surfaced in the 1960s, and standard packet switching protocol, known as X.25, was developed in 1976. To increase network speed, packet switching allows for the parceling of data into smaller chunks, known as packets, prior to transmission. These packets can travel independently via alternate routes, and they are reassembled once they reach their target. Although X.25 remained the most popular WAN packet switching protocol for years, other packet switching protocols used with increasing frequency by WAN developers and administrators include the Internet standard, Transmission Control Protocol/Internet Protocol (TCP/IP), and Frame Relay, used most often by WANs connected via high speed T-1 and T-3 lines.

WANs are used for a variety of purposes. A corporation with offices in several locations may use a WAN to form an intranet. Quite often, the individual offices will use their own LANs for things like internal messaging, data processing functions, and hardware and software sharing. When these LANs are joined together to form a WAN, similar data sharing and messaging capabilities become possible across a much broader geographic area. Businesses wanting to link up with their suppliers or distributors may create a WAN as a means of establishing an extranet. For example, an extranet could provide a sales representative with electronic access to information in about the time it might take to deliver a product, or the availability of a product. Some WANs bring together various types of communications, such as data, video, and voice. Some organizations, including companies, universities, research centers, hospitals, and libraries, use WANs to connect to the Internet.

FURTHER READING:

"Packet Switching." In *Ecommerce Webopedia*. Darien, CT: Internet.com, 2001. Available from e-comm.webopedia.com.

"WAN—Wide Area Network." Tel-Aviv, Israel: Rad Data Communications Ltd., 1994. Available from www.rad.com.

"WAN." In *Techencyclopedia*. Point Pleasant, PA: Computer Language Co., 2001. Available from www.techweb.com.

"WAN (Wide Area Network)." Mumbai, India: Novanet Technologies Private Ltd., 2000. Available from www.novanettechnologies.com.

SEE ALSO: ARPAnet; AT&T Corp.; Communication Protocols; Local Area Network (LAN)

WILDCARDS

Wildcards are symbols that can be used to represent other values or characters during a search for files or other information on a computer system. They also can be used to search for Web sites with search engines—programs that comb the World Wide Web to look for relevant Web sites, based on keywords or phrases entered by a user.

The ability to use a wildcard depends on a computer's operating system—for example, Windows, DOS or Unix—and the search engine being used. In DOS or Windows, a user could search for all files that begin with the letter L by entering "l*." In this case, the asterisk stands for any letter combination after the letter L. Entering "l*.txt" would initiate a search for all text-only files beginning with the letter L. By including a dollar sign after the keyword horse ("horse$"), a search engine would look for Web sites containing different variations of the keyword, such as horse, horsecar, horseshoe, horseman, and so on. Thus, by using wildcards, users are able to broaden the scope of their searches.

FURTHER READING:

"Some Basic DOS Commands." Berkeley, CA: University of California Berkeley Econometrics Laboratory. February 14, 2001. Available from emlab.berkeley.edu.

"Wildcard Character." *Ecommerce Webopedia*, February 10, 2001. Available from e-comm.webopedia.com.

SEE ALSO: Stemming

WINER, DAVID

David Winer is the founder and CEO of User-Land Software, a Burlingame, California-based developer of Internet tools. A member of the World Wide Web Consortium's board of advisors, since 1998 Winer has worked with Microsoft Corp. to create a standard protocol for extensible markup language (XML), which many Internet experts believe will revolutionize the way computers communicate and the ways in which the Internet can be accessed by various devices. In 2000, Winer and Microsoft developed Simple Object Access Protocol (SOAP), a crucial component in Microsoft's plan, known as.Net, to connect all types of computing appliances to each other and to the Internet.

While a student at the University of Wisconsin during the 1970s, Winer began developing an outlining program for the Pascal programming language. In 1980, he moved to California, hoping to sell his program to Apple Computer Co. When Apple proved more interested in the database functions of the program than the outlining functions, Winer took his application to Personal Software, developer of the groundbreaking VisiCalc spreadsheet program. Personal Software hired Winer to work on a program called VisiText, which would be based on the software Winer had developed as a college student. The product never made it to market, but Winer left Personal Software with enough capital to found his own company, Living Videotext, in 1983. At the time, Winer's outlining application—by then named Think-Tank—had begun to gain recognition as presentation software. ThinkTank 128, one of the first business software programs developed for the Macintosh computer, was launched in June of 1984. Two years later, Living Videotext shipped MORE 1.0, an enhanced version of ThinkTank that included an automated bullet chart feature. Winer sold his firm to Symantec Corp. the following year.

After taking some time off, Winer created his second company, UserLand Software, in November of 1988. One of the firm's first major products, the Frontier scripting environment and application server, was offered to Macintosh users in January of 1992. However, Apple's release of AppleScript overshadowed Frontier. Frustrated, Winer left UserLand in January of 1994. Later that year, he launched Dave-Net, an online newsletter that grew popular among technology professionals and later came to be known as a prime example of "blogging." According to an April 2001 article in Government Computer News, "Blogging, as it is sometimes called, entails posting one's thoughts, opinions, and other minutiae on the Web. Several pieces of downloadable software make this process almost too easy—for example, Dan Bricklin's free-on-the-Net Blogger, at www.blogger.com, and UserLand Software Inc.'s Manila, at www.userland.com. UserLand's founder, Dave Winer, is the master of the form.'' Winer also spent the mid-1990s working as a contributing editor for *Hotwired*.

Winer returned to UserLand in 1996 to spearhead the development of Frontier for Windows 95 and Windows NT, believing that a Windows-based version of the application would be well suited to Internet programming. In 1997, Winer was named a Seybold Fellow for his innovations in Web-based publishing. Winer shifted his firm's focus in 1998 to Web development. Frontier 5.1, compatible with both Windows and Macintosh platforms, was enhanced with several Web publishing capabilities including a Web server and an object-oriented database. Throughout 1999 and 2000, UserLand continued to evolve from a scripting software manufacturer into a maker of Web tools for writers, designers, and graphic artists. In 2001, Winer spearheaded the launch of Radio UserLand, a Web application server for desktop computers that includes Web-log and syndicated newsreader functions. He continues to work on Internet standards and Web publishing tools.

FURTHER READING:

Colby, Clifford. "Frontier Heads to Windows." *MacWEEK.* September 9, 1996.

"Dave's Manila Playtown," 2001. Available from daveeditthispage.com.

Fink, R. "Spielberg He Ain't." *Government Computer News.* April 30, 2001.

Markoff, John. "Internet Critic Takes on Microsoft." *The New York Times.* April 9, 2001. Available from www.nytimes.com.

Morgenstern, David. "Frontier Blazing Internet Trail." *MacWEEK.* June 29, 1998.

"Radio Userland Calling." May 3, 2001.

"Userland Software Inc." *Inc.* November 15, 2000.

SEE ALSO: Apple Computer Inc.; Microsoft Corp.; Microsoft Windows; World Wide Web Consortium (W3C); XML

WOMEN AND THE INTERNET

The number of women on the Internet grew from 15 percent of all U.S. Internet users in 1995 to only 17 percent in 1997 and 26 percent in 1998. However, as the Internet became a more mainstream media outlet in the late 1990s, particularly in the U.S., more women began to seek online access. Roughly 60 percent of new Internet users in 1999 were women, and by year's end, the number of women on the Internet nearly equaled the number of men. In 2000, women who accessed the Internet from home did so mainly to find news and information. Some also used the Internet to plan trips and book tickets, and to take care of banking needs online.

Even before women became a leading presence on the Internet—they began to outnumber men in the first quarter of 2000—several World Wide Web sites specifically targeting women, including iVillage.com, Oxygen.com, and Women.com, had emerged. According to a March 2001 article in *San Jose Mercury News*, the fact that women typically make about 80 percent of a household's spending decisions seemed to bode well for these ''women's Web'' sites. ''Dozens of sites offering information, chat, and shopping sprang up in recent years, creating online communities where women could forge relationships and find content created especially for them. Advertisers were then supposed to flock to these sites, eager to parade their wares in front of legions of educated and affluent women online.'' Like most sites reliant on online advertising, however, these women's hubs struggled to secure the amount of advertising needed to produce a profit.

IVILLAGE.COM

With $2 million in backing from America Online (AOL), former Time Warner executive Candice Carpenter and former president and publisher for Doubleday Nancy Evans co-founded New York-based iVillage.com in June of 1995. Developed as the one of the first Internet hubs to serve as a resource for women, the site's first two networks were called About Work and Parent Soup. Carpenter headed up the firm as CEO, while Evans worked as president and editor-in-chief.

Carpenter and Evans spent the next few years expanding iVillage's content and developing e-commerce alliances with companies that sold products specifically for woman. iVillage eventually grew into the leading online destination for women and one of the largest content sites on the Web, with more than five million visitors each month. To serve its target market of women between 25 and 54 years of age, iVillage offered several different channels, including astrology, babies, beauty, books, computing, diet and fitness, food, games, health, home and garden, money, news, parenting, pets, relationships, and work. Along with reading about topics of interest, users could also interact with online experts, participate in discussion and support groups, post messages,

provide links to their own Web sites, enter contests, and shop. Membership was free, as the company chose instead to make money through advertising and sponsorships agreements, as well as from commissions on the products it sold online.

In April of 1999, iVillage conducted its initial public offering (IPO). Like so many other dot.com upstarts, iVillage watched its share prices skyrocket on the first day of trading. Roughly one year later, however, shareholders began to express concern about iVillage's lack of profitability. Stock plummeted from a high of $113.75 in 1999 to roughly $1 per share. In August of 2000, Carpenter was succeeded by Doug McCormick, who immediately put in place a restructuring that included layoffs and budget cuts. The firm bought out rival Women.com Network for $27 million in 2001. When the deal was completed, Hearst Corp. became the firm's largest shareholder with a 25 percent stake. AOL Time Warner and NBC both owned roughly 5 percent.

WOMEN.COM NETWORKS

Prior to its buyout by iVillage, San Mateo, California-based Women.com exceeded iVillage in total site traffic. In fact, Jupiter Media Metrix listed Women.com as third among the most visited Web sites in the U.S. in 2000. Established in 1992 as part of an effort to form an Internet-based meeting ground for women, Women.com also conducted a successful IPO in 1999. That year, it joined forces with the online arm of magazine giant Hearst Corp., gaining access to content from traditional women's magazines such as *Cosmopolitan* and *Good Housekeeping*.. Like iVillage, Women.com saw its advertising revenues start to tumble in 2000. As a result, its stock price plunged to roughly 25 cents per share, compared to a high of $20.25 in 1999.

OXYGEN MEDIA, INC.

Oxygen Media was co-founded in 1998 by world renowned talk show host Oprah Winfrey, television producer Carsey-Werner-Mandabach Co., and Nickelodeon founder Geraldine Laybourne. The startup was dedicated to providing entertainment and information to modern women with its cable television and Internet offerings. Its online arm eventually included Oxygen.com, an Internet gateway for women, as well as Thriveonline, Moms Online, Girls On, ka-Ching, and Oprah.com.

Oxygen has at its roots a 1995 agreement between Winfrey and America Online (AOL), which resulted in the creation of Oprah Online, an AOL site offering information about Winfrey's show. Two years later, ABC Internet Group and Winfrey's company, Harpo Productions, created Oprah.com, the official Web site of The Oprah Winfrey Show, the highest rated talk show in all of television. In August of 1999, Oprah.com joined Oxygen group of Web sites. Oprah.com offered information on Oprah's Book Club and Oprah's Angel Network and vowed to help women ''Live Their Best Life'' by giving advice on relationships, food, mind and body, and lifestyles. Web surfers visiting Oprah.com—the site averaged over 155 million hits per month and 3,000 e-mails per day in 2000—can subscribe to Winfrey's magazine, *O, The Oprah Magazine*; see streaming video of post-show discussions; write in an online journal; interact with other online Oprah fans; and even email Winfrey herself.

Oprah.com was unique in that it was able to use the success of a leading television show to attract an increasing number of female Web surfers. As a result, Oprah.com became one of the most popular online destinations for women. In additional to operating a leading women's site, Winfrey also encouraged women to become Web savvy by promoting ''Oprah Goes Online,'' a 12-part series explaining how she and friend Gayle King learned how to use the Internet themselves.

Despite the name recognition Winfrey brought to both Oprah.com and to Oxygen, the firm's Oxygen.com site drew fewer viewers than both iVillage.com and Women.com in 2000. Believing it might have diversified too broadly, the firm consolidated its online holdings into three major sites—Oxygen.com, Oprah.com, and health portal Thriveonline—in December of that year. The restructuring included cutting 65 positions. Four months later, the firm implemented a second round of layoffs, citing weak advertising sales.

CHALLENGES

Along with a reliance on online advertising, which has yet to prove a dependable revenue source, another main problem with sites like iVillage, Women.com, and Oxygen.com is their attempt to target such a large, highly diverse group of people. According to *BusinessWeek Online* writer Diane Brady, ''Women aren't a terrific niche market. There are too many of us, with too many different tastes, to race toward a portal or network based on gender alone.'' Despite the struggles faced by most of the Web sites targeting women, most analysts believe that women will continue to be a point of focus for new online ventures. According to a study conducted by California-based PeopleSupport, an online provider of customer service, nearly 63 percent of individuals who shop online twice a week or more are women. In addi-

tion, Forrester Research predicts that over 71.2 million women will be online by 2005, as the average annual Internet usage growth rate over the next five years for women will be 19 percent, compared to 13 percent for men.

FURTHER READING:

Brady, Diane. ''Why Oxygen Is Hyperventilating.'' *BusinessWeek Online,* October 16, 2000. Available from www.businessweek.com.

Brookman, Faye. ''An i Toward Profitability; iVillage Inc.'' *Crain's New York Business,* November 27, 2000.

———. ''Millionaires of Silicon Alley: Candice Carpenter.'' *Crain's New York Business.* November 29, 1999.

''Data Zone: Top TV Show Web Sites.'' *Electronic Media,* August 7, 2000.

Donahue, Dick, and Daisy Maryles. ''Oprah Yet Again.'' *Publishers Weekly,* October 18, 1999.

Greenberg, Paul A. ''Gender Gap Narrows As Women Take to the Net.'' *E-Commerce Times,* November 9, 1999. Available from www.ecommercetimes.com.

''Internet Hears Women Roar—Study.'' *Newsbytes,* August 19, 2000.

Kwan, Joshua.''Women on the Web: Specialty Sites Struggle.'' *San Jose Mercury News,* March 11, 2001.

''Need an Oprah Fix? Now She's on Your PC.'' *BusinessWeek Online,* November 5, 1998. Available from www.businessweek.com.

O'Leary, Mick. ''Web Goes Mainstream for Everybody.'' *Online,* November 2000.

''Women Lead Internet Charge.'' *United Press International,* March 23, 2000.

''Women Prove to Be Serious Shoppers in Internet Realm.'' *Crain's Cleveland Business,* October 2, 2000.

SEE ALSO: iVillage.com; Oprah.com; Virtual Communities

WORKFORCE, E-COMMERCE

The e-commerce workforce is a large, indistinct mass of working people that overlaps and blends gradually into other sectors of the economy, such as information technology, manufacturing, and retail. As the 21st century began, the Bureau of Labor Statistics, the Census Bureau, and other government agencies were taking the first halting steps to track the size and extent of the American e-commerce workforce. Part of the problem is definition—what *is* it? Does it consist only of workers at the so-called ''dot-coms''—firms that derive 95 percent or more of their revenues from business on the World Wide Web but that, according to a study by the Center for Research in Electronic Commerce (CREC), make up a mere 9.6 percent of the Internet economy? Or should it include workers at any companies that produce *anything* for the Internet, that do *any* business online, or that have *any* Web presence? The government lumps e-commerce workers in with the Information Technology (IT) sector, which includes manufacturers of computers, computer parts, software, and components; software and applications developers; database managers; hardware and software engineers; as well as the Internet, but tracks only "core IT" workers, namely computer scientists and engineers, systems analysts, and computer programmers. But what about people who design the marketing campaigns, write the Web site content and pack the boxes at Amazon.com? The waters are murky indeed.

According to a 2001 study done by the CREC at the University of Texas, in mid-2000 the Internet economy supported 3.08 million workers, a number larger than the insurance (2.36 million) or real estate (1.5 million) industries. The CREC further broke down the Internet economy into four constituent sectors: an infrastructure sector which employed 932,484; an application sector which employed 740,673; an intermediary sector which employed 468,689; and, an Internet commerce sector which employed a workforce of over 1.03 million. In 2000 dot.coms employed about 360,718.

Despite Census Bureau metrics, e-commerce is more than IT jobs. According to the Web site Internet Economy Indicators, the highest percentage in 2000 of workers in e-commerce were in sales and marketing, who comprised 33 percent of the total e-commerce workforce. IT workers made up only 28 percent. Operations and manufacturing accounted for 17 percent; accounting and finance for 12 percent; and administration, executives, and others for 10 percent of e-commerce workers. The surveys of the Association of Internet Professionals' membership provide a partial breakdown of typical job titles in e-business. They include graphic designers, art directors, copywriters, Web designers, Web production and coding specialists, project managers, content developers, systems administrators, multimedia specialists, technical support, network engineers, database designers, and database administrators. To these mostly Web-specific jobs can be added customer service people, warehouse clerks, shipping and receiving help, accountants, human services departments, and virtually every other job title found in modern retail and corporate life.

Salaries in the Web economy vary by job, size of the firm and location. In late 2000 an *Industry Standard* survey reported that the average annual salary of

Internet workers was $85,000, $54,000 more than the private industry average. Those Internet workers put in 10 hour days on the average, along with one weekend a month. According to the same survey, the median salary of a CEO in a Web firm was $204,000 plus additional bonuses and cash compensation. In contrast, the typical Internet desk jockey earned about $50,000, sometimes with stock options. According to the *Industry Standard,* however, most rank-and-file Internet workers considered the size of their salaries far more important than any stock option plan. According to the government's *Digital Economy 2000,* a webmaster in California earned an average salary of $59,600, while her counterpart in New England earned an average of only $43,800. A company with more than $500 billion in annual revenues paid a webmaster $58,600, more than $10,000 more than a company with less than $100 billion in revenues.

The Internet workforce grew rapidly through much of 2000. During the first half of the year, it added 612,375 new workers, almost as much as entered the industry in all of 1999. Employment in the Web economy grew at a remarkably faster pace during this period than in the economy as a whole. It increased by 29 percent between the first quarter of 1999 and the first quarter of 2000, compared to a meager 6.9 percent for non-Internet workers. As late as October 2000, companies were complaining of a serious shortage in skilled e-commerce help. However, the layoffs that accompanied the dot.com crash were already underway. Between June 2000 and April 2001, according to CREC statistics, some 93,979 Internet workers lost their jobs, about 3 percent of the whole Web economy. They continued through the first half of 2001. It was not as bad as it at first seemed it might be. Dot.coms announced 87,795 layoffs; less than half that number actually lost their jobs, however—about 41,000 between were put out of work between October 2000 and July 2001.

The bust had immediate repercussions on workers—at least in the dot.com sector. Salaries flattened out, and frequent raises and benefits like flex hours and casual workplace all but disappeared. In late 2001, laid-off workers were facing long job searches and to compromising their demands for salaries and perks. Union organizers found Internet workers, at Amazon.com for example, more open to their arguments. On the other hand, many laid-off dot.commers could boast of levels of management experience that others needed years at a traditional companies to acquire.

FURTHER READING:

Mahoney, Michael. "Dot-Com Job Cuts Fall to 12-Month Low." *E-Commerce Times,* August 29, 2001.

———. "E-Commerce Layoffs: Storm on the Tech Frontier." *E-Commerce Times,* May 08, 2001.

"PwC Report Rates Best Recruiting & Retention Practices." *Report on Salary Surveys,* October 2000.

Regan, Keith. "For Dot-Com Workers, Double Trouble Post-Bubble." *E-Commerce Times,* August 24, 2001.

Said, Carolyn. "Dot-Com Disasters Have Opened Door a Crack for Unions." *San Francisco Chronicle,* December 3, 2000.

U.S. Department of Labor. *Digital Economy 2000.* Washington, D.C.: GPO, June 2000.

SEE ALSO: Talent, Recruiting and Retaining

WORLD INTELLECTUAL PROPERTY ORGANIZATION (WIPO)

Headquartered in Geneva, Switzerland, the World Intellectual Property Organization (WIPO) comprises one of 16 specialized international agencies affiliated with the United Nations (UN). WIPO oversees the enforcement of 21 international treaties concerning the protection of intellectual property. By 2000, it possessed 175 member nations and an international staff of 760. WIPO is funded primarily through earnings from its three major intellectual property registration systems.

International safeguards for intellectual property, such as patents and trademarks, began in 1883 with the Paris Convention for the Protection of Industrial Property. The Paris Convention granted protection to inventors for their inventions and ideas in foreign countries, as well as their country of residence. The 14 signatory nations instituted an International Bureau—a forerunner of WIPO—to enforce the Convention's terms. The international protection of artistic intellectual property followed in 1886 with the drafting of the Berne Convention for the Protection of Literary and Artistic Works. It gave artists and other creators control over the use of, and payment for, their works in the fine and performing arts. The Berne Convention also instituted a regulatory bureau. The two bureaus merged in 1893 into the United International Bureaux for the Protection of Intellectual Property (BIRPI), located in Berne, Switzerland. BIRPI formed the nucleus for WIPO.

BIRPI transferred to Geneva in 1960 and in 1970 changed its name to WIPO; it became a UN organization four years later. In 1996, WIPO entered a cooperative agreement with the World Trade Organization (WTO). WIPO's duties have grown from administering four international treaties to administering 21. Its work is conducted through its secretariat and by its member states. Among its primary duties, WIPO attempts to harmonize intellectual property legislation among nations, assist with applications for industrial property rights, arbitrate private intellectual property disputes, and help nations share intellectual property information.

WIPO fosters international intellectual property protection through 11 treaties that delineate common intellectual-property protection standards; all States that sign these treaties agree to enforce them within their own territories. Several WIPO treaties—the Patent Cooperation Treaty (PCT), Madrid Agreement, and the Hague Agreement—directly protect international patents, trademarks, and industrial designs, by guaranteeing that a single international filing is enforced by all WIPO signatory States. These treaties allow a creator or inventor to avoid making individual applications in each country for which they would like to obtain intellectual property protection. Between 1979 and 1999, the number of international patent applications increased nearly 30-fold.

WIPO generated several initiatives to tackle the burgeoning importance of information technology with regard to international intellectual-property issues. WIPO addressed the expanding world of global e-commerce in 1999, when it announced its Digital Agenda—an initiative to develop programs and procedures that encourage the online dissemination and use of intellectual property, such as music, films, and trade marks, while safeguarding the rights of creators and owners. The Digital Agenda also targets the need to integrate developing countries into the global online environment, since they are in danger of falling behind industrialized nations with the growing digital divide. Finally, the Digital Agenda seeks to modify existing intellectual property laws so that they address the particular intellectual property concerns associated with the Web.

In January 2000 WIPO launched the Information Management for the Patent Cooperation Treaty (IMPACT) Project. IMPACT, which constitutes the organization's largest information technology undertaking to date, will fully automate the workings of the PCT by providing electronic filing capabilities for applicants and electronic data transfer between WIPO, patent offices, and the PCT International Searching and Preliminary Examining Authorities.

Another such endeavor is WIPOnet, an online network linking independent intellectual property offices around the globe. Besides permitting the swift exchange of information, the streamlining of application procedures, and the development of common intellectual property standards, WIPOnet seeks to integrate developing countries within the digital environment. To this end, WIPO helps furnish intellectual property offices in such nations with Internet connections and basic information technology equipment. Modernization of intellectual property systems in developing countries is also facilitated through WIPO's

Nationally-Focused Action Plans (NFAPs), which are tailored to the needs of each country.

In 1999, WIPO turned its attention to the increasingly common problem of ''cybersquatting.'' Cybersquatters register domain names that approximate the names of well-known companies, brands, or celebrities. Squatters try to generate profit from the high recognition value of such names by drawing traffic to their sites, reselling the name, or holding the name for ''ransom'' in hopes of accruing a payoff from the entity whose name has been appropriated. The Internet Corporation for Assigned Names and Numbers (ICANN) has authorized WIPO to handle cases filed under the Uniform Domain Name Dispute Resolution Policy. Many media celebrities have taken their cybersquatting complaints to WIPO for arbitration.

FURTHER READING:

D'Amico, Mary Lisbeth. ''First Cybersquatting Case Settled.'' *Computerworld,* January 24, 2000.

''WIPO Tackles the Net.'' *Managing Intellectual Property,* October, 1999.

World Intellectual Property Organization. ''WIPO-World Intellectual Property Organization.'' Geneva, Switzerland: World Intellectual Property Organization, 2001. Available from www.wipo.org.

SEE ALSO: Cybersquatting; Internet Corporation for Assigned Names and Numbers (ICANN)

WORLD WIDE WEB

The World Wide Web is one of several utilities—including e-mail, File Transfer Protocol (FTP), Internet Relay Chat (IRC), Telnet and Usenet—that form the Internet. Based on a 1989 proposal from Tim Berners-Lee, it was developed at the European Center for Nuclear Research as a way to share information about nuclear physics. At the heart of the Web is a system of many Web servers—computers or software programs that make it possible for end-users to view and teleport between Web pages, or specially formatted documents commonly written in Hypertext Markup Language (HTML). The World Wide Web Consortium (W3C) describes the Web as ''the universe of network-accessible information, the embodiment of human knowledge.''

Locations on the World Wide Web, which commonly reside on individual servers, are known as Web sites. Web sites have individual addresses called uniform resource locators (URLs), which must be used to gain access. Upon visiting a Web site, visitors normally begin on its home page. This document often serves as an index to other content within the site, or contains hypertext links to content residing on a different Web site.

Web pages are viewed through software applications called Web browsers. Microsoft's Internet Explorer and Netscape's Navigator were the two popular Web browsers during the 1990s and early 2000s. Web browsers are the essential link between end-users and a vast sea of static pictures, video, sounds, and text. Said differently, they also enable buyers and sellers of goods and services to engage in electronic commerce.

Because of the Web, consumers and companies began to engage in electronic commerce during the 1990s. After an initial boom, some Internet companies folded or watched their stock value drop in the early 2000s. However, the Web's impact on the economy has been significant. According to the U.S. Department of Commerce, the digital economy was a critical factor in the United States' economic growth during the mid-to-late 1990s, accounting for one third of the nation's real economic growth during that period, according to *Nua Internet Surveys.* The growth of e-commerce exceeded the U.S. Department of Commerce's projections during this period, according to Nua. Furthermore, the department predicted ''that almost half of all U.S. workers will work in industries that either produce IT products or use IT products extensively by 2006.

According to *Global Cosmetic Industry,* ''During first quarter 2000, shoppers spent $7 billion at e-commerce sites—merely the tip of the iceberg considering these sales generated an estimated $13.8 billion in offline purchases.'' Citing information from *eMarketer,* the publication also noted that e-commerce sales were expected to reach $303 billion by the end of 2001.

According to data released in late 2000 from the OCLC Web Characterization Project, at that time the Web consisted of 7.1 million unique Web sites, 41 percent of which were available to the public. Twenty-one percent of sites were private (restricted to subscribers or other private parties) and the remainder (38 percent) were considered provisional sites, meaning that they were in an unfinished state. According to the project, while the Web was growing at a rapid pace, growth was occurring more slowly than in past years. Additionally, the amount of private or restricted content was increasing.

Because of its very nature, the Web holds strong potential for international e-commerce. According to data from Jupiter Research reported in *InformationWeek,* by 2005 75 percent of the world's Web market is expected to live outside of the United States, compared to 45 percent in 1999. Additionally, according to International Data Corp. (IDC), total Internet spending amounted to $130.5 billion in 1999, 62 percent of which occurred in the United States. While IDC predicted total e-commerce spending would reach $1.6 trillion by 2003, the United States was expected to account for less than half of this amount ($726 billion).

Along with large companies, a growing number of small businesses also found a place on the Web. However, according to information from the 19th Annual Dun & Bradstreet Small Business Survey, reported in *Community Banker,* more than half of the survey's respondents indicated that the Web has not had a measurable impact on their business. Seventy-one percent of respondents indicated that e-mail was the main reason they used the Internet.

In addition to using the Web for marketing or education, companies also have incorporated other business practices into the online environment. One example is supply chain management (SCM) software, which is used to track inventories, sales, and orders. According to *Network World,* ''retailers, distributors, and manufacturers want to share logistics information by giving trading partners and even consumers direct Web access to their SCM systems. In addition, some industries, such as grocery and apparel retailing, are starting to use shared Web-based online supply chains as hosted business-to-business exchanges.'' Some companies also began to integrate traditional telephone call centers—the places where customer service calls are handled or orders are taken for products or services—with Web pages and other Internet technologies like e-mail and chat rooms.

FURTHER READING:

Gareiss, Dawn. ''Business on the World Wide Web.'' *InformationWeek* December 11, 2000.

''OCLC researchers measure the World Wide Web.'' *OCLC,* October 16, 2000. Available from www.oclc.org.

Saral, Katie. ''http://the.worldwide.web: How To Get Started.'' *Global Cosmetic Industry,* December 2000.

''Small Businesses are Using the Web But are Skeptical.'' *Community Banker,* August 2000.

''U.S. Department of Commerce: Digital Economy Driving U.S. Growth.'' *Nua Internet Surveys,* June 24, 2000. Available from www.nua.ie/surveys.

''World Wide Web.'' *Ecommerce Webopedia,* February 10, 2001. Available from e-comm.webopedia.com.

''World Wide Web.'' *Tech Encyclopedia,* February 10, 2001. Available from www.techweb.com/encyclopedia.

SEE ALSO: Berners-Lee, Timothy; HTML; History of the Internet and WWW; New Economy; Web Site Basics; World Wide Web Consortium (W3C)

WORLD WIDE WEB CONSORTIUM (W3C)

While not a governing body, the World Wide Web Consortium (W3C) was the leading organization devoted to setting a path for the Web's development, settling disputes related to emerging technologies and practices, and implementing standards that companies, organizations, governments, and individuals overwhelmingly adopt. As such, the W3C carries enormous power, even if it chooses to exercise its power in a soft-spoken manner.

The W3C was founded in 1994 by Tim Berners-Lee, the developer of the World Wide Web. Berners-Lee launched the W3C at MIT's Laboratory for Computer Science in collaboration with the Geneva-based Centre Europen de Recherche Nucleaire (European Laboratory for Particle Physics, or CERN), where Berners-Lee had first developed the Web. At the time, the leading organization overseeing the development of the Internet was the Internet Engineering Task Force (IETF). One of Berners-Lee's ambitions was to grow an organization that would be more nimble and effective than the IETF. The IETF, however, was focused on the Internet itself, and when the Web came along in the early 1990s it was unprepared for the new medium. As a result, the IETF and the W3C jointly allocated to the IETF only smaller-scale issues involving the World Wide Web, such as the specifications for the Hypertext Transfer Protocol (HTTP). Thus, the IETF focuses on lower-level technical problems, while the W3C handles a broader range of issues more closely guiding the Web's development.

Over 500 organizations count themselves as members of the World Wide Web Consortium and work on its various task forces. Centered at the Massachusetts Institute of Technology (MIT) and with research centers in France and Japan, the W3C explains its work more in terms of a research and development organization rather than a standards body. The W3C's work extends beyond devising standards to the development of actual technologies, from software to tools to specifications. The World Wide Web Consortium was the leading developer of a number of technical specifications, including such central developments as Extensible Markup Language (XML), which was poised to become a critical part of the e-commerce architecture.

The W3C's activities are organized into five categories: the Architecture Domain, which focuses on the technologies of the Web's basic structure; the Document Formats Domain, which is devoted to the development of technical formats and languages for the presentation of information on the Web; the Interaction Domain, which promotes the Web's capabilities for interaction with users; the Technology and Society Domain, which considers the Web's place in the context of the broader society and develops standards and technologies to address particular social and legal issues; and the Web Accessibility Initiative (WAI), which is devoted to bringing Web access to all people, regardless of particular disabilities.

A major focus of the W3C's activities through the 1990s and early 2000s was the mediation of technical disputes so as to stave off proprietary battles that could lead to the privatization of the Web or the closing off of segments of the Web behind a wall of commercial interests. The organization's goal in this area was to keep the Web a seamless whole freely accessible to all. The development of specifications at the W3C, then, aims to prevent the fragmentation of the Web. Berners-Lee, for instance, worries that without mediated guidance, companies following the commercial incentive to readjust standards to their own advantage could end up causing incompatibility between media-say, between Web televisions and Web browsers-and thereby splinter the Web.

Maintaining the decentralized nature of the Web is another primary area of the W3C's concern, and among the reasons the W3C insists it isn't a governing body. The Web, according to the W3C, is emblematic of the modern distributed system. In addition to avoiding the bottlenecks and other technical difficulties involved in centralizing the Web, the W3C opposes the principle that the Web be controlled by any central governing body, seeing in such a prospect a means whereby the Web's freedom and universality could be compromised. The W3C's role as mediator highlights its aim of keeping the Web a medium that develops by consensus rather than by fiat.

Crucially, then, the W3C is explicitly vendor and market neutral. To ensure this neutrality, the organization invites the public to comment on specifications through their development process and afterwards, and works to build consensus between competing vendors and markets. In the late 1990s, the W3C mediated some of the disputes between Netscape and Microsoft and was successful in providing a forum through which the companies could reach a common platform and avoid fragmenting the Web with competing standards.

FURTHER READING:

Anthes, Gary H. "W3C's World Wide Power." *Computerworld,* September 6, 1999.

"The World Wide Web Consortium." Cambridge, MA: The World Wide Web Consortium, 2001. Available from www.w3.org/.

SEE Berners-Lee, Tim
ALSO:

WORMS

Worms are destructive, self-replicating computer viruses that spread via e-mail. Once a user activates a worm—usually by opening an infected file attachment—the virus makes copies of itself and sends them to some or all of the e-mail addresses in the user's address book. The ability to spread rapidly makes worms especially dangerous, since much damage can be done before infected users know what is happening. By overloading them with messages and eating up system resources like memory, worms cause e-mail servers, computer networks, and standalone personal computers to crash. Some worms also erase or alter files. Among the most well-known worms were Worm.ExploreZip, LoveLetter, NewLove, Prilissa, Melissa, Killer Resume, Bubbleboy, Morris, Code Red, and, perhaps most potentially destructive of all, Nimda, which hit in September 2001.

In the early 2000s, the increasing appearance of polymorphic and metamorphic worms, such as LoveLetter, caused concern among both users and those responsible for administering large computer systems. Polymorphic worms have the ability to change their form through the use of encryption. They are programmed to periodically decrypt themselves, change slightly, and then encrypt again to avoid detection by anti-virus software. Metamorphic worms use special tools called mutation engines to periodically create new, slightly different versions of themselves that avoid detection.

In addition to being a nuisance, the damage caused by worms and other viruses results in real costs for companies doing business on the Web, some of which are passed on to consumers in the form of higher costs for products and services. According to *InfoWorld,* Carlsbad, California-based Computer Economics estimated that companies devoted $7.6 billion to virus attacks in the first half of 1999 alone. Additionally, according to a *Network World,* article by Ellen Messmer, 41 percent of companies surveyed by the International Computer Security Association (ICSA) said the LoveLetter worm ''inflicted a 'disaster' in their networks, shutting down servers and costing companies an average of $120,000 based on productivity and other measures.''

Companies devote an increasing amount of resources to the prevention of worms and other viruses. In the early 2000s, along with using anti-virus software, some organizations formed 24-hour virus response teams, wrote emergency response policies, and used virus scanning servers to check the integrity of incoming e-mail messages before they entered computer networks. According to Fontana's article, Portland, Maine-based Fairchild Semiconductor even dropped the use of file attachments and forbids the distribution of executable files via e-mail within the company. While Fairchild's actions may appear to be extreme, such measures may be necessary in an age when, according to the ICSA, virus infections are increasing rapidly.

FURTHER READING:

Fontana, John. "Defending Against Outlook Viruses." *Network World,* July 3, 2000.

McClure, Stuart, and Joel Scambray. "Virus Threats of Past and Present Reveal Current State of the Digital Immune System." *InfoWorld,* July 12, 1999.

McNamara, Paul. "Worm Outbreak has Managers Fishing for Answers." *Network World,* June 21, 1999.

Messmer, Ellen. "Experts Predict More Mutating Viruses." *Network World,* October 30, 2000.

Riggs, Brian. "New Worm Viruses Threaten Windows PCs." *InformationWeek,* November 29, 1999.

Schar, Steve. "The Last Laugh." *Credit Union Management,* September, 1999.

"Worm." *Techencyclopedia,* February 12, 2001. Available from www.techweb.com/encyclopedia.

SEE ALSO: Computer Crime; Computer Security; Denial of Service Attack; National Information Infrastructure Protection Act of 1996; National Infrastructure Protection Center; Viruses

WOZNIAK, STEPHEN

Stephen "Woz" Wozniak was born on August 11, 1950, in San Jose, California. He grew up in Sunnyvale, California, which is located in the Santa Clara Valley. This area became a center of high-technology research and development in the 1950s and 1960s and acquired the nickname, Silicon Valley. Wozniak's father was an aerospace engineer at Lockheed.

Although Wozniak shared the same interests as other young boys when he was growing up, he also took an early interest in electronics and computers. He read books and magazines about computer innovations, software programs, and electronic products. At age 11 or 12 he built his own amateur "ham" radio and earned an operator's license. As a teenager he designed computers and software programs, although he couldn't afford to make any of the designs a reality.

Wozniak also designed and built a variety of electronic gadgets, some of them for science fairs, others for his own personal use. His ability to create electronic inventions earned him the nickname, "Woz the Wiz." The "Woz" nickname has stuck with him throughout his life.

After graduating from Cupertino's Homestead High School in 1968, Wozniak attended the University of Colorado at Boulder for one year. He then returned to Sunnyvale and began working as a programmer for a small computer company. Although his electronics and computer projects kept him busy, he did not abandon college altogether. After taking some classes at a local community college, he transferred to the University of California at Berkeley to continue his engineering studies.

COMPUTERS INTERRUPT COLLEGE, THE 1970S

After finishing his junior year at UC-Berkeley, Wozniak took a summer job at Hewlett-Packard. The summer job turned into a 10-year career, and Wozniak didn't return to UC-Berkeley until 1981, after he and Steve Jobs co-founded Apple Computer Co.

While working for Hewlett-Packard during the summer of 1970, Wozniak also spent time working on his own computer designs with his friend Bill Fernandez. One of Fernandez's friends was 15-year-old Steve Jobs, who shared Wozniak's fascination with computer technology. Wozniak and Jobs began to share ideas and tinker with electronic projects together. They also shared a love of practical jokes and technological challenges. In one instance, they created an electronic device that could tap into telephone company computers to make free long-distance calls.

Wozniak and Jobs joined the Homebrew Computer Club in 1975. The group consisted of computer programmers and engineers who met informally to discuss computers, software, and electronics. Wozniak was inspired by their enthusiasm for computer technology and decided to design a computer that would incorporate all of the latest technological advances into one simple machine. At the time computers were massive, complex machines that only computer professionals could use.

Wozniak first wrote a detailed software program for the yet-to-be-built computer. Then he found inexpensive and easy-to-find components to build a personal computer for the software to run on. When he showed it to the members of the Homebrew Computer Club, they were impressed, but none more than Steve Jobs. Jobs convinced Wozniak they should establish a company to sell the new computer.

CO-FOUNDS APPLE COMPUTER CO., 1976

Wozniak and Jobs used Jobs' parents' garage in Los Altos for their base of operations to build the new computer. They settled on the name Apple, and in April 1976 Apple Computer Co. officially went into business. Wozniak was responsible for computer and software design, while Jobs handled marketing and sales and other aspects of the business. The company's first computer was called the Apple I. Within a few weeks a local computer shop placed an order for $50,000 worth of computers, forcing Wozniak and Jobs to borrow money to build and deliver the computers on time.

During Apple's first year Wozniak continued to work on improvements to the Apple I while still holding a job at Hewlett-Packard. By the end of 1976, however, Jobs and new business partner Mike Markkula convinced Wozniak, who had recently married, to leave Hewlett-Packard and work full time for Apple. In January 1977 Apple officially incorporated and moved into a new office in Cupertino.

After working full-time on his new computer design for a couple of months, Wozniak completed his design for the Apple II in 1977. The new computer was the first fully assembled programmable computer that was small enough to fit on a desktop. Among its innovative features were a high-resolution color video display, a cassette-tape interface, and a built-in keyboard. The computer also included a plastic case and a built-in speaker for sound.

The Apple II came to be regarded as the world's first personal computer. It was also an immediate success, and Apple recorded $2 million in sales by the end of 1977. Seeking to make even more improvements to the Apple II, Wozniak, together with programmer Randy Wigginton, invented a flexible disk drive to replace the cassette-tape interface. The flexible disk drive read information from a floppy diskette instead of a cassette tape. By mid-1978 all Apple II computers came with a flexible disk drive. The creation of the flexible disk drive was another innovation that is now regarded as an important step in the development of personal computers.

DECADE OF CHANGE, 1980-1990

Apple's success made more than 40 Apple employees and investors millionaires by the start of the new decade, and Jobs, Wozniak, and Markkula became very wealthy as a result. For Wozniak, the 1980s were a time of great changes and new directions. His first marriage ended in divorce in 1980. In 1981 he was seriously injured, along with his new fiancée Candi Clark, when a small plane that he was piloting crashed on the runway. Wozniak suffered head injuries that affected his short-term memory.

As Apple grew into a big company in the 1980s, Wozniak became dissatisfied with his role there. Following the plane crash, he took a leave of absence and, from then on, did only limited engineering work for Apple. While on leave in the early 1980s, Wozniak spent his energy organizing a three-day music festival that was held on Labor Day in 1982 and again in 1983. The US Festival featured top acts such as Fleetwood Mac and the Grateful Dead and was staged by noted rock promoter Bill Graham.

For his work on designing personal computers, Wozniak was awarded the National Medal of Technology in 1985. He resigned from Apple in 1985, the same year Jobs left the company. After selling his Apple stock for an estimated $70 million, Wozniak formed a new company, CL9, to design and market a universal remote-control device that he invented known as Core. CL9 merged with another company, Tech Force, that manufactured toy robots operated by remote-control devices. After failing to turn a profit, Tech Force went out of business in 1990.

By the 1990s Wozniak was out of the business world. His marriage to former Olympic kayaker Candi Clark ended in divorce in 1990. Later that year he married Suzanne Mulkern, an attorney with three children. Together with Wozniak's three children from his marriage with Clark, the family was a big one. When his son Jesse discovered computers at age 9 in 1991, Wozniak was inspired to begin a class for Jesse and some of his classmates in the summer of 1992. He bought them Apple Macintosh PowerBooks and taught them three times a week from his office in Silicon Valley. By 1993 Jesse's computer class had grown to 12 students, and Wozniak began another one with 20 fifth-grade students. The class consisted of hand-picked students and met after school.

During the 1990s Wozniak's connection to the modern computer industry was limited to occasional speeches on technology issues and appearances at Macworld conventions. He established his own Web site where visitors can exchange e-mail with him and read about his views on computer technology. The site also features WozCam video cameras that are installed throughout his seven-bedroom house in Los Gatos. In 2000 Wozniak was named to the Inventors Hall of Fame.

FURTHER READING:

Kendall, Martha E. *Steve Wozniak: Inventor of the Apple Computer.* Los Gatos, CA: Highland Publishing Group, 2000.

Min, Janice. ''Wizard of Woz: Apple's Steve Wozniak Is Reprogrammed—As a Grade-School Teacher.'' *People Weekly,* February 14, 1994.

Picarille, Lisa. ''Apple's Engineering Genius—Steve Wozniak.'' *Computer Reseller News,* November 15, 1998.

Sellers, Dennis. ''Apple Cofounder Named to Hall of Fame.'' *Computer User,* September 2000.

''Steve Wozniak.'' *Biography Today: Scientists and Inventors Series* Vol. 7. Detroit: Omnigraphics, 2001.

SEE ALSO: Apple Computer; Jobs, Steven

X

Palo Alto, California-based X.com served as one of the first online banking sites from its launch in December 1999 through October of 2001, when founder Elon Musk decided to shut down its operations. The firm merged with online payment services provider PayPal in March of 2000, and those operations are what remain of X.com. The largest Internet-based payment network in the world, PayPal offers its services to roughly 8 million customers, many of whom use the online payment provider to conduct person-to-person (P2P) transactions on auction site eBay.

X.com was created by the 28-year-old founder of Zip2 Corp., Elon Musk, in late 1999. Musk envisioned X.com as a full-scale banking and investment services site that offered everything from checking accounts to insurance services, mortgage lending, and bonds. He hired investment banker John Story as executive vice president and former Intuit Corp. CEO Bill Harris as president and CEO. Musk took on the role of chairman. The firm employed 15 staff members when the site-powered by Sanchez Computers Associates' e-PROFILE Internet bank solution—became operational. Roughly $25 million in venture capital had come from Musk and Harris, as well as from Sequoia Capital.

To attract new clients, X.com offered $20 to anyone who opened a free online checking account. Members who referred new customers to X.com were awarded $10 for each referral. Instant credit was also available to those who qualified. To make money, the firm planned to do what traditional lenders did—rely on the interest rate spreads between what it earned on loans and what it paid on accounts. Within two months, X.com had secured 100,000 customers, compared to Etrade Telebank, the largest World Wide Web-based bank, with 130,000 customers. However, according to *Forbes* columnist Elizabeth Corcoran, cash incentives were not enough to ease consumer fears regarding virtual banking, particularly after X.com was forced to admit its initial site design had allowed for fraud. "In January X.com conceded that it had designed its system in a way that made it too easy to siphon other people's money into an X.com account from traditional bank accounts. X.com detected about half a dozen questionable transfers and the money was returned." To prevent this from happening in the future, the firm required new clients to submit a canceled check if they planned to withdraw money from an account.

In March 2000, X.com merged with PayPal, which had been in operation since November of 1999, retaining the X.com name. At the time, PayPal was brining in nearly 15,000 new clients a day with its P2P payment services. To register, PayPal visitors were simply asked to input their name, daytime phone number, home address, and email address. PayPal members were then able to email funds to any other PayPal account holder via an automated email message titled, "You've Got Cash!" The funds could be charged to a credit card via an online form at the PayPal site, or they could be withdrawn from a bank account, providing the user had supplied adequate verification of account ownership.

In June, X.com expanded PayPal services to allow for payments between businesses and consumers (B2C), including those made on cell phones. Clients who deposited funds into an X.com account by electronic fund transfer, credit card transfer, or check, were able to pay bills either at the X.com Web site or by pushing the letter "x" on their cell phones and then entering the email address of the payee. Businesses that accepted payments made via PayPal were assessed no monthly fee, compared to the typical 2.9 percent fee charged by credit card firms. Instead, PayPal levied a 1.9 percent charge for each transaction completed, compared to the industry standard of 30 cents per credit card transaction.

Management differences prompted Harris to leave just six months after joining the new firm. The following month, X.com began offering online payment services on the Evite.com event planning Web site. As a result, Evite users in the U.S. could make a payment at the same time they responded to an online invitation. X.com's P2P customers grew to exceed 3 million in August. It was then that the firm began focusing on business-to-business (B2B) payments, wanting to penetrate that market as well as it had the P2P market. As a result, X.com forged a deal with BuyLink Corp., a San Francisco-based online marketplace that served roughly 8,300 retailers and 3,000 manufacturers. Using the PayPal service, BuyLink users were able to make instant payments to one another. The firm faced more negative publicity when 125 PayPal users who bought computer hard drives at an online auction failed to receive what they had purchased. This, along with the fact that the value of transactions conducted over PayPal were increasing, prompted X.com to begin offering fraud protection, similar to the protection offered by credit card companies. As part of its new Cybersource Fraud Scan, the firm also put in place a member information guide, which allowed buyers to verify that sellers had been reviewed by X.com.

In October, Musk "launched a major redirection of the company's strategy," wrote *American Banker* columnist Megan J. Ptacek. "Rather than offer a wide range of banking and related services, the Palo Alto, Calif., company will become solely a global payment system." By then PayPal was serving 4 million P2P customers and handled roughly 50 percent of the transactions conducted on auction powerhouse eBay. As a result of Musk's decision, X.com reversed its plans to buy First Western National Bank, a purchase that had been planned as a means to gain Federal Deposit Insurance for its virtual accounts. To increase its foothold in the B2C and B2B markets, X.com began working on forging alliances with insurance firms, banks, and other financial institutions. Via a five-year agreement with Intuit Inc., X.com gained exclusive rights to provide online payment services to the three million small business customers using Intuit technology. Eventually, X.com officially changed its name to PayPal.

International expansion efforts, which included allowing Internet users outside the U.S. to open PayPal accounts, began late in 2000. For example, PayPal and financial services powerhouse ING Group began working to extend email payment services throughout Europe. By March of 2001, the firm had expanded its reach to 26 countries. That month, PayPal put together a listing of 5,600 "PayPal Shops," which allowed shoppers to easily locate merchants that accepted PayPal payments. In June, PayPal and Providian Corp. began offering a credit card that rewarded PayPal members with various perks. Efforts to increase B2B and B2C operations continued into 2001.

FURTHER READING:

Carlsen, Clifford. "PayPal Lands $90M in Funding." *TheDeal.com,* March 6, 2001. Available from www.TheDeal.com.

Corcoran, Elizabeth. "Something Better Than Free." *Forbes,* February 21, 2000.

Perry, Joellen. "Settling Debts Online: A New Tool for E-mailers." *U.S. News & World Report,* April 17, 2000.

Ptacek, Megan J. "X.com Scraps Bank Strategy to Focus on PayPal System." *American Banker,* October 11, 2000.

Rosen, Cheryl. "New Services Let Users Pay Bills Via Cell Phone-Analysts Say Instant Payments Through Mobile Devices are the Wave of the Future." *InformationWeek,* June 19, 2000.

Toonkel, Jessica. "Electronic Commerce: X.com Moving In to B-to-B Online Payments." *American Banker,* August 9, 2000.

SEE ALSO: Banking, Online; Musk, Elon; PayPal; Peer-to-Peer Technology

XML (EXTENSIBLE MARKUP LANGUAGE)

By the early 2000s, Extensible Markup Language (XML) was fast emerging as the lingua franca of the World Wide Web, augmenting and superseding Hypertext Markup Language (HTML), the dominant language for encoding content since the Web's inception. HTML was increasingly viewed as too basic and inflexible to effectively transmit and format new forms of Web information, particularly the highly structured data needed for business-to-business e-commerce.

While XML is popularly known as a language, experts call it a metalanguage—a grammar that defines the language's rules and processes. Whereas HTML employs a limited number of set *tags* to define the form of Web-based content, XML is nearly infinite in its capacities to define not only the form but also the content itself. This means there is no single, universal collection of tags that make up XML: individual users, companies, industries, and other groups are able to define new languages and attributes appropriate to their specific needs.

Technically, XML doesn't replace HTML, but envelopes it. XML's flexibility makes it compatible with the existing HTML infrastructure while allowing for greater integration with other forms of electronic data. XML thus streamlines the transfer of data across networks, systems, and computer platforms and defines form and content both on the Web, for hard copies, on CD-ROM, and in other media.

Unlike HTML, XML tags aren't primarily presentation-oriented. Rather, well-formed XML—a phrase insiders use to describe tag schemes that employ XML's full powers and best practices—uses tags to influence the look, function, and meaning of content. The organization of a document is set by a document type definition (DTD), allowing it to appear in formats appropriate to the technological needs and capabilities of whoever is viewing the document. To tailor the document to its required form, it is mediated by parsing software that reads its DTD and translates the document into the medium required. In other words, the parser, rather than the medium (such as a Web browser), actually reads and interprets the document.

The World Wide Web Consortium (W3C) launched its XML Working Group in September 1996 to devise improved methods of organizing and integrating data, and to work towards harmonizing tag-naming conventions to avoid overlap that could confuse XML parsers. XML Version 1.0 was rolled out in December 1997 as a W3C recommendation, and the organization ratified XML as a standard the following February. A revised edition was released in October 2000, still known as XML 1.0. In 2001 the W3C formally adopted a DTD standard replace the existing business-created DTDs developed for the exchange of business documents using XML.

One key benefit of XML that emerged in the early 2000s was facilitating data integration between markets, leading to greater convergence of online marketplaces and business-to-business e-commerce. By allowing a common framework through which different methods of organizing and sharing information over networks are made compatible, XML helps bridge data communication between industry groupings that previously developed their own, mutually exclusive networks.

Speed-bumps to XML adoption persisted in the early 2000s. Some parsers, for instance, remained excessively strict in their translation of XML documents. But most analysts expected these problems to be largely ironed out, and many expected XML to become the document-transfer standard by the mid-2000s.

FURTHER READING:

Abualsamid, Ahmad. "A Metalanguage for the Ages." *Network Computing,* April 3, 2000.

———. "XML: A Metastar is Born." *Network Computing,* April 16, 2001.

Luh, James C. "The ABCs of XML." *Internet World,* March 1, 2000.

Radding, Alan. "XML: The Language of Integration." *Information Week,* November 1, 1999. Available from www.informationweek.com.

SEE ALSO: HTML (Hypertext Markup Language); Programming Language; Web Scripting Language; World Wide Web Consortium (W3C); XML Schema

XML SCHEMA

Hypertext Markup Language (HTML) was widely used to determine how information was displayed on Web pages in the early 2000s. HTML is very similar to Standard Generalized Markup Language (SGML) and a subset of SGML called eXtensible Markup Language (XML). While HTML determines how information is displayed on a Web page, XML deals with the actual information that gets displayed. Its importance to the world of e-commerce centers on its ability to enable information to be shared in a universal way, regardless of the computer systems or applications a company might be using. As *ABA Banking Journal* explained, "XML is a set of simple rules for converting the meaning of a document written in any software into a globally standardized format that any other software can understand." Alternative ways of sharing information often require companies to make special arrangements.

As with HTML, XML involves presenting data within tags. Models called XML schemas are used to determine how these tags are arranged within a document and to ensure the information they contain is valid based on predetermined criteria. They are more effective and expansive than document type definition (DTD) schemas used by SGML, especially for ensuring the validity of a document. Validity is very important to companies engaging in e-commerce because they populate databases with large amounts of information about potential and actual customers. If bad data is entered into databases, the effectiveness and accuracy of these tools are undermined.

In order to understand how an XML schema works, one could use the example of a customer's contact information. A schema for a customer's addresses could require that certain informational elements (such as name, street address, city, state, and ZIP code) be present in order to be valid. Furthermore, the schema might specify exactly what constitutes valid information within these categories, indicating that ZIP codes contain only numbers, and no more than five of them.

In May 2001, the World Wide Web Consortium (W3C) issued its XML schema specification, which standardized XML schemas. The organization's specification consisted of three parts. The first pertained to how XML software manages numbers, dates, and other forms of information. The second proposed ''methods for describing the structure and constraining the contents of XML documents, and defines the rules governing schema-validation of documents.'' Finally, the third part of the specification was a primer explaining ''what schemas are, how they differ from DTDs, and how someone builds a schema.''

FURTHER READING:

''DTD.'' *Ecommerce Webopedia,* June 12, 2001. Available from e-comm.webopedia.com.

Orr, Bill. ''Is XML the Next Big Thing?'' *ABA Banking Journal,* May 2000.

Sliwa, Carol. ''W3C Readies Long-Awaited XML Schema Spec.'' *Computerworld,* October 30, 2000.

van der Vlist, Eric. ''Using W3C XML Schema.'' *O'Reilly XML.com,* November 29, 2000. Available from www.xml.com.

Walsh, Norman. ''Understanding XML Schemas.'' July 1999. Available from www.xml.com.

''World Wide Web Consortium Issues XML Schema as a W3C Recommendation.'' Cambridge, MA: World Wide Web Consortium, May 2, 2001. Available from www.w3.org.

''XML 101.'' *Chain Store Age,* October 2000.

''XML Schema.'' *Ecommerce Webopedia,* May 25, 2001. Available from e-comm.webopedia.com.

SEE ALSO: HTML (Hypertext Markup Language); World Wide Web Consortium (W3C); XML (Extensible Markup Language)

Y

YAHOO! INC.

As one of the early Internet search engines, Yahoo! enjoyed the benefits of being first to market as it evolved from a search engine to an Internet portal. Yahoo! became a strong Internet brand in its first year of operation. It was the first search engine to develop a commercial look and one of the first to attract online advertisers. While the company has developed alternative revenue streams, it has remained dependent on Internet advertising for the bulk of its revenue.

FORMATION OF YAHOO!

Yahoo! began in 1994 as a database for finding Internet resources. The online directory of Web servers was developed by two Stanford University graduate students, Jerry Yang and David Filo, who had Master's degrees in electrical engineering. Their Web search engine was initially made available to the public on Stanford's Web site, where it was an instant hit. Unlike other search engines that would come along, Yahoo! used hierarchical menus to organize Web sites. Yang and Filo soon took a leave from their doctoral studies to devote themselves full-time to Yahoo!.

Yahoo Corp. was formed in April 1995. Tim Koogle, a Stanford graduate in electrical engineering and mathematics, joined as CEO, and the company had 14 employees. By April 1995 Yahoo had about 200,000 daily users who accessed its search engine. The company obtained $1 million in financial backing from venture capital firm Sequoia Capital. Users could search 40,000 Web pages, a small percentage of the 5 million then in existence.

Yahoo hoped to generate revenue by selling advertising space. Web design firm CKS Partners of Portland, Oregon, was hired to redesign Yahoo!'s interface. On July 31, Yahoo was relaunched as an advertising-supported directory. Five advertisers paid $60,000 each for a three-month contract. They included telecommunications giant MCI Communications Corp., a San Francisco-based startup called Worlds Inc., the Internet Shopping Network, MasterCard International, and online retailer NECX. The only competition at the time was InfoSeek, which began in January 1995. InfoSeek also gained revenue from ads, charging $15 for every 1,000 times an ad appeared on someone's computer screen. Yang expected that competition would soon become fierce.

Analysts noted Yahoo's new commercial look and predicted it would become the model for future services on the Internet. The site displayed a newly designed company logo. ''Extra!'' news tag added to some headings suggested more informational depth. *Computer Weekly* predicted, ''Eventually, the company may become a one-step site for all the services an Internet user might want.''

STRONG BRAND HELPS IPO SUCCEED, 1996

After its first year of operation Yahoo! was the best known and most widely used Internet guide. The company had attracted an additional $4 million in financial backing from Ziff-Davis Publishing Co. and Japanese software giant Softbank Corp. It generated

$500,000 in revenue in its first six months. In January 1996 Ziff-Davis and Yahoo! formed a strategic partnership whereby the magazine *ZD Internet Life* would become *Yahoo! Internet Life* and the two companies would publish an online guide for computing resources on the Internet.

At the beginning of 1996 Yahoo! provided links to about 100,000 sites. The company tried to list the most important sites. It worked closely with advertisers and supplied them with demographic information and traffic reports. To broaden its perspective, Yahoo! formed a partnership with the Internet division of Canada's Rogers Communications to develop an Internet search service for Canadian sites. Around this time Rogers also launched CANOE, the Canadian Online Explorer, which enabled users to browse online editions of such Rogers publications as *Maclean's, The Financial Post,* and the *Sun* newspapers.

Yahoo! held its initial public offering (IPO) in April 1996, selling 2.6 million shares at $13 per share on the NASDAQ. By the end of the first week shares more than doubled to nearly $33. Search engines Lycos and Excite also had their IPOs that same month. Following its IPO, Yahoo! Inc. enjoyed a market capitalization of more than $1 billion. It gained a $106 million investment from Softbank and together the two companies launched Yahoo! Japan, which was the first major directory service to contain language and content for a non-English speaking audience. Yahoo! Japan quickly became the most-trafficked site outside of North America. Softbank owned a 37 percent interest in Yahoo!

Yahoo! and Ziff-Davis International Media Group partnered to launch Yahoo! Europe in the United Kingdom, France, and Germany, with other countries to follow in 1997. In the United States Yahoo! began forming online alliances with local print and broadcast media companies to create city guides that organized and indexed sites relating to each city. The first cities to be covered were New York, Los Angeles, and San Francisco.

Yahoo! rolled out many new services in 1996, including My Yahoo!, a personalized service that delivered content from a user's favorite Web sites and provided other personalized information based on user preferences.

Although it was the recognized market leader, Yahoo! lost money in 1996, and its stock fell by 44 percent. Yahoo! planned to become profitable by turning itself into a media company. As Yang told *Fortune,* "The fundamental bet we are making is that we are a media company, not a tools company." The company planned to survive by creating brand loyalty.

ADDS SERVICES AND BECOMES A PORTAL, 1997-1998

Yahoo!'s branding efforts resulted in 39 percent of the general public knowing the Yahoo! name, according to a Yankelovich study. To build its brand recognition Yahoo! was the first Internet-only company to advertise on television. New services launched in 1997 included Yahoo! Finance, which included investment research, market summaries, and financial news as well as links to stock quotes, company profiles, and similar information.

By 1997 Yahoo! was posting profitable quarterly financial results, including $210,000 in the first quarter and $610,000 in the second quarter. Revenue in the second quarter more than quadrupled to $13.5 million from $3.3 million a year ago. First-quarter advertising sales were $9.5 million, compared to $1.7 million in the first quarter of 1996. Third quarter revenue reached $17.3 million, with an operating profit of $222,000 and net income of $1.6 million. Traffic reached an average of 50 million page views per day in September. Wall Street took note and toward the end of 1997 analysts were recommending Yahoo! as being financially sound and likely to benefit from increased Internet spending by advertisers and retailers.

During 1998 Yahoo! developed plans for becoming a portal and developing additional revenue streams from commerce and other sources. In mid-1998 the company acquired Viaweb Inc., an Internet commerce software vendor, for $49 million in stock. The acquisition gave Yahoo! the ability to design, build, promote, and host online storefronts and give merchants tracking and reporting tools. The Viaweb Store was subsequently relaunched as Yahoo! Store. Later in the year Yahoo! acquired Yoyodyne for about $30 million in stock. Yoyodyne specialized in target marketing, and Yahoo! would use its resources to develop ongoing promotional programs for its advertisers.

Yahoo! continued to operate at a profit in 1998. For the first quarter it had revenue of $30.2 million and a net profit of $4.3 million. About 22 percent of its revenue came from commerce and sponsorships. Strong traffic helped Yahoo! report financial results ahead of analysts' expectations for the rest of the year. In May Yahoo! led all Internet sites with 30.6 million unique visitors, followed by America Online with 22.8 million and Netscape with 18.9 million. For September average page views reached 144 million, with the number of registered users increasing by 7 million to more than 25 million. *PC Magazine* named Yahoo! the best Web search engine of 1997, citing its news-searching capabilities and extensively cross-referenced directory. It also praised the company's microsites, including Yahoo! Finance, regional guides, Yahooligans! For Kids, and Beatrice's Web

Guide, a partnership with Women's Wire. Yahoo! also featured chat rooms and a free e-mail service. For fiscal 1998 the company's revenue reached $203.3 million, up from $70.5 million in fiscal 1997.

Yahoo! extended its brand in many ways. Globally it operated sites in 11 countries overseas, including a newly launched Chinese-language Web site based in Hong Kong. Like other search engines, Yahoo! offered extra services such as news, yellow and white pages, free e-mail, chat, and instant messaging. The Yahoo! name was also found on its own magazine, *Yahoo! Internet Life,* and a co-branded Visa credit card. New services launched in 1998 included Yahoo! Small Business and Yahoo! Clubs.

ACQUISITIONS AND NEW SERVICES, 1999-2000

In 1999 Yahoo! enjoyed strong revenue growth and profitability due to its global operations. Its stock joined the Standard & Poor 500 Index. Early in the year the company announced that it would acquire GeoCities, one of the largest domains on the World Wide Web, for an estimated $3.5 to $5 billion in stock. GeoCities hosted personal Web sites and sold ads on those sites. In its most recent quarter GeoCities lost $8.4 million on sales of $7.5 million.

Later in the first half of 1999 Yahoo! made another major acquisition when it paid $5.7 billion in stock for Broadcast.com, a multimedia Internet broadcasting company with the capability to send TV-quality video over the Internet. For 1998 Broadcast.com lost $15 million on sales of $24.4 million. As part of its strategy to deliver content to wireless devices, Yahoo! acquired Online Anywhere in June for about $80 million. Online Anywhere's software would enable Yahoo! to more easily format its content for wireless devices.

Among the many new services introduced during 1999 on Yahoo! were auctions, Yahoo! Radio, Corporate My Yahoo!, electronic bill paying, and Yahoo! Everywhere. A new version of its instant messaging service incorporated live voices, allowing users to talk to each other by pressing a talk button. The company's broad array of services added a great deal of "stickiness" to its site and kept people coming back.

Yahoo!'s fourth quarter profits surged to $57.6 million on revenue of $201 million, due to soaring advertising and e-commerce revenue. During December 1999 traffic increased to an average of 465 million page views per day, compared to 167 million page views per day in December 1998. The company's international operations accounted for 30 percent of its traffic and 13 percent of its revenue.

Yahoo! enjoyed strong revenue growth during the first half of 2000. In the second half of the year

the dot.com shakeout began to affect Yahoo!'s advertising revenue as advertisers cut back on their spending. Yahoo!'s mid-2000 acquisition of eGroups for $432 million in stock enhanced the company's e-mail communications services for its online communities.

At the end of the first quarter Yahoo! had 125 million registered users for its personalized services, an increase of 25 million over December 1999. Page views per day rose to 625 million in March. A promotional arrangement with Kmart's Bluelight.com resulted in 1 million new users for Yahoo! With a network of 10,500 linked merchants, Yahoo! claimed that it enabled more than $1 billion of online transactions in the first quarter of 2000.

Even though Yahoo!'s third quarter earnings exceeded expectations, the company's stock dropped 21 percent following its quarterly report. In spite of Yahoo!'s diversification, analysts noted that page views and site traffic were the most important factors driving the company's revenue. In the first half of 2000, advertising accounted for 91 percent of Yahoo!'s revenue, with business services accounting for the other 9 percent. In the third quarter the company's merchant and advertising base fell to 3,450 from 3,675 in the second quarter.

New services launched in 2000 included the Yahoo! B2B Marketplace, a site designed to help companies find products and suppliers by serving as a portal to other vertical trading communities. Targeting enterprise customers, Yahoo! introduced Corporate Yahoo!, an enterprise information portal that would contain both Yahoo! content and corporate data. Corporate Yahoo! included personalization features taken from the My Yahoo! service for consumers.

During the year Yahoo! upgraded its instant messenger service to let users conduct hands-free conversations by eliminating the talk button. Conversation links were also added to news stories to enable people to talk to other users about a particular story. Yahoo! Finance Vision was a new site that incorporated video interviews, original production, and editorial content from other providers, all on one Internet page.

Consumers interested in conducting their personal finance transactions online were introduced to a new account aggregation service on Yahoo!, where they could consolidate their banking, credit card, investment, and other financial account information using Yahoo!'s online banking center or its My Yahoo! personalization tool.

Yahoo!'s communications initiative and its Yahoo! Everywhere program converged when the company began offering free voice-based services that included Internet content over the telephone, voice mail, and long distance calling. With Yahoo! by

Phone, users could call a toll-free number to check e-mail, weather, news, and other information. Yahoo! Mail was expanded to include voice mail, while Yahoo! Messenger was extended to include the ability to make free PC-to-phone calls.

WEAK AD MARKET RESULTS IN QUARTERLY LOSSES, 2001

Further weakness in the online advertising market affected Yahoo!'s financial performance in 2001. Several stock analysts downgraded the company's stock at the beginning of the year. After a year-long slide, Yahoo!'s stock had lost 90 percent of its value. Profits for the first quarter were down 87 percent from a year ago, and second quarter losses of $48.5 million were accompanied by reduced earnings forecasts. In March chairman and CEO Tim Koogle gave up his CEO title but remained as chairman. Terry Semel, a former entertainment executive who was once co-CEO of Warner Bros., was hired as the new CEO. In April the company laid off 421 employees, some 12 percent of its 3,510 workers. Co-founder Jerry Yang noted that Yahoo! was in a transition from a period of tremendous growth to one of long-term growth in a volatile economy. To sustain that growth Yahoo! sought to balance its revenue from advertising, e-commerce, and services. One analyst speculated that Yahoo! would begin charging subscription fees for services such as multimedia content, enhanced financial services, and enhanced instant messaging.

In an effort to boost revenue and develop new revenue streams in 2001, Yahoo! Auctions began charging listing fees in January. In February it introduced a Sponsored Sites program for B2B and shopping, whereby paid listings would appear in some search results. Later in the year Yahoo! began charging U.S. customers for domestic voice calls made over the Internet as part of an updated version of Yahoo! Messenger. Yahoo! also expanded its B2B efforts by introducing three Industry Marketplaces for computer hardware, software, and electronics.

The addition of multimedia services also appeared to be a key part of Yahoo!'s plan to develop new revenue streams. The company began using streaming media to encourage online shopping on Yahoo! ShoppingVision and entered into a strategic relationship with ValueVision International, the third-largest home shopping network. Yahoo! also added video to its instant messaging service, which ranked third behind America Online and the Microsoft Network. Yahoo!'s $12 million acquisition of Launch.com added streaming music videos and music news as well as an Internet radio station. Yahoo! also entered into a wide-ranging agreement with Sony that included online movie marketing, e-commerce, and Web site development. For corporations, Yahoo! introduced Yahoo! Broadcast Services to give them Internet broadcasting capabilities for videoconferencing.

Despite its financial woes, Yahoo! continued to be one of the most popular Internet destination in 2001. In March it was the number one Internet property in terms of both page views and unique audience, ahead of such sites as eBay, Amazon.com, America Online, the Microsoft Network, and the Lycos Network. According to a mid-2001 study by Jupiter Media Metrix, Yahoo! was one of four Internet sites that accounted for more than half of all the time spent online by Internet users in the United States. With more than 192 million registered users as of mid-2001, Yahoo! had more people using its site than any other company.

FURTHER READING:

Anderson, Jennifer L. "Yahoo!" *PC Magazine,* January 6, 1998.

Hansell, Saul. "Red Face for the Internet's Blue Chip." *The New York Times,* March 11, 2001.

Hodges, Jane. "Winning and Keeping Web Surfers." *Fortune,* May 24, 1999.

Maloney, Janice. "Yahoo! Still Searching for Profits on the Internet." *Fortune,* December 9, 1996.

Moody, Glyn. "The New Yahoo and the Future of the Internet." *Computer Weekly,* September 7, 1995.

———. "Yahoo Brands Itself as an Internet Innovator." *Computer Weekly,* April 9, 1998.

Rupley, Sebastian. "Big Portals Do B2B." *PC Magazine,* May 23, 2000.

Sausner, Rebecca. "Report: Yahoo! Retains Online Ratings Crown." *E-Commerce Times,* May 1, 2001. Available from www.ecommercetimes.com.

Stodder, Gayle Sato. "Unconventional Thinking: Yahoo!" *Entrepreneur,* September 1997.

Taylor, Dennis. "Yahoo Reshaping Continues with Debut of Financial Site." *The Business Journal,* May 5, 2000.

Wilson, Tim. "AOL, Yahoo Jump into B-to-B Services." *InternetWeek,* March 27, 2000.

"Yahoo! to the Rescue." *Business Week,* September 11, 2000.

SEE ALSO: Filo, David; Koogle, Timothy; Portals, Web; Yang, Jerry; Ziff-Davis Inc.

YANG, JERRY

A native of Taiwan, Jerry Yang co-founded Yahoo! Inc. in March of 1995 at the age of 27. What began in 1993 as an effort by two Stanford University doctoral students—Yang and his partner David Filo—to catalog their favorite World Wide Web sites eventually evolved into the world's busiest Internet portal. By the year 2000, the site was logging more than 100 million visitors every month. Yang remains a member of Yahoo!'s board of directors and plays a major role, in conjunction with CEO Tim Koogle, in steering the company's growth strategy. Yang owns roughly eight percent of Yahoo!'s stock.

Yang's family moved from Taiwan to San Jose, California, in 1978, when Yang was 10 years old. He won a scholarship to Stanford University, where he earned both his Bachelor's and Master's degree in just four years. Yang gained his first experience cataloging information with a part-time job at the university's library, where he sorted and shelved books. He was working on an advanced degree in electrical engineering at Stanford when he met Filo in 1989. In the early 1990s, the two began using Mosaic to browse the fledgling World Wide Web. They eventually created a program that would allow them to group Web sites into subject categories. The duo dubbed the resulting list of sites, "Jerry's Guide to the World Wide Web," and posted it on the Web. Positive e-mail responses from Web surfers all over the world prompted Yang and Filo to begin indexing all sites on the Web. They set a goal of cataloging 1000 sites per day, and when subject categories became too large, they added layers of subcategories.

The site's popularity grew rapidly, and Stanford's server began struggling under the increased traffic load. As a result, the university asked Yang and Filo to find another organization to host what they had renamed Yahoo!, an acronym for "Yet Another Hierarchical Officious Oracle." Buyout offers emerged from executives at Netscape, AOL, and what would become other leading Internet firms, but Yang and Filo turned them down. Instead, they agreed to take a leave of absence from their studies to co-found Yahoo! Inc. After securing financial backing from Sequoia Capital, Yang and Filo hired Tim Koogle to run the business. The more outgoing of the pair, Yang focused his attention on turning Yahoo! into a popular brand name, while Filo focused on the technological aspects of the operation. When the company went public in 1996, Yang and Filo found themselves millionaires, and as Yahoo's stock prices soared in the late 1990s, they eventually reached billionaire status.

Yahoo stands apart from most Internet-based ventures because it actually turns a profit. Advertising accounts for most of the company's revenues. Technology that allows the firm to track a visitor's online activity also lets Yahoo! control what banner bars and button ads that visitor sees. Yahoo! is also able to monitor how many hits an advertisement receives as a way of judging an ad's effectiveness. These advertising functions, though, are only a source of profits because of the firm's intense traffic levels. It is Yang who is most often credited for creating a site that attracts more visitors than most others. According to an April 2000 *Advertising Age* article, Yang created a "destination where Web surfers could get whatever they wanted from the site's personalized content, e-commerce offerings, special promotions, and other interactive data." Yang did this by continually forging alliances with companies as a means of offering new products and technology to users. For example, a 1999 alliance with Motorola Inc. allowed Yahoo! to expand into wireless Internet service. At the same time, Yang also worked to expand Yahoo!'s services to include things like e-store management and Web site construction.

In 2001, Yahoo! was forced to pause as declining advertising revenues and tumbling stock prices took their toll on the firm's bottom line. As a result, Yang stepped up his management role, and announced at a March 2001 press conference that Yahoo! was searching outside the company for a new CEO to replace Koogle.

FURTHER READING:

Elkin, Tobi. "Jerry Yang." *Advertising Age,* April 17, 2000.

Mangalindan, Mylene, and Suein L. Hwang. "Yahoo!'s Isolation Plays Into Downfall; The Coteries of Early Hires Made the Company a Hit, But an Insular Place." *Contra Costa Times,* March 11, 2001.

Pepe, Michele. "Number 16: Yahoo—Jerry Yang." *Computer Reseller News,* November 15, 1999.

Schlender, Brent. "How A Virtuoso Plays the Web: Eclectic, Inquisitive, and Academic, Yahoo's Jerry Yang Reinvents the Role of the Entrepreneur." *Fortune,* March 6, 2000.

Stross, Randall E. "How Yahoo! Won the Search Wars." *Fortune,* March 2, 1998.

"Web Crawlers." *Forbes,* October 9, 2000.

SEE ALSO: Filo, David; Koogle, Timothy; Yahoo!

YANKEE GROUP

A subsidiary of Reuters Enterprise, which is a unit of Reuters PLC, Yankee Group is a leading market researcher focused on Internet-related industries such as e-commerce, telecommunications, and wireless. Employees total roughly 200. The Boston, Massachusetts-based firm offers more than 30 different analysis and consulting services covering areas such as

- application infrastructure and software platforms
- Australasian market strategies
- billing and payment application strategies
- Brazilian and Canadian market strategies
- business-to-business (B2B) commerce and applications
- carrier convergence infrastructure
- communications services for the new economy
- consumer market convergence
- convergent communications
- wireless and mobile markets
- Internet strategies in Asia, Europe, and Latin America
- customer relationship management strategies
- e-networks and broadband access
- e-sourcing strategies
- global regulatory strategies
- Internet market strategies
- media and entertainment strategies
- mobile commerce strategies
- security solutions and services
- small and medium business communications
- telecom e-business
- wholesale communications services
- and wireless and mobile technologies and services.

The firm's more than 500 clients receive a combination of research reports, research notes, strategy sessions with Yankee Group analysts, audio conferences, and access to Yankee Group industry forums.

Harvard Business School graduate Howard Anderson founded Yankee Group in 1970 to provide market analysis to companies operating in the rapidly changing communications industry. The new company was the industry's first research and advisory services firm. Eventually, Yankee Group's focus shifted to networking technology, particularly enterprise applications and datacom networks. In 1986, Yankee Group began using the Technologically Advanced Family Survey to query U.S. households with regard to their use and perception of new technology products and services. Four years later, the firm launched its Mobile User Survey, seeking data regarding mobile technology use across North America.

Annual growth during the early 1990s exceeded 20 percent. During that time, the firm expanded into Canada, establishing a research and consulting unit named Canadian Market Strategies in Ontario. The Global Network Strategies Survey was first utilized in 1992 to gather information from corporate network administrators regarding network usage. In August of 1996, Primark Corp. acquired Yankee Group from Anderson for $34 million in cash and additional performance-based payments worth up to another $31 million. Anderson remained at the helm of the firm as the number of employees reached 60, and sales neared the $8 million mark.

Yankee Group expanded its international reach into Brazil by opening an office in Sao Paulo in 1999. The number of World Wide Web users there, estimated to be 3.5 million, was expected to nearly double over the next two years. This growth had prompted firms like MCI Communications Corp., Sprint Corp., and Bell Canada to move into the country, and Yankee Group believed a market for its services would exist there as well. As a result, the firm also launched its Internet Strategies Latin America Planning Service, which analyzed the regional Internet service provider (ISP) strategies, broadband Internet access development, business-to-business (B2B) e-commerce initiatives, and Web hosting services among Latin American businesses.

In November, long-time Yankee Group employee Berge Ayvazian succeeded Anderson as president and CEO, although Anderson remained chairman. It was at roughly the same time that the firm began to reinvent itself as an Internet industry expert. Not only did the Internet become a key focus of Yankee Group's research—along with the wireless and communications industries—but the firm also began working to offer its Internet industry analysis on a global scale, reaching Europe, the Pacific Rim, and Latin America. Also that year, YankeeTek was created to invest in small dot-com startups. The venture would receive strategic planning services from Yankee Group, and have access to the firm's body of research.

Yankee Group overhauled its Web site in early 2000. Rather than complete the redesign work in-house, the company hired InterNoded, an independent Web site designer. InterNoded's improvements included enhancing search capabilities and allowing clients to customize the site via the ''My Yankee'' feature. The new site also included breaking technology news, which made use of content push technology, and a restricted area for members of the press. In May, Yankee Group launched two new programs: Online Financial Strategies (OFS) Planning Service and Online Retail Strategies (ORS) Planning Service. The OFS service analyzed the Internet's influence on the financial services industry in terms of consumer behavior, new products, marketplace requirements, and business issues. The ORS service analyzed the behavior and attitudes of online shoppers, the business models used by online retailers, online shopping services, and fulfillment. Yankee Group also assisted clients within either industry to develop appropriate business strategies.

Primark planned to take Yankee Group public in 2000. However, it instead decided to divest the technological market research arm and focus on its core financial and economic information services operations. Reuters PLC, one of the world's leading information firms with $35 billion in market capitalization, paid $72.5 million for Yankee Group in June. Yankee Group remained an autonomous entity, operating out of its parent's newly created global information business arm, known as Reuters Enterprise. Ayvazian, who remained CEO and president after the takeover by Reuters, commented on the acquisition in the June 2000 issue of *PR Newswire,* stating: "The Reuters purchase acts as a springboard to the Yankee Group's re-branding efforts. These efforts include key sales channel expansion, Web innovation, global expansion, and the 'e-volution' of our research planning services."

In January of 2001 Yankee Group opened an office in Miami, Florida, to better serve the growing Latin American telecommunications and Internet markets there. Two months later the firm released its "Yankee Group Stars" list of the best online retailers, which was based on seven factors evaluated by Yankee Group. The firm also placed its international operations under the name Convergent Communications. Consequently, EuroScope Communications was renamed Convergent Communications Europe, and Latin American and Asian operations were renamed Convergent Communications Latin America and Convergent Communications Asia-Pacific, respectively. A new Global Regulatory Strategies service was created in July, which focused on the regulatory issues surrounding international e-business.

FURTHER READING:

Greene, Tim. "Yankee Group to Focus on e-Business." *Network World.* November 15, 1999.

Hall, Mark. "Yankee Group to Go Public Soon; Parent Company Floats IPO for IT Services Firm." *Computerworld.* November 15, 1999.

McGee, Marianne K. "The Specialists: Finding Their Own Niche." *Information Week.* November 15, 1999.

"Reuters to Acquire the Yankee Group for $723.5 Million." *Information Today.* June 2000.

Tanzillo, Kevin. "Howard Anderson's Forward Thinking." *Communications News.* December 1996.

"The Yankee Group—New Look, Enhanced Strategy." *PR Newswire.* June 12, 2000.

SEE ALSO: E-commerce Consultants; Internet Service Providers (ISPs)

Y2K BUG

The phrase "Y2K bug" stood for the range of potentially adverse effects on computer systems of the rollover from the year 1999 to 2000. Within that definition, however, there were a wide range of questions, concerns, and solutions. The two-digit date-storage system posed its problem in the computer's recognition of time and its logical implications. Computers that already assumed the "19" and read and manipulated only the last two digits would naturally read the new date as "1900." Nobody knew for certain how this rollover would affect various systems, but few were willing to take chances. In the late 1990s, businesses, governments, organizations, individuals, and just about every other entity that depended on computer systems scrambled to render their systems Y2K-compliant, spending billions of dollars in the process.

Fears ranged from the relatively mundane (lost e-mail) to the costly (disruption of service or lost records) to the catastrophic (unpredictable computer responses at air-traffic controls and even nuclear facilities). One factor adding to the concern was the result of the increasingly networked nature of modern life. With computer systems interconnected with each other across state and national boundaries, analysts feared the potential snowball effects of moderate problems in local systems as they spread through wider networks. As wide-ranging as the concerns, however, were the reactions to the event—or non-event—as the crucial date came and went.

ROOTS OF THE PROBLEM

The underlying problem—the inability of computers to read years rendered in four digits—seems almost a foolish and short-sighted blunder, but there was good reason for the two-digit date system. Computer programmers were faced with the daunting task of providing for adequate computer memory at an affordable cost. In the early days of computing technology, memory was expensive and logistically difficult, and thus designers needed to cut corners where they could. In the 1950s and 1960s, the most sophisticated computer-memory systems utilized strips of costly punched cardboard. Programmers at the time opted to save space and money on those cards by rendering dates in only six digits rather than eight (as in "01-01-00" rather than "01-01-2000"). At the time, few programmers considered the possibility that such memory programs would last until the end of the century.

Soon, however, scientists and programmers adapted their own systems to this programming technique, called common business-oriented language (COBOL). In this way, the problem that would eventually be referred to as the Y2K bug spread through computing systems by the sheer act of rendering computers compliant with each other. By the end of the 1960s, IBM, the leading computer maker of the day, had effectively codified the Y2K bug as part of the dominant programming language. Once this de facto standard was set, other computer makers and programmers followed suit.

Ironically, one of the main writers of the COBOL program, IBM programmer Robert Bemer, was among the first to sound the alarm of an eventual Y2K crisis clear back in 1971. However, with the crucial date still nearly thirty years away and the problem so remote from programmers' everyday concerns, Bemers's warning went unheeded. In fact, by that time Bemer had even written a program that allowed eight-digit date listing, but the priorities for programmers and manufacturers were elsewhere, and the six-digit standard blossomed.

Interest in the topic was largely shelved until the early 1990s, when a handful of younger programmers, such as the IBM computer operator Peter de Jager, began speaking and posting Web sites on the topic. By the middle of the decade, awareness of Y2K had reached most major organizations, including corporations and governments, who set about convening task forces to study the problem and ready their systems for it. By the late 1990s, the Y2K bug was a hot topic of popular concern, generating miles of newsprint and far-ranging speculation, some of it reaching the apocalyptic. There was in fact some evidence for the grave predictions. In 1993, nuclear monitors at NORAD rolled their clocks forward to see what would happen on January 1, 2000. To their surprise, the intercontinental ballistic missile (ICBM) alert system crashed.

Popular concern—and occasionally hysteria—with the Y2K bug fed, and was fed by, cultural and religious fears involving the year 2000, which some felt would mark large-scale catastrophes and other shattering phenomena. The mountain of information and rumors circulating on the Internet about Y2K took on a life of its own, generating a small industry devoted to Y2K survival, geared toward a situation in which society's sustaining computer systems were inoperative. Adding to the mix were the conspiracy theorists, who remained skeptical of the whole affair, seeing it as a product of the agenda of powerful forces. While such factors normally don't reach the level of mainstream consideration, the coalescence of these factors with the Y2K bug—which the business world, after all, was certainly taking seriously—produced a second life for the Y2K bug.

THE CRISIS COMES AND GOES

But in the months leading up to the crucial rollover, no one could say with any certainty just what the Y2K bug's effects would be. While some insisted the whole phenomenon was much ado about nothing, others warned of potentially costly and disruptive side effects if companies, organizations, governments, and individuals didn't work to ready their own systems. Most groups chose to play it safe, investing hefty sums to purchase Y2K-compliance software or hire outside consultants to root through their systems and fix any potential trouble spots. In the process, an enormous Y2K industry was spawned. Estimates of total U.S. Y2K expenditures reached into the hundreds of billions of dollars, while the worldwide total topped $600 billion. According to Peter de Jager, the U.S. government alone spent $8.34 billion on year-2000 compliance.

As midnight on December 31, 1999 approached, businesses and governments all over the world maintained staff on-call, ready to respond at a moment's notice should catastrophe strike. Cisco Systems Inc., for example, kept nearly half of their 22,000 employees on call during the rollover.

Finally, the crucial date came and went, and to the surprise of many, virtually nothing happened—certainly nothing on the order of the more dire predictions. The extent to which the Y2K bug's benign effects were the result of vigilant compliance measures or of the bug's relatively benign nature was a matter of debate, and commentators had yet to reach consensus on the matter even two years later. There were glitches, even in some major systems. For instance, a U.S. military satellite surveillance system went down and wasn't recovered for several weeks. But on the whole, the extent of preparation—to say nothing of the newsprint and hysteria—seemed vastly out of proportion with the event itself.

IN HINDSIGHT

As a result, the early 2000s were marked by nearly as much Y2K debate as were the late 1990s, but of a very different nature. Analysts, business executives, and IT experts all offered their own takes on exactly what occurred and why, and assessed the benefits and drawbacks of the extensive technological preparation. Gartner Group, for instance, held that the catastrophe-free rollover was a product of the extensive and successful preparation companies undertook; Gartner Group analyst Dale Vecchio remarked, ''people didn't spend $300 billion on a problem that didn't exist.''

Some commentators noted that, in addition to the economic benefits of the new software expenditures, the phenomenon of businesses moving all at once to upgrade their software was a boon to the emerging Internet economy, since the new systems were vastly more likely to be able to accommodate the Internet's heavy, interactive traffic. In this way, such analysts noted, more or less all at once entire industries were upgraded for e-commerce. In the absence of such a crisis, the pace of such an upgrade would have been much slower, and would not have occurred with such simultaneity—some industries would make the transition much more quickly than others, for example—and thus seamless e-commerce readiness would have been postponed. In addition, some analysts noted that the Y2K crisis forced companies to reconsider the role of technology in their businesses, inspiring executives to involve their information officers in strategic planning to an unprecedented extent. In the wake of the Y2K crisis, companies were also more likely to develop continuity plans that will enable them to continue functioning in the event of technology failures.

By forcing companies to overhaul their information-technology systems and purge antiquated hardware and software, the Y2K bug may have sped IT's evolutionary process along. For instance, *Business Week* reported that, largely as a result of the Y2K crisis, by 2000 hotels such as Marriott International Inc. featured computer and Internet connectivity in each room, where that was seldom the case just a few years earlier. At DaimlerChrysler, meanwhile, the $260 million investment into Y2K fixes resulted in the purging of some 15,000 outdated computers; the replacement of these systems with state-of-the-art technology allowed the company to link two-thirds of its plants to the same network, thereby greatly enhancing internal efficiency and supply chain management. Companies were most likely to have their entire personnel online and feature electronic customer service systems, all of which are essential for readying businesses for the Internet economy.

Not everyone was so charitable or positive about the benign effects of Y2K. *Fortune,* for instance, expressed indignation over the whole affair, insisting that the Y2K crisis was an overblown panic that caused businesses to waste billions of dollars, and going so far as to demand that those responsible for the fervor—the media, financial executives, and computer industry players who capitalized on the crisis, and those "professional Jeremiads" who made their names lecturing and writing on the severity of the problem—be held accountable. To other analysts, the investment was not only a colossal waste, but an indication of the information-technology industry's inability to manage—economically and otherwise—computer-based risks.

Since companies and governments faced the threat of severe short- and long-term consequences if their systems weren't prepared, they had little choice but to devote whatever amounts were required to remedy their Y2K problems; cost wasn't the immediate consideration before making such an investment. As a result, organizations tied up vastly disproportionate percentages of their budgets to Y2K issues. International Data Corporation held that some of the consultants claiming responsibility for Y2K success would prove some of the ultimate victims of Y2K, as business executives reviewed their expenditures in the late 1990s and concluded that too much was spent on Y2K preparation at the expense of more important strategic programs.

FURTHER READING:

Bing, Stanley. "Oh, Sure. Now They're Sorry: Y2K Idiots Cost Business $500 billion! Is No One to be Punished?" *Fortune,* February 7, 2000.

"Bugging People." Economist, December 18, 1999.

Burke, Steven, and Pedro Pereira. "Industry Ponders Impact On Operations, Sales: As the Clock Ticks, Y2K Still a Puzzle." *Computer Reseller News,* November 30, 1998.

Hicks, Matt. "Did Y2K Consultants Cry Wolf?" *PC Week,* January 10, 2000.

Jones, Jennifer. "Y2K Bug Squashed, Feds Say." *Network World,* January 10, 2000.

"Panic Postponed." *Economist,* January 8, 2000.

Peters, Richard, and Robert Sikorski. "Y2K or Bust." *Science,* December 17, 1999.

Rash, Wayne. "Why the Y2K Problem was Good for You." *InternetWeek,* December 4, 2000.

Strassman, Paul A. "The Y2K Ransom." *Computerworld,* January 10, 2000.

"The Y2K Bug Repellent Wasn't a Waste." *Business Week,* January 17, 2000.

Z

ZIFF-DAVIS, INC.

Before the company was dismantled and its separate businesses sold off, Ziff-Davis Inc. reached its target audience of techies through three media: print, cable TV, and the Internet. The company's magazine publishing business produced a range of computer and technologically oriented magazines for the business and consumer market. Ziff-Davis's online service ZDNet went live on the Internet in 1995, and its cable TV channel ZDTV was launched in May 1998. The company also operated Ziff-Davis Events, which produced trade shows and expositions—the best known of which is Comdex—and had other interests.

Ziff-Davis Inc., also known as Ziff-Davis Publishing Co. and a subsidiary of Ziff Communications, went public in 1998. For many years the company was a private business owned by the Ziff family and published a wide range of magazines. In the mid-1980s it sold off 24 off its trade and consumer magazines to CBS Inc. and to Rupert Murdoch to focus on computer, technology, and interactive gaming magazines. In 1994 the company launched two new titles, *Computer Life* and *Family PC*. In October 1994 Ziff-Davis Publishing was sold to buyout specialist Forstmann Litle and Co. for $1.4 billion. A little more than a year later, in December 1995, Japanese software giant Softbank Corp. acquired Ziff-Davis for $2.1 billion. Both of these transactions had the effect of burdening the company with a heavy load of debt.

In 1998 turned out to be a difficult year for the company financially, despite the fact that it went public in May. It shut down three of its titles—*Equip, In-ternet Business,* and *Windows Pro*—and laid off 350 workers, or 10 percent of its U.S. workforce. Parent company Softbank, pursuing an Internet-based strategy, started dismantling Ziff-Davis's assets and selling off pieces of the company that were not related to the Internet. ZDTV eventually went to Paul Allen's Vulcan Ventures and was renamed TechTV. The magazine publishing business was sold in a management buyout backed by venture capital firm Willis Stein & Partners for $780 million in December 1999, and resulted in the creation of Ziff Davis Media, Inc. Even the company's computer and technology portal ZDNet was sold to rival CNET in July 2000 for $1.6 billion.

MAGAZINE PUBLISHING BUSINESS BECOMES ZIFF DAVIS MEDIA, INC.

In December 1999 publishing turnaround expert James D. Dunning, Jr., and Chicago-based venture capital firm Willis Stein & Partners agreed to purchase Ziff-Davis Publishing for $780 million. The deal included more than 80 computer industry publications, including *PC Magazine, PC Week,* and *Yahoo! Internet Life.* Dunning and Willis Stein had previously been successful in turning around magazine publisher Petersen Publishing, selling it after two years for $1.5 billion in January 1999 after paying only $465 million for it. During Dunning's tenure at Petersen, the publisher launched 50 new titles.

At the time of the sale, ZDNet was still owned by Softbank, and Ziff-Davis's magazines were supplying content to the Internet portal. Under existing agreements, ZDNet owned the exclusive online rights to those magazines' content through 2003. For new magazines, through, Ziff Davis Media would control the Web sites. After ZDNet was acquired by rival CNET in October 2000, Ziff Davis Media sought to regain the rights to the online content of its magazines and negotiated an agreement to regain those rights as of March 1, 2002.

New publishing initiatives planned by Ziff Davis Media for 2000 included the relaunch of *PC Computing* as *Ziff-Davis Smart Business for the New Economy* and a new travel magazine co-branded with Microsoft's online travel site Expedia.com. Music technology was another area in which the company hoped to publish. Later in 2000 the company launched *The Net Economy,* a monthly magazine targeted at business and technology managers at companies that provide network-based services. It also changed the name of *Sm@rt Reseller* to *Sm@rt Partner* to better connect with its target audience of information technology (IT) supply chain vendors, systems integrators, and consultants.

In mid-2000 Ziff Davis Media sold its European magazines to Netherlands-based media conglomerate VNU. The ten titles included British, German, and French editions of such titles as *IT Week, PC Magazine, PC Direct,* and *PC Gaming World,* among others.

Ziff Davis Media continued with plans for new titles and new Web sites in 2001 in the face of declining advertising revenue. For its fiscal year ending March 31, 2001, the company reported a loss of $73.4 million on revenue of $440.5 million. In May it announced the launch of *CIO Insight* and then successfully defended the title against a copyright infringement suit from *CIO Magazine* publisher IDG (International Data Group). *CIO Insight* was aimed at senior-level technology executives and hoped to attract major business-to-business advertisers such as IBM Corp., Sun Microsystems Inc., and Oracle Corp. Later in the year the company announced the fall debut of *Baseline,* a new magazine whose content would cover Web-based solutions and focus on the bottom line in information technology. It began with a controlled circulation of 150,000 IT industry professionals.

In the online arena Ziff Davis Media had a three-year plan to create a variety of online sites that were more than replications of its magazines. It launched ZCast.tv, a streaming video news and analysis Web site, in February 2001. Content was taken from Ziff-Davis titles, including *eWeek* (formerly *PC Week*) and *PC Magazine.* However, ZCast did not catch on and was closed at the end of July. In June the company launched ExtremeTech, a Web site that targeted IT professionals and computer enthusiasts with content based on *PC Magazine.*

In May 2001 Ziff Davis Media announced it would lay off 50 employees, or about 5 percent of its workforce. In July the company also folded its *Family PC* magazine. The decline in tech advertising was even more pronounced in 2001 than in 2000. For the first half of 2001 Ziff-Davis's ad pages were down 39 percent compared to the same period in 2000, and its ad revenue for the period was down 31 percent. Even though Ziff Davis Media received an additional $70 million from its venture capital backers, its SEC filings indicated that the company would have a difficult year financially. In August Dunning was fired as chairman, president, and CEO. Ziff-Davis subsequently folded its Internet unit as an independent operation and planned to fold its Web properties back into the company's print operations. The relaunch of InteractiveWeek.com went ahead as planned in September. In October Robert Callahan, former president of ABC's Broadcast Group, was named chairman, president, and CEO of Ziff Davis Media.

As of late 2001, Ziff Davis Media's 12 magazines included four titles devoted to interactive gaming (*Computer Gaming World, Official U.S. PlayStation Magazine, GameNow,* and *Electronic Gaming Monthly*); along with business-to-business publications *Ziff Davis Smart Business, eWeek, Interactive Week, Smart Partner, The Net Economy,* and *CIO Insight.* Its leading consumer publications *Yahoo! Internet Life* and *PC Magazine* each had a paid circulation of more than 1 million.

COMPUTER AND TECHNICAL PORTAL, ZDNET

Before it was acquired by CNET, ZDNet was Ziff-Davis's online service and Internet portal. It was launched in 1995 and hosted electronic editions of Ziff-Davis's magazines. It began accepting advertising in April 1995. For 1996 ZDNet had revenue of $10.2 million. With its high-quality technical news and information, ZDNet was often ranked as the top news, information, and entertainment site on the Internet. In 1997 technology media company CMP Media launched a competing site, TechWeb. For the next two years, ZDNet's revenue increased, from $32.2 million in 1997 to $56.1 million in 1998, but it failed to turn a profit. Parent company Ziff-Davis decided to spin off ZDNet as a separate company in 1999 and offer it as a tracking stock.

When ZDNet was spun off from Ziff-Davis at the end of March 1999, it was losing money and contributing about 2 percent of its parent company's revenue. ZDNet's initial public offering raised $190 million, which Ziff-Davis planned to use to pay down its debt. Following the IPO, Ziff-Davis retained an 83 percent ownership interest in ZDNet.

Later in 1999 ZDNet debuted its redesigned Web site, which made it easier for users to navigate the 60

Web sites in its network. The portal's more than 30 channel headings were consolidated under 10 categories. ZDNet, which featured software downloads as well as news and information, had nearly 500 advertisers. When competing portal CNET launched a $100 million advertising campaign, ZDNet responded with its own $25 million branding campaign that launched on December 30, 1999.

With parent company Ziff-Davis shedding its other business units in 1999, it was decided to eliminate ZDNet's tracking stock in early 2000 and revive it as ordinary common stock. Through a technical merger with a newly formed subsidiary, Ziff-Davis would emerge as the surviving company and adopt the ZDNet name. All of this appeared to be a preliminary move to the mid-2000 sale of ZDNet to its much larger rival, CNET, for $1.6 billion. Following CNET's acquisition of ZDNet, CNET continued to operate ZDNet as a separate brand. According to CNET, CNET and ZDNet had 16.6 million monthly unique users and reached 22 percent of all Internet users. Before the acquisition, Media Metrix figures for January 2000 showed that ZDNet had more than 10 million unique visitors while its ad campaign was running, compared to 9.5 million for CNET. Internationally, ZDNet had syndicated operations in 23 countries and was accessible in 15 languages. Toward the end of 2000 it established an office in Miami, Florida, as a base for expansion into Latin America.

COMPUTER CABLE CHANNEL, ZDTV

Ziff-Davis launched ZDTV, a cable channel devoted to computers and technology, on May 11, 1998, with six hours of programming that were repeated to fill a 24-hour broadcast schedule. As a result of Ziff-Davis's own IPO in April 1998, ZDTV was in fact owned by Ziff-Davis's parent company, Softbank. During its first year of operation ZDTV extended its reach by signing carriage agreements with major cable and satellite TV operators, including TCI and DirecTV.

In November 1998 Microsoft co-founder Paul Allen, through his company Vulcan Ventures, ac-quired a controlling 33 percent interest in ZDTV for $54 million. That same year Allen acquired cable system operators Charter Communications for $4.5 billion and Marcus Communications for nearly $3 billion. A year later Vulcan Ventures acquired Ziff-Davis's remaining 64 percent interest in ZDTV for $204.8 million, with ZDTV executives owning the remaining small percentage of the cable channel.

ZDTV prospered under Allen's ownership. It had about 8.5 million subscribers as of November 1998. ZDTV launched a national branding campaign in mid-1999. At the time it was producing about 30 hours of original programming per week and was on the air 24 hours a day. By November 1999 ZDTV was available in more than 14 million homes. In August 2000 ZDTV was renamed TechTV and added new programs. Through new carriage agreements with AT&T, Time Warner, and Charter Communications, ZDTV reached more than 20 million cable TV subscribers.

FURTHER READING:

Callaghan, Dennis, and Jennifer Saba. ''Ziff-Davis' New Clothes.'' *MC Technology Marketing Intelligence,* January 2000.

Callahan, Sean. ''Ziff-Davis Sells ZDTV.'' *Business Marketing,* December 1, 1999.

''Can Anyone Make Ziff-Davis Sexy?'' *Business Week,* February 14, 2000.

Giebons, Kent. ''Allen's 'World' Keeps Expanding.'' *Multichannel News,* November 23, 1998.

Paikert, Charles. ''ZDTV Tries to Trade in on Modem Frenzy.'' *Multichannel News,* January 26, 1998.

Petrozzello, Donna. ''ZDTV Logs On.'' *Broadcasting & Cable,* May 18, 1998.

Steinert-Threlkeld, Tom. ''Electronoclast: If You Can't Beat 'em.'' *Inter@ctiveWeek,* July 24, 2000.

Weinberg, Neil. ''Geek TV.'' *Forbes,* July 5, 1999.

Ziff Davis Media Inc. ''Welcome to Ziff Davis Media Inc.'' October 24, 2001. Available from www.ziffdavis.com.

SEE ALSO: CNET Networks Inc.

Appleman, Daniel. *How Computer Programming Works,* 2nd ed. APress, 2000.

Berners-Lee, Tim, and Mark Fischetti. *Weaving the Web: The Original Design and Ultimate Destiny of the World Wide Web by its Inventor.* HarperCollins, 1999.

Bick, Jonathan. *101 Things You Need to Know About Internet Law.* Three Rivers Press, 2000.

Borsook, Paulina *Cyberselfish: A Critical Romp Through the Terribly Libertarian Culture of High-Tech.* Public Affairs LLC, 2000.

Breier, Mark, and Armin A. Brott. *The 10-Second Internet Manager.* Crown Publishing, 2000.

Brinson, J. Dianne, and Mark F. Radcliffe. *Internet Law and Business Handbook: A Practical Guide.* Ladera Press, 2000.

Butler, Susan P. and Mark Butler. *Ebusiness Legal Kit for Dummies.* Hungry Minds, Inc., 2000.

Castells, Manuel. *The Information Age: Economy, Society and Culture,* Blackwell, 1996.

Ceruzzi, Paul E. *A History of Modern Computing.* Cambridge: The MIT Press, 1998.

Davenport, Thomas H., and John C. Beck. *The Attention Economy: Understanding the New Currency of Business.* Harvard Business School Press, 2001.

Dowling, Paul J., Jr. *Web Advertising and Marketing.* Prima, 1996.

Downes, Larry, Mui, Chunka, and Nicholas Negroponte. *Unleashing the Killer App.* Harvard Business School Press, 1998.

Emery, Vince. *How to Grow Your Business on the Internet,*3rd ed. Coriolis Group, 1997.

Ezor, Jonathan. *Clicking Through: A Survival Guide for Bringing Your Company Online.* Bloomberg, 2000.

Forester, Tom, and Perry Morrison. *Computer Ethics: Cautionary Tales and Ethical Dilemmas in Computing.* MIT Press, 1993.

Hauben, Michael, and Ronda Hauben. *Netizens: On the History and Impact of Usenet and the Internet.* IEEE Computer Society, May 1997.

Hise, Phaedra. *Growing Your Business Online: Small Business Strategies for Working the World Wide Web.* Holt, 1996.

Korper, Steffano, and Juanita Ellis. *The E-Commerce Book: Building the E-Empire.* Academic Press, 2000.

Kosiur, David. *Understanding Electronic Commerce,* Microsoft Press, 1997.

Loshin, Pete. *TCP/IP Clearly Explained.* Academic Press, 1997.

McCormack, Mark H. *Staying Street Smart in the Internet Age: What Hasn't Changed About the Way We Do Business.* Viking, 2000.

Moon, Michael. *Firebrands!: Building Brand Loyalty in the Internet Age.* McGraw-Hill Professional Book Group, 2000.

Naugle, Matthew. *Network Protocols.* McGraw Hill, 1999.

Negroponte, Nicholas. *Being Digital.* Random House, 1995.

Oberst, Robert D. *2020 Web Vision: How the Internet Will Revolutionize Future Homes, Business & Society.* Upublish.com, 2001.

O'Loughlin, Luanne, et al. *Online Auctions: The Internet Guide for Bargain Hunters & Collectors.* McGraw-Hill, 2000.

Pierce, J.R. *An Introduction to Information Theory: Symbols, Signals and Noise,* 2nd ed. Dover Publications, 1980.

Plunkett, Jack W. *Plunkett's E-Commerce & Internet Business Almanac.* Plunkett Research, Ltd., 2000.

Power, Thomas, Weber, Mike, and Bryan Boswell. *E-Business to the Power of 12: The Principles of Competition.* Financial Times/ Prentice Hall, 2001.

Rheingold, Howard. *Tools for Thought.* MIT Press, 2000.

Rosen, Anita. *The E-Commerce Question and Answer Book.* Amacom, 2002.

Schrage, Michael. *Serious Play: How the World's Best Companies Simulate to Innovate.* Harvard Business School Press, 2000.

Shim, Jae K., Anique A. Qureshi, Joel G. Siegel, and Roberta M. Siegel. *The International Handbook of Electronic Commerce.* AMACOM, 2000.

Sweeney, Susan. *101 Internet Businesses You Can Start From Home.* Maximum Press, 2001.

———. *101 Ways to Promote Your Web Site,* 3rd ed. Maximum Press, 2001.

Szydlik, Sherry and Lamont Wood. *E-trepreneur: A Radically Simple and Inexpensive Plan for a Profitable Internet Store in 7 Days.* John Wiley & Sons, 2000.

Tapscott, Don. *Creating Value in the Network Economy.* Harvard Business School Press, 1999.

———. *The Digital Economy.* The McGraw-Hill Companies, 2000.

———. *Growing Up Digital: The Rise of the Net Generation.* McGraw-Hill Professional, 1999.

Tiernan, Bernadette. *e-tailing.* Dearborn Financial Publishing Inc., 2000.

Walden, Gene and Tom Shaughnessy. *The 100 Best Technology Stocks to Own for the Long Run: Investing in the New Economy and the Companies that Make it Click,* 2nd ed. Dearborn Trade, 2001.

Ziff-Davis, II:793

Allen, Robert, I:38

Alliance Capital Partners, II:602

Alliance for Global Business, I:413

Alliances, strategic, **II:578–580**

Allot Communications, I:49

Ally & Gargano, I:291

Alpha microprocessor, I:202, 203

Altair 8800, II:590–591

AltaVista Company, **I:13–15;** I:425
  Affiliate Network, I:14
  CMGI Inc. and, I:13–14, 132
  Compaq Computer Corporation and, I:13, 132; II:523, 694
  DoubleClick Inc. and, I:218, 219
  Hoover's Online and, I:374
  MSN and, II:507
  shopping section, II:599
  Wetherell, David and, II:763
  Zip2 and, II:523

Alteon WebSystems, II:558

AlterNet, I:2; II:729

Amadeus Travel Commerce, I:237

Amault, Bernard, I:336

Amazing Media, I:385

Amazon.com, **I:15–18;** I:61–64
  Advantage program, I:62
  advertising, I:8, 10
  America Online and, I:62
  Asia and, I:328
  associates programs, I:62, 398; II:504
  auction site, I:16–17, 40, 62, 144, 228, 239–240
  vs. Barnes and Noble, I:15, 17, 18
  brand recognition, I:17, 76, 77; II:612
  business model for, I:93–94
  business plan, I:96, 97, 274
  CDNow and, I:115; II:499
  e-commerce solutions from, I:236
  economies of scale, I:238
  FedEx Corporation and, I:293
  Greenlight.com and, I:354
  history of, I:15–17, 341
  holiday seasons, I:16, 17–18, 62
  Hoover's Online and, I:374
  initial public offering, I:394
  innovations by, I:397–398
  kitchen products, I:63
  market research by, II:490
  market value of, I:341–342
  music, I:16, 62, 63
  Netcenter and, II:598
  one-click shopping, II:656–657
  patent infringement, I:54–55
  PlanetAll and, II:763
  platform, II:597
  product management by, II:612
  profitability of, I:16–17, 18, 62, 63
  ranking of, I:227
  relaunch of, II:755
  software sales, I:239–240
  toys on, I:16–18, 52, 63, 117–118, 274; II:747
  wireless access to, II:593
  Yahoo! and, I:62

AMD, I:405, 406

Amelio, Gilbert, II:444

America Online, I:26–30, 89; II:672–675. *See also* AOL Time Warner; Case, Stephen M.

advertising, I:8
Amazon.com and, I:62
Ameritrade Holding Corporation and, I:22; II:634
associates programs, II:579
Australia, I:331
Barnesandnoble.com and, I:54; II:598
B2B e-commerce initiatives, II:599
Book Link Technologies and, I:131, 296
brand recognition, I:77
business model for, I:95; II:673–674
business plan, I:97; II:673–674
Cassiopeia handheld computers and, I:114
co-branding by, I:77
competition with, I:143
CompuServe Inc. and, II:497
eBay and, I:225, 226; II:764
eToys and, I:275
Europe, I:338
Excite@Home and, I:281, 283
France, I:338
Gateway and, I:320
General Mills alliance, I:78
Gomez Inc. and, II:659
growth of, II:673
history of, I:28–29, 340; II:672–673
initial public offering, I:28, 394
Inktomi Corporation and, I:397
international market for, I:112; II:673
Internet Explorer and, I:112, 143, 317; II:503
Internet service providers and, I:424
iPlanet Enterprise Web Server and, I:270
iVillage Inc. and, I:109
local news, I:112
Loudcloud Inc. and, II:471
marketing by, II:490
merger of, I:29–30, 95, 112; II:497, 651, 674
Microsoft Corporation and, I:112; II:490, 506, 673
Monster.com and, II:514
Motley Fool and, II:519
Netcenter and, II:545, 599
Netscape Communications and, I:25, 53, 95; II:497, 543, 544
Oprah.com and, II:566, 767–768
Shopping Channel, I:92
subscribers to, II:505, 507
Ticketmaster and, II:701
wireless access to, I:112; II:674

America West, II:580, 602, 603

American Airlines, II:540, 601, 602, 603, 710, 745

American Bankers Association, I:195

American Bell Inc., I:37–38

American Classic Voyages Company, II:712

American Express Blue card, I:208

American Federation of Teachers, I:367

American Information Systems, I:285

American Institute of Certified Public Accountants, I:233–234

American Management Association, II:608

American Messenger Company, II:722

American National Standards Institute (ANSI), **I:18–20;** II:532, 533
  on BASIC, I:56
  on C, I:103
  on FORTRAN, I:307
  international standards, I:347
  X12/EDIFACT Alignment Plan, I:245; II:718–719

American Registry for Internet Numbers (ARIN), I:420

American Stock Exchange, I:433

American Telephone and Telegraph. *See* AT&T Corporation

America's Job Bank, II:515

Ameritech, I:423; II:710

Ameritrade Holding Corporation, **I:20–23;** I:76; II:579, 634

Ameritrade Institutional Services Inc., I:21

Ameritrade Online Investor Index, I:22

AmeriVest Inc., I:21

AMFM Inc., I:133, 135

Ami Pro, II:470

AMP Inc., I:294

Amplifiers, operational, I:23

AMR Corporation, II:710

AMR Research Inc., I:88; II:646–647, 667

Analog, **I:23;** I:192–193; II:690

Andersen, Matthew, I:242

Andersen Consulting
 on business plans, I:116–117
 on e-books, I:229
 e-business consulting by, I:233
 on micro-payments, II:500, 727
 on value creation, II:733
 on wireless devices, II:593

Anderson, Howard, II:485, 786

Anderson, Kent, I:312

Andreessen, Marc, **I:24–25;** I:130; II:542, 544, 698
 Global Trading Web Association and, I:350
 Loudcloud Inc. and, I:24, 25, 395; II:471

Andresen, Matthew, I:434

Andrews McMeel Universal, II:519

Angel investors, **I:25–26;** II:669

Animations, flash, II:754

Annan, Kofi, I:324

Annenberg Public Policy Center, I:124; II:608

Anonymity
 auction sites, II:564
 cash cards, II:581
 criminal activity, I:145, 149; II:463–464
 cyberculture, I:171–172
 digital cash, I:194
 electronic communications networks, I:400
 etiquette, II:541
 misinformation, II:511, 512

Anschutz, Philip, II:623, 624, 625

Anschutz Corporation, II:623

ANSI. *See* American National Standards Institute

ANSI character set, II:533

ANSI X12, I:245; II:718–719

AnswerThink Consulting Group, I:302

Anthrax, II:646

Anti-Cybersquatting Consumer Protection Act, I:174, 216

Antique auction sites, I:226–227

Anti-terrorism legislation, II:465

Antitrust litigation
 AT&T Corporation, I:37–38
 browser software, I:53
 IBM Corporation, I:378, 379, 380

interchanges and, I:412
 Microsoft Corporation, I:315–318, 322; II:503, 504–505, 508, 543

Anti-virus software, I:154–155, 358; II:737–738

AnyDay.com, II:578

AOL AAdvantage, II:540

AOL Mobile Messenger, I:112

AOL Time Warner Inc., **I:26–30**. *See also* America Online; Case, Stephen M.; Time Warner Inc.
 vs. Bertelsmann AG, I:58
 Earthlink and, I:224
 formation of, I:27, 29–30, 95, 112
 interactive TV, I:161
 iVillage Inc. and, II:767
 Motley Fool and, II:519
 MusicNet and, II:629
 Napster and, II:529
 small business portal, I:88

AOLTV, I:160

APEC (Association of Petroleum Exporting Countries), I:344

Apex Interactive Inc., II:656

APNIC (Asia Pacific Network Information Centre), I:420

Apollo Computers, I:363

Apparel customization, II:492

Apple Computer Inc., **I:30–32**
 Adobe Systems Inc. and, II:579
 Earthlink and, I:224; II:579
 education market, I:30, 31; II:444
 Ellison, Lawrence J., I:257
 Gates, Bill, I:315–316
 history of, I:30–32; II:443, 444, 591, 592, 774–775
 IBM Corporation and, I:32; II:592
 Jobs, Steven P., I:30, 32; II:443–445, 591, 774
 Lotus Development Corporation and, II:470
 Microsoft Corporation and, I:31, 32; II:444, 502–503, 508, 592
 Mississippi 2000 Project, II:558
 Nortel Networks and, II:558
 Novell and, II:559
 PostScript for, I:3
 PowerPC and, II:522
 Winer, David, II:766
 Wozniak, Stephen G., I:30, 249; II:443, 591; **II:774–775**

Apple Education Foundation, I:30

Apple Language Card, I:31

Apple University Consortium, I:31

Appleman, Daniel, II:617

AppleScript, II:766

AppleTalk, I:31

Applets, II:440–441

Application Expert, I:157; II:675

Application hackers, I:358

Application integration software, I:403

Application servers, I:270

Application service providers (ASP), **I:32–34;** I:48–49; II:573, 640, 648, 664–665

AppSense Technologies Ltd., II:703

Aptis Communications Inc., II:558

Arbitron Company, II:676

Arca Systems Inc., I:285

Archipelago Holdings LLC, **I:34–35;** I:241, 242

Archipelago Investment LLC, I:34

Archipelago Securities Exchange LLC, I:34

Architecture
  business, I:349
  information, **I:386–387**
  open, I:369–370; II:565–566

Archives, I:408

Ardent Communications Corporation, I:128

Arena (software), II:698

Argentina, I:335, 368

Ariba Inc., I:136, 269, 297

ARIN (American Registry for Internet Numbers), I:420

Arista label, I:59

Arithmometer, II:720

Armstrong, Michael, I:36, 38

Army, Navy and Defense Logistics Agency, I:248

Army Standard Information Management Systems (ASIMS), I:247

ARPA. *See* Advanced Research Projects Agency

ARPAnet, **I:35–36;** I:369–370
  in Australia, I:330
  development of, I:416, 419; II:513, 765
  Tomlinson, Ray and, I:257

ArrowPoint Communications Inc., I:129

Article Numbering Association, I:246

Artificial intelligence, I:401

Artnet.com, I:227

Asahi Corporation, I:113

Asbury Automotive Group, I:354

Ascend Communications, II:476

ASCNet (Australian Science Network), I:330

Ascom, I:159

Asea Brown Voberi Inc., I:203

Ashford.com, I:16, 228

Ashton Technology Group, I:351

Asia, **I:326–330;** I:335. *See also* China; India; Japan
  Compaq Computer Corporation in, I:141
  Dell Computer Corporation in, I:188
  digital divide and, I:199, 201
  DoubleClick Inc. in, I:220
  eBay in, I:227
  EDS in, I:248
  FedEx Corporation in, I:291
  Gateway in, I:319
  Internet access in, I:342, 416
  Monster.com in, II:515
  online banking in, I:50
  Yahoo! in, II:783
  Yankee Group in, II:787

Asia Pacific Network Information Centre (APNIC), I:420

ASIMS (Army Standard Information Management Systems), I:247

ASP. *See* Application service providers

ASP Industry Consortium, I:33; II:664

ASP ManagedOps Inc., II:665

Aspect Development Inc., I:104

Asseily, Henri, I:67–69

Assembly languages, I:307; II:616

Assembly lines, I:390; II:491

Assets
  intangible, **I:401–402;** I:407; II:687
  intellectual capital as, I:407
  tangible, I:401, 402

Associated Communications, II:480–481, 691–692

Associated Group, II:480–481

Associates programs, I:62, 398; II:504

Association for Computing Machinery, I:149–150, 214

Association for Information and Image Management (AIIM), **I:387**

Association of Community Organizations for Reform Now (ACORN), II:759

Association of Independent Music, II:529

Association of Information Technology Professionals, I:150

Association of Internet Professionals, II:769

Association of Petroleum Exporting Countries (APEC), I:344

Association of Purchasing Management, I:306

Asymetrix, I:11

Asynchronous transfer mode (ATM), I:127, 128

At Home (company), II:599

Atamp;T, I:281

Atari, II:593

Athletes, II:589

Athlon microprocessors, I:405

Atkinson, Bill, II:698

ATM (Asynchronous transfer mode), I:127, 128

ATMs. *See* Automated teller machines

AT&T Broadband, I:36

AT&T Business, I:36–38

AT&T Consumer, I:36

AT&T Corporation, **I:36–39**
  Africa One and, I:324
  breakup of, I:38
  Dell Computer Corporation and, I:187
  Excite@Home and, I:281, 283–284
  fiber optics and, I:294
  history of, I:36–38
  Internet service providers and, I:419, 423, 424
  Lucent Technologies and, II:475–476
  Mandl, Alex J., II:480
  Microsoft Corporation and, II:504
  Nortel Networks and, II:557
  Sun Microsystems and, II:679
  TechTV and, II:793
  UNIX version, I:316; II:721, 725
  Yahoo! and, II:578

AT&T Global Information Solutions, I:38

AT&T Interactive Group, I:38

AT&T Wireless, I:36

Attention economy, **I:39–40**

AtWeb, II:544

Auction sites, **I:40–42.** *See also* eBay
  Amazon.com, I:16–17, 40, 62, 144, 228, 239–240
  anonymity on, II:564

automobile industry, I:163
    business model for, I:94–95
    business-to-consumer, I:41
    commission-free, I:144
    consumer interest in, I:225
    consumer-to-consumer, I:40–41
    development of, I:40–42, 341, 398; II:564–565
    dynamic pricing, II:606
    Egghead.com, I:239
    fine art, I:40, 226–227
    fraud on, I:41, 176, 227, 308; II:564
    Lycos, I:228
    mediation services for, I:212
    mergers of, II:497
    outsourcing, I:289
    portals, I:41
    private-label, I:226, 289
    procurement systems, I:272
    profitability of, I:228; II:564
    ranking of, I:228
    regional, II:565
    sales on, I:40–41
    software for, I:136
    warehouse clubs, I:290
    Whitman, Margaret, I:225, 227–228; II:564–565, 764
    Yahoo!, I:40, 144, 226–227, 228; II:565, 784

Auction Web, I:94, 398; II:564, 764

Auctions, reverse, I:88, 95, 163; II:603

AuctionWatch.com, I:41

Audiences
    measurement reports, II:447
    target, I:6, 52, 218; II:530

Audio, I:261; II:444, 522–523
    RealAudio, II:627, 628
    streaming, II:530, 676–677
    wireless devices for, II:555

AudioGalaxy, II:528

August Capital, II:614

Australia, I:100; **I:330–332;** II:515, 546

Australian Academic & Research Network (AARNet), I:330–331

Australian Overseas Telecommunications Commission, I:330

Australian Science Network (ASCNet), I:330

Authentication, **I:42**
    digital certificates for, I:195, 196
    digital signatures for, I:204–205
    electronic data interchange and, I:246
    of information, II:512
    RSA Data Security and, II:635
    service level agreements and, II:648

Authoring tools, I:4

Authoritarianism, I:391

Authorization and authorization codes, **I:43–43;** I:108, 196, 204–205, 299

Auto racing sponsorship, I:110

AutoCAD, II:539

Automated clearinghouse, I:193

Automated teller machines (ATMs), I:65, 193, 204, 277

Automatic Sequence Controlled Calculator, I:378; II:590

Automobile dealers, I:353–354; II:482

Automobile industry
    electronic data interchange for, I:245
    marketing by, II:487–488, 489
    marketplaces for, I:137, 162–164

Automobile loans, I:109

Automobile rentals, II:603, 712

Automobile sales
    Amazon.com, I:16, 17
    CarsDirect.com, I:109–111
    channel transparency in, I:119–120
    CitySearch.com, II:701
    complaints about, I:211
    consortia-led, I:87, 88
    Greenlight.com, I:353–355
    by manufacturers, II:482
    Priceline.com, II:601, 602, 603

AutoNation Inc., II:602

AutoTrader.com, I:354

Autoweb.com, I:110

Auto-Xchange, I:163

AVS (Address verification service), II:495, 581

Award Sites!, I:44

Awards, Web, **I:43–45;** II:753

Ayvazian, Berge, II:786, 787

B

Baby boomers, II:686

Baby Center Inc., I:275

Backbone. *See* Infrastructure; Telecommunications infrastructure

Backbone Network Service (vBNS), II:553

Backups, II:510–511

Backus, John, I:306–307; II:590, 617

Backward compatibility, II:679

Ballard, Greg, II:678

Ballmer, Steve, **I:47;** I:314, 317; II:584

Bancroft, David, I:44

BancSystems Association Inc., I:248

Bandwidth, **I:47–48**
    Bluetooth standard for, II:555
    commoditization and, I:138
    Internet2, I:159
    microwave networks, II:692
    multimedia, II:522
    Next Generation Internet Initiative, II:553
    photonics and, II:595
    streaming media, II:676

Bandwidth management, **I:48–49;** I:235

Bandwidth Trading Organization, I:138

Bank of America, II:625

Bank One Corporation, I:109

Banking, online, **I:49–51;** I:277, 278; II:777. *See also* Payment options and services

Banks. *See also* Acquiring banks
    cannibalization in, I:107
    card-issuing, **I:108**
    churn in, I:127
    financing from, I:295–298
    interchanges and, I:412
    kiosks in, II:454–455

Bannan, Karen, II:581

Banner advertisements, I:6–7, 10; **I:51–52;** II:445

brand recognition, I:76
click through rates for, I:6, 9, 10, 51; II:459, 487
privacy, II:607–608
profiling, II:615

Bantam Books, I:59

Barber, Brad, I:432–433

Barbour, John, **I:52–53**

Barksdale, Jim, **I:53–54;** I:130, 340; II:542, 543

Barksdale Group, I:53

Barlow, John Perry, I:249

Barnat, Christopher, I:172

Barnes & Noble Digital, I:55

Barnes & Noble Inc., I:54–55, 61, 92; II:507, 728

Barnes & Noble University, I:55

Barnesandnoble.com, **I:54–55**
    advertising by, I:8, 17
    vs. Amazon.com, I:17, 18
    America Online and, I:54; II:598
    Bertelsmann AG and, I:54, 59, 338
    CDNow and, I:115
    co-branding by, I:77
    e-books, I:229, 254
    initial public offering, I:395
    Lycos and, II:693
    one-click shopping, II:656–657
    patent infringement, I:54–55
    Walt Disney Company and, II:746
    wireless access to, II:593

Barnet, Bruce, I:104

Baron, Talia, II:593

Barrett, Craig, I:356

Barry, Hank, II:529

BASIC, **I:56;** I:314–315; II:502, 590–591

Basic Communications Corporation, I:405

BASYS Automation Systems, I:203

Batch processing, II:513

Batelle, II:690

Bay Networks Inc., II:558

BBB Auto Line, I:211

BBB Philanthropic Advisory Service, I:211

BBBOnLine Inc., **I:56–57;** II:613, 660

BBBOnLine Privacy Seal, I:57

BBN Corporation, I:424

bCentral, I:88; II:505

BEA Systems, Inc., I:267

Bear Stearns, I:185

BearShare, II:528

Beauty products, I:78

Because It's Time Network (BITNET), **I:66–67;** I:310

Bechtel Group, II:761

Bechtolsheim, Andreas, II:494, 679

Becker, Robert, II:448

Beemsterboer, II:723

Beenz.com, II:474, 581

Behavior analysis software, I:155, 358

Beijing International Information Processing Company, I:248

Belief.net, I:287

Bell, Alexander Graham, I:36

Bell, George, I:281

Bell Atlantic, I:424

Bell Laboratories, I:37, 294, 393; II:476

Bell South Corporation, I:248; II:625

Bell Telephone Company, I:36; II:557, 558

Bellcom, I:37

Bemer, Robert, II:788

Benchmark Capital, I:52, 297; II:564, 614, 642

Benhamou, Eric, II:577

Berkeley University BSD4.x, II:725

Berkshire Hathaway, I:82–84

Berne Convention, I:410; II:770

Berners-Lee, Timothy, **I:57–58;** I:371; II:771–772
    Global Trading Web Association, I:350
    HTML, I:376
    protocol development, II:697–698
    on standards, II:773
    vision of, I:58, 197
    W3C, I:343, 371; II:772

Bertelsmann, Carl, I:59

Bertelsmann, Friederike, I:59

Bertelsmann AG, **I:58–60;** I:338
    America Online and, I:29
    Australia, I:331
    Barnesandnoble.com and, I:54, 59, 338
    CDNow and, I:90; II:498–499
    Lycos and, I:59, 115, 282; II:693, 694, 695
    music, I:58, 59, 60
    MusicNet and, II:629
    Napster and, I:58, 60, 338; II:586
    Terra Lycos, Inc. and, I:59, 115, 338; II:499

Bertelsmann eCommerce Group, I:58, 59–60, 114, 115; II:499

Bertelsmann Lesering, I:59

Bessemer Venture Partners, I:297

Best Buy, I:267

Best of the Web Awards, I:43

Better Business Bureau, I:56–57, 125, 211
    Connecticut, II:604, 606
    on PayPal, II:583
    on Priceline.com, II:604, 606

Betty, Garry, I:224

Betty Crocker Web site, I:77, 78

Beyond.com, I:60–61; II:632

Bezos, Jeff, I:15–18; **I:61–64;** I:341. *See also* America Online
    business model, I:93
    business plan, I:96, 97
    innovations by, I:397–398
    market research by, II:490

Bharadwaj, Rajeev, II:728

Bicycles, II:482–483, 614, 722

Bidding strategy, I:40

Bidzos, Joe, I:263, 264; II:635, 636

on retail sales, I:16

Bots. *See also* Shopping bots
  intelligent agents, I:81–81, 410–412; II:604–605, 668
  personal financial, I:411
  vs. spiders, II:668

Bottlenecks, I:48; II:596, 676

Bottomley, Elizabeth, II:561

Bottomline Technologies, II:724

Bouhot and Le Gendre, I:313

Bowers, Ann, II:561

Bowman Capital, II:614

Bozell, Jacobs, Kenyon & Eckhardt Inc., I:218

Bradner, Scott, II:510

Brady, Diane, II:768

Braille writing devices, I:378

Brain Capital, I:184, 434

Brainplay.com, II:497

Brand, Stewart, II:641

Brand building, **I:75–78**

Brand recognition
  advertising for, I:6, 7–8, 75, 76, 77; II:618
  AltaVista as, I:13–14
  Amazon.com, I:17, 76, 77; II:612
  America Online, I:77
  auction sites, I:41
  banner ads for, I:51
  bricks and clicks, I:90
  brokerage services, I:76–77, 278, 279; II:618
  children and, I:123–124
  creating *vs.* supporting, II:488
  domain names, I:173–174
  DoubleClick Inc., I:218
  Dow Jones Internet Index, I:191–192
  eBay, I:76
  E*Trade, I:278, 279
  Levi Strauss, II:466, 467
  loyalty, I:77; II:474
  market research for, II:485
  Monster.com, II:514, 618
  Netscape Communications, I:77
  Priceline.com, I:76, 77
  product management, II:611
  rebranding, II:754
  Yahoo!, I:77; II:782

Brazil
  distance learning in, I:368
  e-commerce in, I:335
  Gartner Inc. in, I:313
  infrastructure of, I:334
  UUNET in, II:731
  Yankee Group in, II:485, 786

Breier, Mark, I:60

Brenton, Flint, I:142

Bressler, R., I:30

Brewer, Charles, I:224

Brewer, Eric A., I:396

Bricklin, Dan, II:451, 766

Bricks-and-clicks
  Australian, I:332
  brand recognition of, I:90
  business model for, I:91, 92

change and, I:116
channel transparency in, I:120
dot com collapse and, II:652
loyalty to, II:650
restructuring, II:631–632

Bridge Information Systems, I:69, 72; II:663

Brigham Young University, II:709

Brisco, Robert, I:109, 110, 111

Bristol-Myers Squibb Company, II:486

Britain. *See* United Kingdom

Britannica.com, II:578

British Post Office, I:37

British Telecommunications PLC, I:14, 38, 39, 127, 294

British Terrorism Act, I:148

Broadband Networks Inc., II:558

Broadband technology, **I:78–80;** I:157–158
  cable TV, I:161
  infrastructure for, I:78–79, 157–158, 419
  Motorola in, II:522
  Napster, II:527
  NTIA, II:537
  Qwest Communications, II:625
  rural areas, I:224
  streaming media, II:676
  Teligent Inc., II:691–692
  United Kingdom, I:337

Broadcast.com Inc., I:94, 165–166; II:599, 743, 783

Broadcom Corporation, I:372

BroadJump, I:79–80

BroadVision Inc., I:237; II:545

Brochure web sites, II:748, 751, 754

Brock, James R., I:235

Brokerage model, **I:80–82;** I:94–95

Brokerage services, I:80–82, 94–95, 430–433. *See also* Electronic
communications networks
  alliances between, II:579
  Ameritrade Holding Corporation, I:20–23
  Bloomberg L.P., I:70
  brand recognition, I:76–77, 278, 279; II:618
  Charles Schwab Corporation, I:121–123
  Datek Online Brokerage Services LLC, I:183–184
  development of, II:634
  discount, I:20–23, 121–123
  E*Trade, I:277–278
  extended hours, I:22, 432; II:612
  Gomez Inc. on, I:431; II:659
  real-time, I:183
  traditional, I:431
  wholesale, I:21
  wireless access to, I:22, 158

Brokers, customs, I:292

Brown, Marc, I:398; II:656

Brown, Richard H., I:246, 248, 249

Browser software. *See also* Internet Explorer; Netscape Navigator
  anti-compete laws, I:53
  bundling, I:24, 53, 84–85, 130, 316–317; II:543
  development of, I:24–25, 130, 340–341; II:542–545, 698, 771
  infomediary model, I:385
  killer apps, II:452
  low-end, II:756
  mergers and, II:497
  Mosaic, I:24, 130; II:542, 543

Security Sockets Layer for, I:264
web scripting languages, II:748

Brusk, Robert, II:721

Brussels Convention, I:344

Brynjolfesson, Erik, II:474, 632

BSD4.x, II:725

BSP (Business service providers), I:33

B2B e-commerce. *See* Business-to-business e-commerce

B2C e-commerce. *See* Business-to-consumer e-commerce

Btrieve, II:559

Budget Rent-A-Car, II:603

Buffett, Warren, **I:82–84**

Building Online Demand (BOLD), II:524, 655

Bulletin boards, I:209; II:609

Bundling, I:24, 53; **I:84–85;** I:130, 316–317; II:543

Bureau of Labor Statistics, II:768–769

Burger King Corporation, II:589

Burma, I:148

Burroughs, William S., II:720

Burroughs Corporation, II:720

Burton, Richard, I:407

Bush, George W., I:252

Business @ the Speed of Thought, I:317

Business architecture, I:349

Business cycles, II:549, 550, 650

Business Desk (software), II:672

Business forecasting, **I:301–303**

Business models, **I:93–96;** II:481–482, 677–678. *See also* Community model
  advertising, I:94, 98–99; II:445
  affiliate, I:10, 77; II:495–496, 619
  Amazon.com, I:93–94
  America Online, I:95; II:673–674
  auction site, I:94–95
  B2B e-commerce, I:91, 94–95
  for bricks-and-clicks, I:92
  brokerage, **I:80–82;** I:94–95
  Click-through, I:10, 68; II:495–496, 619
  Dell Computer Corporation, I:144, 187
  dot com collapse and, II:650
  eBay, I:94–95, 144
  electronic publishing, I:256
  first-to-market, I:144
  incubators and, I:382
  infomediary, **I:384–386**
  information, I:94
  manufacturer, **II:481–483**
  merchant, I:93–94; **II:495–497**
  name-your-price, II:580, 601–602, 603–604, 606, 687
  new economy and, II:551
  online services, I:95
  Priceline.com, I:95
  pure-play, I:92; II:651, 686
  subscription, **II:677–679**
  traditional, I:91, 92; II:482
  utility, **II:727–728**
  Yahoo!, I:94

Business news, II:456

Business plans, **I:96–98**

Amazon.com, I:96, 97, 274
  due diligence and, I:222
  financing and, I:295
  global, I:347
  managing, I:116–117
  strategic, II:672–675

Business service providers (BSPs), I:33

Business Software Alliance, I:239

Business transactions. *See* Transactions

Business Ware integration server, I:267

Business.com, I:77

Business-to-business e-commerce, **I:85–89**
  aggregators for, I:11
  Asian, I:327
  Australian, I:332
  automobile industry, I:137, 163
  Bertelsmann AG, I:61
  business model for, I:94–95
  Central and South American, I:334–335
  Cisco Systems in, I:127
  Commerce One in, I:136–137
  community model for, I:140
  customization and, II:492
  Dell Computer Corporation in, I:189
  digital signatures for, I:204
  dispute resolution for, I:212
  dot com collapse and, II:651
  e-commerce solutions for, I:236–237
  e-mail marketing for, I:259–260
  enterprise application integration for, I:267
  European, I:337
  external integration for, I:402–403
  extranets and, I:428
  financing for, I:295–296
  Firstsource Corporation, I:298
  Global Trading Web Association, I:350
  Gomez Inc., I:352
  intelligent agents for, I:411
  Internet payment providers, I:422
  marketplaces for, I:81, 345
  newsletters, II:552
  payment systems for, I:252; II:523, 580–583, 778
  platforms, II:597
  portals, I:88, 283, 298
  procurement systems for, I:271–273
  real-time transactions for, II:629–630
  sales in, I:85–86, 403
  shipping for, I:292
  storefront builders for, II:672
  vortals, II:740
  Yahoo! and, II:783

Business-to-consumer e-commerce, I:85; **I:89–93**
  business models for, I:91
  development of, I:89–90, 274
  dot com collapse and, II:651
  European, I:337
  integration for, I:403
  payment systems for, II:523, 777–778
  platforms, II:597
  portals, I:89, 91, 92
  profitability of, I:92
  vortals, II:740

Business-to-employee e-commerce, I:142

Butterfield & Butterfield, I:40, 226, 227; II:764

Buy.com Inc., **I:98–101;** I:115, 177, 395; II:651

BuyComp.com, I:99

BuyerZone.com, II:485

BuyLink Corporation, II:778

BuySite, I:236, 269, 350

BuyUSA, I:88

Bytecode, II:440

Bytravel.com, I:100

C

C2B Technologies, I:396

C2it payment service, II:583

C3 Marketplace, I:68

C programming language, **I:103–104;** II:440, 725

Cable & Wireless Inc., I:419, 424; II:648

Cable & Wireless Optus Ltd., I:331

Cable modems, I:78–79, 158, 281, 284; II:452–453

Cable services
    AOL Time Warner, I:29
    AT&T Corporation, I:38–39
    Excite@Home, I:282, 283
    transatlantic, I:37

Cable television
    advertisements, I:77
    AOL Time Warner, I:27
    Bertelsmann AG in, I:59
    bundling services, I:84
    CNET Networks in, I:133–134
    cost of, I:161
    high-speed access from, I:282
    Knight-Ridder, II:456
    Microsoft Corporation, II:504
    narrowcasting on, II:530
    pay-per-view, II:584–585

Cabletron Systems Inc., I:203

Cablevision Systems Corporation, I:282

Caching technology, I:396

CACI Products Company, I:156; II:675

Cadence Designs, II:721

Cahners, Norman, I:104

Cahners Business Information, **I:104–105**

Cahners In-Stat Group, II:593

CAIDA (Cooperative Association for Internet Data Analysis), I:420, 421

Calculators, I:113, 361, 363, 378; II:576, 590

Caliber System, I:292

Call center services, **I:105–106;** I:121, 167; II:724
    web-based, I:105–106; II:772

Callabra Software Inc., II:543

Callahan, Robert, II:792

Call-back, I:105

Camay soap, II:611

Cambrian Systems Corporation, II:558

Cambridge Technology Partners, II:560

Cameras
    digital, I:113, 114; II:613
    disposable, II:715
    video, II:775

Campbell, Alta, I:374

Campbell, Kirk, I:414

Camping products, II:490

Campsites, II:700

Campus Solutions, II:588

Canada, I:340, 416; II:712

Canadian Overseas Telecommunications Corporation, I:37

Canion, Joseph Rod, **I:106;** I:141

Cannavino, James A., II:589

Cannibalization, **I:107–108**

CANOE, II:782

Canon Inc., II:559

Canopy Group, II:556

Cansica, I:291

Capellas, Michael, I:141, 142

Capenter, Candice, **I:108–109**

Capital. *See also* Venture capital
    intellectual, **I:406–407**
    structural, I:406

Capital investment, I:98, 389

Capitalism, II:550

CAPSCO Software Canada Ltd., I:248

Captimark Corporation, I:249

Captus Networks, I:191

Car rentals, II:603, 712

Car sales. *See* Automobile sales

Card Capture Services Inc., I:277

Card verification value (CVV), I:309

Card-issuing banks, **I:108**

Cards
    cash, II:581
    debit, I:41, 124, 193, 206, 252
    greeting, I:54, 258; II:455
    phone, II:603
    SecurID, I:42
    smart, I:42, 65, 195, 299, 309

Career Builder, II:515

Career services, II:493, 514–546

CareTech Solutions Inc., I:156

Carnivore surveillance system, I:253; II:607

Carpenter, Candice, I:280, 435–436; II:767

CarPoint, I:111, 336

CarsDirect.com, **I:109–111;** I:353, 355

Carsey-Werner-Mandabach Company, II:767

Carts, shopping, I:177, 235; II:570; **II:656–657**

Cary, Frank T., I:379

Cascade (virus), I:153

Cascading Style Sheets (CSS), II:751

Case, Stephen M., I:28, 30, 95; **I:111–113;** I:143, 340. *See also* America Online; AOL Time Warner
    strategic planning by, II:673–674

CASE (Computer-aided systems engineering), II:569

Casey, Jim, II:722

Cash, digital, **I:193–194;** II:581

Cash cards, II:581

Casio Computer Co. Ltd., **I:113–114**

Casio Electronic Devices, I:113

Casio Soft Inc., I:114

Cassiopeia handheld computers, I:113–114

Castells, Manuel, I:391

Catalogs, II:490, 688

Catholic Healthcare West, II:589

CAUCE (Coalition Against Unsolicited Commercial E-Mail), I:261; II:666

Cause-and-effect forecasting, I:302

CBS Inc., II:585, 791

CbXML (Electronic Business XML), I:20

CD1 Financial.com, I:109

CDNow Inc., **I:114–116;** II:498–499
Amazon.com and, I:115; II:499
Bertelsmann AG purchase of, I:60, 90, 115
Lycos and, II:693
Napster and, II:528
order fulfillment problems, I:312

CDNow.com, I:18

CD-ROMs
Amazon.com and, I:15, 62
CDNow and, I:114
comparative shopping for, II:474
read-write, II:444
write, II:527

CEFACT (Centre for the Facilitation of Administration Commerce and Trade), II:718

Celarier, Ian, I:400

Celent Communications, I:241

Celeron, I:405

Cellular multiprocessing systems, II:721

Cellular telephones. *See also* Wireless devices
AT&T Corporation, I:38
financial services on, I:50
Home Location Register system for, I:248
Motorola, II:520, 521–522
Nokia Corporation, II:554–556
payment systems for, II:582, 777–778
reviews of, II:613
WAP-enabled, II:555, 654
web-enabled, I:158

Cendant Corporation, I:54

Ceneca Communications, II:674

Censorship, I:147–148, 346; II:464

Census Bureau, II:590, 768–769
on B2B e-commerce, I:86
on B2C e-commerce, I:89
on the digital divide, I:198
on electronic data interchange, I:85
on total sales, I:90, 91

Center for Information Technology and Dispute Resolution, I:212

Center for Research in Electronic Commerce (CREC), II:769

Center for Strategic and International Studies, I:145

Center for Venture Research, I:25–26

Central America, **I:332–336;** I:416; II:786, 787

Central Intelligence Agency (CIA), I:145, 181, 256

Central Limit Order Book (CLOB), I:35

Central processing unit (CPU), II:501, 590, 616

Centre European de Recherche Nucleaire (CERN), I:57; II:698

Centre for the Facilitation of Administration Commerce and Trade (CEFACT), II:718

Centrex, I:37

Centura Software, I:156

Cerent Corporation, I:129

Ceres Securities Inc., I:21; II:579, 634

Cerf, Vinton, I:370

CERN (Centre European de Recherche Nucleaire), I:57; II:698

CERT (Computer Emergency Response Team), I:147, 153, 154

Certificate revocation list, I:196

Certificates, digital. *See* Digital certificates

Certificates, merchant, I:352

Cerulli Associates, I:241

Ceruzzi, Paul E., II:663

CGI (Common Gateway Interface), II:748

Chaebols, I:329

Chain letters, II:541

Champman, Alvah H., Jr., II:456

Champy, James A., II:589

Chandrasekhar, K.B., I:284

Change, managing, **I:116–118**

Change-of-address systems, I:260

Channel cannibalization, I:107

Channel conflict/harmony, **I:118–119**

Channel transparency, **I:119–120**

ChannelFusion Network, I:226

Charge-back, **I:120–121;** II:496, 581, 708

Charitable organizations, I:211

Charles Schwab Corporation, **I:121–123**

Charter Communications, I:12, 39, 223; II:793

Chat
call center services, I:105, 106
etiquette for, II:541
moderated *vs.* unmoderated, II:735
privacy, II:609
technology for, I:209

Cheap Tickets, I:117

CheckFree Corporation, I:252

Checks
electronic, I:193, 225; II:582, 777
paper, I:193

Chemdex, I:11

Chevron Corporation, I:294

ChiefMonster, II:515

Child pornography, I:146, 147, 346; II:464

Children, **I:123–126**
e-books for, I:229, 254
on hacking, I:151
investments by, I:430
privacy and, I:57, 124–125, 146; II:464, 608

Walt Disney Company and, II:746

Children's Online Privacy Protection Act, I:57, 125, 146; II:464, 608

Chile, I:335, 368

Chilton Business Group, I:104

China, I:328–329
    censorship in, I:148
    digital divide and, I:199
    DoubleClick Inc. in, I:220
    EDS in, I:248
    Great Firewall, II:465
    legislation in, I:344
    RSA Data Security in, II:636

China Management Systems Corporation, I:248

Chinese Ministry of Information Industry, I:344

Chips. *See* Microprocessors

Chips and Technologies Inc., I:405

Chissano, Joaquim Alberto, I:200

Chromatis Networks Inc., II:476

Chuang, Alfred, I:267

Churn, **I:126–127**

CIA (Central Intelligence Agency), I:145, 181, 256

CICB (company), I:294

CinemaNow, II:585

Circle.com, II:487

Cisco Systems Inc., **I:127–129**
    customer service site, I:169
    E-Government Web Privacy Coalition, I:241
    home networks, I:372
    Internet2 and, I:159
    market value of, II:739
    Nortel Networks and, II:558
    Qwest Communications and, II:624
    Y2K bug, II:788

CiscoFusion, I:128

CitiCorp, II:598

Citron, Jeffrey, I:183, 434; II:612

CityAuction Inc., II:700

City.Net, I:281; II:598

CitySearch.com, II:523, 699–700, 701

Civil liberties, I:249–250, 346

C.J. Singer, I:313

CL9, II:775

Clarify Inc., II:558

Claris, I:31; II:592

Clark, Candi, II:775

Clark, James H., **I:130–131;** I:340–341; II:542, 698

Clark, Mary Higgins, I:229, 254

Clarke, Ian, II:586

Clarke, Roger, I:330

Classified advertisements, I:6, 228

Classmates.com, I:8

Classrooms, I:366, 367

ClearPath HMP System, II:720, 721

CLEC (Competitive local exchange carrier), II:480–481, 691–692

Click-and-mortar companies. *See* Bricks-and-clicks

Click2Learn.com, I:11

Click-n-Build Web, I:224

ClickRewards program, II:539–540

Click2Talk, II:691

Click-Through Interactive, II:713

Click-through model, I:10, 68; II:495–496, 619

Click-through rates
    advertising, I:6, 9, 10, 51; II:459, 487
    affiliate model, II:495–496
    e-mail marketing, I:260
    newsletter ads, II:487

Clientize, II:552

Client-server systems, I:192, 266, 270, 316; II:587

Clifford, William, I:314

Clinton, Bill, I:195, 198, 204, 205

Clipper chip, I:265; II:635–636

CliqNow, II:713

CLOB (Central Limit Order Book), I:35

Closed-Loop Marketing Solutions, I:219

Clothing customization, II:492

CMD Group, I:104

CMGI Inc., **I:131–133**
    AltaVista and, I:13–14, 132
    Intel Corporation and, I:132, 296; II:763
    Lycos and, II:693, 694, 695
    Novell and, II:560
    @Ventures and, I:132, 296
    Wetherell, David and, II:762–763

CMG@Ventures. *See* CMGI Inc.

CMOS (Complementary metal oxide semiconductor), II:721

CMP Media LLC, II:706

CNBC.com, I:374–375

CNET Data Services, I:133

CNET Networks Inc., **I:133–135;** II:524, 525, 655, 791–793

CNET.com, I:133, 255, 352; II:552

CNN, I:215; II:540, 545

CNNfn.com, I:215

CNW Marketing/Research, I:110

Coalition Against Unsolicited Commercial E-Mail (CAUCE), I:261; II:666

Coalition for Computer Ethics, I:151

Cobalt Networks, II:681

COBOL (Common business-oriented language), **I:135–136;** II:502, 617, 788

Co-branding, I:77, 226; II:514

Code of Online Business Practices, I:57

Code Red, I:154, 358

Codes of ethics, I:149, 150

Codex Corporation, II:521

Cognitive lock-in, II:474

Cohesive Technology Solutions Inc., I:285

ColdFusion, I:52

Coleman, John, II:720

Collaborative commerce, II:666–667, 709, 734

Collaborative planning, forecasting and replenishment (CPFR), I:87

Collectibles, I:40, 226–227

College Marketing Group, I:131; II:762

Colleges, I:364–368; II:690. *See also* names of specific colleges and universities

Collins, Todd, I:354

Collins Radio, I:247

Collyns, Napier, II:641

Colombia, I:335

Colonialization, I:325–326

Colony, George Forrester, I:305, 306; II:485

Color television, II:521

Columbia House, I:115; II:499

Columbia Pictures, I:59

Comcast Corporation, I:281, 282, 284

COMDEX, II:706

Comer, Gary C., II:461, 462

Commerce Department. *See* Department of Commerce

Commerce One Inc., I:81; **I:136–137;** I:163, 236, 269, 350

Commerce Server 2000, II:672

CommerceNet, I:193, 350; II:573

Commercialization, I:360, 367, 371–372, 416

Commission Junction, I:51

Commission on International Trade Law, I:205

Commoditization, **I:137–138;** I:347

Commodore International Ltd., I:111

Common business-oriented language (COBOL), **I:135–136;** II:502, 617, 788

Common Gateway Interface (CGI), II:748

CommQuest Technologies, I:380

Communication protocols, **I:138–139.** *See also* Protocols

Communications Decency Act, I:146; II:465

Communicator (software), II:543

Community Calculator, II:759–760

Community colleges, I:365

Community model, **I:139–141; II:734–736**
    building, II:620–621
    cyberculture, I:171–172
    discussion forums, I:209
    Excite@Home, I:282
    iVillage Inc., I:436
    value creation from, II:734

Community technology centers, I:199

COMNET Conference & Expo, II:706

Company Media LLC, II:705

Company profiles, I:373–375

Compaq Computer Corporation, **I:141–142**
    AltaVista and, I:13, 132; II:523, 694
    Canion, Joseph Rod, I:106
    Cyrix microprocessors, I:405
    vs. Dell, I:187, 189

Digital Equipment Corporation merger, I:142, 202, 203, 359
    dynamic pricing by, II:606
    E-Government Web Privacy Coalition, I:241
    Gateway and, I:320
    history of, I:106, 141–142; II:591, 592
    IBM Corporation and, I:106, 380
    NetZero and, I:385
    Novell and, II:559
    personal computer sales, I:187
    servers, I:142, 187, 189
    Tandem Computers and, I:359

Comparison shopping, I:134–135, 262; II:474, 524–525, 604–605, 655

Compatibility, II:679, 756

Competition, **I:143–144**
    commoditization and, I:137–138
    vs. co-opetition, I:162
    international, I:347
    marketing plans, II:490
    Microsoft Corporation, I:315–317
    price wars, II:496
    regulation of, I:345

Competitive advantage, **I:144**

Competitive local exchange carrier (CLEC), II:480–481, 691–692

Compilers, II:617, 747

Complementary metal oxide semiconductor (CMOS), II:721

Compression formats, II:676

CompUSA, I:224; II:579

CompuServe Inc., I:28, 112, 143, 166; II:507, 673

Computer Accreditation Board, I:151

Computer and Business Equipment Association, II:532

Computer crime, **I:144–148;** II:463–464. *See also* Fraud; Hacking
    anonymity, I:145, 149; II:463–464
    denial-of-service attacks, I:90, 145, 153–154; **I:190–191;** I:358
    distributed denial-of-service attacks, I:190
    global e-commerce, II:464
    history of, I:153
    insider attacks, I:144–145
    international, I:147–148; II:464
    mirror sites, II:510–511
    NIIPA on, II:533–535
    reports on, II:464
    smurf attacks, I:190
    state legislation on, I:147; II:464
    time zones, II:702

Computer Crime and Security Survey, I:144

Computer Economics (company), II:773

Computer Emergency Response Team (CERT), I:147, 153, 154

Computer ethics, **I:149–151;** I:152

Computer Ethics Institute, I:149; **I:151–152**

Computer Fraud and Abuse Act, **I:152;** I:153, 309; II:464, 533

Computer hardware, I:91, 201; **I:359**

Computer integration. *See* Integration

Computer Sciences Corporation, I:86; II:740

Computer security, **I:152–155.** *See also* Authentication; Encryption
    application service providers for, II:664
    biometrics for, I:42; **I:64–65**
    breaches of, I:144
    in Central and South America, I:334
    COBOL and, I:136
    DefCon expo, II:706–707
    digital cash, I:194
    digital certificates, I:195

downloads, I:214

electronic data interchange, I:246

extranets, I:428, 429

Fischer, Addison and, I:299

GUIDEC for, I:321–322

insider attacks on, I:144–145

NIIPA on, II:533–535

online banking, I:50

peer-to-peer networks, II:586

SET for, II:645

spending on, I:358

statements, II:619

of tax information, I:251

terrorist attacks, II:647

Computer Security Institute, I:144, 153

Computer terminology, II:760

Computer viruses. *See* Viruses

Computer-aided systems engineering (CASE), II:569

Computer.com, I:77

Computerland, I:380

Computers. *See also* Handheld computing devices; Personal computers

comparative shopping for, I:262

development of, I:378–380; II:590–592

quantum, II:501

reports on, II:447

scalability of, II:639

standards for, I:19–20

wearable, I:262

Computers4Sure, I:298

Computing-Tabulating-Recording Company, I:377

Compuware Corporation, **I:155–157;** II:675

Comsat, I:37

Comstock, II:662

Concert (company), I:39

Conde Nast Publications, II:694

Condemned.org. *See* Internet Corporation for Assigned Names and Numbers

Confidentiality agreements, I:407

Configurable network computing, II:442

Conflict, channel, **I:118–119**

Connecticut Better Business Bureau, II:604, 606

Connectivity, Internet, **I:157–160;** I:402

Consolidated Freightways, II:654

Consolidated Stores Corporation, I:275

Consortia-led marketplaces, I:87–88

Constitutional issues, II:464–465, 608–609, 687–688

Consultants

e-commerce, **I:232–234**

information services from, I:385

information technology, I:313–314, 392; II:547

International Data Corporation, I:414

network solutions, II:547

Perot Systems Corporation, II:589

Sapient Corporation, II:638

Scient Corporation, II:642–643

Consumer electronics, I:16, 88, 113–114

Consumer Electronics Association, I:199; II:527, 705–706

Consumer Protection in the Global Electronic Marketplace, I:344

Consumer Reports e-Ratings, II:659

Consumer Reports Online, I:94; II:613

Consumer satisfaction. *See also* Customer service

BizRate.com, II:659–660

brand building, I:75–76

Buy.com Inc., II:651

customer relationship management software, I:168–169

customization and, II:492–493

Dell Computer Corporation, I:188

digital wallets, I:208

dot coms and, II:650

e-mail marketing, I:259–260

feedback and, II:756

kiosks and, II:455

loyalty and, II:473–476

PayPal, II:583

with personal computers, I:143, 188

product review services, II:613–614

shipping costs, I:274

shopping bots, II:655

shopping carts, II:656, 657

survey on, I:91, 188

time and, I:238

transaction processing, II:707–708

transparency, II:709

usability, II:755–757

value-added services, II:496–497

web site design, II:753

Consumer Sentinel, I:308

Consumer Wallet 2.1, I:207–208

ConsumerNet, II:713

ConsumerReview.com, II:614

Consumers Union, I:29

ConsumerSearch.com, II:613

Content, I:160; II:620, 687, 755

control of, I:346

delivery software, I:397

filtering software, I:125, 126, 155, 358; II:465

licensing, I:11; II:456

Content Bridge, I:397

Content management systems, II:755

Content Networking Solutions, I:397

Content Partner Program, II:614

Content providers, **I:160**

Continental Airlines, II:580, 601, 602, 603, 745

Continental Cablevision, I:38

Continuing education, I:367

Control Data Corporation, I:379

Control Video (company), I:111

Conventions, **II:704–707**

Convergence, **I:160–162**

Convergent Technologies, II:721, 787

Conway, Craig, II:588

Cookie technology

advertising, I:6, 52

disabling, II:616

DoubleClick Inc., I:218

privacy, II:607, 608

profiling, II:615

Cool Central, I:44

CoolSavings.com Inc., I:74; II:540

Cooperation, I:162, 347

Cooperative Association for Internet Data Analysis (CAIDA), I:420, 421

Coopers & Lybrand, I:296

Co-opetition, **I:162**

Copiers, I:363

CopyJet, I:363

Copyright
content providers, I:160
digital goods, I:214
e-books, I:230, 254
European, I:410
first sale doctrine, I:408, 409
Freenet and, II:586
intellectual property, I:408–409; II:463
international, I:408
Knight-Ridder and, II:456
Lotus Development Corporation and, II:470
music, I:114
Napster and, II:527–529
Sklyarov, Dimitri and, II:706–707
state legislation, I:409; II:463
treaties, I:410; II:463
WIPO on, II:770

Copyright Act, I:146, 408

Copyright Felony Act, I:408; II:463

Copyright Treaty, I:410; II:463

Corcoran, Elizabeth, I:236; II:569, 674, 777

Cordless telephones, II:691

Core Strategies, I:335

Corel Corporation, II:560

CoreTek Inc., II:558

Corning Inc., I:294; II:477

Corporation for Research and Educational Networking, I:67, 310

Cortal, II:579

Cotsakos, Christos, I:278

Council on Higher Education Accreditation, I:365

Counterfeit Access Device and Computer Fraud and Abuse Law, I:146

Country Stores Inc., I:319, 320, 321; II:744

Coupons, I:9, 259

Courseware, I:366, 409; II:680–681

Covad Communications, I:425; II:446, 625

Covation, II:590

Covisint, I:87, 88, 94–95, 137; **I:162–164**

Cowell, Casey, II:577

Cox Communications Inc., I:281, 282, 284

Cox Enterprises Inc., I:38, 294

CPFR (Collaborative planning, forecasting and replenishment), I:87

C-Port Corporation, II:522

CPR Institute for Dispute Resolution, I:216

CPU (Central processing unit), II:501, 590, 616

cPulse LLC, I:314; II:484

Crackers, I:357

Cramer, James J., I:286; II:696, 697

Cray Research Inc., I:203

Creative Good, II:657

CREC (Center for Research in Electronic Commerce), II:769

Credit card fraud
acquiring banks and, I:1; II:581
vs. auction fraud, I:41
card information sales, I:308
charge-back in, I:120
fear of, II:707–708, 709
merchant discount and, II:495
merchant model and, II:496

Credit cards, I:206; II:580–581
in Africa, I:325
in Asia, I:328
auction sites and, I:41
authorization for, I:1, 108; II:580–581
card-issuing banks for, I:108
in Central and South America, I:334
charge-back to, I:120–121; II:496, 581, 708
children and, I:124
vs. digital cash, I:193
digital wallets, I:207–208
encryption for, I:154
Independent Sales Organizations and, I:384
interchanges and, I:412
Internet payment providers and, I:422–423
merchant discount, II:494–495
payment systems for, II:543
real-time transactions for, I:120; II:629
recurring transactions on, II:630
Security Sockets Layer for, I:264
SET for, II:645
utilization of, I:252
wireless devices for, II:593

Crescendo Communications, I:128

Crime, computer. *See* Computer crime

Critical Path, I:14; II:763

CRM (Customer relationship management), **I:166–170;** I:179, 237, 387; II:573

Cross licensing, I:378

Crosspoint Venture Partners, I:300

CrossWorlds Software Inc., I:267

Cruises, II:712

Cryptography, **I:164–165;** I:263, 393. *See also* Encryption

CSI/FBI Computer Crime and Security Survey, I:309

Csikszentmihalyi, Mihaly, I:301

CSnet, I:67

CSS (Cascading Style Sheets), II:751

CSX Transportation Inc., II:624

Cuban, Mark, **I:165–166;** II:743

Cukier, Kenneth Neil, II:546

Culture
Asia and, I:328
cyberculture, I:170–173
digital divide and, I:198
international, I:172, 348
organizational, I:171; II:458, 561, 686

Currency, **I:193–194;** I:349; II:581

Custom Loyalty Network, II:540

Customer co-creation, II:734

Customer relations
churn in, I:126–127

managing, I:117, 166–170

Customer relationship management (CRM), **I:166–170;** I:179, 237, 387; II:573

Customer satisfaction. *See* Consumer satisfaction

Customer service
    B2B e-commerce, I:87
    brand building, I:76
    Buy.com Inc., I:99, 100
    call center services for, I:105–106, 121, 167; II:724, 772
    channel conflict and, I:119
    Charles Schwab Corporation, I:121
    community model for, I:140
    complaints about, I:90
    cost of, I:169
    customers on, II:474, 475
    Dell Computer Corporation, I:117, 188
    direct sales and, I:119
    Egghead.com, I:239
    IBM Corporation, I:377
    intelligent agents for, I:411
    Landsend.com, I:93; II:462, 611
    managing, I:118
    Microsoft Corporation, I:317
    online banking, I:50
    on-site, II:619–620
    outsourcing, II:573
    in product management, II:611
    real-time, II:629–630
    retail sales, I:120
    self-service, I:86, 169
    software for, I:167, 168–169

Customers, weblining, II:758–760

Customization, I:144, 319–320; II:482–483; **II:491–493;** II:605–606, 608. *See also* Personalization

Customs brokers, I:292

Cutting, Allen, I:155

CVV (Card verification value), I:309

Cyber Dialogue, I:50, 127; II:595

Cyberbashers, I:174

CyberCash Inc., I:193, 422

CyberCenter, II:623, 624

Cybercitizen Partnership, I:151

CyberCoins, I:193

CyberCorp Inc., I:122

Cybercrime. *See* Computer crime

Cyber-crime. *See* Computer crime

Cyberculture, **I:170–173**

Cybergeography, I:173

Cyberpersonalities, I:171–172

Cyberpsychology, I:173

Cybersource Fraud Scan, I:120; II:582, 778

Cyberspace, **I:173**

Cybersquatting, **I:173–174;** I:216; II:463, 770–771

Cycles, business, II:549, 550, 650

CYPNET, I:257

Cyrix Corporation, I:405

D

@D:tech, II:706

Daemen, Joan, I:5, 265

Daily Blast, II:746

DaimlerChrysler, I:163; II:789

Daley, Ted, I:399

Dallas Mavericks, I:165–166

Dalvell, Greg, I:49

Daniels, Cal, II:538

DART (Dynamic Advertising Reporting and Tracking software), I:6, 7, 52, 218, 219

Data Broadcasting, II:579, 634

Data centers, II:730–731

Data encryption. *See* Encryption

Data Encryption Standard (DES), I:5, 164; **I:175–176;** I:265; II:636

Data integrity, **I:176–178**

Data marts, I:180

Data mining, **I:178–180;** I:227; II:474

Data Personal Communications Services, I:32

Data Processing Resources Corporation, I:156

Data Protection Directive, I:65

Data Resources (company), II:721

Data warehousing, I:167, 179; **I:180–181**

Data Warehousing Institute, I:168

DataBank, I:219

Database management, **I:181–183**

Database management systems (DBMS), I:181–182
    middleware and, II:509
    Oracle Corporation, I:181–182, 236, 256, 387; II:568–570
    relational, I:181–182, 256; II:568–569
    suites and, II:451–452

Database servers, I:270

Datamonitor
    on customer service, I:90
    on DefCon, II:706
    on hacking, I:358
    on security, I:155

Datapoint, II:538–539

Datapro Information Services, I:313

Dataquest, Inc., I:372–373; II:484, 522

Data-recovery, I:264

DataRover Mobile Systems, I:262

Datek Online Brokerage Services LLC, I:12; **I:183–184;** I:242, 434; II:612

DaveNet, II:766

Davis, Chuck, I:68

Davis, Ziff, I:104

Day trading, **I:184–186;** I:241, 242, 430–431

Dayton, Sky, I:223

DB2 XML Extender, I:182

DBA-XPERT, I:156

DBMS. *See* Database management systems

DDC (Digital Development Centers), I:156–157; II:675

DDOS (Distributed denial-of-service attacks), I:190

DDS (Decision support systems), II:683

de Jager, Peter, II:788

Dead-end pages, II:752

Dealers, automobile, I:353–354

DealTime, II:655

Debit cards, I:41, 124, 193, 206, 252

Debugging software, I:156

DEC. *See* Digital Equipment Corporation

Decentralized management, I:361, 363; II:575, 773

Decision support systems (DDS), II:683

DECUS (Digital Equipment Computer Users Society), I:202

Deeko PLC, II:555

DefCon, II:706–707

Defense Department. *See* Department of Defense

Defense industry marketplaces, I:88, 366, 370

Deja.com, II:614

Delivery services. *See also* Shipping
    air, II:722–723
    dot com collapse and, II:650
    grocery, II:761–762
    history of, II:722–723
    just-in-time, I:303
    order fulfillment, II:571, 572
    overnight, I:291; II:723
    problems with, I:89–90, 312
    residential, I:292

Dell, Michael, I:109; **I:186–187**

Dell Books, I:59

Dell Computer Corporation, I:186–187; **I:187–190**
    Amazon.com and, I:18
    business model, I:144, 187
    competition with, I:143, 144, 187, 188
    customer relations, I:117, 188
    customization by, II:491
    direct sales by, I:186, 188, 189, 210–211; II:482
    disintermediation and, I:210–211
    dynamic pricing by, II:606
    education market, II:444
    Epinions.com and, II:614
    history of, I:187–189; II:592
    restructuring, II:632
    Teligent Inc. and, II:692
    Unisys Corporation and, II:721
    UNIX and, I:186–187, 188

Della.com, I:62

Deloitte Consulting, I:107, 116, 193, 233

Delphi method, I:304

Delta Airlines, II:580, 601, 712, 745

Demandline.com, I:11, 81

Demographics, II:759

Denial-of-service attacks, I:90, 145, 153–154; **I:190–191;** I:358

Dense wave division multiplexing (DWDM), I:129; II:476, 567, 596

Department of Commerce
    on the digital divide, I:199
    on economic growth, II:771
    on encryption, I:5
    Falling Through the Net report, I:197–198
    ICANN and, I:381
    marketplace, I:88

    NIIPA and, II:534
    on privacy, I:280, 345; II:465
    RSA Data Security and, II:635
    Safe Harbor Privacy Program, I:280, 345; II:465, 528, 610, 637–638

Department of Defense
    ARPAnet, I:35
    attacks on, I:153, 357; II:464
    Next Generation Internet Initiative and, II:553
    RSA Data Security and, II:635
    Unisys Corporation and, II:720, 721

Department of Education, I:123, 365

Department of Energy, II:553

Department of Justice
    AT&T Corporation, I:37
    browser software and, I:53
    on computer crimes, I:145, 147, 151
    on encryption, II:600
    IBM Corporation, I:379, 380
    Microsoft Corporation, I:315–316; II:503, 504, 543
    National Infrastructure Protection Center, I:153

Department of Labor, II:515

Deregulation, II:549

DeRose, Gene, I:418

Derringer, Pam, I:180

DES (Data Encryption Standard), I:5, 164; **I:175–176;** I:265; II:636

DeskJet printers, I:363

Destination buttons, II:628

Destination E*Trade, I:278

Detection software, I:153, 155

Detroit Edison Company, I:189

Detrola, II:520

Deutsche Bank AG, II:579

Deutsche Telekom, I:338

Developing countries, I:199, 367–368, 415, 420–421

DHL Airways Inc., II:653

DHL Worldwide Express, II:653, 654

Dialer programs, I:308

Dialog Information Services, II:456

Dialogic Corporation, I:405

Diamond Cluster International, I:163

Diego Broadband Inc., I:12

Differentiation, **I:191–192**

Diffie, Whitfield, I:164

Diffie-Hellman algorithm, I:164

Digex Inc., I:424

Digirolamo, Enrico, I:163

Digital, I:23; **I:192–193;** I:393; II:690

Digital cameras, I:113, 114; II:613

Digital cash, **I:193–194;** II:581

Digital Certificate Authority, **I:196–197**

Digital certificates, I:42; **I:194–196**
    digital signatures for, I:204
    encryption for, I:165
    GUIDEC on, I:321

for payment systems, I:309
privacy, I:240
secure, I:177
timestamping, II:704
VeriSign and, I:263

Digital development centers (DDC), I:156–157; II:675

Digital divide, I:172; **I:197–200;** I:201, 323

Digital Economy 2000, **I:200–202**

Digital Equipment Computer Users Society (DECUS), I:202

Digital Equipment Corporation (DEC), **I:202–204**
AltaVista and, I:13
Apple Computer and, I:31
Compaq merger, I:142, 202, 203, 359
minicomputers, II:590
RSA Data Security and, II:635

Digital fingerprints, II:529

Digital Goods, II:727–728

Digital goods, I:214

Digital Media Audience Ratings, I:418

Digital Millennium Copyright Act (DMCA), I:160, 254, 408; II:463, 528, 706–707

Digital Performance Rights Act, I:408; II:463

Digital Research Inc., II:559

Digital rights management, I:160

Digital Signature Act, I:205

Digital Signature Trust Company, I:241

Digital signatures, **I:204–205**
certificates and, I:195, 196–197
GUIDEC on, I:321
legislation on, **I:205–206**
public-key encryption for, I:165; II:708
standards for, I:20

Digital Style Corporation, II:497, 543

Digital subscriber line (DSL), I:78–79
Australia, I:331–332
bundling, I:84
Earthlink Inc., I:224; II:579
Flashcom Inc., I:299–301
home networks, I:373
killer apps, II:452–453
Qwest Communications, II:625

Digital video disks (DVDs), I:99, 114

Digital wallet technology, I:124; **I:206–209;** II:581–582, 645

Digital watermarks, I:214

Digital World, II:557

Diller, Barry, I:109; II:699

Dimension X Inc., II:497

Din, Attiazaz, I:262

Diplomacy, I:348

Direct mail, I:10, 258; II:488

Direct Marketing Association, I:261

Direct network externalities, II:545–546

Direct response advertisements, I:7–8, 9, 17

Direct sales
customer service, I:119
Dell Computer Corporation, I:186, 188, 189, 210–211; II:482
disintermediation and, I:210–211
Egghead.com, I:239

growth of, II:482
manufacturer model for, II:481–483

Direct Technology Ltd., I:156

Direct Ventures, I:110

Directive on Data Privacy, **I:279–280;** II:464–465, 610

Directory-based search engines, II:644

DirecTV, I:71

Disabled users, II:756

Disclosure, fair *vs.* selective, II:739

Discount brokerage services, I:20–23, 121–123

Discount shopping, I:73–74, 98–100

Discounts
advertising, I:9
coupons for, I:9, 259
e-mail marketing of, I:259
merchant, **II:494–495**

Discovery process, II:668

Discrimination, II:758–760

Discussion forums, **I:209;** I:255; II:621, 735

Disintermediation, I:118–119; **I:210–211**

DiskBASIC, II:502

Disks, II:533, 775

Display phone, II:557

Display resolution, II:630–631

Displaywriter, I:379; II:591

Disposable cameras, II:715

Dispute resolution, **I:211–212;** I:344

Distance Education Demonstration Program, I:365

Distance learning, I:365–367; II:558

Distinction Software, II:588

Distributed denial-of-service attacks (DDOS), I:190

Distributed systems, **I:212–213;** II:586

Distribution, I:118–119; **I:213–215;** II:612

DistriVision Development Corporation, I:136

Dixie-Narco, II:715

DMC Stratex Networks Inc., I:267

DMCA. *See* Digital Millennium Copyright Act

DMS-200 system, II:557

DNS (Domain Name System), I:139, 420, 426

Dobbs, Lou, **I:215**

DOCTYPE tag, II:752

Document type definition (DTD), II:779, 780

Domain Name System (DNS), I:139, 420, 426

Domain names, **I:215–217**
Australian, I:331
brand recognition, I:173–174
cybersquatting, I:173–174, 216; II:463, 770–771
development of, I:370
dispute resolution for, I:211–212
Domain Name System for, I:139, 420, 426
extortion of, I:308
ICANN and, I:381
top-level, I:173–174, 216, 217
trademarks, I:409; II:463

Instinet Group LLC, I:34, 399–401
NASDAQ and, I:34, 35, 241, 242–243, 400–401; II:531–532

Electronic Communications Privacy Act (ECPA), I:146; II:609

Electronic Crimes Task Force, I:147

Electronic data interchange (EDI), **I:243–246**
Census Bureau on, I:85
EDIFACT on, II:718–719
Extensible Markup Language, I:87, 246, 376, 403–404; II:708, 719
integration of, I:402–403
open, I:245, 246, 272
point-to-point, I:272
for procurement systems, I:271–272, 273
for small and medium-sized businesses, II:719
UNCITRAL on, II:716–718
XHTML and, I:376; II:698

Electronic Data Interchange for Administration Commerce and Transport (EDIFACT), I:245; **II:718–720**

Electronic Data Systems Corporation (EDS), I:194; **I:246–249**; II:589

Electronic Document Systems Foundation, I:4, 254

Electronic Frontier Foundation, I:175; **I:249–250**; I:265; II:707

Electronic income-tax filing, **I:250–252**

Electronic mail. *See* E-mail

Electronic money. *See* Digital cash

Electronic payments, **I:252**. *See also* Payment options and services

Electronic Privacy Information Center (EPIC), I:220; **I:252–253**; I:265–266; II:607, 615

Electronic publishing, **I:253–256**. *See also* E-books; E-zines; Newsletters
Adobe Systems Inc., I:4, 254, 339; II:674, 706–707
Barnes & Noble Digital, I:55
business models for, I:256
cannibalization in, I:107
initial public offerings and, I:395
newspapers, I:255–256; II:456–457

Electronic record keeping, I:65, 205; II:704

Electronic signatures. *See* Digital signatures

Electronic Signatures in Global & National Commerce Act, I:204, 205–206, 309; II:564
digital certificates and, I:195, 197
on public-keys, I:165
validation and, II:708

Electronic Trade Practices Working Group, I:413

Electronic Traders Association, I:185

Electronic Transfer Inc., I:422

Electro-optical instruments, II:595

Ellison, Lawrence J. (Larry), I:181–182; **I:256–257**; II:568, 569

E-Loan Inc., I:297, 354

eLogic Corporation, I:104

e-Logistics, II:572, 653

Elstrom, Peter, I:296; II:692

E-mail, **I:257–258**
advertisements, I:6, 9, 257, 258–262; II:488, 713
attachments, II:738, 773
audio, I:261
BITNET for, I:66–67
bombs, I:154, 358
call center services, I:105, 106
customer relationship management software for, I:167
development of, I:36, 66–67, 370

digital cash by, I:193
employee, I:150–151
encryption, II:600
etiquette for, II:541
free access to, II:445
killer apps, II:452
lists, I:67, 260, 310
marketing, I:219, 220; **I:258–262**
MSN, II:507
newsletters, I:255, 259; II:487, 552–553, 619, 621
opt-in, I:219, 259; II:713
opt-out, I:259; II:665
Oracle systems for, II:569
outsourcing, II:544
payment systems, II:569, 582
privacy, II:609
rich media content in, I:261, 376
small business use of, II:772
spam, I:227, 257, 258–262; II:541; **II:665–666**
URLs, II:725
viruses, I:154, 257–258
wireless access for, II:593

E-mail marketing, I:219, 220; **I:258–262**

eMarketer Inc., I:50, 258, 327

Emerging Digital Economy, I:201

EMI Group, II:529, 629

E-mod technology, I:114

Emoticons, II:541

Employees, II:768–770
benefits for, I:378
change and, I:116–117
dot com collapse and, II:650
e-mail use by, I:150–151
flexible schedule for, II:576
information revolution and, I:390
information technology, I:201; II:769
as intangible asset, I:401–402
knowledge management and, I:407; II:458
knowledge workers, I:390; **II:458–459**
layoffs, II:550, 769
privacy, I:149, 150–151; II:608
recruiting and retaining, II:493, 515–546; **II:685–687**
salaries, II:686, 769
scalability of, II:639–640
surveillance of, I:151, 185; II:447
time zones and, II:703
training, I:366; II:680–681

Employer Reports, I:375

Employment services, II:493, 514–546

Emulex Corporation, II:512

En Pointe Technologies Inc., I:236; **I:262–263**; I:298

Encarta, I:316; II:503

Encore Computer Corporation, II:680

Encryption, **I:263–266**. *See also* Public-key encryption
Advanced Encryption Standard, I:5, 164, 176, 265
attachments, II:541
backdoor for, II:647
40-bit, II:636
Clipper chip, I:265; II:635–636
communication protocols for, I:139
for credit cards, I:154
cryptography keys for, I:164–165
Data Encryption Standard, I:5, 164, 175–176, 265; II:636
development of, I:154, 263–264; II:708
digital cash and, I:194
digital signatures, I:204–205
digital wallets and, I:207

on taxes, I:345, 427
  value-added tax, II:689

EuroScope Communications, II:787

Eurosept, I:248

Eurotrade, I:412

Evaluation services, **II:659–660**

Evans, Nancy, **I:280–281;** I:435–436; II:767

Event marketing, II:619

e-Ventures, II:572, 653, 724

Evergreen Internet, II:560

Evite.com, II:701, 778

eWireless Report, I:158, 261

Exactis.com Inc., II:714

Excedrin, II:486

Excel Switching Corporation, II:476

ExchangePath, I:132

Exchanges. *See* Marketplaces

Excise tax, II:688

Excite Inc.
  advertising on, I:8
  Charles Schwab Corporation and, I:121–122
  history of, II:597–598, 694, 758
  initial public offering, I:394
  shopping bot, II:655

Excite Photo Center, I:283

Excite@Home, **I:281–284;** I:424; II:599, 694, 700

Exodus Communications Inc., **I:284–286;** I:424; II:632

Exostar, I:88

Expedia.com, I:104; II:603, 712, 792

Experience Music Project, I:11

Expert reviews, II:613

Expert systems, I:401

Expositions, **II:704–707**

Express Checkout system, I:55

EXPRESSfreighter, I:291

Extended Industry Standard Architecture (EISA), I:106, 141

Extended service contracts, I:110

Extensible Hypertext Markup Language (XHTML), I:376; II:698, 750–751, 752

Extensible Markup Language (XML), I:376; II:750–751, 752; **II:778–780**
  database management systems, I:182
  development of, I:58; II:698
  electronic data interchange, I:87, 246, 272, 403–404; II:708, 719
  enterprise application integration, I:267
  Global Trading Web Association, I:350
  migration to, I:404
  schema, **II:779–780**
  search engines, II:644
  standards for, I:20; II:766
  tags, II:779

Externalities, network, **II:545–546**

Extortion, II:534

ExtraLink, II:729

Extranets, I:48, 122, 245; **I:428–430;** II:765

Eye scans, I:64

Eyewitness (software), I:156

Ezboard Inc., I:209; II:735–736

E-zines, I:104, 255–256, 258; **I:286–287;** II:661. *See also* Magazines

F

F & M Schaefer Corporation, I:247

FAA (Federal Aviation Administration), II:536

Facial recognition, I:64

Faculty, I:367

Fair Credit Billing Act, I:309; II:609

Fair disclosure, II:739

Fair Housing Act, II:759

Fair information guidelines, I:252–253

Fair use, I:160, 367, 408

Fairchild Semiconductor, II:516, 560, 561, 775

FairMarket Auction Place, I:41, 226

Fairmarket Inc., **I:289–290;** II:700

Falling Through the Net, I:197

Family, I:391

Family.com, II:746

Fan Loyalty System, II:700

Fanning, Shawn, II:527–528

FastForward Networks, I:397

Fatbrain.com, I:55; II:728

FBI. *See* Federal Bureau of Investigation

F.C. Consultoria, I:248

FCC. *See* Federal Communications Commission

FDDI (Fiber distributed data interface), I:127, 128; II:468

Feasibility studies, II:684

Federal Acquisitions Streamlining Act, I:244

Federal Aviation Administration (FAA), II:536

Federal Bureau of Investigation (FBI)
  Carnivore surveillance system, II:607
  Computer Crime and Security Survey, I:144
  Computer Emergency Response Team, I:147, 153, 154
  on fraud, I:308
  on hacking, I:357
  NIPC and, II:535
  role of, I:147
  RSA Data Security and, II:635
  Sklyarov, Dimitri and, II:706–707

Federal Communications Commission (FCC)
  on AOL Time Warner, I:29
  on AT&T, II:480
  on the digital divide, I:198
  on fiber optics, I:294
  history of, I:37
  on Knight-Ridder, II:456
  NTIA and, II:536
  on user locations, I:9
  on wireless devices, I:32

Federal Express. *See* FedEx Corporation

Federal government, Office of Electronic Government, **II:563–564**

Federal legislation. *See* Legislation

Ford Motor Company, I:162–163; II:491, 603, 621

FordDirect.com, I:88

Forecasting
    analytic, II:594
    business, **I:301–303**
    cause-and-effect, I:302
    Forrester Research on, I:305–306
    judgmental, I:302–303
    order fulfillment and, I:311, 312
    scenarios for, II:640–642
    simulation software for, II:658
    technological, **I:303–305**
    time-series, I:302

Foreign Corrupt Practices Act, I:150

Foresight studies, I:304

Formant, Chris, II:643

Forrester, Jay, II:590

Forrester Research Inc., **I:305–306;** II:484–485
    on advertising, I:9
    on auction sites, I:40
    on auto sales, I:109
    on brokerage services, I:431
    on Buy.com Inc., I:100
    on Central and South America, I:334, 335
    on change management, I:116
    on channel conflict, I:118
    on customer relationship management, I:168
    on data mining, I:179
    on digital signatures, I:204
    on digital wallets, I:207
    on E-procurement, I:306
    on exchanges, I:88
    on information architecture, I:386
    on integration, I:403
    on investing, I:430
    on kiosks, II:453
    on micro-payments, II:500, 727
    on music sites, I:115
    on newsletters, I:255; II:487, 552
    on online banking, I:50
    on payment methods, I:206
    on platforms, II:597
    on portals, II:740
    on privacy, II:608
    on product design, II:667
    on recruitment, II:686
    on retail sales, I:91
    on Sapient Corporation, II:638
    on site location, II:618
    on subscription-based software, II:678
    on taxes, II:687
    on TheStreet.com, II:696
    on travel services, II:712
    on usability, II:755
    on weblining, II:759
    on women, II:768

Forstmann, Little and Company, II:791

FORTRAN, I:135; **I:306–307;** I:379; II:502, 590, 617

Forum One Communications Corporation, I:209

FotoNation Inc., I:114

Fouress Inc., I:284

Four-Phase Systems, Inc., II:521

Fourth Amendment protection, II:608–609

Frame Technology Corporation, I:4

France, I:31, 338, 346

France Telecom, I:338

Frank, Thomas, II:628

Frankenberg, Robert J., II:560

Franskston, Bob, II:451

Fraud, I:145–147; **I:307–310**. *See also* Computer crime; Credit card fraud
    acquiring banks and, I:1
    auction site, I:41, 176, 227, 308; II:564
    debit card, I:41
    digital cash and, I:194
    in financial services, I:146
    legislation on, I:152
    payment system, II:582
    securities, I:145–146; II:512
    wireless access, I:308

FraudPatrol, I:422

FraudScreenNet, II:495, 581

Freedom of Information Act, I:253; II:607

Freedom of speech, I:249–250, 346; II:465

Freehill, Hollingdale & Page, I:331

Freelancers, II:515

Freeman, Greydon, I:66–67, 310

Freenet, II:586

Freeserve, I:336, 337, 338

Freetrade.com, I:20–21

Freeup, I:142

Freight Transportation and Logistics Industry Report, II:653–654

Frequent flyer program, II:540

Friday the 13th (virus), I:153, 154

Frontier Corporation, II:544, 624, 625

Frontier scripting, II:766

Frook, John Evan, I:399

Frost, Robert, II:515

Frost & Sullivan, I:65; II:691

Fry's Electronics, I:240

FSP platform, I:298

FTC. *See* Federal Trade Commission

FTP (File transfer protocol), I:371; II:725

Fuchs, Ira, I:66–67; **I:310**

Fujitsu Ltd., II:559

Fukuyama, Francis, I:390–391

Fulfillment, order. *See* Order fulfillment

Full-service providers, I:33

Full-text searching, I:13

Furniture, office, I:211

Furukawa Electric Company Ltd., I:293; II:475, 477

Future trends. *See* Forecasting

Fylstra, Dan, II:451

G

G7 group, I:345

Galactic Network, I:369; **II:512–514**

Gale, Grant, II:560–561

FedEx Corporation, I:291
Gateway, I:319
Levi Strauss, II:466, 467
marketplaces for, I:88
Middle East, I:201, 335
North America, I:335; **I:339–343**
outsourcing, II:471–473
PeopleSoft, I:268–269
privacy, II:610
projections for, II:771
regulation of, **I:343–346**
shipping for, II:653
taxes, I:345; II:689
terrorist attacks, II:647

Global EDI Guidelines for Retail, I:245

Global Information Infrastructure, I:415

Global Internet Software Group, I:128

Global Internet Trends service, I:417

Global Network (company), I:380

Global Network Navigator, I:28

Global Online Japan Company Ltd, I:285

Global presence, **I:347–350**

Global Services, I:233

Global Sports Inc., I:74, 100

Global Trading Web Association, I:137; **I:350–351**

GlobalCast Communications, II:560

GlobalCenter Inc., I:285

Globalization
vs. colonialism, I:325–326
cyberculture, I:172
digital divide, I:198, 199–200
information revolution, I:389
information technology, I:391
intellectual property, I:410
ITU, I:415
new economy, II:549

GlobalNetXchange, I:87

GlobalSources.com, I:88

Globo Cabo, I:334

Glushko, Bob, I:350

GNN Select Guide, II:758

Gnutella file sharing system, II:586

Go Network, II:746, 747

Go.com, II:598, 746–747

Golden Retriever Systems, II:540

Golden Web Awards, I:44

Golden Years, II:550

Goldman Sachs & Co., I:34, 90–91, 241; II:506, 614, 696

Goldman Sachs Internet Index, II:649

Goldstein, Mark H., I:73, 74

Golf, I:99

GoLive Systems Inc., I:4; II:579, 674

Gomez, Julio, I:351–352

Gomez Advisors Inc. See Gomez Inc.

Gomez Inc., **I:351–353;** I:385–386; II:659
vs. BizRate.com, I:68

on brokerage services, I:431; II:659
on CarsDirect.com, I:109
on electronic checks, II:582
financing for, I:297
Hoover's Online and, I:375
on MySimon.com, II:524–525
on Webvan, II:761

Gonesilent.com, II:680

Go2Net Inc., I:12; II:440

Gonzales, Tom, I:136

Goodbuy, II:712

Goodman, Joshua, II:524

Goodyear Tire & Rubber Company, II:594

Google Inc., II:579

Gopher, II:725

Gorchels, Linda, II:612

Gore, Al, I:62

Gorney, Jon, II:641

GoTo Auctions, I:226

GoTo.com, II:621

Gott, John Jr., I:147

Government Paperwork Elimination Act (GPEA), II:563–564

Government services
E-Government Web Privacy Coalition on, I:240–241
local, I:240–241
Office of Electronic Government, II:563–564

GPEA (Government Paperwork Elimination Act), II:563–564

Graham, Benjamin, I:83

Graham, John R., II:490

Gramm-Leach-Bliley Act, I:122; II:609, 638

Grand Junction Networks Inc., I:128

Grant, Thomas, II:537

Grant Thornton, I:50

Graphic Services, II:720

Graphical user interfaces (GUIs), II:726–727
Apple Computer, II:443
Clark, James H., I:130
development of, I:340; II:443, 502, 508–509
Motif, II:724

Graphics
dots-per-inch, II:631
Jobs, Steven P. and, II:443–444
resolution of, II:630–631
response time, II:660–661, 750
search engines, II:644
usability, II:756

Graphics, Visualization and Usability Center, I:416–417

Great Plains Corporation, I:318; II:505

Greenberg, Eric, II:642

Greenberg, Jerry, I:192, 295; **I:352–353;** II:517, 638

Greenfield Online, I:91

Greenlight.com, I:16, 17, 109, 111; **I:353–355**

Greenspan, Alan, I:407

Greenwich Electronic Time (GeT), II:703

Greenwich Mean Time, II:702

High-speed Internet access, I:78–79, 157–159. *See also* Bandwidth; Broadband technology; Digital subscriber line (DSL); Telecommunications infrastructure
    access to, II:522
    alliances in, II:579
    AOL Time Warner, I:27, 29
    Australia, I:331–332
    cable TV, I:282
    Earthlink Inc., I:223–224
    electrical power lines for, I:159
    Excite@Home, I:281–284
    hubs for, I:419
    Internet2, I:159; II:523, 624
    killer apps, II:452–453
    multimedia, II:522
    Napster, II:527
    Next Generation Internet Initiative, II:553
    NTIA, II:537
    photonics, II:596
    prevalence of, I:157
    Qwest Communications, II:623–625
    response time, II:661, 750, 755
    United Kingdom, I:337
    UUNET, II:730

Hilbers, Konrad, II:529

Himelstein, Linda, II:486

HiringTools, II:515

History of the Internet and WWW, I:35–36; **I:369–372;** I:416

Hitachi Corporation, I:248, 417

HIWARE AG, II:522

Hobart Manufacturing, I:378

Hoffman, Donna, I:301

Hoffman, Mark, I:136

Holding companies, I:131–133

Holiday shopping season
    Amazon.com, I:16, 17–18, 62
    auction sites, I:41
    B2C e-commerce, I:89
    BizRate.com, I:68
    Buy.com Inc., I:100
    e-tailing, I:274
    growth of, I:92
    Landsend.com, II:461
    order fulfillment problems, I:312
    spending in, I:90–91
    toy sales, I:17–18, 52, 274, 276

Hollywood Entertainment, II:763

Hollywood.com, II:585

Holmes, David, I:172

Home Depot, I:401

Home furnishings, I:74

Home Location Register system, I:248

Home networking, **I:372–373**

Home offices, II:703

Home page, II:749, 752, 771

Home shopping channels, I:109; II:699

Home Shopping Network, II:699

Homebrew Computer Club, II:443, 774

Homegrocer.com, I:16, 62; II:761–762

HomePNA, I:372–373

Honesty, II:709–710

Hong Kong, I:326–327

Hoover, Gary, I:374

Hoover's Inc., I:373, 374

Hoover's Online, I:351; **I:373–375;** I:395

Horowitz, Ben, I:25; II:471

Horton, Sarah, II:751–752

Hosting. *See* Web hosting

HotBot, I:396

HotDispatch, I:81

Hotel rooms, II:601, 603, 712, 789

HotJobs.com, II:515

HotMail, I:13, 14, 317; II:507

HotSync, II:576, 578

Hotwire.com, I:97; II:490, 603–604, 642, 712

HotWired Network, I:282

Houtkin, Harvey, I:185

Howe, Robert, II:642, 643

Howes, Tim, II:471

HP. *See* Hewlett-Packard Company

HP Business Store, II:545, 599

HTML. *See* Hypertext Markup Language

HTTP (Hypertext Transfer Protocol), I:57, 139, 371; II:697–698, 727

Hubs, II:730

Hughes Network Systems, I:224; II:579

Human Code Inc., II:638–639

Human error, I:177

Human resources software, I:268, 387; II:587

Human-computer interaction, II:726–727

Hurwitz Group, II:442

Hush (company), II:601

Hyper encryption, I:264

Hypercard, II:698

Hypertext, II:538–539

Hypertext links, I:173; II:620–621, 644, 750, 753, 782

Hypertext Markup Language (HTML), I:139; **I:375–376;** II:750, 752
    COBOL and, I:136; II:617
    development of, I:58; II:543, 697–698
    tags, II:752
    web scripting languages, II:748

Hypertext Transfer Protocol (HTTP), I:57, 139, 371; II:697–698, 725

I

IAB (Internet Architecture Board), I:420

IADAS (International Academy of Digital Arts and Sciences), I:44

IAF (International Accreditation Forum), I:19

IANA (Internet Assigned Numbers Authority), I:381

iAnywhere Solutions, I:114

IAWMD (International Association of Web Masters and Designers), I:44

iBazar S.A., I:227, 338; II:497

IBM Corporation, **I:377–381**

Apple Computer and, I:32; II:592
BITNET and, I:66, 67
call center services, I:105
Compaq Computer Corporation and, I:106, 380
Consumer Wallet 2.1, I:207–208
co-opetiton by, I:162
CrossWorlds Software Inc. and, I:267
Data Encryption Standard and, I:175
database management systems, I:181, 182
display resolution, II:630–631
distributed systems, I:213
dynamic pricing by, II:606
e-business service providers and, I:231
e-commerce solutions from, I:235
Egghead.com and, I:240; II:498
enterprise resource planning software, I:268
enterprise servers, I:271
Gates, Bill and, I:315, 316
history of, I:377–380; II:590, 591, 592
Intel Corporation and, I:405
intelligent agents, I:411
Lotus Development Corporation and, I:231, 235, 380; II:469, 471
Microsoft Corporation and, II:502, 592
Mississippi 2000 Project, II:558
NOIS alliance, II:543
Nokia Corporation and, II:580
OS/2 operating system, I:306; II:503, 592
personal computers, II:591, 592
PowerPC, II:522
product management by, II:612
Web Services division, I:359
WebSphere Commerce Suite, I:231, 235, 380–381; II:597
Y2K bug, II:788

iBook, I:30, 32; II:444

ICANN. *See* Internet Corporation for Assigned Names and Numbers

iCast, I:132

ICBM (Intercontinental ballistic missiles), II:788

Icon CMT, II:624

ICQ, I:112; II:673

ICS (Internet Connection Sharing), I:372

Idapta, I:88

IDC. *See* International Data Corporation

Idealab, I:109, 296, 382

Identification. *See* Authentication

Identity
cyberculture and, I:171–172
national identity database, II:607
theft of, I:308

IDSL, II:730

IDT, II:481

IEC (International Electrotechnical Committee), I:19

IETF (Internet Engineering Task Force), I:420, 426

iForce initiative, II:680

IIGS System, I:31

iinet Technologies, I:330–331

Illiac IV, II:720

Illustrator, I:3, 4

ILOVEYOU virus, I:358

iMac, I:30, 32, 224; II:444

Image Data Inc., II:607

Images. *See* Graphics

ImageWriter, I:31

ImagingResource.com, II:613

iMail, I:283

IMPACT (Information Management for the Patent Cooperation Treaty), II:770

Imperial Wire and Cable Company, II:557

IMPs (Interface Message Processors), I:416

Impulse! Buy Network Inc., I:396

IMRG (Interactive Media in Retail Group), II:702

IMS Health Inc., I:314

Incentive programs, II:539–540

Income level, I:197

Income taxes, **I:250–252;** II:687

INCORE (Internet Content Rating for Europe), I:346

Incubators, I:131; **I:382–384;** II:669

Independent contractors, II:515

Independent Music Companies Association, II:529

Independent Sales Organization (ISO), **I:384**

Indexes
online community, I:209
search engine, II:758
stock market, I:72–73, 191–192, 221–222, 432–433; II:649

India, I:188, 199, 368, 421; II:546

Indirect network externalities, II:545–546

Industrial designs, II:770

Industrial revolution, **I:387–391;** II:549, 701–702

Industry profiles, I:373

Industry-sponsored marketplaces, I:87–88

Inex Corporation, I:142; II:439

Inflation, II:550

InfoExchange Portal, I:237

Infomediary model, **I:384–386**

Infonetics Research, II:479

Informatics MCAB, I:313

Information. *See also* Personal information
aggregators of, I:10–11
authentication of, II:512
business model for, I:94
capture and sale of, I:94, 385–386
collecting, I:220
distribution of, I:213–215
fair information guidelines for, I:252–253
false, II:511–512
free access to, I:408
glut of, I:391
Grossman's paradox and, I:355
healthcare, I:210
knowledge and, II:457, 458
NASDAQ and, II:532
portals, I:237
product, II:475
transparency, II:709–710
value-added, II:678
volatility of, II:739

Information architecture, **I:386–387**

Information Associates, II:587

international, I:410; II:700–771
legislation on, I:146
marketplaces for, II:690
Napster and, II:527
personal information as, II:609
timestamping, II:704
transfer of, II:689–690
treaties, II:770
WIPO on, II:770–771

Intellifact.com, I:375

Intelligence, artificial, I:401

Intelligent agents, I:81–82; **I:410–412**; II:604–605, 668

Intelligent Interactions, II:713

Intelligent Systems for Retail, II:761

IntelliQuest Inc., I:417

Inter@active, I:221

Interactive Advertising Bureau, I:6

Interactive Imaginations, II:713

Interactive media, I:160–161
television, I:72, 160–161; II:569
voice response, I:105

Interactive Media in Retail Group (IMRG), II:702

InteractiveWeek.com, II:792

Interchange and interchange fee, **I:412**

Intercom Plus system, II:548

Intercomputer Communications Corporation, I:218

Intercontinental ballistic missiles (ICBM), II:788

Interface Message Processors (IMPs), I:416

Intermarket Trading System, I:35

Intermedia Communications, I:424

Intermediaries, I:211; II:482, 769

Internal Revenue Service, I:250–252

Internation Accounting Standards Committee, II:512

International Academy of Digital Arts and Sciences (IADAS), I:44

International Accreditation Forum (IAF), I:19

International Association of Web Masters and Designers (IAWMD), I:44

International Business Machines. *See* IBM Corporation

International Chamber of Commerce (ICC), I:321; **I:412–414;** I:426

International Computer Communication Conference, I:369

International Computer Security Association, II:773

International culture, I:172

International Data Corporation (IDC), **I:414**
on application service providers, II:665
on Asia, I:327, 328
on call center services, I:105
on consultants, I:232
on data mining, I:179
on data warehousing, I:181
on EBPP, I:252
on e-learning, I:364
on enterprise application integration, I:267
on global e-commerce, I:347; II:771
on handheld devices, II:576
on IT spending, I:392
on management service providers, II:480
on Net2Phone, II:691
on online banking, I:50

on portals, II:599
on privacy, II:608
on restructuring, II:631
on search engines, II:644
on shopping bots, I:82
on Y2K bug, II:789

International Electrotechnical Committee (IEC), I:19

International Federation of Information Processing Societies, II:537

International Finance Corporation, I:324

International market. *See* Global e-commerce

International Organization for Standardization (ISO), I:19, 20

International Standards Organization, I:347; II:718

International Telecommunications Union (ITU), I:324, 344; **I:415**

Internet, **I:415–416**
culture of, I:170–173
history of, I:35–36; **I:369–372;** I:416
society and, I:358–361
standards for, I:19–20

Internet2, I:159; II:553, 624

Internet access, I:197–200, 201. *See also* High-speed Internet access
Africa, I:200, 201, 323, 416
Asia, I:342, 416
Australia, I:330, 331–332
Canada, I:416
Central and South America, I:333, 416
Europe, I:201, 337, 342, 416
free, I:73–74, 425; II:445–446, 498
Germany, I:338
India, I:421
killer apps and, II:452
Middle East, I:416
tracking, **I:416–418;** II:447
United Kingdom, I:337, 338
universal, I:415
women and, II:767, 768
worldwide, II:546

Internet Advertising Bureau, I:7, 9

Internet Advisory Board, I:426

Internet Architecture Board (IAB), I:420

Internet Assigned Numbers Authority (IANA), I:381

Internet Auction Co., Ltd., I:227

Internet Brand Study, I:76

Internet Business Solutions Group, I:128

Internet Capital Group, I:295–296

Internet companies. *See* Dot-coms

Internet Connection Sharing (ICS), I:372

Internet connectivity, **I:157–160**

Internet Content Rating for Europe (INCORE), I:346

Internet Corporation for Assigned Names and Numbers (ICANN), I:124, 211–212; **I:381–382**
cybersquatting and, I:174; II:771
regulatory role of, I:343
role of, I:216–217, 420

Internet Data Center facilities, I:284–285

Internet Economy Indicators, II:769

Internet Engineering Task Force (IETF), I:420, 426; II:510, 725, 772

Internet exchanges (IX), I:419

Internet Explorer
America Online and, I:112, 143

Islamic nations, I:148

Island Courier Companies, I:291

Island ECN, I:184; **I:433–435**
    Datek and, I:183, 185
    day trading and, I:241
    development of, I:242, 243, 434–435
    investment in, I:12

ISO (Independent Sales Organization), **I:384**

ISO (International Organization for Standardization), I:19, 20

ISOC (Internet Society), I:216, 420; **I:425–427**

ISP. *See* Internet service providers

i-Supply Service, I:163

Isys Information Architects Inc., II:726

Itanium microprocessor, II:501

IToolbox.com, I:266

iTools, I:32

ITU (International Telecommunications Union), I:324, 344; **I:415**

iTV (Interactive television), I:72, 160–161; II:569

iVillage Inc., I:108–109, 280–281, 338; **I:435–437**; II:736, 767

Ivory soap, II:611

IX (Internet exchanges), I:419

iXL Enterprises Inc., I:231; II:642, 643

J

Jackson, Steve, I:250

Jackson, Thomas Penfield, I:318; II:508

Jacobi, Peter, II:466

Jacobsen, Bruce, II:627

Jaffe, Sam, I:256; II:569

Jagadeesh, B.V., I:284

Jain, Naveen, **II:439–440**

James River Corporation, II:555

Japan
    Amazon.com in, I:17
    America Online in, I:112
    Compaq Computer Corporation in, I:141
    eBay in, I:226
    EDS in, I:248
    E*Trade in, I:278
    Lotus Development Corporation in, II:470
    NASDAQ in, II:532
    Novell in, II:559
    Palm Computing K.K. in, II:578
    Travelcity.com in, II:712

Jargon, II:760

Jarvis, Mark, II:488

Java, **II:440–441**; II:504
    development of, II:494, 679, 680, 681
    Lotus Development Corporation and, II:471
    NetWare and, II:560

Java servlets, II:748

Java Virtual Machine, II:440

JavaScript, II:543, 748

Jazz (software), II:470

Jazz Telecom Inc., II:558

J.C. Penney Company, I:289–290; II:723

JCP, II:680

J.D. Edwards & Company, I:269; **II:441–443**

J.D. Powers & Associates, I:143, 188

Jeans, II:466–467, 606, 611–612

Jennings, Dennis, I:370

Jermoluk, Thomas, I:281, 282

Jewelry, I:297

Job placement services, II:493, 514–546

Jobs, Steven P., I:30, 32; **II:443–445**; II:591, 774–775

John Lewis Partnership, I:100

Johnson, Eric J., II:474

Johnson, Ron, II:444

Johnson, Tod, II:448

Jolt (software), I:267

Jones University, I:366

Journal Storage, I:310

Journalism, II:511–512

Journals. *See* Magazines

Joy, William, II:679, 680

J.P. Morgan Chase, I:34, 241

Judgmental forecasting, I:302–303

Juniper Network Inc., I:129; II:730

Juno Online Services Inc., I:8, 29, 226; **II:445–447**; II:498

Jupiter Media Metrix, I:417–418; **II:447–449**
    on affiliate programs, I:10
    on Amazon.com, I:17
    on auction sites, I:41; II:606
    on Australia, I:331
    on B2B e-commerce, I:85–86, 87
    on Bluelight.com LLC, I:74
    on broadband access, I:80
    on cannibalization, I:107
    on CarsDirect.com, I:110
    on Central and South America, I:333, 334, 335
    on children, I:123
    on consortia-led exchanges, I:88
    on customer loyalty, II:474–475
    on customer relationship management software, I:168, 169
    on customer satisfaction, II:650
    on the digital divide, I:197, 199
    on digital wallets, I:206
    on EBPP, II:546
    on eToys, I:275
    on Expedia, II:712
    Gartner Inc. and, I:313; II:484
    on global e-commerce, II:771
    on holiday sales, I:89, 91
    initial public offering, I:395
    on Internet service providers, I:425
    on licensing, I:11
    on Lycos, II:694
    on marketing, II:618
    on MySimon.com, II:525
    on NetRatings, II:483
    on portals, II:599
    on RealNetworks Inc., II:629
    on scalability, II:640
    on streaming media, II:676
    on subscriptions, II:678
    on X10.com, I:78

on Yahoo!, II:784

on ZDNet, II:793

Justice Department. *See* Department of Justice

Just-in-time delivery, I:303

Just-in-time inventory, II:551

K

K. Aufhauser & Co. Inc., I:21; II:634

Kahn, Robert, I:369

Kairamo, Kari, II:554

Kalpana Inc., I:128

Kana Communications, I:296

Kansas, Dave, II:696

Kapor, Mitchell D., I:249; **II:451–452;** II:469

Karmanos, Peter Jr., I:155

Kashio, Tadao, I:113–114

Katz Millennium Marketing, II:713

KB Holdings, I:274

KB Toys, I:275; II:497

KBKids.com, I:274, 276, 312; II:593

KDD (Knowledge discovery from data), I:178

K2Design, II:713

Kearney, A.T., I:248

Keller, Maryann, II:602, 603

Kelsey Group, I:260

Kemeny, John G., I:56; II:590

Kemna, Wolfgang, II:706

Kenan Systems Corporation, II:476

Kendall, Donald, I:100

Kennard, William E., I:333

Kernighan, Brian, I:103

Key Measures reports, II:447

Key3Media Group Inc., II:706

KeyLabs Inc., I:285

Keynote Systems Inc., II:461, 522, 755

Keystroke dynamics, I:65

Keywords, II:621, 643–644, 668, 757

Khosla, Vinod, II:494, 679

Kidneys, I:40

Kid's Privacy Seal, I:57

Kilby, Jack, I:388; II:561

Killer applications, II:452–453

Kimsey, Jim, I:28, 111

Kinetic Strategies, I:79

King, Kenneth, I:310

King, Stephen, I:229, 254

King, W. Frank III, II:470

Kinsley, Michael, I:255, 286, 317; II:503

Kiosks, **II:453–455**

bookstore, I:387; II:454

Central and South American, I:333

E*Trade, I:279

in-store, I:92; II:453–455

Kmart, I:74; II:454

Kirkpatrick, David, I:316; II:504

Kitchen products, I:63

KIVA Software Corporation, II:497, 544, 710

Kleiner Perkins Caufield & Byer, I:62, 282, 354, 436

Kleinrock, Leonard, I:369

KLM, II:712

Kmart Corporation. *See also* Bluelight.com LLC

alliances, II:579

kiosks, I:74; II:454

Kmart.com, I:73

Knight, Charles Landon, II:456

Knight-Ridder Inc., **II:455–457;** II:515

Knowledge, I:401, 407; II:457

Knowledge discovery from data (KDD), I:178

Knowledge management, **II:457–458**

Knowledge Net Holdings, I:375

Knowledge workers, I:390; **II:458–459**

Koizumi, Junichiro, I:255; II:552

Kokusai Denshin Denwa, I:294

Konare, Oumar, I:325

Koogle, Timothy, I:295; **II:459–460;** II:781, 784, 785

Korea, I:329

KOZ.com, II:763

Kozmo.com, II:760

KPMG Consulting, I:233; II:547

KPNQwest, II:623

Krishnan, M.S., II:734

Krogers, II:603

Krugman, Paul, I:66

Kruse International, I:225; II:764

Kudos Partnership Ltd., II:458

Kurtz, Thomas, I:56; II:590

Kymmene Corporation, II:555

L

La Quinta Inns Inc., II:589

Labor unions, I:390

LAIN service, I:308

Landmark Systems Corporation, I:156

Lands' End Inc., I:93–94, 96, 397; II:461–462, 611

Lands' End Live, I:93

Landsend.com, I:93–94, 96; **II:461–462;** II:490, 594, 611

Lang, Paul, II:621

Language, I:348

LANs. *See* Local area networks

Large scale integration (LSI), I:202

Laser printers, I:31, 362; II:576, 579

Lasers, II:595, 596

LaserWriter, I:31; II:579

Lasseter, Jon, II:444

Last mile, II:553

Latin America. *See* Central America; South America

Launch.com, II:784

Laybourne, Geraldine, II:767

Layoffs, II:550, 769

LCD (Liquid crystal display), I:113

LCI International Inc., II:624

LDDS Communications, I:294

Learning, I:364, 365–367

Learson, T. Vincent, I:379

Leases, automobile, I:109

Legacy systems, II:547, 639, 726

Legal issues, **II:462–466;** II:608–609, 687–688

Legislation. *See also* names of specific acts
  Anti-Cybersquatting Consumer Protection Act, I:174, 216
  anti-spam, II:666
  anti-terrorism, II:465
  Central and South American, I:333
  Chinese, I:344
  Communications Decency Act, I:146; II:465
  computer crime, I:146–147, 152
  Copyright Act, I:146, 408
  Copyright Felony Act, I:408; II:463
  Digital Performance Rights Act, I:408; II:463
  digital signature, **I:205–206**
  Digital Signature Act, I:205
  Draft Model Law on Legal Aspects of EDI and Related Means
    of Communication, II:716–718
  Electronic Communications Privacy Act, I:146; II:609
  e-mail marketing, I:261
  European, I:339
  Fair Credit Billing Act, I:309; II:609
  Fair Housing Act, II:759
  Federal Acquisitions Streamlining Act, I:244
  Federal Wiretap Statute, II:609
  Foreign Corrupt Practices Act, I:150
  fraud, I:309
  Freedom of Information Act, I:253; II:607
  global e-commerce and, I:343–346, 348–349
  Gramm-Leach-Bliley Act, I:122; II:609, 638
  Health Insurance Portability and Accountability Act, II:464
  intellectual property, I:146
  international, II:716–718
  Internet Tax Freedom Act, I:345; **I:427–428;** II:608
  National Information Infrastructure Protection Act, I:146;
    II:533–535
  National Stolen Property Act, I:146
  No Electronic Theft Act, I:146, 408; II:463
  privacy, I:280; II:608–610
  vs. self-regulation, I:125, 280, 343, 360; II:610, 637
  tax, I:345, 427–428; II:687–688
  Telecommunications Act of 1996, I:85, 146, 198
  Uniform Computer Information Transactions Act, I:409; II:463
  Uniform Electronic Transactions Act, I:205

Lehman Brothers, I:63

Lending Tree, II:602

Lenk, Edward, I:274, 275

Lerner, Sandra, I:127

Lesman Instrument Company, II:672

Less-than-truckload shipping, II:652, 653, 654

Level One Communications Inc., I:405

Levi Strauss & Co., I:96; II:466–467, 606, 611–612

Levin, Gerald, I:30

Levine, Daniel, I:94

Levine, Joshua, I:434

Levis.com, **II:466–467;** II:611–612

Levitan, Robert, I:435–436; II:581

Levitt, Arthur, I:407

Lewis, Barbara, I:98

Lewis, Michael, II:696

Lewis, Thomas, II:634

Lewis, Thomas K., Jr., II:634

LG Electronics, I:74

Liability, I:409

Libert, Barry, I:407

Libraries
  catalogs of, I:365
  children in, I:126
  copyright and, I:408, 409
  database management for, I:181
  Internet and, I:360
  misinformation, II:512
  pay-per-view services, II:585
  subscriptions to, II:678

License Online Program, I:100

Licensing
  business plans and, I:97
  courseware, I:367
  cross, I:378
  online content, I:11; II:456
  pay-per-play, II:584
  software, I:100, 136–137
  streaming media, II:627

Licklider, J.C.R., I:35, 369; II:512–513

Life, search for, I:213

Life sciences, I:11

Lightwaves, II:595–596

Linear programming, II:658

Link Resources Corporation, I:414

Links, I:173; II:620–621, 644, 750, 753, 782

LinkShare, I:51

Linux, **II:467–468;** II:565–566
  development of, II:467–468, 709, 734
  MS Windows and, I:12
  Red Hat and, I:395
  Sun Microsystems and, II:681

Liquid crystal display (LCD), I:113

List owners, I:260

LISTSERV (software), I:67, 310

Listserves, I:67, 310; II:541, 620

Little, Brown Publishing, I:27

Live Motion, I:4; II:674

Living Videotext, II:766

Living.com, I:16

Loans, automobile, I:109

Local area networks (LANs), **II:468–469**
    communication protocols for, I:139
    development of, II:468–469, 556–557, 559–560
    DSL for, I:299
    hardware for, I:127–129
    WANs and, II:765
    wireless, I:142

Local governments, I:240–241

Local news, I:112

Local telephone service, I:84, 336; II:480, 481, 691–692

Locke, Gary, I:367

Lockhead, Christopher, II:642

Lockheed Corporation, II:456

Lock-in, **II:469;** II:474

Logic bombs, I:154, 358

Logistics. *See also* Order fulfillment; Shipping; Warehouses
    customization and, II:492
    disintermediation of, I:211
    global, I:349
    manufacturer model and, II:482
    merchant model and, II:497
    outsourcing, II:571, 573
    UPS and, II:723–724

Logo SnapShot, II:462

London Stock Exchange, I:400

Long-distance service
    AT&T, I:36–38
    bundling, I:84
    Cisco Systems Inc., I:127
    fiber optics, I:294
    history of, I:36–38
    Internet service providers, I:423–424
    Nortel Networks, II:557–558
    Priceline.com, II:603
    Qwest Communications, II:623, 624

Loral, II:721

Los Alamos National Laboratory, I:165

Lotus Development Corporation, II:451–452; **II:469–471**
    IBM Corporation and, I:231, 235, 380; II:469, 471
    Novell and, II:559
    RSA Data Security and, II:635

Loudcloud, Inc., I:24, 25, 395; **II:471–473**

Loudcloud Operational Environment, II:472

Love Bug virus, I:147, 154, 358

LoveLetter worm, II:773

Low-end users, II:755–756

Low-income groups, I:197, 201; II:688

Loyalty, **II:473–476;** II:492–493, 599, 620, 650

LSC, II:680

LSI (Large scale integration), I:202

L-Soft International, I:67

Lucas, Donald L., II:568, 569

LucasFilm Ltd., II:443

Lucent Power Systems, II:476

Lucent Technologies, I:38, 372; **II:475–477;** II:558

Lucent Worldwide Services, II:763–764

Luechtefeld, Monica, II:631

Lupien, Bill, I:400

Luxury merchandise, I:297

Lycos Inc. *See also* Terra Lycos, Inc.
    auction site, I:228
    Bertelsmann AG and, I:59, 115; II:693, 694, 695
    financing for, I:296
    history of, I:338; II:597, 598, 599, 693–694
    initial public offering, I:394
    MSN and, II:507
    profitability of, I:282
    shopping bot, II:655
    Ticketmaster and, II:700
    WebShopper, II:695–695

Lynch, Patrick J., II:751–752

Lynx (software), II:698

M

M&SD Corporation, I:248

Mac OS X, I:32; II:445

Machine languages, II:616

Macintosh computers
    history of, I:30, 31; II:592
    Lotus Development Corporation and, II:470
    Nortel Networks and, II:558
    Novell and, II:559
    OS X, I:32; II:445
    UNIX and, II:566

Macro viruses, II:737

Macworld Conference & Expo, II:706

Macys.com, I:312

Madonna (singer), I:216

MAE (Metropolitan area exchanges), I:419

Mafiaboy, I:153, 190, 358

Magaziner, Ira, I:360

Magazines
    advertisements, I:255
    AOL Time Warner, I:27
    Barnesandnoble and, I:54, 55
    Bloomberg L.P., I:71
    Cahners Business Information, I:104–105
    e-zines, I:104, 255–256, 258; **I:286–287;** II:661
    investment, II:661
    out-of-print, I:310
    pay-per-view services, II:585
    subscriptions to, I:255; II:678, 745
    Ziff-Davis, II:791–792

Mahoney, Michael, I:337

Mail, electronic. *See* E-mail

Mail and Telephone Order Rule, I:312

Mail bombs, I:154, 358

Mail Boxes Etc., II:653, 723

Mailing lists, I:67, 310; II:541, 620

Maillefer, II:555

Mail-order companies, I:90, 427; II:688

Mainframe computers, I:155–157, 212, 363

Mainspring Inc., I:50

Malcolm Baldridge National Quality Award, I:291; II:521

Management

business plan for, I:97–98
of change, **I:116–118**
decentralized, I:361, 363; II:575, 773
open-door, I:361, 362; II:575
of staffing, I:116–117

Management and Applications Support, I:380

Management information systems (MIS), II:683

Management service providers (MSP), I:33; **II:479–480**

Manby, Joel, I:354

Mandl, Alex J., **II:480–482;** II:692

Manufacturer model, **II:481–483**

Manufacturing industry
customization, II:491–493
industrial revolution, I:388
information revolution, I:390
marketplaces for, I:104
online sales, I:85
order fulfillment, II:571

Manufacturing Marketplace, I:104

Manugistics Group Inc., I:399

Manzi, James R., II:451, 470, 471

Map technology, II:662–663

MapQuest.com Inc., I:112

MapStation, II:662–663

MarchFirst Inc., I:77, 231

Marcus Cable, I:12, 282

Marcus Communications, II:793

Marengi, Joseph, II:560

Marineau, Philip, II:467

Mark I, I:378; II:590, 664

Market, global. See Global e-commerce

Market makers, I:241, 242, 243; II:531

Market research, **II:483–486**
children and, I:124–125
Forrester Research in, I:305–306
Gomez Inc. in, I:351–352
Grossman's paradox and, I:355
International Data Corporation on, I:414
for market plans, II:489–490
services, I:386

Market Retrieval Service, I:364

Market Site Portal (software), I:136–137, 236

Market value, I:402, 407; II:549

MarketBoomers, I:332

Marketing, **II:486–488;** II:490–491, 617–621
business plans and, I:97
to children, I:123–124
communication services, I:3
data mining and, II:474
e-mail, I:219, 220; **I:258–262**
event, II:619
four P's of, II:611
goals, II:489
history of, II:486–487
magazines for, I:258
newsletters for, I:258; II:487
personalized, I:167; II:474
plans, **II:488–491**
subscriptions, II:678
test, I:41

viral, II:620–621

Marketing plans, **II:488–491**

MarketMaker, I:237

Marketplaces
automobile industry, I:137, 162–164
business-to-business, I:81, 345
business-to-employee, I:142
Commerce One and, I:136–137
consortia-led, I:87–88
defense industry, I:88, 366, 370
e-commerce solutions for, I:236–237
electronic data interchange for, I:245, 272
Extensible Markup Language and, I:403
Global Trading Web Association and, I:350
industry-sponsored, I:87–88
intellectual property exchange, II:690
manufacturing, I:104
private, I:87–88
procurement systems for, I:272
public, I:87–88
small business, I:88; II:545
transparency of, II:709
vortals, II:740

Markets
capitalization, I:128
deregulation, II:549
fragmentation, I:61, 97; II:530
niche, I:382
penetration, II:715–716
speed-to, **II:666–667;** II:702
target, I:96; II:489–490
volatility, II:738–739

Marketwatch.com, I:351; II:659

Markkula, Mike, I:30; II:775

Markup languages, II:752. *See also* specific types of languages
Standard Generalized, I:376; II:698, 779
standards for, I:20

Marriott International Inc., II:789

Marsh, Robert, II:535

Marsh Report, II:535

Marshall Plan, II:550

Martha Stewart Living, I:73

Martin, Kendra L., II:719

Mass customization, **II:491–493**

Mass marketing, I:137–138

Massachusetts Institute of Technology (MIT), **II:512–514;** II:537–538

MasterCard International, I:208; II:543, 581, 630, 645

Match.com, II:700, 701

Matsushita Electric Industrial Company, II:521

Maveron, II:519

MaxMiles Inc., II:540

Mayfield Fund, II:519

Mazu Networks, I:191

Mazzola, Mario, I:128

MBMA America Bank, N.A., I:22

MBX Xpediter/TSO, I:156

McCaw Cellular Communications, II:480

McCormick, Doug, I:109, 436; II:767

McCracken, Edward, I:130

McGovern, Patrick J., I:414

MCI Communications Corporation
    AT&T Corporation and, I:38
    Digital Equipment Corporation and, I:203
    fiber optics and, I:294
    Internet service providers and, I:423
    Microsoft Network and, I:317; II:503
    RealNetworks Inc. and, II:628

MCI Systemhouse Corporation, I:249

MCI WorldCom, I:249; II:691

McKelvey, Andrew J., **II:493–494**

McKiernan, William, I:60

McKinley Group, I:281

McKinsey & Co., I:92

McMaster, John, II:624

McNealy, Scott, **II:494;** II:679–681

McNulty, Lynn, I:264

McVaney, Edward, I:269; II:442

Mecklermedia Corporation, II:760

Medaille d'Or Award, I:44

Media, II:627–629. *See also* Streaming media
    convergence of, I:160–162
    interactive, I:72, 105, 160–161; II:569
    multimedia, II:522–523, 537, 628
    research on, I:305
    rich media content, I:6–7, 261, 376

Media General Inc., I:374

Media Laboratory (MIT), II:537–538

Media Metrix. *See* Jupiter Media Metrix

Media Player, I:322

Media Technologies Inc., I:373

Mediacom Communications Corporation, I:39

MediaMarket Research, I:417

MediaOne Group Inc., I:39, 283–284

Mediation, I:212; II:773

MediaWays, I:60

Medicaid, I:247

Medicare, I:247

Medidian TeleCenter, II:558

Medium-sized businesses
    electronic data interchange for, II:719
    Forrester Research, I:306
    high-speed access for, I:80
    Internet payment providers, I:422–423
    market research for, II:485
    marketplaces for, I:88
    network solutions for, II:547

Melbourne IT, I:331

Melissa virus, I:145

Memorex, II:720

Mercedes Information Technologies, II:721

Mercer Management Consulting, I:75

Merchant banks. *See* Acquiring banks

Merchant Certification program, I:352

Merchant discount, **II:494–495;** II:580–581

Merchant Express LLC, II:581

Merchant model, I:93–94; **II:495–497**

Merchant service providers, I:384

Merchants Parcel Delivery, II:722

Mergers and acquisitions, **II:497–499**

Meridian Research, I:204; II:496

Meritocracy, II:561

Merrill Lynch & Company
    AltaVista and, I:14
    Buy.com Inc., I:100
    on dot-coms, II:649
    electronic communications networks, I:241
    Innovative Market Systems for, I:70
    on IT spending, I:392
    on outsourcing, II:573

Merriman, Dwight, I:218

Messaging systems. *See also* Instant messaging
    killer apps and, II:452
    Lotus Development Corporation, II:452, 469, 470
    MSN and, II:507
    standards for, II:470
    text, II:453

Messman, Jack, II:560

Messmer, Ellen, II:773

Meta tags, II:643, 668

Metacrawler, II:757

Metadata, I:180

Metalanguage, II:751

Metallica, II:528, 529

Metamediaries, I:81

Metcalfe, Robert, II:499–500

Metcalfe's law, **II:499–500**

Metered use, II:727

Metrics, Internet, **I:421–422**

Metropolitan area exchanges (MAE), I:419

Metsa-Botnia Oy, II:555

Meyerson, Morton H., I:247; II:589

MFS Communications, I:2, 424; II:729

Miadora.com, I:231

Mice (Computer), I:315; II:502

Micron Millenna, II:579

Micro-payments, **II:500–501;** II:584, 593, 727

Microportal service, I:14

Microprocessors, **II:501**
    8008, I:404–405; II:516
    Alpha, I:202, 203
    Apple, II:444
    Athlon, I:405
    Cyrix, I:405
    development of, I:141, 203; II:516–517, 561, 591
    Intel and, I:356, 404–406; II:516–517
    Itanium, II:501
    Moore's law on, II:518
    Motorola, II:521
    Pentium, I:405
    photonics and, II:595
    PowerPC, II:522
    silicon, I:388–389; II:518

tracking, I:253

Microsoft Corporation, **II:501–505**. *See also* Gates, William H. (Bill)
    acquisitions by, II:497
    Active Server Pages, II:748
    advertising by, I:8
    Allen, Paul and, I:11–13, 314–315
    AltaVista and, I:13
    America Online and, I:112; II:490, 506, 673
    Ameritrade Holding Corporation and, II:634
    antitrust litigation, I:315–318, 322; II:503, 504–505, 508, 543
    Apple Computer and, I:31, 32; II:444, 502–503, 508, 592
    AT&T Corporation and, II:504
    Australia and, I:331
    Ballmer, Steve and, I:47
    BizTalk platform, II:597
    Central and South America, I:334
    c2it payment service, II:583
    CMGI Inc. and, I:132, 296; II:763
    Commerce Server 2000, II:672
    co-opetiton by, I:162; II:734
    customer service, I:317
    database management systems, I:182
    denial-of-service attacks on, I:190
    Digital Equipment Corporation and, I:203
    eBay alliance, I:227
    e-books, I:229, 254
    e-commerce solutions from, I:235–236
    enterprise resource planning software, I:268
    enterprise servers, I:271
    Expedia.com, I:104; II:603, 712, 792
    e-zines, I:255, 286
    handheld devices, II:577
    Harvard Conference on Internet and Society, I:360
    history of, II:502–505, 591–592
    home banking network, I:50
    home networks and, I:372
    hotel room auctions, II:603
    IBM Corporation and, II:502, 592
    initial public offering, II:502, 592
    interactive TV, I:161
    Jain, Naveen and, II:439
    Java and, II:494
    lock-in products by, II:469
    Lotus Development Corporation and, II:470
    market capitalization of, I:128
    market value of, I:316
    Noorda, Raymond J. and, II:556
    Qwest Communications and, II:624
    RealNetworks and, I:322; II:628
    Secure Transaction Technology, II:543
    servers, I:316, 317; II:503–504, 508
    Simple Object Access Protocol, II:766
    Site Server Commerce, I:142
    small business portal, I:88
    streaming media, II:677
    Ticketmaster and, II:700
    transparency and, II:709
    ubiquity of, II:715
    UUNET and, II:729
    VerticalNet and, II:740
    white papers, II:763

Microsoft Internet Information Server systems, I:154

Microsoft Multimedia Productions, II:506–507

Microsoft Network (MSN), **II:505–508**
    advertising on, I:7, 8
    AltaVista and, I:13, 14
    AlterNet and, I:2
    development of, I:317; II:503
    Inktomi Corporation and, I:396
    Internet service providers and, I:424
    Match.com on, II:700
    ranking of, I:418; II:505

    shopping section, I:92; II:599
    TheStreet.com and, II:696

Microsoft Office, II:501, 505

Microsoft Windows, **II:508–510**
    Apple Computer and, I:31
    CE, II:577
    development of, I:315–316, 318; II:502–503, 505, 508–509, 591
    e-commerce solutions and, I:235–236
    encryption for, I:264
    handheld devices and, II:577
    Internet Explorer with, I:24, 53, 130, 316–317; II:543
    market share of, II:501
    NT, I:316, 317, 318; II:503, 504–505, 508
    XP, I:318

Microsoft Word, I:315; II:502

MicroSolutions, I:166

Microsource Inc., II:559

Microwave Communications Inc., I:37

Microwave networks, II:481, 692

Middle East, I:201, 335, 416

Middleware, **II:509**

MightyWords, I:55

Miles, Alice, I:163

Military (United States), I:88, 366, 370. *See also* Department of Defense

Millenium, II:675

Miller, Heidi, II:603

Miller, Mark, II:538

Millman, Gregory J., I:186

Mills, David, I:370

MIME/SMIME, I:257; **II:509–510**

Mindspring Enterprises, I:224, 424

Miner, Robert, I:181–182, 256; II:568

Minicomputers, I:202, 213, 361; II:576, 590

Minidisc.com, I:312

The Minitel, I:338

Minix, II:468

Minor, Halsey, I:133, 134

Mirror sites, **II:510–511;** II:756

MIS (Management information systems), II:683

Misinformation online, **II:511–512**

Mission Ventures, I:68

Mississippi 2000 Project, II:558

MIT (Massachusetts Institute of Technology), **II:512–514;** II:537–538

Mitnick, Kevin, I:153, 357

Mitterand, Francois, I:338

Mobile Daily Briefing, II:628

Mobile devices, I:114, 158; II:555. *See also* Wireless devices

Mobile Micropayments, II:500, 593, 727

Mobira, II:554

Modahl, Mary, I:305

Model Law on Electronic Commerce, I:205

Modeling, simulation, II:657–658

N

Nacchio, Joseph, II:624

Name recognition. *See* Brand recognition

Name.Net Enterprise Servers, I:271

Name-your-price model, II:580, 601, 602, 603–604, 606, 687

NAPs (Network access points), I:419

Napster, **II:527–530**; II:586
    bandwidth problems, I:48
    Bertelsmann AG and, I:58, 60, 338; II:586

Narrative Communications Corporation, I:282

Narrow band service, I:283

Narrowcasting, **II:530**

NASA (National Aeronautics and Space Administration), II:553

NASAA (North American Securities Administrators Association), I:185

NASCAR, I:110

NASDAQ Stock Market, I:433, 435; **II:530–532**
    electronic communications networks, I:34, 35, 241, 242–243, 400–401; II:531–532
    Island ECN, I:433–434
    Small Order Execution System, I:183, 185, 434; II:530
    SuperMontage, I:243, 400–401; II:532

Nashoba Networks, I:128

National Account Service Company, I:248

National Aeronautics and Space Administration (NASA), II:553

National Arbitration Forum, I:216

National Association of Broadcasters, I:29

National Association of Convenience Stores, II:455

National Association of Purchasing Management, II:485

National Association of Securities Dealers, II:530

National Automated Clearing House Association, I:246

National Automotive Dealers Association, II:482

National Basketball Association, I:165–166

National Bellas v. Illinois, II:687

National Best Bid/Offer (NBBO), I:434

National Bureau of Standards, I:175

National Business Incubation Association, I:383

National Car Rental System Inc., II:603

National Center for Supercomputing Applications (NCSA), I:24

National Center of Education Statistics, I:123

National City Corporation, II:641

National Committee for Information Technology Standards (NCITS), **II:532–533**

National Education Association, I:125

National Football League, II:694

National Homeland Security Agency, I:147

National identity database, II:607

National Information Infrastructure Protection Act (NIIPA), I:146; **II:533–535**

National Infrastructure Protection Center (NIPC), I:147, 153; **II:535–536**

National Institute of Standards and Technology (NIST), I:5, 18, 175–176, 264–265

National Institutes of Health, II:553

National Market System, I:242

National Research Council, I:175, 265, 371

National Resource Commission, I:303

National Retail Federation, I:91

National Science Foundation (NSF), I:370, 416, 423; II:553

National Security Agency (NSA)
    on encryption, I:164, 175, 264, 265
    privacy, I:253; II:600
    RSA Data Security, II:635

National Security Telecommunications and Information Systems Security Committee, II:534

National Semiconductor Corporation, II:724

National Stolen Property Act, I:146

National Telecommunications and Information Administration (NTIA), I:197; **II:536–537**

National White Collar Crime Center, I:309

Nationally-Focused Action Plans, II:770

Navisite, I:132; II:763

Nazi content, I:148, 346

NBBO (National Best Bid/Offer), I:434

NBC, I:375; II:506, 598, 694, 767

NBC Interactive Neighborhood, II:713

NBCi, II:598

NCITS (National Committee for Information Technology Standards), **II:532–533**

NCP (Network Control Protocol), I:369, 370

NCR Corporation, I:38

NCSA (National Center for Supercomputing Applications), I:24

NEC Corporation, II:559

NEC Ready Computers, I:224; II:579

NECX Office, I:320

Nee, Eric, II:579

Neely, C.Richard, I:61

Negroponte, Nicholas, **II:537–538**

Neidorf, Craig, I:250

Nelson, Ted, **II:538–539**

Neo-Nazis, I:148, 346

Net generation, I:171

Net Perceptions, II:594

Netaction, I:235

NetB@nk, I:22

Netbooster, II:644

Netcenter, I:28; II:544, 545, 598, 599

Netcentives Inc., **II:539–541**

Netcom Online Communications Services, I:423

NetDynamics, II:494, 680

Netfish Technologies, II:442

NetGravity Inc., I:219

Netgrocer.com, II:582

NetIQ, I:422

Netiquette, **II:541**

Net2Phone, Inc., II:603, 691

NetPro Computing, II:560

Netquity, II:485

Netratings. *See* Nielsen/Netratings

NetRatings, Inc., I:417; II:448, 483–484

NetReturn system, I:293

Nets Inc., II:589

NetSage, I:411

Netscape Communications Corporation, I:53–54; **II:542–545**
    acquisitions by, II:497, 543, 544, 545
    advertising, I:8
    America Online alliance with, II:543
    Andreesen, Marc and, I:24–25
    AOL purchase of, I:28, 53, 95; II:497, 544
    brand recognition, I:77
    Clark, James H., I:130–131
    Earthlink and, I:223
    Enterprise Web Server, I:270
    Excite@Home and, I:282
    history of, I:340–341; II:543–545, 698
    initial public offering, I:221, 394
    Knight-Ridder and, II:456–457
    market value of, I:342
    Microsoft Corporation and, I:315–316
    Netcenter, I:28; II:544, 545, 598, 599
    Security Sockets Layer and, I:264
    Sun Microsystems, Inc. and, I:25; II:543, 544

Netscape Navigator, I:24, 53, 316–317; II:503, 542–543

Netscape Netbusiness Marketplace, II:545, 599

NetSolve, II:480

Netstructure 7340 Traffic Shaper, I:49

NetSys Technology Inc., I:128

NetVentures Inc., I:134

NetVision, II:560

NetWare, II:559–560

Network access points (NAPs), I:419

Network Associates Inc., I:190, 264; II:560, 600

Network Control Protocol (NCP), I:369, 370

Network externalities, **II:545–546**

Network HotSync, II:576

Network management services, I:284

Network-1 Security Solutions Inc., I:285

Network servers. *See* Servers

Network service providers, I:33

Network solutions, **II:546–548**

Network Solutions Inc., I:216, 381, 420

Network Working Group, I:416

Networks. *See also* Local area networks
    application service providers for, I:33
    architecture of, II:547
    configurable network computing for, II:442
    development of, II:556–557, 559–560
    distributed, I:212–213; II:586
    economic value of, II:500
    Galactic Network, I:369; II:512–514
    hardware for, I:127–129
    history of, I:369

home, **I:372–373**
integration of, II:547
knowledge management and, II:458
maintenance of, II:547
Metcalfe's law for, II:499–500
Microsoft Corporation and, II:508
microwave, II:481, 692
Noorda, Raymond J. and, II:556–557
Novell, II:556–557, 559–560
operating systems for, II:468
optic, II:596
peer-to-peer, II:468, 585–587
radio, II:556
real-time services on, II:546, 547
scalability of, II:639
solutions for, II:546–548
storage-area, I:20
synchronization equipment for, II:702
value-added, I:244–245, 272
wide area, I:36, 48; II:479, 513; **II:765**

NetWorld+Interop, II:706

NetZero Inc., I:211, 385, 425; II:445, 446, 498

Netzip Inc., II:628

NeuLevel, I:217

New Corporation, II:471–472

New economy, **II:548–552;** II:649

New England Telephone Company, I:36

New Internet Computer Company, I:257

New Science (company), II:484

New Sub Services, II:745

New York Stock Exchange
    electronic communications networks and, I:34–35, 241,
      242–243, 400–401, 434
    vs. NASDAQ, II:531
    online investing and, I:433

New York Times, I:255

New York Times Company, II:696

NewHoo, II:544

Newland, Ed, II:641

New.net, I:381

Newport Systems Solutions, I:128

News
    AltaVista, I:14
    America Online, I:112
    Bloomberg L.P., I:70–71
    business, II:456
    CNET Networks, I:133–135
    content providers, I:160
    financial, I:70–72, 215; II:695–697
    local, I:112
    Microsoft Network and, II:506
    opt-in, I:258, 259
    pay-per-view, II:585
    stock market, II:696–697
    Ziff-Davis, II:792–793

News Alert Inc., I:375

News Corporation, II:696

News.com, I:135

Newsgroups, II:541, 614

Newsletters, I:254–255; **II:552–553**
    advertisements in, I:255; II:552
    e-mail, I:255, 259; II:487, 552–553, 619, 621

marketing, I:258; II:487
Motley Fool, II:518–520
personalized, II:595
print, II:552

Newspapers
advertisements in, I:77
Barnesandnoble.com and, I:54
eBay Seller program, I:228
electronic, I:255–256; II:456–457
Knight-Ridder, II:455–457
subscriptions to, II:678

NeXT Computer Inc., II:443, 698

Next Generation Internet Initiative (NGI), **II:553–554**

Next Level, II:522

NexTag, I:88; II:605

NextCard Inc., I:16; II:603

NexTrade Holdings Inc., I:242

NFO Research, I:260

Ng, Elliot, II:539

NGI (Next Generation Internet Initiative), **II:553–554**

Nguyen, Vanchau, II:736

NIC Technologies Inc., I:240, 241

Nicoll, Edward J., I:184

Nielsen, Jakob, II:756–757

Nielsen Media Research, I:417; II:448

Nielsen Norman Group, II:757

Nielsen/Netratings
on auction sites, I:228
on connectivity, I:157
on eBay, I:227
Jupiter Media Metrix and, II:448
market research by, II:483
on MySimon.com, II:525
on portals, II:599
on retail sales, I:91
on the terrorist attacks, II:646
on Toysrus.com, I:18
on travel services, II:712

NIIPA (National Information Infrastructure Protection Act), I:146; **II:533–535**

Nike Inc., I:99

Nike.com, I:120; II:724

Nimda virus, II:773

Ninemsn.com, I:331

NIPC (National Infrastructure Protection Center), **II:535–536**

Nippon Telegraph and Telephone, II:557–558, 560, 692

Nissan, I:163

NIST (National Institute of Standards and Technology), I:5, 18, 175–176, 264–265

NKF Holding NV, II:555

NM Electronics, I:356, 404; II:516

No Electronic Theft Act, I:146, 408; II:463

Noble, Dan, II:521

Nohria, Nitin, I:383

NOIS alliance, II:543

Nokia Corporation, **II:554–556;** II:580

Nomex Inc., I:156; II:675

Nomura Research Institute, I:158

Non-disclosure agreements, II:503

Nonlinear Technologies, I:3

Noorda, Raymond J., I:162; **II:556–557;** II:559–560

NORAD, II:788

Norman, Donald A., II:757

Nortel CRM, I:267

Nortel Networks Corporation, I:159, 294; **II:557–559;** II:624

North America, I:335; **I:339–343**

North American Securities Administrators Association (NASAA), I:185

Northeast Consulting Resources Inc., II:641

Northern Electric Company Ltd., II:557

Northern Lights Technology, I:54

Northern Telecom, I:31; II:521, 558

NorthPoint Communications Inc., I:39, 300; II:579

Northwest Airlines, II:580, 601, 602, 604, 712, 745

Norton Your Eyes Only, I:264

Notary service, II:704

Notebook computers, I:188, 319; II:706

Novack, Kenneth, I:30

Novak, Thomas, I:301

NovaQuest Systems Inc., I:262

Novell, Inc., **II:559–560**
incentive programs, II:540
in Ireland, I:339
Lotus Development Corporation and, II:470
Netscape Communications and, II:543
Noorda, Raymond J. and, II:556
Tuxedo software, I:267

Novell Japan Ltd., II:559

Novonyx, II:543

Noyce, Robert, I:356, 388, 404–405; II:516; **II:560–562;** II:590

NPD Group Inc., I:418; II:447

NSF (National Science Foundation), I:370, 416, 423; II:553

NSFNet, I:370, 419

NTIA (National Telecommunications and Information Administration), I:197; **II:536–537**

NUA Internet Surveys, I:176, 416

Nuclear family, I:391

NuMega Technologies Inc., I:156; II:675

Numeric computations, I:307

Numetrix, II:442

NuvoMedia Inc., I:229, 254

NYNEX Corporation, I:294

NYTimes.com, I:255

O

Oakwood Healthcare Inc., I:156

Object-oriented programs, I:212

Occupations, knowledge-based, I:390; II:458–459

Oceanic, II:555

OCLC Web Characterization Project, II:771

O'Connell, Jennifer, II:537

O'Connor, Kevin, I:218

OCR Systems, I:3

Odd-number pricing, II:604

Odean, Terrance, I:432–433

Odlyzko, Andrew, II:702

O'Donnell, Kevin, I:223

OECD (Organization for Economic Cooperation and Development), I:333, 406, 413; II:689

OEMs (Original equipment manufacturers), I:224

Office Depot, II:598, 631

Office furniture, I:211

Office machines, II:720

Office of Electronic Government, **II:563–564**

OfficeMax, I:292

Offices, home/virtual, II:703

Ogbuji, Uche, I:182

Ogilvy, Jay, II:641

OLAP (Online analytical processing), I:180

Olim, Jason, I:114, 115

Olsen, Kenneth, I:202; II:590

OLTP (Online transaction processing), I:180

Omidyar, Pierre, I:94, 225, 297, 398; **II:564–565;** II:764

Omnibus Crime Control and Safe Streets Act, II:609

Omnimedia, I:73

On Technology Inc., II:451

One World Hosting, II:656

One-click shopping, I:207

O'Neil, Mark, I:354

OneMain.com, I:224

One-to-One Enterprise platform, I:237

One-to-One Retail Commerce Suite, I:237

One-way hash functions, II:704

OneWorld Suite, I:269; II:441–442

Online analytical processing (OLAP), I:180

Online Anywhere, II:783

Online banking. *See* Banking, online

Online Career Center, II:493, 514–515, 693

Online Community Index, I:209

Online Investor Index, II:634

Online Ombuds Office, I:212

Online payments. *See* Payment options and services

Online Privacy Alliance, I:125

Online services, I:95, 143; II:598, 673

Online transaction processing (OLTP), I:180

OnMoney.com, I:21, 22

OnSale Inc., I:239–240, 336; II:498

Ontario Securities Commission, I:400

Opel, John R., I:380

Open architecture, I:369–370; II:565–566

Open Bloomberg, I:71

Open EDI, I:245, 246, 272

Open Messaging Interface, II:470

Open Source Definition (OSD), II:565

Open Source Initiative, II:565

Open systems, I:369–370; **II:565–566**

Open Systems Interconnect Model (OSI), I:138–139

Open-door management, I:361, 362; II:575

Open-source software, II:467, 565

OpenView, I:235, 364

Operating systems, II:664. *See also* Microsoft Windows
    antitrust litigation, II:505
    development of, II:502–503, 508–509
    Java and, II:440
    MS-DOS, II:502, 503, 508–509, 591, 592
    network, II:468
    OS/2, I:306; II:503, 592
    pay-per-play, II:584
    platforms, II:597

Operational amplifiers, I:23

Opinion leaders, II:620

Opinion Research Corporation, I:76, 77; II:602, 618

Oprah.com, **II:566–567;** II:767–768

Optical fiber. *See* Fiber optics

Optical instruments, II:595

Optical switching, **II:567–568**

Optima, I:157

Opt-In Email.com, I:219

Opt-in services
    e-mail, I:219, 259; II:713
    mailing lists, II:620
    news, I:258, 259

Options Research Corporation, I:278

OptionsLines, I:278

Opt-out services
    e-mail, I:259; II:665
    profiling and, II:615

Oracle Complex Systems Corporation, II:569

Oracle Corporation, I:256–257; **II:568–570**
    alliance program, II:568
    Commerce One and, I:136
    Covisint and, I:163
    customer relationship management software, I:167
    database management systems, I:181–182, 236, 256, 387; II:568–570
    e-commerce solutions from, I:236
    E-Government Web Privacy Coalition and, I:241
    enterprise resource planning software, I:269
    interactive TV and, II:569
    in Ireland, I:339
    marketing by, II:488
    Netscape Communications and, II:543
    NOIS alliance and, II:543

Oracle Data Publishing, II:569

Oracle Express Servers, II:569

Oracle Systems Corporation. *See* Oracle Corporation

Oracle Transaction Process Subsystem, II:568

OracleMobile, I:226

ORB Digital, II:578

Orbit Commerce Inc., I:292

ORBit Express, II:578

Orbitz.com, II:712

Order fulfillment, **I:311–312; II:570–572**
    dot com collapse, II:650
    Oracle Corporation systems for, II:569
    outsourcing, II:571, 573
    problems with, I:90, 311–312; II:496, 572
    supply chain management, II:681

Organization for Economic Cooperation and Development (OECD), I:333, 406, 413; II:689

Organizational culture, I:171; II:458, 561, 686

Organizational structure, II:551, 631–633

Organized labor, I:390

Original equipment manufacturers (OEMs), I:224

Ortel Corporation, II:476

OS/2 operating system, I:306; II:503, 592

Oscillators, I:361, 362; II:575

OSD (Open Source Definition), II:565

OSI (Open Systems Interconnect Model), I:138–139

Outfits Online, II:461

Out-of-print books, I:54

Outsourcing, **II:572–573**
    to Asia, I:328
    auction sites, I:289
    customer service, II:573
    e-mail, II:544
    extranets and, I:429
    global operations, II:471–473
    information technology, II:479, 572–573
    inventory management, II:571, 573
    logistics, II:571, 573
    management service providers, II:479
    network solutions, II:547
    order fulfillment, II:571, 573
    procurement systems, I:272
    scalability and, II:640
    service level agreements for, II:648
    shipping, II:571
    software, II:573, 664–665
    technology, II:571
    transportation, II:571, 573
    warehouses, II:571, 573

Overnight delivery, I:291; II:723

Ovum, I:80

Oxygen Media LLC, II:566, 767–768

Oy Kymamo, II:554

Oy Nokia Ab, II:554

Ozzie, Ray, II:451–452

P

@Plan.inc, I:220

P2P. *See* Peer-to-peer technology (P2P)

Pacific Bell, I:423, 424

Pacific Rim, I:327, 344, 416

Pacific Stock Exchange, I:34, 35, 242

Pacific Telesis, I:38

Packard, David, I:361, 362; **II:575–576**

Packard Bell, I:224; II:579, 592

Packet switching, I:369–370, 419; II:513, 765

Packeteer Inc., I:48–49, 235

PacketShaper, I:48–49

PacTel Communications Company, II:558

PacTel Meridian Systems, II:558

PageMaker, II:674

Pages
    dead-end, II:752
    home, II:749, 752, 771

Paging devices, I:113, 158; II:520, 521

Pagliuca, Steve, I:184

Painter, Bill, I:109, 110

PairGain Technologies Inc., I:177; II:511

Palm Computing K.K., II:578

Palm Inc., **II:576–578;** II:593

Palmer, Robert, I:203

Panasonic, II:691

Pantex Plant, II:690

Panttaja Consulting Group Inc., II:540

Papows, Jeffrey, II:471

Paralle computing, I:396

Parana Institute of Technology, I:313

Parent Soup community, I:436

Paris Convention for the Protection of Industrial Property, II:770

Parisi, Dan, I:216

Parity Software Development Corporation, I:405

Parker, Jeff, II:537

Parker, Sean, II:527

Parsons, R., I:30

PartMiner, I:104

Partnerships and alliances, **II:578–580;** II:619, 674

PASS PLUS seal, I:352

Passwords, I:42, 264, 308; II:534

Patel, Marilyn Hall, II:528, 529

Patent and Trademark Office, I:409

Patent infringement
    Apple Computer *vs.* Microsoft, II:444, 502–503, 592
    Barnesandnoble.com *vs.* Amazon.com, I:54–55; II:656–657
    integrated circuits and, II:561
    Juno Online Services *vs.* NetZero, II:446

Patents
    Bell Laboratories, II:476
    intellectual property, I:407, 408, 409
    universities and, II:690
    WIPO on, II:770

Pathvu/2, I:156

PATHWORKS software, I:203

Patriot Computer, I:312

Paul G. Allen Forest Protection Foundation, I:12

Payment options and services, **I:252; II:580–583**. *See also* Credit cards
    business-to-business, I:252; II:523, 580–583, 778
    business-to-consumer, II:523, 777–778
    cellular telephones and, II:582, 777–778
    digital wallets for, I:65, 124, 206–209; II:581–582
    e-mail, II:569, 582
    encryption for, II:636
    fraud, II:582
    global e-commerce and, I:348–349
    hacking, II:523
    interchanges and, I:412
    Internet payment providers, **I:422–423**
    kiosks and, II:454
    micro-payments, **II:500–501;** II:584, 593, 727
    Netscape Communications and, II:543
    PayPal, II:523, 582–583, 656, 777–778
    peer-to-peer, II:523, 582–583, 778
    recurring transactions, II:630
    security for, I:309
    SET for, II:645
    standards for, I:19–20
    X.com and, II:777–778

PayPal, II:523, 582; **II:583;** II:656, 777–778

Pay-per-access, II:676

Pay-per-play, **II:583–584**

Pay-per-view, I:27; **II:584–585**

PC Data Online, I:18

PC Expo, II:706

PC Meter L.P., I:418; II:447

PCS (Personal communications systems), II:558

PCT International Searching and Preliminary Examining Authorities, II:770

PDAs. *See* Personal digital assistants

PDF (Portable document format), I:3

PDF Merchant, I:4

PDP minicomputers, I:202

Peapod Inc., II:498

Peer-to-peer technology (P2P), **II:585–587;** II:680
    networks, II:468, 585–586
    payment systems, II:523, 582–583, 778

Pegasus Networks, I:330

Pender, Lee, II:451

Penney's (retailer). *See* J.C. Penney Company

Penske, Roger, I:110

Pentagon attacks, I:145; II:646–647

Pentium microprocessors, I:405

Penton Media Inc., II:705

PeopleSoft HRMS, I:268

PeopleSoft Inc., I:167, 267, 268–269; II:442, 488; **II:587–588**

PeopleSoft Manufacturing Inc., II:587–588

PeopleSoft PSA, II:588

PeopleSupport, II:768

Peppers and Rogers Group, I:211; II:482

Peretz, Martin, I:286; II:696

Perfect YardSale, II:603

Performance and Phonograms Treaty, I:410

Periodicals. *See* Magazines

Periphonics Corporation, II:558

Perot, H. Ross, I:247; II:589–590

Perot Systems Corporation, I:247; **II:588–590**

Personal communications systems (PCS), II:558

Personal computers, **II:590–592**
    clusters of, I:396
    Compaq, I:106
    competition in, I:143, 144
    convergence of, I:160–161
    customer satisfaction with, I:143, 188
    customized, I:144, 319–320; II:491
    Dell Computer Corporation, I:187
    development of, I:380; II:590–592, 775
    Gateway, I:318–321
    history of, I:141–142
    IBM, I:380; II:591, 592
    inexpensive, I:405
    networked, I:372–373
    ownership of, I:198
    sales of, I:187; II:592
    standards for, II:591
    storage capability of, I:214
    telephone access to, II:691

Personal digital assistants (PDAs), **II:592–594**
    killer apps, II:452
    middleware, II:509
    Palm, II:576–578
    user interface for, II:726
    wireless access from, I:158

Personal financial bots, I:411

Personal financial services, II:661

Personal identification numbers (PINs), I:42, 64, 195, 264

Personal information, II:594–595, 607–611. *See also* Privacy
    children and, I:124–125
    collecting, II:607
    digital certificates and, I:194–195
    DoubleClick Inc. and, I:219–220, 253
    ethics and, I:149
    European Commission on, I:279–280; II:464–465
    fair information guidelines for, I:252–253
    fear of disclosure, II:707–708
    as intellectual property, II:609
    marketing with, II:474
    profiling and, I:52; II:496, 615–616
    protection of, I:308–309
    selling, I:253
    shopping carts and, II:656
    storing, II:672
    theft of, I:307, 308
    weblining, II:758–760

Personal Shopper, I:226

Personal Software, II:766

Personal Technology Center, I:320

Personalities, cyber, I:171–172

Personalization, **II:594–595;** II:734
    customization, I:144, 319–320; II:482–483; **II:491–493;** II:605–606, 608
    Landsend.com, I:93; II:617
    marketing, I:167; II:474
    My Yahoo! program, II:594, 782
    newsletters, II:595
    shopping, I:93; II:496, 594–595, 617
    Starbucks Coffee program, II:672
    viral marketing and, II:620

Pertech Computer Ltd., I:188

Pet supplies, II:651

Peterschmidt, David, I:396

Petersen Publishing, II:791

Peterson, Thane, I:256, 286

Petronella, Michael A., I:191–192, 221

Petry Interactive, II:713

Pets.com, I:16, 62; II:651

PETsMART, II:651

Pew Internet & American Life Project, II:607, 608, 615–616

Pez dispensers, II:564, 565

Pfaffenberger, Brian, II:469

Pfeiffer, Eckhard, I:106, 141

PGP (Pretty Good Privacy), I:264; **II:600–601**

PGP Inc., II:600

Pharmaceutical Electronic Commerce and Communication, I:332

Pharmaceuticals, I:85

Pharmacia & Upjohn, I:422

Philips Medical Systems, I:404

PhoCusWright, II:712

Phoenix Technologies, II:579

Phone cards, II:603

Photographs, I:283

Photonic Technologies, II:558

Photonics, II:553; **II:595–597**

Photoshop, I:4; II:674

Phrack World News, I:250

Pianos, digital, I:113

Picazo Communications Inc., I:405

PictureTel, I:142

Pilot handheld devices, II:576–577, 593

Pinging, I:190

Pinkerton, Brian, II:757, 758

PINs (Personal identification numbers), I:42, 64

Piracy, I:145–146, 408

Pirelli SpA, I:129

Pittman, Robert, I:28, 30, 95, 112, 340; II:673

Pixar, II:443–444

Pixels, II:630–631

Planet Direct, II:763

PlanetAll, II:693, 763

PlanetFeedback.com, I:386

Plans. *See* Business plans; Marketing plans

Plantes, Peter J., I:210

Platforms, **II:597;** II:681, 715–716, 756, 773

Platt, Lewis E., I:363, 364

Plattner, Hasso, I:269

Plewe, Brandon, I:43

PLM (Product Lifecycle Management), II:666–667

Point.com, II:613

Point-to-Point Protocol (PPP), I:139

Polymorphic worms, II:773

Popeyes Chicken, II:703

Pop-up advertisements, I:78

Pornography, I:124, 146, 147, 346; II:464

Portable Bloomberg machines, I:70, 71

Portable document format (PDF), I:3

Portals, **II:597–600**. *See also* Marketplaces
    advertising on, II:740
    auction site, I:41
    B2B e-commerce, I:88, 283, 298
    B2C e-commerce, I:89, 91, 92
    BizRate.com, I:68
    Cahners Business Information, I:104
    Commerce One and, I:136–137
    company profile, I:374
    education, I:126
    e-mail and, I:257
    free Internet access, I:425
    government, I:240–241
    higher edution, I:365, 366
    history of, II:597–599, 693–694
    information, I:237
    leading, II:597
    loyalty to, II:599
    Netscape Communications and, I:53
    shopping, I:283
    supply chain management, II:681
    top-level, II:740
    utilization of, II:599
    vertical, II:739–741
    vs. vortals, II:740
    Walt Disney Company, II:745–746
    wireless access for, II:593

Porter, Bill, I:277

Portfolio management, II:662

Portola Communications Inc., II:497, 543

Post Communications, II:540

Post offices, I:293

Postel, Jon, I:212, 216, 381

PostScript, I:3; II:579, 674

PostX, II:579, 634

Potomac Leasing, I:247

Pour-El, Marian, I:23

Power lines, I:159, 373

Power Mac G4 Cube, II:444

Powerize.com Inc., I:373, 375

PowerNet, I:159

PowerPC, I:32; II:522

PowerRankings, I:306; II:485

PowerShip, I:292

PowWow, I:14

PPP (Point-to-Point Protocol), I:139

Prahalad, C.K., II:734

Predictions. *See* Forecasting

Premiere Technology, II:762

Premisys, II:442

President's Commission on Critical Infrastructure Protection, II:535

Preston, Robert, II:594

Pretty Good Privacy (PGP), I:264; **II:600–601**

Preview Travel, II:693, 710–711

Price, Robert, I:100

Price Watch, II:655

Priceline.com, **II:601–604;** II:606
    advertising by, I:77; II:618
    Allen, Paul and, I:12
    alliances, II:579–580
    brand recognition, I:76, 77
    business model for, I:95
    business plan, I:97
    Hotwire.com and, II:490
    initial public offering, I:394–395; II:602
    Travelcity.com and, II:712
    Walker, Jay and, I:395; II:601, 603, 745

PriceSCAN, II:655

PricewaterhouseCoopers, I:233, 337; II:703

Pricing, **II:604–606**. *See also* Shopping bots
    below cost, II:651
    commoditization and, I:137–138
    comparing, II:524, 604–605, 655
    competitive, II:496
    customization, II:605–606
    dynamic, II:605–606
    markups, II:605
    name-your-price model, II:580, 601, 602, 603–604, 606, 687
    new economy and, II:549
    odd-number, II:604
    search agents for, I:99
    transparency, II:709
    value-based, II:606

Primark Corporation, II:485, 486, 786, 787

Princeton eCom, II:724

Print catalogs, II:490

Printers
    Apple, I:30, 31
    development of, II:590
    dots-per-inch, II:631
    Hewlett-Packard, I:362, 363; II:576
    inkjet, I:363
    laser, I:31, 362; II:576, 579
    multifunction, I:363
    PostScript, I:3; II:579, 674

Privacy, II:464–465; **II:607–611**. *See also* Computer security; Hacking
    Australia and, I:331, 332
    BBB Online seal for, I:57; II:660
    biometrics and, I:65
    certificates, I:240
    children and, I:57, 124–125, 146; II:464, 608
    digital cash and, I:194
    DoubleClick Inc. and, I:218, 219–220
    E-Government Web Privacy Coalition on, I:240–241
    Electronic Frontier Foundation on, I:249–250
    Electronic Privacy Information Center for, I:220, 252–253
    employee, I:149, 150–151; II:608
    ethics of, I:150–151
    European Commission on, **I:279–280;** II:464–465
    legislation, I:280
    National Security Agency and, I:253
    NIIPA on, II:534
    profiling and, II:615–616
    protection of, I:146
    RealNetworks Inc. and, II:628
    reasonable expectation of, II:609
    regulation of, I:345

Safe Harbor Privacy Program, I:280, 345; II:465, 528, 610; **II:637–638**
    standards, I:279–280; II:610
    statements, II:607, 610, 619
    of tax information, I:251
    tracking technology and, II:607
    workplace, I:149, 150–151; II:608

Privacy Seal, II:660

Private marketplaces, I:87–88

Private-key encryption, I:164–165, 175, 204, 264; II:635

Private-label auction sites, I:226, 289

Procter & Gamble, I:78, 244, 273; II:611

Procurement systems, I:238; **I:271–273;** I:298, 306, 399

Prodigy Communications, I:28, 143, 424, 425

Product design, II:666–667

Product information, II:475

Product Lifecycle Management (PLM), II:666–667

Product management, **II:611–613**

Product review services, **II:613–614**

Production process, I:97, 237–238, 388, 390; II:491–493

Productivity Management Group Inc., I:313; II:484

Professional Golf Association, I:99

Professionals, recruiting and retaining, II:685–687

Profiling, **II:615–616**. *See also* Personal information
    for advertising, I:52
    customer-created, II:496
    dynamic, II:734
    industry, I:373
    privacy and, II:607, 608
    weblining for, II:759

Profit sharing, I:362; II:576

Profitability
    Amazon.com, I:16–17, 18, 62, 63
    auction site, I:228; II:564
    business-to-consumer e-commerce, I:92
    dot com collapse, II:651
    due diligence, I:222
    eBay, I:228; II:564
    initial public offerings, I:394
    Lycos Inc., I:282
    projections of, I:98
    speed-to-market, II:667
    toy industry, I:276
    Yahoo! Inc., I:94, 282; II:784, 785

ProfitScape, II:545

Programart Corporation, I:156

Programming languages, **II:616–617**
    assembly, I:307; II:616
    BASIC, I:56
    C, **I:103–104;** II:440, 725
    COBOL, I:135–136; II:502, 617, 788
    FORTRAN, I:135; **I:306–307;** I:379; II:502, 590, 617
    high-level, II:664
    web scripting, II:543, 747–748, 766

Progress & Freedom Foundation, I:241

Progressive Networks, I:322; II:627–628

Project Viable, I:247

Proliant server, I:142

Promotion, II:474; **II:617–621**. *See also* Marketing

Property, intellectual. *See* Intellectual property

Prospero Directory Service, II:725

Protocols, **II:697–699**. *See also* Transmission Control Protocol/
Internet Protocol
    802.11, I:158
    AirPort, I:158
    communication, **I:138–139**
    Ethernet, I:128, 139, 202, 294; II:468, 559
    FTP, I:371; II:725
    HTTP, I:57, 139, 371; II:697–698, 727
    IP, I:129, 215, 370, 419–420; II:465
    NCP, I:369, 370
    PPP, I:139
    SLIP, I:2
    SMPT, I:257; II:510
    SOAP, II:766
    WAP, I:158; II:555, 580, 593, 654
    X.25, II:765

Proton World International, I:5

Protos LLC, II:537

ProWatch, II:480

PSINet, I:223, 423

Psychology, cyber, I:173

Ptacek, Megan J., II:523, 778

Public domain, I:408

Public marketplace, I:87–88

Public relations, II:619

Public schools, I:125

Public-key encryption, I:264
    digital certificates, I:195, 196, 263–264
    digital signatures, I:165; II:708
    GUIDEC on, I:321
    Pretty Good Privacy for, I:264; II:600–601
    RSA Data Security, II:634–636

Publishing. *See also* Books; Electronic publishing; Magazines
    AOL Time Warner, I:27
    Bertelsmann AG in, I:58–60
    Cahners Business Information, I:104–105
    cannibalization in, I:107
    CNET Networks in, I:133
    electronic, I:55
    market fragmentation in, I:61, 97

Punch cards, I:378

PurchasePro, II:545, 599

Purchasing systems. *See* Procurement systems

Pure-play business model, I:92; II:651, 686

Push technology, I:9

Pustilnik, Jerome, I:400

Putnam, Gerald D., I:34

Q

QBASIC, I:56, 315

Q-Metrix Report, II:447

Qpass Inc., II:593

Quantum Computer Services, I:28, 95, 111

Quantum computers, II:501

Quantum cryptography, I:165

Quattro Pro, II:470, 560

Questia, II:678

QuickCheckout, II:471

QuickTime, II:677

Quill Corp v. North Dakota, I:427; II:687, 688

Quote.com Inc., II:599, 694

Qwest Communications International, I:128, 159; **II:623–626**

R

R/3, I:268, 269

Rabin, Michael, I:264

Race, Internet use and, I:197

Radical Communications, II:522

Radio
    advertisements, I:77
    CNET Networks in, I:133, 135
    FM, II:521
    Internet, I:55; II:456
    Motorola and, II:520
    networks, II:556
    two-way, II:520

Radio frequencies, I:213; II:536–537

Radio UserLand, II:766

RadioShack, II:454

Raggett, Dave, II:698

Raging Bull Inc., I:14, 15

Ragunas, Mike, II:756

Railroads, II:654

RAMAC, I:379

Ramaswamy, Venkatram, II:734

Rand Corporation, I:304

Randall, Scott, I:289

Random events, II:658

Random House, I:59, 230, 254; II:710

Ranking. *See* Rating systems

Raptor Systems Inc., I:142

Rare books, I:54

Rating systems, I:67–69, 306, 351
    product review, II:613–614
    search engine results, II:633–634
    site evaluation, II:659–660

Rayport, Jeffrey F., I:81; II:678, 733

RCA, II:720

RCN Corporation, I:12

RDBMS, II:568

ReadyShip, II:672

Real Cities, II:457

Real Decisions, II:484

Real Estate Exchange Network (REXnetwork), I:72

Real Time Online Processing technology, II:581

RealAudio, II:627, 628, 629, 677

Real.com Games, II:629

Real.com Network, II:628

Reality television, II:585

RealJukebox, II:628, 629

RealMarket Research, I:168

RealMoney.com, II:696

RealNames Corporation, I:212

RealNetworks Inc., I:322; **II:627–629**
    CNET Networks and, I:134
    Music.net and, II:529
    Nokia Corporation and, II:555
    pay-per-view services, II:585
    profiling, II:615
    streaming media, II:627–629, 677

RealPlayer, II:628, 629

Real-time transactions, **II:629–630;** II:708–709
    brokerage, I:183
    credit card, I:120
    extranets, I:429
    financial, I:108
    integration for, I:404
    Internet2, I:159
    networks for, II:546, 547
    order fulfillment, I:311
    searches, II:758
    securities information, I:69
    shipping, II:654
    streaming media, II:675–677
    time zones, II:703
    tracking, II:629–630, 654

RealVideo, II:628, 629, 677

Reasonable expectation, II:609

Rebranding, II:754

Record keeping, electronic, I:65, 205; II:704

Recording Industry Association of America, II:528–529

Recruitment, employee, II:493, 515–516; **II:685–687**

Recurring payment transactions, **II:630**

Recursive partitioning regression (RPR), I:178

Red Hat, I:395

Red Herring Communications, I:135

Red Pepper Software Company, I:269; II:587–588

Red Rocket, I:276

Redactron, II:720

Redlining, **II:758–760**

Reduced instruction set computing (RISC), I:130, 363

Reed Elsevier Inc., I:104

Reel.com, II:763

Reference books, I:230, 254, 374; II:569

Reference Press, I:374

Referral advertisements, I:6

Reflect.com, I:78

Regional Bell operating companies, II:623, 624

Regulation. *See also* Legislation
    of global e-commerce, **I:343–346**
    self-regulation, I:125, 280, 343, 360; II:610, 637

Regulation FD, II:739

REI, II:453

Relational DBMS, I:181–182, 256; II:568–569

Relaunching web sites, **II:754–755**

Relevancy searching, II:633

Relevant Knowledge, II:447–448

Reliability Seal, I:56–57

Reminder services, II:620

Remington Rand, I:378, 379; II:590, 720

Remote control devices, II:775

Remote spooling communications system (RSCS), I:66, 310

Renault S.A., I:163

RenderMan, II:443

Renucci SA, II:555

Reruzzi Group, II:555

Research, market. *See* Market research

Research and development, I:201, 365; II:447, 537, 690

Reseaux IP Europeans Network Coordination Centre (RIPE NCC), I:420

ResellerRatings.com, I:99

Resellers
    channel conflict with, I:118–119
    computer, I:262–263
    value-added, I:330–331; II:568

Reservations, II:699–701, 710–712

Reserve America Holdings Inc., II:700

Residential delivery services, I:292

Resolution, **II:630–631**

Resource marketing, I:90

Response time, II:660–661, 750, 755

Restructuring, **II:631–633**

Results ranking, **II:633–634**

Retail sales, I:273–274. *See also* Business-to-consumer e-commerce
    channel transparency in, I:119–120
    e-mail and, I:258
    e-tailing, I:245; **I:273–274;** II:495, 648, 671–672
    holiday season, I:16
    September 11, 2001 terrorist attacks and, II:646

Retail stores, I:92, 279, 320; II:453–455. *See also* Traditional retailers

Retinal scans, I:64

Return Path Inc., I:260

Return systems, I:293

Reuters Enterprise, II:486, 785

Reuters Group PLC
    Bloomberg L.P. and, I:69, 72
    Hoover's Online and, I:374
    Instinet Group LLC and, I:242, 400, 432
    Motley Fool and, II:519
    Yankee Group and, II:486, 785, 787

Reverse auctions, I:88, 95, 163; II:603

Review services, product, II:613–614

Revolution
    industrial, II:701–702
    industrial *vs.* information, **I:387–391;** II:549

REXnetwork (Real Estate Exchange Network), I:72

RFC 1738 policy, II:725

Rhee, Sik, II:471

Rheingold, Howard, II:513, 734–735

SBC Communications Inc., I:29, 38, 425

SBC Warburg, II:589

Scalability, **II:639–640;** II:664, 679

Scale, economies of, **I:237–238;** II:670

Scanners, I:64–65

Scenario planning, I:304; **II:640–642;** II:657–658

Scenario servers, I:386

Schmidt, Andreas, I:60, 115

Schmidt, Eric, II:560

Schoolnet Africa, I:325

Schools. *See also* Education
    digital divide and, I:198
    Internet use in, I:123, 125–126
    Web-based, I:125–126

Schrage, Michael, II:641, 658

Schrock, Rod, I:13, 15

Schwartz, Peter, II:641, 658

Schwartz, Steven, II:661

Science Research Associates, Inc., I:379

Scient Corporation, I:230, 231, 297; **II:642–643**

Scott, Ed, I:267

Scripting language, II:543; **II:747–748;** II:766

Sculley, John, II:443

SDLC (Systems development life cycle), II:683–684

Seaboard Coast Line Industries, II:480

Search engines. *See also* specific search engines
    Boolean operators, I:75
    directory-based, II:644
    Excite@Home and, I:281–282
    full-text, I:13
    Inktomi Corporation, I:396–397
    keyword searches by, II:757
    link-based, II:644
    MSN and, II:507
    placement with, II:619, 621
    portals and, II:597–598, 599
    pricing, I:99
    real-time, II:758
    results ranking on, **II:633–634**
    spiders, II:643–644; **II:667–668**
    stemming, II:670, 765
    strategy of, **II:643–644**
    types of, II:643–644
    utilization of, II:643
    Webcrawler, I:281; II:757–758
    wildcards for, II:670; **II:765**

Sears, Roebuck & Co., I:244, 380

SEC. *See* Securities Exchange Commission

Secret Service, I:147, 307; II:607

Secure certificates, I:177

Secure Courier, II:543

Secure electronic transactions (SETs), I:108; II:495, 580; **II:645–646**

Secure Socket Layer (SSL), I:165, 308; II:580

Secure Transaction Technology, II:543

SecurID cards, I:42

Securities brokers. *See* Brokerage services

Securities Dynamics Technologies, Inc., II:636

Securities Exchange Commission (SEC)
    Archipelago Holdings LLC merger, I:34
    computer crime and, I:145–146
    on consultants and accounting firms, I:234
    on electronic communications networks, I:242–243
    on fraud, I:307
    on Island ECN, I:434
    on order handling protocols, I:34, 400; II:531
    Regulation FD, II:739
    on securities fraud, II:512

Securities fraud, I:145–146; II:512

Security. *See* Computer security

Security Sockets Layer (SSL), I:263–264

Security Traders Association, II:531

Seed money, I:295; II:669

Seidenbert, Ivan, II:706

Selective disclosure, II:739

Self-regulation, I:125, 280, 343, 360; II:610, 637

Semantic Web, I:58

Semel, Terry, II:784

Semiconductor Industry Association, II:561

Semiconductors, I:404; II:516–517, 520

Semtech, II:561

Sendall, Mike, II:698

September 11, 2001 terrorist attacks, **II:646–647**

Sequoia Capital, II:523, 642, 777, 781

Serial Line Internet Protocol (SLIP), I:2

Servers
    application, I:270
    Compaq, I:142, 187, 189
    database, I:270
    Dell Computer Corporation, I:187, 189, 190
    distributed systems, I:212–213
    domain name system, I:215
    enterprise, I:270–271; II:544
    file, I:270
    Hewlett-Packard, I:235, 364
    HotSync, II:578
    integration, I:267
    local area network, II:468
    Microsoft Corporation and, I:316, 317; II:503–504, 508
    mirror sites and, II:510–511
    Netscape Netsite, II:542
    network, I:270
    Novell, II:559–560
    Oracle Express, II:569
    Proliant, I:142
    response time and, II:660
    scalability of, II:639
    scenario, I:386
    Sun Fire, II:681
    Sun Microsystems and, II:679
    Web, I:177, 270; II:750
    WebSphere software for, I:231, 235, 380–381
    Wireless Server, II:544

Service Bureau Corporation, I:379

Service contracts, extended, I:110

Service level agreements (SLAs), II:472; **II:648–649**

Service Merchandise, II:454

Service Metrics Inc., I:285

Service providers, e-business, **I:230–232**

Servlets, II:440

SET Secure Electronic Transaction LLC, II:645

SETI Institute, I:213

SETs (Secure electronic transactions), I:108; II:495, 580; **II:645–646**

Sextant Research, II:667

Seybold, Patricia, I:169

Seybold Seminars, II:706

SGML (Standard Generalized Markup Language), I:376; II:698, 779

Shadow Support Program, II:730

Shaheen, George, II:761

Shake-out, dot-com, **II:649–652**. *See also* Dot-coms

Shamir, Adi, I:263

Shannon, Claude, I:393

ShareData Inc., I:278

Shasta Networks, Inc., II:558

Shattner, William, I:77, 97; II:618, 687

Shaw, David, II:445

Shaw Communications, I:282

Shell, West, III, II:539, 540

Shipping, **II:652–655**
    B2B e-commerce, I:292
    complaints about, I:89–90
    costs of, I:274; II:716–717
    express, II:653
    FedEx Corporation, I:290–293
    global, I:349; II:653
    groceries, II:761
    international trade law on, II:716–718
    less-than-truckload, II:652, 653, 654
    Oracle Corporation systems for, II:569
    order fulfillment, II:571, 572
    outsourcing, II:571, 573
    overnight, I:291; II:723
    tracking, I:292; **II:652–655**

Shockley, William, II:516, 561

Shop@AOL, I:82, 411

ShopBuilder, I:134

Shopping
    barriers to, II:707–708, 709
    comparison, I:134–135, 262; II:474, 524–525, 604–605, 655
    links, I:173
    one-click, I:207; II:656–657
    personalized, I:93; II:496, 594–595, 617
    portal-affiliated, I:283; II:599
    ranking of, II:599

Shopping bots, I:81–82, 411; II:613; **II:655–656**
    independent, II:524–525, 655
    limitations of, II:655
    loyalty and, II:474
    Virtual Learning Agent technology for, II:604–605, 655

Shopping carts, I:177, 235; II:570; **II:656–657**

Shopping Channel, I:92

Shopping Engine, I:396

Shopping.com, I:13, 14; II:599

Shopping.Yahoo!, I:82, 411

Showtime Networks, II:585

Sidgmore, John, II:730

Siebel Systems Inc., I:167, 168, 269

Siemens, I:159

Sift Inc., II:713

Signatures, digital. *See* Digital signatures

Silentype, I:30

Silicon chip, I:388–389; II:518

Silicon Graphics Inc., I:24, 130–131, 340–341

Silknet Software Inc., I:296; II:762, 763

Silver King Broadcasting, II:699

Silver Lake Partners, I:184, 314, 434

Silverberg, Brad, I:317; II:503

Simon & Schuster, I:229, 230, 254

Simpatix, II:515

Simple Mail Transfer Protocol (SMTP), I:257; II:510

Simple Object Access Protocol (SOAP), II:766

Simplex Technologies Inc., I:294

Simulation software, **II:657–659**

Sina.com, I:220

Singapore Telecom, II:694

Site evaluation services, **II:659–660**

Site response time, **II:660–661**; II:750, 755

Site Server Commerce, I:142

SiteZero, I:331

SkillsVillage, II:588

Skipjack algorithm, I:265

Sklyarov, Dimitri, II:706–707

Skoll, Jeff, II:564

Slack, Michele, II:487, 552

SLAs (Service level agreements), II:472; **II:648–649**

Slate, I:255, 286, 317; II:503

Slatkin, Reed, I:223

SLIP (Serial Line Internet Protocol), I:2

Small businesses
    aggregators for, I:11
    auction sites and, I:41
    e-business service providers for, I:230
    electronic data interchange for, II:719
    e-mail marketing for, I:260
    e-terms service for, I:413
    Forrester Research and, I:306
    high-speed access for, I:80
    Internet payment providers and, I:422–423
    market research for, II:485
    marketplaces for, I:88; II:545
    Netscape Netbusiness Marketplace for, II:545
    network solutions for, II:547
    predictions about, I:360
    web presence of, II:772

Small Order Execution System (SOES), I:183, 185, 434; II:530

SmallCap Market, II:530

Smart cards, I:42, 65, 195, 299, 309

Smart Clouds, II:472–473

SmartBook, I:35

SmartDisk Corporation, I:299

SmartMoney.com, **II:661–663**

SmartPortfolio.com, II:696

Smarty, I:299

SMDS (Switched Multi-Megabit Data Services), II:765

SME Commerce, II:671–672

Smiley, Barbara, II:645

Smith, Frederick W., I:290–291

Smith, George D., II:722

Smith, Michael D., II:474

Smithsonian Institution, II:662–663

SMTP (Simple Mail Transfer Protocol), I:257; II:510

Smurf attacks, I:190

Snap Internet Portal Service, II:507, 598, 694

Snap! Online, I:134

SNDMSG, I:257

Sniping, I:40

Soap, II:611

SOAP (Simple Object Access Protocol), II:766

Social Security Administration, I:195

Society
    Central and South American, I:333
    cyberculture and, I:170–173
    egalitarian *vs.* authoritarian, I:391
    industrial revolution and, I:388
    information revolution and, I:388, 390, 391
    Internet and, I:358–361

SOES (Small Order Execution System), I:183, 185, 434

Soft Warehouse Inc., I:188

Softbank Corporation, I:296–297
    Africa and, I:324
    Bluelight.com LLC and, I:73, 74, 296–297; II:579
    Broadcast.com and, II:743
    Buy.com Inc. and, I:99
    CNET and, I:135
    E*Trade and, I:278
    in Europe, I:336
    Gomez Inc. and, I:352
    Motley Fool and, II:519
    Yahoo! and, II:781
    Ziff-Davis and, II:791, 793

SOFTBANK Venture Capital. *See* Softbank Corporation

Softbook Press Inc., I:229, 254

Softcard, I:315; II:502

Software, **II:663–664**. *See also* Database management systems; Wordprocessing software
    anti-virus, I:154–155, 358; II:737–738
    application integration, I:403
    behavior analysis, I:155, 358
    bundling, I:24, 53, 84–85, 130, 316–317; II:543
    customer relations, I:166–170
    debugging, I:156
    detection, I:153, 155
    filtering, I:125, 126, 155, 358; II:465
    forecasting, I:302
    graphics, II:443–444
    history of, II:664
    hosting, II:573; **II:664–665**
    human resources, I:268; **I:387**
    integration of, I:266–267
    licensing, I:100, 136–137
    lock-in, II:469
    mailing list, I:67, 310; II:541

    micro-payments for, II:728
    middleware, **II:509**
    middleware and, II:509
    on-demand, II:728
    online licensing, I:100
    open-source, II:467, 565
    outsourcing, II:573, 664–665
    pay-per-play, II:583–584
    pirated, I:145–146, 408
    price wars in, I:239
    rental companies, I:33
    sandboxing, I:155, 358
    scalability of, II:639
    simulation, **II:657–659**
    spending on, I:392
    spreadsheet, II:451–452, 469–471, 560, 657–658
    storefront builders, **II:670–672**
    subscriptions to, II:678
    suites, II:451–452, 470
    system, I:155; II:663–664
    translation, I:245
    workforce, II:769

Software & Information Industry Association, I:145–146, 343

Software Corporation of America Inc., II:522

Software Engineering Institute, I:147

Software History Center, II:664

Software hosting, II:573; **II:664–665**

Software Spectrum Inc., I:239

Software.net, I:60

Softway Systems, II:763

Solaris, II:679

SoloSurfer, I:300

Solutions4Sure.com, I:298

Sonicport.com, I:300

Sony Corporation, I:115; II:503, 529, 559

Soriano, Paul, I:172

Sotheby's Holdings Inc., I:16, 17, 40

The Source, I:111

Source code, II:465, 565–566, 725

South Africa, I:323, 324

South America, **I:332–336**
    FedEx Corporation in, I:291
    Internet access in, I:201, 335, 416
    UUNET in, II:731
    Yankee Group in, II:485, 786, 787

South Central Bell, II:558

South Korea, I:227, 329

South Pacific Education and Research Network (SPEARNet), I:330

Southern Pacific Transportation Co., II:623

Southwest Airlines, II:712

Sovereignty, II:464

SP Telecom, II:623, 624

Space and Naval Warfare Center, I:145

Space.com, I:215

Spain, Patrick, I:374, 375

Spam
    e-mail, I:227, 257, 258–262; II:541; **II:665–666**
    filtering software, II:666

Amazon.com and, I:17–18, 63, 117–118, 274; II:747
  holiday seasons, I:17–18, 52, 274, 276

Toys.com, I:275

Toysmart.com, I:276; II:607, 747

Toysrus.com, I:52–53
  Amazon.com and, I:18, 63, 236
  BizRate.com on, I:68
  order fulfillment problems, I:312

ToyTomes, I:276

TPS (Transaction processing systems), II:683

Tracking technology
  Adobe Systems, I:4
  for advertising, I:51–52
  blocking, II:608
  FCC on, I:9
  FedEx Corporation, I:292
  firms in, I:417–418
  Intel Corporation, I:253
  Internet access, I:416–418; II:447
  Jupiter Media Metrix and, II:447
  MSN and, II:506
  NetRatings, Inc. and, II:483–484
  order fulfillment, II:571
  privacy and, II:607
  profiling and, II:615
  real-time, II:629–630, 654
  shipping, I:292; **II:652–655**
  traffic-logging systems, II:607
  UPS, II:654, 723
  wireless, II:654

TRADACOMS, I:246

Trade agreements, I:347

Trade Matrix Network, I:87

Trade shows, **II:704–707**

Trade x-change, I:163

TradeCast Ltd., II:634

Trademarks, I:97, 216, 408–409; II:463, 770

Trade*Plus, I:277

Tradepoint Stock Exchange, I:34

Trade-Related Aspects of Intellectual Property Rights Agreement,
  I:410; II:463

Trade-secrets, I:408, 409–410

Tradeware S.A., I:400

Trading networks, electronic. *See* Electronic communications networks

Trading partner agreements, I:244

Trading stocks. *See* Brokerage services

Traditional retailers. *See also* Bricks-and-clicks
  business model for, I:91, 92; II:482
  change and, I:116
  dot com collapse and, II:652
  marketing by, II:487–488
  merchant discount and, II:495
  new economy and, II:551
  restructuring, II:631–633
  sales of, I:90
  Yahoo! advertising by, II:460

Traffic Director, I:359

Traffic Server, I:396, 397

Traffic-logging systems, II:607

Transaction processing systems (TPS), II:683

Transactions, **II:707–709**. *See also* Payment options and services;
  Real-time transactions
    abandoning, II:755
    Draft Model Law on, II:716–718
    EDIFACT on, II:718–719
    electronic data interchange for, I:244–246
    global e-commerce and, I:348–349
    GUIDEC for, I:321–322, 413
    micro-payments for, II:500–501, 727
    Oracle Transaction Process Subsystem for, II:568
    timestamping, II:704

Transistors, II:501, 518, 521, 560–561

Translation software, I:245; II:509

Transmeta, I:12

Transmission Control Protocol/Internet Protocol (TCP/IP), I:138–139
  development of, I:36, 67, 370, 416, 419
  routers for, I:127
  via satellite, I:421

Transmission speed. *See also* High-speed Internet access
  bandwidth management for, I:48
  Next Generation Internet Initiative on, II:553
  optical switching for, II:567
  photonics for, II:596
  response time and, II:600–601, 750, 755

Transora, I:87; II:632

Transparency, **II:709–710**

Transportation, II:571, 572, 573

TransTerra Company, I:21; II:634

Travel Group, I:104

Travel services. *See also* Airline tickets
  alliances between, II:579–580
  business model for, I:81
  business plans for, I:96, 97
  Buy.com Inc., I:100
  comparative shopping for, II:474
  e-commerce solutions for, I:237
  hotel reservations, II:601, 603, 712, 789
  management of, I:117
  marketing plans and, II:490
  sales of, I:91
  Travelcity.com, I:81; II:710–712

Travelcity.com, I:81; **II:710–712**

Treaties
  computer crime, I:148
  copyright, I:410; II:463
  intellectual property, II:770
  international, II:463

Tribal Voice, I:14

Tribune Company, I:112, 436; II:515

Tricon Global Restaurants, I:399

Tricord Systems Inc., I:106

Trilogy Technology Corporation, I:203

TriMark Technologies, II:588

Triple DES, I:175

Trojan horses, I:145, 154, 308, 358; II:737

Truncation, II:670, 765

Trust, Charles F., I:377

Trustbase, II:680

TRUSTe, I:125

Tunisia, II:558

Turner, Ted, I:30

Turner Broadcasting System, Inc., I:27

Tutorials, II:662

Tuxedo (software), I:267

TWA, II:580, 602

Tweney, Dylan, II:761

Two-way radios, II:520

Tyco Submarine Systems Ltd., I:294

Tyson, Laura D'Andrea, II:551

Tyson, Poppe, I:218

U

Ubiquity, **II:715–716**

UCITA (Uniform Computer Information Transactions Act), I:409;
II:463

U.K. Online Strategy, I:337

Ultra Extended Graphics Array (UXGA), II:631

Ultraseek Corporation, I:397

UltraSPARC III, II:681

UltraSparc RISC, II:679

Ultra-wideband technology, II:537

UNCITRAL (United Nations Commission on International Trade
Law), **II:716–718**

UN/EDIFACT, I:245; **II:718–720**

UNESCO (United Nations Educational, Scientific and Cultural
Organization), I:368

UNext.com, I:366

Uni-Data, II:724

Uniface Holding B.V., I:156

Uniform Communication Standard, I:245

Uniform Computer Information Transactions Act (UCITA), I:409;
II:463

Uniform Crime Reporting Statistics, I:144

Uniform Domain Name Dispute Resolution Policy, I:174

Uniform Electronic Transactions Act, I:205

Uniform resource locators (URLs), **II:725–726**; II:749, 750
cybersquatting and, I:173–174, 216; II:463, 770–771
development of, I:57; II:697–698
filtering software for, I:185
profiling and, II:615

Union Bank of California, II:547

Unions, labor, I:390

Unisys Corporation, **II:720–722**

United Airlines, I:100; II:580, 602, 745

United International Bureau for the Protection of Intellectual Property,
II:770

United Kingdom, I:337–338
AltaVista in, I:14
Apple Computer in, I:31
Buy.com Inc. in, I:100
computer crime in, I:148
Dell Computer Corporation in, I:186, 188
EDS in, I:247
E*Trade in, I:278

Internet access in, I:337, 338
NASDAQ in, II:532
Nortel Networks in, II:558
Travelcity.com in, II:712

United Nations
on Africa, I:324
Commission on International Trade Law, I:205
State of the World Forum, I:200

United Nations Commission on International Trade Law
(UNCITRAL), **II:716–718**

United Nations Educational, Scientific and Cultural Organization
(UNESCO), I:368

United Online, I:425; II:446, 498

United Parcel Service, Inc. (UPS), **II:722–724**
e-Logistics service, II:572, 653
e-Ventures, II:572, 653
FedEx Corporation and, I:290, 292, 293; II:723
tracking systems, II:654, 723

United States government departments. *See* the specific department

UNIVAC, I:378; II:590, 720

Universal product code, I:399

Universal resource locators (URLs). *See* Uniform resource locators

Universities, I:364–368; II:690. *See also* names of specific colleges
and universities

University of California at Los Angeles, I:36

University of Michigan, Cool Central, I:44

University of Phoenix, I:366

University of Utah, I:36

UNIX, **II:724–725**
AT&T version, I:316; II:721, 725
Dell Computer Corporation and, I:186–187, 188
development of, I:103, 316
Linux and, II:468
open system, II:566
standards for, II:725
Sun Microsystems and, II:494, 679–680

UNIX System Laboratories, II:559, 560

Unix-to-Unix Copy Protocol (UUCP), I:330

UPC Cable Company, II:504

Uploading, I:409

UPS. *See* United Parcel Service, Inc.

UPS Capital, II:724

Upton, Wayne, I:402

Urban areas, I:389

URLs. *See* Uniform resource locators

U.S. Airways, II:601, 602, 604, 745

U.S. departments. *See* the specific department

U.S. government departments. *See* the specific department

U.S. Navy, I:145

U.S. Postal Service, I:293

U.S. Robotics Corporation, I:128; II:576–577, 593

U.S. Trust Corporation, I:122

US West, II:623, 625

USA Bankcards, II:495

USA Networks, I:12; II:694

USA Today Internet, I:221

Virtual Learning Agent (VLA), II:524, 604–605, 655

Virtual offices, II:703

Virtual private networks (VPNs), I:32, 38, 154; II:729, 731

Virtual teams, II:703

Virtual warehouses, I:262

VirtualCart, I:235; II:656

Viruses, I:145, 147, 154, 358; **II:736–738**
    anti-virus software for, I:154–155
    Bluelight.com LLC and, I:73
    boot-sector, II:737
    Cascade, I:153
    costs of, II:736, 773
    development of, I:153
    e-mail, I:154, 257–258
    fraud and, I:308
    ILOVEYOU, I:358
    legislation on, I:152
    Love Bug, I:147, 154, 358
    LoveLetter worm, II:773
    macro, II:737
    mail bombs, I:154, 358
    Melissa, I:145
    mutation engines, II:773
    NIPC on, II:535
    Novell and, II:560
    peer-to-peer networks and, II:586
    Stoned, I:153
    Trojan horses, I:145, 154, 308, 358; II:737
    worms, I:145, 154, 358; II:737; **II:773–774**

Visa International
    charge-back and, II:496
    digital wallets and, I:208
    FraudScreenNet and, II:581
    interchange fees, I:412
    on micro-payments, II:500
    recurring transactions and, II:630
    Secure Transaction Technology, II:543
    SET and, II:645

VisiCalc, II:451

VisiText, II:766

Visor (handheld device), II:577

Visual BASIC, I:56

Visual BASIC Scripting Edition (VBScript), II:748

Vitria Technology, I:267

Viva Magnetics, II:545

Vivendi Universal, I:336; II:529

Vivo Software Inc., II:628

VLA (Virtual Learning Agent), II:524, 604–605, 655

VLINX.com, I:88

VNU, II:792

Vocaltec Communications Ltd., II:690–691

VOD (Video on demand), II:585

Vodafone AirTouch, II:439–440

Voice mail, II:784

Voice over IP (VOIP), II:691, 783–784

Voice verification, I:64

Volatility, **II:738–739**

Volume Pricing Center, I:88

Voluntary Inter-Industry Commerce Standards, I:245

Vortals, **II:739–741**

VPNs. *See* Virtual private networks

VTech Holdings, II:476

Vulcan Northwest Inc., I:11

Vulcan Ventures, I:11, 12; II:791, 793

Vuorilehto, Simo S., II:555

Vxtreme Inc., II:504

W

@Work, I:282, 283

W3C. *See* World Wide Web Consortium

Wack, Pierre, II:641

Waggoner, Dena, I:144

Wagner, Todd, **II:743–744**

Wagner, Tony, I:166

WAI (Web Accessibility Initiative), II:757

WAIS (Wide Area Information Servers), II:725

Waitt, Ted, I:295, 318, 320; **II:744**

Walgreen Company, II:548

Walker, E. Lee, I:186, 188

Walker, Jay, I:395; II:601, 603; **II:745**

Walker, John, II:538, 539

Walker Digital, II:601, 745

Wall Street Journal Online, I:94, 255; II:661

Wallets, digital, I:124; **I:206–209;** II:581–582, 645

Wal-Mart Stores Inc., I:275, 276; II:709

Walmart.com, I:18

Walt Disney Company, I:29, 58, 276; II:598, 694; **II:745–747**

Walt Disney Internet Group, II:746, 747

WAN Downtime Study, II:479

Wanadoo Group, I:337, 338

Wang, James, I:326

WANs (Wide area networks), I:36, 48; II:479, 513; **II:765**

WAP (Wireless Application Protocol), I:158; II:555, 580, 593, 654

Warehouse Information Network Standard, I:245–246

Warehouse management software, I:311; II:571, 658

Warehouses
    auction sites for, I:290
    merchant model and, II:497
    order fulfillment and, I:311; II:570–571
    outsourcing, II:571, 573
    simulation software for, II:658
    virtual, I:262

Warehousing, data, I:167, 179; **I:180–181**

Warner Books, I:27

Warner Bros., I:226

Warnock, John, I:3

Watches, I:113; II:703

Watermarks, digital, I:214

Waterstone, I:236

WATFIV, I:307

X

X10.com, I:78

X12 (ANSI), I:245; II:718–719

X12/EDIFACT Alignment Plan, II:718–719

X.25 protocol, II:765

XA Systems Corporation, I:156

Xanadu, II:538–539

X-Cell Communications, Ltd., II:558

Xcert International, I:299

X.com, II:523, 582; **II:777–778**

Xerox Corporation, I:202; II:443, 559

XHML (Extensible Hypertext Markup Language), I:376; II:698, 750–751, 752

Xinkuei, Lu, I:344

XML. *See* Extensible Markup Language

Xros Inc., II:558

Xybernaut Corporation, I:262

Y

Y2K bug, I:156, 233; II:442, 484; **II:787–789**

Yahoo! Auctions, I:40, 144, 226–227, 228; II:565, 784

Yahoo! Inc., **II:781–784**. *See also* Yang, Jerry
    advertising, I:7, 94, 295; II:459–460, 781, 784
    advertising revenues, II:487
    alliance program, II:578–579
    Amazon.com and, I:62
    auction site, I:40, 144, 226–227, 228; II:565, 784
    Barnesandnoble.com and, I:55
    brand recognition, I:77; II:782
    Broadcast.com and, I:166; II:743
    business model for, I:94
    discussion forums, I:209
    Filo, David and, I:94, 294–295, 341, 398; II:459, 781
    financing for, I:296
    GeoCities and, I:94, 132; II:599, 763, 783
    Gomez Inc. and, I:352
    history of, I:341; II:597, 781–784
    initial public offering, I:394; II:782
    innovations by, I:398
    Knight-Ridder and, II:457
    Koogle, Timothy and, I:295; **II:459–460;** II:781, 784, 785
    vs. Lycos, II:694
    market value of, I:217, 221, 342
    pay-per-view services, II:585
    personalization on, II:594, 782
    profitability of, I:94, 282; II:782, 784, 785
    ranking of, I:418
    shopping bot, II:655
    shopping links, I:173; II:599

Yahoo!Shopping, I:92

Yahoo!Small Business, I:88

Yakpak, II:582

Yang, Catherine, I:340; II:673–674

Yang, Jerry, **II:784–785**

    advertising model and, I:94
    alliance program and, II:578
    Filo, David and, I:294–295
    Koogle, Timothy and, II:459, 785
    Yahoo! founding by, I:341, 398; II:781, 784–785

Yang, Michael, II:524

Yankee Group, II:485–486; **II:785–787**
    on B2C e-commerce, I:92
    in Central and South America, II:485, 786, 787
    on marketing, II:618
    on UUNET, II:730

YankeeTek, II:786

Yankowski, Carl, II:577, 706

Yebo Net, I:323

Yellow pages, II:493

Yesmail.com, I:259, 261

Yet2.com, II:690

Yeti Cycles, II:483

Yockelson, David, I:246

Youcentric Inc., I:269

Young, John, I:363; II:560

Your Personal Model, II:461

Yoyodyne, II:782

Yun, Yeogirl, II:524

Yung, Yiu-Fai, I:301

Z

ZapMail, I:291

ZapMe! Corporation, I:126

ZCast.tv, II:792

ZDNet.com, I:133, 135; II:791, 792–793

ZDTV, II:791, 793

ZeroPoint, I:385; II:446

Ziff-Davis Inc., I:133, 135; **II:791–793**

Ziff-Davis International Media Group, II:782

Ziff-Davis Publishing Company, II:781–782

Zimmerman, Phil, I:264; II:600–601

Zing.com, I:114

Zions First National Bank, I:195

Zip2 Corporation, I:13, 14; II:523–524

Zisman, Michael D., II:471

Zollar, Al, II:471

Zona Research, I:1; II:661, 755

ZSeries Servers, I:271

zShops, I:16, 62

Zuse, Konrad, II:617